THE *FASTI* OF
ROMAN BRITAIN

THE *FASTI* OF
ROMAN BRITAIN

ANTHONY R. BIRLEY

CLARENDON PRESS · OXFORD
1981

Oxford University Press, Walton Street, Oxford OX2 6DP

London Glasgow New York Toronto
Delhi Bombay Calcutta Madras Karachi
Kuala Lumpur Singapore Hong Kong Tokyo
Nairobi Dar es Salaam Cape Town
Melbourne Wellington

and associate companies in
Beirut Berlin Ibadan Mexico City

Published in the United States by
Oxford University Press, New York

British Library Cataloguing in Publication Data
Birley, Anthony
The Fasti of Roman Britain.
1. Romans — Great Britain
I. Title
936.2'04   DA145   80-41709
ISBN 0-19-814821-6

Printed in Great Britain
at the University Press, Oxford
by Eric Buckley
Printer to the University

patri optimo

PREFACE

Britain was under Roman rule from AD 43 until the Britons expelled their governors in 409. The evidence for the men who served here during those years is patchy, but the fortunate interest taken by Rome's greatest historian, on account of his father-in-law's repeated service in Britain, gives a unique opening to these *Fasti*. Some other writers, notably Ammianus Marcellinus, are also helpful, and epigraphic evidence is plentiful for some parts of the period, even in Britain itself, notoriously infertile in inscriptions. The genre of provincial *Fasti* is well established in the field of Roman imperial history, and this production will, it is hoped, fall a gap. Unlike most other works of its kind, it does not stop with Diocletian, since the obvious utility of including the last century or so hardly needs stating. The criteria for the inclusion of individuals are fairly wide; but *praefecti castrorum*, equestrian officers and centurions, freedmen and slaves of the *familia Caesaris*, and some late Roman officers (such as the German princes Crocus and Fraomarius) are omitted. Governors and *iuridici*, legionary legates and *tribuni laticlavii* (but not legionary prefects), procurators, prefects of the fleet, and the fourth-century *vicarii, praesides, comites*, and *duces*, together with high-ranking visitors to the island, already constitute a substantial body of men, and to cast the net wider would be to inflate the book out of all proportion. By the same token, I have refrained, with some reluctance, from including a systematic examination of the governors' role in dispensing patronage. A number of examples are noted in the entries for individual governors.

The composition of the work has a history of its own. It was originally planned by my father, Eric Birley, shortly after the Second World War, and he wrote draft entries for most of the persons serving here between 43 and the recovery of Britain in 296. He asked me to take over the task in 1965, and I originally hoped to complete it within a few years. The first fruits were an article on the governors, in *Epigraphische Studien* 4 (1967), but the pressure of full-time teaching and other commitments have delayed completion for far too long. It may be added that the subject demands familiarity with the history and institutions of the whole Roman empire and with a vast bibliography, well beyond the normal confines of Romano-British studies. I cannot hope to have noticed every relevant item, even from work published by midsummer of 1979; but the effort has been made, and generous help has been given.

Many debts have been incurred in the preparation of this work. First and foremost is that to Eric Birley, to whom the book is dedicated. His generosity to me, no less than to his other pupils, has been a constant source of inspiration.

My other debts are numerous. On the practical side, I must acknowledge a contribution from the Society of Antiquaries Research Fund towards travelling expenses. I was fortunate to have been taught as an undergraduate by the late C. E. Stevens; and to have been supervised as a postgraduate by Sir Ronald Syme, whose interest in my work has continued, to my great benefit. I likewise owe a great deal to the late John Morris, to H.-G. Pflaum, G. Alföldy, and W. Eck, for their advice, information, and encouragement. Many other friends have helped in various ways in the discussion of particular problems, notably A. K. Bowman, G. P. Burton, the late R. W. Davies, B. Dobson, A. J. Graham, J. G. F. Hind, P. A. Holder, M. G. Jarrett, G. D. B. Jones, J. B. Leaning, J. C. Mann, J. Mottershead, M. M. Roxan, B. E. Thomasson, G. Webster, J. P. Wild, and J. J. Wilkes. To all I record my gratitude, as also to my brother, Robin Birley, whose work at Vindolanda has further enhanced that site's notable contribution to the *Fasti* of Britain; and to my wife and children, for their support in various ways.

Manchester   A. R. BIRLEY
31 July 1979

CONTENTS

List of abbreviations   xi

Note on the citation of sources   xii

I

I.1 Introduction   1

I.2 The senatorial career under the principate   4

     (a) The pre-senatorial stages   4

     (b) The quaestorship   12

     (c) From quaestorship to praetorship   14

     (d) The praetorian career   15

     (e) The consulship   24

     (f) The consular career   26

     (g) Conclusion   32

II

II.1   Governors of undivided Britain   37

II.2   The first division of Britain   168

II.3   Governors of Britannia superior   172

II.4   Governors of Britannia inferior   181

II.5   *Incerti*   201

II.6   King Cogidubnus and the *iuridici*   208

II.7   The legionary garrison of Britain   219

II.8   Legionary legates of the British army   222

II.9   *Tribuni laticlavii* of the British army   267

II.10 *Incerti*   284

II.11 Equestrian procurators of Britain   287

II.12 Junior procurators and census officials   300

II.13 A freedman procurator of Britain   304

II.14 Prefects of the *classis Britannica*   305
II.15 The British emperors, AD 286–296   309
II.16 The second division of Britain   315
        The fifth province   318
        Military command in the last century of Roman rule   319
II.17 *Vicarii*   321
II.18 *Praesides*   329
II.19 *Comites*   331
II.20 *Duces*   344
II.21 A possible *praepositus limitis*   353
II.22 *Comites* of the emperors in Britain, and senior
        officers sent to the island on special missions   354

III

III.1 The origins and careers of the governors of
        undivided Britain   377
III.2 The governors of Britannia superior   401
III.3 The origins and careers of the governors of Britannia
        inferior   402
III.4 The origins and careers of the *iuridici* of Britain   404
III.5 The origins and careers of the legionary legates of
        the British army   407
III.6 The *tribuni laticlavii* of the British army   416
III.7 The procurators of Britain   419
III.8 The prefects of the *classis Britannica*   422
III.9 High officials and senior officers from the last century
        of Roman rule   422

Appendix I: The titulature of governors   425
Appendix II: The titulature of legionary legates   431
Appendix III: A patron of the province of Britain   433
Select bibliography   435
Index   445

ABBREVIATIONS

Periodicals and epigraphical publications are abbreviated as in Liddell–Scott–Jones, *A Greek-English Lexicon*[9] (1940) and *The Oxford Classical Dictonary*[2] (1970), except in the following cases:

A. Ant. Hung.	*Acta Antiqua Academiae Scientiarum Hungaricae* (1951–)
ANRW	*Aufstieg und Niedergang der römischen Welt*, edd. H. Temporini and W. Haase (1972–)
Ant. J.	*Antiquaries Journal*
Arch. Camb.	*Archaeologia Cambrensis*
Arch.-ep. Mitt.	*Archäologische-epigraphische Mitteilungen aus Oesterreich(-Ungarn)*
Arch. J.	*Archaeological Journal*
BCR	*Bulletino della Commissione Archeologica Communale*
BMC	*Catalogue of the Coins of the Roman Empire in the British Museum*, ed. H. Mattingly (1923–)
CW	*Transactions of the Cumberland and Westmorland Antiquarian and Archaeological Society*
EE	*Ephemeris Epigraphica*, 9 vols. (1872–1913)
H-A-C	*Historia-Augusta-Colloquium Bonn* (1963–)
HSCP	*Harvard Studies in Classical Philology*
IGR	*Inscriptiones Graecae ad res Romanas pertinentes* (1906–27)
ILAfr.	*Inscriptions latines d'Afrique* (1923)
ILAlg.	*Inscriptions latines de l'Algérie* (1922–)
ILTun.	*Inscriptions latines de la Tunisie* (1944)
Inscr. It.	*Inscriptiones Italiae* (1931–)
IRT	*Inscriptions of Roman Tripolitania* (1952)
JBAA	*Journal of the British Archaeological Association*
MAAR	*Memoirs of the American Academy at Rome*
MEFR	*Mélanges d'archéologie et d'histoire de l'école française de Rome*
MRR	*The Magistrates of the Roman Republic*, by T. R. S. Broughton (1951–2)
MW	*Select Documents of the Principates of the Flavian Emperors*, edd. M. McCrum and A. G. Woodhead (1961)
PLRE	*Prosopography of the Later Roman Empire*, I, edd. A. H. M. Jones, J. R. Martindale, and J. Morris (1971)
RAL	*Rendiconti dell' Accademia dei Lincei*
RE	*Realencyclopädie der classischen Altertumswissenschaft* (1898–)
REA	*Revue des études anciennes*

RIC	*The Roman Imperial Coinage*, ed. H. Mattingly and E. A. Sydenham (1923–)
RIT	*Die römischen Inschriften von Tarraco*, ed. G. Alföldy (1975)
TLL	*Thesaurus Linguae Latinae* (1900–)
ZPE	*Zeitschrift für Papyrologie und Epigraphik*

NOTE ON THE CITATION OF SOURCES

Inscriptions which directly relate to service in Britain are cited *in extenso*, as well as a few others. I have mostly not sought to indicate the estimated number of letters missing, contenting myself with [. . .], the three dots being purely a convention to show a gap. Line divisions are, however, shown, to make it easier to refer to particular parts of a text. In citing the publication of inscriptions, I have not sought to be exhaustive, omitting many re-publications, but including references to *ILS* where possible. Volumes of *CIL* are cited by volume number in Roman numerals only, except in a few instances where this might cause confusion. In spite of criticism of the practice from an authoritative quarter (J. and L. Robert, *Revue des études grecques* 89 (1976) 442, reiterated ibid. 91 (1978) 386 f.), I have used the sign = to show republication, intending by this not to confer equality of status on each publication, but to show that the same stone, bronze tablet, etc., is in question.

I have cited Tacitus and the *Historia Augusta* in the Teubner editions, Cassius Dio according to the numbering of volumes by Boissevain, and Ammianus Marcellinus in the edition of C. U. Clark. Although, ideally, the relevant sections of Tacitus, Suetonius, and Dio might have been quoted *in extenso* at the head of each entry, it has seemed preferable for the most part to omit them, and to confine verbatim quotation of literary sources to the less familiar ones.

I

INTRODUCTION

The first systematic treatment of the governors of Britain was provided by E. Hübner, later editor of the British volume of the *Corpus Inscriptionum Latinarum*, in an article published in 1857.[1] This was superseded in the 1920s by D. Atkinson's article in the *Journal of Roman Studies.*[2] E. Birley supplied a more accurate list of governors in 1951.[3] In all cases the governors up to Diocletian were included, but not the fourth- and fifth-century officials. These were handled, together with those of the earlier period, in an article which appeared in 1967.[4] In the meantime E. Ritterling included the senatorial officers of the legions which served in Britain in the second half of his *Realencyclopädie* article 'legio' (1925), E. Birley discussed the known *iuridici* in 1947,[5] and H.-G. Pflaum covered the procurators and prefects of the fleet in his *Carrières procuratoriennes* (1960).

The gradual progress of the second edition of the *Prosopographia Imperii Romani*, begun in the early 1930s by E. Groag and A. Stein and now edited by L. Petersen, the virtual completion of the *Realencyclopädie*, the publication of the first part of the *Prosopography of the Later Roman Empire*, and, above all, the appearance in 1965 of the first volume of *The Roman Inscriptions of Britain*, have made the task of compiling British *Fasti* immeasurably easier than would otherwise have been the case. Of equal importance has been the increasingly complete coverage of the other areas of the empire, both in works confined to particular provinces, or groups of provinces, such as those by A. Stein, E. Ritterling, E. Groag, B. E. Thomasson, J. Fitz, and G. Alföldy, and in studies of particular periods, notably those of W. Eck on the years 69–138, G. Alföldy on 138–80, and G. Barbieri on 193–285.

Roman provincial *Fasti* provide a chronological framework for the

---

[1] *Rhein. Mus.* 12 (1857) 46 ff.
[2] *JRS* 12 (1922) 60 ff.
[3] Appendix to G. Askew, *The Coinage of Roman Britain* (1951) 81 f.
[4] A. R. Birley, *Ep. Stud.* 4 (1967) 63 ff.
[5] *Durham University Journal* 1947, 58 ff., reprinted in *Roman Britain and the Roman Army* 48 ff. A revised version is to appear in the *ANRW*.

history of the provinces, and help to link that history with the wider story of the empire as a whole. Where the evidence is sufficiently full, they also have a no less important function, to illustrate the social and administrative history of Rome by examining a cross-section of Roman officials. The bulk of the men whose careers are discussed in parts II and III were of senatorial rank. Many of them are known to have had long careers which took them to other provinces as well as to posts at Rome. Some of the earliest cases had naturally begun their public life well before the invasion of 43. Hence, to avoid excessive annotation, it seems logical to begin this work with a description of the senatorial career under the principate.

Discussion of the origins of Romans who served in Britain is reserved for the individual entries and for the analysis in part III. But some general observations are in place here. For some of the well-known figures, for whom Roman writers supply biographical information, origin and social background are not in doubt, as with Julius Agricola, or, naturally, the future emperors Vespasian and Pertinax, or Septimius Severus' brother Geta.[6] For most, inference has to be used. The method is well known, based on the distribution of inscriptions and the study of nomenclature.[7] Conjectures about origin can easily prove mistaken in individual cases, but the general trend is clear: the provinces increasingly contributed to the membership of the ruling élite which was almost exclusively Italian at the opening of the principate. During the later part of the period covered by these *Fasti* there was also a marked change in social as well as geographical origins. This too can be observed in the *Fasti* of Britain.

It is difficult to discover how men were chosen for posts, whether in Britain or elsewhere in the empire. Inscriptions rarely give detail, nor do our authors tell us much. Vespasian was appointed legate of II Augusta by the *gratia* of the powerful freedmen Narcissus, according to Suetonius.[8] There are a fair number of other examples of imperial favourites securing posts for their friends or clients.[9] Clearly men did not hesitate to press their claims, either directly or through intermediaries. Didius Gallus was made fun of for complaining that he was forced to take up a provincial governorship for which he had canvassed energetically.[10]

---

[6] pp. 73, 225, 143, 278 below.

[7] E. Birley, *Roman Britain and the Roman Army*, 154 ff. To the essential works by W. Kubitschek and W. Schulze there cited may now be added that of I. Kajanto on the *cognomina*.

[8] *D. Vesp.* 4. 1, see p. 227 below.

[9] A few examples must suffice: Suet. *Vit.* 7. 1; Dio 65. 14. 3; *HA Comm.* 3. 8; *HA Pert.* 3. 3; 6. 9–10; Dio 72. 10. 2, 12. 3; *HA Sev.* 4. 4.

[10] pp. 44, 48 below.

Perhaps this was the British post, for his successor Veranius' funerary monument appears to state that he was appointed even though he did not ask to be.[11] Tacitus gives the impression that Agricola, likewise, did not seek the command in Britain which public opinon thought should be his.[12] Merit, and suitable previous experience, certainly played some part, at least on occasion.[13] So too did bribery.[14] But it cannot be supposed that every office was filled, either by a conscientious review of well-qualified candidates, or as the result of backstairs intrigue. For junior appointments, such as military tribunates, the emperors relied, it must be assumed, on the judgement of their generals. For many others, at least at intermediate level—such as legionary legateships and some governorships—one may infer that some kind of regular system developed, even if its workings are in doubt. Even hard-working emperors could not have known personally all the 600 members of the senate, let alone equestrian aspirants to imperial service.[15] Quite how they used their secretariat,[16] and how far they devised patterns of promotion, will doubtless remain *arcana imperii.*[17]

Augustus and his successors continued to operate, in modified form, the republican *leges annales*, which governed the ages at which the traditional magistracies, quaestorship, tribunate of the plebs and aedileship, praetorship, and consulship, could be held. This seems to have meant that the quaestorship could be held in the twenty-fifth, the praetorship in the thirtieth, and the consulship in the forty-second year. The tribunate or aedileship was held between quaestorship and

[11] p. 53 below.

[12] *Agr.* 9. 5.

[13] Cf. Tacitus' comments on the appointment of Corbulo in 54: 'daturum plane documentum, honestis an secus amicis uteretur, si ducem amota invidia egregium quam si pecuniosum et gratia subnixum per ambitum deligeret' (*Ann.* 13. 6. 4); '. . . laeti, quod Domitium Corbulonem retinendae Armeniae praeposuerat, videbaturque locus virtutibus patefactus' (ibid. 8. 1).

[14] Cf. esp. Dio 60. 17. 8 (Messallina and the freedmen of Claudius), 65. 14. 3 (Vespasian's mistress Caenis), 72. 10. 2, 12. 3 (Cleander).

[15] Note the significant case of the schoolmaster Numerianus, who posed as 'a senator sent to collect an army' and defeated the Albinians: Severus thought he was a senator (Dio 75. 5. 1-3).

[16] The role of the *ab epistulis* is emphasized by E. Birley, *Roman Britain and the Roman Army*, 142 ff.; id., *Carnuntum Jahrb.* 1957, 5; and by H.-G. Pflaum, *CP* p. 338 (on no. 142). F. Millar, *The Emperor in the Roman World* (1977) 83 ff. stresses that the holders of this post were mainly intellectuals and literary men. Statius (*Silv.* 5. 1. 83 ff.) describes the military correspondence of the freedman *ab epistulis* Abascantus, including letters of appointment to centurions and equestrian officers. A little later, Pliny appears to state that the first known equestrian *ab epistulis* had a hand in the promotions himself, 'studiosos amat, fovet, provehit' (*ep.* 8. 12. 1)—to be *studiosus* was not necessarily a disqualification for military command.

[17] D. C. A. Shotter, *CQ* N.S. 16 (1966) 323 detects a hint of an attempt to uncover Tiberius' criteria for making appointments to military command in Tac. *Ann.* 2. 36. 1: 'haud dubium erat eam sententiam altius penetrare et arcana imperii temptari'. But Tacitus may simply have in mind the magistracies.

praetorship, with the requirement that there should be a year's interval between offices. The Augustan legislation to encourage a growth in the birth-rate included the privilege of a year's remission, for each child, the *ius liberorum*. This was merely the framework of public life.[18] All 600 members of the senate were expected to go through this series of offices (except for the consulship, to which not all could aspire). Even though the republican magistracies soon became merely ornamental, the circumstances in which they were held provide important clues to the fortunes of particular individuals.

I.2

THE SENATORIAL CAREER UNDER THE PRINCIPATE

(a) THE PRE-SENATORIAL STAGES

Entry to the senate was controlled by the emperor,[1] who could confer the *latus clavus* on suitably qualified aspirants.[2] For the young man in his teens, who would not enter the senate until the age of twenty-four, there were two posts to be held as preliminary stages, the vigintivirate and the military tribunate. The former was compulsory, it appears; but not all future senators served as tribune with a legion.

The vigintivirate

During the principate four boards of minor magistrates constituted the *vigintiviri*: *IIIviri auro argento aere flando feriundo*, or *IIIviri monetales*; *IVviri viarum curandarum*; *Xviri stlitibus iudicandis*; *IIIviri capitales*. In the early part of the Augustan period the moneyers' names appeared on the coinage, as had occurred under the Republic; it is not known whether they continued to have any real role at the mint thereafter. Little is known of the duties of the other three boards: the *IVviri* were concerned with the streets of the capital; the *Xviri* were attached to the Centumviral court; and the *IIIviri capitales* were involved with capital cases—under Domitian they had to conduct book-burning.[3] By a decree

---

[18] Detailed annotation is given in § 2 of this chapter.

[1] A. Chastagnol, *MEFR* 85 (1973) 583 ff. detects a change in the system in the year 38, analysing Dio 59.9.5 and related passages; cf. also his note on the case of Vespasian, *Historia* 25 (1976) 253 ff.

[2] The most obvious qualification was the census of 1,000,000 (Dio 54. 17. 3) or 1,200,000 HS (Suet. *D. Aug.* 41. 1). On *adlectio* see pp. 14 f. below.

[3] See H. Schaefer, *RE* 8A 2 (1958) 2570 ff., esp. 2579 ff. on the imperial period. For the book-burning: Tac. *Agr.* 2. 1.

of the senate placed in 13 BC by Cassius Dio, no one could become a senator without holding one of these posts.[4] In AD 20 special exemption was obtained for the eldest son of Germanicus.[5] A number of *cursus* inscriptions suggest that the vigintivirate was omitted by some senators, but it is impossible to tell whether this was really so, or whether the post was simply not mentioned.[6]

From the early principate until the reign of Severus Alexander patricians seem to have been guaranteed a post as *monetalis*.[7] It follows that plebeians who were made *monetalis* must have been especially favoured, and there are indeed enough examples to suggest that plebeian *monetales* enjoyed particularly successful careers. Quite what was involved is a matter for speculation. The patronage which secured a young man a socially preferable position may well have been powerful enough to ensure continuance of favour in succeeding stages of public life. Examination of the careers of the other *vigintiviri* does indeed confirm that it mattered in some way which of the three posts was held. Clearly the least favoured was that of *IIIvir capitalis*. After L. Coiedius Candidus, quaestor of Claudius *c.*43,[8] only one former *capitalis*, A. Platorius Nepos,[9] is known to have received imperial backing for any of the republican magistracies until the time of Severus Alexander, when the system evidently changed. Furthermore, only three known *capitales* had the favoured 'short' route to the consulship, with just one senior praetorian post, all special cases, it seems; and only five are recorded as governors of consular imperial provinces.[10] This compares with sixteen former *monetales* in such posts:

[4] Dio 54. 26. 5 ff.

[5] Tac. *Ann.* 3. 29. 1.

[6] Cf. the case of C. Memmius Fidus Julius Albius (p. 278 below). There are several examples of men whose vigintivirate is omitted in one inscription but mentioned in another: e.g. L. Funisulanus Vettonianus (*PIR*[2] F 570); C. Octavius Appius Suetrius Sabinus (G. Barbieri, *L'Albo* no. 387). Numerous *cursus* inscriptions commence with the quaestorship, making it impossible to tell whether the man concerned had held either vigintivirate or military tribunate; cf. e.g. A. Claudius Charax (p. 251 below). Some of these may have been late entrants to a senatorial career.

[7] This was established by E. Groag, *Arch.-ep. Mitt.* 19 (1896) 145 f. See also Barbieri, *L'Albo* nos. 1743, 1771, and W. Eck, *ZPE* 18 (1975) 91, who cites another third-century patrician *IIIvir capitalis*, L. Caesonius Ovinius . . . Bassus (*AE* 1964. 223).

[8] p. 354 below.

[9] pp. 101 ff. below.

[10] L. Funisulanus Vettonianus(?) (*PIR*[2] F 570: he may have been *monetalis*); C. Bruttius Praesens (*AE* 1952. 74); A. Platorius Nepos (pp. 101 ff. below); L. Burbuleius Optatus (pp. 271 f. below); C. Caesonius Macer (*PIR*[2] C 210).

The later distinctions of these *capitales* may be explained readily by the changes of dynasty. Vettonianus' earlier career was under Nero, his consular career under the Flavians. Bruttius Praesens was *capitalis* under Domitian; it was probably friendship with Hadrian, in the later years of Trajan, that brought about his change of fortune. This certainly applies to Platorius Nepos, known to have been a friend of Hadrian. Burbuleius Optatus may have obtained a

1. L. Aelius Lamia (*PIR*[2] A 200).
2. L. Apronius (*PIR*[2] A 971).
3. Cn. Calpurnius Piso (*PIR*[2] C 287).
4. P. Calvisius Ruso (*PIR*[2] C 350).
5. L. Dasumius Tullius Tuscus (*PIR*[2] D 16).
6. Q. Hedius Rufus (*PIR*[2] H 42).
7. C. Julius Proculus (*PIR*[2] J 497).
8. C. Julius Quadratus Bassus (*PIR*[2] J 508).
9. Cn. Julius Verus (p. 118).
10. L. Minicius Natalis jr. (p. 244).
11. L. Neratius Marcellus (p. 88).
12. M. Nummius Umbrius Primus (*L'Albo* no. 386).
13. Ti. Plautius Silvanus Aelianus (p. 357).
14. T. Pomponius Proculus Vitrasius Pollio (*ILS* 1112).
15. L. Venuleius Apronianus (XI 1432-3).
16. Q. Veranius (p. 51).[11]

There has been some disagreement about the relative status of the
IVviri and *Xviri*.[12] But, whatever the social cachet attached to the two
posts, it is striking to find seventeen former *IVviri* on record in consular
commands, whereas the *Xviri*, more than twice as numerous, can only

consular command because Hadrian, in his last few years, had grown suspicious of established
figures. Finally, Caesonius Macer was *capitalis* under M. Aurelius and consular governor of
Upper Germany under Severus. Apart from L. Coiedius Candidus (p. 354 below), *capitalis*
under Caligula and quaestor of Claudius shortly after his accession, A. Platorius Nepos (pp. 101 ff.
below) seems to be the only example of a former *capitalis* later receiving imperial backing for
one of the republican magistracies until the system of reserving places among the *monetales* for
patricians was ended under Severus Alexander.

There are only three instances of *capitales* later proceeding to the consulship after a single
praetorian appointment: Bruttius Praesens and Platorius Nepos, already discussed, and L.
Flavius Silva Nonius Bassus (*AE* 1969-70. 183), whose rise was undoubtedly a result of Vespasian's accession.

[11] K. Wachtel, *Arheološki Vestnik* 28 (1977) 292, asserts that *monetales* seldom followed
a military career, and in n. 4 on p. 296 he names the former *monetales* who later governed
consular imperial provinces; but he omits nos. 2, 3, 4, 7, 8, 15, 16 from the list given above.
One might add to the category of *monetales* who had more than the minimum military service
L. Aninius Sextius Florentinus (p. 238 below), who died as governor of Arabia after a military
tribunate and legionary command, P. Metilius Secundus, legate of III Augusta after a similar
earlier career (*ILS* 1053), and Q. Camurius Numisius Junior (pp. 254 f. below), known to have
been military tribune and to have commanded two legions. On the other side, it will be conceded that nos. 4, 11, 12, 14, and 15 were hardly military men in spite of their consular
commands.

[12] S. Brassloff, *JÖAI* 8 (1905) 60 ff., showed that the *IIIviri monetales* and *Xviri* enjoyed
higher social standing than the other two boards. Likewise, S. J. De Laet, *De Samenstelling van
den romeinschen Senaat 28 v. C.-68 n.C.* (1941) 305, followed by Schaefer, *RE* 8A 2 (1958)
2582, attributed greater prestige to the *Xviri* than to the *capitales* and *IVviri*. E. Birley, *PBA*
39 (1953) 201 ff. accepted Brassloff's view, but drew attention to the particular significance of
the *IVviri* among the senators in the emperors' service. See Table 1.

Table 1

Former IVviri in consular commands	Former Xviri in consular commands
M. Aemilius Papus (p. 243)	P. Aelius Hadrianus (PIR^2 A 184)
L. Annius Italicus (PIR^2 A 659)	L. Aemilius Karus (p. 274)
Q. Antistius Adventus (p. 130)	L. Antistius Rusticus (p. 269)
C. Arrius Antoninus (PIR^2 A 1088)	T. Caesernius Statianus (PIR^2 C 183)
P. Cluvius Maximus (*RE* Supp. 14, 105)	M. Claudius Fronto (PIR^2 C 874)
C. Curtius Justus (p. 252)	M. Didius Julianus (PIR^2 D 77)
Sex. Julius Severus (p. 108)	L. Fabius Cilo (PIR^2 F 27)
Q. Lollius Urbicus (p. 113)	Q. Glitius Atilius Agricola (PIR^2 G 181)
L. Marius Maximus (*L'Albo* no. 1100)	M. Herennius Faustus(?) (PIR^2 H 107)
10 Maximus(?) (*ILS* 1062, XVI 99; see Alföldy, *Konsulat* 143)	C. Julius Severus (PIR^2 J 574)
L. Minicius Natalis (*ILS* 1061)	C. Junius Faustinus (p. 163 below)
M. Pontius Laelianus (p. 273)	P. Mummius Sisenna Rutilianus (p. 248)
Rutilius Pudens Crispinus (*L'Albo* no. 1147)	M. Nonius Macrinus (*ILS* 8830)
C. Septimius Severus (*RE* Supp. 14, 662 f.)	C. Plinius Secundus (*ILS* 2927)
M. Servilius Fabianus (*ILS* 1080)	Q. Pompeius Falco (p. 98)
C. Valerius Festus (*ILS* 989)	C. Popilius Carus Pedo (*ILS* 1071)
17 *ignotus* (*ILS* 1022)	T. Prifernius Paetus (*RE* Supp. 14, 484)
	P. Salvius Julianus (*ILS* 8973)
	P. Septimius Geta (p. 278)
	20 T. Statilius Barbarus (*L'Albo* no. 483)
	C. Suetrius Sabinus (*L'Albo* no. 387)
	P. Tullius Varro (p. 239)
	C. Ummidius Quadratus (*ILS* 972)
	24 *ignotus* (*AE* 1957. 161)

muster twenty-four (see Table 1). Perhaps the totals are too small to be statistically significant; otherwise it must be concluded that *IVviri* were more likely to obtain one of the major imperial provinces some twenty to twenty-five years after the vigintivirate than were *Xviri*. It may be unacceptable to infer that the emperors arranged the government of the empire in this way.[13] If so, it might be suggested as an

---

[13] Eck, *Chiron* 3 (1973) 393, comments that about 100 *XXviri* are known from the period 69–138. But of these 21 per cent are *IIIviri monetales*, only 11 per cent *capitales*, while the known *IVviri* form 28 per cent and the *Xviri* 40 per cent. Thus the *monetales* and *IVviri* are 'over-represented', the other two boards 'under-represented'. This doubtless reflects the greater success of the first two in their subsequent careers, and tends to substantiate the conclusions of E. Birley, *PBA* 39 (1953) 201 ff. However, it should be noted that in the unpublished lists

alternative that talented *novi homines* were more likely than sons of senators to hold consular provinces; and that these men would generally become *IVviri* rather than *Xviri*.[14]

The military tribunate

During the Julio-Claudian period service as tribune sometimes preceded the vigintivirate, but this was very rare thereafter.[15] At first sight all twenty *XXviri* might be assumed to have proceeded to a legion, sooner or later, before the quaestorship at about twenty-four. Excluding those commanded by equestrian *praefecti* (in Egypt, and, from *c.*197, the three *legiones Parthicae* formed by Severus), there were over twenty legions in which *tribuni laticlavii* might serve:[16] the number rose from twenty-three in AD 14 to twenty-nine in the later 160s. Yet some future senators clearly did not hold tribunates—perhaps as many as eight out of twenty each year.[17] About thirty cases are known of

prepared by J. Morris for the index to *PIR*[2], there are some 300 *XXviri* from the post-Augustan period (in view of the over-representation of the numismatically recorded *monetales*, the Augustan principate must be excluded from consideration), of whom almost exactly 50 per cent are *Xviri*; the *capitales* are 'under-represented' with only 10 per cent instead of 15 per cent, and the other two boards, particularly the *monetales*, are 'over-represented' (18½ per cent *monetales*, 21½ per cent *IVviri*).

[14] However, of the men listed in Table 1, several *Xviri*, as well as a number of the *IVviri*, were undoubtedly *novi homines*.

[15] See D. McAlindon, *JRS* 47 (1957) 191 ff. Note also the unusual case of the *ignotus AE* 1957. 161, where the XXvirate is listed between two tribunates. C. Julius Proculus (*PIR*[2] J 497) held his tribunate after the quaestorship in the exceptional circumstances of the year 97.

[16] B. Campbell, *JRS* 65 (1975) 18, scouts the possibility that each legion need not always have had a *laticlavius*; or that some might have had more than one at a time. This is of course impossible to demonstrate, but deserves noting. It might, for example, be tempting to suppose that the inseparable brothers Domitii were both tribunes of V Alaudae together (*PIR*[2] D 152, 167). Equally, when a tribune was seconded from one province to another (see n. 18, below), the new man may not always have displaced an existing *laticlavius*: cf. the case of Titus (p. 269 below).

[17] Eck, *ANRW* II. 1 (1974) 175n. 70, is sceptical about E. Birley's view, *PBA* 39 (1953) 200, followed by J. Morris, *Listy fil.* 88 (1965) 25, that only ten to twelve of the *XXviri* each year went on to become military tribunes. Eck's use of the careers in Dessau, *ILS* 987–1072 as a sample, producing thirty-eight who were tribune against twelve who were not (including two careers beginning with the quaestorship), is, however, questionable. Dessau's selection naturally includes a high proportion of careers of outstanding men. The senators in Morris's unpublished thesis, covering the period 70–192, show a somewhat different pattern: about 250 who were tribune, nearly 150 who were not, although the second figure includes over sixty cases where the recorded career begins with the quaestorship. Naturally, the latter category may conceal cases of men who were tribune and did not mention it on their inscriptions, but the figure of 250 is inevitably weighted by cases of men recorded during their service as tribune: these cannot be balanced against cases of men recorded while *not* serving. Further, more detailed, examination of the evidence is required. It would be instructive to see, for example, whether there is any significant correlation between the presence or absence of a military tribunate in a *cursus* and the future offices held, either during the principate as a whole or at particular periods. It may be worth commenting that in the list of praetorian proconsuls between *c.*210 and 250, produced by Eck, *Chiron* 4 (1974) 539 f., only five out of seventeen senators appear

young men who were tribune in more than one legion (see Table 2); two of them, Hadrian and the younger L. Minicius Natalis, served in three. Pliny, no doubt with some exaggeration, speaks of Trajan having served for 'decem stipendia'; he certainly held commissions in the armies of Germany and Syria.[18] It would, indeed, have been inefficient if the *laticlavius* generally stayed for one year only. A term of two or three years is probably to be postulated.[19] The age at which the *laticlavius* entered the service was doubtless generally nineteen or twenty;[20] in spite of his youth, he was second in command of the legion.[21]

Some tribunes are known to have served under close relatives,[22] and a number of other cases may be inferred from epigraphic evidence. The evidence is circumstantial in most cases:

to have been *tribuni militum*, but only six of the remaining twelve record a post in the XXvirate; the other six have careers apparently commencing with the quaestorship. Taking all these factors into account, it might be reasonable to suggest that not more than thirteen or fourteen *XXviri* each year, on average, became *tribuni militum*.

[18] Campbell, *JRS* 65 (1975) 18, states that 'very few tribunes are known to have served in more than one legion', and in his note cites only three examples (nos. 3, 16, 17 in the table). He could have referred to the list in E. Ritterling, *JÖAI* 10 (1907) 310 n. 18; and this can now be extended (see Table 2).

In virtually all cases the two legions concerned were in different provinces, sometimes adjacent (nos. 8, 10, 12, 13, 17, 21, 23, 30), but sometimes far apart (nos. 1, 4, 11, 20, 24). No. 6 appears to be an exception: see G. Alföldy, *Legionslegaten* 61 f., for the restoration [*trib. leg. X et XIIII Ge*] *min. Gordianarum in* [*quo honore vi*]*c. leg. sustinuit*. In several cases one may readily infer what Pliny described in the case of no. 14, the transfer of Junius Avitus with his commander Servianus: e.g. no. 13 (perhaps a commander promoted from Cappadocia to Syria) or no. 17 (perhaps a legate of XXII Pr. becoming governor of Raetia) or no. 21 (a governor of Dacia superior being promoted to Moesia superior). It is suggested on p. 269 below that Titus (no. 8) took reinforcements from Germany to Britain in 60-1; there may have been several other such cases.

[19] This is argued by E. Birley, *PBA* 39 (1953) 200. Eck, *ANRW* II. 1 (1974) 175 f., and Campbell, *JRS* 65 (1975), are sceptical. It must be pointed out that there is no evidence for the view that tribunates were often short, other than Pliny's rhetorical remarks in *Pan.* 15. 2: 'neque enim prospexisse castra brevemque militiam quasi transisse contentus'. Tacitus' often quoted comment, 'nec Agricola licenter, more iuvenum qui militiam in lasciviam vertunt, neque segniter ad voluptates et commeatus titulum tribunatus et inscitiam rettulit' (*Agr.* 5. 1), need not imply a short tenure. Nor, should it be added, is there any justification for supposing that Pliny himself had only a brief stay with III Gallica. None of his comments on this service supports such an inference. Indeed, if he had time to study with Euphrates and Artemidorus (*ep.* 1. 10, 3. 11), as well as to audit the accounts of auxiliary regiments (7. 31. 2), one year would hardly have sufficed.

[20] Vettius Crispinus, son of M. Vettius Bolanus (pp. 47 f. below), was only about sixteen when Statius rhapsodized about his impending military service (*Silv.* 5. 2. 7 ff.). Julius Agricola was nineteen when first in Britain (p. 74 below), Pliny about the same age in Syria (Syme, *Tacitus* (1958) 75). Hadrian, born in January 76, took up the second of three tribunates 'extremis iam Domitiani temporibus', i.e. presumably in 96, and his third after the adoption of Trajan by Nerva, i.e. in October 97 (*HA Had.* 1.3, 2. 2-5). Note also the polyonymous of III 6755, who died at Ancyra at twenty-one years, nine months, and three days, tribune of V. Mac. and I Ad.

[21] A. v. Domaszewski, *RO*[2] LV. 172.

[22] Tac. *Ann.* 1. 19. 24; 2. 57. 76; 3. 21; 12. 31; 15. 23; Pliny, *Pan.* 14 f.; *HA Had.* 2. 5-6; Dio 68. 19. 1; III 3473.

Table 2

tribuni laticlavii who served in more than one legion

1. M. Accenna Helvius Agrippa — XVI Fl., XX V.V. (II 1262; p. 279 below)
2. M. Aelius Aurelius Theo — XI Cl., XII Fulm. (*ILS* 1192)
3. P. Aelius Hadrianus (Hadrian) — II Ad., V Mac., XXII Pr. (*ILS* 308; *HA Had.* 2. 2-5)
4. C. Aemilius Berenicianus Maximus — IV Scyth., VII Gem. (*ILS* 1168)
5. L. Aemilius Karus — VIII Aug., IX Hisp. (*ILS* 1077; p. 274 below)
6. Annianus — X Gem., XIV Gem.(?) (*ILS* 1188) (see p. 9 n.18 above)
7. Clodius Marcellinus — X Fret., II Ad. (III 3472)
8. T. Flavius Vespasianus (Titus) — Germany, Britain (Suet. *D. Tit.* 4. 1; p. 269 below)
9. P. Flavonius Paulinus — X Fret., XII Fulm. (*SEG* VI 555 = *JHS* 1933. 317)
10. P. Julius Geminius Marcianus — X Fret., IV Scyth. (*ILS* 1102-3)
11. A. Julius Pompilius Piso — XIII Gem., XV Apoll. (*ILS* 1111)
12. C. Julius Septimius Castinus — I Ad., V Mac. (*ILS* 1153)
13. [C. Ju]lius [. . .] vianus — XII Fulm., IV Scyth. (*IGR* III 889)
14. Junius Avitus — Germany, Pannonia (Pliny, *ep.* 8. 23)
15. L. Junius Aurelius Neratius Gallus Fulvius Macer — [leg. III Aug.(?)] , XI Cl. (VI 1433, cf. *PIR*[2] J 732)
16. L. Licinius C[. . .] — V Mac., *leg. inc.* (VI 1442)
17. L. Marius Maximus — XXII Pr., III It. (*ILS* 2935)
18. L. Minicius Natalis jr. — I Ad., XI Cl., XIV Gem. (*ILS* 1061 etc.; p. 244 below)
19. Salvius Nenolaus Campanianus cet. — V Mac., I Ad. (III 6755)
20. L. Neratius Proculus — VII Gem., VIII Aug. (*ILS* 1076)
21. A. Platorius Nepos Calpurnianus Marcellus — XIII Gem., VII Cl. (*BCR* 1940, 180)
22. P. Plotius Romanus — I Min., II Ad. (*ILS* 1135)
23. Sex. Quintilius Valerius Maximus — I It., XIII Gem. (XIV 2609)
24. M. Ulpius Traianus — Rhineland, Syria (Pliny, *Pan.* 14-15)
25. Q. Voconius Saxa Fidus — III Cyr., *leg. inc.* (*ILS* 8828)
26. *ignotus* — *leg. inc.*, XIV Gem. (*AE* 1957. 161)
27. *ignotus* — IV Scyth., V Mac. (*ILS* 1553)
28. *ignotus* — IX, XXI[. . .] (XI 5173; p. 267 below)
29. *ignotus* — *leg. inc.*, XII Fulm. (XII 1861)
30. *ignotus* — XXII Pr., XXX U.V. (XIV 4178b)
(?)31. *ignotus* — [*trib. mil. bi*]*s leg. V*[. . .] (*AE* 1922. 38)
(?)32. Haterius Latronianus — *leg. inc.*, II Ad. (*RE* Supp. 15 (1978) 111 f.)
(?)33. P. Marc[. . .] Gallus — X Gem., I Min. (*AE* 1929. 159; perhaps equestrian)
(?)34. P. Metilius Secundus — X Gem., *leg. inc.* (*ILS* 1053, revised by R. Syme, *Gnomon* 29 (1957) 522 = *Danubian Papers* (1971) 186)

1. M. Caecilius Rufinus Marianus IV Fl. (Aquincum) (*ILS* 3638)–
   Q. Caecilius Rufinus Crepereianus governor of Pannonia inf. (*ILS* 3109).
2. L. Calpurnius Proculus XIII Gem. (*IGR* III 180)–P. Calpurnius Proculus governor of Dacia sup. (III 1007).
3. P. Cassius Dexter III Aug. (*ILS* 1050)–P. Cassius Secundus leg. leg. III Aug. (*ILS* 5977, etc.).
4. L. Cassius Pius Marcellinus II Ad. (III 13371), *q. des.* in 204 and hence hardly the same as L. Cassius Marcellinus governor of Pannonia inf. (*ILS* 3925) before *c.* 214.
5. C. Curtius Rufinus XIII Gem. (III 1459)–C. Curtius Justus governor of Dacia sup. (III 1458; p. 000 below).
6. C. Luxilius Sabinus Egnatius Proculus IV Fl. (*ILS* 1187)–Egnatius Marinianus governor of Moesia sup. (*JÖAI* 6 (1903) Bbl. 14).
7. [J]ul. Maximi[a]nus (V. Mac.) (*ILS* 3023)–C. Julius Maximinus governor of III Daciae (III 1127).
8. P. Manilius Vopiscus . . . Julius Quadratus Bassus IV Scyth. (*ILS* 1044)–C. Antius A. Julius Quadratus governor of Syria (*ILS* 8819).
9. C. Julius Severus IV Scyth. (*ILS* 8829)–C. Julius Severus leg. leg. IV Scyth. and acting governor of Syria (*ILS* 8826).
10. Cn. Julius Verus X Fret. (*ILS* 1057; p. 118 below)–Sex. Julius Severus governor of Judaea (*ILS* 1056; p. 109 below).
11. L. Minicius Natalis jr. XIV Gem. (*ILS* 1029 etc.; p. 244 below) –L. Minicius Natalis governor of Pannonia sup. (*ILS* 1029 etc.).
12. L. Neratius Marcellus XII Fulm. (*ILS* 1032; p. 89 below)–M. Hirrius Fronto Neratius Pansa commander of task-force in Armenia (*AE* 1968. 145).
13. Ti. Pontius Pontianus II Ad. (III 3481), perhaps identical with Pontius Pontianus governor of Pannonia inf. (III 3707).
14. C. Salvius Vitellianus V Mac. (IX 6365, cf. *ILS* 1012)–C. Salvius Liberalis leg. leg. V Mac. (*ILS* 1011; p. 211 below).
15. L. Dasumius Tullius Tuscus IV Fl. (*ILS* 1081)–P. Tullius Varro governor of Moesia sup. (*ILS* 1047; p. 239 below).
16. M. Valerius Florus III Aug. (XIII 3162)–M. Valerius Senecio governor of Numidia (*ILS* 2636 etc.).[23]

It must be assumed that army commanders were often able to appoint

[23] More cases could no doubt be found. This slightly extends the list given by Ritterling, *JÖAI* 10 (1907) 310 n. 19.

sons or nephews; otherwise they could have relied heavily on recommendations from their friends. There is no need to suppose that the emperors had to take the initiative in appointing tribunes of senatorial rank, any more than they did with equestrian officers.[24]

Very few cases are known of men returning subsequently to command the legion in which they had served as tribune, or even to the same province. Nor did many men govern provinces in the armies of which they had held tribunates.[25]

(b) THE QUAESTORSHIP

Twenty[1] quaestors were elected[2] each year, which made it possible for all the *XXviri* to proceed to this office in due course. The minimum age, reduced from thirty to twenty-five by Augustus, was evidently modified further to twenty-four,[3] on the principle that 'annus . . . vicesimus quintus coeptus pro pleno habetur'.[4] Any shortfall caused by premature death or loss of property incurred by any of the *vigintiviri* in the interval of about six years could be made good by the addition of late entrants.[5] Ten of the quaestors were allocated by lot to the proconsuls of the senatorial provinces.[6] Although the quaestors entered office on 5 December,[7] the provincial quaestors must be assumed to have spent several months at Rome before accompanying their proconsuls to their provinces to enter office there on 1 July.[8] They will

[24] See E. Birley, *Roman Britain and the Roman Army* 141 ff.

[25] See further pp. 29 ff. below, on the avoidance of specialization.

[1] Tacitus (*Ann.* 11. 22. 5) implies, although he does not state, that Augustus reverted to the Sullan figure of 20, doubled by Caesar in 45 BC (Dio 42. 47. 2; Suet. *D. Jul.* 41. 1).

[2] See A. N. Sherwin-White, *Letters of Pliny*, 119 f. on *ep.* 1. 14. 7 etc., who notes that election to the lesser magistracies was still actively contested in Pliny's day.

[3] Morris, *Listy fil.* 87 (1964) 317.

[4] Ulpian, in *Digest* 50. 4. 8.

[5] Cf. e.g. M. Statius Priscus (pp. 125 below), who became quaestor after service as an equestrian officer and procurator.

[6] For the proconsular provinces, see p. 17, n. 12 below. It is still often stated that Sicily had two quaestors, as it had had in Cicero's day: thus e.g. M. Cébeillac, *Les quaestores* 6; Eck, *ANRW* II. 1 (1974) 177 f. Both cite T. Mommsen, *Staatsrecht* II³ 533, although Eck modifies Mommsen's figure of twelve provincial quaestors to eleven. Yet Mommsen, in n. 2 on p. 533 merely refers to J. Marquardt, and the latter, in his *Römische Staatsverwaltung* I² (1886) 244, is agnostic on the question: 'ob diese Einrichtung unter den Kaisern fortdauerte, ist unbekannt'. It is, indeed, impossible to accept that under the principate the junior proconsul of Sicily was served by two quaestors, while the consular proconsuls of Asia and Africa had only one each.

[7] Mommsen, *Staatsrecht* I³ 606.

[8] Mommsen, *Staatsrecht* II³ 254 ff. on the proconsular year, 258 f. on the provincial quaestors. Thus in most cases quaestors would be attached to one proconsul each, and there is no need to assume that Tacitus (*Agr.* 6. 2), by referring only to Salvius Titianus as Agricola's chief in Asia, is deliberately omitting reference to the more upright Antistius Vetus. Occa-

have had to provide games in late December, along with the other quaestors.[9] Of those who remained at Rome throughout their term of office, some had the title *quaestor urbanus*. There were two such quaestors under the Republic, whose duties included supervision of the *aerarium Saturni*, and it is generally assumed that the number remained constant.[10] This is in fact far from certain, since, apart from the period 44-56,[11] the quaestors lost their role at the *aerarium* under the principate. The emperor himself had quaestors assigned to him, whose duties included the reading of speeches in the senate. It is often stated that there were two of these *quaestores Caesaris* or *quaestores Augusti* each year,[12] but all that is certain is that there was more than one.[13] The title *quaestor Augusti* virtually disappears after the time of Antoninus Pius.[14] In the meantime, from the early second century, the title *quaestor candidatus Caesaris* came into use, and continued into the third century; by the end of the principate the name of the emperor was omitted. In spite of energetic attempts to solve the problem, it is far from clear whether the *quaestores Augusti* and *quaestores candidati* represented the same group, with a change of titulature.[15] Finally, each consul had two quaestors assigned to him from 38 BC onwards.[16]

Patricians were evidently guaranteed election as *quaestor Augusti* or

---

sionally, special circumstances may have caused a quaestor to be retained in office, and there is one case of a man who served three proconsuls (*PIR*[2] J 391).

[9] Mommsen, *Staatsrecht* II[3] 534.

[10] Most recently discussed in full by G. Wesener, *RE* 24 (1963) 811 ff.

[11] See p. 354 below, on L. Coiedius Candidus.

[12] Thus Wesener, *RE* 24 (1963) 818; Cébeillac, *Les quaestores* 6, and *passim*.

[13] From Pliny's phrase in *ep.* 7. 16. 2, 'simul quaestores Caesaris fuimus'; and from *Digest* 1. 13. 1. 2, 4, on which see n. 15 below.

[14] Except for the enigmatic mention in the *Acta* of the Secular Games of 204, *ILS* 5050a etc. (Fulvius Fuscus Granianus).

[15] The evidence is discussed at length by Cébeillac, *Les quaestores*. But she does not convince me that there need have been a distinction. *Quaestor Aug.* disappears after the reign of Pius (except for the man in *ILS* 5050a, of AD 204, perhaps an archaizing titulature), and *quaestor candidatus* begins to appear under Trajan. Why not assume that only a change of titulature is involved, as implied by *Digest* 1. 13. 1. 2, 4, where the 'quaestores ... candidati principis ... qui epistulas eius in senatu legunt' look like *quaestores Augusti*, referred to by Ulpian as *candidati*? Above all, Cébeillac fails to discuss the fact that the younger L. Minicius Natalis (p. 244 below) is called *quaestor candidatus divi Hadriani* in *ILS* 1061 but *q. Aug.* in *ILS* 1029, while on p. 207 her interpretation of a similar variation in the case of Q. Sosius Priscus (*cos. ord.* 169), *quaestori candidato Augg.* in *ILS* 1104, *quaestori Aug.* in X 3724, seems forced. See also Eck, *ANRW* II. 1 (1974) 179 n. 88, who makes this point (without having been able to consult Cébeillac).

[16] Dio 48. 43. 1; cf. Pliny, *ep.* 4. 15 etc. There are a few epigraphic instances, notably *ILS* 412 (Didius Julianus): [*quaes*]*t*[*o*]*ri consulum*. Since the other quaestorships (in Italy) were done away with in the early principate (*RE* 24 (1963) 819), it must be assumed that quaestors who served at Rome and were not *q. urb.* or imperial quaestors, were attached to the consuls. Hence, no doubt, more than two had this function each year.

quaestor candidatus. Hence those plebeians who obtained this distinction were clearly marked out for imperial favour.[17] It should be noted, however, that not many cases can be found of men who were *candidatus* for the tribunate of the plebs and praetorship as well as for the quaestorship.

(c) FROM QUAESTORSHIP TO PRAETORSHIP

Between quaestorship and praetorship there seems to have been a statutory five-year interval, meaning that a man could expect to be elected praetor in his thirtieth year.[1] A few cases are known of men who held a second quaestorship, presumably when a sudden death created a vacancy.[2] By contrast, particularly from the later second century onwards, cases are found of men being *adlecti inter quaestorios*, allowing them to omit holding the office at all.[3] Patricians were of course ineligible to serve as *tribunus plebis* or *aedilis plebis*; and they were also exempted from the other post intermediate between quaestorship and praetorship, that of *aedilis curulis*.[4] Under the Julio-Claudians it was not uncommon for men to command legions before the praetorship, whether as ex-quaestors or as ex-tribunes or ex-aediles. But this practice virtually died out from the beginning of the Flavian period.[5] One senatorial post was available to be filled by an ex-quaestor, the supervision of the proceedings of the senate, the *acta senatus*. The earliest epigraphic record is of Hadrianic date.[6] Young senators or future senators, before or after the quaestorship could serve as *VIvir equitum Romanorum* at the annual review of the knights; the function can only have been honorific, but it was thought to be worth recording by over a

---

[17] This point was stressed by Brassloff, *Hermes* 39 (1904) 618 ff. and *JÖAI* 8 (1905) 60 ff. There are two cases of *quaestores candidati* who served in a province rather than at Rome, Sex. Julius Severus (p. 106 below) and Ti. Claudius Saethida Caelianus (*ILS* 1086). The case of A. Platorius Nepos is uncertain (p. 102 below). The fact that Julius Severus is described as *candidatus* on one inscription but not on another (p. 106 below) does, however, make one wonder whether this distinction may have been omitted in some other cases.

[1] This is generally inferred from Dio 52. 20. 1–2; see Morris, *Listy fil.* 87 (1964) 316 f.

[2] See the list in A. R. Birley, *H-A-C 1968/9* (1970) 69 n. 47: seven cases, including the future emperor Septimius Severus; and add XI 6165, An. Satr[. . .] Sal[. . .] (p. 282 below).

[3] See the list in Alföldy, *H-A-C 1966/7* (1968) 33 ff. (fourteen cases).

[4] See e.g. M. Hammond, *The Antonine Monarchy* (1959) 267 f. n. 19.

[5] See e.g. Alföldy, *Legionslegaten* 103 ff. The latest case of a man commanding a legion before the praetorship seems to be A. Larcius Priscus in the exceptional circumstances of the year 97 (p. 236 below).

[6] viz. L. Neratius Marcellus (pp. 87 f. below). Tacitus (*Ann.* 5. 4. 1) records a case under Tiberius. See also A. Stein, *Protokolle des römischen Senates* (1904).

hundred senators.[7] More serious occupation was provided by the post of *legatus* to a proconsul. Fourteen such *legati* were evidently required every year and although the majority of known cases were men of praetorian rank, a fair number of ex-quaestors and ex-tribunes are found among them.[8]

There were ten tribunes and six aediles in office each year. Of the twenty ex-quaestors from two years earlier, one or two must have failed to secure election, since there can hardly have been as many as four patricians entering the senate every year.[9] Some of those who failed to secure election may have been allowed to omit the office by *adlectio inter tribunicios* or *aedilicios*.[10] At the same time, the emperor might confer this status on equestrians who had not been through the earlier stages.[11] The most favoured in each year were elected with the emperor's backing, as *candidatus Caesaris*. As for the duties of these officials, they were increasingly ornamental rather than functional.[12] After another year's interval, election to the praetorship was the next stage. The number of posts as praetor rose from twelve in AD 14 to eighteen at the end of the first century AD.[13] Early deaths or withdrawal from public life, on the one hand, combined with the return to competition of patricians and the addition of *adlecti* on the other, may well have meant that few who sought office would fail to obtain it. Once again, the most favoured, including all the patricians, were *candidati Caesaris*. Equally, there are a fair number of cases of men already in the senate being allowed to omit the praetorship by adlection, as well as of new men being brought in for the first time with the rank of ex-praetor.[14]

(d) THE PRAETORIAN CAREER

After the praetorship the patricians could look forward to the consulship at thirty-one or thirty-two or a little later, and hence were virtually

---

[7] See Eck, *ANRW* II. 1 (1974) 177, who also discusses the *praefecti feriarum Latinarum*. For examples of *VIviri* who later served in Britain, see Sex. Julius Severus (p. 108 below) and C. Curtius Justus (p. 252 below).

[8] See Eck, *Senatoren* 38 ff.

[9] Eck, *ANRW* II. 1 (1974) 179 f.

[10] Eck, *ANRW* II. 1 (1974) 180 n. 90, cites two cases. One of these, A. Claudius Charax, may in fact be misleading, see p. 251 below. Note also C. Curtius Justus (p. 252 below).

[11] Eck, *ANRW* II. 1 (1974) 180. Cf. e.g. C. Salvius Liberalis (p. 211 below).

[12] See Hammond, *Antonine Monarchy* 294 f. Note how Julius Agricola spent his tribunate of the plebs (p. 75 n. 19 below).

[13] Hammond, *Antonine Monarchy* 292 ff., 307 ff.

[14] Eck, *ANRW* II. 1 (1974) 180 f.

excluded from tenure of any intervening posts.[1] There were a great many of these, reserved for most of the principate for ex-praetors, with occasional exceptions.[2] It is convenient to list them in separate categories:

at Rome

2 *praefecti frumenti dandi*[3]
3 *praefecti aerarii militaris*
2 *praefecti aerarii Saturni*[4]

in Italy

9 *curatores viarum*[5]
uncertain number of *praefecti alimentorum* (a post sometimes held in conjunction with a *cura viae*)[6]
4–5 *iuridici*[7]

in the provinces

(a) *imperial*
24 *legati legionum*[8]
at first 5, then 8, then 12, finally 14 *legati Augusti pro praetore*[9]

---

[1] See Brassloff, *Wien. Stud.* 29 (1907) 321 ff.; Groag, *Strena Buliciana* (1924) 253 ff.; Eck, *ANRW* II. 1 (1974) 218 f., who notes the future emperor Trajan, legate of VII Gemina as a praetorian, as an exception. There are not many others.

[2] Note e.g. Q. Pompeius Falco as a consular *curator viae*, p. 99 below.

[3] The post was created by Augustus in 22 BC for two ex-praetors who had been praetor not less than five years earlier (Dio 54. 1. 4); modified in 18 BC when, Dio records, 54. 17. 1, that four were chosen annually from those who had been praetor three years before. It is generally assumed that the number must have been reduced later: Eck, *ANRW* II. 1 (1974) 102 f., favours two. Further, it is often believed that the post was dispensed with between the time of Claudius and Nerva; thus e.g. W. Ensslin, *RE* 22. 2 (1954) 1306 ff. But see Syme, *JRS* 67 (1977) 49, redating a career. On the *praefecti* and *curatores Miniciae* of the late second and early third centuries, see Pflaum, *Bonner Jahrb.* 163 (1963) 232 ff.

[4] M. Corbier, *L'aerarium*, *passim*.

[5] Eck, *Organisation Italiens* 25 ff.

[6] Eck, op. cit. 146 ff., esp. 166 ff.

[7] Eck, op. cit. 249 ff. The post was not created until the 160s AD.

[8] The number of legateships varied only slightly: AD 14: 23 (25 legions, of which two were commanded by *praefecti* in Egypt); AD 70: 25 (29 legions, less two in Egypt, one each in Numidia and Judaea, commanded by provincial governors); AD 117: 24 (30 legions, less two in Egypt, one each in Numidia, Judaea, Arabia and Pannonia inferior); AD 180: 24 (30 legions, less one in Egypt, and one each in Numidia, Arabia, Pannonia inferior, Raetia, and Noricum); AD 217: 23 (33 legions, less one in Egypt, two in Mesopotamia, and one at Alba commanded by *praefecti*, and one each in Numidia, Arabia, Raetia, Noricum, Syria Phoenice, and Britannia inferior commanded by governors).

See the still useful conspectus given by Ritterling, *RE* 12. 2 (1925) 1265 ff., which naturally requires some correction in a few instances.

[9] See Syme, *JRS* 48 (1958); Eck, *Senatoren* 1 ff. The provinces of the emperor governed by ex-praetors were as follows: AD 14: Lusitania, Aquitania, Lugdunensis, Belgica, Galatia; AD 38:

2 *iuridici* (Tarraconensis, Britain; from *c.*70-114 a third, in Galatia-Cappadocia)[10]

(b) *senatorial*
14 *legati pro praetore*[11]
8 proconsuls.[12]

in Italy and the provinces
curatores civitatium (numbers unknown but variable)[13]
There were in addition a variety of special posts, created on an *ad hoc* basis, not least in time of war.[14]

Simple arithmetic makes it obvious that in practice about half of all the ex-praetors would be required to command a legion. Some held the post more or less immediately after being praetor, others after one or more intervening posts. But with some twenty-four legions that needed *legati Augusti* and only eighteen praetors each year, some of whom would be virtually excluded by their patrician status and others by ill health if not death, and with an average tenure of the post not exceeding three years, probably somewhat less, the logic was inescapable.[15] It is worth observing that few cases are known of men who commanded legions in which they had previously served as military tribune, or even legions in the same army as that in which they had held a tribunate (see

---

legio III Augusta was added as a *de facto* province, eventually Numidia (total 6); AD 45: Lycia was added (total 7); AD 70: Galatia was joined to Cappadocia until *c.* 113; Judaea and Cilicia were added (total 8); AD 106: Arabia and Pannonia inferior were added (total 10); under Trajan Thrace and Galatia were added (total 12); under Hadrian Judaea was made consular but Dacia superior was added, leaving the total unchanged; under M. Aurelius Raetia and Noricum were added and Lycia-Pamphylia was transferred to proconsuls (total 13); under Severus Syria Phoenice was added (total 14); under Caracalla Britannia inferior was added but Pannonia inferior received a consular governor, leaving the total unchanged at 14.

The above figures omit the temporary presence of Dalmatia and Asturia-Callaecia as praetorian imperial provinces.

[10] See Eck, *Senatoren* 3; Alföldy, *Fasti Hispanienses* 236 ff.

[11] viz. one each for the eight provinces listed in the next note and three each in the provinces of Africa and Asia (Dio 53. 14. 7). See further B. E. Thomasson, *Statthalter Nordafrikas* I. 58 ff.; Eck, *Ep. Stud.* 9 (1972) 24 ff., who shows that most *legati* were ex-praetors.

[12] See Eck, *Zephyrus* 23-4 (1972-3) 233 ff. Seven provinces were almost without exception governed by praetorian proconsuls, at any rate after the Julio-Claudian period: Achaia, Baetica, Crete-Cyrene, Cyprus, Macedonia, Narbonensis, Sicily. The eighth place was filled at first by Pontus-Bithynia and later by Lycia-Pamphylia. Sardinia, for brief periods, was substituted first for Achaia and later for Baetica.

[13] See Eck, *Organisation Italiens* 190 ff. The status of the *curator reipublicae* was of course by no means uniform. Many *curatores* were equestrian.

[14] e.g. the charge of recruitment, as in the case of Julius Agricola in AD 69 (pp. 76 f. below), or a military command such as that of Petillius Cerialis at the same time (p. 68) or of Lollius Urbicus in the Jewish war under Hadrian (pp. 113 f. below).

[15] Alföldy, *Bonner Jahrb.* 169 (1969) 237 f., calculates that in practice at least half of all ex-praetors would be needed; similarly Eck, *ANRW* II. 1 (1974) 190.

Table 3

*Tribunate and legionary command in the same army**

		trib. leg.	leg. leg.	
1.	L. Aemilius Karus(?)	IX Hisp.	XXX U. V.	(p. 275 below)
2.	M. Fabius Fabullus	XIV Gem.	XIV Gem.	(*ILS* 996)
3.	M. Fabius Magnus Valerianus	XI Cl.	I It.	(*ILS* 1138)
4.	Cn. Julius Agricola	*leg. Brit.*	XX V. V.	(pp. 74 f. below)
5.	A. Julius Pompilius Piso	XIII Gem.	XIII Gem.	(*ILS* 1111; *BCTH* 1893, 153)
6.	C. Julius Proculus	IV Scyth.	VI Ferr.	(*ILS* 1040)
7.	Sex. Julius Severus	XIV Gem.	XIV Gem.	(p. 108 below)
8.	M. Maecius Celer(?)	*leg. Syr.*(?)	*leg. Syr.*	(Stat. *Silv.* 3. *pr.* and 3. 2. 104 ff., 120 ff.; but the tribunate might have been in Judaea)
9.	L. Marius Perpetuus	IV Scyth.	XVI Fl.	(*ILS* 1165)
10.	Q. Petronius Melior	I Min.	XXX U. V.	(*ILS* 1180)
11.	M. Pontius Laelianus	VI Vic.	I Min.	(p. 273 below)
12.	C. Rutilius Gallicus	XIII Gem.	XV Apoll.	(*ILS* 9499)
13.	P. Tullius Varro	XVI Fl.	XII Fulm.	(p. 239 below)
14.	*ignotus*(?)	X. Gem.	I Ad.	(X 336)

* The whereabouts of IX Hispana when no. 1 served in it is uncertain. No. 11 moved with VI Victrix from Germany to Britain. The date of no. 14 is unknown, but since he was apparently quaestorian legate of I Ad., it is probable that he served in X Gemina before it went to Pannonia superior. Note that C. Minicius Fundanus served in XII Fulminata as tribune in Cappadocia, but was legate of XV Apollinaris when it was still in Pannonia: Syme, *Tacitus* n. 3. L. Julius Apronius . . . Salamallianus was tribune of X Gemina in Upper Pannonia, but legate of I Adiutrix after Caracalla's boundary changes had allocated that legion to Lower Pannonia (*PIR*[2] J 161). C. Popilius Carus Pedo served in III Cyrenaica during the Jewish war, but withdrew from the command of the legion X Fretensis, in the province of Syria Palaestina, to which he was appointed (*ILS* 1071). Q. Voconius Saxa Fidus was tribune of III Cyrenaica under Hadrian and legate of IV Scyth. at the beginning of the reign of Pius (*ILS* 8828); however, it is extremely doubtful whether III Cyr. was ever stationed in Syria.

Table 3). The appointment seems not to have been controlled or influenced by the provincial governor: only a handful of examples can be found of legionary commanders who were close kinsmen of their governor (see Table 4). Some thirty men are known who were legate of more than one legion: where evidence is available, special circumstances can be seen to have brought about the iterated command:

1. Q. Antistius Adventus: VI Ferr., II Ad. (p. 130 below).
2. L. Attius Macro: VII Gem., I Ad. (*ILS* 2290), III 4356 = 11077; identity doubted by Syme, *Historia* 14 (1965) 352 = *Danubian Papers* (1971) 235).
3. Q. Aurelius Polus Terentianus: XXII Pr., II Aug. (p. 262 below).
4. Q. Camurius Numisius Junior: *leg. inc.*, VI Vic. (p. 255 below).

Table 4
Legionary commanders serving under close kinsmen *

	legion	kinsman
1. Annius Vinicianus (*pro legato*)	V Mac.	Cn. Domitius Corbulo (Tac. *Ann.* 15. 28. 2; Dio 62. 23. 6)
2. Titus	XV Apoll.	Vespasian (pp. 228, 269 below)
3. Q. Lollianus Plautius Avitus	VII Gem.	Q. Hedius Rufus Lollianus Gentianus (*ILS* 1145, 1155)
4. Junius Blaesus(?)	*leg. Afr.*(?)	Q. Junius Blaesus (Tac. *Ann.* 3. 74. 2)
5. P. Mummius Sisenna Rutilianus	VI Vic.	P. Mummius Sisenna (pp. 110, 249 below)
6. Pomponius Bassus(?)	*leg. Moes.*	Pomponius Bassus (Dio 78. 21. 3)

* Dio stresses that no. 1 was only permitted to serve under his father-in-law because they were trusted by Nero; Tacitus stresses that he was not yet a senator and hence was *pro legato*—in other words, he presumably went east as *tr. laticl.* No. 4 ought to have been a *legatus*, if not *legatus legionis*, if he was the same son as the one who had been tribune eight years earlier, in AD 14 (Tac. *Ann.* 1. 29, 29). But he had a brother (*Ann.* 6. 40. 2). No. 6 is very doubtful: H. Dessau, *PIR*[1] S 708 took Dio to mean that another man, not the younger Bassus, was *leg. leg.*; but see Stein, *Moesien* 55. There is no need to believe that the younger C. Julius Severus commanded XXX Ulpia Victrix while his father governed Germania inferior: see Alföldy, *Konsulat* 227, 302, who places his command of the legion several years later. E. Birley's statement, *Carnuntum Jahrb.* 1957. 5 f., that 'Es gibt keine Beweise, welche die Vermutung zulassen, dass der Statthalter irgendein Mitbestimmungsrecht bei der Ernennung seiner Legionslegaten hatte' is therefore largely borne out by these figures. For the kind of disagreements between governor and legionary legates to which he refers on p. 6, cf. the case of Trebellius Maximus (p. 61 below).

5. Ti. Claudius Claudianus: XIII Gem., V Mac. (*simul*), I Ad. (*ILS* 1147).

6. M. Claudius Fronto: XI Cl., I Min. (*ILS* 1097).

7. Ti. Claudius Quartinus: II Trai., III Cyr. (pp. 111 f. below).

8. L. Cossonius Gallus: I It., II Trai. (*ILS* 1038).

9. Domitius Antigonus: V Mac., XXII Pr. (*AE* 1966. 262).

10. M. Domitius Valerianus: XII Fulm., VII Cl. (*AE* 1957. 44).

11. M. Fabius Fabullus: XIII Gem., V Alaud. (Tac. *Hist.* 3. 14, *ILS* 996).

12. T. Flavius Secundus Philippianus: XIV Gem., I Min. (*ILS* 1152).

13. T. Julius Maximus Manlianus: I Ad., IV Fl. (*ILS* 1016).

14. A. Julius Pompilius Piso: XIII Gem., IV Fl. (*ILS* 1111).

15. A. Larcius Priscus: IV Scyth., II Aug. (p. 236 below).

16. C. Manlius Valens: XX V.V.(?), I It. (p. 230 below).

17. Martius Macer: IV Scyth., V Mac. (*simul*) (*ILS* 969).

18. Q. Petronius Melior: VIII Aug., XXX U. V. (*ILS* 1180).

19. Cn. Petronius Probatus: XIV Gem., VIII Aug. (*ILS* 1179).

20. Serenus: IV Fl., XXII Pr. (*AE* 1965. 243).

21. Q. Servaeus Fuscus Cornelianus: XIV Gem., I It. (*ILS* 8978)

22. P. Tullius Varro: XII Fulm., VI Vic. (p. 000 below).

23. M. Valerius Maximianus: I Ad., II Ad., V Mac., I It., XIII Gem.
    (*AE* 1956. 124).

24. C. Vettius Sabinianus: III It., XIV Gem. (*AE* 1920. 45).

25. *ignotus*: [. . .] p. f., [. . .] p. f. (VI 1566).

26. *ignotus*: *leg. inc.*, XV Apol. (XIV 2933).

27. *ignotus*: [. . .] tricis, XI Cl. (XIV 3518).

28. *ignotus*: XVI Fl., VI Ferr. (*ILS* 1020).

29. *ignotus*: XVI Fl., VI Ferr. (*IGR* III 558).

30. *ignotus*: leg. inc., leg. inc. (*AE* 1952. 168).

31. *ignotus*: IV Fl., III [. . .] (*BCH* 51 (1927) 272).

32. *ignotus*: [. . .] Victr., leg. inc. (*AE* 1973. 133; p. 217 below).

33(?). *ignotus*: *leg. inc.*(?), X[. . .] (XIII 2662).[16]

Although there are cases from the Julio-Claudian period where men seem to have reached the consulship with no other office after their legion, this later became virtually impossible.[17] However, a number of careers fall into a category that may be characterized as the 'rapid path' to the consulship, namely the legionary command and an imperial province, or its equivalent, as the only two significant posts between praetorship and consulship,[18] Of course, it is only rarely that there is

[16] See the remarks of Syme, *Laureae Aquincenses* 1 (1938) 283 = *Danubian Papers* (1971) 98 f.; id., *Historia* 14 (1965) 345 f. = *Danubian Papers* 228; E. Birley, *Carnuntum Jahrb.* 1957. 6; and above all Alföldy, *Legionslegaten* 77 ff. The list above differs only slightly from that furnished by Alföldy 79 n. 353, together with his German cases. I omit L. Varius Ambibulus, whom he includes hesitantly, following Pflaum, *Bonner Jahrb.* 163 (1963) 224 ff. See *Legionslegaten* 40 ff. on *AE* 1911. 142; but it is far more probable, given the offices recorded, that this is the person known from X 3872, and that he was legate of III, not VIII, Aug. I add nos. 17, 26, 31, 33. No. 32 is now better recorded than in *EE* IX 774. No. 3 is interpreted differently. As Alföldy shows, developing the views of Syme and E. Birley, in many cases the evidence explains the iterated commands: nos. 11 and 16 commanded their second legion in AD 69; the crisis of 97 brought a premature command for no. 15 and a second for no. 28; the second Dacian war explains no. 13, Trajan's Parthian war no. 8; the wars of M. Aurelius' reign nos. 1, 6, 14, 23, 24; those of 193-7 nos. 5 and 12; wars in Britain nos. 3 and 4; and the transfer of VI Victrix to Britain no. 22.

[17] Early examples include T. Flavius Sabinus and his brother Vespasian, pp. 224 ff. below. There may have been a few patricians in this category, such as the future emperor Trajan, legate of VII Gemina in 89, *cos. ord.* 91; Q. Hedius Rufus Lollianus Gentianus is not quite comparable, as he was *curator reipublicae* between legionary command and suffect consulship: Alföldy, *Fasti Hispanienses* 47 f., 118 f. It is still a little doubtful whether Pertinax really held no praetorian post other than the command of I Adiutrix before becoming consul in 175 (p. 144 below); but C. Avidius Cassius looks another probable case (Alföldy, *Konsulat* 181 f.).

[18] See e.g. E. Birley, *PBA* 39 (1953) 203, and Syme, *Tacitus* 655, for this category. Campbell, *JRS* 65 (1975) 11 ff. may be right to reject the label *viri militares* used by these two scholars, and others, to describe men who became consul 'after only two posts, viz. a legionary command and a praetorian province'; and he is certainly justified in treating with scepticism some attempts made to detect 'promotion-patterns'. However, he uses illegitimate arguments to

direct evidence of the chronology and 'rapid' may be an inappropriate label in many cases—there may have been intervals of unemployment,[19] or one or both of the two posts in question may have been held for an unusually long period.[20] But, in general, the praetorian imperial provinces were probably given new governors every three years or a little less,[21] and if the legionary command had lasted for a similar period, a man in this category might gain the *fasces* about eight years after being praetor. If he had already secured one or two years' advantage in holding the republican magistracies through the application of the *ius liberorum*, he might be consul at the age of thirty-six,[22] five years earlier than the prescribed forty-second year.[23] But such men were no doubt in a small minority. Most senators held well over two posts, including, generally as the last one, a praetorian imperial province or its equivalent, between praetorship and consulship. But not all ex-praetors became consul.

The praetorian imperial provinces, only five in number at the time of Augustus' death, were gradually added to with the annexation of new territory and the change in status, or subdivision, of existing provinces.

demonstrate his claim that 'there are no clearly discernible patterns of promotion' (op. cit. 23). In his list of seventy-three senators (op. cit. 28 ff.; they should be reduced to seventy-two, since his no. 37, Cn. Julius Verus, is the same as his no. 72, '*Incertus*'—*ILS* 1057; see p. 121 below), he finds 'only . . . five [who] hold exactly the same combination of praetorian posts . . . a legionary command and a praetorian military province' (op. cit. 23 and n. 131). Even within these narrowly defined limits, he overlooks two cases, M. Nonius Macrinus (his no. 49), to whom he mistakenly attributes praetorian rank as *curator alvei Tiberis* (*ILS* 8830 etc.) and M. Statius Priscus (his no. 65) who surely held his command of *legio* XIII Gemina in conjunction with his governorship of Upper Dacia (p. 125 below). But given the very small number of one-legion provinces for most of his chosen period, AD 69–235, a total of only seven men is not surprising. More illuminating would be a list of the men who held legionary command and one other post, a praetorian governorship or its equivalent; and one could legitimately add, further, cases of men who commanded two legions or who held a brief special mission, recruiting troops or commanding detachments. More than twice as many then fall into the category as defined by Syme, as into Campbell's artificially restricted category (even with the addition to it of Nonius Macrinus and Statius Priscus). Note that Eck finds ten cases of the 'rapid path' to the consulship, within the period 69–138, where the first post was the legionary command, *ANRW* II. 1 (1974) 184 f.

[19] This is of course recommended in the speech of Maecenas in Dio 52. 20. 4, where the reference seems to be ex-praetors, who ought to be made to wait for some time before assuming a legionary command.

[20] Sex. Julius Severus, governor of Upper Dacia from 120 until 126 if not 127, and consul in the latter year, might conceivably have had ten years or even a little more between his praetorship and consulship, even though his only other post was a legionary command (p. 108 below). But such long tenures were unusual (see next note).

[21] This is a legitimate inference from Tac. *Agr.* 9. 5, on Agricola's Aquitanian governorship, 'minus triennium in ea legatione detentus'. Where there is full information in the provincial *Fasti*, this figure appears plausible, cf. e.g. the lists for Lycia-Pamphylia and Thrace in Eck, *Senatoren* 244, 249 f., and for the latter province in Alföldy, *Konsulat* 258 f.

[22] As was Julius Agricola (p. 77 below). Morris, *Listy fil.* 87 (1964) 325 ff., examines the ages of consuls. See also Syme, *Tacitus* (1958) 653 ff.

[23] p. 3 above.

An important development came about in AD 39, when Caligula removed the control of the legion III Augusta from the proconsul of Africa, thereby adding the *de facto* province of Numidia, in which the legionary legate acted as governor.[24] More provinces of this type were created later, Judaea in 70, Arabia and Pannonia inferior under Trajan, Dacia superior under Hadrian, Raetia and Noricum under M. Aurelius, Syria Phoenice under Severus, and Britannia inferior under Caracalla. In the meantime, however, Judaea (Syria Palaestina) became consular, under Hadrian, as did Dacia (Tres Daciae) under M. Aurelius, and Pannonia inferior under Caracalla, so that the total number of provinces of this type never exceeded six at any one time.[25] They had some special importance, as will be indicated below, but it is hard to detect any marked distinction in treatment between men who governed one-legion provinces and other governors of praetorian imperial provinces, or their equivalent, the prefects of the *aerarium Saturni*.

Only one case is known before the reign of M. Aurelius of a man governing two praetorian imperial provinces in succession, namely Q. Pompeius Falco, legate of Lycia–Pamphylia and then of Judaea in the first decade of the second century.[26] A number of cases appear during the 160s and 170s, which may readily be explained as resulting from war and plague. But the majority of cases appear in the period from Septimius Severus to Gallienus,[27] when other factors may have come into play.[28] For most of the principate, the governors of praetorian provinces and the prefects of the treasury of Saturn, whether in the so-called 'rapid' category or not, must be supposed to have gone on to the consulship at the conclusion of their term of office, if not during it, unless some special circumstances intervened.[29]

Less needs to be said about the other praetorian posts in the present context. The *curae viarum* evidently varied in importance: the *viae Aemilia*, *Appia*, and *Flaminia* were given to senior *praetorii*, whereas the other roads generally received curators who had been praetor not long before. No information is available about the normal duration of the post, nor indeed it is certain whether each road always had a

---

[24] Thomasson, *Statthalter Nordafrikas* I 10 ff.

[25] Thomasson, *Opuscula Romana* 9 (1973) 61 ff.

[26] p. 98 below.

[27] See Alföldy, *Fasti Hispanienses* 99 f., with list, to which *AE* 1969–70. 601 (L. Saevinius Proculus) should be added, as interpreted by Eck, *ZPE* 8 (1971) 71 ff., who also shows that the *ignotus* III 254 is not to be identified with C. Julius Saturninus. See now also Alföldy, *Konsulat* 200, 204 n. 285, 254; and on some of the cases, pp. 133 (Caerellius), 163 (C. Junius Faustinus), 175, cf. 34 (Q. Aradius Rufinus) below.

[28] p. 34 below.

[29] Eck, *ANRW* II. 1 (1974) 196 ff.; Alföldy, *Konsulat* 33 ff., esp. 54 ff.

curator.[30] At some periods the *cura viae* was combined with supervision of the *alimenta.*[31] The post of *iuridicus*, whether in the provinces or, from the time of M. Aurelius, in Italy as well, was relatively junior in status (with few exceptions) and was followed by other posts before the consulship.[32]

The *praefectura frumenti dandi* seems, on the evidence available, not to have been held by men with prospects of imperial service, and hence to have been a post of low importance.[33] Equally, only a handful of the known proconsular legates are subsequently recorded holding imperial consular commands. It is significant that almost all of the few who did had been legates to a proconsul of Africa or Asia. Since it appears that proconsuls could select their own legates, this is surely evidence that ambitious men might be prepared, in some cases, to lose a year in a senatorial province in the hope that the patronage of a consular proconsul would bring dividends in the future.[34] As mentioned earlier, the majority of known legates were praetorian, although a few ex-quaestors and former tribunes or aediles, even one or two ex-consuls, are also known to have held the post. Not many of the praetorian proconsuls later governed consular imperial provinces. The moment in a career. when the post was held differed markedly, although a five-year interval after the praetorship, laid down in 52 BC, was still in force. Some men even commanded legions after being proconsul, while others seem to have held the post after a praetorian imperial province, perhaps as an agreeable way of filling in time before becoming consul or obtaining consular employment.[35]

The two treasuries differed in status, as may be seen readily from the fact that a number of men, of whom the younger Pliny is the best-known example, served first in the *aerarium militare* and then in the *aerarium Saturni*. Clearly the three prefects of the military treasury were junior in status to the two prefects of Saturn. A minority of the prefects of the military treasury went straight on to the consulship with no further office intervening. Of those known to have become consul, more held another post between the *aerarium militare* and the *fasces*. By contrast, the prefects of the treasury of Saturn seem to have been

---

[30] Eck, *ANRW* II. 1 (1974) 191 f.; id., *Organisation Italiens* 80 ff. gives complete lists.
[31] Eck, *Organisation Italiens* 166 ff., with list 183 f.
[32] M. Corbier, *MEFR* 85 (1973) 609 ff.; Eck, *Organisation Italiens* 249 ff.
[33] Eck, *ANRW* II. 1 (1974) 192 f.; but see Syme, *JRS* 67 (1977) 38 ff., esp. 49, on the dating of L. Caesennius Sospes.
[34] Eck, *Ep. Stud.* 9 (1972) 24 ff.
[35] Eck, *Zephyrus* 23/4 (1972/3) 233 f.; id., *ANRW* II. 1 (1974) 201 ff.

assured of direct passage to the consulship. The tenure of both treasuries seems generally to have been for three years.[36]

Too few praetorian *praefecti alimentorum* are known for it to be possible to generalize about the status of the post.[37] By contrast very large numbers of *curatores* of towns, with senatorial rank, are recorded, over 100 in Italy alone. A number of leading figures who later governed consular imperial provinces are known to have held such posts. But it is not clear to what extent it was considered as an official position. In some cases it may have been something of a sinecure; and some senators may have enjoyed the title of *curator* of a town without making more than a token contribution to its affairs.[38]

(e) THE CONSULSHIP

Augustus created the suffect consulship as an institution.[1] In many of the years of his long principate one or both consuls resigned half-way through the year, to make it possible for a greater number of men to hold the *fasces*. But in the years when this occurred there were generally only one or two *consules suffecti*.[2] Under his successors the number of *suffecti* gradually increased. Under Nero there were often six or more consuls in a year, and this rose to seven or eight under the Flavians, and a little higher still in the second century.[3] In certain years of crisis, such as 69, 90, 98, and, most notoriously, 190, even more consuls held office: the twenty-five consuls of 190 were no doubt an all-time record.[4] But these exceptional years aside, it must normally have been possible for at most half of each year's intake of praetors to reach the consulship. Besides, the eighteen praetors would have had to compete with the *adlecti inter praetorios*, at any rate from the Flavian period onwards.[5] Any patricians among a batch of praetors presumably proceeded to become consul within two or three years or a little more. Most of the

---

[36] Eck, *ANRW* II. 1 (1974) 195 ff.; Corbier, *L'aerarium, passim*; Alföldy, *Konsulat*, esp. 54 ff.
[37] See Eck, *ZPE* 18 (1975) 89 ff.; id., *Organisation Italiens* 156 ff., 166 ff., 183 f.
[38] Eck, *Organisation Italiens* 190 ff.
[1] Following Caesar's precedent: *MRR* II 304 f., 317.
[2] A. Degrassi, *FC* 3 ff.
[3] Eck, *ANRW* II. 1 (1974) 205; Alföldy, *Konsulat*, esp. 11 ff., 56 ff.
[4] Dio 72. 12. 4. See F. Grosso, *La lotta politica al tempo di Commodo* (1964) 280 ff.
[5] On the *adlecti* see Eck, *ANRW* II. 1 (1974) 180 f., who correctly distinguishes between the men so honoured by Vespasian and others, and the cases found under M. Aurelius (and later). The former were men rewarded with an enhancement of rank for their support in civil war etc.; the latter were outstanding military commanders, made senators so that they could command legions during the Marcomannic wars (or, later, the civil wars of 193-7).

others would have had to serve for ten years or more in the hope of earning the still coveted supreme magistracy, with only a favoured few gaining it in a shorter period, when they were still in their thirties.[6]

Only two men each year could be *consul ordinarius*, and the opportunities for most candidates were reduced further by the occasions when the emperor or his kinsmen held office, or when highly distinguished senators, such as prefects of the city, held a second consulship, or even, in a very few cases, a third.[7] But as was pointed out long ago by E. Groag, the overwhelming majority of *consules ordinarii*, other than those in the categories already mentioned, were sons of former consuls. Patricians naturally figured largely among them.[8] The number of *novi homines* to hold the ordinary consulship seems to have diminished as the principate went on, hardly a surprising development considering the increasing numbers of descendants of consulars brought about by the steady rise in the numbers of *suffecti*. Hence it is of considerable importance to attempt to explain cases of new men who did achieve the ordinary consulship.[9] Most of them were doubtless men who had rendered some conspicuous service, although there may be a few whose elevation was the product of an imperial whim, as seems to have happened with C. Manlius Valens, the eighty-nine-year-old consul of AD 96.[10]

In contrast to the other republican magistracies, the consuls were never described as *candidati Caesaris*, no doubt because it would have seemed to conflict with the status of the supreme office of the Roman state. None the less, it became increasingly common from Flavian times onwards for the consulship to be held *in absentia*, by men governing provinces.[11] On the other hand, adlection *inter consulares* was rarely resorted to, at any rate before the third century.[12]

---

[6] Syme, *Tacitus* (1958) 653 ff.; Morris, *Listy fil.* 87 (1964) 325 ff.; ibid. 88 (1965) 22 ff.; Alföldy, *Konsulat* 33 ff., 327 ff., and *passim*.

[7] Alföldy, *Konsulat* 100 ff.

[8] Groag, *WS* 47 (1929) 143 ff.

[9] Cf. pp. 53, 126 below, on Q. Veranius (*ord.* 49) and M. Statius Priscus (*ord.* 159); the case of P. Mummius Sisenna (*ord.* 133) remains enigmatic, p. 110 below.

[10] p. 230 below. He may well have been a last-minute replacement for a *nobilis* whom Domitian had eliminated.

[11] Syme, *JRS* 48 (1958) 1 ff.; Alföldy, *Konsulat* 103 f.

[12] Barbieri, *L'Albo* 4.

(f) THE CONSULAR CAREER

The number of posts available for consulars was naturally smaller than for the ex-praetors:

at Rome

1 *curator alvei Tiberis*[1]
2 *curatores operum publicorum* etc.[2]
1 *curator aquarum*[3]
1 *praefectus urbi*[4]

in Italy

1 *praefectus alimentorum*[5]

in the provinces

(a) *imperial*
at first 7 *legati Augusti pro praetore*, increased gradually to 10 by *c.* AD 118, to 13 by *c.* AD 180 and to 14 *c.* AD 214.[6]

(b) *senatorial*
2 proconsuls (Africa and Asia)[7]
From time to time consulars held posts otherwise assigned to men of lower rank, for example as *curator viae*,[8] as proconsular legate,[9] or even as *curator civitatis*.[10] Further, special assignments were sometimes

---

[1] J. Le Gall, *Le Tibre, Fleuve de Rome dans l'antiquité* (1953) 137 ff., gives a list.
[2] A. E. Gordon, *Quintus Veranius, Consul A.D. 49* (1952) 279 ff., gives a list. See further Alföldy, *Konsulat* 289 ff.
[3] Eck, *ANRW* II. 1 (1974) 208 f.
[4] G. Vitucci, *Ricerche sulla prefectura urbi in età imperiale (sec. I–III)* (1956) 113 ff.; Syme, *Tacitus* (1958) 644 ff.; Alföldy, *Konsulat* 287 ff.
[5] Eck, *Organisation Italiens* 183 ff. It is not clear whether the post was regular or not; it may have been occupied only sporadically.
[6] The consular imperial provinces at different stages were as follows: AD 14: Hispania citerior, the two Germanies, Pannonia, Dalmatia, 'Moesia' (then part of a larger command), Syria; AD 43: Britain was added; AD 70: Cappadocia was added; *c.* AD 86: Moesia was divided into two consular provinces, making a total of ten; Dacia was a consular province from AD 106 to 117, but then became praetorian until *c.* AD 166. Hadrian added Judaea (Syria Palaestina), M. Aurelius added the reunited III Daciae and Pontus–Bithynia, and Caracalla reorganized the Pannonias, to make Inferior as well as Superior consular.
[7] Thomasson, *Statthalter Nordafrikas* I 10 ff.
[8] Eck, *ANRW* 191, cites a few examples from the Trajanic period.
[9] e.g. Vitellius (Suetonius, *Vit.* 5), Cn. Domitius Lucanus (*ILS* 990), P. Pactumeius Clemens (*ILS* 1067)—in each case the proconsul was a close kinsman and the province was Africa. See Eck, *Senatoren* 46 f.
[10] Eck, *Organisation Italiens* 196 n. 121.

given to consulars, recruiting troops,[11] or conducting a *census*,[12] or other *ad hoc* tasks; and senior senators of course served on the *consilium principis*.[13]

Of the consulars employed at Rome, the *curator aquarum* and prefect of the city were very senior men, whereas the curator of the Tiber and the curators of public buildings and works and of temples held office shortly after their consulship. The holders of these two latter posts seem, where information is available about their careers, to have been particularly favoured, proceeding to major imperial provinces after their urban *cura*.[14] These *curatores* evidently took up their posts a year or two after being consul,[15] and held office for at most two or three years, in the case of the Tiber curator,[16] probably only one year with the curators of public works.[17] In striking contrast to them were the curators of the aqueducts[18] and the prefects of the city,[19] whose term of office seems to have been indefinite, often for life. The *praefecti alimentorum*, at times apparently responsible for the *alimenta* throughout Italy, at times for particular districts only, were appointed at various stages in their careers; and it is not clear how long the appointment lasted.[20]

In theory, what made a province consular rather than praetorian was the size of its legionary garrison: provinces with more than one legion required a consular as commander-in-chief and governor.[21] In practice, there were some exceptions. Thus, Hispania citerior (Tarraconensis), for long garrisoned by several legions, had its establishment reduced to one, VII Gemina, during the 70s, but continued to be given a consular governor, no doubt in recognition of its very large size, not least.[22] When

---

[11] e.g. Cn. Julius Verus, p. 120 below.

[12] e.g. M. Trebellius Maximus, L. Aemilius Karus, pp. 59, 275 below.

[13] J. Crook, *Consilium Principis* (1955).

[14] See the comments of Syme, *Historia* 14 (1965) 358 = *Danubian Papers* (1971) 241 f.

[15] Alföldy, *Konsulat* 289 f.

[16] Eck, *ANRW* II. 1 (1974) 207.

[17] Alföldy, *Konsulat* 26.

[18] Eck, *ANRW* II. 1 (1974) 208 f.: note M.' Acilus Aviola, evidently in office for the years 74–97, according to Frontinus, *de aquis* 102, who himself seems to have held the post from 97 until his death, p. 72 below. However, earlier on more junior men are found, e.g. A. Didius Gallus (p. 47 below), appointed just before his consulship. See also Eck's discussion, loc. cit., of the praetorian *curatores*, presumably assistants to the consular; and p. 90 below, on L. Neratius Marcellus.

[19] Eck, *ANRW* II. 1 (1974) 209 f.; Alföldy, *Konsulat* 23, 109 ff.

[20] Eck, *Organisation Italiens* 166 ff.; id., *ZPE* 18 (1974) 97 f., argues that τρίς in *ILS* 8841 should mean 'on three occasions', not 'for three years'; see pp. 152 (Pollienus Auspex), 369 (C. Julius Avitus Alexianus) below.

[21] See in general Domaszewski, *RO*² lv ff., 175 ff.

[22] Alföldy, *Fasti Hispanienses* 207 f.

the garrison of Dalmatia was similarly reduced, and then removed altogether, under Domitian, that province at first received a praetorian governor; but Trajan soon restored consulars even though it remained without legions.[23] Finally, the often troublesome province of Pontus-Bithynia, governed by annual praetorian proconsuls from the principate of Augustus onwards, had to be given special imperial legates of consular status, of whom the younger Pliny was the first, at several points in the second century, and the arrangement was ultimately made permanent, at latest *c*.180, even though this province never had any legions based in it.[24] But the implementation of the two (or more) legions 'rule' may be seen to have operated elsewhere on a number of occasions. Thus Dacia lost its consular governor when its garrison was reduced to one legion by Hadrian, and regained one when M. Aurelius transferred a second legion there.[25] Likewise, Judaea (Syria Palaestina) was assigned to consular governors when Hadrian added another legion to its garrison,[26] and Pannonia inferior was treated similarly by Caracalla, whose boundary change detached part of the Upper province together with the legion I Adiutrix and assigned it to the Lower.[27]

All the consular provinces could be governed by men who had held their consulship just beforehand,[28] but there was clearly a hierarchy among them. Hispania citerior, Britain, Syria, and (following its re-establishment *c*.166) the III Daciae were generally reserved for men who had already governed one of the other consular provinces first. The other side of the coin was that the two Germanies, Upper Pannonia, the two Moesias, Cappadocia, and Syria Palaestina were generally governed by men fresh from the consulship, or who had been curator of public works at Rome but had had no other office.[29] The reasons for

---

[23] Eck, *Senatoren* 7 f.

[24] Eck, *Senatoren* 12 ff., Alföldy, *Konsulat* 238.

[25] Eck, *Senatoren* 16 f.; A. Stein, *Dazien* 41 ff.; Alföldy, *Konsulat* 222 ff.

[26] Eck, *Senatoren* 17 f.

[27] J. Fitz, *Il soggiorno di Caracalla in Pannonia nel 214* (1961) 12 ff.

[28] For Britain, see pp. 389 f. below; for Spain, Alföldy, *Fasti Hispanienses* 201 ff.; for Syria, Eck, *ANRW* 211 f. n. 264. Pannonia, later Upper Pannonia, seems to have fluctuated: W. Reidinger, *Pannonia*, and the review by Syme, *Gnomon* 29 (1957) 515 ff., reprinted with addenda in *Danubian Papers* (1971) 177 ff. The majority of consular governors held Pannonia (or Superior) as their first consular province, as E. Birley, *Carnuntum Jahrbuch* 1957. 9 ff., points out; but several cases of more senior governors are known.

[29] Eck, *ANRW* 211 f., showing scepticism over attempts to reconstruct over-rigid promotion-patterns. In the early 80s, Syria was evidently regarded by Agricola as *maioribus reservatam* (Tac. *Agr.* 40. 1). The man whose death had created a vacancy there, T. Atilius Rufus, had previously governed Pannonia (Eck, *Senatoren* 127 ff.). Two legates of Britain subsequently governed Syria, Sex. Julius Severus, who first went from Britain to Judaea, and Cn. Julius Verus. One, M. Statius Priscus, governed Cappadocia after Britain, and Sex. Calpurnius Agricola governed the III Daciae. All these appointments were caused by exceptional circumstances.

this distinction are not difficult to discover. Although two of the 'junior' consular provinces, Upper Pannonia and Lower Moesia, had for much of the principate as many legions—three—as Britain and Syria, they, in common with the German and Upper Moesian provinces, Cappadocia, and Syria Palaestina, were less exposed to external threat than were Britain, Syria, and the III Daciae. The governors of those latter provinces must have been expected to take independent action more frequently, whereas the German, Pannonian, and Moesian governors could readily seek assistance from their neighbours; while the governors of Cappadocia and Syria Palaestina were less likely to be affected, in the first instance, by hostile action from Parthia than was the governor of Syria. As for Hispania citerior, its great prestige as one of Rome's oldest and largest provinces presumably ensured that, as senior men were anxious to govern it, men of this rank were generally sent there.[30]

As far as the factors affecting the emperors' choice of men for particular posts is concerned, it looks as if most consular governors had previously commanded a legion.[31] There were, to be sure, times when this was not so, notably during the reign of Antoninus Pius.[32] It may not be illegitimate to infer that one reason for the military crisis which came about on several frontiers immediately after his death was precisely that some of his governors had been inadequately prepared for their tasks.[33] However this may be, it is important to stress that very few governors can be found who had previously served as legionary legate[34] (see Table 5), or even as military tribune (see Table 6), in the army which they later commanded. This may to some extent reflect the vagaries of the evidence, but it certainly appears as if there was no policy of specialization worthy of the name, as far as the military

One former governor of Syria, Pertinax, and one former governor of Syria Coele, L. Alfenus Senecio, later governed Britain: the former in exceptional circumstances, the latter after Syria had been divided. With the possible exception of C. Junius Faustinus and Pollienus Auspex, both perhaps governors of Upper, rather than undivided, Britain, there was no overlap between Britain and Tarraconensis. See pp. 145, 159, 165 f., 152 ff. below.

[30] Campbell, *JRS* (1975) 24 ff., while he clearly appreciates the reasons for Syria's seniority, perhaps neglects to consider Britain and Pannonia with sufficient care, overlooking the very different geographical positions of those provinces.

[31] Eck, *ANRW* II. 1 (1974) 215, with exceptions in the period 69-138; they include L. Neratius Marcellus (p. 89 below).

[32] Namely C. Popilius Carus Pedo (who had turned down a legionary command, *ILS* 1071), P. Salvius Julianus, L. Dasumius Tullius Tuscus; and C. Arrius Antoninus, who held consular governorships under M. Aurelius, is another. See the tables in Alföldy, *Konsulat* 329 ff.

[33] E. Birley, *PBA* 39 (1953) 208.

[34] Thus the comments by P. Lambrechts, *La Composition du senat romain . . . 117–192* (1936) 52 ('Il est dès lors logique de supposer qu'il a été gouverneur de la même province ou il avait commandé une légion') or Stein, *Moesien* 123 ('Häufig schickten die Kaiser ihre Legaten in diejenigen Provinzen, die diese schon früher in anderen Amtstellungen kennengelernt hatten') seem hardly justified. See also Table 6.

Table 5

Men who governed provinces where they had commanded legions

	legion	province
1. L. Burbuleius Optatus	XVI Fl.	Syria (p. 272 below)
2. Iasdius Domitianus(?)	XIII Gem.	III Daciae (Stein, *Dazien* 69 f.; doubted by Eck, *Organisation Italiens* 172 n. 111)
3. Cn. Julius Agricola	XX V. V.	Britain (p. 77 below)
4. Cn. Julius Verus	XXX U. V.	Germania inf. (p. 119 below)
5. Maximus(?)	I Ad.	Pannonia sup. (see Alföldy, *Konsulat* 143, following Fitz, *A. Ant. Hung.* 11 (1963) 260)
6. M. Nonius Macrinus	XIV gem.	Pannonia sup. (*ILS* 8820)
7. Q. Petillius Cerialis	IX Hisp.	Britain (p. 66 below)
8. Q. Pompeius Falco	V Mac.	Moesia inf. (pp. 98 f. below)
9. Q. Pomponius Rufus	V (Mac.?)	Moesia (inf.?) (*IRT* 353)
10. P. Septimius Geta	I It.	Moesia inf. (p. 278 below)
11. L. Tettius Julianus	VII Cl.	Moesia (sup.) (Tac. *Hist.* 1. 79, 2. 85; Dio 67. 10. 1)
12. Q. Venidius Rufus	I Min.	Germania inf. (XIII 7994, 8828)
13. C. Vettius Sabinianus(?)	XIV Gem.	Pannonia sup.(?) (*AE* 1920. 45; *ILS* 3655, which may call him *leg. Aug pr. p* [r.] with reference to his special duties as legate of XIV Gem. *cum iurisdicatu Pannoniae superioris* rather than refer to a later governorship otherwise unattested)
14. Sex. Vettulenus Cerialis	V Mac. (in Judaea)	Moesia (Joseph. *BJ* 3. 7. 22, 6. 4. 3; XVI 22, etc.)

provinces were concerned.[35] In other respects, it is possible to observe some uniformity of policy in the allocation of men to posts, over a long period. Thus a considerable number of governors of Britain previously governed Germania inferior.[36] There was also some kind of specialization in the eastern provinces, in that governors of Syria had often governed another eastern province.[37]

The length of tenure of consular imperial provinces was no more

---

[35] See also Eck, *ANRW* II. 1 (1974) 215 and n. 296.

[36] p. 392 below.

[37] Note e.g. Licinius Mucianus (Lycia), L. Caesennius Paetus, C. Julius Quadratus Bassus, L. Catilius Severus, (all in Cappadocia first), Sex. Julius Severus (Judaea), Arrian(?), L. Burbuleius Optatus, M. Cassius Apollinaris (all in Cappadocia), L. Attidius Cornelianus (Arabia), P. Martius Verus (Cappadocia). See Eck, *Senatoren*, and Alföldy, *Konsulat*, under the relevant provinces; for the first posts of Mucianus and Paetus, *PIR*[2] C 173, L 216.

Table 6

Men who governed provinces in the army of which they had been tribune*

		legion	province
1.	P. Aelius Hadrianus	II Ad.	Pannonia inf. (*ILS* 308)
2.	Q. Antistius Adventus	I Min.	Germania inf. (p. 130 below)
3.	L. Cassius Pius Marcellinus(?)	II Ad.	Pannonia inf. (Fitz, *A. Ant. Hung.* 11 (1963) 286 f. etc.; but the identification is highly doubtful)
4.	Q. Hedius Rufus	VII Gem.	Hispania cit. (*ILS* 1145)
5.	Cn. Julius Agricola	*leg. Brit.*	Britain (p. 74 below)
6.	C. Julius Quadratus Bassus	XIII Gem.	Dacia (*AE* 1933. 268, 1934. 176)
7.	C. Julius Septimius Castinus	V. Mac.	III Daciae (*ILS* 1153, III 7638, etc.)
8.	L. Minicius Natalis jr.	XI Cl.	Moesia inf. (p. 245 below)
9.	Pontius Pontianus(?)	II Ad.	Pannonia inf. (III 3707, 3713)

*M. Statius Priscus (p. 124 below) had been an equestrian officer in Britain, which he later governed. P. Helvius Pertinax (p. 143 below) governed several provinces where he had earlier served as an equestrian. Q. Pompeius Falco, governor of Judaea *c.*108 had been tribune of X Gemina, not X Fretensis (p. 98 below).

subject to rules than was the case with the praetorian provinces, and some examples may be found, even after the reign of Tiberius, notorious for its long commands, of men spending well over three years as consular governor. But such cases were rare, for, even if the number of men available as replacements was limited, it would have created ill feeling if prospects of advancement and distinction were blocked. Likewise, the emperors had to guard against the building up of dangerously close links between a consular and his troops.[38]

Very few senators are known to have governed more than two consular provinces of the emperor.[39] What a high proportion must have looked forward to, after one or two consular commands, was the consular proconsulship of Africa or Asia, held for one year only, as were the praetorian proconsulships, but for most senators the highest distinction to which they could aspire. By the beginning of the second

[38] Eck, *ANRW* II. 1 (1974) 43 ff.; A. R. Birley, *Corolla Swoboda* 43 ff.

[39] Eck, *ANRW* II. 1 (1974) 213 f. cites only three cases in the period 69-138. There are rather more in the succeeding eighty years: note the British governors Sex. Julius Severus, Cn. Julius Verus, M. Statius Priscus, P. Helvius Pertinax, Pollienus Auspex, C. Junius Faustinus, pp. 388 ff. below; further, C. Arrius Antoninus and M. Didius Severus Julianus in the 170s, and perhaps C. Vettius Sabinianus (Alföldy, *Konsulat* 333, 338; but see Table 5 above, on Sabinianus); and the Severan cases of L. Fabius Cilo and Fulvius Maximus (*PIR*[2] F 27; Barbieri, *L'Albo* no. 254).

century the increase in the number of ex-consuls meant that these proconsulships were generally held about fifteen years after the consulship.[40] A corollary of this was that it was almost unknown for a senator to be appointed to an imperial province after he had governed Africa or Asia, as had been possible in the early principate.[41]

As well as governorships there were two posts for senior consulars, the *cura aquarum* and the prefecture of the city of Rome, each of which was sometimes held for life.[42] In times of war, experienced consulars accompanied the emperor on campaign as *comites Augusti*— from the time of M. Aurelius, the title was evidently reserved for ex-consuls, and the emperor's *comites* may perhaps be thought of as general staff officers.[43] In the late second century a civil function was created for senior senators, to hear cases as the emperor's deputy, *vice sacra iudicans.*[44]

Other means of distinction for senators were the priesthoods and the patriciate. The four major colleges, *pontifices*, augurs, *XVviri*, and *VIIviri*, retained their superior social cachet.[45] Not many new men secured entry, for the colleges were dominated by the older families. But lesser priesthoods offered consolation prizes: the *fetiales*, the *sodales Titii*, and the *fratres Arvales*; and a host of sodalities to conduct ceremonies in honour of deified emperors, *Augustales*, *Flaviales Titiales*, *Antoniniani*, and the like.[46] The rank of patrician was sometimes conferred on men who had already entered imperial service. More commonly it was given to those whose families had been established for several generations.[47] Perhaps the most coveted distinction of all was a second consulship, as *ordinarius*, particularly if it was held with the emperor himself as colleague.[48]

(g) CONCLUSION

It is possible to discern several distinct groups among the senators of

---

[40] Thomasson, *Statthalter Nordafrikas* I 14 ff. On Asia, see the lists in Eck, *Senatoren* 234 ff., and Alföldy, *Konsulat* 207 ff.

[41] Eck, *ANRW* II. 1 (1974) 222, cites P. Calvisius Ruso as the latest case, for in his *Senatoren* 232 n. 511 he dismisses the possibility that C. Bruttius Praesens and Sex. Julius Major, named as ὑπατικοί in a Syrian inscription of 138, had governed that province after being proconsuls of Africa (*AE* 1938. 137). Some doubt remains.

[42] p. 26 nn. 3–4 above.

[43] See the list in Pflaum, *Bayer. Vorgesch.-Bl.* 27 (1962) 90 f.

[44] F. Millar, *The Emperor in the Roman World* (1977) 515 and n. 50. But he does not discuss the date of the elder Pollienus Auspex (p. 153 below).

[45] See L. Schumacher, *Priesterkollegien.*

[46] See esp. Pflaum, *Les sodales Antoniniani à l'époque de Marc-Aurèle* (1966).

[47] H. H. Pistor, *Prinzeps und Patriziat in der Zeit von Augustus bis Commodus* (1965).

[48] Eck, *ANRW* II. 1 (1974) 222 f.; Alföldy, *Konsulat* 107 ff.

the principate. A limited number, who had the emperor's favour and confidence, often displayed at the beginning of their career, when they were in their late teens, and continued through their twenties, confined their public life to the emperor's service after the praetorship. At the opposite extreme, the patricians, and men of consular ancestry, generally held no posts in imperial provinces and were content with the republican magistracies and a consular proconsulship. These men were often the sons or descendants of successful generals. It was unnecessary for them to earn their consulship by commanding a legion and holding other posts. The majority of senators fell into an intermediate group. Many never reached the consulship, and those that did had in some cases to serve in a great many posts first, including both imperial and senatorial provincial appointments, and the less favoured posts such as that of *praefectus frumenti dandi*.[1] Without doubt, some posts were pure sinecures, created by Augustus and his successors precisely to satisfy the aspirations of senators: 'quoque plures partem administrandae rei p. caperent, nova officia excogitavit', as Suetonius says of Augustus,[2] or 'quo magis eorum cum exercitio iuris auctoritas cresceret', as the *Historia Augusta* says of M. Aurelius' policy.[3]

Augustus had firmly decided that Rome's armies, except in Egypt, should be commanded by senators. The old republican ideal that a senator should excel *domi militiaeque*[4] long prevailed. Inevitably, this leads to the appearance of a highly professional army of which the generals were amateurs. Yet enough cases are known of senators with many years of military service to correct this impression. It made a particular difference when a number of one-legion provinces were available. This meant that, even if a senator had learned little enough as a military tribune, he could have five or six years, as legionary legate and governor of a province like Numidia, Arabia, Upper Dacia, or Lower Pannonia, during which he commanded troops; and this could be followed by a similar period when he was responsible for more than one legion. Men like Sex. Julius Severus, Q. Lollius Urbicus, M. Pontius Laelianus, M. Statius Priscus, or P. Helvius Pertinax,[5] had a good deal more direct experience of commanding troops than many modern generals. At the same time, the necessity for men like them to return to Rome from time to time prevented the formation of a military caste;

---

[1] A clear statement in E. Birley, *PBA* 39 (1953) 197 ff.; more detail now in Alföldy, *Konsulat*, esp. 33 ff.

[2] Suet. *D. Aug.* 37. 1.

[3] *HA M. Ant. Phil.* 10. 3.

[4] Thus in Cic. *Tusc.* 5. 19, 55, etc.; recurring in *HA M. Ant. Phil.* 3. 3.

[5] pp. 109, 114, 125 f., 144 f., 273 f. below.

while the policy of avoiding narrow specialization ensured that military practices and standards could be maintained at a uniform level throughout the empire.

Thus, in spite of the shocks created by military defeats and enemy invasion during the 160s and 170s, the system of command was sufficiently resilient to withstand them.[6] What contributed largely to its disintegration was the breakdown of mutual esteem between emperor and senate in the reign of Commodus,[7] which was followed by the civil wars of AD 193-7.[8] The process that was to reach its climax with the so-called Edict of Gallienus was by then in motion. Either fewer senators were willing to serve the emperor, or *vice versa*, fewer senators enjoyed the emperor's confidence. But those who did serve him evidently held a greater number of posts. For example, Q. Aradius Rufinus[9] was, after a legionary command, entrusted with a series of posts, the two treasuries at Rome, and the provinces of Galatia and Syria Phoenice, any one of which might have gained him the consulship in the second century. The subdivision of provinces, and the reduced length of tenure of their governorships, which may be observed from the beginning of the third century,[10] may well have reduced the attractiveness of such posts. Besides this, there was the chance (not attractive to most) that the troops might incite their commander to seize the throne[11] —and even if this did not happen, suspicious emperors might mistakenly believe that it would and react accordingly. The steady increase during the first half of the third century of equestrian procurators deputizing for governors of senatorial rank[12] presumably reflects all these factors in some measure.

Whether or not Gallienus issued an edict,[13] he certainly took action

---

[6] Ammianus, writing about the disasters to Rome in the same quarter two centuries later, contrasted the response with that in his own day: 'unanimanti ardore, summi et infimi inter se congruentes, ad speciosam pro re p. mortem, tamquam ad portum aliquem tranquillum properabant et placidum' (31. 5. 14), language which may be commonplace—but rather recalls the monument of M. Claudius Fronto, set up 'quod post aliquot secunda proelia adversum Germanos et Iazyges ad postremum pro r.p. fortiter pugnans ceciderit' (*ILS* 1098). The historian might have read the inscription in the Forum of Trajan.

[7] See e.g. Grosso, *La lotta politica al tempo di Commodo*.

[8] Discussed by A. R. Birley, *Septimius Severus* 144–200.

[9] p. 175 below.

[10] Barbieri, *L'Albo* 554 ff.

[11] Note the behaviour of the British legions towards the governor Pertinax and the legionary legate Priscus, pp. 145, 260 below. This kind of thing was to become endemic in the third century.

[12] Pflaum, *Les Procurateurs équestres* 134 ff.; id., *CP*, nos. 317, 347, etc.

[13] Note the comment by G. Lopuszanski, *MEFR* 55 (1938) 168: 'Du reste, Gallien a-t-il eu besoin d'un édit pour bannir les sénateurs de l'armée? Pour ma part, je penserais que le simple jeu des congés et des mises en retraite des officiers et des gouverneurs sénatoriaux et des nominations en masse des chevaliers aurait suffi pour atteindre ce but.' It must be stressed that

to bar senators from the command of troops, as Aurelius Victor reported a century later: 'quia ipse Gallienus, metu socordiae suae ne imperium ad optimos nobilium transferetur, senatum militia vetuit et adire exercitus.'[14] The men who replaced senators were, so far as the evidence indicates, not the equestrian procurators of the old style, whose background was little different from that of the senatorial order itself, but men who had risen from the ranks, of peasant origin. They alone were evidently thought capable of commanding the new forces which Gallienus created to repel the barbarian onslaughts of the 260s.[15] In the part of the empire which he controlled, the latest example of a senator commanding troops is the governor of Numidia C. Julius Sallustius Saturninus Fortunatianus, still responsible for III Augusta c.262.[16] In the Gallic empire senators evidently continued to command troops, as is revealed by the mention of a senatorial governor of Lower Britain, named on a military inscription from Lancaster.[17] But after the defeat of the last Gallic emperor by Aurelian, it must be assumed that senatorial army commanders disappeared for good.

Until the reign of Constantine provincial governors could still combine civil and military functions in the armed provinces.[18] Thereafter the two roles were finally severed. Writing at the end of the fourth century, Ammianus Marcellinus could comment with evident approval of Constantius II that the proper distinction between civil officials and military commanders had been maintained: 'nec sub eo dux quisquam clarissimatu provectus est. erant enim (ut nos quoque meminimus), perfectissimi: nec occurrebat magistro equitum provinciae rector, nec contingi ab eo civile negotium permittebat.'[19]

---

senatorial governors continued to serve in many provinces; but their armies were placed under separate control.

[14] Aur. Vict. *de Caes.* 33. 33.

[15] See now especially Pflaum, *Historia* 25 (1976) 109 ff.

[16] Thomasson, *RE* Supp. 9 (1962) 377.

[17] p. 200 below.

[18] p. 319 below.

[19] Amm. Marc. 21. 16. 2.

II

II.1
GOVERNORS OF UNDIVIDED BRITAIN,
43–c.213

43–47 A. Plautius A. f. Ani. (*cos.* 29)

Tac. *Agr.* 14; *Ann.* 11. 36. 4, 13. 32. 2; Suet. *D. Claud.* 24. 2, *D. Vesp.* 4. 1; Cassius Dio 60. 19–20, 60. 30. 2.

Eutropius 7. 13: Britanniae bellum intulit [sc. Claudius], quam nullus Romanorum post Julium Caesarem attigerat, eaque devicta per Cn. Sentium et A. Plautium, illustres et nobiles viros, triumphum celebrem egit. Quasdam insulas etiam, ultra Britanniam in Oceano positas, Romano imperio addidit, quae appellantur Orcades, filioque suo Britannici nomen imposuit. Tam civilis autem circa quosdam amicos exstitit, ut etiam Plautium, nobilem virum, qui in expeditione Britannica multa egregie fecerat, triumphantem ipse prosequeretur, et conscendenti Capitolium laevus incederet.

The selection of A. Plautius[1] to command the Claudian invasion force can readily be explained, even though little is known of his previous experience in provincial government and military service.[2] 'A political alliance with the Plautii was good Claudian tradition', as Syme has observed, commenting on the career under Augustus of M. Plautius Silvanus (*cos. ord.* 2 BC), first cousin of A. Plautius' father. It is not known whether these Plautii claimed descent from the great plebeian nobles of the fourth century BC—if so, it would have been with doubtful justification.[3] Their family, as L. R. Taylor showed, came from the Sabine town of Trebula Suffenas, in *regio* IV of Italy, east of Tibur and north of Praeneste, and was enrolled in the Aniensis.[4] After a modest start in the late republic,[5] their star rose rapidly under the principate. It was no doubt to Silvanus' mother Urgulania, a close personal friend of Livia,[6] that they owed much of the favour that they received from

---

[1] He had no *cognomen*, in spite of which he has sometimes been called A. Plautius Silvanus, e.g. by H. Furneaux in his edition of the *Annals*, II[2] (1907), Introd., 132, and by M. T. Griffin, *Seneca. A Philosopher in Politics* (1976) 244.

[2] On 'uterque bello egregius' in *Agr.* 14. 1 see p. 38 n. 16 below.

[3] Syme, *Roman Revolution* 422 with n. 3. Any link with the censor of 312 BC, colleague of Ap. Claudius Caecus (C. Plautius Venox: *MRR* I 160), must be discounted.

[4] L. R. Taylor, *MAAR* 24 (1956) 9 ff.

[5] The earliest certain ancestors are A. Plautius, legate in the Social War in 90 BC, and M. Plautius Silvanus, tribune of the plebs in 89 BC (*MRR* II 29, 34; Taylor, *MAAR* 24 (1956) 25).

[6] Tac. *Ann.* 2. 34. 2, 4. 21. 1, 22. 2.

Augustus. Silvanus' daughter Plautia Urgulanilla was chosen as bride for the young Claudius.[7] The ending of that marriage was no impediment to the family's advance, nor, for that matter, were the domestic upheavals in the household of Urgulanilla's brother.[8] It is notable that A. Plautius' own branch of the family also forged valuable, if less glittering, marriage connections. His mother was a Vitellia; his sister was married to P. Petronius (*cos.* 19),[9] later described as 'an old boon companion of Claudius';[10] a daughter of this match was to marry a son of L. Vitellius.[11] A. Plautius' own wife Pomponia Graecina, presumably daughter of C. Pomponius Graecinus (*cos.* 16) and niece of L. Pomponius Flaccus (*cos.* 17),[12] was a close personal friend, it appears, of Julia the granddaughter of Tiberius.[13]

As the son of a consul, it is probable that A. Plautius was under forty[14] when he held the *fasces* himself, as suffect for the second half of the year 29.[15] But one can only speculate about possible military appointments either as military tribune or as legionary legate: he could have seen active service under Tiberius or under Silvanus during the campaign of 6–9 in Illyricum, under Tiberius or Germanicus in Germany in the years 10–16, or in Moesia under his wife's uncle Pomponius Flaccus.[16] All that is known of his pre-consular career is that he played some part in suppressing a slave uprising in Apulia, as is revealed by the inscription of one Celer, *legatus missus* [*a Ti. Caes. Aug. c*]*um A. Plautio in Apulia* [*ad servos to*]*rquendos*. This was probably in AD 24, as G. Alföldy has shown, when Plautius could well have been praetor.[17]

---

[7] Suet. *D. Claud.* 4. 3, 26. 2, 27. 1.

[8] Urgulanilla was divorced for adultery and suspected murder. Her brother M. Plautius Silvanus, praetor in 24, in that year flung his second wife Apronia to her death; his previous wife, the patrician Fabia Numantina, was acquitted of sending him mad. See nn. 6–7 above, and Taylor, *MAAR* 24 (1956) 27 f. The names of Urgulanilla's other brother, P. Plautius Pulcher, suggest that the family had a link with the Claudii Pulchri: their mother Lartia may have been (e.g.) daughter of a Claudia—note e.g. *PIR*[2] C 1057, the daughter of Clodius.

[9] Syme, *Tacitus* 386 n. 5, citing VI 6866 (*Plautia P. Petroni*) and *SEG* XIV 646, Caunus (Πλαυτίαν Αὔλου θυγατέρα). This lady's mother was a Vitellia (Tac. *Ann.* 3. 49. 1) and, as Syme notes, presumably her father was A. Plautius (*cos.* 1 BC).

[10] Seneca, *Apoc.* 14. 2: 'vetus convictor eius, homo Claudiana lingua disertus'.

[11] Tac. *Hist.* 2. 64. 1.

[12] See now Eck, *RE* Supp. 14 (1974) 439–41. The family probably derived from Iguvium.

[13] Tac. *Ann.* 13. 32. 3. Julia was perhaps a distant kinswoman: her grandmother Vipsania was the granddaughter of T. Pomponius Atticus; Nepos, *Vita Attici* 12. 2.

[14] See p. 21 above, on the consulship.

[15] Degrassi, *FC* 9.

[16] Eck, *RE* Supp. 14 (1974) 439 ff. Tacitus' phrase 'uterque bello egregius' (*Agr.* 14. 1), applied to Plautius and Scapula, may of course perfectly well apply to what they did in Britain, and not, as generally assumed, to their previous experience.

[17] Alföldy, *Fasti Hispanienses* 149 ff., improving on *ILS* 961 = IX 9335, *ager Allifanus*, with full discussion.

The fall of Sejanus in AD 31 seems to have left the family unscathed. His presumed younger brother Q. Plautius was consul in 36, and his brother-in-law P. Petronius succeeded L. Vitellius as governor of Syria soon afterwards.[18] Plautius was certainly holding office as a consular governor himself early in Claudius' reign, for it was in that capacity that he decided on the construction of a road in the *ager Tergestinus*.[19] Although the responsibility for a road in this area might conceivably have fallen on the governor of Dalmatia rather than of Pannonia,[20] the fact that Plautius was to take one of the Pannonian legions, IX Hispana, as part of the invasion force points to the latter province.[21] The latest governor of Pannonia known before Plautius, C. Calvisius Sabinus (*cos. ord.* 26), had been recalled and forced to suicide in 39.[22] It is not improbable that Plautius was his immediate successor and hence that he was in a position of great significance at the time of Claudius' turbulent accession in January 41. Even more significant, no doubt, was his potential role in 42, at the time of the coup by L. Arruntius Camillus Scribonianus, legate of neighbouring Dalmatia.[23]

All these factors—the family tradition, the influence of his cousin through Urgulania's friendship with Livia, Plautius' own connections, especially with the Petronii and Vitellii, and his opportunities for gaining Claudius' gratitude in AD 41-2, combined to make him an ideal choice to carry out an undertaking so vital to the new emperor as was the invasion of Britain. It appears from all the sources that he acquitted himself well, although it may be that the *ovatio* was intended not least to revive Claudius' own glory in the eyes of Rome. Certainly the honour was remarkable in this era, and was never repeated.[24] Plautius left Britain firmly within the Roman orbit: only Wales and Scotland remained to be conquered, for virtually the whole of England was under Roman rule, direct or indirect.[25] But the experience of his

[18] R. Hanslik, *RE* 19. 1 (1973) 1200 f.; Supp. 9 (1962) 1733 ff.; and see 8A. 2 (1958) for Petronius' successor in Syria, from AD 42 to 44, C. Vibius Marsus (*cos.* 17), also related to the Plautii: his daughter was married to P. Plautius Pulcher (*ILS* 964).

[19] *ILS* 5889 = V 698, between Trieste and Rijeka.

[20] The possibility is fully ventilated but rejected by A. Jagenteufel, *Dalmatien* 27 f. See also Reidinger, *Pannonia* 35 f.

[21] As originally pointed out by Ritterling, *Arch.-ep. Mitt.* 20 (1897) 8 f. See also id., *RE* 12. 2 (1925) 1666. Since the road built by Plautius was restored before the death of Claudius, that indicates an early date for Plautius' activity in the area. B. Slapšak, *Arheološki Vestnik* 28 (1977) 125 f., 128, regards it as more likely that he had a special mission, and was not a provincial governor.

[22] Dio 59. 18. 4; see Reidinger, *Pannonia* 34 f.

[23] *PIR*[2] A 1140; Jagenteufel, *Dalmatien* 21 ff.

[24] *RE* 18. 2 (1942) 1890–1903.

[25] When allowance is made for the client kingdoms of the Brigantes and Iceni, and of

successors was to demonstrate how fragile that control was. The dating of
the governorship is firm. He arrived in Britain in the summer of 43 and
was back at Rome for his *ovatio* in 47, according to Dio.[26] It is of course
conceivable that he had left the province in 46 and had had to wait
some months before the ovation was held, but direct evidence is lacking.

As would be expected, his prestige was still immense in 48, sufficient
to rescue his errant nephew Lateranus, one of Messallina's lovers, from
the fate meted out to her and others after the Silius affair; and the first
recorded act of Nero after his accession was to restore Lateranus to the
senate.[27] Plautius was still alive in 57, when his wife was accused of
practising a foreign religion; he was permitted to try her himself, and
found her innocent.[28] Tacitus remarks that Graecina had assumed the
garb of mourning when her friend Julia was killed by Messalina's con-
triving—in AD 43[29]—and that she wore it until her death forty years
later. It may be surmised that Tacitus knew the lady.[30] At about this
time another member of the family, namesake of our governor, was put
to death by Nero. He was evidently suspected of aiming for the throne,
urged by Agrippina, whose lover he was. In spite of the shared *praenomen*, the young A. Plautius is generally thought to have belonged to
the other branch of the family, and not to be the son of our man.[31]
However this may be, it is reasonable to suppose that the conqueror of
Britain may have played a part in the selection of his sister's son P.
Petronius Turpilianus (*cos. ord.* 61), to govern the province after the
Boudiccan revolt and its bloody suppression.[32] But he must surely have
been dead by 65, when his nephew Lateranus, then consul designate,
was killed for his part in the conspiracy of Piso.[33] No direct descendants
are known, but the name was continued for a few generations in the
line of the Plautii Silvani Aeliani.[34]

Cogidumnus, not much of England was left outside the Roman orbit, except perhaps for the
Cornovii. See e.g. G. Webster, *Britannia* 1 (1970) 179 ff.

[26] Dio. 60. 30. 2.

[27] Tac. *Ann.* 11. 36. 4, 13. 11. 2.

[28] There has been much discussion of Pomponia Graecina's religious beliefs and practices. It
would be charitable to regard M. Hofmann's suggestion that she had become a devotee of
Druidism as an attempt at humour (*RE* 21. 1 (1951) 29).

[29] Dio 60. 18. 4.

[30] See Syme, *Tacitus* 532 n. 5.

[31] Suet. *Nero* 35. 4, where he is called 'Aulum Plautium iuvenem'. See Taylor, *MAAR* 24
(1956) 29 (not conclusive).

[32] pp. 57 f. below.

[33] Tac. *Ann.* 14. 49. 3, 53. 2, 60. 1; Arr. *Diss. Epict.* 1. 1. 19. His palace, the Lateran, was
confiscated (Juv. *Sat.* 8. 146).

[34] The last trace is the son-in-law of Antoninus Pius, Plautius Lamia Silvanus (*HA Ant. Pius*

47–52　　　　　P. Ostorius Q.(?) f. Scapula (*cos. a. inc.*)

Tac. *Agr.* 14; *Ann.* 12. 31–40. 1.

Scapula's command in Britain is more fully documented (in the *Annals*) than that of most other governors, but virtually nothing is known of his previous career, except for his consulship. He was suffect, with the ill-famed P. Suillius Rufus as his colleague, in the one of the first years of Claudius' principate. Several records of the pair survive, including an inscription from Phrygia which preserves part of the month: [. . .] ευβρίων,[1] and a wax tablet from a suburb of Pompeii, dated 10 November.[2] Hence they were in office for part of the period August to December. Since Scapula was already in Britain in 47, that year must probably be excluded. Other evidence shows that 42 and 46, and perhaps 44 also, should be ruled out, since there is no room for this pair in the consular *Fasti* of those years.[3] Syme suggested that the year might be 45, 'a notion that could be supported by the guess that Scapula . . . had won merit . . . under Claudius in the campaign of 43.'[4] The new province still required a governor capable of energetic campaigning after Plautius' recall, with Caratacus unsubdued, and it is likely that Claudius and his advisers may have looked for a successor to Plautius among those with some experience of Britain. But Tacitus' phrase *exercitu ignoto* (*Ann.* 12. 31. 1) appears to rule out any possibility that Scapula had in fact served with the army of Britain before his governorship. It is reasonable to assume that he had had some military experience,[5] and he might, after all, have had a brief spell in the island as a *comes* of Claudius in 43.

Not much can be deduced about his standing otherwise. He was

---

1. 7; XI 5171, Vettona). Further, this man's aunt, the much married Plautia, was the ancestress of a large portion of the Antonine dynasty: see Syme, *Athenaeum* 35 (1957) 306 ff.

[1] *AE* 1949. 250; Degrassi, *FC* 12, cites the other evidence.

[2] *AE* 1973. 152: *III id[us] Nov[embres] P. Suillio Rufo Q.* [sic] *Ostorio Scapula cos.* The *praenomen* is presumably an error, since *P.* is given by *Annals* 12. 31. 1; see also Barbieri, *RAL* 30 (1975) 157.

[3] See Degrassi, *FC* 12–13: C. Caecina Largus was consul throughout 42 and C. Terentius Tullius Geminus was in office in October and December 45. The year 44 would also be ruled out if the arguments of Barbieri, *Epigr.* 29 (1967) 3 ff., were accepted; but see p. 225 below. As for 45, A. Antonius Rufus and M. Pompeius Silvanus are now known to have been still in office early in October, as well as in late June (Barbieri, *Epigr.* 29 (1967) 8); but Suillius and Ostorius might have taken over from them for the last two months.

[4] Syme, *JRS* 60 (1970) 28. Eck, *Historia* 24 (1975) 342 n. 120, followed by Barbieri, *RAL* 39 (1975) 156 f., favours AD 41—but with the premiss that AD 44 is excluded, on which see p. 225 below.

[5] See p. 38, n. 16 above, on Tac. *Agr.* 14. 1 ('uterque bello egregius').

probably the son of Q. Ostorius Scapula, one of the first joint commanders of the praetorian guard in 2 BC and later prefect of Egypt.[6] A. Stein regarded our man as the prefect's grandson, which at first sight seems more plausible.[7] But it should be observed that the governor's son M. Ostorius Scapula, who was serving under his father in Britain, was *consul ordinarius* in 59.[8] Such a short interval between the consulships of father and son suggests that the former achieved the *fasces* at a relatively advanced age. But even if P. Scapula were born as late as AD 2, for example, and became consul at forty-two, there is no reason why he should not have been the prefect's son. M. Scapula, as son of a consular, may have been consul in his early thirties. The fact that P. Scapula died in office, 'taedio curarum fessus' need not of course demonstrate that he was then an old man.[9]

Scapula may have been chosen for Britain on merit, but one imagines that the influence of L. Vitellius, then at its height, may have been a factor.[10] The only hint of powerful connections for the Ostorii is supplied by an inscription from Rome, attesting that a certain C. Sallustius Utilis and his brother Phosporus were freedmen of Calvina and sons of P. Ostorius Pharnaces, freedmen of Scapula.[11] Syme has conjectured that Scapula's wife or mother was a Sallustia Calvina, names which evoke powerful and noble families.[12] Scapula's son had estates on the borders of Liguria,[13] but the *nomen* is commonest in *CIL* IX and X, and an origin in eastern or southern Italy seems probable. Ostorius' home might well have been in the mountainous lands of *regio* IV, in the back country of central Italy.[14]

[6] Dio 55. 10. 10; G. Bastianiani, *ZPE* 17 (1975) 268.

[7] A. Stein, *Der römische Ritterstand* (1927) 325.

[8] p. 268 below.

[9] See p. 21 above, on the consulship.

[10] He was consul with Claudius as his colleague in 43 and 47 and censor with him 47–8; further his sons were consuls in 48. See Suet. *Vit.* 2. 4–5 etc.

[11] VI 23601: *P. Ostorius Scapulae l. Pharnaces fecit sibi et Ostoriae P.l. Amme l. suae et C. Sallustio Calvinae l. Utili et Phosporo filiis suis et libertis libertabusque suis omnibus.*

[12] Syme, *Hist.* 17 (1968) 79: 'For parallel to Sallustia Calvina stands Junia Calvina (*PIR*² J 856), daughter of M. Junius Silanus, the consul of 19: his father (unattested) had married a Domitia Calvina, that is the assumption (*PIR*² D 173). The inference is that either Sallustius Crispus or his son Passienus had also married a descendant of the *nobilis* Cn. Domitius Calvinus (*cos.* 53 BC)'. Junia Calvina was daughter-in-law of L. Vitellius, although he readily sacrificed her to appease Agrippina in 48: Tac. *Ann.* 12. 4. 1.

[13] Tac. *Ann.* 16. 15. 1. One may note the amphora stamps PQSCAPVLAE (V 8112⁶⁹) and an Ostorius Eugrafianus at Novaria (V 6547).

[14] Apart from the Ostorii at Rome, mostly libertine (VI 23595 ff.), one may note the following: IV 2508²⁷ (a gladiator at Pompeii: P. Ostorius); IX 3174, 3252 (Corfinium); X 2814 (Puteoli), 4042 (Capua), 5947 (Anagnia); XI 3989 (Capena); *AE* 1975. 317–18 (Marruvium, a P. Ostorius). Further, there are Opsturii in IX 3590–1 (pagus Fificulanus), 3615 (Aveia), and 4187 (Amiternum—the home of the historian Sallust, see Syme, *Sallust* (1964) 8, and n. 12 above). See also Schulze 203, 334, 336.

He arrived in Britain late in the year, presumably 47;[15] indeed, if 'coepta hieme' (*Ann.* 12. 31. 1) may be pressed, it was already past the equinox. His rapid action to deal with the serious situation awaiting him suggests the experienced soldier, as is implied by Tacitus' 'gnarus . . .' in the *Annals* (12. 31. 2). The account of the governorship is there placed under the year 50, although the capture of Caratacus towards its end is assigned to 'the ninth year after the war in Britain began', (12. 36. 1) which should be 51.[16] It is impossible to assign all the items described in 12. 31–6 to particular years with any certainty, but the revolt of the Iceni, in the suppression of which the legate's son M. Scapula won the civic crown, probably fell in 48; the campaigns against the Deceangli and Silures may have occupied 49 and 50 respectively, with the final campaign in Ordovician territory coming in 51. Whether one should ascribe to Scapula any 'frontier policy' involving a Trent–Severn line seems questionable. The phrase in 12. 31. 2 refers only to the prelude to a further advance, not to the establishment of any kind of frontier.[17]

Scapula received triumphal decorations for his success in 51; and Claudius did his best to extract further personal credit from the ceremony at which the captive British king was displayed.[18] In Britain itself, however, hostilities were not ended and the revival of resistance was spreading when Scapula, 'wearied by the irksomeness of his responsibilities', expired. The year was presumably 52.[19] Before his successor could arrive—and there may well have been an interval of many weeks in which the army lacked a commander—the legionary legate C. Manlius Valens was to incur a defeat.[20]

The death of Scapula's son is also dealt with by Tacitus in the

[15] But see p. 40 above.

[16] Syme, *Tacitus* 391 n. 3: 'That is, 51, as generally held (e.g. *PIR*[2], C 418), possibly even 52'. As Syme notes, the incident is placed under AD 50 by Tacitus, 'perhaps because the author needed 51 for a long excursus on eastern affairs (XII. 44–51)'. *ILS* 216 = Smallwood I 43 (b), the inscription of Claudius' triumphal arch of AD 51–2, with reference to the *reges Brit[annorum] XI d[evictos]*, is probably relevant.

[17] As E. Birley points out to me, the phrase emended to 'cis Trisantonam et Sabinos fluvios' in *Ann.* 12. 31. 2 may simply refer to the establishment of a legionary base at Wroxeter, between the *Tern* and the *Severn*, and not, as has long been assumed, to a frontier between the *Trent* and the *Severn*. The concept of a *limes* at this early period is in any case anachronistic, see the remarks of D. J. Breeze and B. Dobson, *Hadrian's Wall* (1976) 13 f.

[18] Tac. *Ann.* 12. 36–8; Dio 61. 33. 3c; *ILS* 216, 222.

[19] i.e. the year after the capture of Caratacus, n. 16 above. But, it has to be conceded (given Tacitus' comment in *Ann.* 12. 40. 5), there is no guarantee that the events described in 12. 38. 3–39. 3 occupied the season after the capture of Caratacus, no more and no less. It is not inconceivable that Ostorius died either in the same year as Caratacus' capture, or as much as two years later.

[20] p. 230 below.

Annals: M. Ostorius Scapula was forced to suicide by Nero in the year 66.[21] The last possible trace of the family comes under Trajan, when a M. Scapula was proconsul of Asia.[22]

52-57   A. Didius Gallus (*cos.* 39)

Tac. *Agr.* 14; *Ann.* 12. 40, 14. 29. 1.

The apointment of Didius Gallus to succeed Scapula when news of the latter's death reached Claudius is described by Tacitus in slightly unusual terms in the *Annals*, fitting the circumstances: *suffecit* (12. 40. 1) is used in its original sense.[1] Gallus was a trusted and senior man, well experienced for the task. Perhaps Claudius remembered, also, that Gallus had once sought the post. Quintilian relates that Gallus complained, when appointed to a province (unnamed) for which he had very actively canvassed, that he had been forced to take it. This won him an ironic comment from the orator Domitius Afer.[2] Some prefer to identify the province as one that Gallus governed earlier in his career.[3] But as the sepulchral inscription of his successor in Britain, Veranius, appears to state that the latter was appointed to the province [*cum non p*]*etierit*, 'although he did not seek it', it is hard to resist applying the story to Britain.[4] There is no need to suppose that canvassing and appointment followed in close succession. Afer knew Gallus well over many years (as will be seen) and it is likely enough that he would have remembered, in 52, canvassing by Gallus several years earlier. It is possible, for example, that Gallus hoped to succeed Plautius in 47 or that he offered himself as Scapula's successor some time before the latter's death. By 52, when the offer came, under rather different conditions, it would be understandable if he had changed his mind: the capture of Caratacus had removed the incentive; and dead men's shoes are not always attractive.

The Didii appear to derive from eastern Italy, specifically from the

---

[21] *Ann.* 16. 15-16.
[22] Syme, *Tacitus* 665; Eck, *Senatoren* 178 and n. 272. The third century consul designate Ostorius Euhodianus (*AE* 1945. 20) was perhaps descended from a freedman of the family.
[1] Cf. e.g. Livy 2. 8. 4, 5. 31. 7, etc.
[2] Quint. 6. 3. 68: 'quid ironia? nonne etiam quae severissime fit, ioci prope genus est? Qua urbane usus est Afer, cum Didio Gallo, qui provinciam ambitiosissime petierat, deinde, impetrata ea, tamquam coactus querebatur, Age, inquit, aliquid et rei publicae causa.'
[3] L. Petersen and L. Vidman, *Eirene Congress 1972*, 655, 666.
[4] The suggestion, derived originally from Sir Ronald Syme, was put forward briefly in *Ep. Stud.* 4 (1967) 102 n. 1. For Veranius' inscription, p. 50 below.

coastal town of Histonium.[5] The *nomen* is of 'a type peculiar to the Sabellian peoples, thickest of all among the archaic tribes of the Marsi and Paeligni, extending thence but growing thinner to Picenum north-wards and south to Campania and Samnium'.[6] Like a possible kinsman and fellow-townsman, Gallus may have sprung from the ancient aris-tocracy of the land, 'or at least from a long line of local magnates'.[7] But in Roman terms he was a *novus homo*, if not necessarily the first of his family to enter the senate. A. Didius Postumus, proconsul of Cyprus in the early imperial period, may be a close relative.[8] The Didii may have been assisted in their rise by another family from Histonium, the Hosidii, also prominent in the early years of Claudius' principate.[9] A fragmentary inscription from Olympia records Gallus' *cursus honorum*; it was evidently erected in his honour shortly before he became governor of Britain. Two other incomplete inscriptions from Greece have been associated with Gallus by J. H. Oliver, but their relevance to him seems highly doubtful,[10] and attention must be concentrated on the stone from Olympia:[11]

> *A. Didius G[allus leg]atus [Ti.]*
> *Claudi Caes[aris] Aug. Ger[mani]*
> *ci tr[i]umphal[ibus o]rnamen[tis]*
> 4 *[cos. XVvir] s. f. proco[s. ?Asia] e et Sicilia[e]*
> *[leg. pr. pr.?A]siae pr[?aefectu]s equitat.*
> *[pr. ?tr. pl. or aed. quaestori impe]ratoris*
>   *[Ti. Caesaris Aug.]*

It seems that Gallus was quaestor in AD 19, when his name appears on a decree of the senate,[12] and, if line 6 of the Olympia inscription has been correctly restored, he had the signal honour, for a new man, of being quaestor of Tiberius.[13] Thus, if he achieved this office at the

---

[5] Syme, *Historia* 17 (1968) 75, adducing IX 2903, a Didia Galla. Note also the grand-mother of the egregious P. Paquius Scaeva, another Didia, at the same town (IX 2845 = *ILS* 915).

[6] Syme, *Roman Revolution* 93.   [7] Ibid. 360 f. on *ILS* 915.

[8] *AE* 1934. 86, mistakenly dated to 22 BC by Petersen and Vidman, op. cit. 654; see *PIR²* D 72 ('non ante a. 22 a.C.').

[9] p. 222 below.

[10] *Hesperia* 10 (1941) 240 = *AE* 1947. 76 (Athens), cf. *AE* 1949. 11; *IG* IX 2. 1135 (Volos) = *GRBS* 8 (1967) 237 ff. See Petersen and Vidman, op. cit. 656 f., 667 and p. 365 below.

[11] Petersen and Vidman, op. cit. 656 ff., improving on III 7247, 12278 = *ILS* 970.

[12] Petersen and Vidman, op. cit. 668, referring to an unpublished inscription.

[13] Petersen and Vidman, op. cit. 665 f., suggest the restoration *[quaestori impe]ratoris* with some reserve, referring to Cébeillac, *Les quaestores* 22-3. Her no. II (*ILS* 928) was *quaestor. imp. Caesaris Aug.*; for her no. XXXI (VI 1572) she restores *q. [imp.] Neronis Ca[esaris] Augus[ti Germanici]*; and her no. XLIV (XIV 4240) was *[q]uaestori imp. Cae[saris]* (Domi-tian). One would therefore need to restore e.g. *[Ti. Caesaris Aug.]* in the missing line 7 of the Olympia inscription.

normal age, twenty-four or twenty-five, his date of birth would be
*c.*8–7 BC, and he might perhaps have seen military service as *tribunus
laticlavius* under Tiberius or Germanicus in the campaigns that followed
the disaster of AD 9. But the inscription seems to have omitted both
military tribunate, if he had one, and vigintivirate.[14] The next two
magistracies were presumably recorded at the start of line 6: the
aedileship or tribunate of the plebs should have come *c.*AD 21 and the
praetorship *c.*AD 23.[15] Of course, either or both of the posts recorded
in the fifth line of the inscription might have preceded the praetorship
rather than followed it. Legates of consular proconsuls might be selected
from senators at almost any stage in their career, but not unnaturally
they were most commonly ex-praetors, since it was men of this rank
who could most readily afford to devote twelve months to a legateship
without jeopardizing their advancement.[16] In normal circumstances it
would be fruitless to speculate on the identity of the proconsul of Asia
under whom Gallus served, but it happens that during the late 20s and
early 30s the post was held for two years by M. Aemilius Lepidus (*cos.
ord.* 6) and then for six years by P. Petronius (*cos.* 19),[17] making it
probable that it was one of these two.

The post of *pr[aefectu]s equitat(us)*, as it may be restored with some
confidence, is more problematic. Only the two Domitii, who were
praef. auxiliorum omnium adversus Germanos as junior ex-praetors,
offer a clear parallel.[18] Gallus has been thought to have held his post
during the invasion of AD 43,[19] but it seems improbable that a consular
of four years standing would have had such a role, especially since he
was already *curator aquarum*. To be sure, he did later receive a provincial posting while retaining this *cura*. But that, if anything, makes it
improbable that he had already been absent from his duties to go on
the British campaign. It is more likely that he commanded the cavalry

---

[14] As the photograph in Petersen and Vidman, op. cit. 658–9, shows, if there was a seventh
line (see previous note), it was incomplete.

[15] Gallus' consular colleague Domitius Afer is described as *recens praetura* in AD 26 (Tac.
Ann. 4. 52. 1).

[16] See now esp. Eck, *Senatoren* 38 ff.; and pp. 15, 23 above.

[17] Syme, *JRS* 45 (1955) 29 f. = *Ten Studies in Tacitus* 42 ff.

[18] *ILS* 990–1, on which see most recently Alföldy, *Die Hilfstruppen der römischen Provinz
Germania Inferior* (*Ep. Stud.* 6, 1968) 131 ff., who argues that the post was held in AD 70,
with some parallels on p. 147. One might note also the commands of Petillius Cerialis (p. 68
below) and Marius Celsus (Tac. *Hist.* 2. 24. 3) in AD 69.

[19] Thus Domaszewski, *Röm. Mitt.* 6 (1891) 163 ff.; but he believed the honorand of the
Olympia inscription was the son of the future governor of Britain. See Groag, *RE* 5. 1 (1903)
410 f. and *PIR*² D 70; Petersen and Vidman, op. cit. 665.

in one of the campaigns of Tiberius' principate, for example in Thrace, Africa, or even Gaul.[20] The first of these has something to commend it, for it would satisfactorily explain the choice of Gallus to command the Moesian army *c.*44–5.

At any rate, Gallus was not inactive between praetorship and consulship. His term as proconsul of Sicily presumably fell in the principate of Tiberius, and, given Tiberius' practice, may well have lasted more than twelve months.[21] It was long assumed that he was consul in 36, since Frontinus informs us that he became *curator aquarum*, normally a consular post, in the second half of AD 38,[22] and no vacancies in the consular *fasti* remain for 37 and 38. Thus he was assumed to have been the colleague of his disgraced predecessor in the *cura aquarum*, M. Porcius Cato.[23] But it has now been recognized that another man was Cato's colleague in 36, while two tablets from Pompeii show Gallus as consul on 13 September with Cn. Domitius Afer, whose unusual elevation to the *fasces* is described by Dio under the year 39.[24] Thus Gallus became *curator aquarum* before being consul, perhaps because of a shortage of consulars at the time of Cato's fall from office. He continued to serve as *curator* until 49, and thus had responsibility for this important service at a crucial time in its history. Caligula had begun the construction of two new aqueducts shortly before Gallus took over, and they were finally completed in 52, three years after he was succeeded by Domitius Afer. Claudius undoubtedly took a keen interest in the work: one of the new aqueducts was named the *Claudia.*[25] Gallus must have been a trusted servant of the emperor, as is confirmed by his membership of the *XVviri*, who would have had special prominence at the Secular Games in AD 47.[26]

However, for some years during the 40s Gallus was evidently absent from Rome, as legate of the emperor, winning the *ornamenta triumphalia*. The Olympia inscription does not specify which province he was governing, but his exploits were certainly recorded by Tacitus in

[20] Thrace was still disturbed in AD 21 (Tac. *Ann.* 3. 38 ff.) and 26 (*Ann.* 4. 44 ff.). For Africa, see *Ann.* 2. 52. 5–6, 3. 20 ff., 3. 74, 4. 25. 2, for actions involving auxiliary troops. For Gaul, proposed by Petersen and Vidman, op. cit. 665, see *Ann.* 3. 40 ff., esp. 45.

[21] Dio 58.23.5; W. Orth, *Die Provinzialpolitik des Tiberius* (1970) 71 ff., 127 ff., gives a convenient list (omitting, however, Munatius Plancus Paulinus: J. Morris, *Bonner Jahrb.* 165 (1965) 88 ff.); see also n. 17 above.

[22] *de aquis* 102. 7; cf. Vidman, *Listy fil.* 96 (1973) 16 ff.

[23] Degrassi, *FC* 10.

[24] *AE* 1973. 138; see Barbieri, *RAL* 29 (1974) 259 ff.; Petersen and Vidman, op. cit. 653 ff.; Dio 60. 20. 3.

[25] Frontin. *de aquis* 13.

[26] J. B. Pighi, *De ludis saecularibus populi Romani Quiritium* (1941) 76 ff.

one of the lost books of the *Annals*, probably the Tenth.[27] Under the year 49 Tacitus refers back to Gallus' installation of the young Bosporan ruler Cotys, when describing subsequent disturbances in the Crimea.[28] Cotys began striking coins as king in the Bosporan year 342, equivalent to October AD 45-6.[29] Dio assigns the breaking up of the great Balkan command created by Tiberius into its constituent provinces of Moesia, Macedonia, and Achaia, to the year 44.[30] Gallus may have carried out this task in addition to his special mission in the Black Sea and, even more important, the annexation of the Thracian kingdom as a province, which involved warfare.[31] He could have been away from his duties at Rome for as long as three years; on his return he was to resume the *cura aquarum* for two or three years at most. An obvious reason for his receiving a successor in that office in AD 49 may have been that he became proconsul of Asia; the space available in the inscription is insufficient to restore *proco*[s. *Africa*]e, and there is room for him in the *fasti* of Asia in the years 49-50 or 50-1.[32]

Finally, in 52, following the news of Scapula's death, Gallus was appointed to Britain. Whether or not it was on this occasion that he complained 'tamquam coactus', he hastened to take up the command. He faced a situation not unlike that which had greeted Scapula in 47, and which was to be faced by more than one later governor on his arrival: Britons living on the fringe of the garrisoned area were attempting to intimidate the new commander.[33] Gallus was evidently not displeased that the enemy were exaggerating their successes and was disposed to encourage the rumours—'to increase his credit if he were successful and to have a better claim for forgiveness if he failed to break the rebels', as one may loosely render Tacitus' comment in the *Annals*. When he did arrive on the scene, the Silures dispersed, and thereafter he had to turn his attention to the Brigantian kingdom, where Queen Cartimandua's divorced husband Venutius was trying to overthrow her.[34] The circumstances were similar in many respects to those which Gallus had had to cope with in the Crimea in 45. But on this occasion, since it was merely a question of repelling a rival claimant, rather than,

[27] Syme, *Tacitus* (1958) 260.
[28] *Ann.* 12. 15. 1.
[29] *BMC Pont.* 52 ff., cf. pp. xxxviii, xliii, for the era.
[30] Dio 60.24.1, cf. Suet. *D. Claud.* 25. 2, 42. 1.
[31] See Stein, *Thracia* 1. ff., who suggests the war should be dated to AD 45.
[32] Petersen and Vidman, op. cit. 662 ff.
[33] Cf. the reception given to Ostorius Scapula and to Julius Agricola (pp. 43 above, 77 below).
[34] Sen. *Apoc.* 12, mentions the Brigantes for no obvious reason. Were they topical because Gallus' intervention there took place *c.*54?

as with the Bosporan kingdom, installing a new Roman nominee, he deemed it sufficient to act through subordinates. First he sent some auxiliary cohorts, and on a subsequent occasion, not necessarily in the same or even in the following year, he sent a legion (probably the IXth), under Caesius Nasica.[35] Tacitus not unreasonably ascribes Gallus' failure to take personal command to two further motives only: his age and incapacity on the one hand ('gravis senectute'), and the fact that he had already won enough personal distinction ('multa copia honorum') on the other. In the *Agricola*, too, Tacitus had stressed Gallus' relative inactivity, although noting his eagerness for fame. The small number of forts 'in ulteriora promotis' will perhaps have included some built for garrisons within the Brigantian kingdom—he had left auxiliary troops in the Crimea to support Cotys after withdrawing his main force. But he doubtless also extended the network of military control further into the Welsh mountains.[36]

In the *Agricola* Tacitus states unambiguously that Gallus was succeeded by Veranius. Neither there nor in the *Annals* is there any hint that Gallus died in office, as has sometimes been stated.[37] If three successive governors of Britain—a province in which the historian had a special interest—had all died at their post, Tacitus would surely have said so. We must take it that Gallus returned to Rome, or perhaps to his estates in the country. His last year in Britain was probably 57, as will be seen from a consideration of the next two governors. Thereafter nothing more is heard of him, although his *tria nomina* were borne by the notorious Fabricius Veiento.[38] That person's career, later so successful under the Flavians, almost foundered in AD 62 when he was expelled from Italy by Nero for libelling people in high places.[39] Veiento may have acquired the names by inheritance or adoption, presumably before his expulsion. Whether C. Pomponius Gallus Didius Rufus, proconsul of Crete-Cyrene in AD 88-9, was also a connection is less certain.[40]

[35] p. 231 below.

[36] See e.g. G. Webster, *Britannia* 1 (1970) 191 f.

[37] Groag, *RE* 5.1 (1903) 411: 'Bis zu seinem Tode?'; likewise Syme, *Historia* 17 (1968) 75; Petersen and Vidman, op. cit. 666.

[38] *PIR*² F 91; Syme, *Tacitus* (1958) 633.

[39] *Ann.* 14. 50.

[40] *AE* 1954. 188. In *PIR*² G 55, Stein suggested that Didius was the Gallus, *XVvir* and *consularis*, whose daughter is honoured on a fragmentary inscription (now lost) from Tarraco, naming others of her kinsmen including a Dolabella (II 4129 p. 972). But see now Alföldy, *RIT* 137, with other suggestions.

57–58   Q. Veranius Q. f. Clu. (*cos. ord.* 49)

A. E. Gordon, *Quintus Veranius Consul A.D. 49* (1952) = *AE* 1953. 251 (Rome):

1 [   ] *quinq* [*ue*] *nnio pr* [*a*] *efui* [*t*]
2 [*in pot*] *est* [*a*] *tem Ti. Claudii Caesaris Aug.*
3 [*Tr*] *acheotarum expugnatum delevit*
4 [*Ti.*] *Claudii Caesaris Augusti Germanici*
5 [   ] *utionem moenium remissam et interceptam*
6 [   ] *b* [.] *pacavit, propter quae auctore*
7 [   ] *consul designatus, in consulatu nominatione*
8 [   ] *ni augur creatus in numerum patriciorum adlectus est*
9 [*Ti. Claudii Caesaris Augusti Germ*] *anici aedium sacrarum et operum*
                                                                    locorumque
10 [*o*] *rdo et populus Romanus consentiente senatu ludis*
11 [*cum non p*] *etierit ab Augusto principe cuius liberalitatis erat*
                                                                       minister
12 [*German*] *ici provinciae Britanniae in qua decessit*
13 [(?)*Veranius filius Q. Ve*] *rani vixit annis VI et mensibus X*
Tac. *Agr.* 14; *Ann.* 14. 29. 1.

Veranius' brief governorship is summarized in the *Agricola* in eight words and at somewhat greater length in a sentence of the *Annals* introducing the account of the great rebellion. The dating of the appointment has to be deduced from that of Paullinus, who, as Syme has demonstrated, must have arrived in 58.[1] It seems virtually certain, therefore, that Veranius came to Britain in 57, the year suggested by his inscription from Rome: the language of the admittedly fragmentary phrase in lines 10–12, associating Veranius' appointment to Britain with an occasion when he was the emperor's *liberalitatis . . minister* can only be referred with any plausibility to Nero's *congiarium* of that year.[2] Whether Tacitus' phrase 'intra annum' means 'before the end of the calendar year' or 'in less than twelve months' is not quite clear. The former is perhaps more probable.[3]

In spite of Veranius' apparently almost negligible contribution to the history of Britain, his career and the circumstances of his appointment have been the subject of considerable attention.[4] Roman policy towards the island and the senatorial *cursus* are both illuminated by inspection of this case, as revealed by the Rome inscription and a variety of other evidence. The origin of the family is not directly attested. The *nomen* is

[1] p. 56 below.
[2] p. 53 below.
[3] A. E. Gordon, op. cit. 266.
[4] C. E. Stevens, *CR* 1 (1951) 4 ff.; E. Birley, *Roman Britain and the Roman Army* 1 ff.; Gordon, op. cit.; etc.

not common and it is tempting to suggest Verona as their home because of the poet Catullus' friend of this name.[5] That person may well be an ancestor. However, the tribe Clustumina, to which our governor may confidently be assigned in view of the provincial Veranii deriving citizenship from him who belong to it,[6] points elsewhere, in the first instance to Umbria. But as Syme has pointed out, no Veranii happen to be recorded there, while several occur in the Sabine country, where Forum Novum, south-west of Reate, seems to be an isolated part of the Clustumina.[7]

The governor's father was undoubtedly the Q. Veranius who served as *legatus* under Germanicus in the east in AD 18 and organized the new province of Cappadocia.[8] Later, in AD 20, he was to play an important part in the trial of Cn. Piso, with P. Vitellius and other members of Germanicus' staff.[9] The earlier part of the younger Veranius' career is recorded in a fragmentary inscription from Cyane in Lycia: Κοίντον Οὐηράνιον Κοίντου / υἱὸν τριῶν ἀνδρῶν ἐπὶ χα/ράξεως νομίσματος χειλι⁴/άρχου λεγιῶνος τετάρτης/ Σκυθικῆς ταμίαν Τιβερίου καὶ / Γα[ί]ου Σεβαστοῦ [δήμ]αρχ[ον . . .][10] His first full magistracy was thus as quaestor of the emperor, a mark of favour;[11] as it turned out, he served both Tiberius and Gaius in that capacity and hence must have held office in 37. This makes it probable that he was born *c*.AD 12.[12] His post in the vigintivirate, as *monetalis*, had been the most prestigious of the four;[13] this favour, like the quaestorship of the emperor, was doubtless the result of his father's services to Germanicus. As tribune of IV Scythica his service would have been in Moesia, where the legion is first firmly attested in AD 33; but he is unlikely to have seen much action.[14] After his quaestorship he had three years without employment, which is a little surprising: he could have held his next magistracy in 39 or 40. On the other hand, it might be wrong to expect anyone's career to have proceeded 'normally' under Caligula: Veranius may simply have preferred to lie low for two or three years.[15]

---

[5] Thus R. J. M. Lindsay, *CP* 43 (1948) 44 n. 16.
[6] D. Magie, *Roman Rule in Asia Minor* (1950) 1394.
[7] Syme, *CQ* 7 (1957) 123 ff.; cf. Kubitschek 270.
[8] Tac. *Ann.* 2. 56. 4.
[9] *Ann.* 3. 10. 2, 13. 3, 17. 4, 19. 1; for his services at the trial he was awarded a priesthood.
[10] *IGR* III 703.
[11] p. 13 above.
[12] p. 12 above.
[13] pp. 5 ff. above.
[14] Ritterling, *RE* 12. 2 (1925) 1557.
[15] It may be worth noting the fall of Calvisius Sabinus in 39 (p. 39 above). L. R. Taylor, *The Voting Districts of the Roman Republic* (1960) 200 f., suggested that the family was from Forum Novum, perhaps the home of the Veranii.

His tribunate of the plebs is firmly dated to the year 41, for as holder of this office he played a minor but significant role in the dramatic transactions of 24 and 25 January in that year. The senate sent emissaries to the camp of the guard, 'men outstanding in virtue', to persuade Claudius to desist from flouting its authority, as Josephus records. After delivering the senate's message Veranius and Brocchus—and both were tribunes of the plebs—prostrated themselves before Claudius in supplication.[16] Claudius rejected the appeal, but the messenger Veranius was to prosper under the new *princeps*. Neither inscription happens to preserve a record of his praetorship, but he was probably designated soon after Claudius' accession to hold office in 42. Dio specifically notes that Claudius varied the number of praetors from year to year and the fact that Veranius would not have had the prescribed year's interval between offices is not a serious difficulty.[17] Exceptions were possible, and they would have been natural enough in the circumstances of 41-2, when there were undoubtedly sudden vacancies in any case, as well as a necessity to reward particular individuals.[18]

Veranius very probably went overseas immediately after his praetorship, for Dio records that Lycia was annexed in 43 and added to Pamphylia, after disturbances involving the deaths of Roman citizens.[19] The surviving portion of the inscription of Veranius' monument at Rome begins with the words *quinq[ue]nnio pr[a]efui[t]*, followed in the next three lines by fragmentary phrases which, however they be restored, must refer to details of his campaigns in this province, where there is abundant record of his governorship.[20] The 'five-year term' attested by the Rome inscription need not, in practice, have meant that he stayed in Lycia later than the autumn of 47, for he could have had five campaigning seasons in the years 43-7 inclusive. No information is available about the size or nature of the forces at his disposal, but doubtless troops were made available from the Syrian army.[21] At all events, even without the evidence of the Rome inscription it would be manifest that Veranius acquitted himself well and acquired a military reputation. He is without doubt the Quintus Veranius to whom

---

[16] Joseph. *Ant. Jud.* 19. 234 ff.

[17] Dio 60. 10. 4. Gordon, op. cit. 245 ff., discusses other possibilities and prefers to suppose that Veranius was adlected among the ex-praetors or that he was praetor for part of 43 only. Note the case of Vespasian, aedile in 39, praetor in 40 (pp. 226 f. below).

[18] Dio (60. 15. 4) notes that a praetor of AD 42 was forced to resign and then put to death.

[19] Dio 60. 17. 3.

[20] *IGR* III 577, 703, 902; etc.; see Gordon, op. cit. 240 f.

[21] Cf. Tac. *Ann.* 6. 41. 1 (p. 59 below); 12. 55.

Onasander dedicated his Στρατηγικός;[22] and on his return to Rome he received high honours from Claudius, perhaps *ornamenta triumphalia*, certainly designation to the consulship as *ordinarius* for 49, patrician rank, and a prestigious priesthood, the augurate. He probably held the *fasces* for the first four months of 49. Thereafter he served as curator of temples, public buildings, and works, at Rome, possibly for a term of several years.[23]

It is perhaps surprising that he did not obtain appointment to a consular province in the early 50s. But the power-brokers of the opening years of Claudius' principate had given way to other forces after the emperor's marriage to Agrippina,[24] and, besides, Veranius may have preferred to stay at Rome or on his estates. This is certainly the implication of the statement in lines 11-12 of the Rome inscription: [. . . *cum non p*]*etierit ab Augusto principe cuius liberalitas erat minister* [*legatus Neronis Caesaris German*]*ici provinciae Britanniae . . .*[25] As was suggested in the discussion of Didius Gallus, the phrase [*cum non p*]*etierit* looks like a deliberately chosen contrast to the known conduct of Gallus, who had sought provincial command 'ambitiosissime'.[26] The language of the inscription indicates that the appointment of Veranius to govern Britain was made at some public ceremony at which Veranius himself had some special role, dispensing the emperor's bounty, perhaps at the *ludi* mentioned at the end of line 10. Since both Tacitus and Dio record spectacles under the year 57 (if not *ludi circenses*) and the former also mentions a 'congiarium', this seems to be satisfactory confirmation.[27]

Ostorius Scapula had been threatening the annihilation of the Silures —'Silurum nomen penitus extinguendum' (*Ann.* 12. 39. 2)—shortly before his death. Didius Gallus had had five years in Britain but, after an initial burst of activity, had made no attempt to carry out the policy of aggression. In 58 Corbulo was to launch a new, forward policy on the eastern border of the empire.[28] It is reasonable to assume that Nero and his advisers had decided, in 57, that action was called for in Britain

[22] *Prooem.* 1; see Gordon, op. cit.
[23] Gordon, op. cit. 254 ff. His restoration of lines 9–10 is questionable; see J. M. Reynolds in her review, *CR* 3 (1954) 313 ff.
[24] See now e.g. Griffin, *Seneca* 81 ff.
[25] Cf. J. H. Oliver for alternative restorations of lines 10–12, in his review of Gordon, op. cit., *AJP* 75 (1954) 206 ff. (not plausible.).
[26] Quint. 6. 3. 68 (quoted above, p. 44 n. 2).
[27] Tac. *Ann.* 13. 31. 1; Dio 61. 9. 5. K. F. Bradley's attempt to date Veranius' supervision of the *ludi* to AD 51, *GRBS* 16 (1975) 308, is not convincing.
[28] Tac. *Ann.* 13. 34. 3 ff.

too,[29] replacing Gallus with a man who enjoyed a 'magna severitatis fama'. Veranius had the right experience of campaigning in mountainous country and he was still relatively young, probably only 45. In the event he did no more than ravage Silurian territory on a modest scale before his death, making in his will claims which Tacitus—with the benefit of hindsight—was able to condemn as exaggerated: that he could have subjugated the province for Nero if he had had another two years.

Veranius had at least two children, twin daughters, one of whom may be the child commemorated in the last line of his funerary monument, who died at the age of six years and ten months.[30] Since one of the twins was called Octavilla,[31] it may be that Veranius' wife was as an Octavia.[32] The other daughter, Verania Gemina, was to marry a figure of some distinction, the ill-fated Piso Licinianus, chosen as son and heir by Galba on 10 January 69 and murdered with him five days later.[33] Gemina survived for many years, and was to be subjected, at the end of her life, to the attentions of the notorious fortune-hunter Regulus.[34]

58-61   C. Suetonius Paullinus (*cos. a. inc.*)

Tac. *Agr.* 5; 14; *Hist.* 2. 37; *Ann.* 14. 29–39; Dio 62. 7–8.

The sudden death of Veranius led Nero and his advisers to extract from retirement[1]—it would seem—another general whose laurels had been won early in Claudius' principate, and another specialist in mountain warfare. C. Suetonius Paullinus[2] had conducted a spectacular expedition in Mauretania, 'overrunning the country as far as Mount

---

[29] E. Birley, *Roman Britain and the Roman Army* 5 ff.

[30] See Gordon, op. cit. 266 ff., for discussion of the last line of the Rome inscription. W. Eck has pointed out to me that the child in line 13 was more probably a son, whose age was given to explain why he held no office, a practice not normally followed with girls when the father, with his career, is commemorated first.

[31] As shown by an unpublished inscription from Xanthus, to be published by A. Balland, to whom I am grateful for permission to refer to it.

[32] If so, perhaps another daughter of C. Octavius Laenas (*cos.* 33), whose son married Tiberius' granddaughter Rubellia Bassa, while a daughter married M. Cocceius Nerva, the father of the emperor. For these people, see Groag, *RE* 17. 2 (1937), 1848 f. (The consulship of 33 is supplied by the *Fasti Ostienses*). But there were other, less distinguished Octavii about as well.

[33] *ILS* 240; *PIR*[2] C 300 (and see pp. 356, 359 below for Piso's father and brother).

[34] Pliny, *ep*, 2. 20. 1. Note also [Cornelius Dola]bella Verania[nus], a *puer patrimus et matrimus* who ministered to the Arvals in 105 (*PIR*[2] C 1352).

[1] Syme, *Tacitus* 387.

[2] For the spelling with double L, see Degrassi, *Inscr. It.* XIII. 1, 314 f., referring to Pais, *Suppl. Ital.* 417 (p. 53): *C. Suetoni[o Pa]ullino cos.* (the consul of AD 66. See further p. 56 and n. 16 below). Note also the lead *tessera* (n. 18 below).

Atlas', according to Dio, before handing over his command to Cn. Hosidius Geta.[3] The elder Pliny records that Paullinus was the first Roman general to cross the summit of this range and that he went as far as the R. Ger.[4] His status at the time, Dio specifically states, was that of ex-praetor, so that he was certainly senior to Veranius, for the campaign is placed under the year 42—although the operations of Paullinus and Geta, not to mention the activities of M. Licinius Crassus Frugi (*cos. ord.* 27), probably occupied several years.[5] Paullinus' date of birth should thus have fallen at the very latest *c.*AD 11, and might have been considerably earlier. Apart from this exploit, virtually nothing is known of him before his arrival in Britain. His family almost certainly derived from the Umbrian town of Pisaurum in the *ager Gallicus*, where Sueto, a cognate form of the exceptionally rare *nomen*, is recorded.[6] Hence one may legitimately speculate that the choice of Paullinus for the Mauretanian mission was due to the influence of the praetorian prefect Arrecinus Clemens, in office in 41, a native of Pisaurum.[7]

His reward for his exploit was probably the consulship and perhaps *ornamenta triumphalia*, but neither are in fact attested directly.[8] A phrase in Tacitus' *Histories*—he is called 'vetustissimus consularium' in 69[9]—is the only real evidence that he attained the *fasces* in the 40s, but he might have had to wait until 47 or later. Another phrase in the same work[10] might perhaps mean that he had been in Britain before his governorship, perhaps as *comes* of Claudius in 43; but 'Britannicis expeditionibus' is more likely to refer merely to his three campaigns as governor. It may well be that his high reputation as a military man in the late 50s was based solely on his Mauretanian campaign and on his first two seasons in Britain. But he might conceivably have governed one of the Germanies, Pannonia, or Dalmatia, in the late 40s or early 50s.[11]

---

[3] Dio 60. 4. On Geta see also p. 365 below.

[4] Pliny, *HN* 5. 14.

[5] Thomasson, *Statthalter Nordafrikas* II 241 ff., see also p. 356 below, on Crassus.

[6] Syme, *Tacitus* 781, is cautious: 'There is a faint chance that the scholar [the biographer] and the consular both derive "moribunda ab sede Pisauri" (Catullus 81. 3)'. On Pisaurum, see *RE* Supp. 11 (1968) 1092 ff.

[7] *PIR*[2] A 1072.

[8] Degrassi, *FC* 12; F. Miltner, *RE* 4A 1 (1931) 592.

[9] *Hist.* 2. 37. 1. The exact significance of the phrase depends on whether the consulars in question are all the surviving ex-consuls or only those involved on Otho's side. But perhaps Paullinus may be assumed to have been senior to e.g. M. Pompeius Silvanus (45) and T. Flavius Sabinus (47?; see p. 225 below).

[10] *Hist.* 2. 37. 1.

[11] See Ritterling, *FRD*15 ff., 48ff.; Reidinger, *Pannonia* 36 ff.; Jagenteufel, *Dalmatien* 24 ff., for vacancies in this period.

His first year in Britain should be 58, rather than 59. In the *Agricola* he is said to have been successful for two years, and the great rebellion fell in the third season. Although Tacitus explicitly assigns the Boudiccan revolt to the year 61 in the *Annals*, Syme has shown that this must be mistaken.[12] Tacitus' own account of the transactions in Britain makes it clear that Paullinus' successor Petronius Turpilianus, *consul ordinarius* in 61, must have arrived in the year after the rebellion. In 58 and 59 Paullinus, no doubt taking up the challenge implied in the testament of Veranius, had subjugated Wales and garrisoned it. There remained Mona, the stronghold of the Druids. He launched his attack on the island at the start of his third season, and it was only after this had been successfully carried out, and the island garrisoned, that the uprising of the Iceni and their allies broke out. After the famous victory against the rebels Paullinus' army was reinforced from Germany and a replacement arrived for the procurator Decianus Catus. It was by then past harvest time, and there followed conflicts between the governor and the new procurator Classicianus.[13] These in turn led to the visit of inspection by the freedman Polyclitus,[14] who was sent from Italy by Nero. The decision to retain Paullinus in office for a short time, before his replacement by Turpilianus, 'qui iam consulatu abierat', when a pretext offered, must be assigned to the spring or early summer of 61.[15]

Although Paullinus was dismissed, he was not disgraced, as is seen by the appearance of a namesake, presumably his son, as *consul ordinarius* in 66.[16] What is more, Mrs M. T. Griffin has pointed out[17] that a lead *tessera* found at Rome, with NERO CAESAR on the obverse and PAVLLINI on the reverse, with symbols of victory,[18] should refer to a donative issued by the emperor to celebrate Paullinus' successes in Britain.[19] In 69, by then 'the oldest of the consulars', he was one of Otho's leading commanders in the campaign against the Vitellians, and was even regarded as a potential emperor.[20] Tacitus comments on his

[12] Syme, *Tacitus* 765 f.

[13] See pp. 288 f. below, for these procurators.

[14] *RE* 21. 2 (1952) 1700.

[15] It may be preferable to assign to this period Nero's alleged hesitation over whether he should abandon Britain (Suet. *Nero* 18), on which much has been written, most recently by Griffin, *Seneca* 230 f.; but the moment when the panic-stricken Catus first brought news of Boudicca's successes seems likelier.

[16] Degrassi, *FC* 12, 18, favours identification with our man; but there is no sign of iteration for the consul of AD 66 (see Miltner, *RE* 4A 1 (1931) 593).

[17] *Scripta Classica Israelica* 3 (1976/7) 138 ff.

[18] M. Rostowzew, *Tesserarum Urbis Romae et suburbi plumbearum Sylloge* (1903) no. 230.

[19] This evidence has been neglected by recent commentators. It could, of course, as Mrs Griffin, op. cit. 145 f., concedes, be connected with victories in 58 or 59.

[20] *Hist.* 2. 37. 1.

'auctoritas' and on his 'fama, qua nemo illa tempestate militaris rei calli-
dior habebatur'. He deftly characterizes him as 'cunctator natura', one
who preferred caution and careful calculation to haste and trust in
providence, noting in particular how he urged vainly before the battle
of Bedriacum that the Othonians should await the arrival of the XIVth
legion, 'magna ipsam fama': it was his old legion, and its great reputation had been acquired with him in the defeat of Boudicca.[21] He is last
heard of defending his service with Otho before Vitellius at Lugdunum:
he and a colleague escaped retribution by the plea that they had
counselled delay as a deliberate betrayal.[22] Thereafter he disappears
from the record, but, if he survived for even a few years more, he may
have had the opportunity of advising the new Flavian regime on its
British policy. Tacitus' portrayal of him is not uncritical, but Paullinus
comes out, in all three works, considerably more favourably than does,
for example, Petillius Cerialis.[23] One may suppose that Agricola's
recollections of the man who gave him his start had some influence on
the historian.[24]

61–63   P. Petronius P. f. Turpilianus (*cos. ord.* 61)

Tac. *Agr.* 16. 3; *Ann.* 14. 39.

P. Petronius Turpilianus[1] bore the same names as the early Augustan
moneyer, some of whose reverse types indicate that the family was
Sabine, while others perhaps suggest that the *cognomen* derived from
the comic poet of the second century BC, Sex. Turpilius.[2] The moneyer
was very probably father of the influential P. Petronius P. f. (*cos.* 19),
proconsul of Asia for six years under Tiberius and governor of Syria
AD 39–42.[3] P. Petronius was labelled 'an old friend' of Claudius by
Seneca[4] and was married to a Plautia, probably the sister of the first

---

[21] *Hist.* 2. 32.
[22] *Hist.* 2. 60.
[23] pp. 66 ff. below.
[24] Tac. *Agr.* 5. 1, see p. 74 below.
  [1] The fact that P. Petronius (*cos.* 19) appears to have dispensed with a *cognomen*, unlike
his presumed father and son, suggests personal preference. Similarly, A. Plautius and the Vitellii, his kinsmen (p. 37 above), and the QQ. Veranii, from the same circle (p. 51 above), seem to
have preferred the old style of nomenclature, without *cognomen*.
  [2] Groag, *RE* 19. 1 (1937) 1227 ff.; *RIC* I, p. xcvi. For Turpilius, see *RE* 7A 2 (1948)
1428 ff.
  [3] R. Hanslik, *RE* 19. 1 (1937) 1199 ff.
  [4] Sen. *Apoc.* 14. 2.

governor of Britain.[5] Although Turpilianus was consul forty-two years after P. Petronius, it is not unlikely that he was his son rather than his grandson. For one thing, he is described by Plutarch as an old man at the time of his death in AD 68. Even if this was exaggerated, it could hardly have been applied to a man much under fifty.[6] At any rate, the shared *praenomen* makes a close relationship almost certain. Hence Turpilianus was a nephew (or grand-nephew) of A. Plautius, which may have been an important factor when Nero and his advisers looked for a successor to Paullinus. Doubtless a kinsman of Plautius would have seemed a suitable person to restore confidence among the natives. What is more, Turpilianus' father (or grandfather) P. Petronius had been characterised, when governor of Syria, as 'kindly and gentle by nature', qualities which Turpilianus himself might be said to have possessed.[7]

Nothing is known of his career before his consulship, but it is possible that he had served as military tribune in one of the Syrian legions when his father governed that province. Evidently his tenure of office in Britain was fairly brief, for, according to Frontinus, he became *curator aquarum* in AD 63, holding the post for a year.[8] He could of course have had three campaigning seasons in Britain, AD 61, 62, and 63; but Tacitus makes it plain that his military activity was minimal.

Soon after his year in charge of the aqueducts he was to render Nero services of a different kind, for which he was awarded the *ornamenta triumphalia*. Presumably he had been of some assistance in unmasking the conspiracy of Piso, or in dealing with its aftermath.[9] In AD 68, as further proof of his loyalty, he was chosen by Nero, together with Rubrius Gallus, to command an army to put down the rising of Vindex;[10] but the force never saw any action. Well before the end of that year Galba ordered his death, 'an old man, unprotected and unarmed'. His undiminished loyalty was apparently the reason;[11] but Galba or his associates may have had old scores to settle, relating to the events of AD 65-6.[12] No descendants are recorded.

[5] p. 38 above.

[6] Plut. *Galba* 15. 2; Griffin, *Seneca* (1976) 454, with nn. 5–6. Mrs Griffin suggests that Petronius' links with the Vitellii caused the delay in his career.

[7] Philo, *Leg.* 243: ἦν γὰρ καὶ τὴν φύσιν εὐμενὴς καὶ ἥμερος; cf. Tac. *Agr.* 16. 3: 'tamquam exorabilior . . . paenitentiae mitior'.

[8] Frontin. *de aquis* 102. 10–11.

[9] Tac. *Ann.* 15. 72. 1. On this episode see now Eck, *Historia* 25 (1975) 381 ff.

[10] Dio 63. 27. 1a (= Zonar. 11. 13) says that he went over to Galba, but see the references to Plutarch (next note). Syme, *AJP* 58 (1937) 12 = *Danubian Papers* (1971) 77 n. 27, suggests that he may have 'deserted Nero without declaring for Galba'.

[11] Plut. *Galba* 15. 2, 17. 3; Tac. *Hist.* 1. 6. 1; 37. 3.

[12] Galba's links with the victims of Nero's last years are perhaps symbolised by the fact that it was Helvidius Priscus who saw to his burial (Plut. *Galba* 28).

Tac. *Agr.* 16. 3-4 (cf. 7); *Hist.* 1. 60; 2. 65. 2.

Trebellius Maximus presumably arrived in Britain in 63, the year when his predecessor Turpilianus received an appointment at Rome. His previous career is not known in full, and such facts as there are have received varying interpretation. In the *Annals*, Tacitus records an exploit by a legionary legate of the Syrian army named M. Trebellius (no *cognomen*), who successfully besieged two native fortresses in the Taurus mountains.[1] It is natural to suppose that this Trebellius was the friend of the agricultural writer Columella, who served as tribune of VI Ferrata.[2] A phrase in the *Agricola*, however, is generally thought to mean that Trebellius had had no military experience before coming to Britain, and hence it might seem impossible that he could be identical with the former legionary legate—unless Tacitus was careless or inadequately informed about the man when he was writing his first work.[3] On the other hand, as will be seen, the phrase 'nullis castrorum experimentis' might mean something quite different.

At any rate, the Trebellius Maximus who was present at the meeting of the senate following Caligula's assassination may be identified with the future governor without hesitation. Josephus records that he removed a ring bearing Caligula's portrait from the finger of the consul Sentius Saturninus, who had just been denouncing the murdered emperor.[4] Some fifteen years later, early in the reign of Nero, Trebellius held the consulship with Seneca as his colleague. The pair was in office on 24 August, almost certainly in the year 56.[5] Seneca himself was well over fifty, and Trebellius, if he was indeed the former legionary legate, must have been in his late forties at the very least. It is not unlikely that the two were friends, although there is no direct evidence.[6] In 61, Tacitus records, a census was conducted in the Gallic provinces by three senators: Q. Volusius Saturninus (*cos. ord.* 56), T. Sextius Africanus (*cos. ord.* 59), and Trebellius Maximus. Trebellius' two noble colleagues were rivals; both despised Trebellius, thereby boosting his

---

[1] *Ann.* 6. 41.
[2] Columella 5. 1. 2, cf. 2. 10. 18; *ILS* 2923. See C. Cichorius, *Römische Studien* (1922) 417 ff., esp. 420 n. 3; *PIR*[2] J 779.
[3] Thus Griffin, *Seneca* 446 f., citing a suggestion of Sir Ronald Syme.
[4] Joseph. *Ant. Jud.* 19 185; see also p. 360 below, on Saturninus.
[5] *Digest* 36. 1. 1 etc.; by 3 Sept. Trebellius had been replaced by P. Palfurius, see Degrassi, *FC* 15; Griffin, *Seneca* 73 n. 6.
[6] Griffin, *Seneca* 89.

position.[7] The anecdote, while demonstrating that Trebellius' birth was relatively undistinguished, does not really help to reveal his origins. Cichorius used the story as an argument for identifying the legionary legate of AD 36 with the consular colleague of Seneca: if the latter were the son of a legionary legate, he argued, he would not have been regarded as a *novus homo*.[8] But as the Sextii affected descent from the consul of 366 BC,[9] and the Volusii were related to the Claudii Nerones,[10] they could well have looked down on Trebellius even if his father had commanded a legion; so the argument will not suffice. In favour of identifying the two, one might point to a whole series of elderly men holding consular governorships in the 60s,[11] including, probably, Trebellius' predecessor in Britain, and to the possibility that Trebellius was a friend and coeval of Seneca.[12] However this may be, it is just possible that his home was in Gaul, which might have made his task as *censitor* easier. There were Trebellii from Tolosa in Narbonensis resident at Athens later in the first century: an inscription there records a Q. Trebellius Rufus who was *archon* there in the reign of Domitian, having perhaps opted out of a senatorial career; and this man's son was named Trebellius Rufus Maximus.[13] This is not enough to prove that our governor was from Gaul, but the possibility must be registered.

Turpilianus had taken some modest military action—'compositis prioribus'—and then stopped, 'nihil ultra ausus'. Tacitus' point about Trebellius in the next sentence of the *Agricola* may be that he did even less: 'segnior'—he was *more* sluggish; and 'nullis castrorum experimentis' could mean, not that 'he had no previous military experience', but that 'he neglected to make trial of the army'.[14] Hence the discipline and morale of the soliders, who had been accustomed to regular campaigning, deteriorated from inactivity ('cum adsuetus expeditionibus

---

[7] Tac. *Ann.* 14. 46.

[8] Cichorius, op. cit. 420 n. 3.

[9] *RE* 2A 2 (1923) 2039.

[10] Syme, *Hist.* 13 (1964) 156, referring to Cic. *ad Att.* 5. 21. 6.

[11] C. Cestius Gallus (*cos.* 42) in Syria (*PIR*[2] C 691); Tampius Flavianus and Pompeius Silvanus in Pannonia and Dalmatia (*divites senes*, Tac. *Hist.* 2. 86. 3); Ti. Plautius Silvanus Aelianus (*cos.* 45) in Moesia (Stein, *Moesien*, 29 ff.); Galba in Tarraconensis; and Vespasian in Judaea.

[12] Griffin, *Seneca* 89.

[13] *IG* II[2] 4193; *AE* 1947. 69. See Syme, *HSCP* 73 (1968) 222; Griffin, *Seneca* 446. The other senatorial Trebellius known from this period, Q. Trebellius Q. f. Ter. Catulus (VI 31771), quaestor of Narbonensis, tribune of the plebs, and legate of legio XVI under Claudius, might be a kinsman of our man. His tribe suggests Italian origin (*regio* I), but Arelate is not excluded (Kubitschek 272). Note that Volusius was assigned as *censitor* to Belgica (Eck, *RE* Supp. 14 (1974) 964), which shows that Trebellius must have worked in Lugdunensis or Aquitania in 61.

[14] For the standard rendering, see Richmond and Ogilvie, *vita Agricolae* 203. But Church and Brodrib (1877), 16, translate: 'never ventured on a campaign', which is perfectly legitimate and fits the context equally well.

miles otio lasciviret'). The outbreak of civil war provided an excuse for the governor's 'segnitia', but he was despised and hated by the troops for his avarice and meanness. The legate of *legio* XX, Roscius Coelius,[15] stirred them up, accusing the governor of 'despoiling the legions'. Trebellius left the province early in 69 and fled to Vitellius, perhaps taking with him the 8,000 men 'e Britannico dilectu' that formed part of Vitellius' expeditionary force.[16]

In fairness to this governor it must be noted that Tacitus does give him credit for a certain 'comitas', 'gentleness', in his administration of the province, a quality that was doubtless still thought necessary after the events of AD 60-1. Further, the ironic comments on the fact that under Trebellius 'the barbarians too now learned to condone alluring vices' recall the somewhat similar remarks about Agricola's measures in his second winter, which resulted in 'a gradual passing over to the blandishments of vice'. (The process could be called 'romanization'.)[17] If the governor Trebellius Maximus had campaigned in his youth in the Taurus mountains, it could be argued that—like Didius Gallus, Veranius, and Paullinus—he was selected for Britain in the hope that he could put this experience to good use in the conquest of Snowdonia. Equally, his appointment might be construed as a gesture towards his presumed 'amicus' Seneca, no longer influential by 63, but perhaps still worth placating.[18] However this may be, the times were not propitious for energetic military action. The war in the east was settled and from AD 64 peace was the watchword throughout the empire.[19] Before long a number of leading men were to lose their lives, including some army commanders.[20] Perhaps Trebellius preferred to practice 'quies' and 'otium' during his governorship, because, like others, he was aware that under Nero 'inertia pro sapientia fuit'.[21] Finally, it should be remembered that c.AD 66 Nero withdrew the crack British legion XIV, which was to have accompanied him on his expedition to the Caucasus, together with the eight cohorts of Batavian auxiliaries.[22]

---

[15] p. 231 below.   [16] Tac. *Hist.* 2. 57. 1.

[17] Tac. *Agr.* 21. 2; see Richmond and Ogilvie, *vita Agricolae* 220 ff.

[18] Griffin, *Seneca* 94.

[19] Tac. *Ann.* 15. 46. 2: 'haud alias tam immota pax'; 16. 28. 3: 'pacem . . . per orbem terrarum'; Suet. *Nero* 13. 2, records the closure of the temple of Janus, which is lavishly commemorated on the coinage: 'pace p. R. ubique parta', or 'pace p. R. terra mariq. parta', followed by 'Ianum clusit'; see *BMC* I p. clxxiv, which dates the beginning of these issues to AD 64.

[20] Dio 62. 17. 2 ff.

[21] Tac. *Agr.* 6. 3 (on Agricola's conduct as tribune of the plebs in AD 66, p. 75 n. 19 below).

[22] Tac. *Hist.* 2. 11; Ritterling, *RE* 12. 2 (1925) 1731. The Batavians may be assumed to have accompanied the legion, see e.g. *Hist.* 2. 27. 2, showing that they had been out of Britain with XIV Gemina in AD 68. See also *Hist.* 1. 6. 2, referring generally to the *multi numeri* from Britain and elsewhere, which he had collected for his Caucasus campaign and then recalled to deal with Vindex.

Trebellius seems to have recovered his position under Vespasian. At any rate, he is recorded as *magister* of the Arval Brethren in AD 72, and may still have been a member of the college in 75.[23] Thereafter he disappears from the record, and no descendants are known.

69-71   M. Vettius Bolanus (*cos*. 66)

Stat. *Silv*. 5. 2. 54-6:

> . . . tu disce patrem, quantusque negantem
> fluctibus occiduis fesso usque Hyperione Thulen
> intrarit mandata gerens . . .

140-9:
> quod si te magno tellus frenata parenti
> accipiat, quantum ferus exsultabit Araxes,
> quanta Caledonios attollet gloria campos,
> cum tibi longaevus referet trucis incola terrae:
> 'hic suetus dare iura parens, hoc cespite turmas
> adfari; vicis speculas castellaque—longe
> aspicis?—ille dedit cinxitque haec moenia fossa;
> belligeris haec dona deis, haec tela dicavit
> (cernis adhuc titulos); hunc ipse vocantibus armis
> induit, hunc regi rapuit thoraca Britanno.

Tac. *Agr*. 8; 16. 5; *Hist*. 2. 65. 2; 2. 91. 1 (cf. 3. 44-5).

Trebellius Maximus presented himself to Vitellius soon after the latter left Lugdunum in April 69 on receiving the news of Bedriacum. Unlike Cluvius Rufus, who had arrived from his Spanish province at the same time, Trebellius was not permitted to retain his command *in absentia*. Vettius Bolanus was sent to replace him, 'e praesentibus'.[1] Bolanus may have gone to join Vitellius from northern Italy, where his home perhaps was. Although Vettius is one of the commoner *nomina*, there are several examples in Cisalpina, including MM. Vettii, and an inscription from Milan records a Bolana Secunda whose daughter was a Vettia.[2] Bolanus may thus be a maternal *nomen* used as a *cognomen*, after the

---

[23] *Acta Arv*. = *MW* 5-6, p. 16.

[1] Tac. *Hist*. 2. 65. 2.

[2] V. 5849: *v. f. Bolana M. f. Secunda sibi et Vettiae Sex. f. Civili f. et M. Bolano M. f. Aniens. Marcello fratri IIIIvir. aedil. potestate h. m. h. n. s.*; cf. 5900, 6118, 6123 (also from Milan); (between Bergomum and Comum), 5272 (Comum). The relevance was pointed out long ago by E. Hübner, *EE* II p. 34. The family clearly had estates in Etruria, to judge from Stat. *Silv*. 5. 2. 1. Cicero's friend M. Bolanus, 'virum bonum et fortem et omnibus rebus ornatum', whom he commended to P. Sulpicius Rufus (*ad fam*. 13. 77. 2-3), may be an ancestor.

Etruscan fashion.[3]

Not much is known of his career before the governorship, but he is mentioned by Tacitus under the year 62 as a legionary legate in the east, sent to Armenia by Corbulo.[4] Statius elaborates on his military prowess at that time in a poem addressed to Bolanus' son Crispinus many years later, describing him as Corbulo's second in command.[5] He was perhaps the senior legionary legate in Corbulo's army, in age at least.[6] To judge from the date of his consulship, held as suffect with M. Arruntius in the later part of 66, he was probably born in the 20s, for he would appear to be a *novus homo*.[7] Thereafter, it is possible that he was proconsul of Macedonia for a year between 62 and 66. That would explain why his memory was honoured in a remote area of that province some thirty years later. One M. Vettius Philo, who presumably owed his Roman citizenship to Bolanus, left money in his will, in AD 95, for the councillors at Derriopus to celebrate Bolanus' birthday every year.[8]

Bolanus' first task after appointment was presumably the difficult one of escorting the refractory *legio* XIV back to Britain, and when he reached the island he must have had trouble from the legions that were still there, particularly from XX. According to *Agricola*, he did not attempt to reimpose discipline. 'Inertia' towards the enemy was still displayed, as it had been by Trebellius, and the troops continued to be restive. But Bolanus' room for manoeuvre was very circumscribed, as the *Histories* reveal. Although he brought back XIV Gemina, Britain had already contributed 8,000 men to Vitellius, and these troops are not known to have returned. Before long Vitellius demanded more.

---

[3] See H. Rix, *Das etruskische Cognomen* (1963) 325 ff.

[4] *Ann.* 15. 3. 1.

[5] *Silv.* 5. 2. 31 ff., esp. 48: 'ille secundus apex bellorum et proxima cassis'.

[6] But *Silv.* 5. 2. 31 f. might appear to contradict this: 'quippe ille iuventam Protinus ingrediens phrateratum invasit Araxen'.

[7] Apart from the item in n. 2 above, one should note as a possible connection M. Vettius Marcellus, an imperial procurator under Nero: R. Hanslik, *RE* 8A. 2 (1958) 1860 f. (add *AE* 1967. 23). The latter, whose wife was Helvidia C. f. Priscilla, lived at Teate Marrucinorum (*ILS* 1377).

[8] Suggested by Syme, *ap.* A. E. and J. Gordon, *Album of Dated Latin Inscriptions* III (1965) no. 278 p. 50, citing *PIR*[1] V 323. Eck, *Zephyrus* 23/4 (1972/3) 240 is sceptical; B. Kreiler, *Statthalter Kleinasiens* 26 f. hesitant. T. C. Sarikakis, *Rhomaioi Archontes tes eparchias Makedonias* (1977) 64 ff. suggests that Bolanus' son, the *cos. ord.* 111, was proconsul —this is not plausible for a patrician. The inscription from Derriopus has been published many times, most recently by N. Vulić, *Spomenici Naše Zemlje, Spomenik* 71 (1931) 186 no. 500 (with photograph). See also B. Laum, *Stiftungen in der griechischen und römischen Antike* II (1914) 39 f., no. 35 (cf. 36 for Philo's *praenomen*). Bolanus' birthday, for the record, was 19 Oct.

Bolanus temporized, for, as Tacitus puts it, 'Britain was never peaceful enough', but he must at least have gone through the motions of sending them. Substantial numbers of men from the British army certainly fought for Vitellius against the Flavians in October.[9] In the meantime, the men in *legio* XIV had been actively canvassed by the Flavian leaders,[10] and the rest of the army, especially Vespasian's old legion, II Augusta, was already leaning in that direction.[11]

At this juncture trouble arose in the north. Venutius, the rejected consort of the Brigantian ruler, attacked Cartimandua again and this time her situation became desperate. Bolanus was able to rescue her, and fought several battles with mixed success. But Venutius had to be left in control of the Brigantes. All this must evidently be placed in 69.[12] Tacitus' account of these transactions in the *Histories*—he makes no mention of them in the *Agricola*—suggests that the 'inertia erga hostis' of which he complains in his first work refers only to the period after Agricola arrived as legate of XX, in AD 70.[13] Hence there is not really a serious conflict with the portrayal of Bolanus' command by Statius. There is of course some poetic licence, with the mention of Thule and the 'Caledonios . . . campos', names which Statius would have heard in the early 80s. Nor can the details in lines 140-9 of the poem be pressed too far. Statius may not have known much more about Bolanus' actions than Tacitus records in the *Histories*, that he fought against a British king. None the less, he does state clearly that Bolanus built forts and signal-stations over a wide area, that he surrounded walls with a ditch, and that he dedicated a breastplate 'torn off a British king'. It may be excessive to claim that he must have besieged Venutius at Stanwick ('cinxitque haec moenia fossa'). But, equally, it would be foolish to deny any possibility that Bolanus garrisoned parts of southern Brigantia and that he operated well within the kingdom.[14]

Early in 70 Agricola arrived to take over *legio* XX, but at about this moment XIV Gemina was withdrawn to the Rhineland.[15] It is thus not surprising that Bolanus was reduced to 'inertia'. Indeed, if, as Josephus appears to state, Petillius Cerialis was actually designated governor of Britain *before* taking command of operations against Civilis and his

---

[9] *Hist.* 2. 57. 1 (the 8,000 men), 97. 1, 100. 1; 3. 1. 2, 22. 2; 4. 46. 2.
[10] *Hist.* 2. 86. 4 (before Vitellius' arrival at Rome in mid-July, ibid. 2. 89 ff.).
[11] *Hist.* 3. 44, cf. pp. 228, 269 below.
[12] The account of the year 69 continues until *Hist.* 4. 37.
[13] But Tacitus fails to mention Bolanus by name in *Hist.* 3. 44-5.
[14] See A. R. Birley, *Britannia* 4 (1973) 188 f., esp. 189 n. 52.
[15] *Hist.* 4. 68. 4; see p. 219 below.

allies,[16] Bolanus would have been very unwise to open a new campaign in that year. Cerialis was still fighting Civilis in late September, so it should no doubt be assumed that he did not take over Britain until the spring of 71.[17]

Soon after his return to Italy Bolanus was honoured by Vespasian with patrician rank, in 73 or 74;[18] and a little later became proconsul of Asia.[19] Both these items may serve to indicate that his achievements in Britain had not been negligible in the eyes of an emperor who knew that province well. Bolanus had probably married rather late in life, perhaps not until the 70s, for his sons were still youths at the time of Statius' poem to Crispinus, the younger of the two, *c.*AD 95.[20] The elder son, named after his father, as a patrician *consul ordinarius*, in AD 111,[21] could have been born as late as AD 78 or 79, while, if the date suggested for Statius' poem is correct, Crispinus was born *c.*80.[22] After Bolanus' death his widow tried to poison Crispinus[23]—presumably in the hope of securing his share of the inheritance. The poet implies that this took place after the elder son has assumed the *toga virilis*, for Crispinus' guardians accelerated the ceremony in his case as a result of his mother's action.[24] Thus Bolanus probably died at about the same time as Agricola, in AD 93.[25]

---

[16] p. 68 below.

[17] *Hist.* 5. 22. 1: 'castra, quae hiematuris legionibus erigebantur'; 23. 3: 'flexu autumni et crebris per aequinoctium imbribus superfusus amnis'.

[18] *Silv.* 5. 2. 28.

[19] *Silv.* 5. 2. 56-8; *BMC Ionia* 272, 294 ff. See Kreiler, *Statthalter Kleinasiens* 26 ff., who suggests AD 75-6.

[20] *Silv.* 5. 3 is on the *via Domitiana*, completed AD 95; and note that 5. 1. 239 ff. describes the *templum Flavium*, first referred to by Martial in AD 94 (9. 3. 34).

[21] Degrassi, *FC* 33.

[22] Crispinus was aged sixteen according to *Silv.* 5. 2. 12-13. This would fit well with a date *c.*AD 95, if he was the *cos. ord.* 113 (n. 24 below).

[23] *Silv.* 5. 2. 76 ff.

[24] See P. White, *CP* 68 (1973) 282 ff., who also points out that the brothers need not have been twins. The younger might be the same as C. Clodius Crispinus (*cos. ord.* 113), perhaps adopted into another family after the murder attempt (*PIR*[2] C 1164).

[25] As it happens, there was allegedly an outbreak of poisoning at about this time (Dio 67. 11. 6; see the comment by Syme, *Historia* 17 (1968) 82). The bronze signet ring now at Madrid inscribed 'SVBSTITVTI M VETTI BOLANI' (II 6259[19]) might refer to Bolanus' *heredes substituti*, rather than to a slave of his named Substitutus. It may be noted that this item, in the Salamanca collection, could derive ultimately from Lombardy. Finally, for completeness, attention should be drawn to the inscription from Rome recording Bolanus' restoration of a shrine of the Bona dea (VI 65 = *ILS* 3500, cf. 66-7 = 3501-1a).

71-73/4   Q. Petillius Cerialis Caesius Rufus
                           (cos. a. inc., II 74, ?III ord. 83)

Joseph. bell. Iud. 7. 82 f.: πολλοῦ δὲ μέρους ἤδη τῶν Γερμανῶν τὴν ἀποστασίαν
ἀνωμολογηκότος καὶ τῶν ἄλλων οὐκ ἄνδιχα φρονησάντων, ὥσπερ ἐκ δαιμονίου
προνοίας Οὐεσπασιανὸς πέμπει γράμματα Πετιλίῳ Κερεαλίῳ τὸ πρότερον ἡγεμόνι
Γερμανίας γενομένῳ, τὴν ὑπατὸν διδοὺς τιμὴν καὶ κελεύων ἄρξοντα Βρεττανίας
ἀπιέναι. 83. πορευόμενος οὖν ἐκεῖνος ὅποι προσετέτακτο καὶ τὰ περὶ τὴν ἀπόστασιν
τῶν Γερμανῶν πυθόμενος ἤδη συνειλεγμένοις αὐτοῖς ἐπιπεσὼν καὶ παραταξάμενος
πολύ τε πλῆθος αὐτῶν ἀναιρεῖ κατὰ τὴν μάχην, κτλ.
Tac. Agr. 8. 2-3; 17. 1-2; Ann. 14. 32. 3 (cf. Hist. 3. 59. 2).

Petillius Cerialis is an important figure in the history of Roman Britain,
but the evidence for his career as a whole and for his record as governor
is difficult to interpret.[1] His full nomenclature is supplied only in the
diploma of 21 May 74 recording his second consulship, with Eprius
Marcellus as his colleague.[2] It seems likely that he owed two of these
names to the Petillius Rufus recorded by Tacitus under the year 28,
as an ex-praetor 'who stooped to a shameful deed' in the hope of gaining the consulship.[3] Cerialis might perhaps have been adopted by this
Rufus, his original names being Caesius Cerialis.[4] In AD 69, when he
presented himself to the Flavian advance guard near Mevania in Umbria,
disguised as a peasant, he had evidently managed to evade the Vitellian
outposts on account of his knowledge of the terrain.[5] Upper-class
Caesii are well attested in Umbria at this period, and one should also
note that the legate of IX Hispana whom Cerialis probably succeeded
was Caesius Nasica.[6] In view of the common practice of allowing
brothers to serve together, or in succession in the same post,[7] it is
highly probable that Cerialis was the younger brother of Nasica.[8]

[1] This account is based on my article in Britannia 4 (1973) 179 ff.
[2] XVI 20. For the correct spelling, with double L, see F. Münzer, RE 19.1 (1937) 1137.
[3] Ann. 4. 68 ff.
[4] Compare M. Macrinius Avitus Catonius Vindex, clearly a close kinsman of the praetorian
prefect M. Macrinius Vindex (Pflaum, CP, nos. 161, 168); and M. Sosius Laelianus Pontius
Falco (VI 1978), clearly a relative of M. Pontius Laelianus cet. (p. 273 below) and of the
Pompeii Sosii Falcones (p. 96 below).
[5] Hist. 3. 59. 2.
[6] Sex. Caesius Propertianus, patron of Mevania (ILS 1447, PIR² C 204); C. Caesius Sabinus
(C 205), from Sassina, decus Umbriae (Martial 7. 97); C. Caesius Aper (C 191), from Sestinum.
Syme, Ath. 35 (1957) 313 ff., suggests Sabine origin. E. Swoboda, RE 19. 1 (1937) 1149
preferred Aquileia, citing a Petillia Q. f. Modesta, wife of a decurion (Not. Scav. 1925. 24,
no. 5) and a Petilius Tironis lib. Cerialis (V 1330). One might, for that matter, point to a family
of QQ. Petillii, freedfolk, in the Alpes Graiae (V 6896). The family might have had estates in
several parts of Italy. For Nasica, see p. 231 below.
[7] The brothers Scribonii (RE 2A 1 (1921) 888 ff.) and Domitii (PIR² D 152, 167) are good
examples from this period. Others could be cited.
[8] See Britannia 4 (1973) 180 for details. The Petillii had produced a consul in the early
second century BC and two or three senatorial Petillii are recorded in the late republic. The last

The ex-praetor Petillius Rufus was to meet a well-deserved fate for his disgraceful conduct, presumably in the 30s or early 40s AD, for Tacitus' account of it is lost.[9] This might have retarded the career of Cerialis, so that it is impossible to be confident about his date of birth. In any case, there are plenty of examples from the early principate of men commanding legions before the praetorship;[10] while the case of Manlius Valens, who was in his forties when commanding a legion under Scapula and Didius Gallus, is a useful warning against undue dogmatism over the question.[11] Cerialis can hardly be said to have done well as legate of IX Hispana. After the destruction of Camulodunum by Boudicca's forces, Cerialis, 'coming to help, was routed and his infantry was slaughtered; he himself with the cavalry escaped *in castra*, where he was protected by the fortifications'. The defeat is referred to as a 'clades', 'disaster'—it was after all the first encounter between the rebels and the Roman army; and the terrified procurator Decianus Catus fled to the continent as a result. Brief though it is, the notice is distinctly unflattering: Cerialis came to help, but arrived too late; he was put to flight and suffered heavy losses, but he himself rode away and sheltered in his fortress. It may be that he had some more solid achievements behind him before the outbreak of revolt, which might justify a favourable interpretation of the laconic phrase with which he is introduced in the *Histories*—'nec ipse inglorius militiae'.[12]

It was perhaps as an indirect result of his débâcle in 60 that Cerialis made the marriage to which he owed his prominence in the 70s. Troops were sent from Germany to restore the depleted ranks of his legion,[13] and it may be surmised that it was the younger T. Flavius Vespasianus, the future Titus Caesar, who brought them.[14] At all events, Cerialis was a close kinsman of Vespasian by the year 69.[15] The nature of the relationship has been carefully examined by Townend,[16] who concludes that he must have been Vespasian's son-in-law, the husband of his only daughter Domitilla. She herself was dead by 69 and there is no means

of these, the mint-master Petillius Capitolinus, in office in the late 40s BC, and probably a banker or financier, might be an ancestor of the Petillii Rufi. See T. P. Wiseman, *New Men in the Roman Senate* (1971) 85, 171.

[9] *Ann.* 4. 71. 1; see Syme, *Tacitus* 256 ff., on the structure of the *Annals*.
[10] p. 14 above.
[11] p. 230 below.
[12] *Hist.* 3. 59. 2.
[13] *Ann.* 14. 38. 1.
[14] p. 269 below.
[15] *Hist.* 3. 59. 2, echoed by Dio 64. 18. 1.
[16] G. Townend, *JRS* 51 (1961) 59.

of telling when the marriage took place. But she had at least one child, a daughter named after herself, and she was later deified; both these facts indicate that Cerialis, if he was indeed her husband, would have enjoyed continuing favour from the Flavian dynasty.[17]

Nothing is known of Cerialis' activities between his legionary command and his appearance before the Flavian advance force in December AD 69; but he might have held one or more posts.[18] The Flavian commanders entrusted him with a thousand cavalry, but he bungled his task: displaying the lack of caution which was his hall-mark,[19] he was heavily defeated by the Vitellians in the outskirts of Rome, and failed to arrive in time to save the Flavian group beleaguered on the Capitol.[20] Shortly afterwards, when a deputation from the senate arrived, he was unable to prevent his men behaving violently towards the envoys.[21]

None the less, a few weeks later, early in AD 70, he was appointed, together with Annius Gallus, to suppress the revolt in the Rhineland, as legate of the Lower German army.[22] Josephus states that he was given consular rank and sent to govern Britain, having previously governed Germany, and that he dealt with the uprising on the Rhine on his way. This looks like a confusion, but it is possible that Cerialis was indeed assured that, when he had dealt with the rebels, he would proceed to Britain, a province in which both he and the new emperor obviously had a special interest.[23] He may, also, have been *adlectus inter consulares*; but he could have taken up his command as consul designate and held office *in absentia*.[24] His operations in the Rhineland are described in detail by Tacitus, who makes it clear that, in his view, Cerialis succeeded in his task more by good luck than by good management.[25] The account in the *Histories* breaks off in the autumn of AD 70, and it may be assumed that Cerialis did not proceed to Britain until the spring of AD 71.[26]

His governorship is described in two places in the *Agricola*, to illustrate

[17] Townend, *JRS* 51 (1961) 58 f.; *PIR*[2] F 417, 418.

[18] It is just worth noting that the name Πετίλιος 'Ροῦφος appears on an inscription from Nicaea as one of a handful of Roman names amongst a long list of Greek ones: A. M. Schneider, *Istanbuler Forschungen* 16 (1943) 23 f. no. 4 (col. a, line 14). Petillius might conceivably have been proconsul of Pontus–Bithynia in the 60s.

[19] *Hist.* 3. 79. 1 f.; cf. 4. 76. 3, 77. 2, 78. 2; 5. 20. 1; *Ann.* 14. 33. 1.

[20] *Hist.* 3. 78. 3.

[21] *Hist.* 3. 80. 1-2.

[22] *Hist.* 4. 68. 1 ff.; Dio 65. 3. 3.

[23] Joseph *BJ* 7. 4. 2.

[24] See *Britannia* 4 (1973) 183 n. 21, 187 n. 41. Of course, it is not impossible that he had been consul in the 60s.

[25] *Britannia* 4 (1973) 183 ff.

[26] See p. 65 and n. 17 above.

Agricola's own career, and in its own right. At first sight, Tacitus appears to give Cerialis credit for a major success, the resumption of an aggressive policy and the partial conquest of the Brigantes, Britain's largest people.[27] Archæological evidence suggests that he penetrated well into the northern Pennines, and it is possible to infer, from Tacitus' account of Agricola's activities, that the latter's immediate predecessors had been involved with some of the peoples of southern Scotland.[28] Throughout, Tacitus can be seen, on close examination, to have viewed Cerialis' career, civil as well as military, in a critical light.[29]

He was back at Rome for a second consulship in May AD 74, and in all probability had left Britain late in 73, after three seasons in the province.[30] There is no certain trace of him thereafter, unless, as seems possible, he is the Q. Petillius Rufus who held the consulship as *ordinarius* with Domitian in AD 83.[31]

73/4-77	Sex. Julius Frontinus
	(*cos. a. inc.*, *II* 98, *III ord.* 100)

Tac. *Agr.* 17. 2.

Julius Frontinus is one of the most important figures of the Flavio-Trajanic era. In addition to his prominence in the political sphere, he was a distinguished writer on technical subjects, and is mentioned in the works of Aelian, Martial, and the younger Pliny. But his governorship of Britain is attested only by a single sentence in the *Agricola*, and his early career and origins are shrouded in obscurity. Aelian, author of a work called *Tactica*, called on him to discuss military studies at Formiae,[1] and Martial wrote of his retreat at Anxur, i.e. Tarracina.[2] But there is no reason to suppose that Latium was his original home.[3]

---

[27] *Agr.* 8. 2-3, 17. 1.
[28] Ogilvie and Richmond, *vita Agricolae* 55 ff.; *Britannia* 4 (1973) 188 ff. Note esp. *Agr.* 20. 2.
[29] *Britannia* 4 (1973) 189 f.
[30] XVI 20.
[31] *Britannia* 4 (1973) 186 f. That the family had died out by the early second century is perhaps implied by the fact that the *domus Petiliana* at Rome was in the possession of Martial's friend Sparsus (12. 57. 19), presumably the same man as Pliny's friend Sex. Julius Sparsus (*cos.* 88): *PIR*² J 586.
[1] Ael. *Tactic.*, *praef.* 3.
[2] Mart. 10. 58. 1-2, 5: 'Anxuris aequorei placidos, Frontine, recessus Et propius Baias litoreamque domum. . . . Dum colui . . .'
[3] Schumacher, *Priesterkollegien* 254 f., regards it as more probable that Frontinus came from Italy—'vielleicht aus Latium (Tarracina?)'. But he fails to grapple with the question in sufficient depth.

The *nomen* suggests provincial origin. Sexti Julii are relatively rare, but are found much more frequently in Gaul, particularly in Narbonensis, than elsewhere;[4] and, as Syme has noted, a senator with the names Q. Valerius Lupercus Julius Frontinus is recorded at Vienna on the Rhone.[5] In the absence of further evidence, it seems most likely that his origin was in southern Gaul. Nothing is known of his career before the praetorship. As urban praetor, in the absence of the consuls, he convened the senate for its first meeting of the year 70, on 1 January; but shortly afterwards resigned the office to make way for Domitian.[6] Since he must have held the consulship little more than three years later, he must, unless he was patrician, which is highly unlikely, have been promoted rapidly because of his age. He may have been given senatorial rank shortly before AD 70, after an equestrian career;[7] and he could have been holding some procuratorial post in Spain in AD 68, and have been rewarded by Galba for rapid adherence to his cause.[8]

Later in AD 70 Frontinus participated in the suppression of the Rhineland revolt. As he records in the *Stratagemata*, he received the surrender of 70,000 Lingones, presumably in the capacity of legionary legate.[9] Which legion is uncertain. The suggestion that it was II Adiutrix, and that he later took it to Britain, is attractive, but cannot be proved.[10] Equally uncertain is his status at the time of the dedication at Vetera on the Lower Rhine.[11]

---

[4] There are nearly thirty Sex. Julii in *CIL* XII, and nine Frontini. Contrast II, V, IX, X, XI. Note also the writer of the Flavian era, Sex. Julius Gavinianus, from Gaul (*PIR*[2] J 331).

[5] Syme, *Tacitus* 790; id., *Gnomon* 29 (1957) 518 f. = *Danubian Papers* (1971) 181. It may also be relevant to note the filiation of T. Julius Sex. f. Volt. Maximus Malianus Brocchus Servilianus A. Quadronius [Verus?] L. Servilius Vatia Cassius Cam[ars?] (*PIR*[2] J 426). This man was a native of Nemausus, whence XII 3656; *Sex. Iulio Servato Frontina uxor posuit.*

[6] Tac. *Hist.* 4. 39. 1-2.

[7] Thus Syme, *Tacitus* 790, who notes that 'that consular author, who was singularly reticent about contemporary warfare, has notices of Corbulo (*Strat.* IV 1. 21; 28; 2. 3), and in particular, an anecdote about Corbulo at Tigranocerta. Frontinus might have begun as an equestrian officer'.

[8] Thus Syme, *Tacitus* 592, 790. One may note that the fragments of Frontinus in the *corpus agrimensorum* display some intimate knowledge of the Spanish peninsula: 1 f. Thulin; 9; 44; as also of Africa, ibid. 45, 48. Frontinus might have served in both Africa and Spain as a procurator in the 60s.

[9] *Strat.* 4. 3. 14 (the authenticity of book 4 used to be disputed; but see G. Bendz, *Die Echtheitsfrage des vierten Buches der frontinschen Strategemata* (1938)).

[10] J. B. Ward-Perkins, *CQ* 31 (1937) 102 ff. L. Petersen prefers XXII Primigenia, *PIR*[2] J 322. Unfortunately Alföldy does not discuss the case in his *Legionslegaten.*

[11] XIII 8624, improved by Ritterling, *Bonner Jahrb.* 133 (1928) 48 ff., who argued that Frontinus was there as legate of Lower Germany in AD 73-4. But see Syme, *JRS* 23 (1933) 97, reviewing Ritterling, *FRD*, where the theory was repeated pp. 57 f. As Syme pointed out, it is easier to suppose that Frontinus was at Vetera as legionary legate or as governor at a later period (after Britain). Ritterling's suggestion seems now to be ruled out by a recently discovered inscription naming A. Marius Celsus (*cos.* 69) as legate of Lower Germany in late 72 or early 73, as G. Alföldy kindly informs me.

However this may be, there can be no doubt that he succeeded Petillius Cerialis as governor of Britain. Before this he must have been consul. His tenure of the *fasces* is not explicitly recorded, and it is hard to accept that he can be identified with the suffect consul of AD 74, apparently in office in June of that year, of whose names only the letters ON are preserved.[12] The major difficulty is that his predecessor in Britain, Cerialis, was certainly back at Rome in May of 74, as *cos. II*.[13] But in any case there are several possible alternative names which include these two letters, and it is preferable to suppose that Frontinus was consul earlier, in 73 or perhaps even in 72.[14]

Frontinus is explicitly credited by Tacitus with the subjugation of the Silures, the warlike people of South Wales who had kept Roman armies busy for over thirty years. But, as Syme pointed out long ago, although 'a single sentence is the only record of his activities . . . that would not be enough to justify the unworthy suspicion that he had neglected both northern Wales and northern England and had failed to consolidate or extend the gains of his predecessors.'[15] Indeed, the phrase 'subiit sustinuitque molem' might well have been intended to convey the fact that Frontinus took on the burden of the war against the Brigantes. The archaeological evidence is certainly consistent with Roman forces having been at Carlisle during his governorship, if not earlier.[16]

Frontinus was succeeded by Cn. Julius Agricola in midsummer of, probably, AD 77.[17] His activities immediately following his return are unknown, but it is fair to speculate that he was with Domitian during the German campaign in AD 83, either as *comes* or as legate of Lower Germany.[18] A few years later he became proconsul of Asia, in which office he is recorded on coins of Smyrna and on a bilingual inscription at Hierapolis in Phrygia datable to the year 86.[19] After his year in Asia

---

[12] *Inscr. It.* XIII. 1, 2. VII, lines 11 ff.

[13] XVI 20.

[14] Even if M. Hirrius Fronto *cet.* is excluded, as urged by M. Torelli, *JRS* 58 (1968) 174 n. 22, there are so many *cognomina* which include the elements ON (e.g. Apronianus, Nonianus, Donatus, Honoratus, Longus, Longinus, etc.), that it would be rash to insist that Frontinus' names must be restored.

[15] *CAH* XI (1936) 152.

[16] G. D. B. Jones, *Northern History* 3 (1968) 6; B. R. Hartley, in R. M. Butler (ed.), *Soldier and Civilian in Roman Yorkshire* (1971) 58.

[17] pp. 77 ff. below.

[18] Syme, *Tacitus* 214. He refers to the campaign three times in his *Stratagemata*: 1. 1. 8; 3. 10; 2. 33; 2. 11. 7.

[19] *BMC Ionia* p. 250 nos. 133-7; Eck, *Senatoren* 77 ff., improved by C. P. Jones, *Gnomon* 45 (1973) 688, with a new fragment. *IGR* IV 847, Laodicea, may also refer to Frontinus. See Eck, op. cit., and Kreiler, *Statthalter Kleinasiens* 42 ff. W. Eck kindly points out to me that

he doubtless occupied himself largely with writing. But on the accession of Nerva he emerged as a leading senior statesman.[20] In 97 he was made *curator aquarum*, a task which he undertook with great conscientiousness, to judge from his book on the subject.[21] In the same year he was one of the two first choices of the senate for Nerva's economy commission.[22] Early in 98 he held a second consulship as suffect in February, with Trajan as his colleague, and two years later he was consul a third time, on this occasion as *ordinarius*, with Trajan, also holding his third consulship, as his colleague again.[23] This exceptional honour underlines the high regard in which he was held, and suggests, further, that Trajan had a debt to repay.[24] The favour in which Frontinus was held is also reflected in the success of his son-in-law, the cultivated Q. Sosius Senecio, who was *consul ordinarius* in 99, and then again in 107.[25] By then Frontinus himself was dead. His death, referred to by Pliny in his *Letters*, seems to have come in 103 or 104. Pliny records with satisfaction that he himself was elected to fill the vacancy in the college of augurs which Frontinus' death had created.[26] Frontinus had doubtless been an augur for many years.[27] Apart from Sosius Senecio, whose own daughter married the future governor of Britain Q. Pompeius Falco,[28] Frontinus' connections included the Calvisii Rusones,[29] one of whom bore the names Julius Frontinus, which he perhaps assumed on receipt of a bequest in Frontinus' will.

Frontinus was certainly in Asia in 86 (perhaps 85–6), since Domitian is *cos.* XII on the Hierapolis inscription.

[20] See Syme, *Tacitus* 17, 35.

[21] The date of his appointment is supplied by *de aquis* 102. 17. Unless there is a lacuna in the text immediately before this, his predecessor had held office since AD 74 (ibid. 102. 16), which may explain why Frontinus found so much neglect and so many abuses (cf. e.g. *de aquis* 110 ff.).

[22] Pliny, *Pan.* 62. 2, cf. 61. 6.

[23] Degrassi, *FC* 29 f.

[24] Syme, *Tacitus* 35, suggests that he approved the elevation of Trajan as Nerva's heir and notes that he was probably a friend of Trajan's father.

[25] *ILS* 1105, 8820 attest the relationship. On Senecio see the still valuable article by Groag, *RE* 3A 2 (1927) 1180 ff.

[26] Pliny, *epp.* 4. 8. 3 and cf. 9. 19 (on his refusal to be commemorated by a monument). For the date, see Sherwin-White, *Letters of Pliny* 272 f.

[27] Schumacher, *Priesterkollegien* 254, suggests that he was made an augur under Vespasian or Titus.

[28] p. 96 below.

[29] Syme, *Tacitus* 793.

77-84 Cn. Julius L. f. Ani. Agricola (*cos.* 77)

ILS 8704a = Wright, *Catalogue Grosvenor Museum* no. 199 = *MW* 283, Chester:
[*i*] *mp. Vesp. VIIII T. imp. VII cos. Cn. Julio Agricola leg. Aug. pr. pr.* AD 79
(other examples: *EE* IX 1039; *Britannia* 2 (1971) 292 f., ibid.).
Ant. J. 36 (1956) 8 ff. = *JRS* 46 (1956) 146 f. = *AE* 1957. 169, Verulamium: [*imp.
Titus Caesar divi*] *Vespa*[*siani*] *f. Ves*[*pasianus Aug. / p. m. tr. p. VIII imp. XV
cos. VII*] *desi*[*gn. VIII censor pater patriae /* [*et Caesar divi Vespas*]*ian* [*i f. Do*]*mi-
[tianus cos. VI design. VII / princeps iuventu*]*ti*[*s collegiorum omnium sacerdos*]
[4]*Cn. Iulio A*]*gric*[*ola leg. Aug. pro pr. /* ...] VEI [... ...]NATA[...]
(In lines 2-3, the restoration [... *tr. p. XI imp. XVII cos. VIII*] *desi*[*gn. VIIII* ...]
and [... *cos. VII design. VIII*] is also possible: Titus was *cos. des.* for 82.[1])
Tac. *Agr. passim*; Dio 39. 50. 4; 66. 20.

Because of the biography by Tacitus, Julius Agricola is the best known
of all the Roman governors of Britain. But he deserves special attention
for several other reasons. He is the only recorded instance of a senator
who served in all three military ranks, tribune, legionary legate, and
governor, in the same province. Even cases of men serving twice with
the same army are relatively rare.[2] Agricola is thus the 'British specialist'
par excellence. Another unusual feature of his career is the length of
the governorship, seven years, longer than that recorded for any other
governor of Britain and not usual in any province.[3] It may also be
noted that Agricola was considerably younger than most of the other
governors.[4] Finally, he is the first governor attested epigraphically in
the province.

Agricola's parents were L. Julius Graecinus and Julia Procilla. Both
grandfathers were imperial procurators.[5] Graecinus achieved senatorial
rank, rising as far as the praetorship, but was put to death by Caligula,
soon after Agricola's birth on 13 June AD 40, at Forum Julii, the
Caesarian colony in Gallia Narbonensis.[6] Tacitus records that Graecinus
had offended Caligula by his refusal to prosecute M. Silanus. Seneca,
more impressively, states that Caligula killed him 'for the sole reason
that he was a better man than a tyrant found it expedient for anyone

[1] Eck, *Senatoren* 127 n. 68. It would be impossible, in this context, to give anything like a
complete bibliography of the literature on Agricola. Reference will, therefore, be confined to
works directly utilized. I rely on my paper in B. Levick (ed.), *The Ancient Historian and his
Materials* (1975) 139 ff.

[2] See Table 3, p. 18, Tables 4-5, pp. 30 f. above.

[3] See pp. 397 ff. below.

[4] See p. 390 below.

[5] *Agr.* 4. 1.

[6] *PIR*[2] J 344 conveniently assembles the evidence. He is presumably the L. Julius L. f. Ani.
Graecinus, *tr. pl.* and *pr.*, recorded on *AE* 1946. 94, set up by M. Julius L. f. Ani. Graecinus,
quaestor, who must be either Graecinus' brother or another son. The tribe, Aniensis, is that of
Forum Iulii, the family home (Kubitschek 270).

to be'.[7] Graecinus had already displayed his independent spirit by declining financial assistance for his games from two powerful but disreputable figures, Seneca records.[8] Elsewhere, Seneca quotes a sarcastic comment of Graecinus about the philosopher Aristo,[9] while Columella refers to his two volume manual on viticulture, written with elegance and learning.[10]

By the time that Agricola was ready to enter public life, in his late teens, the dominant position at Rome was held by Nero's two chief ministers, Seneca and Burrus.[11] Burrus was of Gallic origin, like Agricola, and this, combined with Seneca's admiration for the father of Agricola, would have ensured that the young man had no difficulty in achieving a good start. Tacitus fails to mention the vigintivirate, but Agricola should have held one of these posts, since omission was abnormal[12] except for older men transferring to the senate from an equestrian career. If he held such a post, it would presumably have been before the tribunate, *c*.AD 58, rather than after it.[13] He was given his military tribunate in Britain by C. Suetonius Paullinus, a contemporary of Julius Graecinus.[14] Agricola was in Britain at the time of Boudicca's uprising in AD 60, although he might well have arrived a year or two earlier. But the phrase in *Agr.* 5. 1, 'electus quem contubernio aestimaret' may mean only: 'having been given a commission as tribune', and need not indicate that Agricola had been singled out to serve on the governor's headquarters staff after routine service with his legion. Which legion Agricola was assigned to is, unfortunately, unknown. It might be suggested that it was II Augusta. Tacitus reports the name and fate of that legion's prefect, Poenius Postumus, who disobeyed Paullinus' orders to join him and committed suicide when he learned of the Roman victory. As Syme has observed,[15] both the legate and the *tribunus laticlavius* of II Augusta must have been absent at that time,

---

[7] *Agr.* 4. 1; Sen. *de benef.* 2. 21. 5. M. Silanus is generally regarded as the *cos.* 15 (thus *PIR²* J 832), although as Ogilvie and Richmond, *vita Agricolae* 142, point out, he could be M. Silanus Torquatus (*cos. ord.* 19;*PIR²* J 839). The former's death occurred early in 38, over two years before that of Graecinus.

[8] Sen. *de benef.* 2. 21. 6.

[9] Sen. *ep.* 29. 6.

[10] Columella 1. 1. 14, cf. 3. 3, 4, 7, 9, 11; 4. 3. 1-6, 28. 2. Graecinus is also cited by Pliny, *HN* 14. 33, 16. 241. O. Hirschfeld suggested that Graecinus' interests in farming may have prompted his choice of the *cognomen* Agricola for his son, *Wien. Stud.* 5 (1883) 121.

[11] See Syme, *Tacitus* 591.

[12] *Ann.* 3. 29. 1 and Dio 60. 5. 8 (AD 20 and 41) refer to exemption for members of the imperial family (not granted in the latter case); see also p. 5 above.

[13] See D. McAlindon, *JRS* 47 (1957) 191 ff.

[14] p. 55 above.

[15] Syme, *Tacitus* 764 f., referring to *Ann.* 14. 37. 3.

and Agricola was certainly involved in the battle against the rebels. But this is not enough to rule out any of the three other legions. It should be noted here that while in Britain Agricola may have made the acquaintance of the younger T. Flavius Vespasianus, the future Titus Caesar, whose military service included a term as tribune in Britain, probably at this time.[16]

On his return to Rome Agricola married Domitia Decidiana.[17] He was elected to the quaestorship, evidently in 62, for he was appointed to the province of Asia under the proconsul Otho Titianus, whose proconsular year seems to have been 63-4.[18] The year which fell between quaestorship and tribunate, to which Tacitus explicitly refers, should be 65 and he will have been tribune of the plebs in 66.[19] He presumably had another year's interval, in 67, and the praetorship came in 68—that is certainly the latest year, since, after describing his tenure of the office, Tacitus states that Agricola was appointed by Galba to investigate the temple treasures.[20]

Up to this moment Agricola's career had not been particularly distinguished. Although he had reached the praetorship two years earlier than the normal age, thirty, this was entirely due to the birth of two children, which secured him a year's remission in each case.[21] On the other hand, he was apparently not *candidatus Caesaris* in any of the three republican magistracies. It was the events of the year 69 which led to a radical change in his fortunes. In March or early April the Othonian fleet ravaged the Ligurian coast and killed Agricola's mother on her estate at Intimilium.[22] He set out—presumably from Rome—to fulfil

[16] p. 269 below.

[17] *Agr.* 6. 1, presumably daughter of Domitius Decidius, *quaestor aerarii* in AD 44 (*ILS* 966), probably a Gaul (*PIR²* D 143), and perhaps related also to the Augustan procurator T. Decidius Domitianus (*AE* 1935. 5; *PIR²* D 22).

[18] L. Antistius Vetus and Barea Soranus seem to have been proconsul in AD 64-5 and 65-6 respectively (*Ann.* 16. 10. 2, 23. 1), and 62-3 is excluded by Titianus' presence with the Arvals at Rome on 12 Jan. 63 (*Acta Arv.* = Smallwood I 24). There is no basis for the suggestion that Agricola may also have served under the upright Antistius Vetus (Ogilvie and Richmond, 149, 317). Provincial quaestors did not take up their posts in the provinces until the summer, and served with a single proconsul: see Mommsen, *Staatsrecht* II.1³, 258. But they were of course elected in the previous year—in this case, 62, which adds interest to Tacitus' comments on the elections for that year (*Ann.* 15. 19): the *ius liberorum*, from which Agricola himself benefited, was being abused by fake adoptions.

[19] *Agr.* 6. 3. Agricola had a quiet tribunate: 'gnarus sub Nerone temporum, quibus inertia pro sapientia fuit'—unlike a practitioner of *sapientia*, his colleague Arulenus Rusticus, who was ready to use his veto (*Ann.* 16. 26. 4).

[20] *Agr.* 6. 4-5.

[21] *Digest* 4. 4. 2.

[22] *Agr.* 7. 1, cf. *Hist.* 2. 13. 1, where a similar case is described. The Othonian troops involved went on to engage a Vitellian force dispatched by Valens (2. 14-15); news of their encounter reached Valens at Ticinum well before the battle of Bedriacum (14 Apr.). See Syme, *Tacitus* 676 f. K. Wellesley, *The Histories Book III* (1972) 9, assigns this episode to March.

the *sollemnia pietatis*, and was overtaken by news of Vespasian's bid for empire. His departure may have been delayed by the disturbed conditions, and the news of his mother's fate may not have reached him for some weeks. But even so he must have been one of the very first to join the Flavian party.[23] After all, Vespasian was not proclaimed at Alexandria until 1 July.[24] Agricola may well have been approached by one of the men canvassing for support, such as Antonius Primus or Cornelius Fuscus (perhaps a fellow-townsman), although to judge from the *Histories* they did not begin this work in an active way until late July.[25] Another likely Flavian activist in summer 69 was the procurator of Narbonensis, Valerius Paulinus, a native of Forum Julii and hence certainly known personally to Agricola. This man seized the colony by October at the latest, after inducing several other communities to swear allegiance to Vespasian. Paulinus had been a friend of Vespasian before this; soon after, he managed to capture Fabius Valens, which brought about a general swing to the Flavians.[26]

Tacitus describes how Agricola was given an appointment by Mucianus, after joining the Flavian side as soon as he had heard the news: 'is [sc. Mucianus] missum ad dilectus agendos Agricolam integre strenueque versatum vicesimae legioni . . . praeposuit' (*Agr.* 7. 3). In other words, he was made legate of XX after successful service levying troops. Clearly his activities with the *dilectus* must be assigned to the autumn of 69.[27] Strong elements of the British legions had served in the Vitellian

[23] G. E. F. Chilver, *JRS* 47 (1957) 34 f., emphasizes that Vespasian and Mucianus had been preparing the coup for months, citing *Hist.* 2. 5. 2 and 5. 10. 2. As he notes, 'the penetration of Vespasian's agents into high circles is almost more extraordinary than that of Galba's'. But he is mistaken when he adds that Vespasian 'also succeeded in suborning . . . Vettius Bolanus and his young legionary legate Agricola in Britain'. Agricola probably needed no suborning, and he was certainly neither a legionary legate, nor in Britain, when he joined the Flavians.

[24] *Hist.* 2. 79.

[25] *Hist.* 2. 86. 4, 98. 1. The first item is reported before Vitellius' arrival at Rome (2. 89. 1, presumably 17 July, 2. 91. 1). Primus: *PIR²* A 866; Fuscus: ibid. C 1365, cf. Syme, *Tacitus* 683 f.

[26] *Hist.* 3. 43–4. Paulinus was evidently made prefect of Egypt by Vespasian: see now P. J. Sijpesteijn, *Historia* 28 (1979) 117 ff.

[27] Wellesley, *The Histories Book III* 9, states that Agricola 'did not join Antonius [Primus], for it was by Mucianus that he was appointed to his post as recruiting officer (probably in Northern Italy) and then to his legionary command in Britain. The interval between August and December A.D. 69 Agricola presumably spent at Intimilum or Forum Iulii'. Ogilvie and Richmond, *vita Agricolae* 154, likewise appear to assume that Mucianus appointed Agricola to his recruiting post as well as to legion XX, and hence that the former appointment could not have been made until early 70. But even if the legionary command were not given until Mucianus' arrival at Rome, as is strongly implied by *Agr.* 7. 2, the recruiting mission could even have commenced in the summer. Note that Pompeius Silvanus had raised 6,000 men in Dalmatia, who were transferred to the Ravenna fleet (*Hist.* 3. 50. 2–3); thereupon 'e classicis Ravennatibus legionariam militiam poscentibus optumus quisque adsciti', probably in early November (3. 50. 1).

army.[28] Agricola may have had, among other things, to provide replace-ments for these troops and take them to Britain, where he was to replace the turbulent Roscius Coelius.[29] His first year in command of the XXth was not an active one, under the governor Vettius Bolanus, but, with the arrival of Petillius Cerialis, Agricola was involved in vigorous campaigning in the north of England. His service evidently did not extend into the governorship of Frontinus, for the latter is not mentioned in *Agr.* 8. Hence he was back at Rome in 73, to be made a patrician and then to take up the governorship of Aquitania.[30] As he stayed there for 'less than three years',[31] he presumably relinquished the post before the end of 76. Then came the consulship, the appoint-ment to Britain, the marriage of his daughter to Tacitus, and the pontificate.[32]

The chronology of Agricola's governorship of Britain has been much dicussed.[33] Recently the later dating, 78–85, has been favoured, although the natural implication of the phrase in *Agr.* 9. 6, 'et statim Britanniae praepositus est', ought to be that he went there in 77, the year of his consulship.[34] As Syme has pointed out, the key to the dating lies in *Agr.* 39. 2: 'inerat conscientia derisui nuper falsum e Germania triumphum'. 'Agricola's first (calendar) year must be 78, for the seventh witnessed his great victory, subsequent to Domitian's triumph over the Chatti . . ., which occurred late in 83, the *congiarium* being paid out in 84.'[35] This passage requires close examination. After the battle, which marked the virtual end of the campaigning season ('et exacta iam aestate spargi bellum nequibat'), Agricola led his troops 'in fines Borestorum'. This should mean that it was already after 22 Sep-tember, the end of the summer.[36] Agricola then took hostages, and ordered the fleet to circumnavigate Britain, while he slowly, 'lento

[28] p. 64 n. 9 above.

[29] p. 231 below.

[30] *Agr.* 9. 1.

[31] *Agr.* 9. 5.

[32] *Agr.* 9. 6.

[33] Syme, *Tacitus* 22 and n. 6, lent his authority to 78, and is followed by Ogilvie and Richmond, *vita Agricolae* 318 ff., S. S. Frere, *Britannia* (1967) 104, and myself, *Ep. Stud.* 4 (1967) 67. K. Büchner, *Rhein. Mus.* 103 (1960) 172 ff., favoured 77, and is followed by L. Petersen in *PIR*[2] J 126, but on dubious grounds.

[34] See e.g. J. G. C. Anderson in H. Furneaux, *de vita Agricolae*, 2nd edn. (1922) 167 ff. The year 77 is not directly attested as that of his consulship, but seems to be universally accepted, except by Wellesley, reviewing Ogilvie and Richmond, *vita Agricolae, JRS* 59 (1969) 268 f., who thinks 78 is possible. For that matter, the known facts would not rule out 76.

[35] Syme, *Tacitus* 22 n. 6, referring to his own discussion in *CAH* XI (1936) 164, and to *Inscr. It.* XIII. 1, p. 192 for the *Fasti Ostienses*.

[36] H. Mattingly's translation, *Tacitus on Britain and Germany* (1948) 98 ('the summer was nearly over') is inexact.

itinere', led the army to winter quarters. By then the fleet had returned to base (*Agr.* 38. 2-4). It was on all this, 'Hunc rerum cursum', and not merely the great victory, that Agricola reported in his letter to Domitian. One can only guess how long his measures after the battle lasted, but Tacitus stresses their slow and deliberate nature. It would be reasonable to suggest that, if the battle took place in late September, it would have been the end of October at the earliest before Agricola composed the letter. A journey from Rome to Britain is estimated to have taken 'twenty-five days at normal rate' in summer.[37] In late autumn, when days are shorter and travelling conditions generally less favourable, that time would not have sufficed. Besides which, one must add a further delay before the courier reached a Channel port from the governor's northern headquarters. The letter can hardly have reached Domitian before December.

The exact moment when the emperor's own victory in Germany was claimed is not recorded, although it was clearly some time in the summer of 83.[38] It has been argued that there is no evidence for Domitian having had the title Germanicus until 84. In fact, there is an *aureus* of late 83, now in the Hunterian Museum, Glasgow, on which Domitian is named Germanicus.[39] But the question may not be relevant to the triumph in any case. It is unlikely that Domitian would have accepted the title immediately, for no previous emperor had ever assumed a 'Siegerbeiname'—and the example of Vitellius, *Germanicus imperator*, would have been something of an embarrassment, rather than a useful precedent.[40] It is surely probable that Domitian celebrated his triumph as soon as possible after his return at the end of the campaign; but that he waited for some time, egged on by flatterers, before taking the new title.[41] As for the *congiarium*, the fact that it was not paid out until 84 need not imply that the triumph had only just taken place. Claudius

---

[37] Anderson *ap.* Furneaux, *vita Agricolae*² 168; Ogilvie and Richmond, *vita Agricolae* 318.

[38] B. W. Jones, *Historia* 22 (1973) 79 ff., attempts to show that 'the war was undertaken early in 82 and virtually won by the summer of 83 when Domitian became Germanicus'. But see J. K. Evans, ibid. 24 (1975) 121 ff. The papyri which seem to show Domitian with Germanicus in his second Egyptian year are irrelevant, as shown by P. Kneissl, *Die Siegestitulatur der römischen Kaiser* (1969) 44 ff. (But see next note.)

[39] A. S. Robertson, *Roman Imperial Coins in the Hunter Coin Cabinet*, I. *Augustus to Nerva* (1962) p. 284 no. 13 (*OBV.*: IMP CAES DOMITIAN AVG GERMANICVS, REV.: PM TRP III COS IX DES X PP), I am grateful to Dr P. A. Holder for drawing my attention to this coin.

[40] Kneissl, op. cit. 38. Caligula, Claudius, and Nero had all been called Germanicus by inheritance. Claudius had been granted the title Britannicus, but had passed it on to his son: Kneissl 33.

[41] See Dio 67. 4. 1-2; Mart. 2. 2.

celebrated his British triumph in 44, but the *congiarium* was not distributed until 45.[42]

Thus the evidence for Domitian's German victory celebrations is not an obstacle to the earlier dating of Mons Graupius—on the contrary, a date for that battle in 83 accords better with Tacitus' use of the word 'nuper' in *Agr.* 39. 2. There is no other real evidence to date the governorship precisely.[43] Hence, it must be assumed, in the discussion that follows, that the governorship ran from 77 to 83/4. In many ways, 77 is more satisfactory as the first year. The delay which put off Agricola's arrival until midsummer can be explained as having been caused by his daughter's wedding. May and the first half of June were unlucky times for marriages, and Agricola, as a patrician and a *pontifex*, may well have delayed the ceremony until the second half of June, which was especially lucky.[44]

The first season was spent in the reconquest of North Wales and Anglesey, an achievement which Agricola refused to regard as more than 'victos continuisse'.[45] His second season, 78, seems to have been occupied by a good deal of marching, and harrying of the enemy, but there is no mention of fighting—on the contrary: 'nulla ante Britanniae nova pars <pariter> inlacessita transierit', and the governor covered a

[42] Dio 60. 23. 1, 25. 7-8. There is no reason to assume a lengthy delay between Domitian's return from Germany and his triumph, as does C. M. Kraay, *Amer. Numism. Soc. Notes* 9 (1960) 109 ff. He cites the triumph of 71 as a parallel ('though Jerusalem fell on 8 September 70, Vespasian did not hold his triumph until the end of June 71'), but neglects to note the reason for the delay: Vespasian was waiting for Titus to return. No such circumstances applied in the year 83.

[43] Ogilvie and Richmond, *vita Agricolae* 319 f., add a new item which is claimed as 'decisive for the dating of the governorship to A.D. 78-84'. This is the sestertius of 84 published by Kraay, op. cit., with IMP.VII and a reverse 'highly relevant to the victory of Mons Graupius'. But Kraay's arguments are invalid, since, referring to advice from Richmond, he puts the battle in *mid*summer, neglecting 'exacta iam aestate' in *Agr.* 38. 2. Besides, IMP.VII is found as early as 3 Sept. in 84 (XVI 30), too early for Mons Graupius even if the battle could be assigned to 84 on other grounds. See R. Urban, *Historische Untersuchungen zum Domitianbild des Tacitus* (1971) 42 n. 1—whose view that Tacitus' entire account of Agricola's governorship is largely imaginary I cannot, however, accept. Büchner, *Rhein. Mus.* 103 (1960) 172 ff. once more revives the episode of the Usipi as a dating indication. Here it must suffice to remark, that if the Usipi had been involved in an attack on Mogontiacum in AD 70 (*Hist.* 4. 37. 3), that would be good reason for them to have been the subject of reprisals—including the *dilectus* and dispatch to Britain—at any time in the decade prior to Agricola's sixth season, not merely by Domitian in AD 83. It may be noted, finally, that the arguments of G. Alföldy and H. Halfmann, *Chiron* 3 (1973) 331 ff., to redate the defeat and death of Oppius Sabinus in Moesia to early 85, make it less likely that Agricola returned from Britain at that very time, rather than in 84. Tacitus would surely have pointed the contrast in *Agr.* 39, instead of waiting until *Agr.* 41. 2.

[44] Ovid, *Fast.* 5. 487, 6. 223; Plut. *QR* 284 F.

[45] *Agr.* 18. 6. As noted by A. Gaheis, *RE* 10. 1 (1917) 130, Tacitus' remarks here (esp. 'ne laureatis quidem gesta prosecutus est') accord perfectly with Vespasian's failure to register any new imperatorial acclamation in the year 77. In 18. 1-2 he notes that an *ala* had almost been wiped out before Agricola arrived; the war-party wanted to test the new governor.

large area with forts.[46] In his second winter he began to encourage civilian development. It would be pleasing to think that the inscription from Verulamium might attest Agricola's endeavours 'ut templa fora domos extruerent'.[47] His third season, 79, saw a big push forward, with the 'opening up of new peoples' and the laying waste of the lands as far as the Tay estuary (*Agr.* 22. 1). This is surely an appropriate background for Titus' fifteenth imperatorial acclamation, which belongs to the year 79, and which Dio explicitly ascribes to Agricola's achievements in Britain.[48] In 80, his fourth season, when he may have expected to be replaced, work of consolidation was undertaken: 'omnis propior sinus' south of Clyde and Forth was secured (*Agr.* 23). In 81, having presumably received a fresh mandate for advance, he began a further drive against new peoples, crossing the Clyde—that is unambiguous—and pacifying 'ignotas ad id tempus gentes crebris simul ac prosperis proeliis' (*Agr.* 24). Since in his fourth season 'omnis propior sinus' had been dealt with, these hitherto unknown peoples must have lived beyond the Clyde, and it is conceivable that he drew up his forces on the tip of Kintyre for his celebrated gaze at Ireland.[49]

Just before the end of the fifth season, Titus died (13 September 81).[50] The implications for Agricola were no doubt obvious. He had had two and a half years from Vespasian and two and a half more from Titus. His career had advanced spectacularly with their blessing. Both of them had served in Britain, and doubtless took a keen interest in the progress he was making. With the accession of Domitian a change was inevitable. According to Cassius Dio, within a year, or eighteen months at the most, 'many of the leading men' were put to death or banished; Domitian 'quite outdid himself in visiting disgrace and ruin on the friends of his father and brother'.[51] Agricola undoubtedly came into this category, but, with an army of four legions and a large force of auxiliaries, could not be crushed easily. Besides this, his campaign had been followed with interest at Rome, and he must have been able to

---

[46] *Agr.* 20. 1-3. As noted in *Britannia* 4 (1973) 190, the fact that in this year 'multae civitates, quae in illum diem ex aequo egerant [sc. 'had operated on equal terms against Rome'], datis obsidibus iram posuere, et praesidiis castellisque circumdatae' indicates that he was crossing territory already entered by Cerialis and Frontinus.

[47] *Agr.* 21. 1-2, cf. the conduct of Trebellius Maximus, p. 61 above. The Verulamium inscription may belong either to 79 or to 81, p. 73 above.

[48] Dio 66. 20. 3. One may note in passing that a Caledonian boar, presumably supplied by Agricola, was included in the opening festivities at the Colosseum in June 80: Mart. *Spect.* 7. 3.

[49] Ogilvie and Richmond, *vita Agricolae*, 235; see further N. Reed, *Britannia* 2 (1972) 143 ff.

[50] *PIR*² F 399.

[51] Dio 67. 2. 1-3.

convince the new emperor that the *terminus Britanniae* was within his grasp. During this year, however, Domitian may have called on Agricola's troops to reinforce the Rhine armies for their coming offensive.[52] Agricola clearly hoped to finish off the Caledonians in 82, but narrowly failed: had not the enemy eluded him, 'debellatum illa victoria foret'.[53]

Although, as has been stressed already, the battle at Mons Graupius took place late in the seventh season, Tacitus gives no details about the preliminaries which led up to it during that summer. The account of Agricola's recall in chapter 40 of the biography reads a little curiously, but it may be assumed that it was in the spring (of 84) that he 'tradiderat . . . successori suo provinciam quietam tutamque'. He had been granted the *triumphalia ornamenta*,[54] but came back to Rome modestly. There had been talk of his being sent to Syria, but nothing came of it, and he retired into private life. As the military situation on the northern frontiers worsened, 'poscebatur ore vulgi dux Agricola', without response. When his turn arrived to ballot for the consular proconsulships —probably in the year 90—he was dissuaded by threats from letting his name go forward.[55] Three years later he died, on 23 August 93, in his fifty-fourth year.[56]

Apart from the daughter who married Tacitus, and the two sons who died in infancy,[57] Agricola may have had other children. At any rate, a young man of senatorial rank recorded on an inscription at Ephesus has Julius Agricola among his many names, which also include [Ped]anius Fuscus Sa[linat]or. This suggests that Agricola's family acquired a link with the kinsmen of Hadrian.[58]

---

[52] A. R. Birley, in Levick (ed.), *The Ancient Historian* 145.

[53] *Agr.* 26. 2. The fact that IX Hispana was *maxime invalida* in the sixth season does not need to be explained by reference to the detachment absent in Germany with L. Roscius Aelianus (*ILS* 1025, see p. 270 below). As Syme pointed out, *Germania* 16 (1932) 111 n. 17, that legion's permanent base, York, would require a larger garrison, being more exposed, than those of the other three legions.

[54] The apparent discrepancy in Dio's account, 66. 20. 3, may be overcome by emending the text from παρὰ τοῦ Τίτου to παρ' αὐτοῦ τούτου, as editors have noted.

[55] *Agr.* 40-2.

[56] *Agr.* 44. 1.

[57] *Agr.* 6. 2, 29. 1.

[58] Velleius . . . Sertorius . . . [Ped]anius Fuscus Sa[linat] or Sallus[ti]us Bla[esus] . . . Iulius Agricola . . . Caesonius. See Eck, *RE* Supp. 14 (1974) 878, and E. Champlin, *ZPE* 21 (1976) 79 ff., who argues that the young man may be none other than Hadrian's grand-nephew (later forced to commit suicide in 136). The next recorded governor after Agricola, Sallustius Lucullus (p. 82 below) may also be an ancestor of this person. The only other possible member of Agricola's family, apart from Tacitus, is the Trajanic consular C. Julius M. f. Volt. Proculus, whose *cognomen* recalls that of Agricola's mother Julia Procilla, while his tribe points to an origin in Narbonensis: see *PIR²* J 497. See also p. 151 and n. 12 below.

between 85   **Sallustius Lucullus**
and 96

Suet. *Domit.* 10. 2-3: Complures senatores, in iis aliquot consulares, interemit; ex
quibus . . . 3 . . . Sallustium Lucullum Britanniae legatum, quod lanceas novae
formae appellari Luculleas passus esset.

This governor is otherwise unknown, and even the moment when he
was put to death by Domitian cannot be established with certainty.
Although there were several occasions when Domitian carried out
purges among the upper classes,[1] the two likeliest years are 89 and 93.
In 89, Lucullus might have been suspected of complicity with the
rebellious legate of Upper Germany, L. Antonius Saturninus[2]—but, in
that case, it is difficult to see why Suetonius did not say so. Tacitus
specifically refers to the execution of consulars after Agricola's death in
August 93.[3] If Lucullus' death fell within that period, he might possibly be identical with the P. Sallustius Blaesus who was consul suffect
in 89.[4] Many senators of this period were polyonymous, and it could
be that, while Blaesus was his principal *cognomen*, Lucullus occurred
later in his nomenclature. The *nomen* is uncommon and a man of this
name in the first century AD must be assumed to have been Italian.[5]

Suetonius' use of the subjunctive to give the reason for the governor's
execution shows that this was Domitian's version. It should be noted
that both auxiliaries and legionaries used the *lancea*, and it might well
suggest interference with the emperor's prerogatives, and preparation
for insurrection, if a provincial governor arrogated the credit for an
invention to himself. However this may be, a possible concomitant to
the execution of the governor was the transfer from Britain of the unit
with whose loyalty he was perhaps thought to have tampered. That

[1] Note e.g. Dio 67. 4. 5 (AD 85?); 9. 6 (AD 88 or 89?); 11. 2-3 (AD 89); 12. 1-5 (AD
91?); 13. 1-4 (AD 93); 14. 1-3 (AD 95). Further, the Arvals celebrated on 22 Sept. AD 87 *ob
detecta scelera nefariorum* (VI 2065).
[2] See *PIR*² A 874; Syme, *Tacitus* 596 and *JRS* 68 (1978) 20; G. Walser, *Provincialia.
Festschr. Laur-Belart* (1968) 497 ff.
[3] *Agr.* 45. 1.
[4] As suggested by Syme, *Tacitus* 648. He notes that the *cos.* 89 might have had Velleius as
a second *gentilicium*, referring to 'Velleius Blaesus ille locuples consularis' (Pliny, *ep.* 2. 20. 7).
These names appear to have been inherited by the young man of senatorial rank recorded at
Ephesus (p. 81 no. 58 above). If he is not the *cos.* 89, it is almost certain that his consulship fell
before 87-92, unless it was in 93, for the consuls from the years 87-92 and 94-6 are virtually
all known: see Degrassi, *FC* 26-9. But note that a new consul is now known for the year 88:
F. Zevi, *Akt. 6. Int. Kongr. Griech. Lat. Epigr.* (1973) 438.
[5] Thus Syme, *Tacitus* 648: 'Italian, observe Cicero's faithful friend Cn. Sallustius, who had
a relative P. Sallustius (*Ad Att.* XI. 11. 2)'. Note also the P. Sallustius P. f. Lucullius at Lanuvium—perhaps descended from a freedman of the governor (XIV 2147).

seems a fair inference from the appearance on the Danube a few years later of a unit known as the *pedites singulares Britannici*. The title implies that it had been the guard-battalion of a governor of Britain, which seems the obvious unit to be equipped with the new weapon Lucullus had adopted. His disgrace and death provides the likeliest explanation of its removal from the province and transfer to the scene of active operations.[6]

98   Nepos = ?P. Metilius Nepos (*cos.* 91)

XVI 43, Flémalle: [*Imp. Caesar divi Ne*]*rvae f. Nerva Traianus* / [*Augustus Germa*]*nicus pontifex maximus* / [*tribunic.*] *potestat. cos. II* / [*equitibus et pedi-tib*]*us qui militant in alis* / [*tribus et cohortib*]*us sex quae. . . .* [10] / [*. . . sunt*] *in Britannia sub T. Avidio* / [*Quieto, item*] [12] / *dimissis honesta missione a* / [*Metilio?*] *Nepote . . .*

Although only the *cognomen* Nepos is preserved, there can be little doubt about the identity of the ex-governor named on this diploma. He is patently the consul suffect of 91, P. Metilius Nepos.[1] Unfortunately the exact date in 98 at which the diploma was issued has not been preserved (except that it was before 28 October, when Trajan's tribunician power was renewed),[2] but it is quite probable that Quietus had replaced Nepos in 97. In any case, it is to be presumed that Nepos was appointed by Domitian, perhaps as early as 94; but there is no evidence for his previous career. The *nomen* is relatively well attested in northern Italy. Since the Hadrianic consul P. Metilius P. f. Secundus was enrolled in the tribe Claudia, to which Novaria belongs,[3] a city where slaves of a Metilius are recorded,[4] it seems probable that this was his home.[5]

Unfortunately there remain serious difficulties in charting his further progress.[6] A P. Metilius Sabinus Nepos is listed among the Arval Brethren

[6] XVI 54, from the years 103-7. See E. Birley, *Roman Britain and the Roman Army* 22. R. W. Davies, *Acta Classica* 19 (1976) 115 ff., associates with the overthrow of Lucullus the decorations awarded to an equestrian officer *bello Brittannico* (*AE* 1951. 88); but this must remain no more than a hypothesis.

[1] The *Act. Arv.* (VI 2068) show a P. Met. . . consul in November 91, while the *Fasti Potentini* (*AE* 1949. 23) show one L. Metilius Nep[os] as consul on 1 Sept. of the same year. In spite of the difference in *praenomen*, the two are clearly identical: see A. Garzetti, *Nerva* (1950) 141; Degrassi, *FC* 27; Eck, *RE* Supp. 14 (1974) 281. For the identification of the *cos.* 91 with the governor of Britain see also esp. Syme, *Tacitus* 647 and *JRS* 58 (1968) 138.

[2] See e.g. *RE* Supp. 10 (1965) 1042 f.

[3] *ILS* 1053; see Kubitschek 121 for the tribe.

[4] V 6503.

[5] Thus Groag, *RE* 15. 2 (1932) 1403; Syme, *Tacitus* 647.

[6] See Garzetti, *Nerva* 141; Sherwin-White, *Letters of Pliny* esp. 146 f., criticized by C. P. Jones, *Phoenix* 22 (1968) 124 f.; Syme, *JRS* 58 (1968) 138; Eck, *RE* Supp. 14 (1974) 281 ff.

under their proceedings of the years 105, 110, and 111; and this person died not long before 26 February 118, when a successor was co-opted in his place.[7] On the other hand a P. Metilius Nepos is recorded as *cos. II ord.*, with M. Annius Libo as his colleague, on a papyrus from the province of Arabia—he presumably died before taking office, since the Fasti show another man as Libo's fellow-consul, the year being 128.[8] Further, the younger Pliny wrote several letters to a Nepos[9] and others to a Sabinus.[10] Some assistance is supplied by the fact that P. Metilius Sabinus Nepos was evidently consul suffect in 103.[11] He may reasonably be identified with the Arval Brother who died before February 118, and our governor may be reckoned to have survived until 127, to be designated to the honour of a second consulship. But it must be admitted, given the practices of Roman nomenclature, that our governor might be the Arval Brother, and the consul of 103 might be the man prematurely called *cos. II ord.* for 128 on the document from Arabia.[12]

What of the persons in Pliny? The Nepos who received *ep.* 4. 26 is listed in the index to one manuscript as Maecilius Nepos, and Pliny refers to him as 'maximae provinciae praefuturus'. The *nomen* Maecilius was not borne by any known senator at this period, and the corruption is readily explicable.[13] If our Metilius Nepos were the recipient of this letter, the only conceivable province that he could have been about to govern at the time, *c*.105, is Africa.[14] But this is very uncertain. Both this man, and the Nepos of three other letters, might be identical and also be the same as the Sabinus of 9. 2 and 9. 18. In that case, Pliny's friend would be the *cos.* 103, and the province referred to in 4. 26 would be a military one—the references in 9. 2. 4 make this plain: 'cum castra, cum denique cornua tubas sudorem pulverem soles cogitamus'.

---

[7] VI 2075 32372, *AE* 1964. 69; 2078 = 32374; also in Smallwood II 3–6.

[8] H. J. Polotsky, *Israel Exploration Journal* 12 (1962) 259, on which see Jones, *Phoenix* 22 (1968) 124; Syme, *JRS* 58 (1968) 138.

[9] 2. 3, 3. 16, 4. 26, 6. 19.

[10] 9. 2, 9. 18—the Sabinus of 4. 10 and 6. 18 is certainly not a Metilius.

[11] *Inscr. It.* XIII. 1 pp. 177, 197, 225: only [M] *etiliu* [s] is preserved. Garzetti, *Nerva* 141, proposed that the *cos.* 91 received a second consulship in 103 and the suggestion was favoured by Degrassi, *FC* 31, but in their reviews of *FC* Syme, *JRS* 43 (1953) 151 and H. Nesselhauf, *Gnomon* 26 (1954) 270, dissented; and now that one P. Metilius Nepos is known to have survived until 127, while the other, P. Metilius Sabinus Nepos, died in 117/18, there are no longer good reasons for conflating the consuls of 91 and 103—see Jones, *Phoenix* 22 (1968) 124.

[12] Eck, *RE* Supp. 14 (1974) 282, favours this view.

[13] See Sherwin-White, *Letters of Pliny* 147, who unenthusiastically admits the possibility that 'the scribe . . . has repeated the initial letters from the preceding entry, which was *ad Maesium Maximum*'.

[14] Sherwin-White, op. cit. 306, suggests Asia or Africa, but he is wrong to exclude the possibility of an imperial province, as Jones, *Phoenix* 22 (1968) 124, points out. Jones further notes that Asia at least has no vacancies at this time—see Syme, *Tacitus* 665.

It seems unlikely that an ex-governor of Britain would have returned to military service under Trajan.

The Hadrianic consular mentioned above, P. Metilius P. f. Cla. Secundus, could be the son of either of the two Metilii Nepotes. But it may perhaps be assumed that he had no direct male heirs, since the names Metilius Nepos appear in the nomenclature of two polyonymous senators of the succeeding generation, M. Sedatius Severianus (*cos.* 153)[15] and M. Metilius Regulus (*cos. ord.* 157).[16] The Trajanic governor M. Atilius Metilius Bradua[17] might be a nephew of Nepos.

98   T. Avidius Quietus (*cos.* 93)

XVI 43: see p. 83 above.

There can be no doubt that this man is the governor whose *praenomen* and *nomen* are preserved on the British diploma of AD 98. He had been consul in 93, two years after his predecessor in Britain. But Quietus must then have been somewhat older than the standard age of 42.[1] The younger Pliny, a close friend, mentions that Quietus had been an intimate of the Stoic leader Thrasea Paetus.[2] Since Paetus had died in AD 66,[3] it is reasonable to assume that Quietus was over twenty years of age in that year—he was probably born in the early 40s AD.[4] The Avidii derived from the northern-Italian town of Faventia on the *via Aemilia*, as is clear from literary references to other members of the family;[5] and a freedman T. Avidius is recorded on an inscription there.[6] Quietus is also known to have owned at least two houses at Rome and estates in Sardinia.[7]

Of his earlier career only two posts are recorded. In AD 82 the veterans of the Upper German legion VIII Augusta requested that

---

[15] *ILS* 9487 etc.: M. Sedatius C. f. Quir. Severianus Jul. Acer Metil. Nepos Rufinus Ti. Rutilianus Censor.

[16] *ILS* 1075: M. Metilius P. f. Cl. Aquillius Regulus Nepos Volusius Torquatus Fronto.

[17] p. 92 below.

[1] p. 000 above. For his consulship, Degrassi, *FC* 28.

[2] Pliny, *ep.* 6. 29. 1.

[3] Tac. *Ann.* 16. 35 etc. *PIR²* C 1187.

[4] His son was consul in AD 111 (see below). To judge from numerous cases where an interval of thirty years separates the consulships of father and son, it could be argued that our man was about twelve years late in attaining the *fasces*.

[5] *HA Hadrian* 7. 2-3, 23. 10, *Verus* 1. 9, etc.

[6] XI 660, cf. p. 1237.

[7] *ILS* 6105, a bronze tablet set up *in domu sua*, was found on the Esquiline; lead water pipes bearing his name have been found on the Quirinal: XV 7400. Sardinia: X 8046, 11.

Quietus, described as *leg. Aug. ornatissimo viro* should become a patron of the colony of Deultum in Thrace, where they had been settled. It is not apparent from the inscription (set up at Rome) whether Quietus was still holding the post or not.[8] However, since at least three other men are known to have been legates of VIII Augusta under Vespasian, the last of whom was still in command under Domitian,[9] it seems more likely that Quietus was chosen as a patron of Deultum because he was the legionary legate at the time the men were settled, i.e. in 82.[10] Later, probably in 91-2, he was proconsul of Achaia.[11] It was perhaps while he was serving in Greece that he won the friendship of Plutarch, who mentions him with affection in several of his works.[12]

At first sight it is a little surprising that Quietus held the consulship at all under Domitian, let alone in 93, the very year when Domitian carried out a major purge of the Stoics. On the other hand, the emperor may well have hoped to conciliate the group until the last moment.[13] Early in AD 97, after Domitian's murder, Quietus spoke in the senate in support of Pliny, when the latter attempted to gain revenge for the Stoic leader Helvidius. Quietus urged that Arria and Fannia (the widow and daughter of Thrasea) 'should not be denied their right of protest'.[14] Shortly after this he was appointed governor of Britain, for his predecessor Nepos is also named on the diploma of 98. Although he had had some military experience it was not very recent, and he was no longer young. But the choice of such a man fits the pattern of Nerva's brief principate, when a whole series of elderly figures returned to prominence.[15] Tacitus, who was writing his father-in-law's biography at the very time when Quietus went out to govern Britain, is unlikely to have viewed the appointment enthusiastically, considering his harsh allusion

---

[8] *ILS* 6105.

[9] See now especially Alföldy and Halfmann, *Chiron* 3 (1973) 350 ff. The other legates were Numisius Lupus, A. Bucius Lappius Maximus (*cos.* 86), M. Cornelius Nigrinus Curiatius Maternus (*cos.* 83, see Alföldy and Halfmann 353 ff.), and L. Antistius Rusticus (*cos.* 90, see p. 269 below), the last of whom held the post under Vespasian, Titus, and Domitian.

[10] It should be noted that Quietus could have commanded the legion *c.*69-72. As to the reason why the veterans should have chosen him as *patronus*, it might be argued that he was regarded as particularly well qualified (cf. Pliny, *ep.* 6. 29. 1 for his views on undertaking cases). On the other hand, it must be remembered that the veterans might well have enrolled all their ex-legates as *patroni*, not merely Quietus.

[11] Dittenberger, *Syll.*³ 822, Delphi. For the date, see Eck, *Senatoren* 142.

[12] Plut. *quaest. conv.* 632 A; *de fraterno amore* 478 B.

[13] Groag, writing before the date of Quietus' consulship was know, thought it 'vix credibile . . . Domitianum ultimis principatus temporibus viro, qui Paetum Thraseam coluerat, consulatum impertiisse', *PIR*² A 1410. For the purge, after Agricola's death in August 93, see esp. *Agr.* 45.

[14] Pliny, *ep.* 9. 13. 15. For the date of the debate, see 9. 13. 2.

[15] See e.g. Syme, *Tacitus* 3: 'there was some danger of gerontocracy'.

to the Stoics in the *Agricola*.[16] Quietus' later career, if any, is unknown. He was evidently dead by the time that Pliny wrote the second letter referring to him, *c*.AD 107.[17] His tenure of the governorship may, however, be assumed to have lasted until AD 100 or 101, and he was probably succeeded by L. Neratius Marcellus (*cos*. 95).

His son, of the same names, was consul in AD 111 and proconsul of Asia under Hadrian.[18] His nephew, C. Avidius Nigrinus, consul in 110, was governor of Dacia in the last years of Trajan, but was put to death in 118, at Faventia, on a charge of conspiring against Hadrian—who, many years later, was to adopt the man who married one of Nigrinus' daughters, L. Ceionius Commodus, as his son and heir.[19]

103   L. Neratius M.(?) f. Volt. Marcellus (*cos*. 95, *II ord*. 129)

XVI 48, Malpas: [*Imp. Caesar d*]*ivi Nervae f. N*[*erva Tr*]*aian*[*us Augu*]*stus Germanicus* [*D*]*acicus pontifex maximus tribunic. potestat. VII imp. IIII cos. V p. p.* [*e*]*quitibus et peditibus qui militant in alis quattuor et cohortibus decem quae . . . sunt in Britannia sub L. Neratio Marcello . . . a. d. XIIII k. Febr. M'. Laberio Maximo II Q. Glitio Atilio Agricola II cos. . . .*   (AD 103)

Vindolanda Tablet Inventory nos. 29 + 31:
[9] *. . . hoc enim de / me semper meruisti usque / ad hanc d*[*ignit*]*atem cuius fid*[12]*/ ucia ho*[*nestasqu*]*e te primum* [*ex/ornav*]*er*[*unt nu*]*nc aput il*[*lum Ne/ratiu*]*m Marcellum clarissi*[*mum vi/rum*] *consularem meum . . .*[24] *. . . ha*[*ec ti*]*bi a Vindolan/*[*d*]*a scribo q*[*us sunt*] *hiberna/* [*i*]*am posita . . .*

(I am grateful to A. K. Bowman and J. D. Thomas for supplying me with the above text in advance of their forthcoming publication of the Vindolanda writing tablets, in which the letter from which this extract is quoted will be included. Thanks are due to the Vindolanda Trust, for permission to publish the document. Dr. Bowman informs me that two further writing tablets, Inventory nos. 90 and 188, also contain the term *consularis*.)

IX 2456 = *ILS* 1032, Saepinum: [. . .][6]*/ divi Traiani Aug. prov. / Britanniae curat. aquar.* [8]*/ urbis pr. trib. mil. leg. XII Ful/minat. salio Palat. quaest. Aug. curat.*

---

[16] *Agr*. 42. 4. See on this, Syme, *Tacitus* 24 ff.; also A. R. Birley, in Levick (ed.), *The Ancient Historian* 147. It may be noted here that the elderly Stoic governor gave a post—perhaps a commission as an equestrian officer—to an aged Stoic friend, Q. Ovidius, who was also the friend of Martial. See 10. 44 and *RE* 18. 2 (1942) 1907.

[17] *ep*. 6. 29. 1, cf. Sherwin-White, *Letters of Pliny* 388.

[18] *PIR*[2] A 1409, Degrassi, *FC* 33.

[19] *PIR*[2] A 1408. Nigrinus had allegedly been intended as Hadrian's heir (*HA Hadr*. 7. 1). See on these matters Syme, *Tacitus*, esp. 600 f.

actorum sena/tus adlecto inter patric. / ab divo Vespasiano IIIvir.[12]*/ a. a. a. f. f. / ex testamento Vettillae eius.*

The diploma of 19 January 103 shows L. Neratius Marcellus as governor of Britain almost exactly eight years after he had become consul, replacing Domitian as suffect, on the Ides of January 95.[1] He should also be the consular Marcellus referred to by one of the Vindolanda letter-writers, for the archaeological evidence dates the Vindolanda archive to the period 95–105.[2] It must have been, further, in his capacity as governor of Britain that he acceded to Pliny's request to grant a commission to Suetonius Tranquillus, the future biographer of the Caesars. In a letter written, it would seem, shortly before 103, Pliny told Suetonius that he would arrange for the commission, a tribunate, to be transferred to Suetonius' kinsman Caesennius Silvanus.[3] Finally, a senatorial career which must be that of Marcellus is recorded on an acephalous inscription at Saepinum in Samnium, the home of his family.[4] It was set up in accordance with the will of his wife Vettilla.[5] It is, unfortunately, not clear whether Marcellus himself was still alive at the time, but it is hard to believe that he could have checked the text of his *cursus*. The order of appointments seems to be seriously disturbed, which makes it difficult to reconstruct his pre-consular career with any certainty. These difficulties are compounded by the confusion over his kinsmen the Neratii Prisci. It is, mercifully, certain that his brother was the jurist L. Neratius Priscus, presumably the consul of 97, for a passage in the *Digest* happens to state this: 'Neratius libro quarto epistularum Marcello fratri sui respondit'.[6] But the precise relationship of the brothers to the other L. Neratius Priscus, the consul of 87, remains a matter for speculation. Both Prisci were *L. f.* and the younger was plebeian,[7] unlike Marcellus and the other Neratius of the Flavian period, M. Hirrius Fronto Neratius Pansa.[8] It therefore seems probable

---

[1] Degrassi, *FC* 28.

[2] R. E. Birley, *Vindolanda. A Roman Frontier Post on Hadrian's Wall* (1977).

[3] Pliny, *ep.* 3. 8. For the date, see Syme, *Tacitus* 91 n. and 647, favouring '101, at the beginning of his tenure'. Cf. also Sherwin-White, *Letters of Pliny* 229 f., who prefers 103.

[4] See *RE* 16. 2 (1935) 2539–53 for the numerous members of the family, several of whom were in the Voltinia tribe to which Saepinum and several other Samnite communities belonged (Kubitschek 272), and to which Marcellus may therefore be assigned.

[5] The *cognomen* is rare: Kajanto 170 knows only four other specimens, deriving it from Vettius; note also the even rarer Vettulla, id. 171.

[6] *Digest* 33. 7. 12. 43.

[7] G. Camodeca, *Atti dell' Accademia di Scienze Morali e Politiche* 87 (1976) 1 ff., argues strongly that there were only two men called L. Neratius Priscus, consuls in 87 and 97, and discusses their careers in the light of this; some problems remain, and further clear evidence is required.

[8] Pansa's adlection is recorded by *JRS* 58 (1968) 170 ff. = *AE* 1968. 145, Saepinum.

that Marcellus and his brother Priscus were the sons of Neratius Pansa, and that Priscus the consul of 97 was adopted by his homonym, perhaps an uncle, the consul of 87.

Neratius Pansa governed Lycia *c.* 71-3. Marcellus perhaps accompanied his presumed father to that province, and may be the son of Pansa who was honoured by the people of Xanthus.[9] He was doubtless already of an age to commence his senatorial career, and his year as *IIIvir a. a. f. f.* was probably in the early 70s, perhaps at the time of his adlection to patrician rank, which belonged to the censorship of 73-4. His patrician rank is exemplified in his career by his tenure of the priesthood of *salius Palatinus* and by the omission of aedileship or plebeian tribunate. His military tribunate in the legion XII Fulminata was originally thought to have fallen in the period 77-80, when Neratius Pansa was governor of Cappadocia-Galatia.[10] But now that Pansa is thought to have commanded a special force in that region *c.* 75, before his governorship,[11] it is reasonable to suppose that he could have given Marcellus his tribunate in that capacity.

Marcellus' quaestorship cannot be dated precisely, except that the years 79 and 81 may be excluded for he would then have been *quaestor Augustorum*. But he probably held office in the late 70s, going on to take charge of the *acta senatus* and then to hold the praetorship. Thereafter, however, he appears to have had no further post of any kind before his consulship in 95. Even the consulship, although held as suffect to the emperor, came rather late for a patrician, when he must have been over forty. The reason may be that he and his father were regarded with disfavour by Domitian;[12] but this seems unlikely in view of the careers of their kinsmen, the Neratii Prisci. Still, unless the *cursus* inscription omitted some posts, Marcellus' sole overseas experience before his governorship was his spell with a Cappadocian legion a quarter of a century earlier.[13] The reason for so unexpected a choice

[9] Kreiler, *Statthalter Kleinasiens* 106: but that text does not supply the name of the son of Pansa honoured by the Xanthians. For the relationship see Syme, *Hermes* 85 (1957) 491 f. *IGR* III 1511, Tlos, is also thought to have honoured a son of Pansa; but is even more fragmentary than the Xanthus stone.

[10] Groag, *RE* 16. 2 (1935) 2543, 2546; and M. Torelli, *JRS* 58 (1968) 171 n. 7, following Syme, *Hermes* 85 (1957) 491 f., still favours this view, even to the extent of supposing that Marcellus was military tribune *after* his quaestorship, an anomaly which is inconceivable except in some grave emergency (cf. Syme, *Tacitus* 631 on *ILS* 1040), in spite of the alternative possibility revealed by the inscription he was publishing (see next note).

[11] *JRS* 58 (1968) 170 ff. = *AE* 1968. 145: *leg. pr. pr.* ⌊*imp. Caes. Vespasiani Aug. exercit*⌋*us qui in A*⌊*rmeniam? missus est*⌋.

[12] Torelli, *JRS* 58 (1968) 171 n. 7, suggests disfavour under Domitian, but see now Camodeca, op. cit.

[13] Groag, *RE* 16. 2 (1935) 2543, assumes that he must have had a legionary command, omitted from *ILS* 1032.

must be that there was a shortage of suitable men in the year 101, when the first Dacian war began, and the tried men were needed at the front.[14] Trajan clearly gave Britain low priority.

There is no means of telling whether Marcellus was still in office when the two British diplomas of 105 were issued, for neither preserves the governor's name.[15] But it is *a priori* likely that he had been replaced.[16] It was probably some time after his return that he was appointed *curator aquarum*. It seems unlikely that Julius Frontinus, who was appointed in 97, had resigned in time for Marcellus to have held the post before going to Britain—and, in any case, he was probably preceded as *curator* by L. Silius Decianus, who had been consul a year earlier than himself, and appears to have been holding the post not earlier than 102.[17] Thereafter he probably retired from public life. He might conceivably have had a year as proconsul of Africa, *c*.109–10, but firm evidence is lacking.[18] Nothing more is known of him for many years, although it must be noted that the younger Neratius Priscus was thought of very highly by Trajan, who planned to make him his succes-

---

[14] Thus Eck, *ANRW* II.1 (1974) 217, following Syme, *Tacitus* 648; E. Birley, *Carnuntum Jahrb.* 1957. 9.

[15] XVI 51 (Sydenham); *JRS* 50 (1960) 238 = *AE* 1962. 253 = Roxan no. 8 (Middlewich), the latter from the period May–July.

[16] Assuming that he was appointed at latest in 101, a consideration of known tenures of office under Trajan would suggest that he would not have stayed much over the *triennium*: Eck, *Senatoren* 152 ff.; *ANRW* II.1 (1974) 214 ff.

[17] XV 7302 (Trajan is named Dacicus). See Groag, *RE* 3 A 1 (1927) 77 f.; for the consulship: Degrassi, *FC* 28. Marcellus may of course have been a praetorian *curator*: thus Brassloff, *Wien. Stud.* 29 (1907) 322. See further Eck, *ANRW* II.1 (1974) 208 f.

[18] A Marcellus (no other names recorded) is attested as proconsul of Africa on two inscriptions, *ILAfr.* 591, Aunobaris, and *IRT* 304, Lepcis Magna. But Syme, *REA* 61 (1959) 314 ff., followed by Thomasson, *Statthalter Nordafrikas* II 65 f., Eck, *Senatoren* 213, and others, prefers to identify this man with Q. Pomponius Rufus Marcellus (*cos.* 121), proconsul presumably *c*.136–7. Apart from the lettering—not a very sound criterion—the principal arguments are the presence on the stone adjacent to the Aunobaris inscription, *ILAfr.* 592, of a list of names, presumably the proconsul's *officium*, one of which is a *scriba*, L. Marius Perpetuus, identified as the grandfather of the Severan consular L. Marius Maximus (*ILS* 2935 etc.)—see e.g. Pflaum, *CP* no. 168; and the mention on *ILAfr.* 591 of a senator named Cornutus, to whose decision the proconsul refers. But even if the *scriba* were the grandfather of Marius Maximus, that would not rule out a Trajanic date: cf. *IRT* 412, showing the emperor Severus' grandfather to have been active under Trajan; and the *scriba* could of course have been e.g. great-grandfather of Marius Maximus. Nor need the Cornutus be the *cos.* 100; the *cognomen* is found in half a dozen other senatorial families (cf. *PIR*[2] II, pp. 374 f.). Groag, who inclined to the later dating in *RE* 14. 2 (1930) 1490 and *PIR*[2] C 1508, drew attention in *RE* 16. 2 (1935) 2544, to the presence in the proconsul Marcellus' *officium*, *ILAfr.* 592, of a L. Neratius Bassus. It must at once be conceded that there is also a Pomponius on the list; but that *nomen* is far commoner. L. Neratius points to Saepinum. [Syme, *ZPE* 37 (1980) 1 notes that Pomponius Marcellus is now eliminated, since *AJA* 78 (1974) 122 shows him to have been proconsul of Asia; but Syme prefers another man, M. Vitorius Marcellus (*cos.* 105) as the African proconsul, op. cit. 5.]

sor, according to a dubious anecdote in the *Historia Augusta*.[19] The same source also lists Neratius Priscus as one of the legal experts on whose advice Hadrian relied; this must certainly be Marcellus' brother.[20] Marcellus himself may also have been on familiar terms with Hadrian. At any rate, in 129 he received the rare honour of a second consulship, as *ordinarius*[21]—this perhaps explains the dedication in Hadrian's honour which he made at Saepinum in the following year.[22] But it may be that he came to a sad end soon afterwards, for among Hadrian's close friends whom he 'postea ut hostium loco habuit', the author of the *Historia Augusta* lists a Marcellus, forced to suicide by the emperor.[23]

Marcellus was the owner of estates near Beneventum, as is revealed by the alimentary table of Baebiani Ligures.[24] The Neratii survived into the late empire, attested both at Saepinum and at Rome, and including many holders of high office.[25] But it is not clear whether Marcellus himself left any direct descendants. It has been suggested that Corellius Pansa, *cos. ord.* in 122, might have been his son,[26] for the rare *cognomen* recalls that of Marcellus' father and the association of the two families is demonstrated by the existence of a landowner named Neratius Corellius, named on the *tabula alimentaria* of 101 in close connection with Marcellus himself.[27] In that case, Corellius Pansa may be polyonymous and could be the grandson of Pliny's friend Corellius Rufus, about whom he wrote to Rufus' daughter Corellia Hispulla, describing the boy's grandfather as 'clarus spectatusque' and his father and uncle as 'inlustri laude conspicui', labels which would apply well to the Neratii, Pansa, Marcellus, and Priscus.[28] The only difficulty is that Marcellus' wife, on the Saepinum inscription, is named Vettilla—but he could well have married more than once.[29]

---

[19] *HA Hadr.* 4. 8, see Syme, *Tacitus* 233 f.

[20] *HA Hadr.* 18. 1.

[21] Degrassi, *FC* 37.

[22] *EE* VIII 108.

[23] *HA Hadr.* 15. 4. See Groag, *RE* 16. 2 (1935) 2544 f. Schumacher, *Priesterkollegien* 224, insists that this Marcellus must be C. Poblicius Marcellus (*cos.* 120) but his arguments are weak. The matter cannot be resolved.

[24] IX 1455, col. II, 16, 51, 73; col. III, 60.

[25] Cf. *RE* 16. 2 (1935), Neratii nos. 3–8, 14, 16–21; *PLRE* Cerealis 2 (*cos. ord.* 358), Gallus 1, Scopius.

[26] Syme, *Hermes* 85 (1957) 492, developing a suggestion of Groag, *RE* 16. 2 (1935) 2546, *PIR*² C 1293.

[27] IX 1455, col. II 14.

[28] Pliny, *ep.* 3. 3. 1. Sherwin-White, *Letters of Pliny* 212 f., while accepting the link between Corellius Pansa and the Neratii, believes that 'inlustri laude conspicui' connotes 'exalted equestrian rank'; this is thoroughly implausible for sons of Neratius Pansa.

[29] Syme, *Hermes* 85 (1957) 492; *JRS* 58 (1968) 147.

M. 'Appius' (= Atilius Metilius Bradua) (*cos. ord.* 108)

W. Dittenberger and K. Purgold, *Die Inschriften von Olympia* (1896) 620 = *ILS* 8824a, Olympia: M. Ἄππιον Βραδούαν ταμίαν, στρατηγόν /[. . .] / θεοῦ Ἀδριανοῦ ὑπατικὸν Γερμανίας καὶ Βρεταννίας ποντίφικα⁴ /σοδᾶλιν Ἀδριανᾶλιν τὸν Ῥη[γίλλης πρ]ὸς μητρὸς πάππον τῆς Ἡρώδου / γυναικός ἡ πόλις ἡ τῶν Ἠλείεων.

The governorship of Bradua is known only from this inscription at Olympia,[1] one of a series of monuments[2] to the family of the wealthy Athenian Herodes Atticus (*cos. ord.* 143),[3] whose wife Annia Regilla was Bradua's granddaughter, as lines 4–5 indicate.[4] There is a problem about his nomenclature, but, as Thomasson pointed out, it must be assumed that the stonemason, influenced by the names of Regilla's paternal grandfather Appius Annius Gallus (*cos. ord.* 108), who was honoured on an adjacent stone, carved ΑΠΠΙΟΝ by mistake for ΑΤΙ-ΛΙΟΝ.[5] Bradua can thus be identified with M. Atilius Metilius Bradua, consular colleague of Ap. Annius Gallus in 108, his *consocer.*[6]

His family was certainly Italian and an origin in the Cisalpina, where the *gentilicium* is especially common, seems plausible.[7] His father was doubtless M. Atilius Postumus Bradua, proconsul of Asia under Domitian, and the second *nomen* borne by our Bradua suggests that his mother may have been a Metilia.[8] If so, Bradua could have been the nephew of the governor P. Metilius Nepos.[9] His *cursus* inscription indicates that he went straight from quaestorship to praetorship, with no intervening magistracy, doubtless because he had patrician rank—which accords well with the fact that he became *consul ordinarius* and with his position as a *pontifex.*[10] It must, however, be noted that the inscription also omits mention of any post in the vigintivirate, in which he should have served, as well as a military tribunate, which he might have held, so that it is not completely certain that he was patrician. It is quite possible

---

[1] It is perhaps worth noting that in line 5 most of the first letter of τῶν appears quite clearly in the drawing and hence does not need to be shown between square brackets, as by Dittenberger and Dessau.

[2] See Dittenberger and Purgold, *Inschriften von Olympia*, pp. 617 ff.

[3] *PIR*² C 802.

[4] *PIR*² A 720: her full names, Appia Annia Regilla Atilia Caucidia Tertulla, suggest that her mother, the wife of Bradua, may have been called Caucidia Tertulla.

[5] Thomasson, *Statthalter Nordafrikas* II 103 f.

[6] See now Schumacher, *Priesterkollegien*, stemma IV.

[7] See *CIL* V, *index nominum*. A C. Atilius C. f. Bradua at Libarna might be related (V 7427 = *ILS* 5354), although Schumacher, *Priesterkollegien* 391, doubts this on account of the differing *praenomen.*

[8] *PIR*² A 1303; Schumacher, *Priesterkollegien* 200 f., stemma IV.

[9] p. 83 above.

[10] Schumacher, *Priesterkollegien* 201, dates his co-option to the *pontifices* to the period between 102 and 108.

that Bradua, unlike Neratius Marcellus, held at least one post between praetorship and consulship. Dittenberger supplied for the missing line 2 the restoration [ὕπατον, πρεσβευτὴν καὶ ἀντιστράτηγον], but this is unsatisfactory for more than one reason. It is not very plausible that Bradua governed not only one of the German provinces but also Britain under Hadrian,[11] and, in any case, lines 3 and 4 contain considerably more letters than line 1, where the lettering is much larger.[12] It is probable that in line 2 there were at least fifty letters, so that there must have been more than the consulship and the phrase or word governing θεοῦ ᾿Αδριανοῦ at the beginning of line 3. It is likely that a proconsulship of Africa was mentioned, for the *Digest* includes a rescript of Hadrian to 'Aquillius' Bradua, whom it is plausible to identify with our governor.[13] But the restoration [ὕπατον, ἀνθύπατον ᾿Αφρικῆς] is still too short,[14] and it must be supposed that further posts were mentioned as well. There is hardly room for a legionary command,[15] and the logic of the *cursus*'s phrasing seems to require another, praetorian, proconsulship as well as that of Africa,[16] followed by (for example) the Greek word for *comes*: [ὕπατον, ἀνθύπατον . . . καὶ ᾿Αφρικῆς, συναπόδημον].

Bradua's governorship of Britain must thus be assigned to the last decade of Trajan's reign, commencing *c*.111 at the earliest, to allow time for the governorship of one of the German provinces beforehand. This was probably Germania inferior rather than superior, since at least seven governors of Britain are known to have governed the former province before going to Britain, as against only one who governed Germania superior.[17] At least two governors of Britain must be postulated between Marcellus and Bradua. As with Neratius Marcellus, the choice of governor is a little surprising, although one must bear in mind the possibility that Bradua might have had more experience than is recorded on the Olympia inscription.[18] On the other hand, from 113 to

[11] There is not much room for him in Britain under Hadrian, none at all before *c*.125, and so long an interval after the consulship would have been most unusual.

[12] See Syme, *REA* 67 (1965) 344. The excellent drawing in Dittenberger and Purgold, op. cit., makes this quite clear.

[13] Syme, *REA* 67 (1965) 344, followed by Eck, *Senatoren* 193.

[14] Even allowing for e.g. συναπόδημον to go with Θεοῦ ᾿Αδριανοῦ, see below.

[15] For one thing, the names of legions seem to have been less drastically abbreviated in Greek than in Latin, see e.g. Dessau's selection of Greek *cursus* inscriptions, *ILS* 8818, 8821, 8826, 8828–31, 8834a, 8835.

[16] For the coupling of praetorian and consular proconsulship see e.g. *ILS* 970, also from Olympia (p. 45 above, the inscription of Didius Gallus) and 8970, Miletus (improved by Kreiler, *Statthalter Kleinasiens* 33 ff., the inscription of the elder Trajan).

[17] pp. 388 ff. below. See also p. 201 below, for the possibility that Bradua's name may be restored on *RIB* 419, Tomen-y-Mur.

[18] He might even, e.g., have had a military tribunate in Britain—perhaps under his presumed kinsman P. Metilius Nepos (p. 85 above).

117 there was once again a major war elsewhere in the empire, and Trajan may have been unable to spare a tried military man for Britain.

His presumed proconsulship of Africa should have come *c.*122-3.[19] Either before, or more probably after, this, he may have accompanied Hadrian on one of the emperor's numerous journeys around the empire, as *comes*. Apart from this, all that can be said of his later career is that he outlived Hadrian, and became a *sodalis Hadrianalis*. He seems not to have left male heirs, but his names were perpetuated by the *cos. ord.* 160, Ap. Annius Atilius Bradua, his daughter's son,[20] and by descendants of his granddaughter, the wife of Herodes Atticus.[21]

Ignotus XVI 88

XVI 88, Walcot: [*imp. . . . . equitibus et peditibus qui militaverunt in alis . . . et cohortibus . . . quae appellantur. . . e*]*t I Aq*[*uitanor. et . . . et . . . et coh. I Mo*]*rin. et III e*[*t IV et VI Nervior.* (?) *et sunt in Brit*]*ann. sub I* [*. . . quin. et. vicen. plu*]*ribusve stipe*[*ndis emeritis dimissis hon*]*est. missione* [*quorum nomina subscripta su*]*nt ipsis li*[*beris posterisque eorum civitatem dedit et conubium c*]*um uxo*[*ribus quas tunc habuissent, cum est*] *civitas ii*[*s data aut si qui caelibes essent c*]*um iis quas post*[*ea duxissent dumtaxat sing*]*uli singulas.* [*a.d.*] *XVII k. Octobr.* [*. . .*] *Ti. Lartidio Cele*[*re cos. alae Aug. Gallo*]*r. Proculeian. cui p*[*raest . . . Pro*]*pinquos* [*ex grega*]*le* [*. . .*]

This diploma was assigned to the period 120-33 by E. Birley, whose arguments were accepted by H. Nesselhauf, and, as the governor's name appears to begin with the letter I, it seemed likely that he could be identified with Sex. Julius Severus.[1] However, M. M. Roxan has shown that a slightly earlier period, 114-22, is more likely.[2] It should, furthermore, be noted that the first letter of the governor's name was originally read as C (or O or Q),[3] and that, when the diploma was cleaned and re-read by F. Haverfield, the reading P was proposed.[4] H. Nesselhauf, ad

---

[19] Syme, *REA* 67 (1965) 344; Eck, *Senatoren* 193.

[20] *PIR²* A 636.

[21] e.g. the *cos. ord.* 185, son of Herodes Atticus, who may or may not be the same as the polyonymous proconsul of Africa recorded by *IRT* 517: see Schumacher, *Priesterkollegien* 414. Note also the polyonymous P. Vigellius cet . . . Saturninus cet., *ILS* 1116.

[1] E. Birley, *JRS* 28 (1938) 228, accepted by H. Nesselhauf, XVI Supp. p. 215, followed by *PIR²* J 576 and A. R. Birley, *Ep. Stud.* 4 (1967) 71. [*coh I Mo*]*rin.* is read by R. P. Wright, *JRS* 54 (1964) 150.

[2] M. M. Roxan, *Roman Military Diplomas* p. 24.

[3] *Arch. J.* 34 (1877) 318; *Arch. Ael.²* 8 (1880) 219. The point is stressed by Roxan (previous note), who, however, overlooks the reading of Haverfield (next note).

[4] F. Haverfield, *VCH Somerset* I (1905) 280 f.

loc., noted that there would be room for only about ten letters for the remainder of the name. P[*ompeio Falcone*] and P[*latorio Nepote*] each take up fourteen letters, but remain possible. But clearly there is a wide range of names which might be restored.[5]

122   Q. Pompeius Sex. f. Quir. Falco (*cos.* 108?)

XVI 69 = Smallwood II 347 (Brigetio): *Imp. Caesar divi Traiani Parthici f. divi Nervae nepos Tra/ianus Hadrianus Augustus pontifex maximus tribu/nic. potestat. VI cos. III procos.* [4]/ *equitib. et peditib. qui militaverunt in alis decem et trib. et coh<or>/tib. triginta et septem . . . quae sunt in Britan*[20]/*nia sub A. Platorio Nepote quinque et viginti stipendis / emeritis dimissis honesta missione per Pompeium / Falconem quorum nomina subscripta sunt ipsis libe/ris posterisq. eorum civitatem dedit. . . .*[25] *A. d. XVI K. Aug. / Ti. Iulio Capitone L. Vitrasio Flaminino cos.* [17 July AD 122] . . .

X 6231 = *ILS* 1035 (Tarracina): *Q. Roscio Sex. f. / Quir. Coelio Murenae / Silio Deciano Vibull<i>o*[4] / *Pio Iulio Eury.cli Herc<u>lano / Pompeio Falconi cos. / XVvir. s. f. procos. provinc. Asiae leg. pr. pr./ imp. Caes. Traiani Hadriani Aug. provinc.*[8]/ *Brittanniae leg. pr. pr. imp. Caes. Nervae/ Traiani Aug. Germanici Dacici/ [pr]ovinc. Moesiae inferior. curatori/ [via]e Traianae et leg. Aug. pr. pr. provinc.*[12]/ *[Iudaeae e]t leg. X Fret. leg. pr. pr. prov. Lyciae / [et Pamphyl]iae leg. leg. V Macedonic. / [bello Dacico donis militari]bus donato/* [. . . . .] *a*[16]/ [. . . . . . .]

AE 1957. 336 (Tomi): [*Q. Roscio Murenae Coe/lio Pompeio Falconi / consuli, leg. Aug. pr. pr.*[4] *Lyc]iae et Pamphyliae/ [leg. A]ug. pr. pr. Iudae[ae,/ cura]tori viae Traiana[e, leg.] Aug. pr. pr. Moes[iae*[8]/ *inf]erioris, leg. Aug. [pro / p]r. provinciae / [B]ritanniae,/ [A]nnaeus Vibianus* [12] / *[t]estamento fratris/ Annaei Vibi[ani] posui [t]*

JÖAI 49 (1968-71) Bbl. 29-32 = *AE* 1972. 577 (Ephesus): Κόιντον Ῥώσκιον Μου/ρήνα Κούελλον [*sic*] Πομ/πήιον Φάλκωνα, πρεσ[4]/βευτὴν Σεβαστοῦ καὶ ἀν/τιστράτηγον Λυκίας καὶ / Παμφυλίας καὶ Ἰουδαίας καὶ / Μυσίας καὶ Βρεταννίας [8] / καὶ πολλὰς ἄλλας ἡγεμονίας διατελέσαντα Ἀσίας ἀνθύ/πατον ἐτείμησεν Φλαουι/έων Νεαπολειτῶν Σαμαρέ[12]/ων ἡ βουλὴ καὶ ὁ δῆμος τὸν / σωτῆρα καὶ εὐεργέτην. / Διὰ πρεσβευτῶν καὶ ἐπιμελητῶν / Φλαουίου Ἰούνκου καὶ [16]/ Οὐλπίου Πρόκλου.

Digest 28. 3. 6 (Ulpianus libro decimo ad Sabinum), 7: . . . quam distinctionem in militis quoque testamento divus Hadrianus dedit epistula ad Pomponium [*sic*] Falconem, ut, si quidem ob conscientiam delicti militaris mori maluit, irritum sit testamentum; quod si taedio vitae vel dolore, valere testamentum aut, si intestato decessit, cognatis aut, si non sint, legioni ista sint vindicanda.

The above four inscriptions and perhaps the passage from the *Digest* afford ample testimony for the presence of Pompeius Falco as governor

---

[5] Any names beginning with upright letters—B, D, E, F, H, I, L, etc.—need to be considered.

of Britain early in the reign of Hadrian; and a whole host of other inscriptions from various parts of the empire, together with passages in Pliny's letters and the correspondence of Fronto, combine to make this man's career unusually well recorded. The earlier stages, missing from the Tarracina inscription, are supplied by the dedication in his honour at Hierapolis[1] Castabala in Cilicia, set up by a certain A. Laberius Camerinus and his son, a centurion of the legion V Macedonica, of which Falco had been legate (and which was now once more under his command), in honour of their friend and benefactor:

Q. Roscio Sex. f. Qui. Coelio Po[m/p]*eio Falconi decemviro stli*[tibu]*s iudicandis trib. mil. leg. X* [*Gem. / q*]*uaestori trib. pleb. pr. inter civ*[es[4] */ et*] *peregrinos leg. Aug. leg. V Maced. /* [*le*]*g. Aug. pr. pr. provin. Lyciae et Pam/*[ph]*yliae leg. Aug. leg. X Fret. et leg. pr. pr. /* [*pr*]*ovinciae Iudaeae consularis* [8] */ X Vviro sacris faciundis curator./ viae Traianae leg. Aug. pr. pr. prov. / Moes. inf.* Πομπέιον Φάλκονα Αὗλος Λαβέριος Καμερῖνος καὶ [12] / Λαβέριος Καμερῖνας υἱὸς αὐτοῦ / ἑκατοντάρχης λεγ. ἑ Μακεδονικῆς, / τὸν ἴδιον φίλον καὶ εὐεργέτην, ἐκ του / ἰδίου, τεμῆς ἕνεκεν.

(*JHS* 11 (1896) 253 = *ILS* 1036 = III 12117)

Falco's origin, to be discussed presently, is a matter of some uncertainty, but he was undoubtedly well connected by marriage: his wife was Sosia Polla,[2] daughter of Q. Sosius Senecio (*cos. ord.* 99, *II ord.* 107)[3] and granddaughter of Sex. Julius Frontinus (*III ord.* 100),[4] both prominent figures in the reign of Trajan. Falco himself was to leave distinguished descendants, *consules ordinarii* in 149, 169, and 193.[5] Customarily known by the *tria nomina* Q. Pompeius Falco, he had a whole string of additional names, as may be seen from the Tarracina inscription. The final five of these were no doubt inherited, with a legacy, from C. Julius Eurycles Herculanus L. Vibullius Pius, last representative of the royal house of Sparta, who died in 130 or shortly afterwards.[6] The previous pair of names probably came from L. Silius

[1] Sometimes incorrectly spelt Hieropolis, but see L. Robert in A. Dupont-Sommer and L. Robert, *La Déesse de Hiérapolis Castabala (Cilicie)* (1964) 17–22.

[2] *ILS* 1037 = III 7663 (Samos); *ILS* 1105 = VIII 7066 = *ILAlg.* II 652 (Cirta); *IGR* IV 779, 880 = *OGI* 490 = *ILS* 8820 (Apamea).

[3] *RE* 3A (1927) 1180–93 (Groag); C. P. Jones, *JRS* 60 (1970) 98 ff. (although I have reservations about Jones's view that Senecio is the *ignotus ILS* 1022).

[4] pp. 69 ff. above.

[5] *RE* 21 (1952) 2288–90 (Wolf). See the important article by Pflaum, *Bonner Jahrb.* 172 (1972) 18 ff.

[6] *PIR*[2] J 302. Falco seems to have taken over this nomenclature after 116, as it is not on the Hierapolis inscription. But since it does not feature on the new inscription from Ephesus either, the *terminus post quem* should perhaps be extended to 124, although a desire for brevity may have been decisive. Jones, op. cit. 103, suggests that he may have inherited these names from Sosius Senecio.

Decianus (*cos. suff.* 94)[7] or from a son of his. But in neither case does existing evidence enable us to judge whether there were family connections, or only ties of friendship, to justify the legacies thus attested. As for Murena, it seems likely that it was omitted in error from the Hierapolis inscription, since Falco's grandson, the *cos. ord.* 169, included Roscius Murena Coelius among his 38 names; at all events, Roscius Coelius must have been acquired, by descent, adoption, or inheritance, from the M. Roscius Coelius whom Julius Agricola succeeded in command of the twentieth legion and who rose to the consulship in 81.[8] There remain his *tria nomina*, and the question of his ancestry and origin is still open.[9] The Hierapolis inscription may be of some assistance. Cilicia was not one of the provinces in which he served at any stage in his career; it might be argued that the reason for an inscription being set up in his honour at this place was that it was his home, if not that of the dedicators. The balance is tipped in favour of the former alternative by the conjunction of names of the dedicators, Laberius Camerinus, suggestive of an Italian rather than a provincial origin for them; yet there was no Italian settlement in Cilicia, in which we might expect to find rare Italian names persisting.[10] The *nomen* Pompeius is of course commonly found in the Greek east, and that creates no difficulties. It could well be that an ancestor, a Cilician dignitary, had been granted Roman citizenship by Pompeius Magnus in the 60s BC. An alternative suggestion has been put forward, that Falco's ancestor might be a known client of Pompey, the historian Theophanes of Mytilene, whose descendants still flourished in the early second century, having acquired senatorial rank three or four generations previously.[11] However this may be, Falco certainly had strong links with the Greek east—eastern, perhaps Cilician, origin has been suggested for his father-in-law Sosius

---

[7] Groag, *RE* 3A 1 (1927) 77-9, suggesting that he was the son of the poet Silius Italicus. The consular date there given is now known to be incorrect: Degrassi, *FC* 28.

[8] pp. 231 f. below.

[9] Falco is almost unique. Apart from members of this family only three other cases are recorded: III 8160, VI 17982, and J. Vives, *Inscripciones latinas de la España romana* (1971) 533 (a peregrine). Schulze (272) was hesitant about an Etruscan derivation, and it seems likely that it was a descriptive surname of the traditional kind, referring not only to the bird but to a deformity of the toes: *TLL* VI. 1, 175 f., s. v. 'falco'.

[10] Mommsen made this point long ago, in commentary on III 12117: 'Titulum centurio exercitus Moesiacae videtur dedicasse in patria non sua, sed honorati, quem Graecum hominem fuisse et tribus significat et quod inter vocabula eius Eurycles.' Cilician origin was suggested in *Ep. Stud.* 4, p. 69, regarded favourably by Jones, op. cit. 103. L. Petersen, who regards the two Laberii as natives of Hierapolis (*PIR*[2] L 5), does not consider the difficulties.

[11] Schumacher, *Priesterkollegien* 256, and stemma (Anlage VII), taking up a suggestion of Morris, *Listy fil.* 86 (1963) 42 f.

Senecio[12]—as well as with Italian families; and he may be regarded as a fine specimen of the new cosmopolitan aristocracy.

Pliny's letter (*Ep.* 1. 23) in response to his enquiry whether or not he should continue to practise law during his tribunate ('Consulis an existimem te in tribunatu causas agere debere') is assignable to the year 97,[13] which makes it probable that he was born *c.*70.[14] His initial post in the vigintivirate, as a *Xvir*, shows that Domitian had not specifically marked him out for military advancement,[15] and as tribune of X Gemina, still at that time in Lower Germany, he can have had no opportunity of active service.[16] But after the quaestorship at Rome, tribunate of the plebs, and praetorship,[17] *c.*99 or 100, came the command over V Macedonica and military decorations for what must clearly have been the first Dacian war, of 101-2. He went on to the governorship of Lycia-Pamphylia,[18] and then, unusually, to a second praetorian province, Judaea (combined with command over the single legion, X Fretensis). No precedent is known for such an appointment, and the next recorded parallel comes many decades later. It may well be that the annexation of Arabia in 106 made it desirable to appoint a particularly experienced man to the adjacent province.[19] His consulship seems to have come in September 108: although only the letters

---

[12] Jones, op. cit. 103; Syme, *Hist.* 17 (1968) 101 n. 127. Syme, *ap.* Jones 103 n. 64, cites Falconilla, daughter of the Queen Tryphaena of the *Acta Pauli et Theclae* 27 ff. (for the real queen, see *PIR*² A 900), as a further hint of eastern origin.

[13] See Syme, *Tacitus* 76 n. 1, identifying Falco as the tribune Murena who intervened in the Publicius Certus debate of 97 (Pliny, *ep.* 9. 13. 19), followed by Sherwin-White, *Letters of Pliny* 138 f., 497.

[14] See p. 21 above, on the ages for holding office.

[15] See p. 6 above, on the vigintivirate.

[16] Groag, *ap.* Ritterling, *FRD* 147: 'trib. leg. X Geminae am Ende des I. Jahrhundert.—CIL III 12117, zu berichtigen nach einem unveröffentlichten Inschriftbruchstück aus Ephesos, demzufolge Roscius Pompeius Falco *trib. mil.* in der *leg. X. Gemina* (nicht in der *X. Fretensis!*) gewesen ist (Mitteilung Groags vom 12 Febr. 1927).' W. Eck kindly confirms the accuracy of this report. In *JHS* 1890 *leg. X F*[*ret.*] is read. If the *F* is correct, the legion's title has been given mistakenly, influenced by the mention of *X Fret.* in line 5.

[17] Stein, *Moesien* 64 n. 3, refers to a revision of III 12117 by Keil and Bauer ('Scheden des Wiener Arch. Inst.') according to which Falco was '*pr. inter fisc. . . . peregrinos*' [*sic*: presumably he meant to write *privatos*], hence not before Nerva, cf. *Digest* 1. 2. 2. 32.

[18] See also *IGR* III 739 I, lines 3-4 (Rhodiapolis), for this post, which Syme, *JRS* 48 (1958) 4, suggests began in 103, the year when his predecessor Trebonius Mettius Modestus was consul suffect (*AE* 1954. 223).

[19] Syme, *JRS* 48 (1958) 4; Eck, *Senatoren* 15 n. 69. The next example on record seems to be the unknown *leg. Augustorum pr. pr. prov. Galat. item prov. Ciliciae* (III 254, Ancyra), mistakenly identified with C. Julius Saturninus in *PIR*² J 547 (see now Eck, *ZPE* 8 (1971) 78 n. 27). Syme, op. cit. 4 n. 35, suggests that these provinces 'might have been temporarily conjoined in a season of crisis', i.e. the 160s. See also the list in Alföldy, *Fasti Hispanienses* 99 f., to which add L. Saevinius L. f. Quir. Proculus, *leg. Aug. pro pr. prov. Galatiae item Ciliciae* (*AE* 1969/70. 601, Ancyra), discussed by Eck, *ZPE* 8 (1971) 71 ff. For XIII 6806 (Mainz) see pp. 132 f. below; and see also p. 22 above.

[. . .] *ius F*[. . .] are recorded, the identification looks certain. It may well be that he held office *in absentia.*[20]

After his return to Italy he became curator of the *via Traiana*, probably as the first holder of the post, for the new road, from Beneventum to Brundisium, was commenced in 109 and commemorated on the coinage of 112.[21] (At this stage it seems, he was made a *XVvir sacris faciundis*).[22] His next appointment—perhaps after some years without employment[23] —was as governor of Moesia inferior, where he is attested in 116 and 117.[24] His transfer to Britain must have been one of Hadrian's first acts, and, indeed, since the new emperor must have been in Falco's province soon after his accession,[25] one may postulate that he communicated the promotion personally. The *Historia Augusta* shows that Britain was one of several places where there was a serious military threat at the outset of Hadrian's reign,[26] and the coinage suggests that a war was fought there.[27] The British diploma indicates that it was within a matter of weeks before July 122 that Falco had been succeeded by Platorius Nepos. Thus one may infer that Falco's governorship had commenced not later than 118, and that he had been selected by Hadrian to deal with the troubles in the province. He was by then in his late forties, and a fairly senior man—in terms of the interval since his consulship. No epigraphic record of his British governorship survives, but 'the odds are rather better than four to one' for the rescript of Hadrian to Falco referring to his time in Britain and not to the Lower

---

[20] Schumacher, *Priesterkollegien* 312 n. 77, cites the differing opinions on his consulship. I take the view that he was consul in absence, in 108. There is no need to date Pliny, *ep.* 9. 15, addressed to Falco at Rome, to the year 108.

[21] Stein, *Moesien* 65 n. 6, conveniently cites the evidence; see further Eck, *Organisation Italiens* 34 n. 60, 51 f.

[22] Schumacher, *Priesterkollegien* 313 n. 82, notes that the priesthood is given in chronological order on the Hierapolis inscription.

[23] Syme, *Tacitus* 243. His father-in-law Senecio's friendship with Hadrian (*HA Hadr.* 4. 1-2, quoted below, p. 103) *c.* 113, doubtless furthered Falco's prospects at this stage.

[24] See Stein, *Moesien* 64 f.; Fitz, *Moesia Inferior* 39. His son, the *cos. ord.* 149, must have been born while Falco was in this province, since he died in 180 aged sixty-two years, eight months, and fourteen days, hence was born in May 118 at the very latest.

[25] *HA Hadrian* 6. 6: see now Syme, *Danubian Papers* 102 f., 108 f., 167, for Hadrian's abandonment of transdanubian Moesia inferior in 118. As Eck, *Senatoren* 186 n. 306, comments, the Tomi inscription probably indicates that he was sent direct from Lower Moesia to Britain, perhaps in 118.

[26] *HA Hadrian* 5. 1: 'Adeptus imperium ad priscum se statim morem instituit et tenendae per orbem terrarum paci operam impendit. (2) nam deficientibus iis nationibus quas Traianus subegerat, Mauri lacessebant, Sarmatae bellum inferebant, Britanni teneri sub Romana dicione non poterant, Aegyptus seditionibus urgebatur, Libya denique ac Palestina rebelles animos efferebant'.

[27] See the coins referring to Britain, assignable to the year 119: *RIC* II nos. 577 a and b; 561-2, 572 with Mattingly's discussion; ibid. pp. 315, 322. The fighting did not involve the destruction of the legion IX Hispana, as was once commonly claimed. See below, p. 220.

Moesian command.[28] It has been proposed, on archaeological grounds, that the building of the continuous frontier barrier between Tyne and Solway commenced in 120, and hence under Falco rather than Nepos. The question cannot be decided without further evidence, but deserves serious consideration.[29]

Almost immediately after his return from Britain, Falco was success- ful in the ballot and obtained the proconsulship of Asia, where he is attested in 124, having evidently taken up the post in the previous summer.[30] One may assume that the rest of his life was spent in com- fortable retirement. He is last heard of in a letter of the young M. Aurelius to his tutor Fronto, written in 143 and recalling a visit which he and the emperor had made three years previously to Falco's estate. He had shown his admiring imperial visitors a product of his experi- ments in arboriculture.[31] It might be that Antoninus Pius had availed himself of the opportunity to discuss the situation in Britain—where the frontier was being moved north once more—with the aged former governor:[32] but that is pure speculation.

17 July 122   **A. Platorius Nepos** (*cos.* 119)
15 Sept 124

XVI 69 = Smallwood II 347 (Brigetio), quoted on p. 95 above (17 July AD 122).

XVI 70 (Stannington): (Hadrian *tribunic.* [*potest.*] *VIII* . . . .) *quae sunt in Britanni*[*a*] *sub Pretorio* [sic] *Nepote* . . . *a.d. XVI* [*k.*] *O*[*c*]*t*(?) *C. Iulio Gallo C. Valerio Severo cos.* (15 Sept. AD 124).

JRS 28 (1938) 200 = *RIB* 1340 (Benwell): *Imp. Caes. Traiano / Hadr*[*ia*]*n. Aug./ A. Platorio N*[*epote l*] *eg. Aug. pr. p*[*r.*]*[4]/vexillatio c*[*lassis*] *Britan.*

JRS 27 (1937) 247 = *RIB* 1427 (Haltonchesters): *Imp. Caes. T*[*ra. Hadriano*]*/ Aug. leg. VI V*[*ictrix P. F.*]*/ A. Platorio N*[*epote*]*[4]/leg. Aug. pr.* [*pr.*].

VII 662 = *RIB* 1634 (Hadrian's Wall, M/c 37): [. . .]*/leg. II* [*Aug.*]*/ A. Platorio N*[*epote.* . .].

VII 661 = *RIB* 1637 (Hadrian's Wall, M/c 38): *Imp. Ga*[*e*]*s. Traian./ Hadrian. Aug./ leg. I*[*I*] *Aug.[4] / A. Platorio* [*N*]*epote leg. pr. p*[*r.*]

[28] E. Birley, *Roman Britain and the Roman Army* 50.
[29] C. E. Stevens, *The Building of Hadrian's Wall* 39, 52.
[30] *AE* 1957. 17 (Lydia, provenance unknown), dated by Hadrian's eighth year of tribuni- cian power. See Eck, *Senatoren* 192 n. 332.
[31] Fronto, *ad M Caes.* 2. 6 = Haines I 140 = 29 van den Hout. As Sir Ronald Syme has put it, 'he went in for grafting, an operation that should not have proved arduous or uncongenial to a Roman senator of consular standing' (*Historia* 9 (1960) 379).
[32] A. R. Birley, *Marcus Aurelius* 73. A version of this discussion of Falco was published in *Arheološki Vestnik* 28 (1977) 360 ff.

VII 660 = *RIB* 1638 (ibid.): an identical text to *RIB* 1637, but complete (and with *Caes.*).

VII 663 = *RIB* 1666 (Hadrian's Wall, M/c 42): *Im*[*p. Caes. Traian.*] / *H*[*adriano Aug.*] / *le*[*g. II Aug.*] [4]/ *A. Pla*[*torio Nepote leg. pr. pr.*]

JRS 25 (1935) 16, 224 = *RIB* 1935 (Hadrian's Wall, TW M/c 50): [*Imp. Caes. Traiani / Had*]*ria*[*ni Augusti / leg . . . . . . .A.*] *Pl*[*atorio Nepote*[4] / *leg. pr. pr.*]

?VII 713 + add. = *RIB* 1702 (attributed to Vindolanda): [*Imp. Ca*]*es. Traia*[*no / Had*]*riano A*[*ug. / le*]*g. II Au*[*g.* [4]/?*A. Platorio Nepote leg. pr. pr.*]
The resemblance between this stone and 1637–8 makes the restoration of line 4 very probable.

V 877 = *ILS* 1052 = Smallwood II 220 (Aquileia): *A. Platorio A.f. /Serg. Nepoti/ Aponio Italico* [4]/ *Maniliano/ C. Licinio Pollioni/ cos. auguri/ legat. Aug.* [8]/ *pro praet. provinc. Bri/tanniae leg. pro pr. pro/vinc. German. inferior./ leg. pro pr. provinc. Thrac.* [12]/ *leg. legion. I Adiutricis./ quaest. provinc. Maced. / curat. viarum Cassiae Clodiae Ciminiae novae / Traianae candidato divi* [16]/ *Traiani trib. mil. leg. XXII/ Primigen. p. f. praet. trib. / pleb. IIIvir. capitali / patrono* [20]/ *d. d.*

Copiously attested by the above inscriptions, the governorship of Platorius Nepos is perhaps second only to that of Julius Agricola for its interest to the student of Roman Britain. His tenure of office, firmly dated by the two diplomas, must have commenced at most only a few weeks before 17 July 122, as the reference to his predecessor Pompeius Falco makes clear. Hadrian himself visited Britain at this time[1] and this was also the moment when the VIth legion was brought from Lower Germany, Nepos' previous province, to Britain, where it was to be garrisoned for the remainder of its existence.[2] It is safe to assume that Nepos brought the legion with him.

Nepos' origin must remain a matter of conjecture, but as he is explicitly described as a friend of Hadrian before his accession, and he shares the same tribe, Sergia, it seems not improbable that his home was in southern Spain.[3] The *nomen* Platorius, of Illyrian orgin, is attested in Baetica, at Gades,[4] and the conjunction of names Platorius Nepos is apparently recorded for a *IIvir* of Corduba in the same province.[5]

The inscription from Aquileia, set up by decree of the town-council, *d(ecreto) d(ecurionum)*, to their patron, contains a full record of his

[1] *HA Hadr.* 11. 2.
[2] Ritterling, *RE* 12. 2 (1925) 1605 ff.; A. R. Birley in R. M. Butler (ed.), *Soldier and Civilian in Roman Yorkshire* 81 ff.; see also p. 273 below.
[3] Kubitschek 272 shows only Italica and Tucci, of Baetican towns, enrolled in the Sergia. But see Syme, *Tacitus* 791. Note *RIB* 518 (Chester): *L. Antestius L. f. Serg. Sabinus* [*C*]*orduba*; II 2286, 5523.
[4] Schulze 44 n. 5, 334 n. 3. II 1861: *C. Platorius C. f. Gal. Trebianus.*
[5] A. Balil, in *Les Empereurs romains d'Espagne* (1965) 85. But the inscription to which he refers has not been published.

career, although the order of posts, in the earlier stages, is certainly disturbed. In two important respects the career is an unusual one for a governor of Britain. In the first place, it is only the example recorded before the time of Severus Alexander of a man who had begun his career in the least favoured post in the vigintivirate, the *IIIviri capitales*, later receiving an emperor's backing in his candidature for a higher post (although it is unfortunately not clear, due to the disturbance in the text, for which post Nepos was *candidatus divi Traiani*).[6] Secondly, this is one of only three known instances (the others being those of L. Flavius Silva (*ord.* 81) and C. Bruttius Praesens (II *ord.* 139)) of such men proceeding to the consulship after a single senior praetorian appointment.[7] Reference to the time-scale will help to explain these unusual features. He can hardly have reached the consulship much before his fortieth year, and thus will have been born *c.*79 at latest, and have been serving as tribune of XXII Primigenia at Mainz, under the eye of the governor of Upper Germany, in the closing years of the first century.[8] In that case his allocation to the *IIIviri capitales* will probably have been due to Domitian, and we may take it that Trajan, on the recommendation of his kinsman Servianus, if not from his own estimate of the young man,[9] decided to reverse Domitian's unfavourable judgement of his future capabilities, and give him direct support in his candidature for senatorial offices, with a view to giving him earlier employment in praetorian posts. By the same token, his rapid advancement to the consulship may be attributed with confidence to the friendship of Hadrian, who must have appointed him to Thrace on becoming emperor in August 117. Nepos' full nomenclature shows that his ancestry was not necessarily entirely of Spanish colonial stock. C. Licinius Pollio, the last three of his names, were perhaps inherited from a family attested at Naples, apparently its domicile, in the early years of Vespasian's reign.[10] The source of the three previous names, Aponius Italicus Manilianus, is at present unknown.[11]

---

[6] A. Betz, *RE* 20. 2 (1950) 2546 cites the literature. I share Dessau's scepticism (*ILS* III p. clxxiii on no. 1052) over attempts to show that Nepos could have been *candidatus* as curator of roads.

[7] See pp. 5 f. and n. 10 above.

[8] Ritterling, *RE* 12. 2 (1925) 1803 ff., 1816. But Nepos can hardly have served in the legion with Hadrian (for whose tribunate see *HA Hadr.* 2. 5, *ILS* 308), as Betz, op. cit,, implies ('Als trib. mil. . . . gehörte er zu den *tribuni laticlavii* der Legion und könnte etwa gleichzeitig mit Hadrian in ihr gedient haben'), for each legion surely had only one laticlave tribune at a time, cf. p. 8 n. 16 above.

[9] Trajan was legate of Upper Germany at the moment of his adoption (Dio 68. 3. 4: see Syme, *Tacitus* 11 etc.). Servianus: *PIR²* J 631¹.

[10] *IGR* I 450 (Naples).

[11] But Aponius points to Baetica: Syme, *Tacitus* 785; *PIR²* A 932 ff. Note also the Licinii Nepotes (*PIR²* L 220 ff.), who had Spanish connections. The Manilii Vopisci, resident at Tibur

On the time-scale worked out above it seems a little unlikely that the Pollio attested as tribune of the plebs in 109 could be equated with him. If that were the case, it might be assumed that he had been adopted by a C. Licinius Pollio and for a time was known by his adoptive names, reverting subsequently to his original *tria nomina*, although other interpretations are possible. But if Nepos was really tribune of the plebs as late as 109, his career can hardly have been favoured up till then.[12]

Nepos' friendship with Hadrian is first mentioned by the *Historia Augusta* in a context referring to Trajan's Parthian war: '. . . [Hadrianus] legatus expeditionis Parthicae tempore destinatus est. qua quidem tempestate utebatur Hadrianus amicitia Sosii <Senecionis Aemilii>[13] Papi et Platorii Nepotis ex senatorio ordine' (*Hadr.* 4. 1-2). It seems clear that Nepos too must have participated in the Parthian expedition, as legate of the legion I Adiutrix. One might postulate that he was praetor in 111 and curator of the three roads in Etruria in 112-13,[14] before assuming the legionary command. I Adiutrix, possibly although not certainly part of the original garrison of Dacia, was probably in the east at some point, before moving to its final base at Brigetio in Upper Pannonia.[15]

Nepos' governorship of Thrace seems not to have begun until after Hadrian's accession in August 117,[16] but he was already consul in the spring of 119 since he is recorded as colleague of Hadrian, who was *cos. III ord.* that year and retained the office until 30 April.[17] His next appointment, as governor of Lower Germany, doubtless followed soon afterwards, in 119 or 120. While in this province he will have had to

---

and in the tribe Galeria, look Spanish: Syme, *Tacitus* 602; Kubitschek 270. See Groag, *RE* 14 (1928) 1142 f. on the *cos.* 114.

[12] VI 452 = *ILS* 3620 (Rome): . . . *permissu* . . . . *Pollionis trib. pleb.* A. E. Gordon, *JRS* 48 (1958) 47 f., argues that Nepos was originally C. Licinius Pollio, adopted (after 109) by an A. Platorius Nepos *cet.* More likely, perhaps, that he acquired his nomenclature piecemeal in the manner of the period (by inheritance no less than by adoption), but that he ultimately reverted to his original *tria nomina*. If Nepos is identified with the tribune of 109, he was probably aged about thirty, several years older than the minimum age. It might be noted that c.108 Licinius Sura died (*PIR*[2] L 253), as a result of which Hadrian's influence with Trajan increased (*HA Had.* 3. 11).

[13] See Pflaum, *Klio* 46 (1965) 331 ff.

[14] See Pflaum, *J. des Savants* 1962. 109 ff., for the *curatores*.

[15] Ritterling, *RE* 12. 2 (1925) 1389 ff.; Syme, *Danubian Papers* 94, 98, 107.

[16] Stein, *Thracia* 13; Syme, *Danubian Papers* 234.

[17] *HA Had.* 8. 5: 'tertium consulatum . . . quattuor mensibus tantum egit'. VI 2078 = 32374 = Smallwood II 6 shows Nepos as Hadrian's colleague. Syme, *JRS* 48 (1958) 9, suggests that Nepos may have held office *in absentia.*

receive the emperor, on his rigorous tour of inspection in 121.[18] Evidently Nepos passed muster and he moved on to Britain in early summer of 122, perhaps in the emperor's company, bringing with him the legion VI Victrix.[19]

How long he remained in Britain after September 124 is not clear. Sex. Julius Severus, the next certainly known governor, need not have arrived until 130 or 131. It looks as if there must have been an unknown governor—perhaps the man whose names are ill recorded on the Bewcastle inscription[20]—between Nepos and Severus; and any sober assessment of the evidence for the building of Hadrian's Wall must lead to the conclusion that, while Platorius Nepos may have initiated the work, he must have returned to Rome before it was anything like completed.[21]

Appropriately enough for a man whose name appears on this famous construction, Nepos himself produced bricks, on his property in or near the capital: stamps have been found bearing the legend *ex fig(linis) Plaetor(i) Nepo(tis)* and *ex pr(aedis) Pl(atorii) Nep(otis)* dated to 123 and 134.[22] At some point he attained the honour of the augurate (this may have come already),[23] but he did not go on to further office. The *Historia Augusta* twice records how Hadrian came to detest his old friend. In the first instance his name is linked with those of P. Acilius Attianus and C. Septicius Clarus, the praetorian prefects: 'atque ideo prope cunctos vel amicissimos vel eos, quos summis honoribus evexit, postea ut hostium loco habuit, ut Attianum et Nepotem et Septicium Clarum' (*HA Hadr. 15. 2*). Attianus and Clarus lost office relatively early in the reign,[24] and at first sight one might conclude that Nepos too was out of favour in the 120s—perhaps because the new frontier in Britain was proving not wholly successful.[25] But the biographer then goes on to list nine others who incurred Hadrian's hatred and disfavour, including some who were so treated at the very end of the reign;[26] and the second statement is placed in the context of Hadrian's closing years,

---

[18] *HA Had.* 10. 1-11. 1.

[19] See p. 273 below.

[20] *RIB* 995 (p. 105 below).

[21] Stevens, *The Building of Hadrian's Wall passim*; E. Birley, *Research on Hadrian's Wall*. See also p. 205 below, for comment on *RIB* 1051, which has been assigned to Nepos by some.

[22] XV 1363-6; H. Bloch, *I bolli laterizi* (1947) 177. Products of Nepos' brickworks were used in Hadrian's villa at Tibur and in the great baths at Rome. Bloch argues that Plaetorius, found on the brick-stamps, was the correct form of the name. But although he is called Pretorius on XVI 70, on the four British stones, on XVI 69, and on *ILS* 1052, Platorius appears.

[23] Schumacher, *Priesterkollegien* 47 suggests that it was in the last years of Trajan or early years of Hadrian.

[24] See Syme, *Tacitus* 246, 487 f., 779, with *HA Had.* 9. 3-4, 11.3; also pp. 365 ff. below.

[25] See n. 21 above.

[26] *HA Had.* 15. 3-8; see Pflaum, *H-A-C 1968/9*, 180 ff.

when the emperor, after his long peregrinations were over, contracted a serious illness, and put to death his brother-in-law Servianus and grand-nephew Pedanius Fuscus Salinator. This seems to belong to the year 136.[27] Then, the biographer continues, 'in summa detestatione habuit Platorium Nepotem, quem tantopere ante dilexit ut veniens ad eum aegrotantem Hadrianus impune non admitteretur, suspicionibus adductus' (*HA Hadr.* 23. 4). A vivid picture is thus conjured up, of Nepos, who once, when he was ill himself, had refused to let Hadrian in to see him, now, when Hadrian was ill, somehow arousing Hadrian's suspicions and being 'held in the greatest abhorrence'.[28]

Nothing more of him is known, but we shall be justified in assuming that the A. Platorius Nepos Calpurnianus (Marcellus?) who was curator of the Tiber in 161 (and hence consul a year or two earlier) was his son;[29] and it is legitimate to speculate, from the name, that Nepos' wife was a Calpurnia Marcella.[30]

Ignotus *RIB* 995 (Bewcastle)

VII 978 = *RIB* 995 (Bewcastle): [*Imp.*] *Caes. Tra*[*iano/Hadriano Aug.* / *le*]*g. II Aug. et XX V.* [*V.* [4]/...]*IICNC. IR*[.../ *leg. A*] *u*[*g.*] *pr. pr.*

The inscription is now lost and the drawing in *RIB* is reproduced from Horsley's *Britannia Romana*. Horsley identified the governor in line 4 as M. Statius Priscus Licinius Italicus (*cos. ord.* 159), but there is no doubt that the stone is Hadrianic.[1] Although Wright, in *RIB*, comments that 'the recorded letters require some emendation, and Nepos is not necessarily to be excluded', the traces do not really fit the names either of

---

[27] Pflaum, *H-A-C 1963*, 95 ff.; *H-A-C 1968/9*, 187 ff.; A. R. Birley, *Marcus Aurelius* 44 ff.

[28] Bloch, op. cit. 181, argues from the bricks made by Nepos' works in AD 134 that were used for imperial constructions that Nepos was not yet out of favour in that year, since Hadrian's officials would not purchase bricks from a disgraced man. P. Setälä, *Private Domini in Roman Brickstamps of the Empire* (1977) 160 ff., suggests that he was dead by 138, when his *officinator* A. Antistius Thallus appears in a stamp of L. Ceionius Commodus, indicating that Nepos' land had been confiscated.

[29] VI 1241 = 31554 = *ILS* 5933. If his names are correctly restored in the fragmentary inscription from Rome (*Bull. Comm.* 1940, 180)—[*Platorio Ne*]*poti Calpur*[*niano M*]*arcello*— he had an additional *cognomen*. The same inscription appears to record service as tribune of two legions, [*trib. mil.*] *leg. XIII* [*Gem. et*] *VII C* [*l. p. f.*].

[30] Note Calpurnius Salvianus of Corduba, named together with one Marcilius Tusculus in 48 BC (*bell. Alex.* 5. 3. 2) and the former's namesake and presumed descendant mentioned by Tacitus under AD 25 (*Ann.* 4. 36; see *PIR*[2] C 315).

[1] The suggestion made in *Ep. Stud.* 4 (1967) 70, 91, that the emperor might be Decius, must be abandoned. Apart from other difficulties, Decius normally has Traianus at the end of his official nomenclature. For the Hadrianic date of Bewcastle and this inscription, see E. Birley, *Research on Hadrian's Wall* 230 ff.

Nepos or of the other three governors definitely attested under Hadrian, Falco, Julius Severus, and Sisenna. Likewise, the governor apparently recorded on *RIB* 1998 (Castlesteads) of whose names only *dio* survives, must be excluded.[2] Among known consulars, the names of C. Nonius Proculus would perhaps fit best; a restoration might read: [*C.*] *Nonio Pr*[*oculo / leg. A*]*u*[*g.*] *pr. pr.* Unfortunately Proculus' consulship is only approximately dated within the general period 50-150, so the suggestion is very tentative at best.[3]

Sex. Julius Severus (*cos.* 127)

VII 275 = *RIB* 739 (Bowes): *Im*[*p.*] *Caesari divi Traiani* [*Parthici f.*] */ divi Nervae nepoti Traia*[*no Hadria*]*/no Aug. pontifici maxi*[*mo tr. pot. - - - -*]^4*/ cos. I*[*II*] *p. p. coh. IIII B̦* [*reucorum / sub Sex. Iul*]*io Sev*[*ero leg. Aug. pr. pr.*]

?VII 620a = *JRS* 34 (1944) 87 = *RIB* 1550 (Carrawburgh): [. . . ?*Sex. Iulio Se*]*v*[*er*]*o leg. /* [*Aug. pr. p*]*r. coh. I Aquit/* [*anorum*] *fecit* ^{4}*/* [*sub* . . .]*io Nepote/* [*prae*]*ef.*

III 2830 9891 = *ILS* 1056 add. = Smallwood II 217 (Burnum): [*Cn.*] *Minicio Faustino /* [*Sex.*] *I*[*uli*]*o* [. . . *f*]*il. Serg. Severo* [*v. c., / se*]*v*[*iro*] *t*[*u*]*rma*[*e*] *V eq.* [*R. I*]*IIIviro* ^{4}*/* [*v*]*iarum c*[*ura*]*nd*[*ar*]*um XVviro /* [*s.*] *f.* [*tr*]*ib. m*[*il. leg. XII*]*II Geminae /* [*q*]*uaestor. pro*[*vin*]*cia*[*e*] *Macedoniae /* [*c*]*andida*[*t*]*o div*[*i Tr*]*ai.* [*P*]*art<h>ici trib. pleb.* ^{8}*/ candidat*[*o ei*]*usdem praetor. leg. / leg. XIIII Geminae leg. pr. pr. imp. Traiani / Hadria*[*n*]*i Aug. p*[*r*]*ovinciae / Dacia*[*e*] *cos., leg. pr. p*[*r.*] *provinciae* ^{12}*/ Moesia*[*e*] *inferioris, leg. pr. pr. pro/vinciae Britanniae leg. pr. pr. /* [*pr*]*ovinciae Iudeae* [*l*]*eg. pr. pr. /* [*provi*]*nciae Suriae. Huic* ^{16}*/* [*senatus a*]*uctore* [*imp.*] *Caes. /* [*Tra*]*iano Hadrian*[*o Au*]*g. / ornamenta triu*[*mp*]*halia decrevit ob res in* [*Iu*]*dea* ^{20}*/ prospere ge*[*st*]*as/* [*d.*] *d.*

Dio 69. 13. 2.

Sex. Julius Severus,[1] as he was normally known,[2] was suffect consul,[3] with L. Aemilius Juncus, in the last three months of 127. Thereafter, as his *cursus* inscription shows, he became governor of Lower Moesia,

---

[2] pp. 110 ff. below. Stevens, *The Building of Hadrian's Wall* 66 n. 255, proposes that this governor is M. Appius (Atilius) Bradua; restoring the *cognomen* in line 4 of *RIB* 995, but commenting that 'the *nomen* seems hopeless'. See also his n. 213a on p. 53. Reasons are given above for placing Bradua under Trajan (p. 93).

[3] VI 1473: 'II metà del sec. I–I metà del sec. II,' Degrassi, *FC* 131; and note C. Nonius Var(. . .) Proculus, *Epigraphica* 11 (1949) 61 ff., 'I metà del. sec. II?'.

[1] This man's origin and career have been thoroughly handled by Alföldy, *Ep. Stud.* 5 (1968) 116–19. I differ from his views in one small particular only (see p. 108 n. 14 below).

[2] As consul, *Sex. Iulio Severo* in XVI 72, [*Se*]*x. Iulius Severus* in *Inscr. It.* XIII.1 p. 204, although *AE* 1904. 9 (Aequum) has *Cn. Iulio S*[*evero*] ; elsewhere *Iulius Severus*, with *Cn. Minicius Faustinus* preceding in *AE* 1950. 45 (Aequum); the Burnum *cursus* presumably read as given above (so Alföldy, op. cit. 116 n. 93) and not [*Se*]*x. Minicio Faustino Cn. I*[*uli*]*o* etc., as given by editors; see also Syme, *Danubian Papers* 120.

[3] A *senatus consultum* passed during that period is quoted in *Digest* 40. 5. 28.

before going on to Britain, which he can thus hardly have reached before 130. His departure from here to take command against the Jewish insurgents led by Bar-Kokhba is recorded by Cassius Dio, who describes him as 'the first' of Hadrian's 'best generals'. The outbreak of the Jewish rebellion may be dated to 132,[4] and hence Severus' tenure of the British governorship is unlikely to have lasted for more than two years at the most. Three fragmentary inscriptions found in Britain itself are assignable to him, one with some certainty, the other two with varying degrees of probability. The first, a building inscription from the fort of Bowes on the Stainmore road, is datable only within the general period 128–38 from Hadrian's title p(atri) p(atriae), but can hardly be referred to any other governor.[5] The second is another building inscription, from the Hadrian's Wall fort of Carrawburgh, which was a late addition to the original series of Wall forts, and it would be no surprise, on archaeological grounds, to find that Julius Severus was its builder.[6] However, it might be that this inscription should be restored to show the name of Cn. Julius Verus, a generation later.[7] Finally, there is the Walcot diploma, formerly assigned to the period after 124 and before 133. However, recent research has shown that this document should be placed earlier.[8]

Julius Severus, whose home was Aequum, is a good example of an outstanding general of colonial stock,[9] in certain respects not dissimilar to Julius Agricola, although the evidence suggests that he, unlike Agricola, was the first senator in his family; and, again in contrast to Agricola, he came from a province, Dalmatia, which was to produce a relatively small number of senators in comparison with Gallia Narbonensis.[10] His nomenclature suggests that, at latest by the end of the 130s, he had been adopted by Cn. Minicius Faustinus (*cos.* 116) or otherwise acquired his nomenclature.[11] At all events, he was clearly

[4] See now E. Schürer, *History of the Jewish People*[2], rev. F. Millar and G. Vermes (1973) 519 ff., and S. Applebaum, *Prolegomena to the Study of the Second Jewish Revolt* (1976) esp. 25 ff. (but his dating of Severus' arrival in Judaea is surely much too late).

[5] Groag, *RE* 15. 2 (1932) 1814, is sceptical, however: 'doch könnte ebensogut der Name eines Kohortenpräfekten ergänzt werden'.

[6] B. Swinbank and J. E. H. Spaul, *Arch. Ael.*[4] 29 (1951) 221 ff.; E. Birley, *Research on Hadrian's Wall* 176 f; D. J. Breeze, *Arch. Ael.*[4] 50 (1972) 81 ff.

[7] R. W. Davies, *Ep. Stud.* 4 (1967) 108 ff.; p. 118 below.

[8] See p. 94 above.

[9] See the exemplary analysis of Alföldy, *Ep. Stud.* 5 (1968) 118 f.

[10] See the comments of Syme, *Danubian Papers* 112 ff. Alföldy, improving on J. J. Wilkes, *Bonner Jahrb.* 166 (1966), 653, shows that he was probably a descendant of Sex. Julius Ani. Silvanus, *summus curator civium Romanorum* at Aequum and later first aedile of the town when it became a colony; and that Silvanus himself may well have derived from Forum Julii in Narbonensis, Agricola's home town.

[11] In Groag's view, *RE* 15. 2, 1813, Faustinus is more likely to have been, e.g. a maternal uncle; but he was assuming that the *praenomen* Sex. went with Minicius rather than with Julius

marked out for distinction early. Service as a *sevir equitum Romanorum* was an honour of a purely formal kind, but his appointment as a *IVvir viarum curandarum* perhaps indicates that he was one of those for whom a military career was intended.[12] In the Burnum inscription his membership of the *XVviri sacris faciundis* is mentioned next, before the military tribunate with XIV Gemina.[13] If he did indeed obtain entry to one of the four great priestly colleges at such an early age, this would have been a startling distinction for a *novus homo*. It therefore seems probable that the placing of the priesthood at this point in the text was influenced by the desire to put the three posts ending -*viro* together, and that it is not in chronological order.[14] Trajan's backing for the quaestorship and tribunate of the plebs shows that the emperor did not wish his promotion to be delayed; but it was not often that a senator returned as praetorian legate to command the legion in which he had served as tribune, no doubt because his *dignitas* might suffer if there were too many centurions and other ranks who remembered him in the junior grade a dozen years or so earlier.[15]

It is unfortunately not clear whether he owed his appointment to command XIV Gemina to Trajan or to Hadrian.[16] But, at all events, by June 120 he was already in Dacia; a diploma shows him as the first governor of the newly created Upper province.[17] Hadrian had given this area personal attention soon after his accession,[18] and Severus'

(cf. n. 2 above). Alföldy, op. cit. 117 f., regards adoption by Faustinus as probable. As he points out, C. Minicius Fundanus, legate of Dalmatia under Trajan or early in Hadrian's reign (Syme, *Gnomon* 31 (1959) 515 f. = *Danubian Papers* 199) is a probable kinsman: he was an influential figure, with a wide circle of friends (Pliny, *ep.* 5. 16. 3; and see Groag, *RE* 15. 2, 1819–25).

[12] pp. 6 ff. above.

[13] *AE* 1950. 45, line 4, has *trib. leg. XIIII* [. . .] which permits the restoration given in line 4 of the Burnum *cursus*.

[14] I accept the view that Schumacher, *Priesterkollegien* 240 f., who points out that the XV-virate is not mentioned in *AE* 1950. 45, Aequum, which, like the Burnum inscription, lists his career in ascending order as far as the legionary legateship. In Schumacher's view, Severus (whom he prefers to call Minicius Faustinus) probably became a XVvir under Hadrian (not before his legionary command). Alföldy, op. cit. 116, regards the order on the Burnum inscription as accurate, and hence the priesthood as further evidence that Severus was 'warm gefördert' by Trajan even before his military tribunate.

[15] See pp. 17 f. and Table 3 above.

[16] But it is probable that he served for a time at least under the governorship of L. Minicius Natalis (*cos.* 106)—no relation of the other Minicii, apparently—and hence that the latter's son was *tribunus laticlavius* of the legion while Severus commanded it; some ten years later, it would seem, the younger Natalis commanded VI Victrix in Britain at about the time when Severus was governor. See p. 245 below.

[17] XVI 68, confirmed by *AE* 1958. 30 = *AE* 1959. 31 = Roxan no. 17, both diplomas of 29 June 120.

[18] See p. 99 above.

appointment is therefore of particular importance. It may conceivably reflect not only his military capacities but his especial suitability to govern a province with a considerable Dalmatian immigrant population.[19] He was to remain there for an unusually long period, over six years, since another diploma reveals that he was still in the province in 126.[20]

After his consulship, at the end of 127, and the governorships of Lower Moesia and Britain, came the command in Judaea, which, as the Burnum inscription shows, he conducted with success, receiving the highest military honours then open to a senator, the *ornamenta triumphalia*.[21] Dio's account gives some details of his operations. Julius Severus suppressed the rebels with relentless efficiency, picking them off in small groups. He is credited—if that is the right word—with the destruction of 'fifty of the Jews' most important outposts and 985 of their most famous villages'; and 580,000 men are said to have been killed on the Jewish side. Dio (or his epitomator) does not record details of the Roman casualties, which were however substantial.[22] That he was given yet another governorship, Syria,[23] is further evidence for the satisfaction with which Hadrian regarded him. Likewise, the rapid and distinguished career in the emperor's service of Cn. Julius Verus,[24] his son or nephew, indicates that imperial favour continued under the next two reigns. As G. Alföldy rightly comments, his length of service was almost unequalled before the Marcomannic Wars.[25]

14 April 135   P. Mummius Sisenna (*cos. ord.* 133)

XVI 82 (Wroxeter): ([Hadrian] *trib. pot. XVIIII*) .... *et* [*sunt in Brit. sub Mummio*] *Sisenna A. d. XVIII K. Mai. L. Tutilio Pontiano P. Calpurnio Atiliano cos.* ... (14 April 135)

There is little doubt, given the rarity of the name,[1] that the governor

---

[19] C. Daicoviciu, *Dacia* 2 (1958) 263 ff.

[20] Syme, *Historia* 14 (1965) 343 = *Danubian Papers* 226. During the period of less than half a century of Dacia superior's existence as a separate province, two more of its governors are known to have gone on to Britain at a later stage in their career: Cn. Papirius Aelianus and M. Statius Priscus, pp. 117, 125 below; see also p. 123.

[21] This is the more striking in that Hadrian was otherwise unusually mean with *dona*: see p. 113 n. 7 below.

[22] Dio 69. 13. 3-14. 1.

[23] *ILS* 1056; omitted in *PIR*² J 576.

[24] pp. 118 ff. below.

[25] *Ep. Stud.* 5 (1968) 117. It may be noted that three future governors of Britain, Q. Lollius Urbicus, Cn. Julius Verus, and M. Statius Priscus, served under Severus in the Jewish war (pp. 113, 118, 124 below).

[1] See further on the name and origin p. 249 below.

Sisenna must be the same as the *consul ordinarius* of 133 P. Mummius Sisenna. Nothing further is known of his career, except that he was to be proconsul of Asia in 150–1.[2]

He must have been a close kinsman, probably the father, of P. Mummius P. f. Gal. Sisenna Rutilianus (*cos.* 146), whose career is known in detail from two *cursus* inscriptions at Tibur and from Lucian's mocking description of his conduct as an old man. Rutilianus' career included service as legate of VI Victrix, conceivably while Sisenna was governor.[3]

The interval of less than two years—exceptionally short for this period[4]—between consulship and governorship suggests that special circumstances may have affected the choice. It is possible that the sudden departure of Sex. Julius Severus left no other suitable replacement; and Sisenna may, indeed, have been given the ordinary consulship not least as a means of rendering him eligible more rapidly,[5] with the added prestige of a *consul ordinarius* perhaps compensating for his lack of seniority. But this is very speculative, and it is safer to confess ignorance. The fact that Rutilianus, whose nomenclature suggests that he was Sisenna's son, was consul only thirteen years later, at about the normal age, creates a problem in any case. The answer could be that Sisenna held the office unusually late in life, possibly having commenced his career as an equestrian.

The family's origin is not directly attested, but the tribe Galeria and the residence of Rutilianus at Tibur, hint strongly at a Spanish connection.[6]

? ----dius---- (?Ti. Claudius Ti. f. Pal. Quartinus *cos.* 130)

VII 895a, b = *RIB* 1997, 1998 (Castlesteads): (a) [*Imp. Caes. Trai*]*ano* / [*Hadriano Aug. p. p. c*]*os III sub* / [. . .] (b) [. . .] *dio*[4] / [. . . *leg. Aug. pr. pr. leg.*] *II* [*Aug.*]

Both the fragmentary stones, combined above in accordance with a suggestion of E. Birley,[1] are now lost. R. P. Wright, in *RIB*, who prefers to treat them as parts of separate inscriptions, offers no restoration of (b), but for (a) conjectures the following: [*Imp. Caes. T. Aelio Hadri*]*ano*

---

[2] *IG* XII 3. 325–6 show that he was the successor of Popillius Priscus, in office on 18 July 149 and hence for the year 149–50. See Groag, *RE* 16. 1 (1933) 529 and Alföldy, *Konsulat* 214. Sisenna might perhaps have been governor of Thrace before his consulship, if he were the Publius . . . of *IGR* I 785, belonging to the period 128–36; see Eck, *Senatoren* 232 n. 513.

[3] See pp. 249 f. below.

[4] See pp. 388 ff. below.

[5] Compare the case of P. Petronius Turpilianus (*ord.* 61), p. 58 above.

[6] See further on Rutilianus pp. 249 f. below.

[1] *CW*² 52 (1953) 184 f.

/ [*Antonino Aug. Pio p. p. c*] *os III sub* [. . .] This would provide a date between 140 (Pius' third consulship) and 144 (the fourth consulship being in 145). It would, however, be surprising to find what looks like a building slab being erected at a Hadrian's Wall fort during these years. On archaeological grounds a late Hadrianic date seems appropriate for the first stone fort at Castlesteads.[2] Hence, if E. Birley's hypothesis be accepted, this provides a governor whose term of office ought to fall between those of Sisenna and Q. Lollius Urbicus.

The only known consular from the period with a *nomen* ending in -*dius* is Ti. Claudius Quartinus, governor of Germania Superior on 16 October 134[3] and presumably identical with the Quartinus who was suffect consul on 19 March 130.[4] Although only one other man is known to have proceeded from the Upper German province to Britain[5] and Quartinus would have been consul three years before his predecessor in Britain, neither point is sufficient to create a serious obstacle to the identification. Quartinus was certainly back at Rome by 15 October 138, when he was a witness to the *senatus consultum Beguense*.[6]

His career, known from two fragmentary *cursus* inscriptions, was reconstructed by E. Groag,[7] and significant improvements have been supplied by G. Alföldy.[8] He began as an equestrian tribune of III Cyrenaica before acquiring senatorial rank from Trajan and proceeding through the republican magistracies as urban quaestor, plebeian aedile, and praetor, followed by a year as legate to a proconsul of Asia.[9] He was then appointed by Trajan to the post of *iuridicus* in Tarraconensis, which he was still holding on 9 October 119[10] and, as G. Alföldy has proposed, may have retained until the time of Hadrian's visit to that province in 122, when he evidently had the task of conducting a levy of recruits.[11] He then took up a special command over the two eastern

---

[2] *CW*[2] 34 (1934) 159 f. R. P. Wright, ad *RIB* 1997-8, argues that 'As Hadrian does not quote the consulship on Hadrian's Wall, the Hadrianic authorship of this slab . . . seems doubtful'. But in fact we have no comparable late Hadrianic inscriptions from the Wall, while the inscription of Julius Severus from Bowes (*RIB* 739) does indeed give Hadrian the style *cos. I*[*II*]*p.p.*

[3] XVI 80.

[4] VI 2083 = Smallwood II 9, cf. Degrassi, *FC* 36 f.

[5] The *ignotus* XIII 6805 (Mainz), pp. 132 f. below.

[6] VIII 11451 + 23246.

[7] *PIR*[2] C 990.

[8] *Fasti Hispanienses* 79 ff.

[9] These items are quite clear from the fragmentary *cursus* inscription XIII 1802 (Lugdunum).

[10] XIII 1802, and, for 119, II 2959 (Pompaelo: a letter of his to the *duoviri*).

[11] Alföldy restores the end of the even more fragmentary *cursus* inscription VI 1567 = XIV 4473 as [*leg. Aug. iur. Hisp. cit. Tarraconen*]*sis ubi iussu* [*imp. Caes. Traiani Hadriani Aug. dilectum egit . . .*].

legions II Traiana and III Cyrenaica, presumably accompanying Hadrian with this force on his eastern mission in 123. No evidence exists for his employment during the remainder of the 120s, but it is reasonable to assume that he went on to govern a praetorian province or to hold a post of equivalent status at Rome.

Quartinus' membership of the Palatina, one of the four *tribus urbanae*, coupled with his *nomen* and *praenomen*, suggests that he may have been a descendant of a freedman of Claudius or Nero.[12] However this may be, he or an ancestor may be identified with the *duovir* of Puteoli of the same names, since, as at Ostia, the Palatina is found there frequently.[13] Some doubt attaches to Quartinus' membership of a priestly college. It may be that he was only a *curio*, and not a *VIIvir epulonum*.[14]

139, 140, 142   Q. Lollius M. f. Quir. Urbicus (*cos. a. inc.*)

JRS 26 (1936) 264 = *AE* 1936. 75 = *RIB* 1147, Corbridge: [*Imp.*] *T. Aelio Ani-onino* [sic] / [*Au*]*gusto Pio II cos.* / [*sub*] *cura Q. Lolii* [sic] *Urbici* 4/ *leg. Aug. pr. pr. leg. II Aug. f.* (AD 139)

EE IX 1146 = *RIB* 1148, Corbridge: *Imp. Caes.* [*T.*] *Ael*[*io*] / *Antonino A*[*ug.*] *Pi*[*o*] / *III co*[*s. p. p.*] 4/ *sub cura Q.* [*Lolli Urbici*] / *leg. Au*[*g. pr. pr.*] / *leg. II A*[*ug. fecit*] (AD 140)

VII 1041 = *RIB* 1276, High Rochester: *Imp. Caes. T. Aelio* / *H*[*a*]*d. Antonino Aug. Pio p. p.* / *sub Q. Lol. Urbico* 4/ *leg. Aug. pro prae.* / *coh. I Ling.* / *eq. f.*

VII 1125 = *RIB* 2191, Balmuildy: [*Imp. C. T. Ael. Hadr.* / *Antonino Aug. Pio* / *p. p.*] *leg. II Au*[*g. sub*] 4/ *Q. Lollio Ur*[*bico*] / *leg. Aug. pr. pr.* [*fec.*]

EE IX 1390 a, b = *RIB* 2192, Balmuildy: [*Im*]*p. C.* [*T. Ael. Hadr. Anto/nin*]*o* [*Aug. Pio p. p. leg.*] / *II* [*Aug. fec. sub Q. Lo*]*llio* 4/ [*Urbico leg. Aug. pr.*] *pr.*

HA Ant. Pius 5. 4: *per legatos suos plurima bella gessit. nam et Britannos per Lollium Urbicum vicit legatum alio muro caespiticio summotis barbaris ducto* ...

The epigraphic record in Britain bears out well the brief statement in the *Historia Augusta* that Lollius Urbicus defeated the Britons and built the (Antonine) Wall. Since Pius is already *imp. II* on one inscription of AD 142,[1] the victory may be assigned to the end of that year. Urbicus'

---

[12] On the Palatina, see e.g. the remarks of C. Koch in *RE* 18. 2 (1942) 2529 f.

[13] Alföldy, op. cit. 79, identifies our man with the *IIvir* (X 1783 = *ILS* 5919). The inscription at Ostia might however suggest a connection there.

[14] Schumacher, *Priesterkollegien* 134 f., rejects the restoration of [*VIIvir epul*] *oni* in line 5 of XIII 1902 on the grounds that there is insufficient space for more than four letters: hence [*curi*] *oni*.

[1] *ILS* 340, originally from Puteoli.

origin and career are well attested, principally by three inscriptions from the *ager Cirtensis* in Numidia. He himself erected one of them, near Tiddis, from which we learn that his parents were M. Lollius Senecio and Grania Honorata, his brothers M. Lollius Honoratus and L. Lollius Senis, and his maternal uncle P. Granius Paulus.[2] None of the other members of the family appears to have had senatorial rank, and Urbicus may confidently be described as a *novus homo*. What is more, the nomenclature of his brother M. Lollius Honoratus suggests that he, rather than Urbicus, was the eldest son, which makes Urbicus' rise the more remarkable.[3] His career before the British governorship is set out on two more or less identical inscriptions in his honour from the same area, and it will be convenient to set out the text of the better preserved one here:

Q. Lollio M. fil. / Quir. Urbico cos. / leg. Aug. provinc. Germ. [4] / inferioris fetiali legato / imp. Hadriani in expedition. / Iudaica qua donatus est / hasta pura corona aurea leg. [8] / leg. X. Geminae praet. candidat. / Caes. trib. pleb. candidat. Caes. leg. / procos. Asiae quaest. urbis trib. / laticlavio leg. XXII Primigeniae [12] / IIIIviro viarum curand. / patrono / d. d. p. p. (VIII 6706 = *ILAlg.* II 3605, Castellum Tidditanorum)[4]

The chronology of his career is based on his service in the Jewish war of AD 132-5,[5] in which he served as a staff officer. It is reasonable to suppose on the basis of this that his quaestorship came in the early 120s and that his vigintivirate and military tribunate with the Mainz legion XXII Primigenia were also held under Hadrian. Since it was after his year as legate to a proconsul of Asia that his career began to show signs of imperial favour, with Hadrian's backing for both tribunate and praetorship, it might be postulated that Urbicus had acquired a power-ful patron in the proconsul under whom he served.[6] His first important position in the emperor's service was in command of X Gemina at Vindobona (Vienna) in Upper Pannonia, where he must have acquitted himself well to be selected for the special appointment as *legatus Augusti* in Judaea, perhaps as, in effect, second in command to Sex. Julius Severus. It is a little surprising that his decorations for this campaign were so scanty, but it seems that Hadrian was particularly sparing with *dona* for the Jewish war.[7] At all events, here too he

---

[2] VIII 6705 = *ILAlg.* II 1 3563.

[3] The name of one brother was formerly read as L. Lollius Senecio, leading to the view that Urbicus was the youngest of three brothers (e.g. *RE* 13. 2 (1927) 1392, reproduced in *PIR*[2] L 327, although the name is correctly supplied under L 324).

[4] *ILAlg.* II 3446, Caldis, is slightly fragmentary and the abbreviations are different.

[5] p. 107 above.

[6] This might conceivably have been Q. Pompeius Falco (p. 100 above).

[7] See Domaszewski, *RO*[2] 138.

presumably won approval, for his consulship, mentioned out of order on the *cursus* inscription, followed, *c.*135 or 136, and he was no doubt made a *fetialis* at the same time.[8] Then came the appointment to govern Lower Germany, certainly before Hadrian's death—since the emperor is not called *divus* on the inscription—and probably immediately after the consulship.

The appointment to Britain came very shortly after Hadrian's death since he was already active in his new province in 139, as the first Corbridge inscription demonstrates. Although the promotion from Germania inferior to Britain had precedents and was to become common,[9] Urbicus' mission in Britain was far from routine. He was the agent of a radical change in policy. It is fair to assume that his former chief in Palestine, Sex. Julius Severus, who had tried shortly before this to make the Hadrianic frontier policy in Britain work, may have been influential in recommending Urbicus for the task of dismantling it. At all events, it is clear that Urbicus must have had ample occasion, during the early 130s, to have discussed the British problem with Julius Severus.

There is no means of telling how long his governorship lasted, but it is probable that he was replaced soon after his victory in 142, having made a start with the construction of the new frontier Wall in Scotland.[10] Later in the reign of Antoninus Pius he reached the pinnacle of the senatorial career with the appointment as *praefectus urbi*. It is worth noting that by the 140s men from Urbicus' home region were coming to the fore in greater numbers than ever before, thanks not least to the influence of the orator M. Cornelius Fronto (*cos.* 143) of Cirta, tutor to M. Aurelius and an intimate member of the imperial court.[11] The *Fasti Ostienses* record the death in February or March of 146 Sex. Erucius Clarus, *cos. II ord.* in that year and prefect of the city,[12] and it is not unlikely that Urbicus succeeded him. How long he held this post is unfortunately unknown. He is recorded in office on two undated inscriptions from Rome[13] as well as on the family monument in Numidia, and he is referred to in that capacity in Justin's *Apology*, *c.*150.[14] But two later references, in the (very different) *Apology* of Apuleius, *c.*158,[15] and in one of Fronto's letters from the 160s, do not

---

[8] For the grant of a priesthood with the consulship cf. Tac. *Agr.* 9. 6, and p. 000 above. In Urbicus' case it was not, however, a major priesthood.

[9] p. 390 below.

[10] As indicated by the inscriptions from Balmuildy.

[11] M. G. Jarrett, *Ep. Stud.* 9 (1972) 147.

[12] *Inscr. It.* XIII. 1 204 f.

[13] VI 28 (= *ILS* 3220), 10707.

[14] Just. *Apol.* 2. 1. 2 (= Eusebius, *HE* 4. 17).

[15] Apul. *Apol.* 2. 381, 3. 382 f.

necessarily prove that he was still alive or in office at the time.[16] It is not impossible that he is the city prefect whose death appears to be recorded in the Fasti Ostienses for 160,[17] but if he was still in office as late as that year he ought to have received a second consulship. A gap of well over twenty years between first and second consulships was certainly not infrequent, but the urban prefects seem to have received the honour relatively soon after assuming office.[18]

No descendants are recorded, and the 'Lollius Urbicus' who is alleged to have written a history of the events of Macrinus' reign must be regarded as an invention of the *Historia Augusta*.[19]

Ignotus *RIB* 2313

VII 1085 = *RIB* 2313 = *Britannia* 4 (1973) 336 f., near Cramond: [*imp. Caes.* / *T. Ael. Hadr. Anto*]/*nino Aug. Pio p. p. cos.* [*I*] *II* [4] / [[. . . / . . .]] *co*] *h. I Cugernor.* / [*Tri*] *monti. m. p.* [8] / [. . .]

In *RIB* this inscription was recognized as belonging to a milestone, but the fragmentary imperial name and titulature were restored as referring to Caracalla. The names and titles of Severus were supplied in the missing top part of the stone, while the erasure in lines 5-6 was assumed to be of the names and style of Geta. However, the discovery of the missing top of the stone revealed that it had not been inscribed, and hence that it could not be Severan.[1] There is no alternative but to assign it to Antoninus Pius. Either *cos. II* or *cos.* [*I*] *II* must be read in line 3, and the former must be ruled out, for the erasure must be of the name of a governor, and it is inconceivable that the name of Lollius Urbicus was so treated.[2] Thus the inscription must be not earlier than 140, when Antoninus was *cos. III*, and before 145, when he was *cos. IV*. But, since Urbicus may be pretty certainly assumed to have remained in Britain at least until 142, the milestone should belong to the years 143 or 144.

The reign of Antoninus Pius is at first sight an unlikely time to find a governor suffering *damnatio memoriae*. As an alternative, a man

[16] *ad amicos* 2. 7 = 183 v. d. Hout.

[17] *Inscr. Ital.* XIII. 1 571 f.

[18] Cf. the list of *coss. II* in Alföldy, *Fasti Hispanienses* 31. Vidman, *Arheološki Vestnik* 28 (1977) 373 ff. argues in favour of Urbicus being the prefect who died in AD 160.

[19] See Syme, *Emperors and Biography* 4, 35 f.

[1] As was pointed out by E. Birley, reviewing *RIB*, *JRS* 56 (1966) 230, and confirmed by the discovery of the missing top part of the stone, *Britannia* 4 (1973) 336 f.

[2] I cannot accept the arguments of R. W. Davies, *Chiron* 7 (1977) 390 ff., that the name of Lollius Urbicus was deleted because it had been inscribed on the stone contrary to regulations.

condemned in a later reign might have had an ancestor in Britain, whose names were removed through misdirected zeal. But it does so happen that the *Historia Augusta* names two men who conspired against Pius, Atilius Titianus and Priscianus.[3] The first of these appears to be T. Atilius Rufus Titianus (*cos. ord.* 127),[4] whose seniority makes it almost inconceivable that he could have been governor of Britain in the early 140s. The second is clearly the Cornelius Priscianus, who, as the *Fasti Ostienses* reveal, was condemned at a meeting of the senate on 15 September 145; *XVII k. Oct. de Cornelio Prisciano in sen.* [*iud. / cor*]*am factum quod provinciam Hispaniam hostiliter / * [*inq*]*uietaverit.*[5] The circumstances of the man's downfall are baffling and defy conjecture.[6] But it would not be impossible for him to have succeeded Lollius Urbicus in Britain in 142 or early 143, and then to have been transferred to govern Tarraconensis in 145. In that case his governorship of Britain would have been rather brief.[7]

The names are exceedingly uninformative, but it has been suggested that he was a kinsman, perhaps the son, of (L.) Cornelius Priscus (*cos. c.* 104); or that he was a native of Baetica.[8]

146   Cn. Papirius Gal. Aelianus Aemil[ius] Tuscillus (*cos. a. inc.*)

XVI 93, Chesters: [*Imp. C*]*aesar* ... *T. A*[*e*]*lius Hadrianus Antoninus* [*Aug.*] *Pius* [*p*]*ont. max. tr. pot. VIIII imp. II cos. IIII p. p. eq. et pedit. qui militaver. in alis III* [*et cohort. XI qu*]*ae* ... *sunt in Brittannia sub Papirio Aeliano* ... (AD 146)

II 2078, Iliberris: [. . . *l*] *eg. Au*[*g. pr. pr. prov. B*]*rittan*[*iae* . . .]

Aelianus is clearly the same man as the governor of Dacia superior

---

[3] *HA Ant. Pius* 7. 3, cf. *epit. de Caes.* 15. 6.

[4] *PIR*[2] A 1305. His name was erased in the *Fasti Ostienses* for 127: *Inscr. It.* XIII. 1 p. 205, cf. 233.

[5] *Inscr. It.* XIII. 1 p. 205, cf. 235.

[6] See A. R. Birley, *Marcus Aurelius* (1966) 117 f. *Digest* 48. 21. 3. 1 cites a rescript of Pius, confiscating the property of a defendant who commits suicide before sentence in cases where the penalty is death or deportation: aimed at Priscianus, according to R. A. Bauman, *Zeitschr. Sav. St.* 94 (1977) 56.

[7] Alföldy, *Fasti Hispanienses* 28, regards him as having been governor of Tarraconensis at the time of his downfall. But it may be that he lived there, which would allow him longer in Britain.

[8] Alföldy, *Fasti Hispanienses* 28, mistakenly ascribes to Groag the view that Priscianus was a descendant of the consul of *c.*104 as well as being a Spaniard. In *PIR*[2] C 1418 Groag refers to XIV 3516, II 1172-3, 1175 (the family of the Aemilii Papi, in whose nomenclature the names recur: see also p. 243 below). Syme, *Tacitus* 805, suggests north Italy (?Brixia) for the home of the consul of *c.*104; see also id., *JRS* 58 (1968) 147. The Cornelius Priscianus who appeared before M. Aurelius as an *advocatus* in 166 (*Digest* 28. 4. 3) could have been a son of the man condemned in 145.

named on a building inscription of the year 132 at Sarmizegetusa.[1]
There seems ample justification for regarding him as identical also with
the homonym whose fragmentary *cursus* inscription was found at
Iliberris: *Gn. Papirio* [*Gn.*(?) *fil.*] / *Gal. Aeliano Aemil*[*io*] / *Tuscillo
q. prov*[*inciae*] [4]/ *Achaiae tribuno plebi*[*s* . . .] / *pr. leg. Aug. leg. XII*
[. . .] (II 2075). Further, it seems reasonable to suppose that the even
more fragmentary inscription from the same place, quoted above, may
have formed part of the same stone.[2] Aelianus was doubtless a native
of the town, which was enrolled in the tribe Galeria.[3]

Although neither vigintivirate nor military tribunate are mentioned
on the longer inscription, it is perfectly possible that mention of them
was simply omitted, rather than that he entered on a senatorial career
belatedly. There seems to have been space at the end of line four,
perhaps for the words *cand. Caes.* The legionary command could have
been either with XII Fulminata in Cappadocia or XIV Gemina in Upper
Pannonia.[4] He had been succeeded in Dacia by December 135, when C.
Julius Bassus is recorded as governor.[5] Bassus was not consul until the
end of 139,[6] so he probably did not succeed Aelianus until *c.*135;
hence Aelianus' consulship probably fell *c.*136.[7] During the ten years
or so between his tenure of the *fasces* and his appearance in Britain, it
is reasonable to assume that he held one or more additional posts, for
example as curator of public works or of the Tiber, and a consular
governorship. He could well have been governor of Germania Inferior
*c.*139–42.[8] Had it not been for the apparent existence of another
governor as the successor of Lollius Urbicus in 143 or 144,[9] it would be
natural to assume that Aelianus had gone to Britain *c.*143 and that he
was near the end of his term at the time when the Chesters diploma was
issued. As it is, the question may be asked whether he might not be the
governor whose *cognomen* terminated -anus on the Colchester diploma.

---

[1] III 1446 (Hadrian's sixteenth tribunician power); see Stein, *Dazien* 21 f.

[2] Stein, *Dazien* 21, regards the governor of Upper Dacia and Britain as 'sicher nähe ver-
wandt, vielleicht sogar identisch' with the man on II 2078, likewise Groag, *Achaia* 117.

[3] Kubitschek 1875.

[4] It is highly improbable that the Dacian governorship was expressed in the form *leg. Aug.
leg. XII*[*I Gem. et prov. Daciae*], since the limited evidence available suggests that governors of
that province commanded a legion elsewhere before their appointment: Sex. Julius Severus
(p. 108 above), XIV Gemina; C. Curtius Justus (p. 253 below), XX Val. Vic.; M. Sedatius Severianus (Stein, *Dazien* 24 ff.), V Mac.; L. Annius Fabianus (p. 272 below), X Fretensis; M. Statius
Priscus (p. 125 below), XIV Gemina. In the last case Priscus was described as *leg. Aug. prov.
Daciae leg. leg. XIII G. p. f.* on his *cursus* inscription: see p. 125 and n. 8.

[5] *ILS* 2301, Apulum (13 Dec. 135).

[6] XVI 87 (22 Nov. 139).

[7] Degrassi, *FC* 38.

[8] See Alföldy, *Konsulat* 227, for the vacancy.

[9] p. 113 above.

But that document looks as if it should be dated well after the year 149.[10]

Nothing further is known of Aelianus after 146, but it may be presumed that the homonymous *cos. ord.* 184[11] was his grandson.

158   Cn. Julius Cn. f. Verus (*cos. a. inc., des. II ord.* 180)

EE IX 1163 = *ILS* 9116 = *RIB* 1322, Newcastle upon Tyne: *Imp. Antoni/no Aug. Pio p./ p. vexilatio* [4]/ *leg. II Aug. et leg./ VI Vic. et leg./ XX V. V. con(t)r(i)/buti ex(ercitibus) Ger(manicis) du* [8] /*obus sub Iulio Ve/ro leg. Aug. pr. p.*

EE IX 1108 = *RIB* 283, Brough-on-Noe: *Imp. Caesari T.* [*Ael. Hadr.* / *An*]*ntonino Au*[*g. Pio p. p.*] / *coh. I Aquitan*[*orum*] [4]/ *sub Iulio V*[*ero leg. Aug.*] / *pr. pr. inst*[*ante*] / [*C*]*apitoni*[*o Pri*]*sco prae.*

EE IX 1383 = *Arch. Ael.*[4] 21 (1943) 178 = *JRS* 34 (1944) 85 = *RIB* 1132 = *Britannia* 3 (1972) 363, Corbridge: *ve*[*x. leg.*] / *VI* [*Vic. p. f. sub*] / *Cn. Iul.* [*Vero leg. Aug. pr. pr.*] *per L. Q*[. . .] [4]/ *trib.* [*mil.* . . .]

EE IX 1230 = *RIB* 2110, Birrens: *Imp. Caes. T. A*[*el. Hadr.*] / *An*[*to*]*nino Aug.* [*Pio po*]*nt.* / *max.* [*tr*]*ib. pot. XXI cos. IIII* [4]/ *coh. II* [*Tung*]*r. m*[*i*]*l. eq. c. l.* / *sub Iu*[*lio Vero*] *leg. Aug. pr. pr.* (AD 158)

III 8714 + 2732 = *ILS* 8974 + 1057 + add., Aequum: *Cn. Iulio Cn.* / *fil. Vero cos.* / *desig. II augur.* [4]/ [. . .] / *leg. A*[*ugg.*] *pr. pr.* / *provinc. Syriae* / *leg. Aug. pr. pr.* [8]/ *provinc. Brittaniae* / *leg. Aug. pr. pr.* / *provinciae German.* / *inferioris praef.* [12]/ *aerari Saturni* / *leg. leg. XXX VIpiae* / *praetor. tribuno* / *plebis quaestori* [16]/ *Aug. tribuno lati/clav*[*i*]*o leg. X Freten/sis triumviro* / *a. a. a. f. f.* [20]/ *Aequenses* / *municipes.*

Common origin at Aequum in Dalmatia, identity of *nomen*, and part of Julius Verus' career, combine to demonstrate that this governor must have been a close kinsman, in all probability the son, natural or adoptive, of Sex. Julius Severus (*cos.* 127). Julius Severus also bore the *praenomen* Gnaeus, so that a son of his could have been *Cn. f.*, and it seems certain that Julius Verus served as tribune in X Fretensis in Judaea while Julius Severus was governing that province, *c.* 132–5.[1] The only doubt might arise from the absence of any military *dona* for the Jewish war.[2]

The rapidity of his career, with only two posts between praetorship and consulship, together with the auspicious start as *monetalis* and

---

[10] XVI 130 (pp. 122 ff. below).
[11] Degrassi, *FC* 51.
[1] See p. 109 above.
[2] Hadrian was however very ungenerous in this respect. (p. 113 n. 7), although C. Popillius Carus Pedo, tribune of III Cyrenaica in this war, received unspecified decorations (*ILS* 1071).

quaestor Augusti, and his membership of the college of augurs, all suggest that his parent or kinsman Sex. Julius Severus exerted a favourable influence on his behalf, and lead to the conclusion that he probably attained the *fasces* before the age of forty. In that case, his birth probably fell *c.*112, which would accord well with his presumed service in the Jewish war as military tribune, *c.*133, at the age of twenty or twenty-one. It seems improbable that any retardation is indicated by the fact that he did not receive the emperor's backing as tribune of the plebs or praetor.[3] His command over the Lower German legion XXX Ulpia victrix should belong to the early 140s,[4] followed by the prefecture of the treasury of Saturn, a post equivalent in standing to a governorship of a praetorian province.[5] It so happens that no fewer than six other men are attested who were prefects of this treasury in the second half of the 140s, two consul in 146, one in late 147, two in 148, and one in 152.[6] It is possible that Julius Verus and one other, unknown, prefect, together with these six, formed four successive pairs of prefects. Verus may well have been consul in 151.[7]

In that case he probably had a year or two without employment before proceeding to his first consular governorship, in Lower Germany. His presumed predecessor there, the jurist Salvius Julianus (*cos. ord.* 148), who had also served as prefect of the treasury of Saturn, was still curator of public works at Rome in September 150,[8] and is unlikely to have gone to Lower Germany before the spring of 151. If he had a *triennium* as governor, he will have been succeeded by Verus in 154.[9] It may be noted that Verus' dispatch to govern a province where he had commanded a legion a decade or so earlier is relatively unusual.[10]

Verus' governorship of Britain is datable to the year 158 by the inscription from Birrens, north of the western end of Hadrian's Wall, but there is little doubt that he must have arrived there some while earlier. The inscription from Newcastle upon Tyne, revealing the arrival of reinforcements from the two German armies for all three British

[3] Cf. Carus Pedo (*ILS* 1071).

[4] Alföldy, *Legionslegaten* 31 f., suggests *c.*148, which looks a little too late. E. Birley, *ap.* L. Petersen, *PIR²* J 618, prefers *c.*144–6.

[5] p. 22 above.

[6] See now Alföldy, *Konsulat* 292.

[7] 152 is now complete, P. Cluvius Maximus being attested as the missing colleague of M. Servilius Silanus (*AE* 1971. 183); 153 was already complete, while for 154, where Degrassi, *FC* 43, supplied the name of [Cn. Julius Ve]rus as the first in the second pair of *suffecti*, Alföldy now urges [M. Valerius Etrus]cus, *Konsulat* 164 f., and places Verus in 151, ibid. 158.

[8] VI 855.

[9] Ritterling, *FRD* 68 ff., preferred *c.*155.

[10] Table 5, p. 30 above.

legions,[11] indicates that his appointment was in response to an emergency. Coins of the year 155 show Britannia subdued, suggesting that there had been military problems in the province at that time.[12] In that case, it seems likely that Julius Verus, who, as governor of Lower Germany was well placed to go to Britain with extra troops, was appointed to deal with the trouble after only a short stay in the Rhineland.

The epigraphic record of his activity extends from the southern Pennines, at Brough-on-Noe, to the outpost port of Hadrian's Wall at Birrens. He was also active at Corbridge on Tyne, while another inscription, not mentioning his name, is dated by the consuls of 158 to his governorship, and records building work on Hadrian's Wall itself.[13] This evidence strongly suggests that the troubles in Britain involved an insurrection among the Brigantes of the Pennines, while the archaeological evidence from the Antonine Wall indicates that it was evacuated at this time.[14]

Quite when Verus was replaced is difficult to establish; his successor is slightly tenuous.[15] We lose sight of him for a few years, but he reappears in the early 160s. In the meantime dramatic developments had taken place at the other end of the empire. Soon after Pius' death and the accession of M. Aurelius and L. Verus, in 161, the Parthians invaded the eastern provinces. In 162 L. Verus went to the east with an expeditionary force, with M. Aurelius' cousin M. Annius Libo (*cos.* 161) as governor of Syria. But Libo died soon after his arrival,[16] and, in 163 or soon after, Julius Verus, who had perhaps accompanied the emperor to Syria in 162 as his *comes*, is recorded as legate of the province, ordering the reconstruction of a road at Abila.[17] The literary sources do not mention his name among the generals who fought against the Parthians, and it is probable that his major role was to reorganize the Roman base in Syria. By 165 he had been recalled for a further post in Italy. The inscription of an equestrian officer found at Lambaesis reveals that he was assigned *ad dilectum cum Iulio Vero per Italiam tironum II leg. Italicae.*[18] In this task, which must be dated

---

[11] I owe to J. J. Wilkes the expansion *ex*(*ercitibus*) *Ger*(*manicis*) *duobus* rather than the ungrammatical *ex Ger*(*maniis*) *duobus* of *RIB* and earlier editors.

[12] *BMC* IV *Ant. Pius* 1971 ff., 1993 ff.

[13] *RIB* 1389, between Benwell and Rudchester: *leg. VI V. p. f. ref. Ter. et Sac. cos.*

[14] B. R. Hartley, *Britannia* 3 (1972) 36 ff., argues that the Antonine Wall was evacuated *c.*154–5, but reoccupied briefly *c.*159–60.

[15] pp. 121 ff. below.

[16] See A. R. Birley, *Marcus Aurelius* 160 ff.; further, Eck, *Chiron* 2 (1972) 459 ff., on the consulship of Libo (February 161).

[17] *ILS* 5864 (163–5: both M. Aurelius and L. Verus are Armeniacus).

[18] *AE* 1956. 123, see Pflaum, *CP* no. 164 *bis.*

166, Julius Verus also had the assistance of one or more senatorial colleagues.[19] His career was to continue almost until the end of the reign of M. Aurelius, for it is now known that the second consulship to which he was designated was for the year 180. A papyrus at Dura-Europus in Syria actually records him in office, but he must have died in 179.[20] In that case, it must be assumed that the inscription at Aequum which records his career had had a further section, now lost, in which there was reference to his recruiting mission and, very probably, to his position as *comes* of the emperors.[21] It is not impossible that he even had a year as proconsul of Africa, twenty years or so after his consulship, since the plague which arrived at Rome in 166 caused heavy casualties,[22] and this, combined with the demands of the Danubian wars of the late 160s and 170s, meant that several men held consular proconsulships after an unusually long interval.[23] But it is more likely that he served as *comes* of M. Aurelius on the Danube.

There is no trace of any descendants of this remarkable figure.

[. . .] anus

XVI 130, Colchester: [*Imp.* . . . *equitibus et peditibus* . . . *et*] *sun*[*t in Britannia sub* . . .]*ano leg.* [*XXV pluribusve s*]*tipend. eme*[*rit. dimiss. honest. mission.*] *quor. nomi*[*n. subscr. sunt. civit. Rom*]*an., qui eor. n*[*on hab., ded. et conub. cum u*]*xor., quas tun*[*c habuiss., cum e*]*st ci*[*vit. is da*]*t., aut cum is,* [*quas*] *post. du*[*xiss. dumtaxat sin*]*gulis.* [*a. d.*] *VIII k. Iul.* [. . . *S*]*evero* [. . .] *Flavo cos.* [*coh. I fid. Va*]*rdul.* ∞ *cui praest* [. . .] *Verus* [. . . *Satu*]*rnino, Glevi.* [*descript. et recog*]*nit. ex tabul. aer.* [*quae fixa est Romae*] *in mur. post* [*templ. divi Aug. ad*] *Minervam.*

The Colchester diploma can confidently be assigned to Britain, since the cohort there named was regularly part of the army of the province, while the recipient was a native of Glevum.[1] It is harder to be sure

---

[19] M. Claudius Fronto was *misso ad iuventutem per Italiam legendam* after service in the Parthian war, *ILS* 1098. A. Junius Pastor (*cos. ord.* 163), if V 7775 belongs to him, as Ritterling, *FRD* 93 suggested, may also have been involved, see Alföldy, *Legionslegaten* 35 n. 191.

[20] Degrassi, *FC* 50; for details see C. B. Welles *et al.*, *Dura Europos Final Report* V. 1 (1959) 126, *P. Dura* 25. 1, lines 1 and 2.

[21] Alföldy, *Ep. Stud.* 5 (1968) 121 n. 123 notes that 'es fehlen wohl die Hinweise auf die Würde des comes Augusti im Partherkrieg und auf die Rolle bei der Aufstellung der legiones II und III Italicae'; it may also be assumed that Verus was *comes Augustorum bello Germanico et Sarmatico.*

[22] *HA M. Ant. Phil.* 13. 5.

[23] e.g. Salvius Julianus (*cos. ord.* 148), proconsul in 168 and C. Aufidius Victorinus (*cos.* 155), proconsul *c.*173-4. See Thomasson, *Statthalter Nordafrikas* II 82 ff. There are vacancies in the *Fasti* before 168 and *c.*171.

[1] See Nesselhauf, *CIL* XVI 130, ad loc.

about the date. The editor of *CIL* XVI assigned it to the years 139–90, since the privileges for children are omitted, and the dating is by suffect consuls. But, as E. Birley pointed out in his review,[2] certain aspects allow us to be more specific. The cohort-commander is not given an *origo*, which was a regular feature of diplomas during the years 133–49, while in a diploma of 154[3] and frequently thereafter the *origo* is omitted. Various readings of the governor's name have been offered, but E. Birley's version, reproduced above, gives the title *leg.* instead of the beginning of a second name. If this reading is accepted, it provides another yardstick, since the governor's or commanding officer's status was not mentioned on diplomas before the year 150. Finally, the amount of abbreviation in the closing formula *ex tabul. aer.* [*quae fixa est Romae*] *in mur. post* [*templ. divi Aug. ad*] *Minervam* is exactly paralleled in XVI 110, which seems to belong to 154,[4] and almost exactly in XVI 112, from a year which may be narrowed down, with considerable probability, to 159.[5] It is also very similar to that in the new Upper Moesian diploma of 161 and to XVI 185, from AD 164, although the abbreviation in these two is even more extreme.[6] The years immediately after 161 must be ruled out, since the governors Statius Priscus and Calpurnius Agricola must be accommodated; and from soon after 165 the drastic abbreviation of the closing formula seems to disappear.[7] AD 160 must apparently also be excluded, since there is no room in the consular *fasti* of that year for a pair of *suffecti* called Severus and Flavus in June.[8] Hence it looks as if the years 159 and 161 are the most likely. One further consideration arises from the name of the cohort-commander on the diploma. Although the

---

[2] *JRS* 28 (1938) 228.

[3] XVI 104.

[4] See pp. 127 f. below.

[5] Syme, *Historia* 14 (1965) 354 = *Danubian Papers* 237.

[6] Roxan no. 55 has *ex tabul. ae. quae fix. est Romae in mur. post tem. divi Aug.*, and XVI 185 has *ex tabul. aer. quae fix. est Rom. in mur. post temp* [*l. divi Aug.*].

[7] XVI 120, from AD 165, has *ex tabula aerea* [*quae* j[i]] *xa est Romae in muro post* [*templ. di*] *vi Aug.*, and XVI 123, from 167, has *ex tabul. aerea quae fixa est Romae in muro post templ. divi Aug.* Cf. also XVI 128 (AD 178) and 133 (AD 192), both with minimal abbreviation. (XVI 121, from AD 166, has [. . .] *quae fix. est Rom. i*[*n* . . .] and some of the imprecisely dated diplomas [XVI 124, 125, 126, 129, 131] contain above average abbreviation.)

[8] See now Alföldy, *Konsulat* 174 ff., on the consuls of this year. It is, however, worth asking whether FLAVO might not be an error for FESTO. In that case, the diploma would be dated by the consulship of [M. Post]umius Festus and [C. Septimius S]everus. The latter appears to have replaced the original colleague of Festus, which could explain why Severus appears before 'Flavus'.

Mrs M. M. Roxan has kindly shown me the typescript of a forthcoming note, in which she shows that XVI 130 may be dated, with a very strong degree of probability, either to 154 or to 159. Thus the governor -anus will have been either the immediate predecessor, or the immediate successor, of Cn. Julius Verus.

cognomen Verus is common, it is reasonable to identify him with the Trebius Verus named as commander of the same cohort on an altar to Neptune at Castlecary on the Antonine Wall.[9] If Trebius Verus was serving under the successor of Julius Verus when the altar was dedicated, it would be surprising, to say the least, since it appears probable that Julius Verus evacuated most of Scotland. However, it is perfectly possible that the altar was set up a year or two before the Colchester diploma was issued and that Trebius Verus continued to command the Vardulli under Julius Verus' successor. Alternatively, the Antonine Wall may have been reoccupied[10] and the Castlecary dedication may date to *c.*159–60.

The termination -anus is found very frequently, but there happen not to be many possible candidates, in other words men known to have been consul in the decade or so before AD 159 whose principal *cognomen* ended thus. The two most likely are perhaps M. Servilius Silanus (*cos.* 152, *II ord.* 188),[11] and Minicius(?) Opimianus (*cos.* 155).[12] Nothing further is known of the career of either of these two men. A third possibility is Calpurnius Julianus, not yet attested as having held the consulship, but apparently on record as governor of Upper Dacia.[13] It is striking that three out of the ten or so men known to have governed that province during the four and a half decades of its existence later became governor of Britain—Sex. Julius Severus, Cn. Papirius Aelianus, and M. Statius Priscus.[14] Unfortunately there is as yet no firm dating evidence for Julianus.[15]

M. Statius M. f. Cl. Priscus Licinius Italicus (*cos. ord.* 159)

JÖAI 12 (1909) Bbl. 149 = *AE* 1910. 86, Viminacium: [*Pro sal*] *ute imperato* [*rum Caesarum M. Aureli* / *Ant*] *onini Aug. et L.* [*Aureli Veri Aug.* / *M. Stati*] *us Priscu* [*s Licinius Italicus* [4] / *leg. Augusto*] *r. provin* [*c. Moesia*] *e sup* [*erioris* / *item leg. August*] *or.* [*provin*] *c. Britan* [*niae* / ...] *f.*

[9] *RIB* 2149.

[10] Hartley, *Britannia* 3 (1972) 36 ff. On the date of XVI 130, see also Roxan, *Roman Military Diplomas* p. 26 and n. 8 above.

[11] Degrassi, *FC* 43, 52.

[12] Degrassi, *FC* 44; see Eck, *Historia* 24 (1975) 324 ff. for a probable reconstruction of his nomenclature.

[13] Once reckoned governor of one of the Moesias, see *PIR*[2] C 270, on the basis of *ILS* 3891, Ad Mediam, but a new reading shows: *leg. Aug. pr. pr.* [*pro*] *v.* [*Da*] *ciae* [*sup*] *er* [*iori*] *s*, I. Piso, *Röm. Österreich* 3 (1975) 178. Some doubt remains.

[14] See Syme, *Historia* 14 (1965) 357 f. = *Danubian Papers* 241: 'It would be a temptation to look for some of the missing legates of Britain in the roll of Dacia'.

[15] He might be a kinsman of Sex. Calpurnius Agricola, see p. 127 and n. 2 below.

VI 1523 = *ILS* 1092, Rome: [*M. Stati*]*o M. f. Cl. Prisco* / [*L*]*icinio Italico leg. Augustorum* / *pr. pr. prov. Cappadociae leg. Aug*[*g.*] [4] / *pr. pr. prov. Brittanniae leg. Aug*[*g.*] / *pr. pr. prov. Moesiae super. curato*[*ri*] / *alvei Tiberis et cl*[*o*]*acarum urbis, c*[*os.*] / *leg. Aug. prov. Daciae leg. leg. XIII G. p. f. leg. leg.* [8] / [*X*]*III Gem. Martiae Victridis sacerdoti Titiali* / [*Fl*]*aviali pr. inter cives et peregrinos tr. pl., quaes*[*t.*] / *proc. Aug. XX hereditatium prov. Narbones, et Aquita*[*n.* / *p*]*r. eq. alae I pr. c. R. tr. mil. leg. I Adiutr. p. f. et leg. X* [*G.*] *p.* [*f.* [12] / *e*]*t leg. IIII* [sic] *Gallicae praef. coh. IIII Lingonum vexillo mi*[*l.* / *d*]*onato a divo Hadriano in expeditione Iudaic*[*a*] *Q. Cassius Domitius Palumbus.*

Statius Priscus' governorship must have been of very brief duration: consideration of the details of his activities elsewhere indicate, as will be seen below, that it cannot have lasted more than a year at the most, *c.*162. But not least for this reason, his whole career is of considerable interest, and throws a good deal of light on the workings of the Roman military system.

The name Statius is fairly common, and the other items in his nomenclature are also too indistinctive to indicate his origin, except for the tribe Claudia, which is found more frequently than elsewhere in *regio* X of Italy and in certain communities of the northern provinces.[1] Northeastern Italy, where a good many Statii are attested,[2] or one of the cities of the Dalmatian coast,[3] look likely areas for his home.

He was certainly a *novus homo*, for he began his career as an equestrian officer, serving his first *militia* as prefect of the fourth cohort of Lingones in Britain. This was followed by three spells of duty as a legionary tribune, in one of which, it may be presumed, III Gallica, he was decorated for service in the Jewish war of AD 132-5. It would be logical to suppose that he was taken from Britain to the Jewish war by Sex. Julius Severus, and hence that the three legions are named in the correct order, descending, as are the other posts on the inscription. It might then be significant that he then obtained a post in the legion which Q. Lollius Urbicus, another general in the Jewish war, had been commanding, perhaps on his recommendation. But the relative slowness

---

[1] Kubitschek 270.

[2] Schulze (37) comments on its frequency as a *praenomen* in north Italy. There are over seventy examples of the *nomen* in V (including several MM., M.1., etc., and two Statii Prisci, 1385 and 4098), more than twice as many as in IX and X and more than three times as many as in XI.

[3] The tribe Claudia and the *nomen* are both found there, as G. Alföldy kindly reminds me. See now his *Konsulat* 314 f., where he proposes an origin in Dalmatia. It should, however, be considered whether Priscus could not have been of British origin, from Colchester. A Statius is known to have derived from there, with the tribe Claudia (III 11233), and Priscus' first appointment in Britain might well accord with origin in the province. No clues are afforded by the listing of his name with that of other senators on an inscription at Ostia, presumably the patrons of a *collegium* (XIV 249).

of his career at this stage suggests that neither Julius Severus nor Lollius Urbicus exerted themselves unduly on his behalf. It was only after a third tribunate, in another Upper Pannonian legion, that he entered the third *militia*, as prefect of an *ala* in Cappadocia; and he then entered the procuratorial career with a rather lowly post as a *sexagenarius*, in charge of the *vicesima hereditatium* in two Gallic provinces.[4]

Thereafter he changed course markedly by entering the senate. No details are provided, but it must be assumed that it was Antoninus Pius who granted him the *latus clavus*.[5] Priscus may have owed his advancement to the patronage of Lollius Urbicus, whose influence in the 140s was no doubt considerable. But, significantly, Priscus did not receive any remission (except that he was excused the vigintivirate), unlike many who transferred from the equestrian career to the senate at other periods, such as the reign of Vespasian or during the Marcomannic wars. This reflects the conservatism of the reign of Antoninus Pius. Priscus must have been well over thirty when he entered the senate as quaestor, and well over fifty when he finally became consul. On the other hand, once he had been through the compulsory republican magistracies, he had the type of career associated with men like Julius Agricola and Julius Severus, holding only two praetorian posts, the first of them a legionary command.[6] It is not possible to be certain whether this type of career was necessarily always as rapid as it was in the case of Agricola, for firm chronological details are lacking for the various stages. Only his governorship of Upper Dacia, which immediately preceded his consulship, is dated closely, to 158 by one diploma and to 156 or 157 by another.[7] Before that he had commanded the Carnuntum legion XIV Gemina, perhaps when Claudius Maximus, the friend of M. Aurelius, was governing Upper Pannonia (he is attested there in 150 and 154).[8]

---

[4] See Pflaum, *CP* no. 136, for the equestrian part of his career. Fitz, *A. Ant. Hung.* 9 (1961) 182 f., assumed that he was decorated by Hadrian while prefect of IV Lingonum, but see Pflaum, citing Domaszewski, *RO* 138, who points out that Hadrian reduced the number of decorations, hence that Priscus could have received his *vexillum* for service as tribune of III Gallica. However, Pflaum assumes that that legion was the last of the three in which he served, which does not allow for the likelihood of Priscus being taken from Britain to Judaea by Julius Severus.

[5] If Pflaum, *CP* no. 136, is correct in supposing that III Gallica was the third, not the first, legion in which he served, it would just be possible for him to have received the *latus clavus* from Hadrian. But see previous note.

[6] See pp. 20 f. above.

[7] See Stein, *Dazien* 27 ff., and Alföldy, *Konsulat* 245.

[8] Fitz, *A. Ant. Hung.* 9 (1961) 182 f., assumes that after being legate of XIV Gemina, Priscus commanded XIII Gemina outside Dacia before becoming governor of that province. This is unnecessary: see the inscriptions of Pompeius Falco describing him as *leg. Aug. leg. X Fret. et leg. pr. pr. [pr]ovinciae Iudaeae* (pp. 95 f. above). Likewise in VIII 5349 one might read *leg. Auggg. [p]ro pr. [prov.] Pan. in<f>er. et l[eg. II] Adiut.*

Priscus' tenure of the *fasces* as *ordinarius* for 159 was a remarkable honour for a *novus homo*—only one other man of comparable background, the jurist Salvius Julianus, received similar distinction during the entire reign.[9] One reason for his being marked out may be straightforward enough: he undoubtedly had some military success in Dacia, as a number of inscriptions from that province reveal.[10]

After his consulship he had a brief spell as curator of the Tiber, but before the end of 160 he must have been assigned to govern Upper Moesia, where he is attested in office by a diploma of February 161.[11] He was still there, not surprisingly, after the death of Pius the following month, as is demonstrated by his dedication in honour of the new emperors M. Aurelius and L. Verus at Viminacium. That inscription was set up after he had received the assignment to govern Britain.[12] The difficult military situation in the north of the province probably prompted the emperors to transfer Priscus there soon after their accession. But he may only have spent a few months in Britain when a more serious crisis occurred, in the east—the defeat and death of the governor of Cappadocia and the invasion of Syria by the Parthians.[13] Priscus was clearly chosen to deal with this crisis, and the scanty literary sources for the period reveal that he won the victory which permitted L. Verus to assume the title Armeniacus in 163.[14] The satirical writer Lucian alleges that one of the incompetent contemporary historians of the eastern wars described 'how Priscus the general merely shouted out and twenty-seven of the enemy dropped dead'.[15] It is foolhardy to try to squeeze some truth out of evidence of this kind, but one might perhaps suppose, at least, that Priscus was a man with an aggressive and boisterous

[9] See Alföldy, *Konsulat* 100 ff.

[10] XVI 108 (diploma of 158, showing reinforcements from Mauretania Caesariensis and Africa in the province); III 1061 = *ILS* 4006 (*pro salute imperii Romani et virtute leg. XIII G.*), 1416 (*Victoriae Aug.*).

[11] *Chiron* 2 (1972) 449 ff. = *AE* 1972. 657 = Roxan no. 55.

[12] For parallel cases of such inscriptions see pp. 95 (Q. Pompeius Falco), 132 (Caerellius), 261 (Q. Aurelius Polus Terentianus). I read [*leg. Augusto*]*r.* in line 3, rather than [*leg. Augustor.pr.p*]*r.*, and prefer a different expansion of the missing portions in the first two lines, relying on the drawing in the original publication. (Cf. Alföldy, *Konsulat* 219 n. 67, for an alternative reading.) It may be noted here that the equestrian officer Licinius Clemens, found in Britain under Priscus' successor Calpurnius Agricola (*RIB* 1792, 1809) may have owed his appointment to Priscus, perhaps a kinsman, cf. also the officer named Licinius Nigrinus who served under Priscus in Dacia (XVI 108).

[13] Dio 71. 2. 1, *HA M. Ant. Phil.* 8. 6; Lucian, *Alexander* 27; etc. See A. R. Birley, *Marcus Aurelius* 160 ff.

[14] *HA M. Ant. Phil.* 9. 1: 'Gestae sunt res in Armenia prospere per Statium Priscum Artaxatis captis, delatumque Armeniaci nomen utrique principum'; *Verus* 7. 1: 'duces autem confecerunt Parthicum bellum, Statius Priscus et Avidius Cassius et Martius Verus per quadriennium, ita ut Babyloniam et Mediam provenirent et Armeniam vindicarent'; Dio 71. 3. 1¹. See A. R. Birley, *Marcus Aurelius* 172, 175 f., on the title Armeniacus.

[15] Lucian, *quom. hist. conser.* 20.

style of leadership. He is not heard of again, and may have died soon afterwards.

No children are recorded, but M. Statius Longinus, governor of Moesia inferior under Macrinus,[16] was probably his grandson.

163   Sex. Calpurnius Agricola (*cos.* 154(?))

VII 225 = *RIB* 589, Ribchester: *Imp. Ca[es. M. Au]rel. A[ntonino . . . et] / imp. Ca[es. L. Aur]el. Ve[ro . . . Augg.] / vex. leg[ionis sex]tae [Victricis . . .] 4/ sub Se[x. Calpu]rn[io Agricola leg. Augg. pr. pr.]*

EE VII 1050b = *RIB* 1703; Vindolanda: [. . .] *su[b Sex. Calpurnio] Ag[ricola leg. Augg. pr. pr.]*

VII 773 = *RIB* 1809, Carvoran: [. . . *sub Calpur/ni] o Agri/cola cos./ Licinius Cl[e] 4/mens p[raef.]*

VII 758 = *RIB* 1792, Carvoran: *Deae Suri/ae sub Calp/urnio Ag[r] 4/ico[la] leg. Au[g.] / pr. pr. Lic[in]ius / [C]lem[ens praef. / co]h. I Ha[miorum]*

EE IX 1381 = *RIB* 1137, Corbridge: *Soli invicto / vexillatio / leg. VI Vic. p. f. 4/ sub cura Sex. / Calpurni Agrico/lae leg. Aug. pr. pr.*

VII 473 *EE* IX 1382 = *JRS* 34 (1944) 87 = *RIB* 1149, Corbridge: *Imperato[ribus Caesaribus] / M. Aurelio An[tonino Aug. tribuniciae] / potestati[s XVII] cos. [III et L. Aur4/elio Vero Aug.] A[rmeniaco trib/uniciae potestati]s I[II] co[s.] II / [vexillatio leg. XX] V. V. fecit su[b c]ura / [Sexti Calpurni] Agrico[l]ae / [legati Augustoru]m pr. pr.*

VII 334 = *RIB* 793, Hardknot: [. . . *A]gric[o]la coII[. . .]*

HA M. Ant. Phil. 8. 8: et adversus Brittannos quidem Calpurnius Agricola missus est.

Nothing is known of Calpurnius Agricola's career before his consulship. His origin is nowhere attested, but, although the *gentilicium* is extremely common all over the empire, the combination Sex. Calpurnius is found very infrequently.[1] Hence he might be a kinsman of Fronto's friend Sex. Calpurnius Julianus,[2] and, if so, he may have been a native of Cirta or one of the neighbouring communities in Numidia.

Agricola's consulship is known from the diploma XVI 110, showing him in office on 27 September with Ti. Claudius Julianus. Thanks to

---

[16] Stein, *Moesien* 90 f.; Barbieri, *L'Albo* no. 486 (and see nos. 1163–4 for his presumed sons).

[1] There are none in II, V, VIII, X, XII, XIII, and XIV; one each in III, VI, and IX, and one or perhaps two in XI.

[2] The MS has 'Sextii': Fronto, *ad Ant. Pium* 9 = 162 van den Hout. He was an *eques Romanus*, described by Fronto as his *contubernalis*. The relationship was suggested by Groag, *PIR²* C 249.

the discovery of a new fragment, with the names of the witnesses, the diploma can now be dated with some confidence to the year 154, rather than 159, as once seemed probable;[3] and indeed, the names of Agricola and Julianus may be restored in the *Fasti Ostienses* for the earlier year: [*Ti. Claudius Julia*]*nus Sex.* [*Calpurnius Agricola*].[4] Agricola's colleague is recorded as governor of Lower Germany in 160,[5] and it seems probable that he himself governed a consular province before coming to Britain, although there are not many vacancies in the years 155-62.[6] At any rate, the dedication at Corbridge to M. Aurelius and L. Verus firmly dates his governorship to the year 163 and had already disposed of the possibility that he was the predecessor of Priscus, rather than his successor.[7] The context of the sentence in the *Historia Augusta* which refers to his dispatch 'against the Britons' suggests that he was appointed governor in 162 at the very latest.[8] The distribution of the inscriptions which record his presence in Britain, at two sites closely linked to Hadrian's Wall, as well as at Corbridge and at Ribchester in north-west England, indicates that the Pennines were reoccupied at this time, and, *a fortiori*, that the Antonine Wall was no longer held. Whether, however, there had been a brief second occupation of the Antonine Wall during the years 158 to 161 is another matter.[9]

The exact length of his governorship is unknown, but *c.*166 he had moved to the Lower Danube region, as is shown by the inscription of a soldier of V Macedonica, who served 'in the German expedition' under Agricola and another general, and received his discharge from a third, in

---

[3] See B. Lörincz, *Arheološki Vestnik* 28 (1977) 369 ff. and Roxan, *Roman Military Diplomas* no. 47.

[4] Cf. Alföldy, *Konsulat* 164 ff., for another restoration.

[5] XIII 8036 = *ILS* 2907 (Bonn).

[6] See Alföldy, *Konsulat* 220-42.

[7] See the comments of Syme, *Danubian Papers* 171. The dating of *RIB* 1149, assigned by R. P. Wright ad loc. to 'A.D. 163 (autumn-9 Dec.)', depends on the reading *A*[*rmeniaco*] in line 4, as a title for L. Verus, while M. Aurelius clearly did not have it. M. Aurelius assumed the same title in 164 (see A. R. Birley, *Marcus Aurelius* 172, 175 f.). Perhaps the Corbridge inscription, where the tribunician power of both emperors is restored, [*XVII*] and *I*[*II*], might belong to the first half of that year, but, if so, the careful spacing shown in R. P. Wright's drawing would have been spoiled. J. C. Mann, in D. E. Johnston (ed.), *The Saxon Shore* (1977) 15, assigns the inscription to 'the period between 161 and 166', presumably doubting the reading *A*[*rmeniaco*]. Yet were it later than the first half of 165, both emperors would surely have been called *Armeniacus* and L. Verus would have been Parthicus Maximus also (A. R. Birley, op. cit. 189).

[8] E. Champlin, *JRS* 64 (1974) 155 f., argues that Aufidius Victorinus' despatch against the Chatti, referred to in the same sentence of the *HA* as Agricola's against the Britons, must be dated to the summer, or at latest the autumn, of 161.

[9] p. 123 and n. 10 above. For some evidence of fighting in the 160s, see A. R. Birley, in Butler (ed.), *Soldier and Civilian in Roman Yorkshire* 86. See also pp. 202 f. below, for an inscription from Caerleon perhaps assignable to Agricola—it records building work of some kind.

the year 170.[10] It seems reasonable to suppose that Agricola, like the other two men under whom the soldier served at the end of his career, was governor of the newly reunified province of the Three Dacias, to which V Macedonica was transferred on its return from the east *c.*166. It is, however, possible that Agricola was governor of Lower Moesia.[11] Nothing further is heard of him, and he may well have lost his life, like so many, of all ranks, at this time, either from the plague or in battle.[12] No descendants are recorded although one or more of the senatorial Calpurnii of the later second and early third centuries might be from the same family.

Q. Antistius Q. f. Quir. Adventus Postumius Aquilinus (*cos.* 167?)

VII 440 = *RIB* 1083, Lanchester: *Num. Aug. et / Gen. coh. I f. Vardullorum / c. R. eq. sub An⁴/tistio Adven/to leg. Aug. pr. p*[r.] */ F. Titianus trib. / d. s. d.*

Antistius Adventus' governorship is attested only by the dedication at Lanchester, in the hinterland of Hadrian's Wall, but his origin and previous career are amply documented by other evidence. The most important item is a *cursus* inscription from Thibilis in Numidia, his home,[1] which it is convenient to set out in full here:

[*Q. Antistio Advento*] */ Q. f. Quir. Postumio Aqu*[*i*]*/lino cos. sacerdoti fetia ⁴/ li leg. Aug. pr. pr. provinc. Ger/maniae inferioris leg. Aug. / at prae*[*t*]*enturam Italiae et / Alpium expeditione Germa⁸/nica cura. operum locorumq. / publicorum leg. Aug. pr. pr. / provinc. Arabiae leg. Aug. leg. / VI Ferratae et secundae Ad¹²/iutricis translato in eam ex/peditione Parthica qua do/natus est donis militaribus / coronis murali vallari au¹⁶/rea hastis puris tribus ve/xillis duobus praetori leg. / pr. pr. provinc. Africa.* [*t*]*r. pl., se/viro eq. R. q. pr. pr. provinc. ²⁰/ Macedoniae tribuno*

[10] *ILS* 2311 (Troesmis).

[11] Stein, *Dazien* 41, argued that Agricola had V Macedonica under his command in his capacity as *comes Veri Aug.* Syme, *Danubian Papers* 171, 176, favours the governorship of the III Daciae. I am not convinced by the arguments of Fitz, *Moesia Inferior* 19 ff., that Agricola must have governed Lower Moesia, from 167 (or even 166) to 168 or 169. He does not allow for the possibility that serious Roman reverses, perhaps including the death of Agricola, may have made it necessary for M. Claudius Fronto to take over part of Dacia, viz. Apulensis, before the death of L. Verus, and then to become governor of the III Daciae(*ILS* 1097-8, cf. *PIR*² C 874: he was legate of Moesia superior and Dacia Apulensis *simul*, as *leg. Augg. pr. pr.*, i.e. before L. Verus' death in late 168 or early 169—see *PIR*² C 606 for the date). Claudius Fronto's inscriptions by no means prove that he must have been 'der letzte praetorischer und . . . der erste konsularische Legat Daziens', since his consulship came several years earlier (before the triumph of 166, for his *dona* were consular). See also A. R. Birley, in *Provincialia* (1968) 218 f., and Alföldy, *Konsulat* 222 f.

[12] See e.g. *HA M. Ant. Phil.* 13. 5, 22. 7, and the inscription of Claudius Fronto, who *ad postremum pro rep. fortiter pugnans ceciderit* (*ILS* 1098).

[1] See now F. Bertrandy, *Karthago* 17 (1973/4) 195 ff.

mil. / leg. I Minerviae p. f. IIIIvir. / viarum curandarum / Sex. Marcius Maximus ob in[24]*/signem eius in se benivolen/tiam s. p. p. d. d. (ILS 8977)*

From this and from further inscriptions the chronology of his career can be calculated with some precision. He was holding his second legionary command in March 164 and was probably consul *c.*166. Hence his birth probably fell in the 120s. He seems to have been a *novus homo*,[2] although a member of a wealthy landowning family, and it may be suspected that his path to a senatorial career was opened by his marriage to the governor's daughter. At any rate, his wife was Novia Crispina, whose father was presumably the L. Novius Crispinus (*cos.* 150), *de facto* governor of Numidia as legate of III Augusta in the years 147-9.[3] After the vigintivirate Adventus was tribune of the Bonn legion I Minervia, receiving his commission—on the chronology here suggested —from either Salvius Julianus or Cn. Julius Verus.[4] Thereafter he went through the three republican magistracies as quaestor, tribune of the plebs, and praetor, the intervals being punctuated by two additional posts, as *sevir equitum Romanorum* at Rome and as legate to a proconsul of Africa. The latter posting could have given him another powerful patron, although the identity of the proconsul under whom he served is not known. After the praetorship came the command over the Palestine legion VI Ferrata. The outbreak of the Parthian war led to the dispatch of additional units to the east, and Adventus was transferred to command one of these, the Lower Pannonian legion II Adiutrix, probably in 162. During his legateship of this legion, on 1 March 164, his freedman Q. Antistius Agathopus made a dedication to the *genius domus* for his welfare, at Thibilis.[5] He evidently saw some active service, in view of his *dona militaria*, but was probably appointed *c.*164 to govern Arabia. An inscription from Bostra describes him as consul designate, and another, from Gerasa, called him ὕπατος.[6] Thus he held the *fasces* in his province, in 166 or 167.[7] There followed, as was not infrequent, an appointment at Rome, as curator of public buildings and works.

His next appointment was an extraordinary command, as *leg. Aug. at prae*[t]*enturam Italiae et Alpium expeditione Germanica.* The 'German

---

[2] L. Antistius Asiaticus, *praefectus montis Berenicidis* in AD 90 (III 13580, *IGR* I 1183) may be an ancestor, cf. VIII 18931 (Thibilis): *Civilis Q. Antisti Asiatici f. v. a. VIIII*; the possibility is not noted by Bertrandy, op. cit.

[3] *ILS* 1091 (*Noviae Crispinae eius*) etc. for L. Novius Crispinus see Thomasson, *Statthalter Nordafrikas* II 174 f. and Alföldy, *Konsulat*, esp. 351 ff.

[4] Ritterling, *FRD* 68 f., and p. 119 above.

[5] *ILS* 1091.

[6] III 92, *IGR* III 1368. His successor in Arabia, L. Claudius Modestus, was in the province before 169: G. W. Bowersock, *Hommages Préaux* (1973) 573 ff.

[7] Alföldy, *Konsulat* 183 f., prefers 167.

expedition' was launched by M. Aurelius and L. Verus in 168, and their initial inspection of the military situation north of Italy was followed by precautionary measures: 'denique transcensis Alpibus longius processerunt composueruntque omnia, quae ad munimen Italiae atque Illyrici pertinebant'. It is difficult to resist identifying the measures 'ad munimen Italiae atque Illyrici' described in this sentence in the *Historia Augusta* with Adventus' mission in the *praetentura Italiae et Alpium*. His duties will have included the command over the two new legions II and III Italicae, and the protection of the passes through the Julian Alps from Pannonia into Italy. In due course, perhaps in 170, the German tribes were indeed to break through, but they failed to capture Aquileia. Adventus may have been involved in the city's defence, but it is not improbable that he had been transferred, before the Marcomanni and Quadi invaded, to govern Lower Germany.[8]

His governorship of that province is the latest post recorded on the *cursus* inscription from Thibilis. The priesthood, as *fetialis*, was very likely obtained earlier, perhaps at the time of his consulship. His presence is recorded in Germany by a fine dedication at Vectio to a series of deities appropriate to the troubled times.[9] If Adventus did go to Germany *c.*170, he might be expected to have moved on to Britain—by this period a sequence of offices for which there was ample precedent —about three years later. But the times were far from normal. It is fair to assume that some two or three unknown governors must be postulated in the interval between Calpurnius Agricola and Adventus, and the latter's governorship may be very tentatively assigned to the period *c.*173-6.[10] In that case, he will have had the task of absorbing into the army of the province the 5,500 Sarmatians sent to Britain following M. Aurelius' armistice with that people in 175.[11]

The high esteem in which Adventus was held by M. Aurelius is demonstrated by the patrician rank of a young kinsman, probably his son or nephew, revealed by an inscription of 178, and by the selection of L. Antistius Burrus, probably his son, as *consul ordinarius* for 181.[12]

[8] See A. R. Birley, *Provincialia* 219 ff. There is now an extensive literature on the *praetentura Italiae et Alpium*. It must be noted that the view here taken, that the invasion of Italy came in 170, after the *praetentura* was established, is not the orthodox one. See J. Šašel, *Mus. Helv.* 31 (1974) 225 ff. for a recent discussion.

[9] XIII 8812.

[10] But it must be noted that even on *ILS* 1091, from a joint reign, Adventus is called *leg. Aug.*, not *leg. Augg.*, so that the Lanchester inscription need not necessarily belong to the period 169-76 or to the sole reign of Commodus (a point missed by Bertrandy, *Karthago* 17 (1973/4) 197, who also assigns the inscription to Lancaster by error).

[11] Dio 71. 16. 2. See e.g. Jarrett and Mann, *Bonner Jahrb.* 170 (1970) 192, A. R. Birley, *Soldier and Civilian in Roman Yorkshire* 86 f.

[12] *PIR*[2] A 758 (L. Antistius Burrus Adventus, *salius* in 178), 757 (L. Antistius Burrus *cos.*

Burrus was also to marry M. Aurelius' youngest child, Vibia Aurelia Sabina, although this union can hardly have taken place before M. Aurelius' death in 180 since it seems that Sabina was only born in 170.[13] Burrus later fell foul of his brother-in-law Commodus, and was put to death *c.*189.[14] The family appears to have died out thereafter, although Sabina survived for many years.[15]

It seems possible that our governor may have been the Adventus to whom C. Julius Solinus dedicated his *Collectanea rerum memorabilium*, including the often quoted reference to the use of mineral coal in a temple of Minerva in Britain—one of the few original items in that work, such as Antistius Adventus might well have passed on to the author as a result of his tour of duty in Britain.[16] It is not known whether he held any further appointments.

(Caerellius) (*cos. a. inc.*)

XIII 6806, Mainz: [. . . *leg.* / *Aug.* or *Augg.*] *pr. pr. pro* [*vi*] *n* [*c.*] / *Thrac. Moes. sup. Rae* [*t*] [4] / *Germ. sup. et Britt.* / *et Modestiana eius* / *et Caerellii Mar* /*cianus et Germa* /*nilla filii*

The inscription at Mainz, capital of Upper Germany, was presumably set up by the governor of that province, together with his wife and children, on the occasion of his promotion to Britain.[1] Although there is no emperor's name or obvious form of dating, and the governor's name is missing, consideration of the other offices which he held allows the period to be narrowed down considerably. In the first place, Raetia was governed by equestrian procurators at least until 167 or 168, when

---

ord. 181: the two might be identical. Bertrandy, *Karthago* 17 (1973/4) 197 f., identifies the *cos. ord.* 181 with L. Antistius Mundicius Burrus, brother of Adventus (*PIR*[2] A 762), which is not convincing. There is no difficulty in supposing that Adventus and Novia Crispina could have had a son *c.*148.

[13] Pflaum, *J. des Savants* 1961. 37 ff.; A. R. Birley, *Marcus Aurelius* 321 and n. 1.

[14] *HA Comm.* 6. 11, *Pert.* 3. 7. see Grosso, *La lotta politica* 253 ff., for the date.

[15] See Pflaum, *J. des Savants* 1961. 38 f., who also comments on her second marriage, to L. Aurelius Agaclytus. She was still alive in 211, after the death of Severus (*ILAlg.* I 241, Calama).

[16] Solinus 22. 11. Herodian (4. 12. 1) and Dio (78. 14) make it clear that M. Oclatinius Adventus (*cos. ord.* 218) who was also in Britain, as procurator (p. 298 below), was hardly likely to be the dedicatee of a literary work, however inferior. H. Walter argues that Solinus should be dated to the mid-third century at the earliest: *Die 'Collectanea rerum memorabilium' des C. Julius Solinus* (Hermes Einzelschr. 22, 1969), esp. 73 f. But his arguments, derived from the mention of the Blemmyes in Solinus, are not compelling.

[1] For parallels see the inscriptions set up by Pompeius Falco (p. 95 above) and Statius Priscus (p. 123 above) on their appointment to govern Britain.

the latest is recorded.[2] Soon after that, it was assigned to *legati Augusti pro praetore*, of whom the earliest datable case is found in 179 or 180.[3] Secondly, the governorship of Britain must come before the division of the province, since both *Germ(ania)* and *Moes(ia)* are labelled *sup(erior)*, but *Britt(annia)* is not. The order of appointments is, however, puzzling. If it is chronological, the status of one or more of the provinces concerned must have been temporarily altered. Thrace was regularly governed by ex-praetors, and this presents no difficulties, as the first province that the man governed. Moesia superior, on the other hand, as a two legion province, was normally governed by ex-consuls. But from 179/80, at any rate, Raetia was a one legion province, regularly governed by ex-praetors. Hence it seems out of place between two consular provinces. The solution may be that during the early 170s more than one legion was stationed there, during the Marcomannic wars, and that it had consular governors at this period.[4] For that matter, it is not unlikely that Moesia superior was temporarily downgraded at the same time, when one of its legions was removed.[5] Several other governors of Moesia superior are known from the 170s, and the likeliest time to place our man there seems to be *c.*170-2.[6] His governorship of Britain would then fall *c.*178-80. He might conceivably be the unknown governor killed by invading tribes early in the reign of Commodus. It is perhaps more probable to suppose that this fate overtook a new and inexperienced legate.[7]

E. Groag suggested that our governor might be identified with Asellius Aemilianus, proconsul of Asia 192-3 and Pescennius Niger's principal lieutenant in his war against Severus 193-4.[8] Aemilianus is said to have governed many provinces,[9] one of which, Thrace, is the same as one of those of which our man was legate. On the other hand, Aemilianus also governed Syria, and it is not easy to fit in four other provinces, Raetia,

---

[2] *AE* 1961. 174 (Abusina).

[3] III 11965 (Regensburg).

[4] This was suggested by S. E. Stout, *The Governors of Moesia* (1911) 30 f. See now J. Fitz, *Bayerische Vorgeschichts-Blätter* 32 (1967) 42 ff., G. Winkler, ibid. 36 (1971) 75 f.

[5] I suggested this in *A. Ant. Philip.* 102 ff. G. R. Stanton, *ANRW* 2. 1 (1975) 508 f., points out that it is not necessary to suppose that Upper Moesia was praetorian, if it is realized that Raetia could have been consular. This I had of course appreciated, and the change of status for Upper Moesia must now in any case be regarded as less certain (see p. 123 n. 13 above on Calpurnius Julianus, and p. 144 n. 17 below on Pertinax). See p. 22 and n. 27 above, for other cases of men governing two praetorian provinces in this period.

[6] The other governors known are M. Claudius Fronto (till *c.* 169, p. 129 n. 11 above), M. Macrinius Avitus *cet.* and Pertinax, both before 177 (p. 144 and n. 17 below): see now Alföldy, *Konsulat* 235, 246.

[7] p. 135 below.

[8] Groag *ap.* Ritterling, *FRD* 34 f.

[9] Dio 74. 6. 2.

Upper Moesia, Upper Germany, and Britain, between 176/80, when he was in Thrace, and the mid- to late 180s, when he was in Syria.[10] Besides, this involves the assumption that Raetia is out of place on the Mainz inscription, and leaves the difficulty that his children had a different *nomen*, Caerellius, not Asellius. Although parallels can be adduced,[11] and Aemilianus might have been polyonymous, Groag's theory must be regarded as implausible.

It is also tempting to seek to identify the man from Mainz with C. Caerellius Sabinus, legate of XIII Gemina in Dacia shortly after 185 and then legate of Raetia.[12] But this possibility is very dubious; not only must the order of governorships on the Mainz inscription once again be regarded as erroneous, but it would be necessary to suppose that he went from Raetia, a province with a legion, to Thrace, a *provincia inermis*, before going on to his three consular provinces. Such an order would be unexampled. There is the further difficulty that Caerellius Sabinus is known to have had a different wife, Fufidia Pollitta.[13] Although it is conceivable that he had married a second time and produced two children by the time he got to Mainz, it is preferable to reject this identification also.

A dating in the 170s therefore still remains the most likely. In that case our governor may be identical with Caerellius Priscus, *praetor tutelaris* under M. Aurelius and L. Verus, i.e. during one of the years 161–9.[14] Equally, the son named on the Mainz inscription, Caerellius Marcianus, may be the same as 'Cerellius Macrinus', included by the *Historia Augusta* in the list of those put to death by Severus.[15] C. Caerellius Sabinus, who could well be a kinsman, was certainly an Italian. While he was in Dacia he made a dedication to Juno Regina Populonia, *dea patria*, an Italian deity,[16] and his son was enrolled in the Oufentina tribe, not found outside the peninsula.[17] But, as G. Alföldy has shown, these Caerellii had links with Africa,[18] and the

---

[10] *PIR*[2] A 1211. If, as is possible, Aemilianus was already in Syria by 185 or 186, his governorship of Britain would have been very brief indeed, between those of Marcellus and Pertinax (pp. 140 ff. below).

[11] To the examples given by Groag, op. cit., add Flavius Catulus Munatianus, *c. p.*, son of Claudius Gallus and Flavia Silva Prisca (*AE* 1957. 123).

[12] *PIR*[2] C 161 gives the evidence, supplemented by *AE* 1965. 40 = *Dacia* 16 (1972) 295 ff. (Apulum), which attests his appointment to Raetia.

[13] *PIR*[2] F 507—she was from Saepinum, cf. *PIR*[2] F 501–6.

[14] *Frag. vat.* 244; *PIR*[2] C 160.

[15] *HA Sev.* 13. 6; *PIR*[2] C 158.

[16] *ILS* 3086 (Apulum), cf. *RE* 21 (1953) 95 ff.

[17] *ILS* 1160 (Rome), cf. Kubitschek 271.

[18] Alföldy, *Bonner Jahrb.* 168 (1968) 138 f. (but he is mistaken in regarding Fufidia Pollitta as African, in view of her family's links with Saepinum, *PIR*[2] F 501-6).

nomenclature of our governor's wife and children also evoke that province.[19]

Ignotus

Dio 72. 8. 1-2: μέγιστος δὲ [sc. πόλεμος] ὁ Βρεττανικός. 2. τῶν γὰρ ἐν τῇ νήσῳ ἐθνῶν ὑπερβεβηκότων τὸ τεῖχος τὸ διόριζον αὐτούς τε καὶ τὰ τῶν Ῥωμαίων στρατόπεδα, καὶ πολλὰ κακουργούντων, στρατηγόν τέ τινα μετὰ τῶν στρατιωτῶν οὓς εἶχε κατακοψάντων, φοβηθεὶς ὁ Κόμμοδος Μάρκελλον Οὔλπιον ἐπ' αὐτοὺς ἔπεμψε.

There is some disagreement over the status of the στρατηγόν . . . τινα killed by the invading northern tribes. It has been assumed that he was merely a legionary legate,[1] but consideration of Dio's usage makes it virtually certain that he was referring to a governor. Elsewhere he employs the term ὑποστράτηγος to describe a legionary legate. There are several examples in different parts of his work, one of which occurs very shortly after this passage.[2] His most frequent term for governor is ἄρχων, but he has alternative expressions, including ἡγεμών and various phrases,[3] and he does use the word στρατηγός where the governor concerned is referred to in a military context. For example, Julius Agricola was maltreated by Domitian ἅτε καὶ μείζονα ἢ κατὰ στρατηγὸν καταπράξας (66. 20. 3). Much more telling, immediately after the passage under discussion, the governor Ulpius Marcellus is described as being ἀϋπνότατος . . . τῶν στρατηγῶν and is called τὸν στρατηγόν (72. 8. 4).[4]

[19] Germanilla is very rare: Kajanto 201 notes that eight out of the eleven epigraphic examples are in VIII. Modestiana is even rarer: Kajanto 263 knows only six cases, of which two are in VIII. Marcianus is commoner and has no special link with Africa, but note two senatorial Geminii, Marcianus and Modestus, from the Cirta region (VIII 5528, Thibilis and 7054, Cirta) and the senator's wife [P]omponia Germanilla from Rusicade (*ILS* 1146).

[1] R. P. Wright, ad *RIB* 1320, comments that 'Dio's phrase . . . is more likely to refer to a less important officer, probably a legionary legate', but offers no arguments. Likewise Frere, *Britannia* (1967) 163: 'the tribes . . . slew a general (no doubt a legionary legate) at the head of his forces', with no discussion. Contrast Grosso, *La lotta politica* 450 n. 2: 'Nel nostro caso l'allusione al governatore sembra evidente', with reference to G. Vrind (see n. 4 below).

[2] 72. 9. 2a (see pp. 139, 260 below); see also 60. 20. 3 (pp. 224 ff. below), 62. 26. 6, probably 78. 21. 2 and 79. 7. 2, where the meaning is also legionary legate. The sense is not certain in 68. 30. 2 and is less precise in 71. 3. 2 and 74. 6. 2.

[3] ἄρχων and related forms are found too frequently to list here. Note also ἡγεμών etc. (56. 18. 3, 58. 25. 4, 60. 25. 6, 62. 7. 1, 71. 2. 2, 71. 23. 3, 72. 11. 4, 72. 12. 3) and other alternatives in 63. 17. 3, 71. 3. 1a.

[4] Note also 69. 19. 2 (ὁ Πλαύτιος στρατηγήσας), 60. 30. 4 (ἐν τῇ Κελτίκῃ στρατηγῶν), 69. 13. 2 (τοὺς κρατίστους τῶν στρατηγῶν . . . ὦν πρῶτος Ἰούλιος Σεουῆρος ὑπῆρχεν), 71. 3. 1¹ (ἥπερ ἐστὶ στρατηγῶν ἀλκή), 75. 6. 2 (τῶν τοῦ Σεουήρου στρατηγῶν ὄντα), all of which refer to governors. Compare too 64. 4. 1: οἱ ἐν ταῖς Γερμανίαις στρατιῶται, οὓς εἶχε Ῥοῦφος, which recalls τῶν στρατιωτῶν οὓς εἶχε in this case. Herodian uses the phrase στρατηγὸς καὶ ἡμεμών to refer to a governor of Pannonia at this period (2. 9. 9). H. J. Mason, *Greek Terms*

Apart from this, what was the position of Ulpius Marcellus? Reference to parallel cases described by Dio indicates that when he says that Commodus Μάρκελλον . . . ἐπ᾽ αὐτοὺς ἔπεμψε, he must mean that Marcellus was appointed governor by Commodus and sent to Britain from outside. Thus Augustus τὸν Τιβέριον . . . ἐς τὴν Δαλματίαν . . . ἔπεμψε (56. 12. 1), and Nero Παῖτον ἐς τὴν Καππαδοκίαν . . . ἀπέστειλεν (62. 20. 4) and ἐπ᾽ αὐτοὺς [sc. the Jews] τὸν Οὐεσπασιανὸν ἔπεμψε (63. 22. 1a).[5] *A fortiori*, of course, if Marcellus had been in Britain already, which has been argued,[6] the στρατηγός who was killed by the invaders could not be the governor. But the examples cited show that Dio's normal usage requires the interpretation that Marcellus came to Britain after the death of the unnamed στρατηγός.

Hence there is no difficulty in regarding the στρατηγός as the governor. There are no clues to his identity, except that one might suspect that he was one of the low-quality governors appointed by Commodus soon after his accession,[7] rather than that he was, for example, an experienced commander such as 'Caerellius'. The date of the episode can be calculated fairly closely. The outside limits are Commodus' accession in March 180 and the British victory won by Marcellus in 184. But the account of the British war is placed after the death of the Quintilii, which may be assigned to 182,[8] and it is prefaced by a reference to fighting against 'the barbarians beyond Dacia'.[9] Hence it seems reasonable to assign the death of the governor to AD 182 or 183.

The question remains, which was τὸ τεῖχος that the barbarians crossed? Dio later uses a similar phrase to refer—it seems clear—to the Antonine Wall.[10] Hence there is a slightly greater likelihood that that

for Roman Institutions. *A lexicon and analysis* (1974) 154 ff., does not offer much help. See also D. Magie, *De Romanorum iuris publici sacrique vocabulis sollemnibus in Graecam sermonem conversis* (1903) 84 f., 122 f., G. Vrind, *De Cassii Dionis vocabulis quae ad ius publicum pertinent* (1923) 52 n. 119, 143 n. 360.

[5] Cf. also 56. 23. 2, 63. 27. 1, 67. 6. 5, 69. 13. 2, 73. 4. 2.

[6] e.g. by D. Atkinson, *JRS* 12 (1922) 68; R. P. Wright, ad *RIB* 1329. See also p. 137 and n. 12 below.

[7] *HA Comm.* 3. 8 (just after his return to Rome in 180): 'misit homines ad provincias regendas vel criminum socios vel a criminosis commendatos.' It may also be remembered that both Ostorius Scapula and Julius Agricola had to face sudden attacks by natives beyond the frontiers immediately after their arrival (pp. 43, 79 above). There may however have been reasons other than the advent of a new legate to provoke attack on this occasion, see below and n. 12.

[8] Dio 72. 5. 3-7. 2; see Grosso, *La lotta politica* 157 ff.

[9] Dio 72. 8. 1; see Grosso, op. cit. 516 ff., who argues that this war ended in 183.

[10] Dio 76. 12. 1: the Maeatae lived next to αὐτῷ τῷ διατειχίσματι ὃ τὴν νῆσον δίχη τέμνει, and the Caledonians lived beyond them. Frere, *Britannia*² (1974) 188, asserts that the Maeatae lived in southern Scotland, because he believes that the διατείχισμα must be Hadrian's Wall. But see K. A. Steer in I. A. Richmond (ed.), *Roman and Native in North Britain* (1958) 92, and I. A. Richmond, *Roman Britain*² (1963) 57, for the other evidence which points firmly to Strathmore and Strathearn, north of the Antonine Wall, as the home of the Maeatae.

Wall was in question here too, although it may not necessarily have been in full commission at the time.[11] The unknown governor may, for example, have been planning to reoccupy it, thus provoking a barbarian attack.[12]

M. Antius Crescens Calpurnianus (*cos. a. inc.*)

VI 1336 = *ILS* 1151, Rome: *M. An*[*tio* . . .] / *Crescent*[*i*] / *Calpurniano* [*cos.*?] [4]/ *proc*[*o*]*s. prov. M*[*aced.*] / *XVvi*[*ro s.*] *f. iurid. Brit.* / *vice leg. leg. pr. pr.* / *prov.* [. . . *cur.*] *r. p.* [8]/ *Mars*[*orum Marruvior.*] / *pr*[*aet.* . . .]

The acting-governorship of this man is attested only by an undated and fragmentary *cursus* from Rome, but an approximate chronology may readily be obtained, for he is also known from three other, dated, inscriptions. Two at Ostia show his presence there in his capacity as *pontifex Volcani* of the colony in the years 194 and 203,[1] while the third, the *Acta* of the Saecular Games of 204, attests his participation in them as one of the *XVviri sacris faciundis*.[2] His tenure of that priesthood is recorded on his *cursus* inscription, apparently in chronological order, which has led to the almost universal—but not wholly compelling—conclusion that his service in Britain, which is mentioned next, must have come not long before. The year 203 is excluded, since he was at Ostia on 24 March in that year, and it has been assumed that he was in Britain *c.*200, serving as acting governor on the death or sudden departure of Virius Lupus.[3]

Further reflection must lead to the conclusion that this dating is far from certain. Given that the XVvirate is indeed listed in chronological order, in other words that Calpurnianus was elected to the college after his service in Britain and before his proconsulship of Macedonia, it does not necessarily follow that he had held these posts

---

[11] Jarrett and Mann, *Bonner Jahrb.* 170 (1970) 193, believe that τὸ τεῖχος in 72. 8. 1 was Hadrian's Wall, but agree that the matter cannot be proved.

[12] See A. R. Birley in *Soldier and Civilian* 87.

[1] XIV 325 (= *ILS* 4176), 324.

[2] VI 32326, line 50, 32327, line 10, 32332, line 3.

[3] See e.g. Atkinson, *JRS* 12 (1922) 60, Barbieri, *L'Albo* no. 34. Hesitation was expressed by A. J. Graham, *JRS* 56 (1966) 103, and J. Morris, *ap.* Jarrett and Mann, *Bonner Jahrb.* 170 (1970) 197 n. 2. In *Ep. Stud.* 4 (1967) 75 f. I suggested that a Commodan date was more satisfactory. Schumacher, *Priesterkollegien* 158 f., 163, prefers the Severan dating on the grounds that the *XVviri* are listed in order of seniority in the *Acta* of the Saecular Games. But his argument depends very largely on the case of Antius Crescens himself, and hence is not compelling.

only a short while before the Saecular Games of 204. If he held his praetorship at the normal age, thirty,[4] his service in Britain presumably came when he was in his mid-thirties (since the *cura* of an Italian community and the legateship in a proconsular province would not occupy more than three years or so). Hence he probably entered the college of *XVviri* at about the age of thirty-eight. There is no reason why he could not have remained alive and an active member for at least another twenty years.

Acting governorships were the product of special circumstances, in most cases (before the third century) resulting from the sudden death of the governor. Sometimes an imperial procurator assumed the governor's role,[5] but there are several cases where a legionary legate took over.[6] The only precedent in Britain is from the year 69, when the legionary legates governed the province jointly after the flight of the governor Trebellius Maximus.[7] At that time, of course, there was no *iuridicus* (so far as is known). Since there is evidence that a governor of Britain was killed in the far north of the province *c.*182-3, it is surely unnecessary to look any further for the occasion when Calpurnianus was *vice leg.* There is no difficulty in supposing that he was still able to participate in the Saecular Games some twenty years later, when he would still have been well under the age of sixty. It so happens that a *XVvir* is known to have died *c.*185, namely C. Aufidius Victorinus (*cos. II ord.* 183).[8] Calpurnianus may well have been elected to replace him—a distinction that might be construed as his reward for meritorious service in Britain. That might also explain his relatively rapid progress to the consulship,[9] after only one further post, as proconsul of Macedonia. By contrast, C. Sabucius Major Caecilianus, after being *iuridicus* of Britain not long before Calpurnianus, had to serve as governor of Belgica, prefect of the military treasury, and proconsul of Achaia, which must have occupied at least seven years, before becoming consul in 186.[10]

Further evidence will be needed before this dating of Calpurnianus'

---

[4] p. 21 above.
[5] e.g. *ILS* 1374, and of course numerous examples from the third century. B. Rémy, *Historia* 25 (1976) 466 ff., gives a list (omitting Crescens Calpurnianus among others).
[6] e.g. *ILS* 1055 and *AE* 1908. 237 (p. 235 below), *IGR* III 175 and 190.
[7] Tac. *Hist.* 1. 60 (pp. 61 above, 231 below).
[8] Dio 72. 11. 1, cf. Grosso, *La lotta politica* 214; Schumacher, *Priesterkollegien* 83, 322.
[9] It must be observed, however, that [*cos.*] is restored on *ILS* 1151, although [*c.v.*] is equally possible, cf. 1150 (another *XVvir*). On the other hand, if Antius Crescens was indeed *iuridicus* in the 180s, he no doubt did achieve the consulship eventually, whether or not it was recorded on *ILS* 1151.
[10] p. 216 below.

acting governorship can be regarded as definite. In the meantime it is worth pointing to another possibility. There are several surprising pieces of information about the British army at this period. An extract from Cassius Dio describes how one Priscus, a legionary legate (ὑποσ-τράτηγος), was invited by the British troops to become emperor, but refused.[11] The *Historia Augusta* states that at the time that Commodus was named Britannicus, the Britons wanted to choose a rival emperor, which suggests that the Priscus affair belongs to 184.[12] The same work also records that during the British war Perennis had removed senators from the command of the legions and replaced them with equestrians—and that this led to his downfall at the hands of the soldiers; this was in 185.[13] Cassius Dio describes how 1,500 men from the British army arrived outside Rome and successfully demanded the right to lynch Perennis.[14] Finally, Dio states that Ulpius Marcellus, who won the British victory of 184, narrowly escaped being sentenced to death after it.[15] It is not impossible that the British legions attempted to make a legionary legate named Priscus emperor; that the legionary commanders were thereupon dismissed on the orders of Perennis; that the governor Marcellus was recalled and put on trial; and that the *iuridicus* was left as acting governor—being the only senator left in the province. But this reconstruction must remain purely hypothetical.

There is no way of telling whether or not Calpurnianus went on to hold further posts after his consulship. But it would not be surprising if he preferred to devote himself to his private or local concerns, for example at Ostia, which was presumably his home.[16] The times were precarious, and many suffered, although there is no good reason to

[11] Dio 72. 9. 2a (pp. 260 f. below).

[12] *HA Comm.* 8. 4: 'appellatus est Commodus etiam Brittannicus ab adulatoribus, cum Brittanni etiam imperatorem contra eum deligere voluerint'. For the date at which the title was assumed (184) see p. 140 and n. 1 below. The affair might be later, while Pertinax was governor; or earlier, if 'ab adulatoribus' may be taken to imply that the title had not been taken officially: see the discussion p. 145 below.

[13] *HA Comm.* 6. 2: 'hic tamen Perennis, qui tantum potuit, subito, quod bello Brittannico militibus equestris loci viros praefecerat amotis senatoribus, prodita re per legatos exercitus hostis appellatus lacerandusque militibus est deditus'. This action must thus antedate the conclusion of the war in 184.

[14] Dio 72. 9. 4, discussed by Grosso, *La lotta politica* 185 ff. P. A. Brunt, *CQ* 23 (1973) 172 ff., quite rightly points out that ὑπάρχοντες has been misinterpreted on several occasions, e.g. by G. M. Bersanetti, *Ath.* 29 (1951) 151 ff., by Grosso, *La lotta politica* 186, and by myself, *Septimius Severus* 121 (and, I must add, in *Soldier and Civilian* 88), to mean 'legionary legates', whereas in fact it is merely a synonym for ὄντες, and must mean 'the soldiers'. Likewise, as Brunt shows, *legatos exercitus* in *HA Comm.* 6. 2 should refer to 'envoys of the army', not *legati legionum.*

[15] Dio 72. 8. 6 (p. 142 below).

[16] There are no other clues to his origin. For the priests of Vulcan at Ostia, who seem to be local worthies, see R. Meiggs, *Roman Ostia*² (1973), esp. 177 ff.

believe that Calpurnianus was related to M. Antonius Antius Lupus, one of Commodus' victims.[17] No certain relatives or descendants are in fact on record, but M. Antius Grat[il]lianus, quaestor of Sicily in the year 213, could be his son.[18]

184   Ulpius Marcellus (*cos. a. inc.*)

VII 504 = *RIB* 1329, Benwell: *Deo Anocitico / iudiciis optimo/rum maximorum* [4] / *que impp. n. sub Ulp. / Marcello cos. Tine/ius Longus in p* [re] / *fectura equitu* [m] [8] / *lato clavo exorna/tus et q. d.*

EE IX 1171 = *RIB* 1463, Chesters: *aqua adducta / alae II Astur. / sub Ulp. Mar-cello* [4] / *leg. Aug. pr. pr.*

VII 592 = *RIB* 1464, Chesters: [. . . *ala*] *II Ast* [*urum / sub*] *Ulpio* [*Marcello leg. / Au*]*g. pr. pr.*

Dio 72. 8. 2–6.

At first sight Ulpius Marcellus appears to be as well attested as one might wish. Two complete inscriptions and another fragmentary one record his name as governor, his tenure of office is described in some detail by Cassius Dio, and external evidence allows the successful conclusion of his campaign to be dated precisely to the year 184.[1] But closer inspection reveals a serious difficulty. The Benwell inscription has the phrase *iudiciis optimorum maximorumque impp. n.*, which must mean that it was set up during, or at least very shortly after, a joint reign. Yet Dio's account and a study of his usage elsewhere combine to show that Marcellus must have been sent to Britain by Commodus as sole emperor, while the British war which led to his dispatch there seems not to have begun until well after Commodus' accession. Hence it is quite impossible to argue that Marcellus was already in Britain under the joint reign of M. Aurelius and Commodus—besides, it has been shown earlier that the unnamed στρατηγός whose death made the appointment of Marcellus necessary must himself have been the governor.[2] Hence, either Marcellus must have been governor of Britain twice,[3] for which there is no precedent or parallel—and which

---

[17] *ILS* 127, *HA Comm.* 7. 5, *PIR*[2] A 812.

[18] X 7228 (Lilybaeum).

[1] *BMC* IV 797 nos. 550 f.; Grosso, *La lotta politica* 518 f. M. G. Jarrett, *Britannia* 9 (1978) 289 n. 1 states that 'Presumably victory had been achieved by 183', which is implausible.

[2] p. 135 above.

[3] As proposed by Atkinson, *JRS* 12 (1922) 68, but he preferred the view that Marcellus was governor *c.*179–84, which has been followed widely. See also Jarrett and Mann, *Bonner Jahrb.* 170 (1970) 192 ff. Jarrett, *Britannia* 9 (1978) 290 f., fails to explain this difficulty.

would have required a mention even in the abbreviated version of Dio —or the Benwell inscription must be referred to another man. The only solution which caters adequately for the present evidence appears to be that there were two governors called Ulpius Marcellus, one under Commodus and a second in the next generation, datable to the years 211–12.

Clearly the Benwell inscription must belong to the second Ulpius Marcellus. The two Chesters inscriptions could be assigned to either. In favour of the second it may be noted that the *ala II Asturum* is not otherwise recorded at Chesters before the third century.[4] The very identity of the Commodan governor is subject to some uncertainty, but on balance it seems highly improbable that he could be the Antonine jurist, described by the *Historia Augusta* as a legal adviser to Antoninus Pius and cited in the *Digest* for a decision of M. Aurelius of AD 166.[5] Dio's description of his habits conveys an impression of a stern and eccentric character, but this does not of itself demonstrate even that the governor was an old man, let alone that he was the celebrated jurist. The governor might, on the other hand, be the L. Ulpius Marcellus recorded as legate of Lower Pannonia on an undated inscription at Sopianae, which has been assigned to the 170s.[6]

His nomenclature is rather indistinctive, but the imperial *gentilicium* does suggest provincial or perhaps libertine extraction. At Rome one may note an Ulpius Marcellus, grandson of a centurion in the *vigiles* who was first commissioned in Syria,[7] and a M. Ulpius Aug. lib. Marcellus;[8] and, more promising in view of his senatorial rank, C. Ulpius Marcellus Polybianus, *c. i.*, whose second *cognomen* evokes Greek or freedman origin.[9] Finally, attention should be drawn to Ulpius Tatianus Marcellus of Pisidian Antioch[10] and to Ulpia Marcella, wife of P. Aelius Paullus, high priest of Asia, a native of Thyateira.[11] The apparent existence of a second governor of Britain named Ulpius Marcellus has already been referred to. It may be noted now only that the interval is

---

[4] The *coh. I Dalmatarum* was at Chesters in the later second century: *JRS* 47 (1957) 229. For the *ala II Asturum*, see *RIB* 1462–7, 1480. Jarrett, *Maryport, Cumbria: A Roman Fort and its Garrison* 23 f., explains the evidence otherwise; see also id., *Britannia* 9 (1978) 291.

[5] *HA Ant. Pius* 12. 1; *Digest* 28. 4. 3. See W. Kunkel, *Herkunft und soziale Stellung der römischen Juristen* (1952) 213 ff., who doubts the identity of the jurist and the governor.

[6] *ILS* 3795. See Fitz, *A. Ant. Hung.* 11 (1963) 273 f.; but he is more doubtful about the date in *Alba Regia* 10 (1969) 179 f., and ibid. 11 (1970) 148 f. and 16 (1978) 369 f. favours a third-century date. See also n. 12 below.

[7] *ILS* 2173 (Rome).

[8] *AE* 1908. 230 (Rome).

[9] VI 1542 = 31676 (also mentioning his brother C. Ulpius Aelianus Severus).

[10] *IGR* III 299 *JRS* 3 (1913) 287 ff.

[11] *IGR* IV 1225, cf. 1254. Note also another Ulpia Marcella, honoured at Lystra (W. M. Ramsay, *The Social Basis of Roman Power in Asia Minor* (1941) 185 no. 171); an Ulpia Marcella near Theveste (VIII 27994); and Q. Ulpius Marcellus in Mauretania Sitifensis (VIII 20524).

exactly right, about thirty years, which is often found to be the gap between tenure of office by father and son.[12] Further discussion may be reserved to the appropriate place.[13]

It must be noted in conclusion that after Marcellus' 'ruthless suppression of the barbarians', for which Commodus took his seventh imperatorial acclamation and the title Britannicus in AD 184, the governor was 'very close to the point of being put to death because of his peculiar excellence, but was nevertheless pardoned'. Dio does not make it clear whether or not there was any appreciable interval between Marcellus' victory and his recall, but it is plausible to suppose that it was the governor's harsh methods which provoked the outbreak of mutiny among the legions. Hence there is no need to postulate a further governor before the arrival of Pertinax.[14] It now appears that Marcellus' pardon was sufficiently complete to permit him to go on to the proconsulship of Asia, evidently in 189.[15] In that case, it is reasonable to suppose that he had been consul *c.*174.[16]

P. Helvius Pertinax (*cos. II ord.* 192)

Dio 72. 9. 2[2]; 73. 5. 1.

HA Pert. 3. 5–4. 1: occiso sane Perenni Commodus Pertinaci satisfecit eumque petit per litteras, ut ad Brittanniam proficisceretur. 6. profectusque milites ab omni seditione deterruit, cum illi quemcumque imperatorem vellent habere et ipsum specialiter Pertinacem. 7. tunc Pertinax malivolentiae notam subit, quod dictus est insimulasse apud Commodum adfectati imperii Antistium Burrum et Arrium Antoninum. 8. et seditiones quidem contra Commodum ipse conpescuit in Brittannia, verum ingens periculum adit seditione legionis paene occisus, certe inter occisos relictus. 9. quam quidem rem idem Pertinax acerrime vindicavit. 10. denique

---

[12] See e.g. the Acilii Glabriones, consuls in 91, 124, 152 (Degrassi, *FC* 143 f.); Bruttii Praesentes in 217 and 249 (ibid. 159); Ceionii Commodi in 78, 106, and 136 (ibid. 165)—many more examples may be found. Note the third-century consular named Ulpius Marcellus in an inscription from Side: *AE* 1966. 460 (AD 256). Fitz, *Alba Regia* 16 (1978) 369 f., identifies this man with the Pannonian governor of *ILS* 3795.

[13] pp. 165 f. below.

[14] Grosso, *La lotta politica* 183 ff., argues that Marcellus was dismissed and tried late in 184, which seems unnecessary. I am puzzled by the remarks of Brunt, *CQ* N.S. 23 (1973) 176 n. 3: 'we do not know when or why he was tried for his life (Grosso's date of 184 . . . seems too early to me), but he was perhaps blamed for the breakdown of discipline; he was hardly still governor in 185'. It is certainly reasonable to suggest that he was tried for allowing the troops to become undisciplined. But there seems no need to postulate a long interval between his recall from Britain and his trial. However, it is possible that there was an acting governor for a short period between his departure and the arrival of Pertinax; see p. 139 above, on Antius Crescens.

[15] As revealed by an inscription from Aphrodisias in which Marcellus is referred to, apparently as proconsul. I am grateful to Miss J. M. Reynolds for this information.

[16] The inscription is dated by Commodus' fifth consulship and fourteenth *trib. pot.* to 10–31 Dec. 189. For the proconsular interval, see p. 32 above.

postea veniam legationis petit dicens sibi ob defensam disciplinam infestas esse legiones. 4.1 accepto successore alimentorum ei cura mandata est.

The career of Pertinax is one of the most remarkable in the history of the principate.[1] He is exceptional, although not of course unique, among governors of Britain in being the subject of an ancient biography, a distinction which he owed to his brief reign as emperor. The *vita* in the *Historia Augusta*, although not free from contamination, is one of the more factual in that unsatisfactory work, and the details of his career which it supplies have been authenticated by a number of inscriptions. These include a stone from Brühl, near Cologne in Lower Germany, recording most of his career before he entered the senate.[2] Further confirmation of some items, not least of his British governorship, is supplied by Cassius Dio.

He was born on 1 August 126 at his mother's villa at Alba Pompeia in Liguria, his father being a freedman named Helvius Successus.[3] Initially Pertinax took up the career of schoolmaster, following in the footsteps of his own teacher Sulpicius Apollinaris.[4] Finding this profession insufficiently lucrative, he applied for a centurion's commission, using the good offices of his father's patron Lollianus Avitus (*cos. ord.* 144). This application was evidently unsuccessful[5] and he had to be content with the less permanent, if more honorific, status of equestrian officer, which he gained with the assistance of another patron, Ti. Claudius Pompeianus (*cos. II ord.* 173).[6] He took command of the *cohors VII Gallorum equitata* in Syria, before the death of Antoninus Pius.[7] He distinguished himself in the Parthian war, which broke out soon afterwards, and he was promoted to a tribunate in the British legion VI Victrix.[8] This was followed by a second post in Britain and then the command of an *ala* in Moesia.[9] It may be suggested that his

---

[1] Hence it has been the subject of copious attention by modern scholars. I refrain from giving a full bibliography here. See Alföldy, *Situla* 14/15 (1974) 199 ff., with reference to modern studies.

[2] H.-G. Kolbe, *Bonner Jahrb.* 162 (1962) 410 ff. = *AE* 1963. 52.

[3] Dio 73. 3. 1; *HA Pert.* 1. 1-2.

[4] *HA Pert.* 1. 4.

[5] *HA Pert.* 1. 5: There is no trace of the centurionate on the Brühl inscription, but it is in any case likely that he did not obtain it, cf. *PIR*² H 73: 'non impetravit, ut videtur'.

[6] Dio 73. 3. 1; *HA Pert.* 1. 6.

[7] *AE* 1963. 52; see M. M. Roxan, *Ep. Stud.* 9 (1972) 246 f. for this unit.

[8] *HA Pert.* 2. 1; *AE* 1963. 52.

[9] *HA Pert.* 2. 2. Kolbe, *Bonner Jahrb.* 162 (1962) 415, interprets the Brühl inscription as [. . . *trib. leg. VI Vi*]*ct.* [*p*]*rae*[*f. coh. Tungr. pr*]*aef.* [*a*]*lae* [. . .], since the two Tungrian cohorts were the only milliary cohorts of which the commanding officers were called *praefectus* instead of *tribunus*. His major reason for favouring this view is that Pertinax's first procuratorial appointment was sexagenary, and therefore too lowly for his last appointment in the *militiae equestres* to have been a prefecture of a milliary *ala*. However, as I pointed out in *Provincialia* 223 f. n. 49, Pertinax might have received higher pay than normal in his first

posting to Britain may have been on the recommendation of Cn. Julius Verus, who was governor of Syria *c.*163, while the transfer from Britain to the Danube may reflect the career of Sex. Calpurnius Agricola, who made this move himself *c.*166, and may have taken Pertinax with him.[10]

Pertinax now began a procuratorial career, in charge of the *alimenta* along the *via Aemilia*, a particularly important region at that time, *c.*168, when there were major concentrations of troops taking place there for the German war.[11] He was then dispatched to the Rhine as prefect of the *classis Germanica*.[12] But he cannot have held this post for long, since he was transferred to a procuratorship in Dacia before 170.[13] His career met with a brief setback at this point, and he was dismissed as the result of an intrigue against him, but shortly afterwards he was recalled to assist Pompeianus—who had now become a son-in-law of M. Aurelius—in the urgent task of clearing the German invaders out of Italy.[14] His conduct won him adlection to senatorial rank, followed before long by promotion to the rank of ex-praetor and the command of the legion I Adiutrix.[15] In this post he achieved a remarkable victory in barbarian territory, *c.*172.[16] During the remainder of the 170s he went on to govern both Upper and Lower Moesia, the III Daciae, and Syria, obtaining the consulship, which he held *in absentia* as the colleague of Didius Julianus, probably in 175.[17]

procuratorial post, and thus could have commanded a quingenary *ala* in Britain, followed by a milliary *ala*, *in Moesia*. Dio says that 'he became a χιλίαρχος in the cavalry through his association with Ti. Claudius Pompeianus'. The phrase ἐν τοῖς ἱππεῦσι χιλιαρχήσας could be an exact translation of *praefectus alae milliariae*. Note *ILS* 407, Sirmium, a dedication made by Pertinax as *praef.* of an unspecified unit. Sirmium is in Lower Pannonia, of which Pompeianus was governor in 167 (XVI 123). The *ala* may then have moved to Upper Moesia. At present, the question must remain undecided.

[10] pp. 120, 129 above.

[11] Pflaum, *CP* no. 179, regards the procuratorship as sexagenary. But see n. 9 above. For the importance of the area in 168, see above, p. 131 on Antistius Adventus.

[12] *HA Pert.* 2. 4; *AE* 1963. 52.

[13] *HA Pert.* 2. 4; *AE* 1963. 52—set up on the occasion of his transfer. For the nature of the Dacian post see now Alföldy, *Situla* 14/15 (1974) 202 n. 12.

[14] *HA Pert.* 2. 4; Dio 71. 3. 2. See A. R. Birley, *Provincialia* 214 ff.; Alföldy, *Situla* 14/15 (1974) 203 f.

[15] *HA Pert.* 2. 5-6.

[16] Eusebius-Jerome *Chron.* under the year 173 ascribes the command over Roman forces at the battle of the Rain Miracle to Pertinax, not M. Aurelius. See A. R. Birley, *Marcus Aurelius* 326 on the chronological problems.

[17] *HA Pert.* 2. 10-11. I argued in *A. Ant. Philip.* 109 ff. that Pertinax, along with several other men, governed Upper Moesia before the consulship (following a suggestion of E. Birley). Alföldy, *Situla* 14/15 (1974) 208 f., is sceptical in the case of Pertinax, and another possible praetorian governor is now rather more doubtful (see p. 123 n. 13 above). The matter must therefore remain doubtful, although I am not convinced that *HA Pert.* 3. 2 (*post quattuor provincias consulares*, the two Moesiae, Dacia, and Syria) necessarily proves that Pertinax governed Upper Moesia after his consulship. The source of the *HA* may have been unaware of a temporary change of status.

He seems to have been governing Syria at the time of M. Aurelius' death in 180, and to have remained there for some two years,[18] returning to Rome *c*.182 to enter the senate-house for the first time after governing four consular provinces.[19] The praetorian prefect Perennis was now dominant, and he compelled Pertinax to withdraw from public life to his father's estate in Liguria.[20] He remained there for three years, engaging in business, and it was only after the death of Perennis in 185 that he was recalled, when Commodus wrote to him with the request that he assume the governorship of Britain.[21] The army of the province was in a mutinous state. Due to the influence of Perennis the legionary legates had been dismissed and replaced by equestrian officers, perhaps as a result of the Priscus affair, when a legionary commander of that name had been offered the purple by the troops. A detachment of 1,500 troops from the British army was directly instrumental in bringing about the overthrow of Perennis, whom they lynched outside Rome.[22] But the British legions were still not satisfied. Cassius Dio records in two separate places merely that Pertinax suppressed the mutiny. The biographer in the *Historia Augusta* adds details, the veracity of which may be a little suspect. Apparently the troops still wanted another emperor, preferably Pertinax himself,[23] but he managed to repress them, although with difficulty, and he nearly lost his life in a riot at the hands of one of the legions. He then requested the emperor to send a replacement, since the legions resented his restoration of discipline.

His return to Rome was probably in 187.[24] He was evidently given a new appointment at once, as prefect of the *alimenta*.[25] This was followed, probably in 188-9, by a year as proconsul of Africa.[26] Soon after this he reached the pinnacle of the senatorial career with the prefecture of the city of Rome, in addition to which—as was customary for city prefects—he was given a second consulship, as *ordinarius* for the year 192 with the emperor as his colleague.[27]

In the course of 192—at the latest—a conspiracy was hatched by the

[18] *HA Pert.* 3. 1-4.
[19] *HA Pert.* 3. 2.
[20] *HA Pert.* 3. 3.
[21] *HA Pert.* 3. 5.
[22] p. 139 above.
[23] Some would date the Priscus affair to this period, rather than to 183 or 184: see p. 260 below.
[24] Grosso, *La lotta politica* 254 ff. (with a discussion of Pertinax's involvement in the downfall of Antistius Burrus and Arrius Antoninus).
[25] *HA Pert.* 4. 1.
[26] *HA Pert.* 4. 2; see Thomasson, *Statthalter Nordafrikas* II 91 f.
[27] *HA Pert.* 4. 2-3.

praetorian prefect Q. Aemilius Laetus which resulted in the murder of Commodus and the proclamation of Pertinax as his successor on the last day of the year.[28] But Pertinax's reign lasted only until 28 March 193, when he himself was murdered.[29] His career had been truly astonishing. In this context it must be noted that his governorship of Britain was the product of very exceptional circumstances.

His son of the same names survived him, to be murdered by Caracalla in 212.[30]

192-197   D. Clodius (Septimius) Albinus (*cos. II ord.* 194)

Dio 73. 14. 3; Herodian 2. 15; 3. 6. 6; 3. 7. 1.

Aur. Vict. *de Caes.* 29. 8-9: Pescennium Nigrum apud Cyzicenos, Clodium Albinum Lugduni victos coegit mori . . . alter Pertinacis auctor occidendi, cum eo metu in Britannos, quam provinciam a Commodo meruerat, transmittere niteretur, in Gallia invaserat imperium.

HA Clod. Alb. 3. 4: cum Brittannicos exercitus regeret iussu Commodi . . .

Like Pertinax, Albinus is the subject of a *vita* in the *Historia Augusta*; in this case, unfortunately, a very high proportion of the contents is pure fiction.[1] There is, however, a little evidence from elsewhere. Albinus is revealed governing Britain immediately after the murder of Pertinax, in late March 193, as one of the three principal contenders against Didius Julianus, along with Pescennius Niger in Syria and Septimius Severus in Pannonia. Since the *Historia Augusta* specifically states in the biography of Pertinax that that emperor did not remove any of those 'quos Commodus rebus gerendis inposuerat',[2] it may safely be taken that Albinus was already in Britain in 192, confirming the garbled remarks in Aurelius Victor, as well as in the *vita Albini*, that he was appointed to the province by Commodus. It is unlikely that he was the direct successor of Pertinax in the governorship, for the latter's tenure terminated abruptly, at his own request, hardly later than 187. Otherwise, Albinus would have been in the province for over five years by the

---

[28] I have discussed this at length in *Bonner Jahrb.* 169 (1969) 247 ff. and *Septimius Severus* (1971) 131 ff.

[29] *PIR*[2] H 73.

[30] *PIR*[2] H 74. Pertinax's wife was Flavia Titiana: *PIR*[2] F 444.

[1] This was demonstrated by J. Hasebroek, *Die Fälschung der Vita Nigri und Vita Albini in den Scriptores Historiae Augustae* (1916). See also *PIR*[2] C 1186 and most recently Alföldy, *H-A-C 1966/7* (1968) 19 ff. T. D. Barnes's comment in *H-A-C 1968/9* (1970) 55, that Alföldy 'wishes to rescue his [Albinus'] bogus career', can only be based on an inadequate study of that article. See now Alföldy, *Konsulat* 62 n. 4.

[2] *HA Pert.* 12. 8: 'sane nullum ex his, quos Commodus rebus gerendis inposuerat, mutavit'.

time of Commodus' death, which does not conform with the practice of the period.[3]

His origin is clearly stated in the *vita*: 'familia nobili, Hadrumetinus tamen ex Africa'.[4] Doubt has been cast on this, understandably enough, since the biography contains so much blatant invention. On the other hand, the information does appear to be confirmed by the coinage struck for Albinus, which portrays the deity Baal-Hammon, under the Roman name Saeculum Frugiferum.[5] Although Baal-Hammon was worshipped elsewhere in Africa as well as at Hadrumetum,[6] that city, the *colonia Ulpia Traiana Frugifera*,[7] can be seen from its Roman title to have had special links with the deity, and the fifth-century-BC relief found there bears a remarkable resemblance to the figure on Albinus' coins.[8] Thus it seems possible to accept that in this instance the *vita* supplies an authentic fact, perhaps derived from the biography of Severus by Marius Maximus.[9]

It is another matter with the career which the *vita* ascribes to Albinus. Neither the chronology nor the appointments themselves can be accepted as authentic, although it is probable enough that he held the praetorship,[10] and there may be some basis in another statement. Characteristically, the biographer is quite ignorant of the item transmitted by Cassius Dio, that Albinus (along with Pescennius Niger) won distinction in a war with 'the barbarians beyond Dacia' at the beginning of Commodus' reign.[11] If, as is probable, he was then serving as a legionary legate, V Macedonica is the likeliest of the legions in question.[12]

[3] Note especially the rapid turnover in Syria: Pertinax (p. 145 above), C. Domitius Dexter (*PIR*[2] D 144), C. Julius Saturninus (*PIR*[2] J 547), Asellius Aemilianus (pp. 133 f. above), and Pescennius Niger (Dio 73. 14. 3 etc.). The *fasti* of the other consular provinces are too incomplete for certainty, but note also Thrace (at least five governors: Stein, *Thracia* 32 ff.) and Egypt (ten or more prefects: Bastianini, *ZPE* 17 (1975) 299 ff.).

[4] *HA Clod. Alb.* 1. 3, 4. 1.

[5] *BMC* V pp. lxxxix–xl and 134, Severus no. 539, etc.

[6] A point stressed by H. Dessau, *Phil. Wochenschr.* 35 (1918) 319 f., referring especially to A. Merlin, *Notes et documents* 4 (1910) 17, pl. II, and 39 ff.

[7] VI 1687 = *ILS* 6111.

[8] P. Cintas, *Revue africaine* 91 (1947) 1 ff.

[9] See further A. R. Birley, *Bonner Jahrb.* 169 (1969) 265 f., Alföldy, *H-A-C 1966/7* (1968) 20 ff. Barnes, *H-A-C 1968/9* (1970) 51 ff., remains unconvinced, although he concedes (p. 55) in the coins 'the temptation to see an allusion to Albinus' supposed Hadrumetine origin, or, less specifically, proof that he came from Africa. And it is hard to produce any other reasonable explanation for the type of these coins'. But to conclude that 'as concerns Albinus' *origo* there is still a gap in the argument: how particular types (or even legends) came to be put on the Roman coins is utterly unknown' is a counsel of despair. (The prominence given to the god Elagabalus by the emperor normally given that name may be recalled.)

[10] But not at the date or the stage in his career given by *HA Clod. Alb.* 6. 7. See Alföldy, *H-A-C 1966/7* (1968) 26.

[11] Dio 72. 8. 1. For the date see Grosso, *La lotta politica* 512 ff.

[12] Alföldy, *H-A-C 1966/7* (1968) 26, regards this as probable but notes that he might have fought in this war with one of the Moesian legions.

Thereafter he may have gone on to govern a praetorian province or to hold an equivalent post at Rome, followed by the consulship, *c.*187.[13] The *vita* alleges that he was 'per Commodum ad Galliam translatus, in qua fusis gentibus Transrenanis celebre nomen suum et apud Romanos et apud barbaros fecit'.[14] G. Alföldy has re-examined the fragments of a building inscription from Cologne, assignable to the period 184-92, on which the governor's name may be restored as [*D. Clo*]*dio* [*Albin*]*o*.[15] Since at least five, and probably more, of Albinus' predecessors as governors of Britain had previously governed Lower Germany (and two of his successors were to come from there),[16] it is at least highly plausible that he did likewise. The biographer may have obtained from Marius Maximus a brief statement that Albinus had campaigned against the Germans on the right bank of the Rhine before going to Britain.[17] At any rate, if the possibility that Albinus governed Lower Germany be accepted, it makes it highly improbable that he arrived in Britain before 191.

The sequence of events after the assassination of Commodus has been much discussed and cannot be analysed again in detail here.[18] But it must be noted that there is no warrant for the *Historia Augusta*'s wilful assertion that Albinus was offered the title Caesar by Commodus.[19] Another dubious story, that he was behind the murder of Pertinax, is also found in Aurelius Victor and Eutropius, and may derive from Severan propaganda, designed to discredit Albinus after the breach between himself and Severus. It may have been given some plausibility by some indirect links between Albinus and Pertinax's successor Didius Julianus.[20]

Albinus received the title Caesar from Severus in the period immediately after the latter's proclamation as emperor on 9 April 193. It would not be rash to assume that he was using it within a matter of weeks. Coins were struck in his honour and he was the colleague of Severus as *cos. II ord.* for 194, *in absentia*.[21] The biography mentions

[13] Alföldy, *H-A-C 1966/7* (1968) 27.

[14] *HA Clod. Alb.* 6. 3, cf. 5. 5.

[15] XIII 8598, see Alföldy, *H-A-C 1966/7* (1968) 28 ff.

[16] See p. 390 below.

[17] Barnes, *H-A-C 1968/9* (1970) 55 n. 91, notes that 'the only real possibility seems to be Marius Maximus', on whom see also A. R. Birley, *Septimius Severus* 308 ff.

[18] See e.g. A. R. Birley, *Bonner Jahrb.* 169 (1969) 247 ff.; *Septimius Severus* 144 ff.

[19] *HA Clod. Alb.* 13. 4 etc.

[20] Aur. Vict. *de Caes.* 20. 9; Eutrop. 8. 18. 4; *HA Clod. Alb.* 1. 1, 14. 2. 6; see A. R. Birley, *Bonner Jahrb.* 169 (1969) 266.

[21] See *PIR*² C 1186 for references; further, A. R. Birley, *Septimius Severus* 187 ff.

this, although unaware that it was a second consulship.[22] The inscriptions and coins give him a second *nomen*, Septimius, which he clearly assumed in honour of his senior colleague. He does not appear to have received any additional powers, and there is no good evidence for his activities between the spring of 193 and winter of 195. It seems to have been then that the breach with Severus came, a move adumbrated by the honours given to Severus' son Caracalla. Albinus crossed into Gaul, with, no doubt, a large part of the British garrison, and was proclaimed emperor there. He issued coins as Augustus, but did not claim the tribunician power or other items which could only be granted at Rome. He won some successes in the course of 196, seizing Lugdunum, and defeating at least one of Severus' generals, Virius Lupus, probably governor of Lower Germany. But he himself was defeated and killed at the battle of Lugdunum on 19 February 197.[23]

The name of his wife is unknown—she may have been an Asellia, since Cassius Dio says that Asellius Aemilianus, proconsul of Asia in 192-3 and Pescennius Niger's principal lieutenant, was related to Albinus.[24] A suspect passage of the *Historia Augusta* supplies another kinsman, Clodius Celsinus.[25] He is said to have had either one son or two sons, put to death at the same time as himself.[26] Not surprisingly no descendants are known, although the fourth-century Ceionii Albini may have claimed him as an ancestor.[27]

197   **Virius Lupus** (*cos. a. inc.*)

VII 210 = *RIB* 637, Ilkley: [*Imp. Caes. L. Sept*]/*im*[*ius*] *Severus. P.* / *Aug. et Antoninus*[4]/ *Caes. imp. destinatus res*/*tituerunt curante Vir*/*io Lupo leg. eorum pr. pr.*

VII 273 = *RIB* 730, Bowes: *D*<*e*>*ae Fortunae* / *Virius Lupus* / *leg. Aug. pr. pr.* [4]/ *balineum vi* / *ignis exust*/*um coh. I Thr*/*acum resti*[8]/*tuit curan*/*te Val. Fron*/*tone praef.* / *eq. alae Vetto.*

---

[22] *HA Clod. Alb.* 6. 8.
[23] *PIR*[2] C 1186. For Lupus, see below. On the battle, see now A. J. Graham, *Historia* 27 (1978) 625 ff.
[24] Dio 74. 6. 2; see A. R. Birley, *Bonner Jahrb.* 169 (1969) 266.
[25] *HA Sev.* 11. 3. Syme, *Ammianus and the Historia Augusta* 155 f., and Barnes, *H-A-C 1968/9* (1970) 51 f., may be right in regarding this passage as fictional and the person as spurious. I attempted a justification in *Septimius Severus* (1971) 198.
[26] *HA Sev.* 10. 1, cf. 11. 9, *Clod. Alb.* 9. 5. The son 'Princus' in *Clod. Alb.* 7. 5 is clearly fictitious.
[27] This would explain the *HA*'s references to Ceionii in *Clod. Alb.* 4. 1 ff. etc. But perhaps it is more likely that the author of the *HA* was 'amusing himself with mild parody of the pretension advertised by the Roman aristocracy' in an age when 'gross genealogical fantasies' abounded, as Syme, *Ammianus and the Historia Augusta* 163, pointed out.

EE IX 1384 = *RIB* 1163, Corbridge: *vexi*[*llatio*] / *leg. V*[*I Vic. p. f.*] / *sub c*[*ura Viri*] ⁴/ *Lup*[*i v. c. cos.?*]

Dio 75. 5. 4.

Digest 28. 6. 2. 4: Prius autem sibi quis debet heredem scribere, deinde filio substituere et non convertere ordinem scripturae: et hoc Iulianus putat prius sibi debere, deinde filio heredem scribere: ceterum si ante filio, deinde sibi testamentum faciat, non valere. quae sententia rescripto imperatoris nostri ad Virium Lupum Brittanniae praesidem comprobata est, et merito.

Virius Lupus' origin cannot be established with certainty, but the *gentilicium* is particularly common in nothern Italy.[1] His *praenomen* is nowhere attested, but was very probably the same as that of the *consules ordinarii* of 230 and 232, L. Virius Agricola and L. Virius Lupus Julianus, who may be assumed to be his sons;[2] and it may be noted that there are more LL. Virii in northern Italy than elsewhere.[3]

The inscription from Ilkley recording Lupus as governor should belong to 197, since Caracalla, who became Augustus in January 198, is called *Antoninus Caes. imp. destinatus.*[4] This leaves no doubt that Lupus was sent to Britain immediately after the defeat of Albinus. His first appearance in the historical record comes just a little before this, since he must be the general Lupus who was defeated by Albinus before the battle of Lugdunum.[5] It is reasonable to assume that he was then governor of Lower Germany, although this is nowhere made explicit.[6] In that case, he was certainly consular in status when in Britain, and was operating in the area that later belonged to the praetorian province of Lower Britain. Hence, either Herodian was simply mistaken in stating that Britain was divided in 197, or the boundaries were different from those found later and Lower Britain was consular.[7]

The fragment of Cassius Dio recording Lupus' dealings with the two principal hostile tribes suggests that the Roman position in the north of the province was weak. From the mention of prisoners it can be inferred that the Maeatae had already invaded the province, and the reference to 'large sums of money' to buy the Maeatae off permits the

[1] Over seventy examples in V (compared with nine in II, sixteen in III, eighteen in VIII, two in IX, sixteen in X and XI, thirteen in XII, one in XIII, and one or two in XIV S).

[2] Barbieri, *L'Albo* nos. 1186–7. The latter is known to have been patrician: ibid. p. 487 no. 72.

[3] Eight examples in V, against four in X, no more than two elsewhere (not counting VI).

[4] See e.g. *RE* 2. 2 (1896) 2440 f. For the date of Caracalla's assumption of the title Augustus (28 Jan. 198) see J. Guey, *REA* 50 (1948) 60 ff.

[5] Dio 75. 6. 2.

[6] Groag, *ap.* Ritterling, *FRD* 76 f., following J. Hasebroek, *Untersuchungen zur Geschichte des Septimius Severus* (1921) 96.

[7] pp. 168 ff. below.

conclusion that there was a threat of renewed attack. The inscriptions at both Ilkley and Bowes record rebuilding, that at Corbridge building.[8] There is no indication of what had necessitated the work, for the reference to 'destruction by fire' at Bowes is uninformative, but it is perfectly possible that either Brigantian tribesmen from the Pennine hills or invaders from Scotland had caused the damage.[9] Not much can be done with the rescript in the *Digest*, pleasant though it is to be reminded that Lupus also had to attend to the governor's non-military functions.

While the Ilkley inscription, which should be early, calls Lupus *leg. eorum*, he is *leg. Aug.* on the stone from Bowes. It may at least be suggested that this implies that it was not much later than 198, before the army had become accustomed once more, after an interval of nearly twenty years, to having joint Augusti. Lupus is not heard of again, but there is no particular reason to suppose either that he died in office or that he expired soon after his governorship ended. In the absence of other information it will be safest to assume that he was replaced some three years later, in 200.

As already mentioned, the consuls of 230 and 232 were presumably his sons, and later Virii Lupi are also attested, including the *cos. II ord.* of 278 and a *consularis Campaniae* of the 360s.[10] Lupus was in fact one of several Severan generals to found noble houses which lasted into the fourth century.[11] The *cognomina* of his presumed sons, Agricola and Lupus Julianus, encourage the speculation that Lupus might have been married to a descendant of Cn. Julius Agricola. However, several other explanations of this nomenclature are possible.[12]

Pollienus Auspex (*cos. a. inc.*)

Arch.-Ep. Mitt. 19 (1896) 147 ff. = *AE* 1897. 78 = *IGR* III 618 = *ILS* 8841 = *TAM* II 278, Xanthus: [...] ε / [...] μι [...] αυιατ/[... Πολλήνια] ν Ὀ[ν]ωράταν ἐκγόνη[ν]

---

[8] Jarrett and Mann, *Bonner Jahrb.* 170 (1970) 196, claim that as only LV can be read of the governor's name in *RIB* 1163 the attribution is uncertain. However, R. P. Wright, ad loc., is confident about the reading LVP; he also notes that only [*v. c. cos.*] will fit the space at the end of line 4. If this can be accepted, it is of course important as confirmation of the rank of Lupus.

[9] I have discussed the events of 196–7 in Britain elsewhere, *Arch. Ael.*[4] 50 (1972) 179 ff., and therefore refrain from a detailed re-examination here.

[10] See *PLRE* Lupus nos. 5–7.

[11] Q. Anicius Faustus is the most notable example: see *PLRE* stemma no. 7.

[12] For a second-century bearer of the names Julius Agricola see p. 81 n. 58 above. But note that Sex. Calpurnius Agricola may have had a kinsman called Sex. Calpurnius Julianus (p. 123 above).

*⁴/ΦΛ. Λατρωνιανοῦ ὑπατικοῦ / ποντίφικος ἐπάρχου Ῥώμης / [κ]αὶ Αὖσπικος ὑπατι-
κοῦ Βρι/ταννίας Μυσίας Δακίας Σπα⁸/νίας ἐν χώρᾳ Σεβαστοῦ δικά/σαντος προεκ-
γόνην Αὖσπι/κος, ὑπατικοῦ ἀνθυπάτου / Ἀφρικῆς ἐπάρχου ἀλειμέν ¹²/ των Ἀππίας
καὶ Φλαμιν[ί]ας / τρὶς κυινδεκεμουίρου ἐν χώρᾳ Σεβαστῶν διαγνόν/τος ὑπατικοῦ
Δαλματίας ¹⁶/ θυγατέρα Τιβ. Πο[λληνίου] Ἀ[ρ]μ[ενίου / Περεγρίνου . . .]*

The inscription from Xanthus in Lycia, in honour of Pollienus Auspex's
granddaughter Honorata, is the only evidence for his governorship of
Britain, and it is extremely difficult to interpret. The lady was the
daughter of Ti. Pollienus Armenius Peregrinus, *consul ordinarius* in
244;[1] granddaughter of Auspex, consular governor of Britain, Moesia,
Dacia, and Spain, and *vice sacra iudicans* for a single emperor,[2] and of
Flavius Latronianus, consul, pontifex, and prefect of Rome; and great-
granddaughter of another Auspex, consul, proconsul of Africa, prefect
of the *alimenta* three times,[3] *XVvir, vice sacra iudicans* for more than
one emperor, and governor of Dalmatia. The great-grandfather should
be the *XVvir s. f.* who participated in the Saecular Games of 204,[4] a
man noted for his sarcastic wit.[5] But the real key to the dating seems to
be provided by coins from Lower Moesia which show Pollienus Auspex
as governor in the 190s under Severus, before Caracalla became co-
emperor in 198.[6]

The first and most obvious problem arises from the great gap in age
between Honorata's father, consul in 244, and her grandfather, the
younger Auspex, who, if he governed Lower Moesia—which was not his
first consular province—in the mid-190s, cannot have been consul much
after 190. Hence there must have been an interval of at least fifty years
between the consulships of father and son. This seems rather unlikely,
although the case of the Volusii Saturnini, consuls in AD 3 and 56,[7]
demonstrates that it is not impossible.

A second difficulty concerns the younger Auspex's other offices. If
Britain was his first consular post—even though governors of Britain

---

[1] *IGR* III 556 = *ILS* 8840 = *TAM* II 572 (Tlos); see Barbieri, *L'Albo* no. 1696 (where, however, it is suggested that the man in the Xanthus inscription was the father of the *cos. ord.* 244;
see below, n. 14).

[2] See p. 153 below.

[3] Eck, *ZPE* 18 (1975) 97 f., shows that τρίς should mean 'on three occasions' rather than
'for three years'.

[4] VI 32327 = *ILS* 5050a.

[5] Dio 76. 9. 2 ff.

[6] B. Pick, *Die antike Münzen Nord-Griechenlands,* I. *Dacien und Moesien* 1898) 198
no. 543, 355 ff. nos. 1252–63. See the comments, 186 n. 1, 331 n. 1. The legend ΥΠΑΠΟΛ-
ΑΥΣΠΙΚΟΣ should be understood as ὑπα(τεύοντος)Πολ. Αὖσπικος and not as evidence for the
man having the *praenomen* A., a view unfortunately perpetuated by Schumacher, *Priesterkollegien* 210 ff.

[7] Eck, *Hermes* 100 (1972) 461 ff.

were generally rather more senior men[8]—he must have been there before Albinus, not later than 192. The governorship of Dacia is very difficult to fit in, since five other governors must be accommodated within the years 198–209,[9] and Hispania citerior is only a little less crowded, with four governors in the same period.[10] If the order is assumed to be descending, the position is a little less awkward. No governors of Hispania citerior are known under Commodus until the year 192,[11] so that Auspex's tenure of the post could be assigned to the period *c*.186–9, while there is also room for a governorship of the III Daciae *c*.190–2.[12] His governorship of Britain would then fall into place at the end of the 190s, after his tenure of Moesia inferior, and he could be regarded as the successor of Virius Lupus.[13]

This latter chronology would of course mean that this consulship would have to be placed even earlier, *c*.185, in other words some sixty years before that of his son Peregrinus in 244. A way out of that difficulty may be found if it is assumed that Peregrinus was the adopted son of the younger Auspex, his natural father being L. Armenius Peregrinus, praetor in 213.[14] It has been suggested that a third member of the family, Ti. Julius Pollienus Auspex, governor of Numidia in the early third century,[15] was the natural son of the younger Auspex, and that on this man's death the younger Auspex adopted an Armenius Peregrinus in order to perpetuate the family name.[16]

There remains the question of the office which both Auspices held, as judge of appeal. The elder Auspex is described as ἐν χώρᾳ Σεβαστῶν διαγνούς, the younger as ἐν χώρᾳ Σεβαστοῦ δικάσας. This function is not otherwise found before the early third century. The earliest securely datable example is C. Octavius Ap. Suetrius Sabinus (*cos. ord.* 214), *iudex ex delegatione cognitionum Caesarianarum*, or [*iudex ex*] *delegatu principum in provincia* [. . .], presumably before 212.[17] If the distinction between Σεβαστῶν and Σεβαστοῦ is accurate, the elder

---

[8] p. 390 below.

[9] Stein, *Dazien* 58 ff.

[10] Alföldy, *Fasti Hispanienses* 45 ff. (although the first of the four cannot be assigned to this period with complete certainty).

[11] Alföldy, *Fasti Hispanienses* 42 f.

[12] Stein, *Dazien* 51 ff.

[13] See n. 18 below for further problems with the elder Auspex.

[14] *PIR*[2] A 1059. The suggestion was made by Stein, *Arch.-ep. Mitt.* 19 (1896) 150, followed by R. Egger, *JÖAI* 19–20 (1919) Bbl. 311 ff. Barbieri, *L'Albo* no. 1696 preferred to suppose that Honorata was sister of the *cos. ord.* 244. Pflaum, *RPh.* 30 (1956) 79 f., and Schumacher, *Priesterkollegien* 210 ff., show the difficulties of this alternative.

[15] Thomasson, *Statthalter Nordafrikas* II 209.

[16] See Schumacher, *Priesterkollegien* 211 f. with stemma.

[17] X 5398 (= *ILS* 1159), 5178; see Barbieri, *L'Albo* no. 387, Eck, *ZPE* 8 (1971) 92; Schumacher, *Priesterkollegien* 290 n. 374.

Auspex must have carried out these duties either under the joint rule of M. Aurelius and Commodus, 176-180, or under Severus and Caracalla, 198-211.[18] The younger Auspex must have functioned either before 198 or after 211—in the latter case after a considerable interval since his last provincial governorship.

A radical solution to the whole problem was proposed by A. Stein, namely that the elder Auspex was the governor of Lower Moesia in the 190s, but that this post was omitted in error from the Xanthus inscription.[19] The younger Auspex could then be identical with Ti. Julius Pollienus Auspex, legate of Numidia under Caracalla or Elagabalus,[20] who would then have gone on to govern his four consular provinces in the period *c.*215-35. Βριταννία on the Xanthus stone would refer to Upper Britain, while Μυσία could refer to either of the Moesian provinces, since both were consular. It is probable that Upper Britain occupied a lower place among the consular provinces than undivided Britain had done,[21] and hence that the younger Auspex governed it soon after his consulship, i.e. not later than *c.*225, on this interpretation. The functions as judge of appeal could then be dated without difficulty to the joint reign of Severus and Caracalla (Σεβαστῶν) in the case of the elder Auspex and to the reign of Severus Alexander (Σεβαστοῦ) in the case of the younger. But, unfortunately, no decision is possible until further evidence is forthcoming.[22]

---

[18] See Alföldy, *Fasti Hispanienses* 106 ff. for the third-century judges of appeal. It is noteworthy that none (excluding the elder Auspex) is known from the second century. (According to Eck, *ZPE* 18 (1975) 90, all were consular; but this seems rather over-confident in view of the scanty evidence.) If the younger Auspex was consul *c.*190, his father should have held the *fasces* not later than *c.*170. His governorship of Dalmatia should then be placed in the reign of M. Aurelius, where it can certainly be accommodated, see Jagenteufel, *Dalmatia* 43 f., with Syme, *Gnomon* 31 (1959) 514 = *Danubian Papers* 196 f. The claim by I. Piso, *Revue roumaine d'histoire* 15 (1976) 480, that new evidence for Arrius Antoninus having governed Dalmatia in the later 170s makes it impossible for the elder Auspex to have done so as well, is unfortunately not completely justified; but it certainly strengthens Stein's case.

[19] Stein, *Moesien* 82 ff.

[20] Thomasson, *Statthalter Nordafrikas* II 209; cf. id., *SPQR* (1975) 56 ff., for a convenient conspectus of the problem.

[21] But real information is lacking: p. 402 below.

[22] There is of course room for manoeuvre over the offices of 'the two troublesome homonyms' (Syme, *Danubian Papers* 197). Stein, *Moesien* 82 ff., took the order of the younger's offices to be: Moesia, Dacia, Spain, Britain (Upper). I followed this view in *Ep. Stud.* 4 (1967) 80 ff., where I also favoured Stein's basic hypothesis. But Alföldy (another adherent of Stein) argued that the chronological order was correct: Britain (Upper) could come first, since the divided province was probably less prestigious than the undivided had been; while Tarraconensis probably remained high in status. Those who reject Stein's hypothesis must tackle the question of the supposed Severan division of Britain (pp. 168 ff. below): Auspex is described as ὑπατικοῦ. Further permutations are possible—e.g. the Spanish post might have been praetorian, as *iuridicus*, illegitimately lumped together with consular provinces. J. B. Leaning points out to me that Stein's solution could be simplified by supposing that on the Xanthus inscription Μυσίας was assigned erroneously to the younger Auspex, by mistake for the elder, an error

Finally, some comment is required on the origin of the family. The *gentilicium*, which should be spelled Pollienus, rather than Pollenius (the Greek version)[23] is exceedingly rare, and there are only two specimens known (apart from the men under consideration and their immediate kin), one from Spoletium in Umbria and one from Sicily.[24] The *cognomen* is also uncommon, being found once in Italy, twice in Celtic provinces, and twice with equestrians in the imperial service abroad.[25] Although it appears Latin in type, it might have a Celtic basis, as has also been claimed for the unique *cognomen* of a kinsman, Pollienus Sebennus—but that name has also been regarded as Etruscan.[26] Rare Italian *nomina* like Pollienus are sometimes found in the provinces,[27] and other elements, including the Ti. Julius of the governor of Numidia, suggest provincial connections.[28] Caution is therefore requisite, although Italian origin still looks likely.

205   C. Valerius Pudens (*cos. a. inc.*)

JRS 51 (1961) 192 = *AE* 1963. 281 = Alföldy, *Hommages M. Renard* II 3 ff., Bainbridge in Wensleydale: *Imp. Caesari Lucio Septimio / Severo pio Pertinaci Aug. et / imp. Caesari M. Aurelio* 4/ *Antonino pio felici Aug. et/* ⟦*P. Septimio Ge*⟧ *tae no/*⟦*bilissimo Caes. Augg.*⟧ */ nn. imp. Antonino II et* 8/ ⟦*Geta Caes*⟧ *are cos., centuriam / sub cura C. Valeri Pudentis / amplissimi cosularis coh. / VI Nervior. fecit, cui praest* 12/ *L. Vinicius Pius praef. coh. eiusd.* (AD 205)

The nomenclature of this governor is too indistinctive to provide any clues to his origin, in the absence of any direct evidence. Valerius is one of the commonest *gentilicia*, and Pudens is attested by several hundreds of examples all over the empire.[1] The combination Valerius Pudens, and even C. Valerius Pudens, is found in a variety of widely scattered places, the bearers of the names being of differing social status.[2]

perhaps caused by the letters Δα with which both Δακίας and Δαλματίας begin; and hence that the younger Auspex did not govern either Moesia at all, only Britain (Upper), the III Daciae, and Hispania citerior.

[23] This is clear from the *Acta* of the Saecular Games, VI 32327 = *ILS* 5050a.

[24] XI 4874, X 7349 f.

[25] Kajanto 318 cites only III 5173 (Noricum), VII 1068 (= *RIB* 2100; the same man in 2104, 2108), XI 4751, XIII 3012. Add *RIB* 650 and Tac. *Hist.* 4. 69. 1 (see next note).

[26] For Auspex, note Tac. *Hist.* 4. 69. 1: 'Iulius Auspex e primoribus Remorum'. On Sebennus, cf. Holder, *Alt-Celtische Sprachschatz* 1421 and Schulze 277.

[27] Cf. the comments of Syme, *Tacitus* 784 f., on the nomenclature of Roman Spain.

[28] The 'princeps Remorum' Julius Auspex (Tac. *Hist.* 4. 69. 1) could have been a Ti. Julius.

[1] Kajanto 264.

[2] Alföldy, *Bonner Jahrb.* 168 (1968) 153, hesitantly suggests African origin, 'jedoch erlaubt der häufige Name keine sicheren Schlüsse'. Valerii Pudentes are found in II, III, V, VI, *RIB*, VIII, IX, X, XIII, XVI. The name was of a type common among the military. For the

His career is known almost entirely from inscriptions in the four provinces which he governed.[3] Several undated stones from Lower Pannonia describe him as *leg. Aug. pr. pr.*[4] Presumably he climbed to the consulship from that position[5] and then went on to govern Lower Germany, where an inscription records his presence under Severus and Caracalla, before the latter's promotion to the rank of Augustus.[6] Hence it seems likely that he was the immediate successor there of Virius Lupus, in 197.

It may be supposed that he served in Lower Germany from 197-*c*.200, but, as the Bainbridge inscription shows that he was in Britain in 205, it is far from certain whether he proceeded there direct from the Rhine. He may have had a year or two out of office. He was probably the predecessor, rather than the successor, of L. Alfenus Senecio, although the closest available dating for the latter is an inscription which could belong to either 205, 206, or 207,[7] so the alternative is just possible. It may be noted that the equestrian officer at Bainbridge, L. Vinicius Pius, served under both Pudens and Senecio, making it virtually certain that the two governors followed one another. On balance it appears probable that the barrack-block set up under Pudens would have preceded the [*vallum cum*] *bracchio caementicium* that was built when Senecio was governor.[8] 205 was not necessarily Pudens' last year in the province, but it is tempting to assign him to the years 202-5, with Senecio succeeding him in 205-8.[9]

He is last heard of as proconsul of Africa, evidently in 210-11 or 211-12.[10] In this capacity he refused to hear a case against a Christian, as Tertullian told his successor Scapula.[11] Since the latter was *consul ordinarius* in 195, it is fair to assume that Pudens had been consul

---

praenomen C., note III 6166 (Troesmis), a Hadrianic veteran of V Macedonica, C. Val. Pud(ens), and XIII 6850 (Mainz), a soldier of II Adiutrix, from Savaria, C. Valerius C. f. Cla. Pudes.

[3] He might also be the Pudens who was proconsul of Lycia-Pamphylia: *AE* 1929. 85. The date is probably late second or early third century, but there are several other candidates. See Barbieri, *L'Albo* no. 2087 + *Agg.* (cf. 514), and Grosso, *La lotta politica* 484 f.

[4] Fitz, *Epigraphica* 23 (1961) 71 ff., *A. Ant. Hung.* 11 (1963) 281 f.

[5] Fitz, *A. Ant. Hung.* 11 (1963) 218 f. (who also suggests that he may have served as *comes* of Severus *c*.195-7).

[6] XIII 8824 = *ILS* 9178, see Ritterling, *FRD* 77.

[7] *RIB* 1234 (Risingham), see p. 159 below.

[8] See *Ep. Stud.* 4 (1967) 79.

[9] See also p. 204 below, for the suggestion that Pudens' name may be restored on *RIB* 591. Pudens, rather than Senecio, may have been the governor on the fragmentary inscriptions *RIB* 1151 (Corbridge) and *JRS* 57 (1967) 205 f. = *AE* 1967. 260 (Housesteads). But there are a great many Severan building stones which lack the name of a governor; see pp. 160 n. 18, 204 ff. below. See also pp. 168 ff. below on the division of Britain.

[10] Thomasson, *Statthalter Nordafrikas* II 110 f., discussing VIII 12006.

[11] Tert. *ad Scapulam* 4. 3 cf. p. 264 n. 4 below.

earlier, in 193 or 194.[12] This leads to the conclusion that he had been governing Pannonia inferior in April 193, at the moment when his neighbour and senior colleague the governor of Pannonia superior, L. Septimius Severus, was proclaimed emperor. Ready and rapid support for Severus' coup may then be invoked to explain Pudens' later success.[13] It may be noted that he is the only former governor of Lower Pannonia known to have gone on to govern Britain.[14]

between   **L. Alfenus L.(?) f. Quir. Senecio** (*cos. a. inc.*)
205 and 207

VII 269 = *RIB* 722 = Alföldy, *Hommages M. Renard* II 4 ff., Bainbridge in Wensleydale: *Imp. Caesari L. Septimio [Severo] / pio Pert[i] naci Augu[sto et] / imp. Caesari M. Aurelio A[ntonino] 4/ pio feli[ci] Augusto et P. S[eptimio] / ⟦Getae nobiliss. Caes.⟧ vallum cum] / bracchio caementicium [fecit coh.] / VI Nervio[ru]m sub cura L. A[lfeni] 8/ Senecion[is] amplissimi [cos., institit] operi L. Vin[ici]us Pius praef. [coh. eiusdem / . . .]*

VII 270 = *RIB* 723 = Alföldy, *Hommages M. Renard* II 4 ff., ibid.: *[. . . sub cura L. Alfeni] Seneçioṇis amplissimi [cos. coh. VI Nerviorum / fecit cui praeest L.] Vịṇịç[ius] Pius [praef. coh. eiusd.]*

JRS 18 (1928) 212 = *JRS* 19 (1929) 218 = *RIB* 740, Bowes: *Impp. Caess. L. Septim. / Severo pio Pertinaci / Arab. Adiab. Part. Maxi. 4/ et M. Aur. Anton. pio Augg. / ⟦et P. Sept. Getae nob. Caes.⟧ ius/su L. Alfeni Senecionis leg. / Augg. pr. pr. coh. I Thrac. eq.*

VII 279 add. = *RIB* 746, Greta Bridge: *Impp. Caess. L. Sep. Severo / pio Pert. et M. Aur. Antoni/no pio Augg. et ⟦P. Sept. Getae⟧ 4/ nob. Caes. sub cura L. / Alfeni Senecionis / leg. eorum pr. pr.*

VII 1003 add. = *ILS* 2618 = *RIB* 1234, Risingham: *[Impp. Caess. L. / Sept. Severo pio Pertin/aci Arab. Adi]ab. Part[i]co Maxi. 4/ cos. III et M. Aurel. Antonino pio / cos. II Augg. ⟦et P. Sept. Getae nob. Caes.⟧ / portam cum muris vetustate di/lapsis iussu Alfeni Senecionis v. c. 8/ cos. curante Oclatinio Advento proc. / Augg. nn. coh. I Vangion. eq. / cum Aem[i]l. Salviano trib. / suo a solo restit.*

VII 513 = *RIB* 1337 = Davies, *Chiron* 6 (1976) 357 ff., Benwell: *Victoriae / Augg. Alfe/no Senecio4/ni cos. felix / ala Asto/[ru]m prạ(etoria?)*

VII 1346 + *EE* VII 1020 + *EE* VII 1028 = E. Birley, *Arch. Ael.*[4] 16 (1939) 240 ff. = *RIB* 1462, Chesters: *[Impp. Caess. L.] Sept. / [Severo pio Pertin]ace / [et M. Aur. Antonin]o pio / [Augg. et ⟦P. Sep. Get]a⟧ e 4/ [nob. Caes. ala II Ast. cu]-rante / Alf[eno Senecione co]s. et / Oc[latinio Advento p]roc. / ins[tante . . .]*

E. Birley, *CW*[2] 30 (1930) 199 = *RIB* 1909, Birdoswald: *Impp. Caess. L. / Sept.*

---

[12] As pointed out by Fitz, *Epigraphica* 23 (1961) 71 ff.; *A. Ant. Hung.* 11 (1963) 282.
[13] Fitz, *A. Ant. Hung.* 11 (1963) 281 f.
[14] See p. 141 and n. 6 above, on L. Ulpius Marcellus.

Severo pio / Pert. et M. Aur. A [*nt*] *o/nino Augg.* [[*et P. Sep.* [4] / *Getae nob. Caes.*]] *hor/reum fecer. coh. I Ael. / Dac. et I Tracum c. R. sub* [8] / *Alfeno Senecione cos. / per Aurel. Iulianum tr.*

Britannia 8 (1977) 432, Vindolanda: [. . . *S*] *eneci* [*o* . . .]

More British inscriptions name Alfenus Senecio than any other governor, although his governorship is not attested outside the province and not much is known of his previous career. However, his origin is certain: he was from Numidia, the third governor, after Lollius Urbicus and Antistius Adventus,[1] who is known to have derived from that province. Four inscriptions record the career of a homonymous equestrian procurator. Two from Italy show him as sub-prefect of the Misenum fleet[2] and sub-prefect of the *vigiles*;[3] a dedication honoured him at the *municipium* of Auzia in Mauretania Caesariensis when he was presidial procurator of that province;[4] and a fourth was set up by decree of the council at Cuicul in Numidia, *quod promptissima benignitate sua utilitates coloniae suae splendidissime iuvit nuper cum provinciae Mauretaniae praesset*—showing that he was a native of the colony. The last inscription also describes him as *proc. Aug. provinciae Belgicae* and gives his filiation and tribe, *M. filio Quir.*[5]

The procurator's career must be assigned to the period between the reign of Nerva, when Cuicul became a colony, and the reign of Severus, when Auzia received that status. It is generally supposed that he was the father of our governor, and that he held these appointments in the reigns of M. Aurelius and Commodus.[6] It is, however, possible that the procurator himself was given senatorial rank. If, for example, he was in Belgica in the year 193, his role as paymaster of the German armies would have been particularly vital, and could have resulted in his adlection to the senate as a reward.[7]

However this may be, a senatorial Alfenus Senecio, who must be regarded as identical with our governor, is named as *leg. Augg. pr. pr.*

[1] pp. 113, 130 above.

[2] *ILS* 8391 (Misenum): *Alfenio Senecioni subpraef. class. pr. Mis.*

[3] XIV 4509 (Ostia): *subprefecto Senecione.*

[4] VIII 9046.

[5] *AE* 1911. 112 = *ILS* 9489.

[6] Pflaum, *CP* no. 176, cf. also Barbieri, *L'Albo* no. 25, where Spanish origin is unconvincingly suggested.

[7] This was suggested in *Ep. Stud.* 4 (1967) 80. It may be worth adding parallels for advancement of this kind. Although it was commoner for equestrian officers or junior procurators to transfer to the senate, cf. M. Statius Priscus (p. 125 above), or Ti. Claudius Candidus (Pflaum, *CP* no. 203), the career of Pertinax, (p. 144 above), who, in his mid-forties, having been a ducenary procurator, moved to a long and active senatorial career, is a reminder that such a thing is conceivable with Senecio. Claudius Gallus, another Severan general, is silent about his early career in *AE* 1957. 123, and may be another *adlectus.*

on two inscriptions from the province of Syria Coele in the reign of Severus. The titulature of Severus and Caracalla is given inaccurately, but it has been shown convincingly that they must belong to the year 200.[8] He is the only governor of that province known from the years 194-207 inclusive, and it is thus quite impossible to tell how long he was there. But it may be noted that the emperor and his family were in the east from 197-202, spending some time in Syria, and that Severus and Caracalla entered their joint consulship of 202 at Antioch in January of that year.[9] Senecio would thus have had ample opportunity to ingratiate himself with the emperor.

Syria had been divided after the defeat of Niger in 194, and it is not clear what the rank of the two legion consular province of Syria Coele was.[10] However, the next recorded legate, L. Marius Maximus (*cos. II ord.* 223), was a man of considerable seniority by the time he is attested in office there, in 208,[11] and at a period of reconstruction, when the emperor was himself in the area, it is fair to assume that Syria Coele was in the hands of a fairly experienced ex-consul. Hence it should be supposed that Senecio had already had a considerable amount of service, including military command in the civil wars and perhaps in the Parthian wars, and at least one previous governorship.[12]

His governorship of Britain was almost certainly after that of C. Valerius Pudens, who was still in Britain in 205.[13] The Risingham inscription gives Caracalla the title *cos. II*, and must therefore belong to 205, 206, or 207, but none of Senecio's other inscriptions are dated more closely than to the joint reign of Severus and Caracalla. It is reasonable to suppose that he was in Britain from 205, or soon after, until 208. The Benwell inscription,[14] dedicated to the 'Victory of the emperors', might suggest either that Senecio was one of those mentioned by Dio,[15] who were winning victories in Britain shortly before Severus came here himself, or even that he remained as governor after the

---

[8] Pflaum, *CP* no. 176, J. B. Leaning, *Latomus* 30 (1971) 386 ff.

[9] A. R. Birley, *Septimius Severus* 201 ff., esp. 210 ff.

[10] J. F. Gilliam, *AJP* 79 (1958) 225 ff.

[11] Gilliam, *AJP* 79 (1958) 230, A. R. Birley, *Septimius Severus* 308 ff.

[12] Fitz, *Alba Regia* 10 (1969) 180, suggests that he may have governed Upper Germany during the period 193-7, or part thereof. The opportunity must be taken here of correcting an unfortunate misunderstanding by Dr Fitz. In the note cited, a discussion of *Ep. Stud.* 4 (1967) 63 ff., he takes 'by' in the phrase 'by 192', 'by 196', etc. (77 ff.) to mean the same as the German 'um' or 'etwa', i.e. *circa*, rather than, as I intended, in the sense of 'not later than'. Not surprisingly, Dr Fitz finds room for disagreement with the interpretation which he believed had been put forward in a number of cases.

[13] p. 155 above.

[14] See now Davies, *Chiron* 6 (1976) 357 ff., whose reading *pra(etoria)* in line 6 is, however, rather uncertain, to say the least.

[15] Dio 76. 10. 6.

emperor arrived. On the other hand, it need not necessarily refer to events in Britain at all.[16] One must be equally cautious with Herodian's story of the governor of Britain appealing for assistance to Severus following a barbarian invasion. Examination of Herodian's methods shows that this was a rhetorical τόπος, and there is no reason to believe either that there was an invasion *c.*207, or that the governor, whether Senecio or another man, appealed to Severus for help.[17] On the contrary, Dio's story suggests that the governor was dealing with the situation comfortably.

The impressive array of inscriptions[18] reveals Senecio building an annexe to the fort at Bainbridge, carrying out unspecified work at Greta Bridge and Bowes a little further north, more work at Chesters on Hadrian's Wall, rebuilding a granary at another Wall fort, Birdoswald, and reconstructing a gate and walls at the outpost fort of Risingham on Dere Street. An unusual feature of two of these inscriptions, those from Chesters and Risingham, is that they record the involvement of the provincial procurator, M. Oclatinius Adventus. At Risingham Adventus took charge of the work, together with the tribune, Aemilius Salvianus, on the orders of Senecio; at Chesters Senecio and Adventus were both (ungrammatically) described as [*cu*]*rante*, while another man, presumably the garrison commander, was *ins*[*tante*]. It is difficult to explain Adventus' involvement, although other procurators are known to have been in the frontier area from time to time,[19] and in other provinces procurators' names are found on building inscriptions.[20] It may be that Adventus, whose background was rather unusual for a financial procurator—he had been an officer in the *frumentarii* after rising from the ranks[21]—had been specially ordered by Severus to inspect the state of the northern frontier at a time when the emperor was contemplating a personal intervention in Britain.[22]

Nothing is heard of Senecio after his British governorship. He may

---

[16] Cf. III 4354 = 11082, Arrabona: *Victoriae Augg. nn. et leg. I Adi, p. f. Antoninia.*, set up on 9 June 207; interpreted by Fitz, *A. Arch.* 11 (1959) 255, as a commemoration of Severus' fifteenth year. It might also commemorate the tenth year from the *victoria Parthica* of 198.

[17] Herodian 3. 14. 1, see A. R. Birley, *Arch. Ael.*[4] 50 (1972) 186 ff Earlier, in *Septimius Severus* (1971) 244, I had followed the standard view which accepts this story as factual.

[18] Davies, *Chiron* 6 (1976) 358 n. 14, conveniently lists a series of inscriptions from elsewhere recording building activity for which Senecio may have been responsible—but cf. p. 156 n. 9 above, where it is pointed out that the other Severan governors must also be considered. See also pp. 168 ff. below, where it is argued that Senecio was governor of undivided Britain.

[19] pp. 294, 299 below.

[20] Graham, *JRS* 56 (1966) 98 ff., gives some examples, the validity of which is dismissed without argument by Mann and Jarrett, *JRS* 57 (1967) 64 n. 39. See also A. R. Birley, *Septimius Severus* 248 n. 1.

[21] p. 298 below.

[22] Mann and Jarrett, *JRS* 57 (1967) 64 n. 39; A. R. Birley, *Septimius Severus* 248.

have continued in office during the imperial expedition, but the inscriptions provide no definite clues to this question. It may, however, be mentioned here that there is no reason to believe that a governor—or two governors if the province was already divided—would not have been retained during the imperial expedition. Further, there is no need to interpret Herodian's statement that while Severus was in Britain 'he left Geta to exercise jurisdiction within the part of Britain subject to Rome and to administer the affairs of the empire, giving him advisers from his senior friends'[23] to mean that Geta was actually governor of Britain at the time.[24]

No descendants of Senecio are known; the other senatorial Alfeni of the third century belong to a different family, probably of Spanish origin.[25]

C. Junius Faustinus Postumianus (*cos. a. inc.*)

EE V 270 = (*CIL*) VIII 11763, Gelat es-Senam: *memoria* / *C. Iuni Faus* [*ti*] *ni Postumiani cos. praesidis provinciaru* [*m* / *His*] *pani* [*ae*] *et Britanniae Iuni P* [*l*] *ac* [*id*] *us et Paulina filii* [4] / *indu* [*lg*] *entissimo pa* [*t*] *ri*

This governor is known only from the funerary inscription erected by his son and daughter, near Thugga in the northern part of proconsular Africa. The family clearly had their home there, as will emerge. All that can be said about the date, in the first instance, is that the expressions *memoria*[1] and *praeses*[2] both suggest the third century. However, another inscription found near by gives the *cursus* of a virtual homonym, the only discrepant item in whose nomenclature seems to match the *cognomen* of our governor's son.[3] It will be convenient to set out the text in full, following the revised version of G. Alföldy:[4]

[*C. I*] *unio Faustino* [*Pl*] *a*/[*ci*] *do Postumian* [*o*] *c. v.* / [*c*] *os. adlecto inter co* [*m*] *i*[4]/ [*t*] *es Augg. nn. sacerdoti* / [*F*] *laviali Titiali leg. Augg.* / *pr. pr. provinciae Mysi/ae*

[23] Herodian 3. 14. 9.

[24] Graham, *JRS* 56 (1966) 94 n. 33; Davies, *Chiron* 6 (1976) 359 n. 26 (but he mistakenly attributes to Graham the view that they both refute, n. 27).

[25] *PIR*[2] A 519, cf. 518; Barbieri, *L'Albo* nos. 1799, 1800.

[1] R. Cagnat, *Cours d'épigraphie latine*[4] (1914) 282 n. 3.

[2] Barbieri, *L'Albo* pp. 562 ff.

[3] In *PIR*[2] J 752 this is restored as '[Fl] ac[c] us *vel* [Pl] ac[id] us', but see Alföldy, *Fasti Hispanienses* 50 n. 225. For similar variation by a man with three *cognomina* cf. L. Marius Maximus Perpetuus Aurelianus, who uses all three in *ILS* 2935–6 and X 6764, but the first and third only in X 6567 and *AE* 1955. 188.

[4] Alföldy, *Fasti Hispanienses* 50 (note particularly the revision of the legion in lines 12 f.), revising VIII 597 (cf. 11754 and p. 2729).

inferior [*is leg.*] *Augg.* [8] / *pr. pr. provinc* [*iae Be*] *l/gica* [*e leg.*] *Augg. pr. pr./ provinciae Luseta ni* [*ae leg. Augg. leg*] *ion* [*i*] *s* [12] / [*pri*] *ma* [*e Ad*] *ia* [*t/r*] *icis*(?) [*pi*] *q* [*e*] *fidelis iu/* [*r*] *idico* [*pe*] *r Aemili/am et Etruriam et Tus* [16] */ciam praetori* [*c*] *andi/* [*dato leg. pr*] *ovinciae /* [*Africae dio*] *eceseos /* [*K*] *ar* [*tha*] *g.*(?) [*tri*] *buno pl* [*e*] *b.* [20] */ candida* [*to qu*] *ae* [*s*] *tori / provinc* [*iae . . .*] *ae d* [*ec*] *em/viro stlitibus iud* [*ic. /* *pat*] *rono perpetuo* [24] / [*. . .*]

Most scholars are content to identify this man with our governor, assuming that he went on to govern Spain and Britain after the last post on the *cursus* inscription, and that his children chose simply to record his consulship and his last two commands on his funerary monument. It has been objected that his first consular governorship could hardly have been omitted,[5] but since on any reckoning only a brief selection of his offices are supplied,[6] the case for identifying the two looks the stronger alternative, in the absence of any firm evidence to the contrary.

All but one of those who have tackled the *cursus* inscription assign it to the third century, and most prefer the Severan period in view of the repeated appearance of *Augg.* in connection with Postumianus' various offices is supplied,[6] the case for identifying the two looks the stronger long enough period to accommodate this series of appointments. The argument is not completely compelling, since *Augg.* was sometimes applied abusively, on inscriptions set up under a joint reign, to posts held earlier under a single emperor; but such cases are exceptional.[7] J. Fitz, however, objects that from the mid-190s until the early 220s, and again from 238 to 246, all governors of Moesia inferior were named on the coins of the cities of Nicopolis and Marcianopolis. Further, he argues that if the early career was largely Severan, the consular governorship of Britain would have fallen after the division of the province, yet the province is not denoted *superior*. Hence he urges that the career should be dated to the reign of M. Aurelius. But this in turn creates grave difficulties and must be rejected.[8]

[5] *PIR*[2] J 752: 'in nostro titulo vix omissum esset eum tribus provinciis consularibus . . . praefuisse'. The further objections are that Moesia inferior–Hispania–Britannia is 'singulari quidem ordine' and that *praeses* was not common in the Severan period. For the order of provinces see Alföldy, *Fasti Hispanienses* 50 f. and 201 ff. *Praeses* is found even in the second century, although much commoner in the third: Barbieri, *L'Albo* pp. 562 ff. But in any case, the inscription was not set up until after the man's death, which might have been at least twenty years after the end of his career.

[6] Alföldy, *Fasti Hispanienses* 51 n. 225 compares the inscriptions of M. Nummius Umbrius (*cos. ord.* 206), quoted ibid. 48. Cf. also *ILS* 1160-1, 2935-6 (and X 6764, *AE* 1955. 188) for analogous cases.

[7] Cf. L. Fabius Cilo (*PIR*[2] F 27), described on *ILS* 1142 as *leg. Augg. pro pr.* of Pannonia superior, which he governed 197-201—but also of Galatia, which he must have governed under Commodus. (By contrast the same man is called *leg. Aug. pr. pr.* of all his provinces on *ILS* 1141.)

[8] Fitz, *Moesia Inferior* (1966) 25 ff. (and an earlier version in Hungarian, *Antik Tanul-*

If the two Augusti are assumed to be Severus and Caracalla, the career may be reconstructed with some plausibility on the following lines.[9] Postumianus will have been born in the 160s and have entered the senate as quaestor in the reign of Commodus after preliminary service as *Xvir*—but apparently not as *tribunus laticlavius*. Both as tribune of the plebs and as praetor he was *candidatus* of the emperor, with a year as legate to a proconsul of Africa in between. His praetorship should have fallen *c.*192, followed by the Italian juridicate and command over I Adiutrix in Upper Pannonia. Then came two praetorian governorships, leading to the consulship *c.*204. His governorship of Moesia inferior can be accommodated in the period 205-8 (not necessarily for as long as three years), followed by service as *comes* in the British campaign of 208-11. The *cursus* inscription should have been erected immediately after his appointment, or at least not later than 209, since otherwise *Auggg.* would have been required. The two final governorships have been generally supposed to have come in the order given on the inscription, but he may have gone to Spain after Britain, as G. Alföldy has argued. It could even be the case that he governed Britain—either the undivided province or a consular Lower Britain—during the imperial expedition, as the successor of Alfenus Senecio, going on to govern Hispania Tarraconensis *c.*211-14. Otherwise one must assign his British governorship to the reign of Caracalla. He could hardly have been left in Britain after the return of Caracalla and Geta to Rome, since the

mányok 12 (1965) 82 ff.; the same view is defended against criticism offered in *Ep. Stud.* 4 (1967) 84 in *Alba Regia* 10 (1969) 180). The second argument can easily be countered, since the labels *superior* and *inferior* were not infrequently omitted, cf. the inscription of Pollienus Auspex (p. 152 above) and here Hispania is not called citerior (which Fitz attempts to explain by special pleading in *Alba Regia* 10 (1969) 180). As a matter of fact, it is possible that Postumianus governed an undivided Britain even as late as 213, see below. As for the first argument, there is no evidence to explain why the two Moesian cities put governors' names on their coins, nor why they stopped. At least one man known to have been in office during the 'coining period' is not on the coins (Stein, *Moesien* 94 f.) and Postumianus may have been another. See Fitz 49 ff. for a revision of Stein 82 ff. (But L. Mantennius Sabinus is now known to have been in Moesia as early as October 227: Eck, *ZPE* 18 (1975) 159 n. 24—hence some further revision is needed.) A further objection to Fitz's dating is the *cursus* itself, which is difficult to accommodate in the reign of M. Aurelius. Fitz is obliged to assign the governorship of Belgica to the years *c.*168/9-171/2 and the consulship to *c.*174/5—allowing a gap of at least two years—to leave room for Didius Julianus, in Belgica *diu* (*HA Did. Jul.* 1. 7), before his consulship, in 175 (*PIR*[2] D 77). This means that the legionary command and governorship of Lusitania must go in the period *c.*162-9, and hence the Italian juridicate which preceded them would have to be put at the very beginning of the reign. Yet Eck has shown good reason to believe that the juridicate was not established until *c.*166/7: *ZPE* 8 (1971) esp. 76 f. Alföldy, *Fasti Hispanienses* 51 n. 228 also notes that the successive governships of the two praetorian provinces are less likely in the 160s than under Severus.

  [9] See esp. Alföldy, *Fasti Hispanienses* 50 ff., whose discussion, with full references to earlier work, enables me to dispense with detailed documentation here.

younger Ulpius Marcellus appears to have been consular governor in 211-12.[10] Assuming that Britain was first divided *c.*213 (or that the division reached its final form then[11]), he might have been sent back as first consular governor of Upper Britain.[12] But it is not completely excluded that he could have been the last consular governor of undivided Britain (or of a consular Lower Britain) as successor of C. Julius Marcus,[13] *c.*214-15.

None the less, it must be stressed that this whole reconstruction rests on rather fragile foundations. The formula *adlecto inter comites Augg. nn.* might even refer to Valerian and Gallienus, and the various posts as *leg. Augg. pr. pr.* could have been held under those two emperors and their predecessors in the 240s and 250s.[14] In that case, he could have been consular governor of Upper Britain and of Spain in the mid- to late 250s.

Apart from his children, various kinsfolk and descendants can be identified,[15] the latest of whom is Junius Postumianus, holder of two priesthoods in the late third or fourth centuries.[16]

Ulpius Marcellus (*cos. a. inc.*)

VII 504 = *RIB* 1329, Benwell: *Deo Anocitico / iudiciis optimo/rum maximorum* 4/ *que impp. n. sub Ulp. / Marcello cos. Tine/ius Longus in p[re] /fectura equitu[m]* 8/ *lato clavo exorna/tus et q. d.*

?*EE* IX 1171 = *RIB* 1463, Chesters: *Aqua adducta / alae II Astur. / sub Ulp. Mar-cello* 4/ *leg. Aug. pr. pr.*

?VII 592 = E. Birley, *Arch. Ael.*4 16 (1939) 243 f. = *RIB* 1464, Chesters: [. . .*ala*] *II Ast[urum / sub]* Ulpio [*Marcello / leg. Au*]*g. pr. [pr.*]

VII 963 = *RIB* 976, Netherby: [. . .] *Iuliae Au[g.] /<M>matri Au[g. / nostri M. Aur]*4/*eli<i> Anton[ini] / et castr. [et] / senatus et / patriae pro* 8 / [*pietate ac*] */ devotione / [communi] / num. eius* 12/ [*curante Ulpio?*] / *Marcello [leg. / Aug.] pr. pr. coh. [I] Aelia / [Hisp. ∞ eq.]posuit.*

---

[10] See below.   [11] pp. 168 ff. below.

[12] A view favoured by Davies, *Klio* 59 (1977) 168. See pp. 168 ff. below, on the date of the division.   [13] pp. 166 ff. below.

[14] It must be assumed that *Augg. nn.* refers to living emperors. But it might of course abusively apply to a single Augustus and a Caesar., a consideration which also affects the other uses of *Augg.* in the *cursus* inscription. See Stein, *Dazien* 61 n. 2.

[15] I[un]i[us F]austinus, *puer senatorius* at the Saecular Games of 204 (*PIR*2 J 750) might be one, [Iu]nia Faustinilla *c. f.* (Barbieri, *L'Albo* no. 2176) another, if they were Junii. Q. Junius Caturicus Faustinus (*PIR*2 J 743) appears to come from a Celtic area.

[16] VI 2151: *Junius Postumianus v.c. p.p. dei Solis invicti Mithre XVvir s. f. pontif. dei Solis.* Not in *PIR*2, *RE*, or Barbieri, *L'Albo*. *PLRE* Postumianus no. 4 notes that he cannot be earlier than Aurelian. The other Postumiani in *PLRE* are probably linked with the Postumii Rufii Festi rather than with the family of our man.

The first three inscriptions set out above have already been discussed in connection with the Commodan governor of this name. It was pointed out that the Benwell inscription, at least, cannot refer to the Ulpius Marcellus who was 'sent against the Britons' by Commodus, since it mentions two emperors.[1] The solution may be that a second Ulpius Marcellus was consular governor, either of Britannia inferior or more probably of a still undivided Britain, in 211, and the two emperors would then be Caracalla and Geta.[2] The promotion of the cavalry officer Tineius Longus to senatorial rank can be construed as the bestowal of a favour designed to win support.[3] It may be noted further that the first *p.* of *impp.* appears to have been damaged, which may represent an erasure following the death and *damnatio* of Geta at the end of 211.[4] The Chesters inscriptions could then be assigned to 212, when Caracalla was sole emperor.[5]

The inscription from Netherby in honour of Julia Domna, which certainly belongs to the sole reign of Caracalla, is lost, and the text is known only from an early manuscript reading. But the governor's name is there given as Marcellus, and it is reasonable to wonder whether this may not be the same man as the governor on the Benwell stone.[6] E. Birley suggested[7] that the reading should be amended to *Marco leg.*, regarding this as another inscription of C. Julius Marcus, who was certainly in office in 213.[8]

It was evidently very seldom that men were sent to govern military

---

[1] pp. 140 f. above.

[2] The theory was first put forward by E. Birley, *Arch. Ael.*[4] 16 (1939) 243 f., who proposed a date of 217-18. In *Ep. Stud.* 4 (1967) 81 f. I argued that the years 211-12 would fit the evidence better. See now Jarrett, *Maryport, Cumbria* (1976) 23 f., and *Britannia* 9 (1978) 289 ff., against, and Davies, *Chiron* 6 (1976) 367 ff., in support. On the date of the division, see pp. 168 ff. below.

[3] Cf. Herodian 3. 15. 1, cited in *Ep. Stud.* 4 (1967) 82, and Davies, *Chiron* 6 (1976) 370.

[4] Davies, *Chiron* 6 (1976) 369, discusses the point and concludes that it must remain uncertain whether the damage occurred in Roman times or is modern. Note also his discussion of the date at which the temple of An(ten)ociticus was destroyed, 370 f., showing that it need not have happened in the late second century as the excavators assumed. This point is conceded by Jarrett, *Britannia* 9 (1978) 290.

[5] See p. 141 and n. 4 above, and Davies, *Chiron* 6 (1976) 373 ff., discussing *RIB* 1466, which, as he shows, could also be dated to 211.

[6] Davies, *ZPE* 27 (1977) 241 ff., suggests that Marcellus' name might have occurred in *RIB* 2060(b) (Bowness).

[7] E. Birley, *Arch. Ael.*[4] 11 (1934) 129; in *CW*[2] 53 (1954) 21 f. he allows for the possibility that it was the second Ulpius Marcellus. The Netherby inscription is not discussed—or even mentioned—by Jarrett, *Britannia* 9 (1978) 289 ff.

[8] See below, p. 167. *Arch. Ael.*[5] 8 (1980) 65 ff. (Newcastle) has a fragmentary text resembling *RIB* 976; the editor restores the erased governor's name as that of Marcus. Gordianus cannot be excluded, cf. *RIB* 590 (p. 182 below).

provinces of which their fathers had been legate, but there are precedents,[9] and the possibility cannot be ruled out for Britain. In the circumstances of the year 211, or shortly before, the appointment of a son of the Commodan governor might have been a particularly astute move.[10] That general had given the northern tribes a memorable battering, and they may have been expected to react respectfully to the appearance of another bearer of the name.[11] If the existence of a second Ulpius Marcellus be accepted, as an hypothesis at any rate, it may be assumed that he was the son of the Commodan governor. He could well have served under his father as *tribunus laticlavius* at that time. Equally, he might have come to Britain as a *comes* of the emperors during the *expeditio Britannica.*[12]

213   C. Julius Marcus (*cos. a. inc.?*)

VII 1186 = E. Birley, *Arch. Ael.*[4] 16 (1939) 255 ff. = *RIB* 2298, near milecastle 17, Hadrian's Wall: *Imp. Caes. M. Aur/[elio A]ntonino / [pio feli]ci Aug. Arab.* [4]/ *Adiab. P[a]rt. Maxim/o Brit. Maximo / trib. p[ot.] XVI cos. IIII / im[p.] II C. Iul. Marco* [8]/ *leg. Aug. pr. [pr.]* (AD 213).

?VII 963 = *RIB* 976, Netherby: [. . .] *Iuliae Au[g.] /.<M> matri Au[g. / nostri M. Aur]*[4]*/eli<i> Anton[ini] / et castr. [et] / senatus et / patriae pro* [8]/ *[pietate ac] / devotione / [communi] / num. eius* [12]/ *[curante(?) C. Iul.] / Marco(?) leg. [Aug.] / pr. pr. coh. [I] Ael. / [Hisp. ∞ eq.]* [16]/ *posuit.*

VII 967 = *RIB* 977, Netherby: [. . . coh. I / Ael. Hisp. ∞ eq.] *Anto/[ninian]a ex solo* [4]/ *[exstruxit] sub cur. G. Iul. / [Marci le]g. Aug. pr. pr., instante / [. . .]r. Maximo trib.*

EE VII 963 = *RIB* 1205, Whitley Castle: [. . .] *restit. / [sub C. Iul. Mar]co leg. / [pr. pr. eiu]s pr. Br.*

VII 995 *add.* = *RIB* 1265, High Rochester: *Deo Matuno / pro salute / M. [A]ur[eli . . .* [4]/ . . .] / *bono generis / human. impe/rante C. [[Iulius* [8]/ *Marcus]] leg. / Aug. pr. pr. posuit / ac dedicavit / c. a. Caecil. Optato trib.*

[9] Namely the Neratii Prisci in Pannonia (p. 88 and n. 7 above). But Sex. Julius Severus and Cn. Julius Verus, who were probably father and son, each governed both Britain and Syria in the second century (pp. 109, 119ff above). Note also that Petronius Turpilianus, governor of Britain 61–3, was nephew of the first governor Plautius (pp. 40, 58 above). The Cassii, Apronianus and Dio, both in Dalmatia (*PIR*[2] C 485, 492), are hardly a proper parallel, since that province no longer had any legions. Likewise, the equestrian prefects of Egypt are hardly comparable, although several such cases may be observed there (cf. Pflaum, *CP* no. 5; nos. 99 and 154; *PIR*[2] A 394–5).

[10] A. R. Birley, *Septimius Severus* 269 ff.

[11] Cf. the appointment of Petronius Turpilianus, nephew of A. Plautius, at an even more difficult moment (when different qualities were required, but the prestige attaching to the family was doubtless equally valuable: p. 58 above).

[12] That the Commodan governor had descendants is suggested by the inscription from Side of AD 256, an Ulpius Marcellus, ὁ λαμπρότατος ὑπατικός: *AE* 1966. 460.

VII 351 = *RIB* 905, Old Carlisle: [. . . *pro sal. imp. do*]*mini nos*[*tri M. / Aur. Antoni*]*ni pii felicis* [*Aug. / sub C. Iul. Ma*]*rco leg. eius. cur.* [4]*/* [. . .] *pra(e)f., ala Aug. /* [. . . *posui*]*t imp. Antoni*[*no / Augusto IIII et*] *Balbino II c*[*o*]*ss.*

The names of C. Julius Marcus appear on a milestone of the year 213 from near milecastle 17 on Hadrian's Wall. Another stone of the same year, from Old Carlisle, was set up [*sub C. Iul. Ma*]*rco*, an inscription from Netherby records building *sub cur. G. Iul.* [*Marci le*]*g. Aug. pr. pr.*, and a fragmentary one from Whitley Castle may also be assigned to him. His complete names may be read, although they were deleted in Roman times, on a dedication for the health of Caracalla at High Rochester. On another inscription, now lost, from Netherby, the governor's name was read as *Marcello*, but could perhaps be restored as *Marco leg.*[1] Further, at least five dedications, four of them from the year 213, but with no legible trace of the governor's name surviving, were set up in honour of Caracalla with the formula *pro pietate ac devotione communi.* As E. Birley pointed out, it looks as though C. Julius Marcus and the army of northern Britain felt a particular need to affirm their loyalty to Caracalla.[2] From the fact that Marcus' names were effectively deleted on two of these stones and erased on the High Rochester inscription also, it would appear that his actions failed to convince the emperor, and that he incurred *damnatio.*

It is still not clear how much of Britain Julius Marcus governed. His title *leg. Aug. pr. pr.* could have referred equally to a consular or praetorian governor. R. P. Wright reads [*C. Iul. Mar*]*co leg.* [*Aug. pr. pr. . . . v. c. c*]*os. pr. Br.* on the inscription from Whitley Castle, but in fact the traces at the beginning of the surviving portion of the last line are too indistinct to allow *o* or any other letter to be read with confidence. The reading [*leg. pr. pr. eiu*]*s* is equally possible. Hence Julius Marcus may have been either consular governor of a still undivided Britain, or of Britannia inferior; or he may have been praetorian governor —perhaps the first—of Britain inferior. Until more information is forthcoming, 216 must be regarded as the earliest date at which the province was certainly divided.[3]

Marcus, although one of the standard *praenomina*, was also frequently

---

[1] But see p. 165 and n. 7 above, where it is argued that the MS reading may be correct.

[2] E. Birley, *Arch. Ael.*[4] 11 (1934) 129 ff. The inscriptions are *RIB* 928, 1202, 1235, 1278, 1705; the very fragmentary 1018, 1551, 1741, may have had similar dedications. See now also E. Birley, *Ep. Stud.* 4 (1967) 106 f. and *Arch. Ael.*[5] 8 (1980) 65 ff. (not unambiguous, p. 165 n. 8 above).

[3] pp. 181 ff. below. See also p. 206 below, for the suggestion that *RIB* 8, London, was set up by [*C. Julius Mar*]*cus for Caracalla's* [*vi*]*ctoriam* [*Germani*]*cam.*

used as a *cognomen*,[4] and, as the names C. Julius were exceptionally common, it is not surprising that a number of homonyms are known, none of whom need have any links with our man.[5] However, Marcus as a *cognomen* was rare among the upper orders—only one other senator is known to have used it[6] —and attention must be drawn to a friend of the sophist Hermogenes of Tarsus, Julius Marcus, ὁ κράτιστος, who could be the father of our governor.[7] It is possible that he himself was the Marcus who received a rescript from Caracalla in the year 205. The details indicate that the recipient of the rescript was a provincial official, perhaps a governor. That would of course support the view that Julius Marcus was a consular legate in 213, but the identification must remain uncertain for the time being.[8]

II.2
THE FIRST DIVISION OF BRITAIN

Cassius Dio, listing the distribution of the legions in his own time, states that VI Victrix was in Lower Britain, while he places XX Valeria Victrix as well as II Augusta in the Upper province.[1] The account was written after the redistribution of legions in the Pannonian provinces, which is known to have already taken place by 217,[2] for he puts I Adiutrix in Lower Pannonia in the same passage.[3] Epigraphic evidence confirms

[4] Kajanto 173 knows of over 200 epigraphic examples.

[5] III 389 (Sarmizegethusa), 7658 (Napoca), VI 389 (an *evocatus Augusti*), 32624 d 8 (a praetorian guardsman, third century).

[6] Barbieri, *L'Albo* 2212: P. Aelius Aelianus Archelaus Marcus, patron of an Italian town, but of eastern extraction, to judge from the other items in his nomenclature.

[7] Hermog. *de inventione* 3. 1 (p. 126 Raabe); *PIR*[2] J 404. For the sophist, see H 149: he was at his peak as a youth in the reign of M. Aurelius.

[8] *Cod. Iust.* 4. 15. 2: 'Imp. Antoninus A. Marco, Si in causa iudicati Valentis, quem tibi condemnatum esse proponis, nihil est, quod sine quaestione pignoris loco capi et distrahi possit, debitores eius conventi ad solutionem auctoritate praesidis provinciae compelluntur.' The Marcus here is evidently in a position to have passed sentence ('tibi condemnatum'), but it is not clear whether he himself is the 'praeses provinciae'.

[1] Dio 55. 23. 2, 6.

[2] This is made certain by the career of C. Octavius Ap. Suetrius Sabinus, *cos. ord.* 214 and sacked as governor of Lower Pannonia by Macrinus in 217 (Dio 78. 13. 2): see Barbieri, *L'Albo* no. 387; Fitz, *A. Ant. Hung.* 11 (1963) 287 ff., who places the change a few years earlier, as does A. Mócsy, *RE* Supp. 9 (1962) 587 ff. The change in status of the governor makes it certain that the legionary garrison had been increased (see pp. 27 f. above).

[3] Dio 55. 24. 2. There is no means of telling exactly when Dio wrote this passage. All that we have is Dio's own statement (72. 23. 5) that he began writing after the death of Severus, having spent ten years in research up till then; and that the writing took twelve years, which should be 211-22 or 223. See A. R. Birley, *Septimius Severus* 8 f. n. 1, criticizing F. Millar, *A Study of Cassius Dio* (1964), who arbitrarily sets aside this information. If Dio wrote at uniform speed, he would have reached book 55 in the year 218.

that VI Victrix was in Britannia inferior[4] and XX Valeria Victrix in superior.[5] Under this arrangement, it may be assumed, for as long as *legati Augusti pro praetore* served in Britain, the governors of the two legion Upper province were of consular, those of the one legion Lower province were of praetorian status.[6] But none of the epigraphically recorded governors name their province on inscriptions within Britain, while the single legate recorded outside Britain,[7] Ti. Claudius Paulinus, is unhelpfully described as *leg. Aug. pr. pr. prov.* [*B*]*ritanniae* on the famous Thorigny inscription. Elsewhere on that stone, however, the phrase describing how Sennius Sollemnis was *assessor* to Paulinus *in Brit. ad legionem sext*[*am*] implies that Paulinus' province had only that one legion.[8] A further possible clue is provided by the identification, which seems very plausible, of the governor attested in the northern frontier area on two inscriptions of the year 216, and on a third stone from Ribchester, with the future emperor Gordian I. Since Gordian was proconsul of Africa 237–8, it is almost certain that his consulship fell after 216,[9] which would indicate that the northern province of Inferior, with a praetorian governor, was already in existence by that year.

As far as the earlier period is concerned, the evidence for the governors under Severus indicates that the province was still undivided. The three firmly attested legates, Virius Lupus, C. Valerius Pudens, and L. Alfenus Senecio, were all of consular rank, although recorded exclusively in what was later to be the far end of the praetorian province of Inferior. Pudens and Senecio are actually called *co(n)sularis* or *cos.* on several inscriptions, while in a passage of the *Digest* Lupus is described as *Brittanniae praesidem.*[10] But in any case all three men are known—in the case of Pudens without a shadow of doubt—to have governed a consular province before coming to Britain. Prima facie, therefore, an impressive volume of evidence suggests that Britain remained undivided until some time between the governorship of Senecio, datable to the years between 205 and 207, and the year 216, or at latest 220, when Paulinus is attested.

But a complication is introduced by the explicit statement of Herodian, that Britain was divided into two provinces by Severus immediately after the battle of Lugdunum in 197. After sending Albinus' head to

---

[4] VIII 5180 + 17266 = *ILAlg.* I 539. 1 (see on this A. R. Birley, in Butler (ed.), *Soldier and Civilian in Roman Yorkshire* 95 n. 92).

[5] VIII 2080.   [6] Cf. p. 28 above on analogous cases.

[7] This excludes the doubtful cases of Pollienus Auspex and C. Junius Faustinus (pp. 151 ff., 161 ff. above), who may have been consular governors of Upper Britain after the division.

[8] p. 189 below.   [9] p. 184 below.   [10] pp. 149 ff., 155 ff., 157 ff., above.

Rome on a pole, Severus 'arranged matters in Britain, dividing the governorship of the province into two commands'—and this was before his return to Rome.[11] Various expedients have been put forward to reconcile the evidence. E. Ritterling suggested that the division at first left two legions under a consular governor of Superior, while Inferior was assigned to a presidial procurator, whose legion, VI Victrix, would have been under an equestrian *praefectus*. The presence of consular governors in the territory of Inferior was to be explained as a temporary measure, and the theory was held to be a satisfying explanation of what seemed anomalous otherwise, the presence side by side of the consular legate Alfenus Senecio and the procurator Oclatinius Adventus.[12] A modified form of this hypothesis was put forward by E. Birley (who had earlier urged that Herodian was simply mistaken[13]), suggesting that the procuratorial province of Inferior excluded York and VI Victrix, and had its capital at Carlisle.[14] Ritterling proposed that it was Severus' arrival in 208 which caused the arrangements to be altered to those described by Dio, while Birley put this change *c.*213. A further solution was devised by J. C. Mann and M. G. Jarrett, that the division of 197 left two legions, XX Valeria Victrix as well as VI Victrix, under a consular governor of Inferior, with a praetorian governor of Superior having only II Augusta under his command. This scheme could then have been modified, they argued, at about the time that Caracalla adjusted the boundaries of the two Pannonian provinces, altering the status of Pannonia Inferior thereby. Thenceforward, from *c.*213, Chester and the XXth legion were transferred from the Lower to th Upper province.[15]

In the meantime A. J. Graham had argued firmly against accepting Herodian's statement.[16] In particular, he showed good reason to doubt that the presence of a procurator alongside the legate was in any way exceptional, and hence that this need not mean that Adventus was the presidial procurator, supervised by his senior colleague from the other province. He also cited an inscription from Ephesus, recording the travels of a local man to see Severus in Britain and Caracalla in Upper Germany. From this he argued that at the time of the Severan expedition Britain was still a single province—for while Germany was specified

---

[11] Herodian 3. 8. 2.   [12] *RE* 12. 2 (1925) 1609.
[13] *Arch. Ael.*[4] 11 (1934) 131 ff.
[14] *CW*[2] 53 (1954) 52 ff.
[15] *JRS* 57 (1967) 61 ff. I accepted their arguments in Butler (ed.), *Soldier and Civilian in Roman Yorkshire* 89 f., and *Septimius Severus* 247 f.
[16] *JRS* 56 (1966) 92 ff.

as τὴν ἄνω, Britain had no such label.[17] But Mann and Jarrett effectively explained away this item, by pointing out that 'Britain' was 'merely a geographical description', while 'Germany' unqualified could have led to confusion with free Germany.[18]

The above summary will serve to indicate that the problem still remains unresolved. Yet it must be doubtful whether Herodian deserves to be taken so seriously. A number of recent studies have demonstrated his unreliability in important questions of fact and chronology.[19] It is curious that he does not mention, for example, the division of Syria after the defeat of Niger, which is attested by Cassius Dio and confirmed by epigraphy.[20] What is more, when he comes to mention Britain again, in preparation for his description of the Severan expedition, he refers to an appeal for help to the emperor from 'the governor of Britain'.[21] The appeal is in any case of dubious historicity;[22] yet, whatever the facts of that matter, he had apparently forgotten that he had recorded the division of the province into two.

There is a further piece of evidence which appears to have been neglected. One of the consuls of 212, C. Julius (Camilius Galerius) Asper, received an honorific inscription at Tusculum, giving him the title *cos.* as the first item in his *cursus*, hence not earlier than 212, set up by *provincia Britannia* to him as *patronus.*[23] Since another province of which the same senator was also patron is specified as Mauretania Tingitana—and not just as Mauretania[24]—it is difficult to avoid the conclusion that in 212 Britain was still undivided. It may be added that the most natural interpretation of an inscription from near the Wall, combined with other evidence, shows the presence in the far

[17] *SEG* XVII 505, discussed by Graham, op. cit. 100 f.

[18] *JRS* 57 (1967) 61.

[19] See e.g. E. Hohl, *Kaiser Commodus und Herodian* (1954); id., *Kaiser Pertinax und die Thronbesteigung seines Nachfolgers im Lichte der Herodiankritik* (1956); Alföldy, *Historia* 20 (1971) 84 ff., id., *Rhein. Mus.* 114 (1971) 360 ff.; id., *Hermes* 99 (1971) 429 ff.; id., *Bonner Jahrb.* 171 (1971) 367 ff.; id., *Latomus* 32 (1973) 345 ff.; A. R. Birley, *Arch. Ael.*[4] 50 (1972) 179 ff.; F. Kolb, *Literarische Beziehungen zwischen Cassius Dio, Herodian und der Historia Augusta* (1972) *passim.*

[20] In 3. 5. 1 he merely states that Severus 'settled the affairs of the east in what he thought was the best manner, and the most advantageous to himself'. There is no mention of this in what survives of Dio's account of 194 (book 74), but he has the information in 55. 23. 2 and probably referred to it in 74. 8 or 9, although Xiphilinus does not include it in his *epitome*. The date is supplied by *AE* 1930. 141, showing Ti. Manilius Fuscus to have been praetorian governor of Syria Phoenice in 194.

[21] 3. 14. 1: ὁ τῆς Βρεττανίας ἡγούμενος.

[22] For the dubious nature of this story, which is merely a rhetorical τόπος, see A. R. Birley, *Arch. Ael.*[4] 50 (1972) 186 ff., comparing 6. 1. 2 and 6. 7. 2.

[23] XIV 2508, discussed on p. 433 below.

[24] XIV 2509, cf. also 2516, referring to 'three Spanish and two Mauretanian provinces' of which this man or a kinsman was patron: see p. 433 below.

north, well within what was later the Lower province, of a legate of the Caerleon legion II Augusta.[25]

Thus the most likely solution seems to be that Herodian was simply wrong. Perhaps, having read Dio,[26] he muddled up the division of Syria with the division of Britain. It therefore seems probable that it was Caracalla who divided Britain, perhaps as a consequence of the British army's hostile reaction when he murdered his brother Geta. The governor Julius Marcus manifestly attempted to protest their—and his— loyalty with a series of dedications *pro pietate ac devotione communi*; but in vain, as the deletion of Marcus' name clearly demonstrates.[27] It is tempting to restore Marcus' name in an inscription from London: [. . . / C. *Julius Mar*] cus [*leg. eius pr. pr. prov. Bri*] tann [*i*] ae / [*fecit ob vi*] ctoriam / [*Germani*] cam. Certainly, no better candidate is known as dedicator, and few better occasions can be found than Caracalla's German victory of the year 213.[28]

The precise boundary line between the Upper and Lower provinces has not been worked out, but its approximate position can be seen from the fact that, while Chester was in Superior, Lincoln was in Inferior.[29] It may be noted, further, that there is evidence of agents of the Upper province's governor operating in Inferior, at unknown dates.[30]

II.3

GOVERNORS OF BRITANNIA SUPERIOR

Pollienus Auspex (*cos. a. inc.*)

IGR III 618 = *ILS* 8841 = *TAM* ii 278, Xanthus: see pp. 152 ff. above, for discussion

---

[25] L. Julius Julianus: see pp. 265 f. below.   [26] See Kolb, op. cit., esp. 25 ff., 160 f.

[27] In 77. 1. 3 Dio indicates that 'the troops' were particularly well disposed towards Geta, especially as he resembled Severus. The context shows that this was before the brothers returned to Rome; note also Herodian 3. 15. 5–6. From these passages one might legitimately infer that the British army reacted with hostility to the news of Geta's murder (as II Parthica at Alba certainly did: *HA Carac.* 2. 6 ff.). For C. Julius Marcus and the loyalty dedications of 213 see p. 167 above.

[28] See p. 206 below, for further discussion of this inscription (*RIB* 8).

[29] As shown by *AE* 1922. 116, Bordeaux (AD 237: a *sevir* of York and Lincoln). Frere, *Britannia*[2] (1974) 219 n. 29, pronounces the Felixstowe seal, 'being a portable object', to be irrelevant; it is in any case only by a conjecture that it is supposed to refer to *inferior* (*PB* [*I*], *p*(*rovinciae*) *B*(*ritanniae*) [*I*(*nferioris*)] : *JRS* 45 (1955) 147).

[30] *RIB* 745, ?747, Greta Bridge; 1696, Vindolanda; all three attest *bf. cos. provinciae superior.* in more or less similar terms. Note also *RIB* 980, Netherby (quoted on p. 186 below): men from the two Upper British legions building north of Hadrian's Wall, apparently in the year 219.

of the identity of this governor, whose province may have been either undivided Britain or Superior.

C. Junius Faustinus Postumianus (*cos. a. inc.*)

EE V 270 = (*CIL*) VIII 11763, Gelat-es-Senam: see pp. 162 ff. above, for discussion of this text, which might refer to a governor of Britannia superior, although his province might equally have been undivided Britain.

-r-ius Rufinus (*cos. a. inc.*)

Ant. J. 41 (1961) 22 = *JRS* 51 (1961) 191 = *AE* 1962. 258, cf. *JRS* 55 (1965) 220, Reculver: *aedem p[rinci]piorum / cu[m b]asilica / su[b . . .]r[. . .]io Rufino* [4]/ *cos. / [. . .Fo]rtunatus / [. . .]it*

The inscription from Reculver records the construction of a major portion of the headquarters building of the fort there.[1] Unfortunately the governor's name is incompletely recorded, but enough survives to permit informed conjecture, if not certainty, about his identity. The traces of the *nomen*, and the space available for it, show that it included the letter R soon after the beginning and that it was relatively short. The archaeological evidence for the fort's date of construction is limited and not very helpful;[2] but it could be said to make it, if only slightly, more likely that the province of which Rufinus was consular governor was Britannia superior.[3] I. A. Richmond restored *su[b A. T]r[iar]io Rufino*, identifying the governor with the *cos. ord.* 210 of that name. To make the name fit the space he was obliged to suppose that the first I of the *nomen* had been carved at a smaller size than the other letters and that it had been inserted between the first R and the A, above the line.[4] This was perfectly legitimate, given that several

---

[1] As pointed out by the editors, the emperor will have been named on another slab, cf. e.g. the inscriptions of Modius Julius and Octavius Sabinus (pp. 187, 200 below).

[2] Frere, *Britannia* (1967) 185, suggests a date *c.*220. S. Johnson, *The Roman Forts of the Saxon Shore* (1976) 47, notes that a series of well-bottoms to the west of the fort were all of late-second- or early-third-century date. Unfortunately the presumed date of this inscription seems to have been relied upon to date the fort.

[3] Very few senatorial Rufini from the second century had suitable *nomina* in any case. The only conceivable known person is C. Curtius Rufinus (see pp. 251 ff. below, for his father), whose career is not recorded beyond a laticlave tribunate (*PIR*[2] C 1617).

[4] *Ant. J.* 41 (1961) 225. The stone did not necessarily give a *praenomen*—J. S. Johnson's drawing, *The Roman Forts of the Saxon Shore* (1976) 17 fig. 11, based on Richmond, omits it (see further below, n. 19, on this drawing).

other vowels elsewhere in the inscription were treated in this way.[5] On the other hand, it has been argued that it is improbable that a former *consul ordinarius* would have governed a military province at this period.[6] There is perhaps some force in this view, but on second thoughts it should be noted that M. Nummius Umbrius *cet.* (*cos. ord.* 206),[7] C. Octavius Ap. Suetrius Sabinus (*cos. ord.* 214),[8] M. Munatius Sulla Cerealis (*cos. ord.* 215),[9] and perhaps Pomponius Bassus (*cos. ord.* 211(?))[10] governed imperial consular provinces at precisely this period. Hence Triarius Rufinus cannot be excluded. In that case, it is not impossible that he was governor of undivided Britain; but on balance the governorship of consular Britannia superior, some time in the reign of Caracalla, seems to be indicated.[11] The Triarii appear to have been an Italian family[12] and Rufinus' father is thought to have been Triarius Maternus (*signo*) Lascivius (probably the *cos. ord.* 185, Maternus), who evaded an attempt by the guard to proclaim him emperor against Pertinax in early January 193.[13]

A second strong candidate must be L. Prosius Rufinus, recorded as legate of Thrace in the year 222.[14] The restoration *su*[*b L. P*]*r*[*os*]*io Rufino* would fit the space admirably. Prosius Rufinus is, admittedly, not known to have become consul, but this is not surprising, for the names of relatively few *suffecti* are known from the third century. On the other hand, the governorship of Thrace had frequently led to the consulship, and certainly did so in the case of several other governors from this period.[15] His *nomen* is peculiar and extremely rare,[16] but another prominent bearer of it was Prosius Tertullianus, governor of Lower Moesia under Gordian III and very probably the son of this

[5] Viz. the *o* and *u* in *p*[*rinci*]*piorum* in line 1, the *o* of *Rufino* in line 3, and the second *u* in [*Fo*]*rtunatus* in line 5.

[6] R. P. Harper, *Anat. Stud.* 14 (1964) 166 n. 18, followed by A. R. Birley, *Ep. Stud.* 4 (1967) 83, and Mann, in Johnston (ed.), *The Saxon Shore* 15.

[7] Hispania citerior: Barbieri, *L'Albo* no. 386, Alföldy, *Fasti Hispanienses* 48.

[8] Pannonia inferior: Barbieri, *L'Albo* no. 387, Eck, *RE* Supp. 14 (1974) 290.

[9] Cappadocia: Barbieri, *L'Albo* no. 377.

[10] One of the Moesias: Barbieri, *L'Albo* no. 421, Stein, *Moesien* 55, 90.

[11] See pp. 163 ff. above.

[12] Barbieri, *L'Albo* no. 504, noting Pliny's friend (*ep.* 6. 23); cf. Schulze 375, citing Cic. *ad fam.* 8. 7. 2 etc., X 3021 (Naples), 6242 (Fundi).

[13] *HA Pert.* 6. 4. 5. See Barbieri, *L'Albo* no. 503, cf. 2108, Alföldy, *Fasti Hispanienses* 87 f.

[14] Stein, *Thracia* 53 ff., id., *Serta Hoffilleriana* (1940) 214; Barbieri, *L'Albo* no. 437.

[15] Stein, *Thracia* 52 ff. Note Q. Atrius Clonius (*PIR*[2] A 1322), Rutilius Pudens Crispinus (Alföldy, *Fasti Hispanienses* 59 f.), D. Simonius Proculus Julianus (Barbieri, *L'Albo* no. 1159), Ti. Clodius Saturninus Fidus (ibid. no. 1008), L. Catius Celer (*RE* Supp. 14 (1974) 87 f.).

[16] Schulze 90 n. 5 knew no other examples and uncharacteristically stated that 'über dessen Etymologie ich nichts auszusagen wage'. Note also however II 5927 = 3434, VIII 18694, 18703, 19207, IX 2282, X 4306, 5513, 6695, XIV 4242 = *ILS* 1044; 27. *Bericht der R.G.K.* 150 (P. Prosius Celer, *praef. cast.* of VIII Augusta, from Teanum Sidicinum).

Rufinus.[17] If the Reculver governor turned out to be Prosius Rufinus, a date in the mid- to late 220s would seem probable, and the province that he governed would certainly have been Britannia superior.

However, the favoured candidate hitherto, first proposed by R. P. Harper,[18] has been Q. Aradius Rufinus Optatus Aelianus. The restoration *su[b A]r[ad]io Rufino*[19] would certainly fit without difficulty. A large part of this man's career is preserved on an inscription from Bulla Regia in Africa, which seems to be his home town: *Q. Aradio Rufino / Optato Aeliano cos. / sodali Augustali agenti 4/ vice p[r]ocos. prov. Afrik. / leg. Aug. pr. pr. provinciarum / [Syriae] Coelae item Phoe/[nices ite]m Galatiae praef. 8/ [aerar. Satu]rni praef. aera[r. / militaris l]eg. leg. [.] II[...]*[20] The priesthood in line 3 gives some ground for identifying . him with the Q. Aradius Rufinus who was co-opted into the *sodales Augustales Claudiales* in 219,[21] but even this cannot be regarded as certain and it would give little specific guidance to dating the remainder of the career. What is more, either this man—or perhaps his father—was the founder of a family which enjoyed prominence for many generations. Consequently, even if the Reculver inscription could be confidently restored to show that an Aradius Rufinus was consular governor in Britain, there would still be a wide range of possibilities over the date.[22]

[17] Stein, *Moesien* 101 f.; Barbieri, *L'Albo* no. 1707.

[18] *Anat. Stud.* 14 (1964) 166 n. 18, followed by A. R. Birley, *Ep. Stud.* 4 (1967) 83, et al.; see now Rémy, *Historia* 25 (1976) 472 f.

[19] See Johnson, *Roman Forts of the Saxon Shore* 17 fig. 11, for a revised version of Richmond's drawing. But it must be pointed out that Johnson appears to have no warrant for showing a small trace of the second A in *[A]r[ad]io* as if it were on the stone: Richmond's drawing, and the photograph in *JRS* 51 (1961) pl. XXII, show that this is impossible.

[20] The inscription was first noted by R. P. Duncan-Jones, who kindly communicated it to the author and to R. P. Harper (see n. 18 above). I was able to study the stone at Bulla in June 1965, and, with the kind permission of Dr A. Beschaouch, I published the text in *Ep. Stud.* 4 (1967) 83, whence *AE* 1971. 490. The career has now received a lengthy re-examination from Rémy, *Historia* 25 (1976) 458 ff. (see n. 22 below). I give here a slightly improved reading, based on further study of the photograph taken at my request by Mr C. M. Daniels, to whom I must record my thanks. It should be noted that the principal difference is that I now regard the identification of the legion in line 9 (of which only the tops of the letters are preserved) as being even less certain than I did before. Besides this, I now allow for more letters at the beginning of lines 7, 8, and 9.

[21] VI 1984 = *ILS* 5025 (*PIR*² A 1016).

[22] Mann, in Johnston, *Saxon Shore* 15, points out that the Reculver governor is unlikely to have been a *consularis* of Maxima Caesariensis, since by the time that Constantine revived *consulares*, civil and military government were being separated, and the *consularis* of Maxima Caesariensis is never likely to have commanded troops.

For the fourth-century descendants of Aradius Rufinus see *PLRE* I pp. 749, 775 f. One of the Aradii Rufini was the patron of the 'translator' of Dictys Cretensis, who is generally dated to the fourth century (thus *PLRE* I p. 821). The man in the Bulla Regia *cursus* appears to have been married to one Calpurnia Fidiana Aemiliana, doubtless identical with Julia Memmia Calpurnia Aemiliana Fidiana, daughter of C. Memmius Fidus Julius Albius (p 278 below), also

In these circumstances, it is safest to leave the identity of this governor open, pending the discovery of further evidence.[23]

M. Martiannius Pulcher

Britannia 7 (1976) 378 f., London: *in h. d. d.* / *M. Martian/nius Pulch/er v. ç. leg.* [4] / *Augg. pro* / *praet. ṭẹmpḷ(u)m̲* / *Isịḍis c*[. . .] /*ṭịs vetustate* [8] / *collabsum* / *restitui praẹ/cepit*

This governor is otherwise completely unknown and his remarkable *nomen* appears to be unique. Curious though it is, however, it is of a well-known type, formed from a *cognomen*, in this case Martianus. Attempts to explain it as, for example, Mar(ius) Ti. Annius,[1] are thus unnecessary. Numerous parallels might be cited, e.g. Martialius, Annianius, Vibianius.[2] The best known perhaps is the *nomen* of the Gallic emperor Postumus, Cassianius.[3] One would have expected, by analogy with the last three examples, Martianius with a single N. An error on the part of the stone-mason is possible.[4] But there are enough cases of variant spellings of both *nomina* and *cognomina*, with single or double consonant,[5] to make it plausible that our governor preferred the form Martiannius.

a native of Bulla: see Eck, *RE* Supp. 14 (1974) 54. Since Memmius Fidus was *cos. des.* 191, it seems plausible to put his son-in-law's tenure of the office about twenty or thirty years later. Rémy, *Historia* 25 (1976) 465, suggested the year 228 on the grounds that Rufinus might have been *cos. suff.* in the year when another man thought to have been his father-in-law was *cos. II ord.*, namely Q. Aiacius Modestus Crescentianus. This relationship was deduced from XV 8088, a signet inscribed *Q. Aradi Rufini et Iunie Aiacie Modeste* (thus Syme, *Emperors and Biography* 140, Rémy, *Historia* 25 (1976) 460 f.). It would now seem preferable to assume that this couple belonged to a different generation. There is no means of dating the Q. Aradius Rufinus described as consul who made dedications to Sol and Luna at Thuburnica (VIII 14688 = *ILS* 3937, VIII 10602 = 14689 = *ILS* 3938). As with the *sodalis Augustalis* of 219 (n. 21 above), identity with Rufinus Optatus Aelianus cannot be assumed. Finally, the suggestion made in *Ep. Stud.* 4 (1967) 83—followed with some enthusiasm by Rémy, op. cit. 465 ff.—that the latter's post *agenti vice procos. prov. Afrik.* might have fallen in 238, cannot be regarded as compelling. Further evidence is required, and may indeed be forthcoming when all the inscriptions of this family from Bulla are published. A possible ancestor of Optatus Aelianus is Aelius Optatus, legate of V Macedonica, probably in the late 150s (*AE* 1960. 337): see Alföldy, *Konsulat* 299, for the date.

[23] The recent discovery of an inscription naming as governor a person hitherto totally unknown, with a unique *nomen* and no detectable kinsfolk (below) is a salutary warning against premature identification of --r--ius Rufinus.

[1] Thus J. R. Martindale, *ap.* J. M. Reynolds, *JRS* 66 (1976) 187. No Ti. Annii appear to be extant. M. Marti(us) Annius might also be possible, in theory, although *nomina* were not frequently abbreviated after a vowel.

[2] VI 22264 (Q. Martialius Frontinus, *patronus* of Q. Frontinius Mercator), XII 765, V 746 + add. See Schulze 51 ff. on 'Gentilnamen aus cognomina' and note also his discussion of one category on pp. 17 f.; further, 487 on Martialius.

[3] *PIR*[2] C 466. Not discussed by Schulze.

[4] Thus the editors in *Britannia* 7 (1976) 378 n. 4.

There are few clues to his origin. The *cognomen* Pulcher, rendered familiar by the great republican house of the Claudii Pulchri, seems actually to have been little favoured in the imperial period, just over forty epigraphic examples being on record.[6] Martianus, from which his *nomen* derives, was even less common, some twenty examples being known.[7] However, 'fabricated' *nomina* such as Martiannius were particularly popular in the Celtic parts of the empire.[8] Hence the balance of probability points to an origin in northern Italy, Gaul, or the Rhineland; indeed, Britain itself cannot be excluded.[9]

As far as dating is concerned, the only real clue is provided by the governor's style, *v. c. leg. Augg. pro praet.*[10] Of joint reigns, the earliest, those of M. Aurelius and L. Verus, and M. Aurelius and Commodus, can probably be excluded, since there are barely any vacancies —although the period *c.*166-9 is not completely impossible.[11] If Britain was not divided until *c.*213, there is scarcely any room under Severus and Caracalla either, except perhaps *c.*200-3.[12] If, on the other hand, as has been postulated, there was a praetorian province of Britannia superior from 197 to *c.*213, Pulcher could have been its governor some time in the years 198-209, or in 211. Otherwise, he must be regarded as a consular governor of Upper Britain.[13] Possible dates are 221-2, 235-8, and most of the period 238-60[14]— hardly later, for although senatorial governors continued under the *imperium Galliarum*, there seem to have been no joint *Augusti*

[5] See Schulze 422 ff. on 'Consonantengemination', with numerous examples. Petil(l)ius and Paul(l)inus are familiar from the annals of Roman Britain. See also the index to VI for Fan(n)ius and Man(n)ius.

[6] Kajanto 231: thirty-three men, nine women.

[7] Kajanto 150: nineteen men, two women.

[8] Schulze 56 ff.; E. Birley, *Roman Britain and the Roman Army* 165 f., 176 f.

[9] The spread of Martiani may be worth noting: there are four in XIII, three each in II and in Dalmatia (III 2023, 14250[1], 14276[2]), two in Lower Pannonia (III 3560, 3651), one in Lower Moesia (III 7566), and a cavalry decurion in the *ala I Thracum* at Alexandria (III 14 = 6581)—in other words two-thirds of them derive from northern and western provinces. Note also XIII 7655 (*inter confluentes*): M. Marlianius(?) Ripanus.

[10] The editors are uncertain about the *c*, for the letter closely resembles an *e*. But *v(ir) e(gregius)* seems quite impossible. *V. c.* is found with governors only in third-century inscriptions in Britain: *RIB* 1234 (AD 205/7), 1553 (AD 237), 334 (AD 253/8), 605 (AD 262/8).

[11] p. 131 above.   [12] pp. 151, 156 above.

[13] Eck, *RE* Supp. 15 (1977) 131, makes him a consular governor of Britannia inferior, which cannot be right.

[14] It should perhaps be noted that the Pulcher who received a rescript from Aurelian (in January of a year 271/5) might conceivably be our man, e.g. as proconsul of Africa or Asia, or as *vice sacra iudicans*. The case concerned a senator (*Cod. Iust.* 5. 72. 2) but the status of the recipient is not clear. One might perhaps also note the Martiani (9.21, 2. 13. 6), Marcianus and Martinus (*Cod. Iust.* 8. 13[14]. 7, 4. 57. 5) who received rescripts in AD 222, 223, 238, and 240, for the names might be corrupt—as for that matter might be that of the governor Marcianus or Martianus by whom martyrs were sentenced in Pisidia under Decius (Barbieri, *L'Albo* no. 1652 + Agg.).

there; and subsequently it must be assumed that equestrian *praesides* governed both British provinces for the remainder of the third century.[15]

| between 253 and 258 | Desticius Juba |

VII 107 = *ILS* 537 = *RIB* 334, Caerleon: *Impp. Valerianus et Gallienus / Augg. et Valerianus nobilissimus / Caes. cohorti VII centurias a so⁴/lo restituerunt per Desticium Iubam / v. c. legatum Augg. pr. pr. et / Vitulasium Laetinianum leg. leg. / II Aug. curante Domit. Potentino ⁸/ praef. leg. eiusdem*

This man's governorship must fall within the years 253–8, for Valerian and Gallienus became emperors in 253 and the latter's elder son Valerian junior was associated with them as *nobilissimus Caesar* until his death in 258.[1] Desticii, with the *praenomen* Titus, and several with the *cognomen* Juba, are attested by various inscriptions from Concordia in northern Italy. The founder of the family's fortunes was T. Desticius Severus, who rose to become praesidial procurator of Raetia in the year 166.[2] The first Desticius Juba, presumably his son, acquired senatorial rank,[3] and seems to have been the father of Desticius Sa[l]us[tius] Juba and of [Dest]i[c]i[a] Sallustia Plotina,[4] whose names suggest that their mother was a Sallustia Plotina. Our governor is thus likely to have been at least a third-generation senator, a matter of some interest, since he is the latest known instance of a consular governor of Upper Britain, and indeed of any consular governor with senatorial legates and legions under him. Gallienus was shortly to exclude senators from military posts,[5] although the *imperium Galliarum* did not follow him in this policy.[6]

| (?) | L. Septimius |

EE IX 997 = *ILS* 5435 = *RIB* 103, Cirencester:
Face: *I. O. [M.] / L. Sept[.../ v. p. pr. B̦[r...] ⁴/ resti[tuit]/ civis R̦[...]*

---

[15] pp. 200 f. below.

[1] *PIR²* L 258, 184.   [2] *PIR²* D 57, Pflaum, *CP* no. 167.

[3] *PIR²* D 54. There is no clue to explain the choice of *cognomen*, which is non-Latin and evokes the king of Mauretania (*PIR²* J 65); cf. Kajanto 111.

[4] V 7473, Industria, cf. *PIR²* D 54, 56, 58. Note also the polyonymous *Xvir stlitibus iudicandis*, D 55. See now on the Desticii G. Alföldy, *Aquileia Nostra* 28 (1980).

[5] Consular legates are of course found elsewhere after Gallienus, but none of them is specifically associated with legions. See pp. 34 f. above.

[6] See p. 200 below.

Back: [*si*]*gnum et* / [*e*]*rectam* / [*p*]*risca re*[4]/[*li*]*gione co*/[*l*]*umnam*
Left: *Septimius* / *renovat* / *primae* [4]/ *provinciae* / *rector*

Primae provinciae rector in the second line of verse is generally thought
to be the equivalent of *praeses provinciae* (*Britanniae*) *primae*. In that
case, L. Septimius must belong to the period after the Diocletianic
reorganization, and the inscription would provide useful evidence for
the location of one of the four British provinces which already existed
when the Verona list was drawn up, between 312 and 314.[1] Further,
the renovation of a column *erectam prisca re*[*li*]*gione* is thought to be
a product of the pagan revival in the reign of Julian.[2]

However, as E. Birley has pointed out, it seems likely that 'the
Diocletianic restyling *Prima* and *Secunda*, wherever we meet it (in place
of *Superior* and *Inferior*) represents the adoption officially of what had
become general informal usage'; and further, 'the fact that the verse
uses the non-technical term *rector* should be sufficient to warn us not
to take *primae provinciae* as necessarily official terminology—*superioris*
would not scan.'[3] *Primae* might well have been used as a poetic equivalent of *superioris*, and it should be noted that the restoration of line 3
of the prose inscription as *v. p. pr. Ḅ*[*r. pr.*] is far from certain. To
judge from the setting out of the surviving left-hand part of the inscription, lines 2 and 3 ought to have been as long as line 5, where a total of
ten letters seems to be required. Hence *v. p. pr. Ḅ*[*r. sup.* or even *super.*]
is perfectly possible.[4] The fact that the governor has a *praenomen* is
also in favour of a third-century date. Although old-style *praenomina*
were still sometimes used in the fourth century, they are found very
infrequently in inscriptions of this type, as study of the fourth century
provincial *Fasti* reveals.[5]

As for the apparent reflection of the ideology of Julian the Apos-
tate, it must be pointed out that numerous inscriptions of all periods
record the restoration of temples and other buildings, with from
time to time reference to their *pristinus status* or the like.[6] *Erectam*

---

[1] p. 316 below.

[2] Thus Wright, *RIB* 103, ad loc., who cites the literature. See now also *PLRE* I p. 822.

[3] E. Birley, *Quintus Congressus . . . 1961* (1963) 84, followed by A. R. Birley, *Ep. Stud.*
4 (1967) 85.

[4] Or indeed *Ḅ*[*rit. sup.*].

[5] See *PLRE* I pp. 1072 ff. For example, of the proconsuls of Africa, more than two-thirds
of those from the years 260–300 have known *praenomina*, only one in six of those from the
fourth century. In other provinces far fewer governors' *praenomina* are known, after 300.

[6] Inscriptions simply recording the reconstruction of a temple *vetustate conlapsum* or the
like are of course too numerous to need citing (cf. e.g. p. 176 above) and do not provide an
adequate parallel. But one can find a variety of cases where the restorer was slightly more
specific. Cf. e.g. *RIB* 152, Bath: *Locum religiosum per insolentiam erutum virtuti et n. Aug.*

prisca·re[li]gione appears more specific, but it is after all part of a verse couplet.

If these arguments are accepted, the likeliest period at which a *v. p. praeses* of Upper Britain might be expected to have held office would be the years 274–86 after the recovery of Britain by Aurelian and before the usurpation of Carausius.

However this may be, a valuable clue to the governor's origin is provided by R. P. Wright's reading of line 5 of the prose dedication, *civis R[emus]*. As he points out, 'the Remi belonged to an area in Gaul where many Jupiter-columns were set up', and it may be regarded as probable that our governor was himself a native of those parts. In view of the commonness of the *gentilicium*, speculation about his identity would be unproductive; but his *cognomen* (unless also abbreviated) must have been a short one, of four or five letters.[7]

Ignotus

Zos. *Hist. Nov.* 1. 66. 2: ἔπαυσεν δὲ καὶ ἄλλην ἐπανάστασιν, ἐν τῇ Βρεττανίᾳ μελετηθεῖσαν, διὰ Βικτωρίνου Μαυρουσίου τὸ γένος, ᾧπερ πεισθεὶς ἔτυχεν τὸν ἐπαναστάντα τῆς Βρεττανίας ἄρχοντα προστησάμενος. καλέσας γὰρ τὸν Βικτωρῖνον πρὸς ἑαυτὸν καὶ ἐπὶ τῇ συμβουλῇ μεμψάμενος τὸ πταῖσμα ἐπανορθώσοντα πέμπει· ὁ δὲ ἐπὶ τὴν Βρεττανίαν εὐθὺς ἐξορμήσας περινοίᾳ οὐκ ἄφρονι τὸν τύραννον ἀναιρεῖ.

Ibid. 1. 68. 3: ὅσους δὲ ζῶντας οἷός τε γέγονεν ἑλεῖν, εἰς Βρεττανίαν παρέπεμψεν· οἳ τὴν νῆσον οἰκήσαντες ἐπαναστάντος μετὰ ταῦτά τινος γεγόνασι βασιλεῖ χρήσιμοι.

Zonar. 12. 29: ἕτερος δέ τις ἐν Βρεττανίαις ἀποστασίαν διεμελέτησεν, ὃν ἐπὶ τῆς ἀρχῆς ὁ βασιλεὺς ἐποιήσατο. Βικτωρίου Μαυρουσίου ᾠκειωμένου αὐτῷ τοῦτο

repurgatum reddidit G. *Severius Emeritus 7 reg.* In VIII 8826 = *ILS* 4452 (Sertei) a man *monitus sacra religione templum simul cum area et aras summa cum diligentia restituit* (AD 247). VIII 21665 = *ILS* 4501 (Albula) records how an official *tempulu[m d]eae Maurae ad pristinum statum reformavit* (AD 299). Cf. also *ILTun.* 868 (Maxula), 1568 (Turris Rotunda). In the mid-second century a legate of III Augusta adorned a shrine to Isis and Serapis *ab antecessoribus [suis i]nstitutam.* VI 222 = *ILS* 2161 describes how an *aedicula facta cum Genio* in AD 111 was extended in AD 156, *vetustate corruptam.* III 4796 = *ILS* 4197 (Virunum) records that a *v. p. p(raeses) p(roviniciae) N(orici) M(edi)t(erranei) a novo restitui fecit* a *templum vetusta. conlabsum quot fuit per annos amplius L desertum.* The date for the building is given as AD 311, which should date the governor's restoration, not the original construction: see Alföldy, *Noricum* (1974) 344 n. 24. Finally, cf. the language of VI 773 = *ILS* 626: Diocletian and Maximian *Tiberino patri aquarum omnium et repertoribus admirabilium fabricarum priscis viris honori dederunt,* on the completion of dredging and reconstruction of *fontium rivis et itineribus eorum.*

[7] Of the commonest *cognomina* (Kajanto 29 f.) only Felix and Rufus are short enough. Note a Septimius Rufus *magister summae (rei)* in the third century(?): *PLRE* I p. 785. The other known Septimii of the third and fourth centuries (listed ibid. pp. 822 f.) have longer *cognomina.*

αἰτησαμένου. καὶ τοῦτο μαθὼν ὁ Πρόβος ἠτιᾶτον τὸν Βικτωρῖνον. καὶ ὃς πεμφθῆναι πρὸς ἐκεῖνον ἠτήσατο, καὶ ἀπῄει ὡς δῆθεν φεύγων τὸν αὐτοκράτορα, καὶ ἀσπασίως ὑπὸ τοῦ τυραννήσαντος ὑπεδέδεκτο. ὁ δὲ διὰ τῆς νυκτὸς ἀνελὼν αὐτὸν ἐπανῆλθε πρὸς Πρόβον.

Anon. Hist. Ecloge, Anec. Gr. 2. 291: Βικτωρῖνος δὲ φίλος τοῦ Πρόβου ᾔτησε φίλον αὐτοῦ [ἄρχοντα] γενέσθαι εἰς Βρεττανίαν, ὁ δὲ ἀπελθὼν ἀντῆρεν· ὀνειδιζόμενος οὖν ὁ Βικτωρῖνος δι' αὐτὸν ἀπεστάλθη παύσων τὴν ἀνταρσίαν, προσποιησάμενος ἀπὸ προσώπου φεύγειν τοῦ βασιλέως, ὡς φίλος τοῦ ἀντάρτου ἀπεδέχθη καὶ ἀνεῖλεν αὐτόν. (Cf. Georg. Monachus Harmatolus, *Chron.* 3. 168. 2 and Georg. Cedrenus, Migne, *PG* 121, 505.)

This governor's tenure falls within the reign of Probus, AD 276-82.[1] A slightly closer dating may be arrived at from Zosimus' second mention of his coup in 1. 68. 3, where it emerges that his main account in 1. 66. 2 is out of chronological order. The prisoners sent to Britain who later helped to suppress 'a certain insurgent' there had been captured at the end of Probus' German campaign, in 277 or 278.[2] Probus himself had appointed the man to Britain, on the recommendation of one Victorinus, a Moor, a friend of both the emperor and of the governor;[3] and Victorinus was given the task of overthrowing him. The date of this can hardly be earlier than the end of 277 and could be a year or two later.[4]

It only remains to comment that the governor was most probably an equestrian *praeses* and that his province was presumably Britannia superior.[5]

II.4
GOVERNORS OF BRITANNIA INFERIOR

216   M. Antonius Gordianus Sempronianus Romanus (*cos. a. inc.*)

EE VII 986 = *RIB* 1049, Chester-le-Street: [. . .] *eqq.* / [*alae* . . . [[*Antoni/nianae*]] *t*] *errito⁴*/[*rium* . . . *aquam*] *induxit* / [*balneum* . . . *a s*] *olo in/*[*struxit sub cura* M. Antoni Gor] diani leg. / [Aug. pr. pr. Sabino II et An] ullino cos. (AD 216).

---

[1] *PIR²* A 1583.   [2] F. Miltner, *RE* 8A 1 (1955) 302 f.; *PIR²* I 19.
[3] This friendship is insufficent basis to deduce Moorish origin for the governor himself.
[4] Victorinus is sometimes identified with the *cos. ord.* 282 of that name, cf. Barbieri, *L'Albo* no. 1760. In that case the story in *Anec. Gr.* 2. 291, that after accomplishing his mission in Britain he asked μηκέτι ἄρξαι πράγματος and was granted ἡσυχίαν and δωρεὰς πολλάς, could hardly be accurate in the strict sense, although the consulship might have seemed like *quies* in comparison to provincial commands (and it might have been a reward for crushing the revolt, which could then be dated to 281).
[5] Lower Britain, with only one legion and separated from the rest of the empire by a two legion province, can surely be ruled out.

VII 1043 = *RIB* 1279, High Rochester: *imp. Caes. M. Aurelio / Severo Antonino / pio felici Aug. Parthic.* [4]*/ max. Brit. max. Germ. / max. pontifici maxim. / trib. potest. XVIIII imp. II / cos. IIII procos. p. p. coh. I* [8]*/ fida Vardul. c. R. eq.* ∞ *Anto/niniana fecit sub cura* ⟦*M. / [Antoni Gordiani]*⟧ ⟧ *leg. Aug. pr. p*[*r.*] (AD 216).

VII 226 = *RIB* 590, Ribchester: *pro salute / et victoria / invicti imp. Mar.* [4]*/ Aur. Sever. Ant/onini p. f. Aug. et Iul. / Aug. matri d. n. et cas. /* ⟦⟦*?su*[*b cura M. Antoni* [8]*/ Gordiani*⟧ ⟧ *Se(m)pr/[oniani Romani / leg. Aug. pr. pr.*]

Britannia 1 (1970) 307 = *AE* 1971. 218, York: [*genio?*] *collegi /* [. . .*o*] *b p(romotionem?) bf. Gordian.*

On an inscription from High Rochester of the year 216 the governor's name has been deleted. The traces that remain,[1] and the space available,[2] make it clear that it cannot have been that of C. Julius Marcus;[3] while a fragmentary inscription of the same year from Chester-le-Street preserves part of the governor's *cognomen*, [. . .]*diani*. Cognomina with this termination are not of course uncommon, particularly Claudianus.[4] But E. Birley divined[5] that the governor was the future ephemeral emperor of AD 238, M. Antonius Gordianus, invested with the purple while serving as proconsul of Africa.[6] The erasure will have taken place in that year, for several of the western provinces remained loyal to Maximinus until his death.[7] The hypothesis received confirmation from the inscription at Ribchester, where SEPR may be read at the end of line 8, after an erasure, on a dedication for the safety and victory of Caracalla and Julia Domna.[8] Gordian's full name was M. Antonius Gordianus Sempronianus Romanus,[9] and it seems clear that on this stone, where the mason employed elaborate ligatures, his complete

[1] E. Birley suggests to me that M. may be detected in the erasure at the end of line 9.

[2] There is ample room for [ANTONI. GORDIANI] at the beginning of line 10, especially if ligatures are allowed for.

[3] See p. 167 above, for the numerous cases where his name was erased.

[4] See e.g. Barbieri, *L'Albo*, index on p. 687 for third-century senatorial Claudiani. Note further Canidianus (*L'Albo* no. 1989a), Clodianus (no. 640), Herodianus (no. 156), Uttedianus (no. 499).

[5] E. Birley, in Askew, *The Coinage of Roman Britain* 82, without discussion; followed by Pflaum, *Rev. de phil.* 30 (1956) 73; R. P. Wright, ad *RIB* 1049, 1279; A. R. Birley, *Britain and Rome* 59; etc. (see below).

[6] *PIR*[2] A 833. See now esp. Syme, *Emperors and Biography* 163 ff.; X. Loriot, *ANRW* II. 2 (1975) 688 ff.

[7] Loriot, *ANRW* II. 2 (1975) 697 ff.

[8] The editors comment on *RIB* 590 that 'the deletion presumably removed the name of a governor whose memory was condemned. C. Julius Marcus . . . does not fit the space or match the letters'. They read *Se(m)pr(oni-)* after the deletion, without discussion. *Se(m)pr/[oniani Romani]* is required, as I first noted reviewing *RIB* in *Erasmus* 18 (1966) 101; see also *Ep. Stud.* 4 (1967) 87. Earlier editors read SV. . . at the beginning of line 7, presumably *su*[*b cura* . . .].

[9] Loriot, *ANRW* II. 2 (1975) 696 n. 309.

nomenclature was set out.[10] When the erasure was ordered, those responsible presumably overlooked the last two *cognomina.*[11] Finally, an inscription recently discovered at York is thought to refer to the promotion of his *beneficiarii.*[12]

As Gordian was proconsul of Africa for the year 237-8,[13] his consulship was very probably held some fifteen to seventeen years earlier, in one of the years 220-2.[14] Hence there is little doubt that he was praetorian governor of Britannia inferior. This makes it pretty certain that the division of Britain described by Cassius Dio, with the Lower province having only one legion, VI Victrix, had been implemented by 216 at the latest.[15]

The three Gordians are the subject of a *vita* in the *Historia Augusta,* but most of what is there retailed is entirely bogus, except for a little taken from Herodian.[16] The latter, writing not long after Gordian's death, asserted that he was in his eightieth year at the time of his proclamation,[17] and that he had governed several provinces besides Africa.[18] Apart from Lower Britain, one of these was probably Achaia,

[10] Every word in the inscription is ligatured except *pro* in line 1. Note that in line 3 *Mar.* is given instead of the usual *M.* for the emperor's *praenomen,* as if to demonstrate the mason's skill.

[11] The stone is broken off after line 8.

[12] See R. P. Wright, *Britannia* 1 (1970) 307 n. 11, citing G. Alföldy's comments.

[13] J. R. Rea, *ZPE* 9 (1972) 7, shows that the news of the Gordians' recognition by the senate was known at Oxyrrhynchus between 7 Apr. and 13 June 238, making it clear that the proconsular year was 237-8.

[14] Thomasson, *Statthalter Nordafrikas* I 14 ff. There is little precise information on the interval for third-century proconsuls, but M. Aufidius Fronto, *consul ordinarius* in 199, was due to be proconsul for 217-18 (Dio 78. 22. 4-5) and Cassius Dio, praetor in 193 and hence probably consul in 205 or 206, was evidently proconsul for 223-4 (see F. Millar, *A Study of Cassius Dio* (1964) 17 ff., 214 ff.). Hence an interval of seventeen years looks plausible for Gordian.

[15] pp. 166 ff. above.

[16] See e.g. Syme, *Emperors and Biography* 163 ff.; F. Kolb, *Literarische Beziehungen zwischen Cassius Dio, Herodian und der Historia Augusta* (1972) 8 ff.

[17] Herodian 7. 5. 2; πρεσβύτης δὲ ἐς ἔτος ἤδη περί που ὀγδοηκοστὸν ἐληλακὼς . . ., followed by the *HA Gord.* 9. 1: 'erat autem iam octogenarius'. Zonar. 12. 17. 11 makes him seventy-nine. K. D. Grasby, *CQ* N.S. 25 (1975) 123 ff., sets out to controvert the evidence of Herodian. He very properly castigates that author's slovenly habits with chronology, but it stretches the imagination too far to believe that Herodian made an error of twenty years (Grasby would have Gordian born *c.*178) in the age of an emperor who died only a few years before his time of writing, cf. 1. 1. 5, 1. 2. 5, 2. 15. 7, and C. R. Whittaker, Loeb. edn. I pp. ix ff. 6 f., 247 (a date soon after 250). Besides, a major plank in his argument is to deny that Gordian II was an ex-consul in 238: this was attested only by the *HA Gord.* 18. 5, and by various coins, which Grasby rejects as hybrids, with some justification. But he was unaware of the milestone from Caesarea Maritima, *AE* 1971. 475: *Imp. Caes. M. Antonio Gordiano filio Aug. Semproniano Romano Africano pio fel. Aug. pontif. trib. pot. cos. pro*[*cos.*], which demonstrates that Gordian II had been consul after all. The *HA* perhaps derived the information from Dexippus, as suggested by Barnes, *Latomus* 27 (1968) 591 f.

[18] Herodian 7. 5. 2: πολλῶν δὲ πρότερον ἄρξας ἐθνῶν ἔν τε πράξεσι μεγίσταις ἐξετασθείς . . . ἐκ πολλῶν ἡγεμονιῶν ὥσπερ κατ' ἀκολουθίαν ἐπὶ τοῦτο ἐλθόντα, once again followed by

as E. Groag pointed out,[19] for Philostratus, who dedicated his *Lives of the Sophists* to Antonius Gordianus, τῷ λαμπροτάτῳ ὑπάτῳ, refers to him at the end of the preface as ἄριστε ἀνθυπάτων. Gordian may thus be supposed to have held the *fasces* during or shortly after his year as proconsul of Achaia.

His career, however incompletely recorded, can thus be seen to have been slightly peculiar. He must have been born in 158 or 159, and was thus in his late fifties as governor of Lower Britain. It may be that he had suffered some retardation, perhaps under Commodus, or as a result of supporting the wrong side in the civil wars of 193-7.[20] His appointment to govern Britannia inferior might, indeed, have been the result of the sudden downfall of C. Julius Marcus.[21] But, in any case, if, as seems possible, the division, or re-division of Britain followed in 213 or 214,[22] an elderly man like Gordian may have seemed a suitably harmless person to place in command of the still powerful army of the Lower province.[23] It might even be surmised that Gordian was one of those whom, Dio says, Caracalla tried to do away with by sending them 'to uncongenial provinces, the climate of which was deleterious to their health, exposing them to excessive heat or cold on the pretext of giving them great honour.'[24]

Gordian might still have failed to achieve the consulship but for the death of Caracalla and the disturbed conditions which prevailed during the years 217-22. During the reign of Elagabalus men from the east were specially favoured: Gordian might have been one such. On the other hand, it might be argued that he was exactly the sort of person to have received favour from Alexander, particularly during the brief period after the latter's accession, when the praetorian prefect Ulpian was at the helm.[25] It may even be that he achieved even more surpris-

the *HA, Gord.* 9. 1: 'et plurimis provinciis, ut diximus, ante praefuerat' (*ut diximus* is inaccurate: the biographer had given Gordian a purely urban career, 3. 5 ff.).

[19] Groag, *Achaia* 87 f.

[20] Barnes, *Latomus* 27 (1968) 593 ff., suggests that he may have paid the penalty for supporting Niger or Albinus, comparing the case of Ti. Claudius Attalus Paterculianus (Dio 79. 3. 5, 4. 3; Barbieri, *L'Albo* no. 140 + *Agg.*, where the correct *praenomen* is given). Loriot, *ANRW* II. 2 (1975) 695 n. 297, draws attention to Maximinus' speech attacking Gordian (Herodian 7. 8. 7) and suggests that 'on pourrait également songer à un scandale des moeurs'. One might add a reference to Dio 76. 6. 4 on the large number of adultery trials under Severus (discussed by P. Garnsey, *JRS* 57 (1967) 56 ff.).

[21] p. 167 above.   [22] pp. 168 ff. above.

[23] See E. Birley, *Ep. Stud.* 4 (1967) 103 ff., for evidence of Caracalla's continuing concern about north Britain in the period after 213.

[24] Dio 77. 11. 6-7.

[25] See the comments of Syme, *Emperors and Biography* 167: 'Gordian got the honour at last [sc. the consulship] from Elagabalus or from Alexander . . . Gordian may have become consul before 222. The reign of Elagabalus was propitious for senators from the East'. Note also

ing eminence. Philostratus recalls in his preface how he and Gordian once discussed the sophists in the temple of Daphnaean Apollo at Antioch. As T. D. Barnes has pointed out,[26] although there are various possibilities to explain Gordian's presence at the Syrian capital, it is not excluded that he was made governor of Syria Coele early in the reign of Alexander. Another elderly man, Cassius Dio, was pressed into service at this time to govern consular provinces.[27]

Gordian's origin has been the subject of some interest in recent years.[28] Philostratus speaks of him as a descendant of Herodes Atticus, the Athenian sophist and millionaire, *consul ordinarius* in 143.[29] In spite of this pointer to the Greek east, credence was long given to the fraudulent assertions of the *Historia Augusta*, that Gordian was descended from the Gracchi and from Trajan.[30] But the name Gordianus proclaims a link with Asia Minor. The first person of senatorial rank to bear it was Ti. Claudius Gordianus, consul under Commodus, a native of Tyana in Cappadocia.[31] Both Gordius and Gordianus are well attested in Anatolia.[32] Further, a lady named Sempronia Romana, daughter of Sempronius Aquila, *ab epistulis Graecis*, and wife of an unknown senator, is attested by an inscription from Ancyra. She might

his discussion, 146 ff., of the reign of Alexander, esp. 153 f. on the death of Ulpian (in 223).

[26] Barnes, *Latomus* 27 (1968) 595 f.

[27] Dio 80. 1. 3.

[28] The subject was first ventilated in my contribution to *Britain and Rome* (1966) 56 ff., with arguments in favour of eastern origin, which have won general acceptance. (For bibliography see Loriot, *ANRW* II. 2 (1975) 694 f., 783 f.; to which add Grasby, *CQ* N.S. 25 (1975) 123 ff., discussed above, n. 17). Note however the lofty dissent of J. Gagé, *ANRW* II. 2 (1975) 832: 'nous ne croyons pas qu'il soit tout à fait raisonnable de ramener ces grands patrons des bourgeoisies italiennes et africaines à une origine cappadoce'. He does not cite an evidence.

[29] *PIR*[2] C 802.

[30] *HA Gord.* 2. 2: 'originem paternam ex Gracchorum genere habuit, maternam ex Traiani imperatoris'. Pflaum, *Le Marbre de Thorigny* 61: 'issu d'une grande famille italique'. Barbieri, *L'Albo* p. 194: 'senza dubbio di antica famiglia italica, forse romana'. Von Rohden, *RE* 1. 2 (1894) 2629 went further than the *HA* suggesting descent from the Triumvir Antonius, whence the possession of the House of Pompey, once owned by Antony (*HA Gord.* 2. 3 etc.). The *cognomen* Romanus was held to have been assumed after accession, in deliberate contrast to the unRoman nature of Maximinus, according to *CAH* XII 77 and Barbieri, *L'Albo* p. 194; etc. P. Lambrechts, *La Composition du sénat romain . . . (193-284)* 44, on the other hand, pronounced Gordian 'probablement originaire de l'Afrique', citing *ILS* 493, Bordeaux, perhaps misunderstanding Dessau's comment, ad loc., on the provenance of that inscription. Herodian 7. 5. 8 explicitly states that the Africans gave him the name Africanus after his coup. Cf. A. R. Birley, *Britain and Rome* 58 f., for parallels.

[31] *AE* 1954. 138, Lambaesis, adduced in *Britain and Rome* 58 ff.

[32] L. Robert, *Les Noms indigènes dans l'Asie Mineure gréco-romaine* (1963) 526, 548 (on Ζεὺς Γόρδιος at Caesarea in Cappadocia). For further documentation see Loriot, *ANRW* II. 2 (1975) 694 n. 295, to which add *Anat. Stud.* 22 (1972) 225 nos. 3, 10; *Epigraphica* 27 (1975) 69 f. no. 2 (a Cappadocian Gordios at Rome to study law).

be the mother or grandmother of Gordian.[33] His *praenomen* and *gentilicium* attest descent from persons enfranchised by the Trimvir Antonius, or by one of his daughters. Several such persons, of eastern origin, were in the senate in the second century,[34] and there is no difficulty in regarding Gordian as the son of a senator—which is the very least that is implied by Herodian's statement that he was *ἄνδρα εὖ γεγονότα*.[35]

He had a son of the same names as himself, who was his legate in 238, and his colleague as emperor.[36] The younger Gordian was already of consular rank, according to the *Historia Augusta*. The statement has been doubted, but it receives confirmation from an inscription at Caesarea in Palestine.[37] It might be, of course, that the younger Gordian was the proconsul and consul to whom Philostratus dedicated the *vitae sophistarum*.[38] That would certainly simplify the problem of how that person could be a descendant of Herodes. If Philostratus' phrase is interpreted literally, the elder Gordian could only have been a grandson of the famous sophist, through a daughter. The elder, Elpinice, is not known to have married.[39] But it is just possible that she was old enough to have had a child in the late 150s.[40] The question must remain open for the time being.

---

[33] *IGR* III 188: [δήμαρχ]ον δήμου ῾Ρωμαίων πραίτορα ἀποδεδειγμένον Σεμπρωνία ῾Ρωμάνα θυγάτηρ Σεμπρωνίου ᾽Ακύλου γενομέ[ν]ον ἐπὶ ἐπιστολῶν ῾Ελληνικῶν [Σε]β. τὸν γλυκάτατον ἄνδρα. The link was suggested in *Britain and Rome* 58 f., where the *rhetor* Aquila Romanus (*PIR*[2] A 983) and the Galatian sophist Aquila, pupil of a pupil of Herodes (A 981), and another *rhetor*, Antoninus Aquila, a friend of Fronto (A 792), were also noted. Syme, *Emperors and Biography* 167 n. 7, adds T. Flavius Sempronius Aquila (*AE* 1937. 257, Isaura). Barnes, *Latomus* 27 (1968) 593, notes that the Galatian sophist is only mentioned by Philostratus, *en passant* (2. 11. 1 K), but that 'surely the recipient of a treatise on sophists should be told more about those sophists who were among his relatives'. It should be added, further, as a slight reservation against origin in Cappadocia, rather than in another Anatolian province, that Philostratus makes some unflattering comments about the Cappadocians' uncomely Greek accent (*v. soph.* 2. 13. 1; also *v. Apoll.* 1. 7).
[34] See e.g. *PIR*[2] A 812, 837, 859, 883 (the prime example, M. Antonius Zeno (*cos.* 148), descended from Pontic kings).
[35] Herodian 7. 5. 2.   [36] *PIR*[2] A 834.
[37] *HA Gord.* 18. 5; *AE* 1971. 475, see n. 17 above.
[38] As suggested tentatively in *Britain and Rome* 58 ff.; urged strongly by Barnes, *Latomus* 27 (1968) 581 ff., and Syme, *Emperors and Biography* 168. G. W. Bowersock, *Greek Sophists in the Roman Empire* (1969) 8, prefers Gordian I. See now also I. Avotins, *Hermes* 106 (1978) 242 ff.
[39] *PIR*[2] A 706; but see R. Stiglitz, *RE* 8A 2 (1958) 2465 f.
[40] If she was born *c.*144, she could have been married *c.*158. My suggestion in *Britain and Rome* 59 that Gordian might have married 'a certain Claudia Regilla, widow of M. Antonius Lupus' was misguided; as pointed out by Barnes, *Latomus* 27 (1968) 587 n. 2, and Syme, *Emperors and Biography* 168 n. 7, Regilla predeceased her husband (*ILS* 1127; *PIR*[2] C 1117). In any case, as Schumacher, *Priesterkollegien* 251 ff., shrewdly suggests, this Regilla was quite possibly no connection of Herodes, but a granddaughter of Commodus' praetorian prefect Regillus.

219(?)   Modius Julius

VII 964 = *RIB* 980, Netherby: *Im*[*p. Caes. M. Aur.*] *Antoṇi*[*no*] / *p. f. Ạug. b*[*i*]*s cos. vẹxil.* / *leg. II Aug. et XX V. V.* ⁴/ *item coh. I Ael. Hisp.* / *eq. sub cura M*[*o*]/ *d*[*i*] *Iuḷị ḷeg. Aug.* / *pr. pr. instante Ṭ. Ael.* / *N*[. . . *trib. coh. eiusdem?* ⁸/ . . . / . . .] / *temp*[*lum*. . .] (AD 219?).

VII 838 = *RIB* 1914, Birdoswald: *sub Modio Iu/lio leg. Aug. pr.* / *pr. coh. I Ael. D*(*a*)*c.* ⁴/ *cui praeest M.* / *Cl. Menander* / *trib.*

The stone from Netherby was recut in modern times, and R. P. Wright doubts the possibility of deriving a valid reading from it. The first line of the original text, still visible in places, 'contains evident traces of an ancient erasure'. In the second line the recut letters PIISVBBSCOS do not make any sense as they stand and it is reasonable to suppose that they were recut in accordance with what could be read at the time. To interpret this as P Ḟ ẠVG̣ B[I]S COS is thus fairly convincing, and, combined with the evidence for an emperor's name having been erased, points to the year of Elagabalus' second consulship, 219.[1]

Modius Julius is not recorded elsewhere. He might conceivably be a son, or more probably grandson, of C. Modius Justus, legate of III Augusta in 171.[2] Another possible kinsman is the Severan procurator L. Julius Victor Modianus.[3] But, given Elagabalus' known tendency to give high rank to men of the humblest origins,[4] it is equally likely that he was connected to, if not even identical with, the Modius Julius who was a member of a *collegium fabrum tignuariorum* at Ostia in 198.[5] It may be noted that the tribune of the Dacians at Birdoswald, who may have owed his commission either to Modius or to his predecessor, had a Greek nomenclature, suggesting eastern origin.[6]

This governorship presumably began before 219, since another man was in office in the following year. It is therefore not unlikely that Modius Julius was the direct successor of Gordianus, in one of the years 216-18.

---

[1] Admittedly, *iterum cos.* (or *cos. iterum*) is required by normal Latin usage, but *bis consule* is found in this sense, e.g. in Martial 10. 48. 20 ('bis Frontino consule'), and the MSS of Tac. *Agr.* 44. 1, have 'Gaio Caesare ter consule', emended by editors to 'tertium'. The mason may well have expanded a draft which read *II cos.* to *bis cos.* for stylistic reasons. (Elagabalus was *cos. III* the following year.)   [2] Thomasson, *Statthalter Nordafrikas* II 184.
[3] *ILS* 1438 = *ILAlg.* II 668, Cirta, on which see Pflaum, *CP* no. 275, *PIR*² J 626. He was clearly a native of Africa.
[4] Dio 79. 7. 2-3, 15. 2-3; Herodian 5. 7. 6-7 (cf. the notes by C. R. Whittaker, Loeb edn. II 63 ff.); *HA Elag.* 6. 1-4, 12. 1-2.   [5] XIV S 4569 dec. IIII, 3, Ostia.
[6] The tribune M. Cl. Menander may have been a connection of the senator Claudius Val. Menander from Paros (Barbieri, *L'Albo* no. 1529).

220   Ti. Claudius Paulinus

EE IX 1012 = *RIB* 311, Caerwent: [*Ti. Claudio*] / *Paulino* / *leg. leg. II* ⁴/ *Aug. pro-*
consul. / *provinc. Nar/rbonensis* / *leg. Aug. pr. pr. provin.* ⁸/ *Lugudunen.* / *ex*
decreto / *ordinis res/publ. civit.* ¹²/ *Silurum*

VII 1045 + 1044 = *RIB* 1280, High Rochester: *imp. Caes. M. Aurelio* / [[*Antonino*]]
pio fel. Aug. / *trib. pot.* [[*III*]] *cos.* [[*III*]] *procos.* ⁴/ *p. p. ballist. a sol*[*o*] *coh. I f.* /
Vardul. [[*A*[*ntonin.*]] *s*] *ub cura* / *Tib. Cl. Paul*[*ini le*]*g. Aug.* /*pr. pr. fe*[*cit insta*]*nte*
P Ael[*io Erasino trib.*] (AD 220)

?*EE* VII 1021 = *RIB* 1467, Chesters: [. . .] *per Cl.* [*Paulinum* or *Xenephontem*] /
leg. pr. [*pr. instante*] / *Sep. Nil*[*o praef. eqq.*]¹

XIII 3162 = Pflaum, *Le Marbre de Thorigny* 7 ff., Vieux:

i *main face*

T. Sennio Sollemni Sollem/nini fil. IIvir. sine sorte quater aug. / [*o*] *mnib. honorib.*
mun. [. . .] *VII* ⁴/ [. . .]*us in* / [*s*]*ua c*[*i*]*vitate eodem tem*[*po*]*re sacerdo*[*s*] /
R[*om*]*ae* [*et Augusti ad aram omn*]*e genus spec/taculorum e*[*did*]*it;* [*fu*]*erunt*
gladia[*to*]⁸/*r*[*um c*]*ertam. n. XXXII, ex quibus per qua*[*d*]/*riduum* [*n.*] *V*[*III*]
s[*ine*] *missione edideru*[*nt*]./[*Bal*]*neum quod* [*pop*]*u*[*lar*]*ibus coloniae s*[*uae*] /
pr[*ofutu*]*rum S*[*ollemninus . . .*]*ribus* ¹²/ *funda*[*me*]*ntis inst*[*itutis reli*]*querat* /
consumm[*av*]*it* [*item legavit . . .*] *fructum unde* / *in perpetuum instauraretur. Is*
Sollemnis / *amicus Tib. Claud. Paulini leg. Aug. pro pr. pro*¹⁶/*vinc. Lugd. et cliens*
fuit, cui postea / [*l*]*eg. Aug. p. p. in Brit. ad legionem sext*[*am*] / *adsedit,* [*q*]*uique*
e[*i*] *salarium militiae* / *in auro aliaque munera longe pluris missi*[*t*]. ²⁰/ *Fuit cliens*
probatissimus Aedini Iuliani / *leg. Aug. prov. Lugd., qui postea praefectus praet.* /
fuit, sicut epistula, quae ad latus scripta es[*t*], / *declaratur. Adsedit etiam in pro-*
vincia Num[*id.*] ²⁴/ *Lambense* [sic], *M. Valerio Floro trib. mil. leg.* / *III Aug.* /
iudici arcae ferrar. / *tres prov. Gall.* ²⁸/ *primo umquam in sua civitate posuerunt.* /
Locum ordo civitatis Viducass. liber. dedit. / *P. XVII K. Ian. Pio et Proculo cos.*
(AD 238).

ii *right side*

Exemplum epistulae Aedin[*i*] / *Iuliani praefecti praet.* / *ad Badium Comnianum*
pr[*o*]⁴/*cur. et vice praesidis agen*[*t.*] / *Aedinius Iulianus Badio* / *Comniano sal. In*
provincia / *Lugduness. quinquefascal.* ⁸/ *cum agerem, plerosq. bonos viros per-*
spexi, inter quos / *Sollemnem istum oriundum* / *ex civitate Viduc. sacerdote*[*m*],
¹²/ *quem propter secta. gravitat*[*em*] / *et honestos mores amare coep*[*i.*] / *His*
accedit, quod, cum Cl. Paulin[*o*] / *decessori meo in concilio* ¹⁶/ *Galliarum instinctu*
quorund[*am*], / *qui ab eo propter merita sua laes*[*i*] / *videbantur, quasi ex con-*

---

¹ The same prefect, Septimius Nilus, is recorded at Chesters under the governorship of
Marius Valerianus in October 221 (*RIB* 1465, see p. 190 below). There is no means of telling
whether the governor *Cl.* on this stone was Paulinus or Valerianus' successor Cl. Xenophon.
R. P. Wright, ad loc., restores [*Xenephontem*], but too little of the stone survives to be sure
of the length of line. In line 3 he reads *Sep. Nil*[*o praef. equit.*], but *praef. eqq.* is equally possible, both here and in line 8 of *RIB* 1465, indeed preferable, cf. *RIB* 1470, the only case from
Chesters where the relevant phrase is extant: *curante Aelio Longino praef. eqq.*

sensu provin[*c.*] */ accussationem instituere temtar*[*ent*], [20]/ *Sollemnis iste meus proposito eor*[*um*] */ restitit, provocatione scilicet inte*[*rpo*]/*sita, quod patria eius cum inter ce*[*ter.*] */ legatum eum creasset, nihil de ac*[24]/*tione mandassent, immo contra laud*[*as/se*]*nt, qua ratione effectum est, ut* [*omnes / a*]*b accussatione desisterent: que*[*m*]/ *magis magisque amare et compro*[*bare*] [28]/ *coepi. Is certus honoris mei er*[*ga se*] */ ad videndum me in urbem venit* [*atq.*] */ proficiscens petit, ut eum tibi* [*com*]/*mendarem. Recte itaque feceris,* [*si*] [32]*de*[*si*]*d*[*e*]*rio illius adnueris. Et r.*

iii *left side*

[*E*]*xemplum epistulae Cl. /* [*Pa*]*ulini leg. Aug. pr. pr. prov. /* [*B*]*ritanniae ad Sennium Sollem*[4]/*nem. A Tampio. / Licet plura merenti tibi h*[*aec*] */ a me pauca tamen quonia*[*m*] */ honoris causa offeruntu*[*r*], [8]/ *velim accipias libente*[*r*] : */ chlamidem Canusinam, / dalmaticam Laodiciam, fibulam / auream cum gemmis, rachanas* [12]/ *duas, tossiam Brit., pellem vit*[*uli*] */ marini. Semestris autem epistulam, / ubi propediem vacare coeperi*[*t*], */ mittam, cuius militiae salarium* [16]/ [*i*]*d est HS XXV n. in auro suscip*[*e, /d*]*is faventibus et maiestate sanct*[*a*] */ Imp. deinceps pro meritis / adfectionis magis digna* [20]/ *consecuturus. Concordit.*

There are several elements of special interest in the brief governorship of Claudius Paulinus. First, he is attested by the dedication at Caerwent as a former legate of II Augusta, and is thus the first example for many generations of a former British legionary legate returning to be governor.[2] What is more, the Caerwent inscription is the nearest approach to a senatorial *cursus* inscription in the epigraphy of Roman Britain. Besides this, he is the first—indeed the only—governor for whom there is indisputable evidence that he was praetorian legate of the Lower province. That evidence is supplied by the celebrated 'marbre de Thorigny', which is also unique, as yet, in providing a letter from a British governor. Paulinus is also the only governor of Lower Britain recorded outside the province. He is described in the heading of his letter simply as *leg. Aug. pr. pr. prov.* [*B*]*ritanniae*, with no mention of *inferior*. But in lines 15–16 of the inscription on the main face his client Sollemnis is described as *amicus Tib. Claud. Paulini . . . cui postea* [*l*]*eg. Aug. p. p. in Brit. ad legionem sext*[*am*] *adsedit.* This neatly indicates that the legate of VI Victrix has become legate of the Lower province, where Cassius Dio registers its presence.[3]

The inscription from High Rochester shows that he was governor in 220. His term of office must have begun soon before, since Modius Julius was governor in 219, and it must have been short in duration, for Marius Valerianus had already taken over by October of 221. Before governing Lower Britain he had been legate of Gallia Lugdunensis, as

---

[2] He is the first since Cn. Julius Agricola (pp. 76 f. above).   [3] Dio 55. 23. 3, cf. 23. 2. 5.

the inscriptions from Vieux and Caerwent show. In view of the irregularity in appointments that prevailed in the period 217-22, under Macrinus and Elagabalus,[4] it is probable that his term of office there too had been short. His command over II Augusta and proconsulship of Narbonensis, the other posts recorded on the dedication by the *ordo* of the Silures, presumably were held during the reign of Caracalla. Paulinus may have succeeded L. Julius Julianus[5] as legate of II Augusta.

E. Groag suggested that he might be the grandson of a homonym from Cibyra in the province of Asia, who was of consular rank in AD 184.[6] However, it seems improbable that the grandson of an ex-consul should have had a career of this kind, and the names are too colourless to permit any certainty over his origin.[7]

Tampio in Paulinus' letter to Sennius Sollemnis presumably represents an otherwise unknown place in Britannia inferior, perhaps named after its garrison the *ala Tampiana*, which is recorded in the army of Britain.[8] It would be beyond the scope of the present work to go closely into all the details of the inscription of Sollemnis,[9] but it should be noted that at the end of the letter Paulinus expressed the hope that 'with the favour of the gods and of the emperor's sacred majesty' his client 'would obtain rewards more fitting to his loyalty'. Sollemnis was only to serve as *assessor* to Paulinus, who was soon replaced as governor, and the emperor—Elagabalus—was violently overthrown soon afterwards. Since Sollemnis would certainly have recorded any further favours he received, it may be that Paulinus had no further employment and hence no patronage to offer. He might, of course, have died in office; or he might have fallen from grace under the new regime of Alexander.

221, 222   Marius Valerianus

VII 585 = *Arch. Ael.*[4] 16 (1939) 244 ff. = *RIB* 1465, Chesters: *Imp. Caesar M. Aurel.* [[*Antoninus p. f.*]] / *Aug.* [*sacerdos ampliss. dei invicti Solis Elagabali*] p. [m. tr]*ib. p.* [IIII] *cos.* [III] *p. p. div*[*i Anton. f.*] [4]/ *divi Sever. nep. et M.* [Aur]el. [[*Alexander nobiliss.*]] / *Caesar imper*[*i* [*consors*] . .] / *alae II Astur.*

[4] See p. 187 n. 4 above, for Elagabalus' practices. For irregularities under Macrinus see Dio 78. 13. 1-15. 1, 22. 1, 35. 1.
[5] p. 265 below.   [6] *IGR* IV 911, cf. *PIR*[2] C 954-5.
[7] See Barbieri, *L'Albo*, index pp. 687 ff., 737, with some fifty Ti. Claudii and over thirty Paulini of the senatorial class, mostly third century. Our man might even have been a Briton.
[8] XVI 48 (AD103), 69 (AD 122). It was transferred to the Danube later in the second century, see now Alföldy, *Noricum* 257.
[9] See above all the magistral study by Pflaum, *Le Marbre de Thorigny.*

[[*Anton.*]] *v*[*et*]*ustate* [*dilapsum restitu*] / *erunt per Marium Valer*[*ianum leg. Aug. pr. pr.*] *8*/*instante Septimio Ni*[*l*]*o prae*[*f. eqq.*] / *dedicatum III Kal. Novem. Gr*[*at*]*o et Sele*[*uco cos.*] (30 October AD 221)

VII 965 = *ILS* 2169 = *RIB* 978, Netherby: *Imp. Caes. M. Aurelio* / *Severo Alexandro pio eel.* [sic] *Aug.* / *pont. maximo trib. pot. cos. p. p. coh. I Ael. 4*/ *Hispanorum ∞ eq. devota numini* / *maiestatique eius baselicam* / *equestrem exercitatoriam* / *iam pridem a solo coeptam 8*/ *aedificavit consummavitque* / *sub cura Mari Valeriani leg.* / *Aug. pr. pr. instante M. Aurelio Salvio trib. coh. imp. d. n. 12* / *Severo Alexandro pio fel.* / *Aug. cos.* (AD 222)

EE IX 1140 = *ILS* 5759a = *RIB* 1060, South Shields: *Imp. Caes. divi Severi* / *nepos divi Magni Antonini fil.* / *M. Aurel. Severus* [[*Alexander*]] *4*/ *pius felix Aug. pontif. max.* / *trib. pot p. p. cos. aquam* / *usibus mil. coh. V. Gallo. in*/*duxit curante Mario Valeriano 8*/ *leg. eius pr. pr.* (AD 222)

The three inscriptions of Marius Valerianus are useful, for they illustrate the fact that the praetorian governor of the Lower province was responsible for the whole of the northern frontier of Roman Britain, from the North Sea to the western outpost north of Carlisle. Valerianus was presumably the immediate successor of Claudius Paulinus and predecessor of Claudius Xenophon.[1] Nothing further is known of his career,[2] but it is worth noting E. Ritterling's suggestion that he is the same man as the Marius Valerianus attested as a centurion in the praetorian guard, not earlier than the reign of Severus.[3] The rise of such a man to senatorial rank, 'von der Pike', would not be a surprise during the reign of Elagabalus.[4]

223   Claudius Xenophon

EE VII 1108 = *RIB* 2299, Crindledykes: *imp. Caes.* [*M.*] *Aurel.* / *Severo Al*[*e*]*xandro* / *pio fel. Aug. p. m. tr. p. II 4*/ *cos. p. p. cur. Cl. X*[*e*]*noph.* / *leg. Aug. pr. praet.* / *m. p. XIIII*

[1] He presumably took over from Paulinus in the spring or summer of 221. His inscriptions are datable to 30 Oct. 221 and to the period 12 Mar.–9 Dec. 222 inclusive. Claudius Xenophon is attested during Alexander's second tribunician power, 10 Dec. 222–9 Dec. 223. See *PIR*² A 1610.

[2] Of the two rescripts in the *Code* of Justinian to a Valerianus, status not specified, from the year 223, that of 26 Apr. might have been addressed to our man as governor of Britain (*Cod. Just.* 8. 22 (23). 2); but that of 26 Nov. must fall after his replacement by Xenophon (7. 19. 3).

[3] VI 32536 c: see Ritterling, *RE* 12. 2 (1925) 1611. On the governor of Numidia Macius (=?L. Magius) Valerianus to whom Ritterling also refers, see now Thomasson, *Statthalter Nordafrikas* II 220 f. Both Marius and Valerianus were of course exceedingly common—the latter scores over 300 in Kajanto 157.

[4] Cf. p. 187 and n. 4 above.

EE VII 1115 = *RIB* 2306, Cawfields: *imp. Caes. M. Aurel. / Sever. Alexandro / p. f. Aug. p. m. tr. p. II* [4] */ cos. p. p. cur. Cl. Xenophon/te leg. Aug. pr. pr/aet. m. p. XVIII*

VII 715 = *RIB* 1706, Vindolanda: [. . . *coh. IIII*] *Gallor. /* [⟦ *Severiana Alexandriana*⟧ *de*]*vota nu/*[*mi*]*ni eius por*[*tam cum tu*]*rribus* [*a*] [4]*/fundamen*[*tis res-titu*]*erunt sub / Cl. Xenepho*[*nte l*]*eg.* [*Aug.*] *n. pr.* [*pr.*] */ curante* [. . .]

EE VII 1021 = *RIB* 1467, Chesters: see p. 188 above.

Claudius Xenophon was presumably the son of the Commodan and Severan procurator T. Claudius T. f. Papiria Xenophon, whose career is known from an inscription at Ephesus.[1] The *cognomen* suggests eastern origin,[2] but no town in a Greek-speaking province is known to have been enrolled in that tribe except perhaps the colony of Cassandrea (Potidaea) in Macedonia.[3] By contrast, some twenty towns in Africa were in the Papiria, and it may be noted that the procurator's last known appointment was as *procurator ad bona cogenda in Africa*; hence African origin is not to be excluded. No connection need be supposed with Ti. Claudius Xenophon of Cos,[4] another man of this name at Pisidian Antioch,[5] or with the philosopher Claudius Xenophon of Cyzicus.[6] Nor, for that matter, is there a strong reason to identify either the procurator or the British legate with the novelist Xenophon of Ephesus, although it must be remarked that the procurator's service as *epistrategus* in Egypt (where much of the action of the novel takes place) and in Asia (he was honoured at Ephesus) make him as good a candidate as any.[7]

His governorship presumably followed that of Marius Valerianus, and must have terminated by 225 at the latest, when a new governor is attested. Nothing further is heard of him.

---

[1] *ILS* 1421. See Stein, *Der römische Ritterstand* 340, *PIR*[2] C 1054, and Pflaum, *CP* no. 222, who cites *P. Cornell* 14, 5, which shows he was *epistrategus* in Egypt in 180. Pflaum comments that 'le prénom aberrant nous parait résulter d'une double erreur du lapicide ephésien, lequel a dû oublier le I de Ti(berius) aussi bien dans le prénom que dans la filiation', which is certainly probable. It may be remarked, similarly, that the spelling of the *cognomen* as Xenephon on two out of three of our governor's inscriptions must also be regarded as an error.

[2] Pflaum, *CP* no 222, is positive on the matter: 'certainement originaire de la partie grecque de l'Empire, comme l'indique son surnom de Xenophon'. He does not discuss the tribe.

[3] Kubitschek 241, with a mark of interrogation—the evidence is minimal.

[4] *PIR*[2] C 1053.   [5] *Anat. Stud.* 17 (1967) 110 no. 20.

[6] *JHS* 24 (1904) 27 no. 25.

[7] On the novelist see H. Gärtner, *RE* 9A 2 (1967) 2055 ff. He suggests a date in the second or third century AD, but has no identification to offer. But, in any case, as Syme, *Emperors and Biography* 263, points out, the novelist may well have written under a pseudonym.

225   Maximus

VII 732 = *RIB* 1738, Greatchesters: *imp. Caes. M. Aur. Seve/rus Alexander p. fel. / Aug. horreum vetu* ⁴/ *state conlabsum mil. / coh. II Asturum S. A. / a solo resti-tuerunt / provincia. regente* [. . .] ⁸/ *Maximo leg. Aug. pr. p*[*r. cur.*] / *Val. Martiale 7 leg.* [. . .] / *Fusco II et Dext*[*ro cos.*] (AD 225)

There appears to be space at the end of line 7 of this inscription for no more than two letters, suggesting that the governor's *nomen* was either Cl(audius) or Fl(avius). However, there are several ligatures elsewhere in the inscription,[1] so other common *gentilicia* such as Ael(ius), Jul(ius), Ulp(ius), Val(erius), etc., cannot be ruled out.[2] Further conjecture would thus be almost fruitless.[3] It may be recalled that Maximus is the sixth governor recorded in the ten years from 216 to 225 inclusive. In 225 he was presumably at the beginning of his tenure, which should have lasted into 226, if not longer.

between 225   Calvisius Ru[fus]
and 235

VII 324 = *JRS* 18 (1928) 212 = *RIB* 929, Old Penrith: [. . . *coh.*] *II Gal.* [⟦*S.*⟧*A.*⟧ *ampl*[*iavit* . . .] / *sub Calvisio Ru*[*fo leg. Aug. pr. pr.* ⁴/ *curante Aureli*[*o* . . . *praef.*]

There is no sure means of dating this man's governorship within the reign of Alexander, to which the erased but still legible letters *S. A.* in line 1 point, except that the years 222–25 appear to be fully occupied by the governors Valerianus, Xenophon, and Maximus. Indeed, 226 may reasonably be excluded also, since it should probably be allocated to Maximus; and the last year or two of the reign also appear to be ruled out.[1] But he might well be the successor rather than the predecessor of the next governor to be discussed, Valerius Crescens Fulvianus.

[1] e.g. *Caes.* in line 1, *restituerunt* in line 6, *regente* in line 7. Further, in several instances letters of smaller size are tucked in.

[2] Barbieri, *L'Albo*, index pp. 728 f., shows some eighty senatorial bearers of this excep-tionally common *cognomen*, mostly third century in date. Names such as Alfius Maximus (*L'Albo* no. 635, a *puer senatorius* in 204) cannot be excluded.

[3] M. Ulpius Maximus, governor of Numidia early in the reign of Alexander is particularly tempting. E. Birley, *JRS* 40 (1950) 63, argued that he should come *c.*221–4, since the cen-turion in VIII 2753 was already *primus pilus* later in the same reign, *AE* 1917–18. 51. See Thomasson, *Statthalter Nordafrikas* II 209 f. Governorship of two one-legion provinces in succession is paralleled later in the century, see Thomasson II 221 f. (Numidia and Noricum). However this may be, it may be noted, finally, that one or other of the legates, of Britannia inferior and Numidia, might be the recipients of rescripts from Severus Alexander in the years 223–7, addressed to a Maximus, with no indication of status: *Cod. Iust.* 8. 27 (28). 2 (AD 223), 5. 62. 6 (224), 5. 62. 8 (225), 6. 53. 5 (226), 9. 22. 3 (4) (227).

[1] See p. 195 below, on Cl. Apellinus.

The *gentilicium* was borne by a senatorial family of the first century AD, the Calvisii Rusones,[2] and it might therefore at first sight be tempting to restore *Ru*[*sone*] in line 2. But even if the family had survived into the third century—for which there is no other evidence[3]— it is hardly likely that a descendant of patrician consulars would be governing a praetorian province. More plausible is the possibility that our man was descended from the younger Pliny's friend C. Calvisius Rufus, a decurion of Comum.[4] At any rate, the *nomen* Calvisius is relatively uncommon outside Italy, which was presumably our governor's home.

between 225   **Valerius Crescens Fulvianus**
and 235

VII 222 = *RIB* 587, Ribchester: [. . .*p*]*ro* / [*sa*]*l. im*[*p. Caes.* [[*Al*] *ex* [*andri*]] *Aug. n. et* / *Iul. Mamaeae ma*]*t*[*r*]*is d. n. et castr. su*[*b cura*] [4]/ *Val. Crescentis Fulviani leg. eius pr.* [*pr.*] / *T. Floridius Natalis 7 leg. praep. n. et regi*[*onis*] / *templum a solo ex responsu* [*dei re*]/*stituit et dedicavit d*[*e suo*]

As already mentioned in the discussion of Calvisius Ru[fus?], there is no way of determining which of these two governors held office first. All that can be said is that this man ought to belong somewhere in the period 227–33 inclusive. He is not certainly identifiable elsewhere, but it may be noted that one of the senatorial ladies who took part in the *ludi saeculares* of 204 was a certain . . .*illa* (*uxor*) *Valeri C*[*res*]*centis*.[1] These might be the parents of our man. Both *nomen* and first *cognomen* are very common, and there are a fair number of other Valerii Crescentes attested at Rome and in different parts of the empire; but in no case need any connection with our man be supposed. On the other hand, the prefect of cavalry M. Valerius Fulvianus, who dedicated to Fortune at Binchester,[2] could well be a kinsman of the governor, given a commission on his recommendation. It is, further, tempting to detect some link in an inscription from Mustis in proconsular Africa, set

[2] *PIR*[2] C 344, 350, 357.
[3] Cf. the Catilii Severi, *PIR*[2] C 556–8, descended from the *cos. II ord.* 120.
[4] *PIR*[2] C 349. Sherwin-White, *Letters of Pliny* 202, oddly refers to the 'possible military tribunate in Britain' of Pliny's friend, citing the original publication of the Old Penrith inscription. Groag, *PIR*[2] C 348, mistakenly regarded our man as *praefectus cohortis*. (In *RE* 3. 1 (1897) 1410 f. he had correctly identified him as a governor, following Hübner ad VII 324, but took him to be a Ruso, perhaps identical with the Trajanic governor of Cappadocia.)
[1] Barbieri, *L'Albo* no. 508 (who regarded this senator as perhaps identical with our governor, which is improbable, if not completely out of the question).
[2] *RIB* 1029. It is not excluded that this was our governor earlier in his career, and that he was later adlected into the senate.

up in honour of an emperor and empress whose names were later erased. The dedicators were *Maria Lucina flam. et L. Fulvius Kastus Ful[vianus? fisci advocatus patrimoni tr]act. Kart. et Galliae Narbo-[nensis . . . et . . .] Britanniae inferioris fili eius.*[3] It is not impossible that the second son of Maria Lucina was M. Valerius Fulvianus, and that the post that he held in Britannia inferior was that of cavalry prefect. In that case, our governor might have been a native of Mustis;[4] but alternatives are possible.[5]

(?)235   Claudius Apellinus

VII 1046 = *RIB* 1281, High Rochester: *Imp. Cae[s. M. Aur. [[Seve]/ro Alex-[andr]o]] p. f. [Aug. et / [[Iuliae Aug.] matr. i[mp. Caes. et ca]s]] coh. I f. Vard.*
⁴/ *[[∞ S. A.]] ballis. a solo re[sti] t. / sub c. Cl. Apellini le[g.] Augg. / instante Aur. Quinto tr.*

This governor is likely to have been related to the Claudii Apellini of Perge in Pamphylia, as was pointed out by E. Groag.[1] The date of his governorship is at first sight no more precisely datable than those of Calvisius Ru[fus?] and Val. Crescens Fulvianus, in other words it belongs in the reign of Alexander and should come after 225. But it is curious that Apellinus is called *leg. Augg. pr. pr.*, which is certainly inaccurate for this reign—it is quite out of the question that *Augustorum* could have been intended to refer to the emperor and his mother, the Augusta.[2] Even for Julia Mamaea, that would have been excessive. The second G is in fact smaller than the first and is inserted inside it, suggesting that it could have been added later. It is therefore possible that Apellinus was governor in 235, at the time of Alexander's murder, and that the second G was added—at the same time that the names of Alexander and his mother, and the title *S. A.* of the Vardulli, were erased—to signify that Apellinus was now the legate of Maximinus and his son Maximus. Although the latter was only *nobilissimus Caesar*, he

---

[3] VIII 1578. However, Pflaum, *CP* no. 311, restores the names of Elagabalus and Soaemias.

[4] For Valerii at Mustis see VIII 1610, 1611, 15633; further A. Beschaouch, *Karthago* 14 (1967/8) 141 f. (25 f.) nos. 1, 10, 11, who notes that they had migrated from Carthage.

[5] Barbieri, *L'Albo* pp. 543, 653, draws attention to Val. Maternus *c. i.*, brother of Val. Crescentia(nus), *eq. R.* (V 5729, *ager Mediolanensis*) as possible kinsmen of our man (his no. 2111 + *Agg.*, where he is mistakenly regarded as consular), who would thus have been Italian.

[1] Groag, *PIR*² C 780, referring to *IGR* III 397.

[2] As suggested in *RIB*, following Richmond, *Northumberland County History* 15 (1940) 146. Parallels seem to be lacking.

was sometimes abusively called *Augustus*,[3] and there are some cases of governors from the years 235-8 who are called *leg. Augg. pr. pr.*[4] If this hypothesis be accepted, Apellinus must be assumed to have been in office in 234, if not earlier, for Alexander was murdered well before 25 March 235.[5] Equally, he was very probably replaced by a nominee of Maximinus later in 235.

237   [?T]uccianus

VII 621 = *RIB* 1553, Carrawburgh: *[imp. Caes. [[C. Julio Ver]o / [Maximino]] p. f. Aug. Ge]r. max. / [Dac. max. Sarm. max. pont.] max.* [4]/ *[tr. p. III imp. VI cos. p]r(o)cos. / [p. p. et [[C. Iulio Vero] Maxi/[mo]] Ger. max. Dac. max. S]arm. / [max. nob.] Caes. n. sub* [8]/ *[. . .?T]ucciano v. c. leg. / [Aug. pr. pr.] coh. I B[a]tavorum / [fecit cur]ante Burrio / [. . .]sto prae[f.* [12]/ *Perpetuo et C]orneliano [cos.]* (AD 237)

The restoration *[T]ucciano* may be regarded as reasonably certain, since Tuccius seems to be easily the commonest of the *gentilicia* ending in -uccius, from one of which the *cognomen* must have been formed.[1] This would leave about six letters at the beginning of line 8 for the *nomen*, which provides an enormous range, especially as it could well have been abbreviated. But one may note the Diocletianic senator Egnatius Tuccianus, *curator* of Thugga in proconsular Africa, where he is attested by two inscriptions;[2] he might have been the grandson of our governor. The question of his origin must remain open. Tuccius appears to be an Etruscan *nomen*,[3] but that need not exclude provincial extraction for a third-century Tuccianus.[4] One may note also the *Latin Anthology* poet Tuccianus, thought to be from Africa.[5] Since three governors are attested during the reign of Gordian III, 238-44, it

---

[3] *PIR²* J 620.

[4] See *ILS* 490 (Bracara Augusta) and Stein, *Moesien* 98, legates of Tarraconensis and Moesia inferior.

[5] X. Loriot, *ANRW* II. 2 (1975) 670 f. Note that Apellinus restored a *ballistarium* at High Rochester (*RIB* 1281): if it was the same one that was built by Ti. Claudius Paulinus in 220 (*RIB* 1280, p. 187 above), this would be an additional argument for dating Apellinus at the very end of Alexander's reign.

[1] In fact, Kajanto only has one other specimen in -uccianus in his section on 'cognomina derived from *gentilicia*', pp. 139 ff., namely Luccianus (p. 149, with a single example, IX 2249).

[2] VIII 26566, 25673 + 26567 = *ILAfr.* 532.   [3] Schulze 375, 425.

[4] Egnatius Tuccianus is not in Kajanto 157, who has three examples only: X 6400 + *add.*, XI 3208 and VIII 2396 = *ILS* 2752, Cornelia Valentina Tucciana, wife of M. Plotius Faustus, an equestrian officer, at Thamugadi in Numidia. From the third century onwards the *curator civitatis* was increasingly a native of the town in question (see e.g. E. Kornemann, *RE* 4. 2 (1901) 1809 f.); but this was not necessarily the case when a senator was appointed.

[5] F. Lenz, *RE* 7A 1 (1939) 765 f.

seems probable that [T]uccianus was replaced on the downfall of Maximinus. He may well have governed Lower Britain virtually throughout the latter's reign, replacing Claudius Apellinus in the spring of 235.

| between 238 and 244 | **Maecilius Fuscus** |

VII 446 = *ILS* 2621 = *RIB* 1092, Lanchester: *imp. Caesar M. Antonius / Gordianus p. f. Aug. / principia et armamen⁴/taria conlapsa restit/uit per Maecilium Fuscum leg. / Aug. pr. pr. curante M. Aur. / Quirino pr. coh. I L. Gord.*

Except for a lead water-pipe at Rome which bears his name and senatorial rank, doubtless indicating his possession of property in the city,[1] this governor is otherwise unknown. But his *gentilicium* is rare, virtually confined to Italy and Africa,[2] so that we may be justified in suspecting that he came from one or the other. It seems probable that he preceded Egnatius Lucilianus, since the reconstruction of the headquarters building and armouries, attested in the above inscription, must surely have taken priority over the building of a bath-house for the garrison, which we find the latter governor entrusting to the same prefect of *coh. I Lingonum.*[3]

| between 238 and 244 | **Egnatius Lucilianus** |

VII 445 = *ILS* 2620 = *RIB* 1091, Lanchester: *imp. Caes. M. Ant. Gordia/nus p. f. Aug. balneum cum / basilica a solo instruxit ⁴/ per Egn. Lucilianum leg. Aug. / pr. pr. curante M. Aur. / Quirino pref. coh. I L. Gor.*

VII 1030 = *RIB* 1262, High Rochester: *G. d. n. et / signorum / coh. I Vardul[l.] ⁴/ n. explora/tor. Brem. Gor. / Egnat. Lucili/anus leg. Aug. pr. pr. ⁸/ curante Cassio Sabiniano trib.*

Egnatius Lucilianus is otherwise unknown, but it seems not improbable that he was the father of the Lucillus who was *cos. ord.* 265, and a kinsman of Gallienus, whose mother seems to have been an Egnatia.[1] His place in the series of Gordianic governors is not known for certain, but he may be supposed to have followed Maecilius Fuscus—for the

---

[1] Barbieri, *L'Albo* no. 1642.   [2] Schulze 185, 204.

[3] If R. P. Wright's conjecture that *RIB* 1751, Great Chesters, refers to the reign of Gordian III, is correct, Fuscus' name could be restored in line 4; [. . .]v/ [. . . G]ord. / [. . . provinciam] regente / [Maecilio Fus]c[o . . .].

[1] The conjecture goes back to Borghesi; see e.g. *PIR²* E 23.

reasons set forth above—and hence to have preceded Nonius Philippus, for the latter is datable to the year 242, and there is hardly time for two more governors between that time and the death of Gordian III in 244.

242   Nonius Philippus

VII 344 = *ILS* 502 = *RIB* 897, Old Carlisle: *I. O. M.* / *pro salu*[*te*] *imperatoris* / *M. Antoni Gordiani p.* [*f.*] [4]/ *invicti Aug. et Sab*[*in*]*iae Fur*/*iae Tranquil*(*lin*)*ae coniugi eius to*/*taque domu divin. eorum a*/*la Aug. Gordia ob virtutem* [8]/ *appellata posuit cui praest* / *Aemilius Crispinus pref.* / *eqq. natus in pro. Africa de* / *Tusdro sub cur. Nonii Ph*[12]/*ilippi leg. Aug. pro pre*[*to.* / *At*]*tico et Praetextato c*[*os.*] (AD 242)

There is no other record of this governor, but it may be noted that a Nonia Phili[ppa] is attested on an inscription from Rome.[1] The *cognomen* has a respectable Italian record, in the family of the Marcii Philippi of the late republic, so that there is no need to suppose that Nonius Philippus himself came from an eastern province or of freedman stock; he could well have been an Italian. There were several senatorial families with this *nomen*. Our man is unlikely to have had any connection with the first two or these, the Nonii Asprenates, already prominent under Augustus, and the Cisalpine Nonii who reached their apogee in the Severan period.[2] But he might have been a kinsman of the *cos. II ord.* of 279, Nonius Paternus.[3]

As was noted above, the other two Gordianic governors presumably preceded Philippus, whose first year is therefore likely to have been 242, or 241 at the earliest.[4] It should be mentioned that the cavalry prefect Aemilius Crispinus is at pains to draw attention to his origin—

---

[1] VI 16237.

[2] Schumacher, *Priesterkollegien* 199 f., 208 ff., with Stemma Anl. IV and VI.

[3] *PLRE* I p. 672; several other third- and fourth-century Nonii are listed on p. 633.

[4] Note VII 415 + *EE* III p. 130 = *ILS* 2635 = *RIB* 883, Papcastle: [. . ./*l*] *eg. Aug. in c*[*u*]/*neum Frision*[4]/*um Aballav*/*ensium* ⟦*Philip*⟧/*p. XIIII kal. et XIII kal.* / *Nov. Gord. II et Pompei*[*ano*] [8]/ *cos. et Attico et Pre*[*te*]/*xtato cos. v.s.l.m.* (VII 416 = *RIB* 882, ibid., is an even more fragmentary version of a very similar text.) The reference is to dedications made on 19 and 20 Oct. 241 and 242, and to some action by a legate (who must be the governor, not a legionary commander—in spite of the absence of *pr. pr.*—for whom there was no room in Lower Britain). Although not set up until after the accession of Philip in early 244 (*PIR*² J 461), the governor ought to be Nonius Philippus, and indeed the surviving traces in the middle of line 1 would accord with the restoration [*Noni*]*o Ph*[*ilippo*]. Aballava, from which the *cuneus Frisionum* took its title, was Burgh-by-Sands on Hadrian's Wall (see E. Birley, *CW*² 39 (1939) 190). Perhaps the unknown dedicator made a vow in 241 when appointed by the governor to the *cuneus Frisionum*, renewed a year later, and fulfilled on his transfer to Papcastle in 244 or soon after.

the towns of Thysdrus in proconsular Africa being the scene of Gordian I's proclamation as emperor in the year 238.[5] It is reasonable to surmise that Crispinus' career may have been furthered, if not launched, by participation in that transaction.

Aem[ilian]us

EE VII 941 = *RIB* 741 = *Ep. Stud.* 4 (1967) 91 f.; Bowes: [. . . / . . . / . . .]*us Aem*[*ilian*]*us* [*leg.* [4]/ *Aug. pr. pr. co*]*h. I Thrac*[*um*] *ins.* / [. . .]*llo praef.* [*coh.*] *fecit*

This inscription, which is mutilated through the stone's reuse as a quern, is expanded in *RIB* as follows: [. . ./ . . . / . . . *us Aem*[*ilian*]*us* [*pr*[4]/*aef. eq. co*]*h. I Thrac*[*um*] *ins.* / [. . .]*llo praef.* / [. . .] *fecit*. The editors comment as follows: 'In 1. 3 ---us Aemilianus is presumably the *praefectus equitum* from Binchester (cf. *RIB* 730) rather than the provincial governor, who, on a building-inscription such as this appears to be, could hardly be`mentioned except in an oblique case.' However, in *RIB* 730, also from Bowes, the governor Lupus is mentioned in the nominative: *D(e)ae Fortunae* / *Virius Lupus* / *leg. Aug. pr. pr.* [4]/ *balineum vi ignis exust/um coh. I Thr/acum resti*[8]/*tuit curan/te Val. Fron/tone praef.* / *eq. alae Vetto.*. Hence the expansions proposed in *Epigraphische Studien* seem perfectly plausible. There is no real certainty about the original length of the lines. As noted by the editors of *RIB* the first two lines contained an erasure, still visible in spite of the retooling. About the last five letters of line 1 and virtually the whole of line 2 (at least twelve letters) have been erased. This points to a third century date, as does also the garrison, *cohors I Thracum*, first attested on *RIB* 730 at Bowes, from AD 197 or soon afterwards. If this conjecture is correct, Aemilianus ought to have been praetorian governor of Britannia inferior, for there is hardly room for him during the early third century when consular governors were still in charge of northern England. The probable dates may be narrowed down still further, since for the period 216–44 no fewer than thirteen governors are already attested, making it a little unlikely that this man could be fitted in anywhere there. But since the names of so many of the emperors from 244 until the late third century were erased, there is little possibility of closer dating. Nor does the *cognomen* help, being extremely

---

[5] Herodian 7. 4. 1 ff., esp. 6. 1.

common.[1] It should, finally, be noted that Aemilianus might have been an equestrian *praeses*, rather than a senatorial *legatus Augusti pro praetore*, if the inscription belongs after the recovery of the western provinces by Aurelian.

between 263 and 268   Octavius Sabinus

VII 287 + p. 307 = *ILS* 2548 = *RIB* 605, Lancaster: [. . ./ *ob*] *balineum refect. / [et] basilicam vetustate conlapsum* [4]/ *a solo restitutam eqq. alae Sebussian. / [[[Po]s[t]u[mi]anae]] sub Octavio Sabino v. c. / praeside n. curante Fla. Ammau/ sio praef. eqq. d. d. XI kal. Septem.* [8]/ *Censore II et Lepido II cos.*

As Dessau first pointed out, the consuls Censor and Lepidus held office in Postumus' *imperium Galliarum*, a view confirmed by R. P. Wright's reading of traces of the deleted title *Postumiana* for the *ala Sebosiana*; the year in question must be one of those between 263 and 268.[1] It is noteworthy that Postumus continued to employ senators to govern military provinces, at a time when the emperor against whom he had seceded had replaced them by equestrian *praesides*.[2]

Octavius Sabinus is otherwise unknown and there is no particular reason to regard him as connected with the handful of recorded homonyms.[3]

between 296 and 305   Aurelius Arpagius

JRS 19 (1929) 214 = *AE* 1930. 144 = *RIB* 1912, Birdoswald: [*dd.*] *nn. Dioc*[*letiano*] *et / M*[*axim*]*iano invictis Augg. et / Constantio et Maximiano* [4]/ *nn. CC.*

---

[1] Barbieri, *L'Albo*, index p. 665, lists over twenty senatorial bearers of the *cognomen*, mostly third century. The future emperor M. Aemilius Aemilianus (*L'Albo* no. 1417, *PIR*[2] A 330) and the *praeses* of Tarraconensis in 259 (*L'Albo* no. 1415, *PIR*[2] A 259) are particularly promising possibilities.

[1] Dessau, *Mélanges Boissier* 165 ff. For the consuls see *PIR*[2] C 653. L 151 (also attested by XIII 6779, Mainz and *AE* 1930. 35, Bonn). Postumus himself inaugurated the Gallic empire in 260, rather than 259: see *PIR*[2] C 466 and, for detailed discussion of the chronology, J. Lafaurie, *ANRW* II. 2 (1975) esp. 907, who shows that Postumus himself was *cos. II* in 261, *cos. III* in 262 and *cos. V* in 269, while his fourth consulship was probably in 268 but might have been in 267. Thus 263–6 and either 267 or 268 remain vacant for Censor and Lepidus, and for the other consuls of the Gallic empire, discussed by E. Birley, *Roman Britain and the Roman Army* 58 ff. (whose chronology requires adjustment).

[2] pp. 34 f. above.

[3] Cn. Octavius Sabinus, *Cvir* of Veii in AD 26 (*ILS* 6579), L. Octavius Sabinus, a soldier in *coh. III vigilum* in 166 (XIVS 4499), the Dalmatian veteran L. Oc. Sabinus (*AE* 1902. 8) and C. Octavius Ap. Suetrius Sabinus *cos. ord.* 214, *II ord.* 240 (*RE* Supp. 14 (1974) 290). Note also the *cos.* 160, [?Octa]vius Sabinus.

sub v. p. Aur. Arpagio pr. / praetor. quod erat humo copert. / et in labe conl. et
princ. et bal. rest. / curant. Fl. Martino cent. pp. c[oh. . . .]

Senatorial *legati Augusti pro praetore* have now gone for good, and
Aurelius Arpagius (who is otherwise unknown) is an equestrian *praeses*,
with the appropriate grading of a *v(ir) p(erfectissimus)*.[1] It seems not
unlikely that the restoration of the Wall and its forts was one of the
first tasks undertaken by Constantius Chlorus after his reconquest of
Britain from Allectus in 296. However this may be, the inscription
cannot be later than the year 305, when Diocletian and Maximian
abdicated. It is not absolutely certain which province Arpagius governed,
but it is quite possible that Britannia inferior still existed at this time,
and that the new province of Britannia Secunda had not yet been
created.[2]

The name Arpagius suggests eastern origin, although a homonym is
recorded at Aquincum in Lower Pannonia,[3] and there are three examples
of an almost identical *cognomen* known from Africa.[4]

II.5

INCERTI

INSCRIPTIONS WHICH APPEAR TO RECORD GOVERNORS
WHOSE NAMES ARE MISSING OR FRAGMENTARY
AND WHOSE DATES ARE UNCERTAIN

1. VII 145 = *RIB* 419, Tomen-y-Mur: [. . .] ḄỊ[. . . / . . . *leg. Aug.*] *pro* [*pr.*]

This miserable fragment formed part of the last two lines of a substantial building inscription, and it therefore seems reasonable to
restore the title [*leg. Aug.*] *pro* [*pr.*]. The traces which are rendered
ḄỊ in the line above[1] should belong to the governor's name. Of known
governors, M. Tre*b*ellius Maximus[2] can presumably be excluded, which

---

[1] Cf. p. 35 above.   [2] Cf. pp. 315 ff. below.
[3] III 10542 (wrongly indexed as Arpagio).
[4] Fl. Arpacius v. c. (VIII 989 = *ILS* 9043, Missua–Dessau reads Arpa*g*ii); Harpagius (VIII
13391, Carthage); Petronius Gallianus *qui et* Harpagius (VIII 23274, Ammaedara). Note also
Arpagius Lupus *v.* [*c.*] (XIV 300, Ostia) and the sixth-century inscription from Mascula, VIII
2245 = *ILS* 9350, recording *Arpag. duci*. See I. Kajanto, *Onomastic Studies* (1963) 40, id.,
Supernomina (1966) 63, 83.
[1] In VII 145 something closer to OL is printed. R. P. Wright's drawing shows such a minute
fraction of each letter that it is hard to feel much confidence in his ḄỊ. However this may be, it
could represent, if correct, *be* or *br* as well as *bi*.
[2] pp. 60 ff. above.

leaves M. Atilius Metilius *Bradua*[3] and Q. Lollius Ur*bicus*.[4] Since there is no trace of occupation at the site after *c.*140,[5] and Urbicus was in any case heavily engaged in the far north of the province, the former appears a more likely candidate on present evidence.[6]

2. *CW*[2] 65 (1965) 169 ff. = *JRS* 55 (1965) 222, Hardknot: [*imp. Ca*]*es. d*[*ivi Traiani*] *Part*[*hici / fil. div*]*i Ner*[*vae nep. Tr*]*aian*[*o / Hadrian*]*o* [*Augusto pont.*] *m*[*ax.* [4]*/ . . . / . . . le*]*g. Aug. p*[*r.*] *pr. / coh. II*[*II De*]*lmatar. /* [*fecit*]

This inscription is fully discussed by R. P. Wright, ad loc., who points out that the space available could have been filled by the names of any of the already known Hadrianic governors.

3. *EE* IX 1388a = *RIB* 1932, Hadrian's Wall milecastle 50 (stone wall): *leg. II Aug. / [coh.] VII su*[*b / cu*]*ra* [. . .]

C. E. Stevens, who regards this stone as Hadrianic, comments that 'it is unique in mentioning the name (though we have lost it) of the officer 'under whose care' (*sub cura*) the job was done'.[1] Thus, by implication, he excludes the possibility that a governor was named; and this is not discussed by the editors of *RIB*. The first example of the formula *sub cura* with the governor's name occurs with Q. Lollius Urbicus, whereas A. Platorius Nepos' name simply appears in the ablative case on the building inscriptions from Hadrian's Wall.[2] The question must remain open, but it is not impossible that this was one of a pair of stones, one of which named Hadrian, the other the legion and the governor, who might be Nepos or one of his successors.

4. *Arch. Camb.* 119 (1970) 37 ff. = *Britannia* 1 (1970) 305 f. = *AE* 1971. 213, Caerleon:
(a) [. . .]*G/*[. . .]*um/* [. . .] *et* [. . .*A*]*ugg.* [4]*/* [. . . *a so*]*lo /* [. . .]
(b) [. . .]*N*[. . ./ *l*]*eg. A*[*ugg. /p*]*r. p*[. . .]

The editors print the following text: [*I. O. M. et*] *g. /* [*imperator*]*um / [Antonini] et [Commodi A]ugg.* [4]*/ [aedem a so]lo / [restituit] Ṭ. Es*[. . . / . . . / . . .]*N*[. . .[8]*/ l*]*eg. A*[*ugg. / p*]*r. p. ḍ.* [*d.*]. However, the traces of the tops of three letters in line 5 are really too insignificant to inspire any confidence in the reading. The same criticism applies to the ḍ in the last line, where only part of the upright stroke survives. In line

---

[3] p. 92 ff. above [4] p. 112 ff. above.
[5] M. G. Jarrett (ed.), V. E. Nash-Williams, *The Roman Frontier in Wales*[2] (1969) 113.
[6] See Jarrett, op. cit. 21 f., summarizing the evidence for building work in Wales under Trajan.
[1] Stevens, *The Building of Hadrian's Wall* 59. [2] p. 429 below.

7, on the other hand, the N appears to be justified, although only the top left hand tip of the letter is left. In these circumstances, any interpretation is hazardous. The editors expand [*p*] *r. p.* as [*p*] *r(imus) p(ilus)*, comparing VIII 12579. But it is implausible to suppose that these letters would have followed [*l*] *eg. A* [*ugg.*], when they would naturally be understood in such a context as *pr(o) p(raetore)*[1] —this abbreviation is found with the Antonine governor Cn. Julius Verus, who is *leg. Aug. pr. p.* on *RIB* 1322. On the other hand, the stop after the *p.* may be misplaced—compare *Urbic.i* in line 3 of *RIB* 1147—and the letter following the stop could be an *r*. The editors, taking the last letters to refer to the *pr(imus) p(ilus)*, regard the [*l*] *eg. A* [*ugg.*] as the legionary legate, of whose name they detect the letters *T. Es* in the traces in line 5, suggesting *T. Es* [*uvius*].[2] But it is preferable to disregard these letters, however they be read—and the first one may be the *t* with which the verb, for example *restituit* or *refecit*,[3] ended. The second and third letters may indeed have formed part of a governor's name.[4] At any rate, the letter *n* in line 7 probably does belong to the governor. But the choice is fairly open, even among known governors who served under two emperors: Sex. Calpurnius Agricola, Q. Antistius Adventus, C. Valerius Pudens, L. Alfenus Senecio—and one must also consider Pollienus Auspex, C. Junius Faustinus Postumianus, and two governors of Upper Britain, Rufinus and M. Martiannius Pulcher. G. C. Boon, ad loc., cautiously notes that the letter following the *n* appears to have been an upright; but this would, if correct, exclude only Auspex and Rufinus.[5] The question must remain undecided.

(?)5. *EE* IX 1248b = *RIB* 2212, Ardoch: [. . .] E (or L) / [. . . *leg.* (?)] *Aug.* / [*pr. pr.* (?)]

The word *Aug.* in line 2 might well have referred to *leg. II*, or perhaps to a procurator, as well as to an imperial legate, as restored without discussion in *RIB*. In view of its provenance, the stone was presumably inscribed during one of the limited periods when substantial portions of

---

[1] B. Dobson, who supplied the editors with their parallel, now regards the expansion *pr(imus) p(ilus)* as 'völlig falsch', *Die Primipilares* (1978) 156.

[2] G. C. Boon, *Arch. Camb.* 119 (1970) 37 ff., suggests that this might be an ancestor of the Gallic emperor Esuvius Tetricus.

[3] The editors concede this, but prefer not to suppose that any of the lines were inset.

[4] Study of the photograph and drawing suggests that *f* and *c*, *o*, or *q* cannot be ruled out.

[5] C. Valerius Pudens would still be possible if his name appeared in an oblique case, Pudentis, Pudente; and indeed [*Pollie*]*n*[*i*] or [*Rufi*]*n*[*i*] are theoretically possible. Alföldy, *Konsulat* 219 n. 68, suggests [*Calpur*]*n*. [*Agricola*], which would be ruled out, but [*Calpur*]*n*[*ius*] would still fit.

Scotland were in Roman hands, of which the reign of Antoninus Pius seems the most probable.

6. VII 482 = *EE* IX 1156 = *RIB* 1151, Corbridge: *Imp. Caes. L. Sep.* [S]*everus pi.* / *Pertinax et imp.* C[a]*esar. M. Aur. Antoninu*[s] *pius Aug⁴/usti* [[*et P. Septimius Geta* / *Caesar* ‖ *horre*[u]*m* [*per*] / *vexillatione*[*m leg.* ...] / *fecerunt su*[*b* ... *leg. Augg. pr. pr.*]

This Severan building inscription is assigned by the editors of *RIB* to the governorship of L. Alfenus Senecio, whose names they therefore restore in line 6. However, neither of the other two Severan governors who are epigraphically attested in Britain can be ruled out, namely Virius Lupus and C. Valerius Pudens.[1] Lupus perhaps deserves the preference among the three, since he is already known to have had building work carried out at this site.[2]

7. *EE* IX 1114 = *RIB* 591, Ribchester: [. . .] / *Aug.* [. . .] / *Aug.* [. . .] ⁴/ [[*Ca*[*es.*]] . . .]/*riç*[. . .] / *Au*[*g.* . . .]

The repeated *Aug.* in lines 2 and 3 and the erased but still partially legible *Ca*[*es.*] in line 4 make it legitimate to assign this inscription to the period 198-209, as does R. P. Wright, ad loc. In lines 4-6 he restores [[*Ca*[*es*]] . . . *vexillatio legionis sextae Vict*]/*ric*[*is* . . . *leg.*] / *Aug*[*g.* . . .]. But it is not particularly common to find *sexta victrix* written out in full, although there is an apparent example from Ribchester dating to the 160s.[1] Here, however, the *c* in line 5 could well be an *o*. In that case it is possible that it refers to [*C. Vale*]/*rio* [*Pudente leg.*] *Au*[*gg. pr. pr.*]. Valerius Pudens is recorded as governor on an inscription at Bainbridge of the year 205.[2]

8. VII 142 = *RIB* 430, Caernarvon: [*Impp. Caess. L.*] *Sept. Severus pius Per*/[*tinax et M. A*]*urel. Antoninus* / [*pius Augg.*] *et* [[[*P. Sep*]*t.* [*Geta no*]*b.* C[*aes.*]]] ⁴/ *rivos*] *aquaeductium vetus*/[*tate conla*]*bs. coh. I Sunic. restit.* / [. . .] ARE [. . . / . . .]NL[. . .]

There is no difficulty in dating this stone to the period 198-209, but the last two lines are so fragmentary[1] that there is little prospect of

---

[1] Jarrett and Mann, *Bonner Jahrb.* 170 (1970) 207, favour Pudens or Senecio.
[2] *RIB* 1163: see p. 151 n. 8 above.
[1] *RIB* 589, quoted p. 127 above.   [2] p. 155 above.
[1] The complete text was first published by J. Foster, *Arch. Camb.*² 4 (1853) 71 and fig., who showed VIPF in line 6. See *RIB* for other conjectures. (It should be noted that Foster read the *aq* of *aquaeductium* on a fragment subsequently lost, a point evidently overlooked by R. P. Wright, who prints [*aq*]*uaeductium*; and that the fragment containing line 7 was also lost between the publication of 1853 and subsequent readings of the stone.)

recovering the governor's name. R. P. Wright's reading of the traces in line 6 as AR̞E̞ would perhaps permit the restoration [*co*(*n*)*sul*]*ar̞e̞*, towards the end of the line (these letters come below the *nic. r* in line 5). *Co*(*n*)*sularis* written out in full otherwise occurs only on the Bainbridge inscription of C. Valerius Pudens,[2] although *cos.* is found on several other third-century stones.[3] This possibly makes Pudens a little more likely, as the governor here, than Virius Lupus or L. Alfenus Senecio.[4] The number of letters in each of the lines above varies between twenty-two in lines 2 and 4 to twenty-six in lines 3 and 5 and twenty-eight in line 1 (if the restoration *Impp.* and *Caess.* with double letters is allowed for). A restoration such as [*sub Valerio Pudente cosul*]*ar̞e̞* [*per*] would therefore be possible, perhaps with the *nomen* abbreviated *Valer.*, although ligaturing could have provided more space. The last line would then have carried the name of the subordinate commander, of which N̞L̞ (or I̞V̞L̞) would have formed part.[5]

9. VII 498 b,a = *Arch. Ael.*[4] 21 (1943) 93 = *RIB* 1051, Jarrow:
(a) [. . .] *omnium fil*[. . . / . . .] *Hadr*[*ian* . . . / . . .] *a necessitat*[. . . [4] / . . .] *vati divino pr*[. . . / . . . *c*] *os. II*[. . .]
(b) *diffusis* [. . .] / *provinc*[*ia* . . .] / *Britannia ad* [. . .] [4] / *utrumque O*[*ceani*(?) . . .] / *exercitus pr*[. . .] / *sub cur*[*a* . . .]

I. A. Richmond and R. P. Wright, ad loc., restore these two stones as part of a Hadrianic war-memorial marking the construction of Hadrian's Wall under the supervision of A. Platorius Nepos,[1] whose name is supplied in their reconstruction in line 6 of fragment (b). The principal objection to this interpretation lies in the fact that the lettering of Hadrian's name in line 2 of fragment (a) is somewhat smaller than that in all the lines of fragment (b). It is therefore prudent to leave open the alternative possibility that this was an early third century inscription, referring back to Hadrian as the Wall's original builder.[2] In support of this view, it may be recalled that Aurelius Victor, referring to Severus' British expedition, has a phrase which echoes that apparently contained

[2] See pp. 426 ff. below for the list.   [3] Quoted on p. 155 above.
[4] pp. 149 ff., 157 ff. above.
[5] These two letters are shown by Foster, op. cit., a little to the left of the letters in line 6. For a similar formula cf. *RIB* 1909, Birdoswald: *sub Alfeno Senecione cos. per Aurel. Iulianum tr.* Alternatively one might supply *cur.* or *inst.*, with the unit commander's name in the ablative.
[1] p. 104 above.
[2] E. Birley, *Research on Hadrian's Wall* 159, who also comments that the lettering 'has manifest affinities with that of early 3rd century inscriptions.' Jarrett and Mann, *Bonner Jahrb.* 170 (1970), 199, note that the monument could have related either to the campaigns of 208–11 or to the reign of Caracalla. Note further that the formula *sub cura* is not found before Lollius Urbicus (p. 429 below).

in line 4 of fragment (b).[3]

10. *JRS* 45 (1955) 145 = *RIB* 8, London: [. . .] G[. . . / . . .] *cus* [. . . / . . . *Bri*] *tann* [*i*] *ae* [4] / [*ob vi*] *ctoriam* / [. . .] *cam*

R. P. Wright, ad loc., restores as follows: [. . . *le*] g. [*Augusti iuridi*] *cus* [*pro/vinciae Bri*] *tann* [*i*] *ae* / [*ob vi*] *ctoriam* / [*Daci*] *cam*. He comments that *Dacicam* is the only adjective short enough to fit the spacing. But the length of the lines cannot really be estimated accurately without a certain restoration of any of them, which is not available. As G. Alföldy has pointed out,[1] an alternative version would be [. . .] *cus* [*leg.* / *Aug. pr. pr. prov. Bri*] *tann* [*i*] *ae* / [*fecit ob vi*] *ctoriam* / [. . .*i*] *cam*, leaving the first two lines, and the last, unrestored. The only known governors whose names included the element *-cus* are Q. Lollius Urbi*cus*, M. Statius Pris*cus* Licinius Itali*cus*, and C. Julius Mar*cus*. Of these, M. Statius Priscus may be ruled out, since he was in Britain very briefly, at a time of Roman disasters rather than victories.[2] Q. Lollius Urbicus could only have celebrated the *victoria Britannica* won for Antoninus Pius by himself.[3] Perhaps more satisfying is the possibility that C. Julius Marcus is the man here, commemorating Caracalla's German victory in 213,[4] in which year he is attested as governor in the north of Britain. There he certainly made a systematic attempt to ingratiate himself with the emperor.[5] A possible restoration would then be [. . . *C. Julius Mar*] *cus* [*leg.* / *Aug.* or *eius pr. pr. prov. Bri*] *tann* [*i*] *ae* / *fecit* or *ded.*, etc. *ob vi*] *ctoriam* / [*Germani*] *cam*. The G in the first line would presumably have been part of the imperial titulature, e.g. [*Au*] g.

11. *JRS* 57 (1967) 205 f. = *AE* 1967. 260, Housesteads: [⟦ *P. Sep. Get*] *ae*⟧ [*nob. Caes.* (?) / *coh. I Tungr. m. restit*] *uit pra* [*etor.* (?) / . . . *l*] *eg. A* [*ugg. pr. pr.*]

Even if the name of Geta is correctly restored, it is far from certain that L. Alfenus Senecio[1] is the governor whose name must be supplied in line 3. One of the other Severan governors is equally possible. The restoration *pra* [*etor*(*ium*)] is supported by the fact that the fragment was discovered in the commandant's house. But the erased letters *ae*

---

[3] Aur. Vict. *de Caes.* 20. 18: 'His maiora aggressus Britanniam, quod ea utilis erat, pulsis hostibus muro munivit per transversam insulam ducto *utrimque* ad finem *Oceani*.' E. Birley, op. cit. 159, cites *HA Severus* 18. 2: 'Brittaniam, quod maximum eius imperii decus est, muro per transversam insulam ducto *utrimque* ad finem *Oceani* munivit.' This passage derives from Victor; and it should be noted that the *HA* MSS reading is *utrumque*.

[1] In his review of *RIB*, *Bonner Jahrb.* 166 (1966) 639.

[2] p. 126 above.   [3] p. 114 above.

[4] The Arval *Acta* show that Caracalla was already called Germanicus by 20 May of that year, while the *victoria Germanica* was celebrated on 6 Oct. (*ILS* 451).

[5] p. 167 above.   [1]pp. 151 ff. above.

could also belong to *Juliae Mammaeae*, whose name was treated in this way on *RIB* 949 and 1281, the latter being a building inscription.[2]

12. VII 1191 = *RIB* 2060, Bowness on Solway:
(a) MARC. AVRELLIVS / IMPERA. TRIVMPH. / PERSA.
(b) MARC. AVREL. / PHILO.

It is clear that the reading of this now lost inscription must be faulty, but if PERSA in line 3 of fragment (a) is correct, it might contain the first part of a governor's name: *per Sa*[. . . *leg. Aug. pr. pr.*]. The use of *per* with the governor's name in the accusative is characteristic of third-century inscriptions in Britain.[1] There are several *nomina* which are known to have been borne by third century senators beginning with these letters, Sabinius, Saenius, Sallius, Salvius, Sallustius, etc.[2] The form Aure*ll*ius, although not found on other British inscriptions, was shown by A. Degrassi to be a feature peculiar to Caracalla, Elagabalus, and Severus Alexander.[3] The *Fasti* of Britannia inferior are rather congested at that period,[4] but the reading is so uncertain that further speculation would be fruitless.[5]

13. VII 833b = *EE* IX p. 600 = *RIB* 1922, Birdoswald: [. . .] CM[. . . / . . .] *imus* DI[. . . / . . .] *es a solo fe*[*c* . . .[4] / *Maximino*] *et Africano c*[*os.*] (AD 236)

There is no guarantee that this stone recorded the name of a governor, although [*praes*]*es* might possibly be restored in line 3. In that case, [(?) *Max*]*imus*(?) *Di*[. . .][1] ought to be part of his names, and he would then be the predecessor of [T]uccianus, attested in the year 237.[2]

14. VII 741 = *RIB* 1751, Great Chesters: see p. 197 n. 3 above, for the suggestion that this may refer to the governor Maecilius Fuscus, from the reign of Gordian III.

15. VII 415 + *EE* III p. 130 = *ILS* 2635 = *RIB* 883, Papcastle: see p. 198 n. 4 above, for a discussion of this stone and of VII 416 = *RIB* 882, ibid. The governor whose name is missing was probably Nonius Philippus.

16. VII 894 = *RIB* 1999, Castlesteads: IV[. . .] / M[. . . *sub*] / *cura L*[. . .] [4]/ *leg. Aug. p. p. coh. II* / *Tung. posuit*

---

[2] p. 195 above.
[1] p. 430 below.   [2] See the index in Barbieri, *L'Albo* 752 ff.
[3] Degrassi, *Athenaeum* 9 (1921) 292 ff. = *Scritti vari di Antichità* I (1962) 467 ff.
[4] pp. 181–196 above.
[5] Cf. Davies, *ZPE* 27 (1977) 241 ff., for the suggestion that the name of Ulpius Marcellus (senior or junior) might be concealed in (b), with PHILO a misreading of *bello*.
[1] [*Max*]*imus* is not the sole possible name; it might be e.g. [*Dec*]*imus*; and DI[. . .] could be a name beginning *De*, *Di*, or *Dr*.
[2] p. 196 above.

This inscription, now lost, ought to belong to the first three-quarters of the third century, to judge from the mention of *coh. II Tungrorum*[1] and of a senatorial governor. The only known man from the period whose names begin with L is L. Alfenus Senecio, but this one letter is insufficient to restore [*Alfeni Senecionis*].[2]

17. *EE* IX 1180 + p. 588 = *RIB* 1596, Housesteads: *Deo* / [*M*]*arti et* / *Victoriae*[4] / *et numinib. Augg.* / *sub cura* L*ịc*[*i*]*ṇi*(?) / . . . VLCA . . II . / . . VMSVAILVTI [8] / ALPIBAIIRISI / . I . I . . . SIC . . . /VS . . . VIVI OB / . . . VINDICII [12] / . . . *cus. arm.* / . . SD . . T

The lettering on this stone is so weathered that no satisfactory reading may be recovered for the last eight lines. The text offered above differs only slightly, after careful examination of the altar and of R. G. Collingwood's drawing, from that printed in *RIB*. In line 5, the reading *sub cura* seems certain, but the name that follows, while it clearly began with *L* and ended with *i*, is otherwise very doubtful. There is no guarantee that a governor is in question, but the formula *sub cura* is one of those most frequently found with governors.[1] It is just possible that the traces in line 6 might have included the title *l*[*e*]*g̣. Ạ*[*ugg.*] *p̣ṛ.* [*pr.*], perhaps preceded by [*c.*] *v.* Nothing more can be said to date the inscription, other than that it should not be earlier than AD 161, in view of *Augg.* in line 4. Nor is it worth speculating about senators called Licinius, in view of the commonness of that *nomen*[2] and the uncertainty of the reading.

18. *EE* IX 1172 = *RIB* 1468, Chesters: [. . . *l*]*e*[*g.*] *Aug. p̣ṛ. pr.* / [. . .] RVVRAE

Too little is recorded of this now lost inscription to give any clue to its date. Nothing is shown on the drawing between *e* and *A* in line 1, but a *g* may perhaps be restored. The letters following *Aug.* are shown simply as RR, but may have been a ligatured *pr. pr.* Likewise, the last three letters in line 2 might represent *prae*[*f.*], with ligatured *pr.*

II.6
KING COGIDUBNUS AND THE *IURIDICI*
Ti. Claudius Cogidubnus

VII 11 + p. 305 = *RIB* 91, Chichester: [*N*]*eptuno et Minervae*/ *templum*/ [*pr*]*o*

---

[1] See *RIB* 1983 for the unit at Castlesteads in the year 241; also 1981-2 (undated). In the second century it was at Birrens (2107-10, 2115), while *coh. IV Gallorum* is recorded at Castlesteads, perhaps under Hadrian (1979-80).

[2] pp. 157 ff. above. Virius Lupus (p. 150 above) may also have had the *praenomen* L.

[1] p. 429 below.   [2] See *PIR*[2] L 171-258.

salute do [*mus*] *divinae* [4]/ [*ex*] *auctoritat* [*e*/ *Ti.*] *Claud.* /[*Co*]*gidubni r. lega* [*ti*|
Aug. in Brit./ [*colle*]*gium fabror. et qui in eo* / [*sun*]*t d.s.d. donante aream* [8]/ [. .
.]*ente Pudentini fil.*

J. E. Bogaers, *Britannia* 10 (1979) 243 ff., proposes in line 5: [*Co*]*gidubni re* [*g.*
m]*agni Brit.*

Tac. *Agr.* 14. 1.

There seems no good reason to question the identification of king Cogidumnus, mentioned by Tacitus in the *Agricola*, with the man named on
the Chichester inscription.[1] In view of this, the 'quaedam civitates'
granted to him must have been in essence the kingdom created by
Commius and his heirs, the rulers of which had shown themselves to
be pro-Roman in the period from Caesar to Claudius. It had been one
of their princes, Verica, who had provided Claudius with a *casus belli* in
the year 43.[2] Nothing is known of Cogidubnus' antecedents, but he
may be assumed to have been a member of the Commian house and to
have received citizenship from Claudius or Nero.

His titulature on the Chichester stone is the matter which particularly concerns the present work. There is no exact parallel for the
combination read in *CIL* and *RIB*, *r(egis) lega* [*ti*] *Aug(usti) in Brit(an-*
nia), but analogies can be found. E. Hübner aptly compared the rulers
of the Cottian Alps.[3] Augustus made Donnus, enfranchised as C. Julius
Donnus, *rex*.[4] His son, M. Julius Cottius, became *praefectus civitatium*,
apparently losing the appellation of king.[5] But Cottius' own son, of
the same names, after succeeding to the position of *praefectus civita-*
tium, had the royal rank and style restored by Claudius.[6] Hübner, not
unreasonably, suggested that it was likewise Claudius—'ut solebat
imperator ille modum excedere'—who gave king Cogidubnus, or perhaps his son, the title of *legatus Augusti* and the senatorial rank that
went with it.[7]

Yet so remarkable a departure as the admission of a British dynast
to the Roman senate should not have passed unmentioned by Tacitus,
describing Claudius' laboured manoeuvres to gain senatorial acceptance
for the entry of the Aedui into that body in 48,[8] let alone by the
author of the *Apocolocyntosis*. E. Birley, struck by this problem, has

---

[1] A. Stein, who in *RE* 3. 2 (1899) 2696, had cautiously accepted the identification, already
found plausible by E. Hübner in *CIL* VII, ad loc., was sceptical in *PIR*[2] C 841.
[2] See e.g. Frere, *Britannia*[2] 56 ff., 75 f., 84.
[3] *CIL* VII p. 18 f.
[4] *PIR*[2] J 295.   [5] *PIR*[2] J 274.
[6] *PIR*[2] J 275.
[7] *CIL* VII p. 19.   [8] Tac. *Ann.* 11. 23–25.

stressed the significance of Tacitus' words about Cogidubnus' loyalty, 'ad usque nostram memoriam fidissimus mansit'.[9] That ought to refer, as he points out, 'to a more recent period than the Claudian invasion'. Vespasian is known to have been generous with the award of senatorial rank to his supporters in 69, and Cogidubnus could be expected to have come out early for the Flavian *partes*—Vespasian had campaigned precisely in the territory which was assigned to his kingdom.[10] Further-more, it was Vespasian who created a post of assistant-governor, a *legatus Augusti*, to serve alongside the *legatus Augusti pro praetore*, the consular governor of Cappadocia-Galatia.[11] There already existed a comparable post, that of the *iuridicus* of Hispania Tarraconensis,[12] and before long, probably on the death of Cogidubnus, an official was appointed with this title in Britain,[13] perhaps initially to supervise the territory of the former kingdom.

J. E. Bogaers has produced a neat solution to the problem of Cogi-dubnus' anomalous titulature. His version of line 5 of the Chichester inscription has the merit of strong support from the early reports of antiquaries. Unfortunately, the present condition of the stone means that only the discovery of new evidence can make his reading com-pletely certain. Grossly inflated though the style *rex magnus* might appear for a British prince whose realms comprised a rather modest tract of southern England, the parallels cited by Bogaers (two eastern client-kings of the first century AD)[14] demonstrate that it is quite possible.[15]

Whether 'Great King' or 'king (and) legate of the emperor', Cogidub-nus can hardly have survived later than the 70s. Nothing in the archaeo-logical evidence would conflict with the view that the person for whom the great palace at Fishbourne, near Chichester, was erected, died in the late 70s.[16]

---

[9] E. Birley, *Britannia* 9 (1978) 243 ff.

[10] p. 227 below.

[11] See Eck, *Senatoren* 3 and n. 9.

[12] See Alföldy, *Fasti Hispanienses* 236 ff. It should be noted that none of the seven legates who held office in the period from Tiberius to Domitian are recorded with the title *iuridicus*. The earliest such case is T. Julius Maximus Manlianus (*ILS* 1016) *c.* 100–103, Alföldy, op. cit. 78.

[13] pp. 212 f. below, where it is shown that the years 78, 79, and 81 are all possible starting-points for the first recorded *iuridicus*.

[14] *ILS* 8957 (Agrippa I or II: [*regi*] *magno*), 8958 (C. Julius Sohaemus: *regi magno*).

[15] I am grateful to J. J. Wilkes for giving me the opportunity to refer to Bogaers's article, in advance of its publication in *Britannia.*

[16] B. Cunliffe, *Excavations at Fishbourne* (1971). Cogidubnus remains, in my view, a strong candidate for the ownership of the Fishbourne palace, whether as *rex magnus* or as *r(ex)* and *legatus Aug.*, although in *Life in Roman Britain* 20 I suggested that the place might have been constructed as the residence of the *iuridicus*. Further evidence is required.

C. Salvius C. f. Vel. Liberalis Nonius Bassus

IX 5533 = *ILS* 1011, Urbs Salvia: [*C. Salv*]io *C. f. Vel. Liberali* / [*Nonio*] *Basso cos. procos. provin*/[*ciae Ma*]*cedoniae legato Augustorum* [4]/ [*iuridi*] *c. Britann. legato leg. V Maced.* / [*fratri A*]*rvali allecto ab divo Vespasiano* / [*et divo Ti*]*to inter tribunicios ab isdem* / [*promoto*] *inter praetorios quinq. IIII p. c. Hic sorte* [8]/ [*procos. fac*]*tus provinciae Asiae se excusavit*

The career is given in descending order, except that admission to the senate in the grade of ex-tribune is mentioned before promotion to that of ex-praetor.[1] There follows the record of municipal honours, chief magistrate of Urbs Salvia, his home, in four separate census years (that is to say, a minimum of fifteen years separate the first from the last tenure of that office). Finally comes the record of selection by lot for the proconsulship of Asia, and of withdrawal, by permission of the emperor, from taking up that office. This was perhaps not an unusual occurrence,[2] although there seems to be only one other epigraphic record of it.[3] No details are supplied of any career before his entry to the senate, probably, although not necessarily, during the censorship of AD 73-4. But as he received the same initial seniority and subsequent promotion as C. Caristanius Fronto (*cos.* 90),[4] he had probably also held equestrian military appointments and been on the right side in the year 69. Otherwise, his command over V Macedonica would be rather surprising.

Pliny's letters, a passage in Suetonius, and the records of the Arval brethren, combine to give a good deal of evidence for the character of Liberalis and the timetable of his career. He was an outstanding advocate, fluent and forcible, whether prosecuting or for the defence. His outspokenness won Vespasian's approval,[5] but under Domitian he was in trouble, perhaps in exile; this may explain the absence of his name from the Arval *Acta* of the years 89 to 91.[6]

He was co-opted to the Arval brethren on 1 March AD 78, and, since his *cursus* apparently lists this priesthood in chronological order, his command over V Macedonica should have begun later than that date, or

---

[1] The restoration [*promoto*] at the beginning of line 7 is preferable to Dessau's [*allecto*], in the light of the inscription of Caristanius Fronto (p. 233 below).

[2] Cf. the case of the orator Fronto, *ad Pium* 8, detailing his preparations and the ill health which obliged him to withdraw.

[3] VI 31719, C. Julius . . . Paternus (*cos. ord.* 269), *procos. pro*[*v. Asiae p*]*ost excusat. praef. urbi.* Cf. also *ILS* 1071, C. Popilius Carus Pedo, *legato legionis X Fretensis a cuius cura se excusavit,* and T. Flavius Sabinus' apparent withdrawal from taking the Gallic census (p. 225 n. 11 below).

[4] p. 234 below.   [5] Suet. *D. Vesp.* 13.

[6] Pliny, *ep.* 3. 9. 33, on which see Groag, *RE* 1A 2 (1920) 2028.

rather, later than May, when he was at another meeting of the college.[7] He is not named in the *Acta* for 80 and most of 81, but was present again on 30 September of the latter year.[8] It would be natural to suppose that he had just returned from his legion, after a tour of duty of about three years.[9] But some difficulty arises from lines 3-4 of his inscription, where he is described as *legato Augustorum* [*iuridi*] *c. Britann.* Titus had died on 13 September 81, so the two emperors should not, strictly, be Titus and Domitian. On the other hand, if he had been appointed *iuridicus* by Vespasian and continued in office by Titus, his legionary command can hardly have lasted more than a year, from late May 78, at the earliest, until, at latest, shortly before Vespasian's death on 23 June 79.[10] Equally, his post as *iuridicus* would have lasted just over two years at the most. It is reasonable to suppose that he was in fact appointed *iuridicus* by Titus, but that he had not left to take up the appointment when the latter died. Besides, it would readily explain the use of the term *Augustorum* if one of the emperors were Domitian.[11] But another interpretation of the *cursus* also deserves consideration, namely to suppose that Liberalis' co-option as a *frater Arvalis* immediately followed his legionary command. Although the order of the *cursus* is in the main descending, the adlection *inter tribunicios* precedes the promotion *inter praetorios*. If the priesthood was in some sense a reward for meritorious service as legionary legate, it would be intelligible that it should have been mentioned after it.[12] In that case, the command over V Macedonica could be assigned to the period 74-8, and the appointment as *iuridicus* to the period 78-81; and it could then be explained as an innovation designed to compensate for the consular governor's increasingly lengthy absences each campaigning season, far from the southern part of the province, at a time when—as seems probable—the death of Cogidubnus, and the incorporation of his client kingdom in the province, had given rise to complex legal problems.[13]

On this third chronology, Liberalis' proconsulship of Macedonia could be assigned to 82-3, and his consulship to 84.[14] It would then

---

[7] VI 2056 = *ILS* 5027; VI 32362.

[8] VI 2060, cf. 32363.

[9] See pp. 407 n. 4, 411 f. below, on the tenure of legionary commands.

[10] This conclusion is cheerfully accepted by H. Petersen, *CPhil.* 57 (1962) 32 f., evidently followed by Eck, *Senatoren* 133 n. 97.

[11] This is the interpretation of Groag, *RE* 1A 2 (1920), 2027, followed by E. Birley, *ANRW* (forthcoming).

[12] For the bestowal of a priesthood on a legionary legate, cf. the case of Q. Aurelius Polus Terentianus (p. 261 below).

[13] p. 210 below.

[14] Eck, *Senatoren* 133 n. 97, points out that since he was in Rome on 1 Oct. 81 and 3 Jan.

be necessary to suppose that another man held office as *iuridicus* in Britain between Liberalis and Javolenus Priscus, whose tenure must have begun in 84. Certainty unfortunately remains unattainable in the absence of further evidence, and the possibility must remain open that Liberalis was *iuridicus*, either 78-81, or 79-81, or 81-4.

His wife was Vitellia C. f. Rufilla, and their son was C. Salvius Vitellianus, whose own career included service as tribune of V Macedonica and legate to the proconsul of Macedonia, in both cases no doubt with Liberalis.[15] L. Flavius Silva Nonius Bassus (*cos. ord.* 81), also from Urbs Salvia, must have been a close kinsman of Liberalis and no doubt assisted his career.[16] Pliny's letters show that Liberalis was attending the senate in 100, when he unsuccessfully defended Marius Priscus at his trial, against Pliny himself and Tacitus;[17] and he was present at meetings of the Arval brethren in 101.[18] But his name does not feature in the *Acta* of 105, and he may be assumed to have died before that year.[19]

Between 83 and 86 C. Octavius Tidius Tossianus L. Javolenus Priscus (*cos.* 86)

III 2864 = *ILS* 1015 + *add.*, Nedinum: *C. Octavio / Tidio Tossia/no L. Iaoleno* [4]/ *Prisco leg. leg. IV Flav. leg. leg. III Aug. iuridic. provinc. Brittaniae leg. / consulari provin*[c.] *Germ. superioris / legato consulari provinc. Syriae / proconsuli provinc. Africae pontifici* [8]/ *P. Mutilius P. f. Cla.* [C]*rispinus t. p. i. / amico carissimo*

The *cursus* inscription of Javolenus Priscus is unusual in that no offices are mentioned earlier than the legionary command. It could be argued that Javolenus' friend, who no doubt established a link with him when Javolenus was commanding IV Flavia at Burnum, not far from Nedinum, was not interested in, or informed about, the earlier career. But there is a strong possibility that Javolenus had been adlected to senatorial rank, *inter praetorios*, and that the legionary legateship was the first senatorial post that he held.[1] Several of his other offices are

86, his proconsulship must be assigned to one of the years 82-3, 83-4, or 84-5. He favours 83-4. His consulship must have been before 87, since all the consuls are known from then until 92 inclusive. There appears to be only one vacancy in each of the years 85 and 86 (on the former year see now S. Modugno, S. Panciera, and F. Zevi, *Riv. stor. ant.* 3 (1973) 87 ff., esp. 108 n. 20).

[15] IX 5534 = *ILS* 1012; see Groag, *RE* 1A. 2 (1920) 2055 f.
[16] See especially Eck, *Senatoren* 93 ff.
[17] Pliny, *ep.* 2. 11. 17.
[18] VI 2074, cf. 32371.
[19] VI 2075, interpreted thus by Groag, *RE* 1A. 2 (1920) 2028.
[1] See Alföldy, *Ep. Stud.* 5 (1968) 108 f.

precisely dated, so there is little doubt about the chronology of his stay in Britain. He was legate of III Augusta in 83,[2] and consul during the last four months of 86.[3] Since he can hardly have taken up the former post earlier than 82,[4] it seems probable that he came to Britain in 84, and remained for two years.

His later career was distinguished, for he became governor of Upper Germany, where he is attested in 90,[5] and of Syria, evidently at the beginning of Trajan's reign,[6] proconsul of Africa shortly afterwards, and was also a *pontifex*. But his principal claim to fame was his reputation as a jurist. Although a harmless gaffe which he perpetuated at a literary gathering at Rome *c.*106 prompted Pliny to cast unworthy doubts on his sanity,[7] he must have continued active leadership of the Sabinian school well into the reign of Hadrian, since he was the teacher of the great Salvius Julianus (*cos. ord.* 148).[8] Of the numerous citations of his legal opinions in the *Digest*, one concerns the will of Seius Saturninus, *archigubernus ex classe Britannica*, whose son, Seius Oceanus, had died before attaining the age for inheritance.[9] The case must have come before him when he was *iuridicus* in Britain.

The names Javolenus, Tidius, and Tossianus all point to Umbria, and specifically Iguvium as the *origo* of our man.[10] But G. Alföldy has pointed out that he ought to be connected with the Octavii of Nedinum in Dalmatia, where he was honoured, a family which was well established in that province before Javolenus served there.[11] It therefore seems quite probable that he was born a C. Octavius, and that he received his other names by adoption into an Umbrian family.[12]

The fact that he had already commanded a legion, and had been the *de facto* governor of Numidia, before going to Britain, underlines the importance of the post of *iuridicus* when it was first created, already revealed by the career of Salvius Liberalis. The second century holders of the post were junior ex-praetors.

[2] VIII 23165; see Eck, *Senatoren* 131 n. 90.

[3] Degrassi, *FC* 26.

[4] His predecessor was there in 81, Eck, *Senatoren* 129, and, more fully, Thomasson, *Statthalter Nordafrikas* II 157 f.

[5] XVI 36.

[6] See now especially Alföldy and Halfmann, *Chiron* 3 (1973) 362 ff.

[7] Pliny, *ep.* 6. 15. For differing views see E. Laughton, *CQ* 21 (1971) 171 f., J. C. Yardley, ibid. 22 (1972) 314 f.

[8] *Digest* 40. 2. 5.

[9] *Digest* 36. 1. 48.

[10] See e.g. *PIR²* J 14.

[11] *Ep. Stud.* 5 (1968) 110 ff., followed by Schumacher, *Priesterkollegien* 239 f.

[12] But Syme, in an *addendum* to the reprint of his article on 'Roman Senators from Dalmatia', *Danubian Papers* 119, remains sceptical (see also his remarks ibid. 113, and *Tacitus* 761).

M. Vettius M. f. An. Valens

XI 383, Ariminum: *M. Vettio M. f. / An. Valenti / quaestori provinc. ⁴/ Macedon. quaestori* [sic] *pleb. / seviro eq.* [R] *om. praet. / leg. provinc.* [N] *arbonens. /* [iuri-dic.] *provinc. Britan. ⁸/* [leg.] *leg. XV Apollinar. / provincia Brittannia / patrono*

This man may be identified without hesitation as the Valens mentioned twice by Arrian as legate of XV Apollinaris,[1] hence his service as *iuridicus* can be dated to the late 120s or early 130s.[2] He was probably the grandson of the man of the same names and tribe also honoured at Ariminum, clearly the home of the family, who was decorated for service in the praetorian guard during the Claudian invasion and rose to be procurator of Lusitania.[3] The intervening generation is repre-sented by the M. Vettius M. f. Valens who acted as *praefectus* for Trajan when the emperor was honorary *duumvir* of Ariminum late in his reign.[4]

In line 4 of the *cursus* inscription, *quaestori* has evidently been repeated in error, instead of *tribuno* (or perhaps *aedili*). There are no other special features of the career, but it should be noted that Vettius Valens was a junior senator in comparison to the two earlier *iuridici*, who received the appointment after a legionary command. The inscription was put up by the province of Britain, in other words the *concilium provinciae*. Valens is one of two known patrons of the province.[5]

Ignotus *Inscr. It.* IV 137

XIV 4248 = *Inscr. It.* IV 137, Tibur: [. . .] *Q. f. Quir.* [. . ./ . . .p] *roconsu* [li / prov.] *Cypri leg. le* [g. . . . ⁴/iuri] *dic. Britan* [niae . . .]

The inscription gives the career in descending order, with command over a legion and the proconsulship of Cyprus following the post of *iuridicus*. The man does not appear to be identifiable with any known senator. His tribe, Quirina, shows that he was not a native of Tibur.[1]

---

[1] *Ectaxis* 5, 24.

[2] Arrian governed Cappadocia from 131 to 137, see Eck, *Senatoren* 204 ff. His measures taken against the Alani cannot be precisely dated within this period, but were probably near the end of it.

[3] *ILS* 2648; see Pflaum, *CP* no. 32 + *add.*

[4] *ILS* 6662. Note also the doctor Vettius Valens: Tac. *Ann.* 11. 30 ff., one of Messallina's lovers, executed in 48; see R. Hanslik, *RE* 8A. 2 (1958) 1869 for further references.

[5] The other one is C. Julius Galerius Asper (*cos. ord.* 212), on whom see p. 433 below.

[1] Kubitschek 50: Tibur was in the Camilia; but it was a favoured residence for provincial senators, particularly Spaniards, cf. pp. 243 and n. 6, 245 ff., 249, 270, 279 below.

C. Sabucius C. f. Quir. Major Caecilianus (*cos.* 186)

VI 1510 = *ILS* 1123, Rome: *C. Sabucio C. f. Quir. Maiori | Caeciliano cos. | sodali August. Claudial. procos. prov. ⁴| Acha. leg. Aug. pr. pr. prov. Belgicae | praef. aerari mil. leg. iurid. prov. | Britanniae iurid. per Flamin. | et Umbriam curat. viae Salar. et ⁸| alimentorum praet. candid. tr. pleb. | [. . .]*

This man's consulship is now firmly attested for the year 186,[1] which allows his service as *iuridicus* in Britain to be dated approximately. His proconsulship of Achaia should belong to 184–5, the governorship of Belgica *c.*180–3, and the prefecture of the *aerarium militare c.*176–9.[2] Thus his service in Britain may be assigned to the period *c.*172–5. It is interesting to note that he had already held two administrative posts in Italy, after the praetorship, the second of them as one of the newly created Italian *iuridici*, but that he did not hold a legionary command. During the 170s several former equestrian officers, whose military capability had already been demonstrated, were adlected to senatorial rank to enable them to become legionary legates,[3] in preference to men like Sabucius, who were thus allowed to specialize in other spheres.

Although Sabucius is a rare Etruscan *nomen*, not found outside Italy, the family could have been provincial.[4] Other Sabucii are C. Sabucius Perpetuus at Lanuvium, and S. Sabucius Sabinus, *v. c.*, named on a bronze seal from Florence; and the grandson of our man, C. Sabucius Major Plotinus Faustinus, set up an inscription in his memory.[5]

M. Antius Crescens Calpurnianus (*cos. a. inc.*)

VI 1336 = *ILS* 1151, Rome: see p. 137 above.

---

[1] He has long been recognized as the C. Sab---, suffect consul of 186 named in the Arval *Acta*, VI 2100; thus Degrassi, *FC* 52. But M. M. Roxan has now deciphered his name on the Palestinian diploma of 186: see her *Roman Military Diplomas* no. 69.

[2] See also Corbier, *L'aerarium* 398 ff., who places his prefecture *c.*180.

[3] Especially P. Helvius Pertinax (p. 144 above) and M. Valerius Maximianus (*AE* 1956. 124; see Pflaum, *CP* no. 181 *bis* + *add.*).

[4] Schulze 170, 223. The tribe Quirina is, however, found in Etruria only at Forum Clodi: see the list in Kubitschek 271 f. Provincial origin is therefore not to be excluded. The *cognomina* Major, Caecilianus, and Faustinus (his grandson's name, see next note) were favoured in Africa, see Kajanto 18, 142, 272. For Perpetuus (see next note), see A. R. Birley, *Bonner Jahrb.* 169 (1969) 276 n. 209, showing that the name is very well represented in Africa (add *CRAI* 1962, 55 no. 1, C. Marius Perpetuus of Thugga). I owe this point to Morris, thesis S 3. Although Sabucius appears not to be attested in Africa, the comments of Syme, *Emperors and Biography* 141, should be noted: 'By its nomenclature Africa attests ancient immigration. *Nomina* crop up that are of rare enough occurrence in the Italian regions or towns of their ultimate origin.'

[5] *EE* IX 629; XI 6712; *ILS* 1123a.

Ignotus *AE* 1973. 133, Praeneste

EE IX 772 + 774 = *Chiron* 2 (1972) 405 ff. = *AE* 1973. 133, Praeneste:
(a) [. . .*pr*]*ovinc*[*iae* . . ./ . . .*Mac*]*edonia*[*e*. . ./. . .]*ar. proco*[*s*. . . .
(b) [. . .]*l̦ia*[. . .] / *eiusd̦e*[*m* . . .] / *prov. B*[. . .] [4]/ *Victr. eț* [. . .] / *praef. aer.*
m[*il.* . . .]

H.-G. Kolbe has shown that the two fragments originally published separately must belong to the same *cursus* inscription of an unknown senator.[1] The letters formerly taken to be part of a name at the beginning of an inscription, ---*lius D*---,[2] now prove to be the word *eiusde*[*m*] at the start of the second line of fragment (b). Of the surviving letters, doubt attaches only to those in line 1 of fragment (b), where -*cia*- or -*eia*- are also possible,[3] while -*ar.* in line 3 of fragment (a) can be restored in several different ways.[4] The order of the career is clearly ascending, with the prefecture of the *aerarium militare* the most senior post,[5] preceded by two legionary commands, the first over a legion with the title Victrix. This might be either VI Victrix or XX Valeria Victrix or XXX Ulpia Victrix or even XIV Gemina Martia Victrix.[6] An upright stroke follows the *B* in line 3, which excludes Baetica. Belgica can almost certainly be ruled out, since the governorship of that province would be completely out of place before a legionary command. The proconsulship of Bithynia–Pontus is theoretically possible—in which case *proco*[*s.*] in line 3 of fragment (a) would have to be construed as referring to another person—but the province was almost always referred to as *Pontus et Bithynia* rather than vice versa. On balance, therefore, the post of [*iuridic.*] *prov. Br̦*[*itanniae*] appears to be the most probable restoration.[7]

As far as the earlier part of the career is concerned, a provincial quaestorship seems required in line 1 of fragment (a), followed presumably by the mention of tribunate of the plebs or aedileship, then the post of legate to a proconsul of Macedonia in line 2. -*ar.* in line 3 could refer to a second such appointment, e.g. [*leg. prov. Cretae Cyren*]*ar.*, or to the post of [*curator viae Sal*]*ar(iae)*; but the curatorship

---

[1] *Chiron*, loc. cit. On p. 408 he notes that the last line of (a) could have been from the same line as the first line of (b).
[2] Thus e.g. Ritterling, *RE* 12. 2 (1925) 1610; Alföldy, *Legionslegaten* 79 n. 353.
[3] Kolbe, op. cit. 410, notes [*iuridic. per Aemi*]*l̦ia*[*m*] as a possible restoration.
[4] Kolbe, op. cit. 409 f., lists various possibilities.
[5] Kolbe, op. cit., esp. 420 ff.; Corbier, *L'aerarium* 390 ff.
[6] E. Birley, *ANRW* (forthcoming), prefers a non-British legion. But there is a good example of a Spanish *iuridicus* becoming legate of the Spanish legion VII Gemina, *ILS* 1155; see Alföldy, *Fasti Hispanienses* 94 ff., 243 ff.
[7] See Kolbe, op. cit. 411.

of a town with a name terminating -*ar*. should not be excluded.[8] Then came a proconsulship, clearly of a praetorian province, unless a legateship to a proconsul be understood.[9]

The large number of posts held after the praetorship makes a second century date rather more likely than the first century, while the third century appears to be excluded, since *iuridici* were probably no longer appointed after the division of Britain.[10]

INCERTI

1. Nera[tius] M[. . .]

VI 1471, Rome: [. . .] P[. . .] / *Nera*[*tio* . . .] / M[. . .] [4]/ *leg. Aug.* [. . .] / *iuridic* [. . .] / *Firman*[. . .] / *pr. k. trib. p*[*leb.* . . .] [8]/ *seviro e*[*q.* . .] / *trib. lati*[*cl.* . .] / *bi*[. . .] / *patron*[. . .] [12]/ *Nerat*[. . .]

2. **T. Sextius T. f. Vot. . . . M. Vibius Qui[etus(?)] . . . Secundus cet.**

VI 1518, Rome: *T. Sextius T. f. Vo*[*t.* . . .] / *M. Vibius Qui*[*etus?* . . .] / *Secundus Luc*[. . .] [4]/ *Vestinus* [. . .] / *Africani con*[. . .] / *filius saliu*[*s* . . .] / *Hadrianalis iu*[*rid(icus)?* . . .] [8]/ *praetor in con*[. . . *imp.*] / *Caesaris L. Aur*[. . .] / *provinciae Afr*[*icae* . . . / *T. Sextius Magi*[*us* . . .] [12]/ *patri*

3. **Ignotus VI 1551**

VI 1551, Rome: [. . .] *leg. Aug. p*[*r. pr.* . . . .] / *leg. Aug. pr.* [*pr.* . . . *leg. Aug.*] / *pr. pr. pro*[*v.* . . . / *XI Claud.* [. . .] / *IIXX Pri*[. . ./ *i*]*uridico* [. . . *cura*[8]/*t*]*ori Sol*[. . .

In all three cases, it is doubtless more probable that the juridicate was of an Italian region rather than of Britain or Hispania Tarraconensis.

4. **Ignotus *RIB* 8**

See p. 206 above for discussion of this inscription, which, it is there suggested, may refer to a governor, perhaps [*C. Julius Mar*]*cus*, rather than to a [*iuridi*]*cus*, as restored by R. P. Wright, ad loc.

---

[8] Kolbe, op. cit. 409 f., discusses various possibilities. One might add [*curator rei p. Ammaed*]*ar., vel sim.*

[9] Kolbe, op. cit. 409 f., notes the possibility of restoring this as [*leg. pro pr. prov. Cretae et Cyren*]*ar. procos.* [*patris sui*].

[10] See p. 405 below.

II.7

THE LEGIONARY GARRISON OF BRITAIN

Four legions arrived with the army of invasion in 43, II Augusta and XIV Gemina from Upper Germany, XX from Lower Germany, and IX Hispana from Pannonia.[1] All four evidently remained in the island until XIV Gemina, by now bearing the additional titles Martia Victrix for its part in 60, was withdrawn by Nero, c.66-7, for his projected Caucasus campaign.[2] This legion returned for a brief period in 69-70, but then left to join the Roman forces in the Rhineland, never to return to Britain.[3] In 71 Q. Petillius Cerialis arrived as governor, evidently bringing with him the recently formed II Adiutrix. This remained in Britain until c.85.[4] Thenceforward there were only three legions in Britain, with the possible exception of a brief period under Trajan, when IX Hispana may have been absent at Nijmegen in Lower Germany; and the years 122-c.133, after VI Victrix had arrived. IX Hispana certainly left Britain at latest in the early 130s, and its former base at York was occupied by VI Victrix. The details of the last years of IX Hispana's existence are still somewhat uncertain and require further discussion. But first it will be convenient to summarize what is known of the other legions' movements within Britain during the years 43-122.

II Augusta   first base: south-west England: at Gloucester(?) from c.65; at Caerleon from c.74.[5]

IX Hispana   first base: east Midlands(?); at Lincoln from the 50s; at York from c.71; perhaps at Nijmegen in Lower Germany under Trajan; perhaps at Carlisle under Hadrian.[6]

XIV Gemina   first base: Midlands (Leicester?); at Wroxeter from the 50s until c.65; in Italy c.66-9; back in Britain at unknown base 69-70.[7]

XX Val. Vic.   first base: Colchester(?); at Gloucester from 49; at Wroxeter from c.66(?); thereafter moved, perhaps after

---

[1] Ritterling, *RE* 12. 1 (1924) 1249 f.

[2] Tac. *Hist.* 2. 11. 1. Ritterling, *RE* 12. 1, 1260, dates the move to autumn 67, but an earlier date is required, since it is difficult to place the foundation of I Italica, raised by Nero for the same purpose, later than 66, as shown by Dobson, *Die Primipilares* 204, discussing the career of L. Antonius Naso (*ILS* 9199).

[3] Ritterling, *RE* 12.2 (1925) 1732, citing Tac. *Hist.* 2. 66. 1-3, 4. 68. 4; see also pp. 232 f. below, on the legate M.(?) Fabius Priscus.

[4] Ritterling, *RE* 12. 2, 1440 f.; see also p. 70 above, on Sex. Julius Frontinus.

[5] See esp. Jarrett, *Arch. Camb.* 113 (1964) 47 ff.; also Frere, *Britannia*[2] 89 ff., 96, 106, 109, 118.

[6] Frere, op. cit. 86 f.; and see below.

[7] Frere, op. cit. 87 f., 94 f., 100, 109.

a stay elsewhere, to Inchuthil for a brief period, *c*. 83–7; at Chester from *c*. 87.[8]

II Adiutrix   first base: Lincoln, *c*. 71–*c*. 74; at Chester *c*. 74–*c*. 85.[9]

IX Hispana was once thought to have been destroyed in Britain early in the reign of Hadrian, but the careers of several of its officers made this theory highly implausible.[10] First there are two former *laticlavii*, L. Aemilius Karus (*cos.* 144) and L. Novius Crispinus (*cos.* 150).[11] Although the latter's promotion may not have been very rapid in comparison to some of his contemporaries, this does not apply to Karus, whose favour with Hadrian was demonstrated by his being *quaestor Augusti*. Neither can have served earlier than the mid-120s. Then there is the ex-legate, L. Aninius Sextius Florentinus, who proceeded via the proconsulship of Narbonensis to the imperial province of Arabia, and is now known to have been in the latter post in 127. Hence he is unlikely to have resigned his command of the legion much before 124.[12] Above all, the career of another former *laticlavius*, Q. Camurius Numisius Junior, strengthens the case for the legion's survival long after the accession of Hadrian. If, as seems virtually certain, he is identical with the Numisius Junior who was suffect consul in 161, he can hardly have served with IX Hispana earlier than *c*. 140, for his later offices show him to have been a trusted and favoured senator.[13] IX Hispana's final disappearance can thus reasonably be assigned to the disaster at Elegeia in 161, when an unnamed legion of the Cappadocian army was destroyed with all its officers.[14] IX Hispana might well have gone to the east with Sex. Julius Severus, initially to Judaea to fight in the Jewish war, *c*. 133–5, later to be transferred to Cappadocia, perhaps *c*. 137, when trouble threatened from the Alani.[15]

But this still leaves unresolved the moment of its departure from

---

[8] See esp. Jarrett, *Arch. Camb.* 117 (1968) 77 ff.; also Frere, op. cit. 87, 95 f., 109, 118, 129, 137.

[9] The presence of II Adiutrix on the Danube is not specifically attested until the Suebo-Sarmatian war of 92, in which a tribune of the legion was decorated (*ILS* 2719); but there seems little doubt that it was summoned by Domitian soon after the disaster of Oppius Sabinus, now dated to early 85 by Alföldy and Halfmann, *Chiron* 3 (1973) 331 ff.

[10] As pointed out by Ritterling, *RE* 12. 2 (1925) 1669, and in more detail by E. Birley, *Roman Britain and the Roman Army* 25 ff.

[11] pp. 275, 277 below.

[12] p. 238 below.

[13] p. 255 below.

[14] Dio 70. 2. 1. The suggestion was first put forward by E. Birley, *ap.* J. E. Bogaers, *Numaga* 12 (1965) 30 = *Studien zu den Militärgrenzen Roms* (1967) 75. See now Eck, *Chiron* 2 (1972) 462, exploiting the consulship of Numisius Junior.

[15] Thus Eck, op. cit. 462, who suggests as an alternative the Parthian threat at the end of the reign of Pius.

Britain. Its latest datable record here is an inscription of 108 at York.[16] At some stage in the early second century it seems to have been at Nijmegen, but its stay there is not precisely defined.[17] Possible occasions might be during the second Dacian war, $c.104$-6,[18] or during the Parthian war, $c.113$-17.[19] J. E. Bogaers, the excavator of Nijmegen, favours the years $c.121$-30,[20] but it seems barely credible that Hadrian would have moved VI Victrix from Lower Germany to Britain in 122, rather than sending back IX Hispana from the same province, when more troops were required.[21] As far as the two possible periods in Trajan's reign are concerned, it has been observed that there is no firm evidence for the legion earlier in garrison at Nijmegen, X Gemina, having moved to Pannonia until $c.114$. It is logical to suppose that Trajan might have switched X Gemina from Rhine to Danube, when XV Apollinaris moved from Carnuntum to the east, and that IX Hispana was brought from Britain to plug the gap.[22] However, when trouble broke out in Britain on Hadrian's accession, he will then have sent IX Hispana back to the province. It may then have moved further north than York, and its presence near Carlisle may be inferred from tile-stamps.[23] Although it is not yet attested as having taken part in the building of Hadrian's Wall, it must be noted that at the western end no stone building inscriptions have been found, the Wall there being built of turf.[24] The addition of VI Victrix to the garrison can then be

[16] *RIB* 665. It is not listed on *ILS* 2288, drawn up before $c.165$.

[17] Bogaers, op. cit. 10 ff. = 54 ff.; id., *Studien zu den Militärgrenzen Roms II* (1977) 93 ff. In spite of Bogaers's arguments, I remain not wholly convinced that the Nijmegen evidence, consisting solely of one tile-stamp and one mortarium-stamp, demonstrates that the whole legion was there, rather than, for example, a vexillation forming part of the *vex. Brit.*, for which there is much more ample evidence. On the Aachen inscription, see n. 19 below.

[18] This period is favoured by Jarrett and Mann, *Bonner Jahrb.* 170 (1970) 184 f., and by E. Birley, in Butler (ed.), *Soldier and Civilian in Roman Yorkshire* 75 f., who argues that the military situation in Britain was too precarious in the period $c.108$-17 for a legion to have been withdrawn then. However, the evidence which he cites is not inconsistent with a brief period of trouble soon after 103, and renewed disturbances $c.117$—perhaps caused precisely by the absence of IX Hispana.

[19] Thus H. Nesselhauf, *Bonner Jahrb.* 167 (1967) 268 ff. Nesselhauf's discussion is centred on the inscription of L. Latinius Macer, *praefectus castrorum*, formerly *pp.* of IX Hispana, found at Aachen (now *AE* 1968. 323). But the inscription is undated, and H. v. Petrikovits, ibid. 278 comments that the style of carving suggests a much earlier period. There is no necessity to invoke the presence of Macer's legion in the immediate vicinity: he may be supposed to have been on furlough at Aachen, taking the waters—perhaps in or soon after 43.

[20] Bogaers, *Studien zu den Militärgrenzen Roms II* (1977) 95.

[21] As pointed out by Nesselhauf, op. cit. 272 ff., followed by Dobson, *Die Primipilares* 233 f. Whence Nesselhauf argues that IX Hispana must have already moved to the east $c.119$ (from Nijmegen).

[22] Nesselhauf, op. cit. 272 ff.

[23] See Bogaers, *Studien* (1967) 68 ff. and fig. 7. The stamps from Carlisle (and nearby Scalesceugh) and those from Nijmegen all have *VIIII*, rather than *IX* as on those from York.

[24] E. Birley, *Roman Britain and the Roman Army* 28. Stevens, *The Building of Hadrian's Wall* 84, suggested that a Turf Wall milecastle (no. 73) might be the type of IX Hispana.

construed not as the response to renewed hostilities but rather as the result of the heavy demands of the frontier construction on military manpower.[25] VI Victrix was perhaps ensconced in the Ninth's old fortress at York, which was to become its permanent base.[26] The permanent departure of IX Hispana from Britain perhaps did not occur for a further ten or eleven years.[27]

II.8

LEGIONARY LEGATES OF THE BRITISH ARMY

43   C. Hosidius Geta (*cos. a. inc.*)

IX 2847 = *ILS* 971, Histonium: CIV[. . .*Hos*]*id*[*io* . . .*Arn. Getae cos.* . . .] / *regi sac*[*ror.*] *flam.* [. . . *a divo Claudio lecto inter*] / *patric. leg. Caesaris pro* [*pr.* . . . *divi*] [4]/ *Claudi in Britannia a d*[*ivo Claudio misso legato* / *p*]*ro pr. in Hiberia ad sed*[*andas turbas*(?) . . . *huic senatus auctore divo Claudio*] / *ornamenta triumph*[*alia decrevit*]

Dio 60. 20. 4.

There can be little doubt that the Hosidius Geta mentioned in Dio's account of the Claudian invasion was a legionary legate, but some have preferred to read his *praenomen* as Γνάϊος rather than the MSS Γάϊος,[1] identifying him with the Cn. Hosidius Geta who succeeded Suetonius Paullinus in the Mauretanian campaign,[2] and who was to be Flavius Sabinus' consular colleague later in the 40s.[3] However, the *cursus*

---

[25] E. Birley, *Roman Britain and the Roman Army* 27 f.

[26] For the history of this legion in Britain, A. R. Birley, in Butler (ed.) *Soldier and Civilian in Roman Yorkshire* 81 ff.

[27] Dobson, *Die Primipilares* 234, objects that if IX Hispana and VI Victrix were both stationed in Britain together for a while from 122, the latter, as the more recent arrival, would have been the legion selected to go to the east. But if the transfer did not take place until Julius Severus' departure c.133 (p. 107 above), and VI Victrix by then had occupied York for some years while IX Hispana was in a new but incomplete base (at Carlisle?) which was by then regarded as superfluous, the choice of the IXth is perfectly intelligible. For the sake of completeness one must note, finally, the inscription of a soldier of IX Hispana buried at Misenum (X 1769), whose Cilician origin coupled with his *gentilicium* Aelius surely point to the presence of the legion in the east not earlier than the reign of Hadrian, as urged by Bogaers, *Studien* (1967) 73. Alternatively, and rather more plausibly, one might suggest that the man in question had been in the Misenum fleet and was transferred to the legion c.133, as was the case with other men from that fleet put into the Judaean legion X Fretensis at the same time (XVI, app. 13).

[1] See *PIR*[2] II 217.

[2] *PIR*[2] H 216. It must however be conceded that CIV at the beginning of line 1 might be a misreading of CN. See also p. 365 below, on Cn. Hosidius Geta.

[3] p. 225 below.

inscription, now lost, from Histonium, cannot be assigned to Gnaeus, although it clearly refers to a native of this town (the home of the Hosidii),[4] who participated in Claudius' British expedition. As Groag pointed out,[5] the traces of the name could be restored to read [*Hos*]*id*[*io ... Arn. Getae*]. The restoration and interpretation of line 3 is difficult. *leg. Caesaris pro* [*pr. ...*] might refer to some post held under Caligula.[6] *Claudi* at the beginning of line 4 appears to require at least [*legato divi*] at the end of line 3;[7] mention of a legion may not have been deemed necessary.[8] Since Dio specifically records that Geta was given *ornamenta triumphalia*, although he had not been consul, it is not improbable that there was a phrase such as *ob res in Britannia prospere gestas* at the end of the inscription.[9]

The Hosidii survived at least into the Antonine period,[10] but our man's name was perpetuated through the female line. His daughter married M. Vitorius Marcellus,[11] friend and pupil of Quintilian and friend of Statius, who dedicated his fourth book of *Silvae* to him. The fourth poem in this book, published not earlier than 95, was addressed to Marcellus himself, and mentions his son Geta, by his full names C. Vitorius Hosidius Geta,[12] stressing the example of the boy's warlike grandfather, *belliger. . .avus*, who is now already demanding worthy feats from the boy and grants him to know the triumphs of the

---

[4] *PIR*[2] H 214–19.

[5] *RE* 8. 2 (1913) 2490, followed by De Laet, *De Samenstelling*, nos. 639, 1170; *PIR*[2] H 217, etc.

[6] Groag, *RE* 8. 2 (1913) 2490, and others. But the choice is rather limited in this period: one of the *tres Galliae*, Lusitania (probably occupied for most of Caligula's reign, see Alföldy, *Fasti Hispanienses* 136 f.), Galatia—and 'Numidia', or III Augusta, taken over precisely at this time, see Thomasson, *Statthalter Nordafrikas* I 10ff. At all events, if our man had indeed governed a province of the emperor before going to Britain, he was presumably a little senior to Vespasian, praetor in 39 or 40 (p. 227 below) and probably to Sabinus as well (p. 225 below).

[7] D. E. Eichholz, *Britannia* 3 (1972) 151 n. 18, comments that since Geta was a legionary legate, '[*com*(*iti*) *divi*] *Claudi in Britannia* seems an unpromising way of supplementing *ILS* 971.' [*leg. leg.*. . . . *et comiti divi*] *Claudi in Britannia* might be preferable. [*legato legionis*. . . *divi*] *Claudi* etc. seems an unusual order, but cf. lines 3–4 of the *cursus* inscription of Eprius Marcellus, p. 228 below. See also next note.

[8] Several *cursus* inscriptions from the early principate have *leg*(*atus*) of Augustus or Tiberius without mentioning a legion, although a command seems probable, e.g. *ILS* 937, *leg. divi Aug. et Ti. Caesaris Aug.*, 947, *legatus Ti. Caesaris Aug.*, 8967, *leg. Ti. Caesaris Aug.*, *EE* IX 385, *leg. Augusti.*

[9] Thus Groag in *RE* 8. 2 (1913) 2490; omitted in *PIR*[2] H 217.

[10] *PIR*[2] H 218–20.

[11] R. Hanslik, *RE* Supp. 9 (1962) 1744 f.

[12] *RE* Supp. 9, loc. cit. The *praenomen* is supplied by VI 2079. This Geta's use of the *praenomen* C. may be regarded as further evidence for the existence of two brothers in the 40s. Cn. Hosidius Mauricus (*PIR*[2] H 220) will be a son or descendant of the Mauretanian commander. Schumacher, *Priesterkollegien* 119 f., argues that C. Vitorius Geta was *cos. suff.* 130.

house.[13] A little earlier, speculating where Marcellus may be sent by Domitian, Statius speaks of the command over legionaries, and service on the Rhine, in Britain (*litora Thyles*), the Danube and the Caspian Gates.[14] It is legitimate to wonder whether the poet was thinking of the career of Geta, who, if he commanded a legion in Britain in 43, had probably served on the Rhine first,[15] and was to operate—if the identification with the honorand of *ILS* 971 may be accepted—in the area of the 'portae limina Caspiacae'. However this may be, Statius certainly appears to indicate that the former legionary legate of 43 was still alive over fifty years later.[16]

43   T. Flavius Sabinus (*cos.* 47?)

Dio 60. 20. 3.

Flavius Sabinus, like his younger brother Vespasian, served in the army of invasion. Dio's text has been taken to mean that Sabinus was in a subordinate capacity to Vespasian, but it has long been recognized that he must have been a legionary legate as well,[1] and attention should have been paid to Vrind's simple emendation, making both brothers ὑποστρατηγοῦντά<ς> οἱ [sc. τῷ Πλαυτίῳ].[2] There is no means of deciding which of the three legions not commanded by Vespasian, IX Hispana, XIV Gemina and XX, was under Sabinus.

Tacitus, after describing Sabinus' violent death in December 69, assigns him an obituary notice in which he mentions his thirty-five

[13] *Silv.* 4. 4. 72 f.

[14] Ibid. 61 ff.

[15] Mention of the Rhine might exclude IX Hispana, thus narrowing down Geta's legion to XIV or XX. The reference to the Danube remains unexplained.

[16] J. P. Postgate, *CQ* 20 (1906) 307 (who conflates C. and Cn. Hosidius Geta), regards the warlike grandfather as dead. Likewise L. Håkanson, *Statius' Silvae* (1969) 120: 'This should not, with Vollmer, be taken too literally, meaning that the grandfather impatiently presses the little boy with reference to his own triumph; such a bore of a grandfather can hardly be implied by Statius. The words mean: "when already <the thought of> his glorious grandfather spurs on to worthy deeds".' None the less, the case of Manlius Valens (p. 230 below) is a useful reminder that such longevity would not be unexampled. It is worth remarking that Geta's daughter, the mother of C. Vitorius Hosidius Geta, is unlikely to have been born much before the 60s, if her son was *parvus* c. AD 95 (*Silv.* 4. 4. 72). (R. Hanslik, *RE* Supp. 9 (1962) 1744, confuses the issue by calling the lady the granddaughter of C. Hosidius Geta.) The *frater Arvalis* of the 160s (VI 2091) was presumably son or grandson of Vitorius Hosidius Geta.

[1] e.g. Groag in *PIR*² F 352: 'immo videtur Sabinus ut vir tum temporis sine dubio iam praetorius haud secus ac Vespasianus legioni cuidam praefuisse.'

[2] G. Vrind, *De Cassii Dionis vocabulis quae ad ius publicum pertinent* (1923) 90: 'Voce οἱ Plautius designari videtur; casu enim dativo legatum provinciae designari cetera quoque exempla illustrant. . . Apparet autem hoc loco Sabinum quoque, fratrem Vespasiani maiorem, legatum legionis fuisse. Quam ob rem legere velim ὑποστρατηγοῦντάς οἱ, cui lectioni Xiphilinus favet, a quo Vespasianus τῶν ὑποστρατηγούντων ὢν τῷ Πλαυτίῳ dicitur.'

years of public service.[3] He had presumably entered the senate in 34, when he must have already passed the minimum age for the quaestorship.[4] But nothing is known of his pre-consular career other than the command in Britain, and the date of his consulship is not quite certain. He is attested in office on an inscription from Rome, as colleague of Cn. Hosidius Geta, on 1 August.[5] The latter had two other known colleagues, L. Vagellius (on 22 September)[6] and C. Volasenna Severus.[7] Geta and his colleagues are customarily assigned to 45, or 44,[8] but 47 is surely much more likely. The inscription set up during the tenure of Sabinus and Geta contains a specimen of one of the new Claudian letters of the alphabet, introduced when the emperor was censor;[9] while the inscription from Herculaneum quoting the *senatus consultum* passed during Geta's continued tenure of the *fasces* refers to the *felicitas saeculi instantis*, an expression rather more appropriate to 47 than to 44.[10]

However this may be, Sabinus' career after the consulship was distinguished. He governed Moesia for seven years, probably from 53 to 60, and was prefect of the city, evidently from 61 until his dismissal by Galba in 68, and again from 15 January 69 until his death.[11]

43   T. Flavius Quir. Vespasianus (*cos.* 51 etc.)

Joseph. *BJ* 3. 4: [ὁ Νέρων] μόνον εὑρίσκει Οὐεσπασιανὸν ταῖς χρείαις ἀναλογοῦντα καὶ τηλικούτου πολέμου μέγεθος ἀναδέξασθαι δυνάμενον, ἄνδρα ταῖς ἀπὸ νεότητος

---

[3] Tac. *Hist.* 3. 75. 1: 'Hic exitus viri haud sane spernendi: quinque et triginta stipendia in re publica fecerat, domi militiaeque clarus.'

[4] p. 12 above, and see A. Chastagnol, *Historia* 25 (1976) 255. Sabinus could not have been born later than the year 8, for Vespasian was born on 17 Nov. AD 9 (p. 226 below).

[5] *AE* 1953. 24.

[6] *ILS* 6043; *AE* 1969/70. 94.

[7] *AE* 1973. 151.

[8] Barbieri, *Epigraphica* 29 (1967) 7 f., followed by Eck, *Historia* 24 (1975) 341 with n. 113 (cf. 340 and n. 103).

[9] See Tac. *Ann.* 11. 13-14 etc. I am most grateful to Dr Jean Mottershead for pointing this out to me, and for drawing my attention to the difficulties in the standard interpretation of *saeculi instantis* (see next note).

[10] *ILS* 6043. If *saeculi instantis* means 'the approaching (new) age', then it should be noted that this would only begin on 21 Apr. AD 48, see J. Gagé, *Recherches sur les jeux séculaires* (1934) 87 f. But in any case, in normal usage *instans* frequently meant *praesens*: see *TLL* VII.1, 2004 f.

[11] *PIR*[2] F 352. See now Griffin, *Seneca* 456 f. for a sensible discussion of the textual difficulty in Tac. *Hist.* 3. 75. 1, and a review of the other evidence for his later career, including the post mentioned in *ILS* 984 + *add.*, [*cur. census*] *Gallici*, which, from its position between the provincial governorship and the urban prefecture, ought to refer to the Gallic census of 61. Sabinus presumably withdrew, on appointment as *praefectus urbi*, in favour of one of the three men known to have carried out this task (Tac. *Ann.* 14. 46; see p. 59 above).

στρατείας ἐγγεγηρακότα καὶ προειρηνεύσαντα μὲν πάλαι Ῥωμαίοις τὴν ἑσπέραν ὑπὸ Γερμανῶν ταρασσομένην, προσκτησάμενον δὲ τοῖς ὅπλοις Βρεττανίάν τέως λανθάνουσαν, (5) ὅθεν αὐτοῦ καὶ τῷ πατρὶ Κλαυδίῳ παρέσχε χωρὶς ἱδρῶτος ἰδίου θρίαμβον καταγαγεῖν.

Sil. Ital. 3. 597-8:   Hinc pater ignotam donabit vincere Thulen,
                            Inque Caledonios primus trahet agmina lucos.

Val. Flacc. 1. 7-9:   tuos o pelagi cui maior aperti
                            Fama, Caledonios postquam tua carbasa vexit
                            Oceanus Phrygios prius indignatus Iulos.

Tac. *Agr.* 13. 3; *Hist.* 3. 44; Sueton. *D. Vesp.* 4. 1; Dio 60. 20. 3; 60. 30. 1; 65. 8. 3[2]; Eutrop. 7. 19. 1.

Not surprisingly the career of the future emperor is better recorded than that of most other British legionary legates, and his command in Britain more copiously than any. The principal source is Suetonius' biography, to which other writers add a little precision and great deal of embroidery. He was born on 17 November AD 9 at the village of Falacrina on the *via Salaria*, close to the Sabine *municipium* of Reate, which counted as his *patria*, as the younger son of Flavius Sabinus and Vespasia Polla. Sabinus, whose own father Petro had been in business as a debt-collector after serving in Pompey's army, had also devoted himself to finance, first as a tax-farmer in Asia and then as a money-lender 'apud Helvetios'. Polla, daughter of an equestrian officer from Nursia, had a brother who entered the senate and attained the rank of praetor, and she seems to have been the driving force behind her sons' rise.[1] The elder, T. Flavius Sabinus, evidently became a senator at the earliest opportunity, while Vespasian 'sumpta virili toga latum clavum, quamquam fratre adepto, diu aversatus est'.[2] A. Chastagnol argues that at this period only sons of senators could wear the *latus clavus* after taking the toga of manhood; others could only do so after election to a republican magistracy.[3] If this is right, Vespasian's service as military tribune, in Thrace, will have been as *angusticlavius*; and the reason why Suetonius does not mention any post in the vigintivirate will be because he did not hold one.[4] As he was apparently aedile in 38,[5] his quaestorship was presumably in 35-6, in the province of Crete-Cryene.[6] He

---

[1] Suet. *D. Vesp.* 1-2. 1.

[2] Ibid. 2. 2.

[3] A. Chastagnol, *Historia* 25 (1976) 253 ff.

[4] Suet. *D. Vesp.* 2. 3. See Chastagnol, op. cit. 255, who points out that the tribunate was probably held c.AD 30, rather than at the time of the campaign of AD 26 (Tac. *Ann.* 4. 46 ff.), as was once thought—the only known occasion when Roman troops had to operate in Thrace at this period—for Vespasian would only have been sixteen years old then.

[5] Dio 59. 12. 3, cf. Suet. *D. Vesp.* 5. 3.

[6] Suet. *D. Vesp.* 2. 3. Chastagnol, op. cit. 255, points out that Vespasian's brother Sabinus

was praetor in 39 or 40.[7] Soon after the accession of Claudius in 41 came his first, and for a long time his only chance to shine, with the appointment as commander of II Augusta, then stationed at Argentorate (Strasbourg) in Germania superior.[8] Only Tacitus, in the *Histories*, supplies the name of the legion. Suetonius says that the post was obtained 'Narcissi gratia'. The powerful freedman seems to have taken a direct interest in the British expedition,[9] which was no doubt already being planned when Vespasian was sent to Germany. Vespasian's close links with the court continued: his elder son Titus, born in 39,[10] was to be a playmate of Britannicus Caesar, born in 41.[11] Further, Vespasian was described by Tacitus as having been a client of Vitellius, 'cum Vitellius collega Claudio fuit'. This could refer to 43 as well as to 47.[12]

II Augusta went to Britain with Plautius and Vespasian commanded it with distinction at the two-day battle thought to have been at the crossing of the R. Medway,[13] going on to further exploits, listed by Suetonius (followed almost verbatim by Eutropius) in the manner of an honorific inscription: the capture of the Isle of Wight and over twenty *oppida*, and the defeat of two 'very strong peoples'. The award of triumphal *ornamenta* need not, as Eichholz has shown, imply that he returned to Rome in 44. He probably stayed in Britain until 47.[14] But although he fought many engagements (*tricies* is perhaps a round number), it is questionable whether the high-flown language of the Flavian poets Silius Italicus and Valerius Flaccus should be interpreted to refer to any exploits in North Britain, let alone to naval activity off Scotland or a mission to the 'Caledonian groves' and 'unknown Thule'. These poetic flights of fancy are on a par with Josephus' flattering attribution of the entire success of the expeditionary force to Vespasian. Tacitus' language is more convincing: 'adsumpto in partem rerum

---

evidently entered the senate (as quaestor, presumably) in 34 (p. 225 above). Hence Vespasian's own quaestorship should be later than this. But as he was aedile in 38, at the second attempt (Suet. *D. Vesp.* 2. 3), he must have attempted election the first time in 36; hence he could hardly have been quaestor as late as that year, as Chastagnol thinks possible (p. 256: 'fut élu en 35 ou 36')—especially since, as a provincial quaestor, his term must have run from summer to summer (p. 12 above).

[7] Suet. *D. Vesp.* 2. 3: as praetor he proposed *ludos extraordinarios* for Gaius' *victoria Germanica* etc., which must refer to the end of 39 (Dio 59. 22 ff.).

[8] Ritterling, *RE* 12. 2 (1925) 1459.

[9] Dio 60. 19. 2.

[10] *PIR*[2] F 399.

[11] Suet. *D. Titus* 2; *D. Claud.* 27. 2 (cf. *PIR*[2] C 820).

[12] Tac. *Hist.* 3. 66. 3, cf. Degrassi, *FC* 12 f.

[13] See e.g. Frere, *Britannia*[2] 79 ff.

[14] Eichholz, *Britannia* 3 (1972) 149 ff.

Vespasiano'. It should be noted that a tenure of the legateship lasting four or five years would help to explain why the legion so readily adhered to Vespasian's cause in 69, as Tacitus. reports—there will have been a number of men still serving, particularly centurions, who had been in the legion in the 40s.

Vespasian had to wait, without further employment, until 51 for his consulship, which does not indicate abnormal retardation: he held the *fasces suo anno*, although he might have legitimately hoped for two years' remission for his two elder children;[15] the two priesthoods he received were some compensation. But it was soon after 51 that his patron L. Vitellius died,[16] while Narcissus' influence declined markedly. Agrippina's hatred of Narcissus' friends even after the freedman's death long kept Vespasian out of public life,[17] presumably until she too died, in 59. His term as proconsul of Africa thus probably fell in the early 60s.[18] Finally, when he was fifty-six, came the appointment to command the army in Judaea,[19] from which his rise to the purple followed.

(?) T. Clodius M. f. Fal. Eprius Marcellus (*cos.* 62, *II* 74)

T. B. Mitford, *Report of the Department of Antiquities, Cyprus* 1940-8 (1954) = *AE* 1956. 186 = *SEG* XVIII (1962) 587, Paphos: ['Ἀπόλλ]ωνι['Υλάτηι(?) / Τίτῳ Κλωδίῳ 'Επρίῳ] Μαρκέλλῳ [ταμίᾳ δημάρχῳ / στρατηγῷ πρεσβ]ευτῇ λεγιῶνος τε[σσαρακαιδεπάτης(?)⁴ / Τιβερίου Κλαυδ]ίου Καίσαρος Σεβαστοῦ π[ρεσβευτῇ ἀντι-/ στρατ]ήγῳ Λυκίας Τ(ι)βερίου Κλαυδίου Καίσαρος Γερ⁶/μανι]κοῦ καὶ Νέρωνος Κλαυδίου Κα[ίσαρος Γερ/μανι]κοῦ ἀνθυπάτῳ Κύπρου ⁸/ 'Αριστοκ[λῆς / 'Αρισ]τοκ-[λ]έους τιμῆς χάρω.

Eprius Marcellus, born in humble circumstances at Capua, and rising to a second consulship and a position of remarkable influence in the 70s, figures largely in the writings of Tacitus.[1] But his legionary command is known only from a dedication at Paphos in Cyprus, of which he was proconsul under Nero. Unfortunately, it is not certain which legion he commanded, since τε[τάρτης] and τε[σσαρακαιδεκάτης] are both possible restorations of line 3.[2] At all events, whichever the legion,

---

[15] p. 21 above.
[16] Last mentioned by Tac. *Ann.* 12. 42. 3 (AD 51); cf. Suet. *Vit.* 3. 1.
[17] Suet. *D. Vesp.* 4. 2.
[18] Thomasson, *Statthalter Nordafrikas* II 42 (who however leaves uncorrected Pallu de Lessert's dating of Agrippina's death to 58, instead of 59, Tac. *Ann.* 14. 4. 1).
[19] *PIR²* F 398.
[1] See *PIR²* E 84.
[2] T. B. Mitford, *Report of the Dept. of Ant.*, *Cyprus, 1940-48* (1954) 4, notes that τε[τάρ-ρης Μακεδονικῆς] is equally admissible epigraphically. *AE* 1956. 186 prints τεσ[σαρακειδεκάτης],

there is no reason to accept Mitford's assertion that Marcellus must have commanded it as a quaestorian. Although there are a number of examples from the Julio-Claudian period of men serving as legionary legate before the praetorship, there are also plenty of cases of ex-praetors, including most of the handful known to have commanded legions in Britain before 69.[3]

There is some uncertainty about the early stages of Marcellus' career,[4] but he was praetor at the end of 48, for one day only, a curious episode mentioned in the *Annals*.[5] Tacitus later records that he was prosecuted unsuccessfully by the Lycians for *repetundae*, in 57.[6] The Paphos inscription reveals that he was legate of Lycia under both Claudius and Nero, in other words in the year 54. Hence his legionary command must have fallen during the period 49-53, in the governorships of Scapula and Didius Gallus,[7] if the legion was indeed XIV Gemina.

His first consulship was in 62,[8] hence the proconsulship of Cyprus must be placed in the period 57-62.[9] During the latter part of Nero's reign he was active as a *delator*—but he was also the dedicatee of Columella's *de cultura vinearum et arborum*.[10] Active in the senate in 69 and 70, he was soon made use of by Vespasian, serving as proconsul of Asia for three years, 70-3,[11] and having the honour of a second consulship, as the colleague of Cerialis, in 74.[12] He was

without justification. τε[τάρτης Σκυθικῆς] is of course also possible, as is urged by K. R. Bradley, *Symbolae Osloenses* 53 (1978) 175 ff. (who prefers this to IV Macedonica).

[3] Mitford, op. cit. 4, states that 'this much is certain: he was *legatus legionis* as a quaestorian—the normal arrangement under the early principate—and not as a praetorian; and such legionary commands were of one or at the most of two years' duration'. He is followed e.g. by Kreiler, *Statthalter Kleinasiens* 21 ff., but J. Devreker, reviewing Kreiler, *Epigraphica* 38 (1976) 180, points out that this is mistaken, citing Morris, thesis (C 343). Hence in line 4 it is permissible to restore [Τιβερίου Κλαυδ]ίου Καίσαρος Σεβαστοῦ—and Bradley, op. cit. 175, notes that Γ[ερμανικοῦ] can be read instead of π[ρεσβευτῆ].

[4] The chief difficulty is to make sense of the fragmentary inscription from Tusculum, XIV 2612, assumed to refer to Eprius because of the words *procos. Asiae per tri[ennium]*. It includes the sentence *hic lectus est ab divo Claud[io . . .]*. Mitford, op. cit. 3 f., argues that [*inter praetorios*] may be restored, but this conflicts with *Ann.* 12. 4. 3. *PIR²* E 84 suggests 'inter tribunicios, vix inter patricios'. Bradley, op. cit. 173 ff., urges the view that Marcellus entered the senate by adlection *inter tribunicios*. Yet, although not much can be made of the other fragments, [*qu*]*aesto[ri]* seems a possible restoration of one; and it may also be noted that MIN might have belonged to [*leg. XIV Ge*]*min[ae*].

[5] *Ann.* 12. 4. 3, cf. Suet. *D. Claud.* 29. 2; he replaced L. Junius Silanus (p. 356 below).

[6] *Ann.* 13. 33. 3.

[7] pp. 41 ff. above.

[8] Degrassi, *FC*, Aggiunte.

[9] Kreiler, *Statthalter Kleinasiens* 21 and n. 4, gives no reasons for his assertion that Eprius was proconsul 58-9.

[10] *PIR²* E 84.

[11] *ILS* 992, cf. XIV 2612; Kreiler, op. cit. 21 ff.

[12] Degrassi, *FC* 21. He was also augur and curio maximus (*ILS* 992).

put to death for alleged conspiracy in 79, before the death of Vespasian.[13]

52   C. Manlius Valens (*cos. ord.* 96)

Tac. *Ann.* 12. 40. 1.

C.[1] Manlius Valens was commanding one of the British legions at the moment when Ostorius Scapula died, hence presumably in the year 52.[2] Unknown circumstances led Domitian to make him *consul ordinarius* for the year 96, when, as Cassius Dio informs us,[3] he was in his ninetieth year. Had it not been for Dio's evidence, it would have been natural to regard the consul of Domitian's last year as the son, or even as the grandson, of the Claudian legionary legate. The case is a salutary reminder that the senatorial *cursus*, while certainly subject to *leges annales*, was also liable to unpredictable variations, above all in its later stages.[4] The whims of successive *principes* and the dictates of some emergency could readily create what appear to be anomalies. Manlius Valens was already forty-five or forty-six years old when commanding his legion in Britain, a good many years older than other legionary legates whose age is known, such as Vespasian (aged thirty-three in AD 43) or Agricola (aged twenty-nine in AD 70)—while there are several examples from the pre-Flavian era of men who commanded legions before their praetorship.[5] Yet seventeen years later he appears in command of another legion, I Italica, with Vitellius at Lugdunum:[6] at sixty-two or sixty-three he is by far the oldest known legionary legate.

The British legion in question in AD 52 was once thought to have been II Augusta, later to be stationed permanently in Silurian territory.[7] But it now seems more likely that Valens was commanding the XXth, by then newly quartered close to Gloucester.[8]

His origin is unknown, and the names are too indistinctive to encourage speculation.

---

[13] *PIR*[2] E 84.

  [1] The *praenomen* is finally confirmed by the *Fasti Ostienses: Inscr. It.* XIII 1, pp. 195, 223.

  [2] p. 43 above.

  [3] Dio 67. 14. 5.

  [4] pp. 24 ff. above.

  [5] p. 14 and n. 5 above.

  [6] Tac. *Hist.* 1. 64, cf. 59.

  [7] Jarrett, *Arch. Camb.* 113 (1964) 47 ff. He duly notes, p. 50, that the legion commanded by Valens is 'not likely to have been II Augusta'.

  [8] Frere, *Britannia*[2] 95 f., argues that the XXth was at Gloucester from 49.

Caesius Nasica

Tac. *Ann.* 12. 40. 4.

The context shows that Caesius Nasica's operation against the Brigantian insurgents under Venutius came in the latter part of Didius Gallus' governorship.[1] Such a task must clearly have been delegated to the legate of IX Hispana, then stationed somewhere to the south-east of Brigantian territory, if not already at Lincoln.[2] Nasica himself is otherwise unknown, but it seems possible that he may have been an elder brother of the next known commander of this legion, Q. Petillius Cerialis Caesius Rufus.[3] There are several instances in the early principate of close kinsmen following one another in military appointments.[4] If so, he must have been Italian, probably from Umbria or the Sabine country.[5]

60   Q. Petillius Cerialis Caesius Rufus (*cos.* 70?, *II* 74)

Tac. *Ann.* 14. 32. 3: see p. 66 above.

69   M. Roscius Coelius (*cos.* 81)

Tac. *Agr.* 7. 3; *Hist.* 1. 60.

By the spring of 69, the governor Trebellius Maximus[1] was despised and hated by his army, whose feelings were stirred up by Roscius Coelius, legate of the XXth legion, according to the account in the *Histories*. Roscius was said to have been *olim discors*, implying that he had held his command for some while. Presumably he had been appointed by Nero. After Trebellius' flight, in April 69,[2] the legionary legates ruled the province with shared authority, but Roscius was *audendo potentior*.[3] He must have remained at his post after the arrival of

---

[1] p. 49 above.
[2] Frere, *Britannia*[2] 86 f., 101.
[3] p. 67 above.
[4] p. 66 and n. 7 above.
[5] Nasica is very rare: only seven instances according to Kajanto 237.
[1] pp. 59 ff. above.
[2] p. 62 above.
[3] There were at this moment three legions in the province, II Augusta, IX Hispana, and XX Valeria Victrix, since XIV Gemina had been withdrawn by Nero (p. 219 above). *Potentior* might imply that there were only two *legati*, hence that one of the legions had no commander at the time; but this interpretation is not mandatory.

Trebellius' successor Bolanus, for his legion, as the account in the *Agricola* shows, was late in swearing allegiance to Vespasian ('vicesimae legioni tarde ad sacramentum transgressae') and had made Bolanus, as well as Trebellius, nervous,[4] the legate—unnamed in the *Agricola*— being unable to restrain it, 'incertum suo an militum ingenio'.

Roscius was presumably replaced early in 70 when Agricola took over. Nothing further is heard of him until 81, when he was consul.[5] The fact that he did not achieve the *fasces* until four years after his successor as legionary legate suggests that his progress may have been a little impeded on account of his conduct in 69.[6]

In the *Histories* he is called Roscius Caelius, and Caelius. But the *Acta Fratrum Arvalium* call him M. Roscius Coelius.[7] He may have used the second *gentilicium* as a *cognomen*, in the Etruscan fashion, as was done by Vettius Bolanus;[8] but he may have had additional names, including Murena, since Q. Pompeius Falco, governor of Britain under Hadrian, includes the items Roscius Coelius Murena in his nomenclature,[9] and there are several senatorial Roscii Murenae of the second century, perhaps his descendants.[10]

70   Fabius Priscus

Tac. *Hist*. 4. 79. 3, cf. 4. 68. 4.

XIV Gemina was withdrawn from Britain by Nero, *c*. 66 or 67, and was to have participated in his projected expedition to the Caspian Gates.[1] After the battle of Bedriacum in April 69, where only detachments of XIV were represented, on Otho's side,[2] Vitellius decided to send the legion back to Britain.[3] The men of the XIVth were already being canvassed by letter to join the Flavians in the summer of 69,[4] with

---

[4] *Agr*. 7. 2: 'quippe legatis quoque consularibus nimia ac formidolosa erat?

[5] Degrassi, *FC* 24, citing VI 2059, 32363.

[6] Groag, *RE* 1A 1 (1914) 1121, on the contrary, reckons that he did not suffer any retardation; and indeed, since Agricola was consul well before the age of 42, Roscius probably held office *suo anno*. [See also Addendum, p. 434 below.]

[7] VI 2059.

[8] pp. 62 f. and n. 3 above.

[9] pp. 96 ff. above.

[10] *ILS* 8834a, on which see Groag in *RE* 1A 1 (1914) 1125–6; Schumacher, *Priesterkol-legien* 224 ff.

[1] Tac. *Hist*. 2. 11. 1, see p. 219 and n. 2 above.

[2] Tac. *Hist*. 2. 43. 2, 66. 1.

[3] Tac. *Hist*. 2. 66. 1–3.

[4] Ibid. 86. 4.

what success is not known—it was to be II Augusta which took the lead in bringing the province over to Vespasian.[5] Early in 70 XIV was summoned to assist in suppressing the revolt in the Rhineland, where its legate is named as Fabius Priscus. Although this man might have been appointed only after the legion left Britain (for the last time), it is possible that he had been in command since the summer of 69, and hence deserves inclusion in the present work.[6]

Although the names are very common, there is a chance that our man is identical with a young senator known from an inscription from Tarraco, now lost: *M. Fabius / Priscus / IIIIvir viarum curan⁴/darum trib. mil leg. I / q. provinciae Achaiae / C. Apronio*(?) */ Secundo f.*[7] The absence of title for *leg. I* pretty well guarantees that this is a Julio-Claudian career, and the find-spot suggests that Tarraco may have been his home.[8] There is no means of telling whether he had held any other post—if identical with the commander of XIV Gemina—after his quaestorship and before taking over the legion. At that time it was still not uncommon for men to command legions before the praetorship, sometimes as *quaestorii*.[9]

70-73   Cn. Julius L. f. Ani. Agricola (*cos.* 77)

Tac. *Agr.* 7. 3–9. 1: see pp. 76 f. above.

(71)   (?) Sex. Julius Frontinus (*cos. II* 98, *III ord.* 100)

See p. 70 above for discussion of the possibility that it was Frontinus who took the legion II Adiutrix to Britain as its legate.

C. Caristanius C. f. Ser. Fronto (*cos.* 90)

ILS 9485 = *JRS* 3 (1913) 260, Antioch (Pisidia): *C. Carist[a]nio C. f. Ser. F[ron]/ toni trib. mil. p[raef.] eq. al. Bosp. adl[e]/cto in senatu inter ⁴/ tribunic. promoto*

---

[5] Ibid. 3. 44.
[6] Alföldy, *Legionslegaten* 10 f., appears (by implication) to exclude the possibility that Priscus served with XIV Gemina in Britain.
[7] II 4117 = *RIT* 134.
[8] Alföldy, *Legionslegaten* 10 f.; id., *RIT*, ad 134.
[9] Alföldy, *Legionslegaten* 11, regards it as improbable that Priscus was still *quaestorius* in 69–70: 'im Bataverkrieg hat man das Legionskommando vielmehr einem älteren und erfahrenen Senator anvertraut, der bereits praetorius war.' See p. 14 above, for discussion of the rank of legionary legates at this time.

in/ter praetorios leg. pro / pr. Ponti et Bithyn. leg. imp. / divi Vespasian. Aug. leg. [8] */ IX Hispanae in Britann. / leg. pro pr. imp. divi Titi / Caes. Aug. et imp. Domitian. Caes. Aug. provinc. Pam* [12] */phyliae et Lyciae patro/no col. T. Caristanius Cal/purnianus Rufus / ob merita eius h. c.*

Caristanius Fronto was one of Vespasian's officers, rewarded for his support in 69 by elevation from equestrian to senatorial status;[1] the grant of tribunician rank at first, and then promotion to praetorian, is exactly matched in the case of Salvius Liberalis.[2] The timing of his legionary command can be worked out from the fact that he mentions Vespasian only as the emperor whose legate he was, while both Titus and Domitian are mentioned for his succeeding post. It is probable that he was legate of IX Hispana *c.* 76-9, under both Frontinus and Agricola, at an important period in the Roman military advance in the north.[3] His predecessor in Lycia-Pamphylia, T. Aurelius Quietus, is attested in the province by an inscription datable to the second half of 80 or the first half of 81.[4] The latter year was presumably Fronto's first in the province. A new governor was in office in 85, and Fronto had probably been replaced in 84, after a *triennium*. But he had to wait until 90 for the consulship.[5]

His home was at Antioch in Pisidia, and he was a descendant of one of the Augustan colonists, C. Caristanius Fronto Caesianus Julius.[6] His wife, Sergia L. f. Paulla, was presumably a daughter of the Claudian proconsul of Cyprus.[7] Two sons, Fronto and Paulinus, are recorded, but their careers are unknown.[8] C. Caristanius Julianus, proconsul of Achaia *c.* 101 who had also been promoted to senatorial rank after service as *praefectus equitum*, was either a younger brother or a cousin.[9]

T. Pomponius T. f. Gal. Mamilianus Rufus Antistianus Funisulanus Vettonianus (*cos.* 100)

VII 164 = *RIB* 445, Chester: *Fortunae reduci / [A]esculap. et saluti eius / libert. et familia* [4] */ [T.] P[o]mponi T. f. Gal. Mamilian[i] / Rufi Antistiani Funisulan[i] / Vetton[i]ani leg. Aug. / d.*

[1] *PIR*[2] C 423.
[2] p. 211 above.
[3] pp. 71, 79 ff. above.
[4] IGR III 690; see Eck, *Senatoren* 125 f. and n. 64, Kreiler, *Statthalter Kleinasiens* 110 f.
[5] Kreiler, *Statthalter Kleinasiens* 111 f.;
[6] See G. L. Cheesman, *JRS* 3 (1913) 260; B. M. Levick, *Roman Colonies in Southern Asia Minor* (1967) 111; *PIR*[2] C 425.
[7] *PIR*[2] C 423.
[8] *PIR*[2] C 424, 427.
[9] *PIR*[2] C 426. For the date, see Eck, *Senatoren* 156 f. and n. 192.

At the legionary fortress of Deva, a man described as *leg. Aug.* without further addition can only be the legionary commander.[1] T. Pomponius Mamilianus (as he was normally known) was suffect consul in 100, with L. Herennius Saturninus as his colleague. The latter was governing Moesia superior a few years later,[2] and our man is presumably Pliny's friend Mamilianus, who was evidently governing a military province when Pliny wrote to him, *c.* 107-8.[3] His legionary command presumably came when he was in his early thirties, in the early 90s, and he must have owed this appointment to Domitian.

He was clearly connected with the Flavian general L. Funisulanus L. f. Ani. Vettonianus,[4] perhaps assuming his names as the result of a legacy. Our man's own tribe, Galeria, could indicate Spanish origin, but there are numerous senatorial Pomponii,[5] and his home cannot be established certainly. Pliny describes him as 'vir gravissimus, eruditissimus ac super ista verissimus'—but then he had been praising Pliny's verses.[6] The consul suffect of 121, T. Pomponius Antistianus Funisulanus Vettonianus, was presumably his son.[7]

A. Larcius A. f. Quir. Priscus (*cos.* 110)

AE 1908. 237, Foum–Merial: *I. O. M. A. Larcius A. f. Quir. Priscus sevirum* [sic] / *decemvirum* [sic] *stlitibus iudicandis quaestor provinciae Asiae* [4]/ *legatus Augusti leg. IIII Scythicae / pro legato consulare provinc. Syriae / tribunus plebei* [sic] *praetor / leg. provinciae Hispaniae Baeticae* [8]/ *praefectus frumenti dandi / legatus Augus. legionis II Aug. / legatus Aug. pro pr. exercitus Africae / v. s. l.*

VIII 17891 = *ILS* 1055, Thamugadi: *A. Larcio A. filio Quirina Prisco VIvir. equitum / Romanor. Xvir. stlitib. iudicand. quaestor. / provinciae Asiae leg. Aug. leg. leg. III* [sic] *Scythicae* [4]/ *ped* [sic] *leg. consulare provinciae Syriae trib. pleb. / praetori praef. frumenti dandi ex s. c. leg. pro/vinciae Baeticae Hispaniae procos.*

---

[1] The legion in question was undoubtedly the XXth by this date. See Jarrett, *Arch. Camb.* 117 (1968) 78.

[2] XVI 46. Saturninus' Moesian command is known from XVI 54, see Syme, *JRS* 49 (1959) 27.

[3] *ep.* 9. 25, assigned by Sherwin-White, *Letters of Pliny* 500, to the period 107-8.

[4] *PIR*[2] F 570 (and note *AE* 1946. 205, improving on XI 571).

[5] See *RE* 21. 2 (1952) 2334 ff. Sherwin-White, *Letters of Pliny* 500, calls him a 'relative of Pliny's elderly friend T. Pomponius Bassus', but gives no evidence. R. Hanslik, *RE* 21. 2, 2342, regards our man as the son of Funisulanus, adopted by a Pomponius Mamilianus, which seems impossible (as pointed out by Syme, *JRS* 47 (1957) 132 n. 7). Hanslik also goes seriously astray in regarding him as a governor of Britain. Syme, *JRS* 58 (1968) 142 and n. 30, suggests Spanish origin, on the basis of the tribe.

[6] *ep.* 9. 25. 2.

[7] Degrassi, *FC* 35. Frere, *Britannia*[2] 142, identifies the *cos.* 121 with the legionary legate at Chester, although only the *cos.* 100 has the *cognomen* Mamilianus. Likewise Jones, *Phoenix* 22 (1968) 127.

provin/ciae Galliae Narbon. leg. Aug. leg. II Aug. leg. [8]/ Aug. pr. pr. exercitus
provinciae Afric. VIIvir. / epulonum cos. design. patrono col. d. d. p. p.

The second text is the later of the two, since it describes Larcius Priscus
as consul designate and records his priesthood, as *VIIvir epulonum*. His
tenure of the *fasces* is now known to have come at the end of 110.[1] On
the face of it this inscription suggests that he only received command of
II Augusta after serving as proconsul of Narbonensis, seven or eight
years after the praetorship; but the absence of the proconsulship from
the earlier dedication, set up by Priscus himself while serving in
Numidia, can only mean that he went on from there to Narbonensis,
and was designated consul while in the latter province.[2] In the Thamugadi inscription the proconsulship is placed out of order, to make a
block of senatorial appointments, followed by two posts in the emperor's
service. He was presumably proconsul in 109-10, legate in Numidia as
immediate predecessor of L. Minicius Natalis,[3] and in Britain immediately before that, c.104-6. By dead reckoning,[4] his praetorship will
have come c.101, and his quaestorship c.96-7. That emphasizes and in
part explains the unusual features of his early career. He had presumably been excused service as *tribunus laticlavius*, and was serving as
quaestor in Asia, when Domitian's death and the accession of Nerva
brought wholesale changes in commands and staffs in the cast, including Priscus' own appointment as legate of IV Scythica and acting
governor of Syria, doubtless replacing the man referred to by the
younger Pliny, acting in a menacing and ambiguous fashion.[5] Priscus'
tenure of this lofty position was presumably short-lived, and seems
to have had no influence on his later career. The two posts which
he held immediately after the praetorship, as legate to a proconsul of
Baetica and as *praefectus frumenti dandi*, presumably occupied the
years 102-4, and can hardly be regarded as evidence of rapid promotion.[6] No consular posts are recorded for him, although he may have
had one or more.[7]

[1] *Inscr. It.* XIII. 1, 200, 229. See *PIR²* L 103 for a summary of his career.
[2] E. Birley, *JRS* 52 (1962) 224 f.
[3] Eck, *Senatoren* 164 f. n. 226.
[4] p. 14 above.
[5] Pliny, *ep.* 9. 13. 11, discussed and interpreted by Groag, *JÖAI* 29 (1935) Bbl. 190 ff.,
Syme, *Philologus* 91 (1936) 238 ff., *Tacitus* 8, 631 f., and most recently by Alföldy and
Halfmann, *Chiron* 5 (1973) 331 ff.
[6] Alföldy, *Fasti Hispanienses* 176, puts his prefecture before the legateship in Baetica,
although in the earlier inscription, set up by Priscus himself, the legateship clearly comes first.
[7] Groag, *JÖAI* 29 (1935) Bbl. 193, followed by Schumacher, *Priesterkollegien* 131, suggested
that he might have been governor of Cappadocia and Armenia; against, Syme, *JRS* 60 (1979)
35 f. (Did the poor literacy, shown on Priscus' two inscriptions, hinder his advancement?
Note Suet. *D. Aug.* 88, a consular legate sacked for bad spelling.)

His father was evidently A. Larcius Lepidus Sulpicianus, who commanded a legion in Judaea in 70, among other posts, and was a native of Antium.[8]

(?) C. Calpurnius Quir. Flaccus (*cos. c.* 124)

IGR III 991, Salamis (Cyprus): [Γ. Καλπούρνιον . . . υἱὸν] Κυρείνα Φλάκκον / [ὕπατον, ἀνθύπατον Κύπρου, πρεσβευτὴν] καὶ ἀντιστράτηγον αὐτοκ[ράτορος / Καίσαρος Τραιανοῦ ᾽Αδρ]ιανοῦ Σεβαστοῦ ἐπαρχείας Λου[σιτανίας [4]/ ἡγεμόνα λεγ. β´(?) Σεβ]αστῆς ἐπιμελητὴν ὁδῶν Αὐρηλίας κα[ὶ τριουμφάλης (?) / στρατηγὸν δήμαρ]χον ταμίαν ῾Ρωμαίων χιλίαρχον [λεγ. . . ./ ἀρχὴν ἄρξαντα]τῶνδ᾽ ἀνδρῶν ὁδῶν ἐπιμελητή[ν . . ./ ἡ βουλὴ καὶ ὁ δῆμος Σα]λ[α]μινίων τιμῆς χάριν.

The nomenclature of this legate and the chronology of his career are now confirmed by another inscription from Salamis, set up διὰ Καλπουρνίου Φλάκκου ἀνθυπάτου in the year 123.[1] His proconsulship of Cyprus followed the governorship of Lusitania, preceded by the command of one of the legions with the title Augusta. G. Alföldy, in his study of the legionary legates in the Rhine armies, argues that II Augusta is more likely to have been Flaccus' legion than VIII Augusta, since legates of the latter are not known to have gone on to govern praetorian provinces after the Flavian period.[2] However this may be, he presumably commanded his legion *c.* 116-19.

As Alföldy points out elsewhere,[3] he was perhaps the son of Pliny's friend Calpurnius Flaccus, who might be identifiable with C. Calpurnius P. f. Quir. Flaccus, *flamen provinciae Hispaniae.*[4] The *flamen* may have been in office at the time of Hadrian's visit to Tarraco, precisely in the year when our man was proconsul of Cyprus.[5] He went on to the consulship, *c.* 124, one may assume, although the inscription recording this is not precisely dated.[6]

L. Aninius L. f. Pap. Sextius Florentinus

III 87 + 14148[10], Petra: *L. [A]ninio L. fil. Pap. Sextio Florentino IIIviro aur. arg.*

---

[8] *PIR*[2] L 94, cf. 90. Cf. p. 274 n. 8 below for possible descendants.
[1] *BCH* 86 (1962) 404.
[2] *Legionslegaten*, 65. See pp. 412 ff. below, for the careers of British legionary legates.
[3] *Fasti Hispanienses* 140; see also Syme, *HSCP* 73 (1968) 231.
[4] Pliny, *ep.* 5. 2; II 4202 = *ILS* 6946 = *RIT* 260.
[5] G. Alföldy, *Flamines Provinciae Hispaniae Citerioris* (1973) 66 f.
[6] *ILS* 7912, Rome: December of an unknown year, with Trebius Germanus as his colleague (mentioned in *Digest* 29. 5. 14).

flando trib. milit. / leg. I Minerviae quaest. prov. A[c]haiae trib. pleb. leg. leg. VIIII Hisp. procos. / pr[ov. N]arb. leg. Aug. pr. pr. prov. Arab. patri piis[sim]o ex testamento ipsius

Florentinus' *cursus* is inscribed on the façade of 'the finest of all the tombs in the necropolis at Petra'.[1] His governorship of Arabia is now dated by a payrus found in the 'Cave of the Letters', showing that he was in office on 2 December 127.[2] Further, his predecessor and successor are also attested, on 12 October 125 and in 130, respectively.[3] Hence he can hardly have taken up the post earlier than 126. His year as proconsul of Narbonensis might have immediately preceded the Arabian command, occupying the period from summer 124 to summer 125; but there may have been an interval between the two appointments.[4] At all events, his legateship of IX Hispana can be firmly dated to the first few years of the reign of Hadrian. There is, however, some doubt over the location of the legion at this time. It may be that it had already been withdrawn from Britain and that it was stationed in Germania inferior.[5]

Florentinus' career opened with service as a *triumvir monetalis*, the most prestigious of the four appointments in the vigintivirate,[6] followed by a tribunate with the Lower German legion I Minervia, probably *c.*110.[7] It is a little surprising that he then became quaestor of Achaia, rather than *quaestor Augusti*, and that he followed this by the post of *tribunus plebis*, rather than *aedilis curulis*.[8] Perhaps the patronage which had secured him a start as *monetalis* was no longer available. The praetorship is omitted on the Petra inscription, presumably in error;[9] it was probably held *c.*120 or a little later, being followed by the legionary command.

No kinsmen are to be found, and his origin must remain uncertain; although the tribe Papiria is more commonly found in Africa than elsewhere, it seems to have been Trajan who was responsible for this,[10]

---

[1] R. E. Brünnow and A. v. Domaszewski, *Die Provincia Arabia* (1909) 169.

[2] Still unfortunately unpublished, but referred to by Polotsky, *Israel Exploration Journal* 12 (1962) 259. In the papyrus, it seems that the *praenomen* is given as *T.*, whereas *L.* (and *L. fil.*) is firmly attested on the Petra tombstone.

[3] See previous note, and L. Petersen, *Klio* 48 (1967) 159 ff., Eck, *Senatoren* 200.

[4] Eck, *Senatoren* 195, prefers 123-4.

[5] pp. 220 ff. below.

[6] p. 5 above.

[7] He might possibly have served under M. Atilius Bradua, later governor of Britain (p. 93 above).

[8] pp. 12 ff. above.

[9] Note that *aer.* and *feriundo* are also omitted, from line 1.

[10] Kubitschek 271.

and our man is perhaps unlikely to have derived from a newly enfranchised community.

P. Tullius Varronis f. Stel. Varro (*cos.* 127)

X 3364 = *ILS* 1047, Tarquinii: *P. Tullio / Varronis fil. / Stel. Varroni cos. [4] / auguri procos. provinc. / Africae leg. Aug. pro pr. / Moesiae superior. curat. [8] / alvei Tiberis et riparum / et cloacarum urbis praef. / aerari Saturn. procos. prov. [12] / Baeticae ulterioris Hispa/niae leg. leg. XII Fulminatae / et VI Victricis p. f. / praetori aedil. Ceriali [16] / quaestori urb. tribuno / milit. leg. XVI Fl. Xviro stlitibus / iudicand. praetori Etruriae quin/quennali Tarquinis [20] / P. Tullius Callistio / posuit*

If Tullius Varro was commanding VI Victrix at the time of its transfer to Britain, in 122,[1] he cannot have remained there long, since he served for a year as proconsul of Baetica, and then as prefect of the *aerarium Saturni*, before his consulship in April 127.[2] But examination of his career and background makes it likely that he was the man entrusted with the delicate task of uprooting the legion from its base at Vetera in Lower Germany and moving it to York. A native of Tarquinii in Etruria, he had excellent connections in high places, for his elder brother had been adopted, it would seem, by the influential Spaniard Dasumius, taking the names P. Dasumius Rusticus, and had been colleague of Hadrian as *consul ordinarius* in 119.[3]

Varro's initial career had not been particularly remarkable, but after his praetorship he had commanded the Cappadocian legion XII Fulminata, possibly at the tail end of Trajan's Parthian war. It was very rare for a man to command more than one legion, and the recorded cases can mostly be explained as the product of some unusual circumstances.[4] On this occasion, the impending transfer of VI Victrix to a new province would be deemed good cause for placing at its head a man with more than the usual experience. Added to this, his Spanish links no doubt made him a particularly favoured choice for Hadrian and welcome to Platorius Nepos. It looks as if he may have been proconsul of Baetica while Hadrian was visiting the Iberian peninsula.[5]

After the treasury prefecture and the consulship, he was curator of the Tiber, legate of Moesia superior, presumably in the early 130s, and

---

[1] For the date of transfer, see p. 273 below.
[2] Degrassi, *FC* 37.
[3] For his family, see now especially Schumacher, *Priesterkollegien* 190 ff.
[4] pp. 18 ff., above, 411 f. below.
[5] Alföldy, *Fasti Hispanienses* 167; Eck, *Senatoren* 195 f. n. 346.

proconsul of Africa early in the reign of Pius.[6] His social standing is
demonstrated by his having been an augur.[7]

[L. Valerius . . .G] al. [Propinquus?] Grani[us ---] Grattius [Cerealis?]
Geminius R[estitutus?] (*cos.* 126?)

II 6084 = *RIT* 140, Tarraco: [*L. Valerio . f*(?) / *G*]*al.* [*Propinquo*(?) / *Grani*[*o*
. . .] [4]/ *Grattio* [*Cereali*(?)] / *Geminio R*[*estituto*(?)] / *praetori XV*[*vir. sacris*] /
faciundis lega[*to Aug.*] [8]/ *leg. VI Victricis* [*piae fid.*] / *legato provinc. A*[*qui-
tanic.*(?)] / *consuli curator*[*i alvei*] *Tiberis et cloaca*[*rum leg.*] [12]/ *Germaniae
inferio*[*ris procos.*] *provinciae Asiae ex* [*testamento*] / *Sex. Pompei Ter*[*tul-
liani*(?)] / *amico op*[*timo*]

G. Alföldy's reconstruction of this fragmentary *cursus* inscription is
based on the close connection, revealed by the surviving portions of the
man's nomenclature, with several members of the Spanish upper classes
attested during the late first and early second centuries, two of them
equestrian officers.[1] No magistracies or other posts earlier than the
praetorship are mentioned, making it not improbable that the man had
been adlected into the senate with tribunician or aedilician rank.[2] The
dating of the career depends on the assumption that his first and
principal *cognomen* was Propinquus.[3] There are three brick-stamps of
the early second century dated *Propinquo et Ambibulo cos.*, one of
which bears the same formula in the first line as a stamp of the *consules
ordinarii* of 126, *Vero III et Ambib(ul)o cos.*[4] A careful study by L.
Schumacher has demonstrated that there is no need to doubt that
Propinquus was suffect to Verus, in spite of being named before Ambibulus.[5] In that case, it is uncertain whether Propinquus commanded

---

[6] Eck, *Senatoren* 205 n. 376; Thomasson, *Statthalter Nordafrikas* II 71; Syme, *REA* 61
(1959) 313, assigns his governorship of Moesia superior to *c.*135, his proconsulship of Africa
to 141-2. Alföldy, *Konsulat* 208, prefers 142-3 for Africa.

[7] Schumacher, *Priesterkollegien* 49 f.

[1] Syme, *ap.* Eck, *Senatoren* 45 n. 15; Alföldy, *Die römischen Inschriften von Tarraco* 82,
citing M. Valerius M. f. Gal. Propinquus Grattius Cerealis, an equestrian officer of the Flavian
period (*RIT* 311), L. Valerius L. f. Gal. Propinquus, a second-century *flamen* of Hispania
citerior (*RIT* 310), C. Cornelius Q. f. Gal. Restitutus [Gra] ttius Cerealis from Saguntum, an
equestrian officer of the Flavian or Antonine period (II 3851), and [G] emin[i] a C. f. Restituta
from Ebusus (II 3659); he also notes the equestrian (with senatorial descendants, cf. p. 274
below) Q. Licinius M. f. Gal. Silvanus Granianus, from Tarraco (*RIT* 288-9, 321).

[2] As suggested by Alföldy, loc. cit.; but see also n. 9 below.

[3] The *cognomen* is not very common: Kajanto 303 knows thirty-eight examples, of which
three are senators.

[4] XV 127, 375, 1288b, the last of which carries the same first line as 1288a (*Vero et
Ambib(ul)o cos.*), *Pila Her. Iun.* [*Sulp. C. Petr. Tr*]*an.*

[5] Schumacher, *ZPE* 24 (1977) 155 ff.

VI Victrix after its transfer to Britain in 122, and whether he was the predecessor or the successor of P. Tullius Varro.[6] As the latter was consul in 127, it would be logical to suppose that Propinquus preceded him. On the other hand, Varro held two posts, the proconsulship of Baetica and the prefecture of the *aerarium Saturni*, between the legionary legateship (which was his second legion) and consulship, which may have delayed his tenure of the *fasces*, whereas Propinquus held only one, the governorship of a province beginning with the letter A. Aquitania looks rather more probable than Arabia.[7]

After the consulship came the *cura alvei Tiberis* and the governorship of Germania inferior, *c*.129. No other posts in the emperor's service followed, and his career concluded with the proconsulship of Asia, *c*.141.[8] His co-option as *XVvir s. f.* immediately after the praetorship is an indication that he had influential support at a crucial stage in his career.[9]

---sius ---ppi f. (*cos.* 130?)

A. M. Schneider, *Istanbuler Forsch.* 16 (1943) no. 2 = *REG* 59–60 (1946–7) 350 f. no. 189 = *AE* 1950. 251 = H.-G. Pflaum, *Arch. Esp. Arq.* 39 (1966) 15 ff., Nicaea:
[. . .] σιον[. . . / . . .]ππου υἱόν[. . . ἀνθύπατον Ἰσπα/νίας] Βαιτικῆς πρεσ[βευτὴν αὐτοκράτορος ⁴/ λεγ]ιῶνος κ´ Οὐαλε[ρίας Νικηφόρου στρατηγὸν] / πρεσβευτὴν καὶ ἀντι[στράτηγον ἐπαρχείας] / Κρήτης καὶ Κυρή[νης δήμαρχον (?) ταμίαν] / ἐπαρχείας [. . . χειλίαρχον] ⁸/ λεγιῶν[ος . . .]

This man has generally been identified as the *cos.* 130, [Ca]ssius Agri[ppa] (or Agri[ppinus]), and his names are restored on this stone as [Γάιον(?) Κάσ]σιον Ἀγρίππαν(?) Μάρκου(?) Κασσίου Ἀγρί]ππου υἱόν.[1] H.-G. Pflaum has forcibly pointed out that Ἀγρίππου is incorrect as the genitive of Ἀγρίππας, and that the man's father's name should

[6] p. 239 above.
[7] Eck, *Senatoren* 45 n. 15, who dates the consulship to 132 or 133, regards Arabia as just possible in the period 127–30. See L. Petersen, *Klio* 48 (1967) 159 ff., on the governors at this period: Julius Julianus is attested for 12 Oct. 125, and L. Aninius Sextius Florentinus (p. 238 above) for 2 Dec. 127. Theoretically our man could have governed Arabia *c*. 122–5, but the dates of Julianus and Florentinus make it likely that the former took up his governorship in 124 at latest.
[8] See Schumacher, op. cit. 162 f., who shows that the *Fasti* of Asia are complete for the years 145–54, which is a further argument against dating our man's consulship—if he was indeed a Propinquus—to *c*. 132 rather than to 126. By contrast there is room for him to have been proconsul a few years before 145. Cf. for a different interpretation Alföldy, *Konsulat* 212 f.
[9] Schumacher, *Priesterkollegien* 234, suggests that he may have been patrician, to explain his rapid career. This is, however, not very plausible at this period.
[1] See Alföldy, *Fasti Hispanienses* 168.

have ended in -πποϛ, e.g. Φίλιπποϛ.[2] However, the form 'Αγρίππου is otherwise attested,[3] and the identification may be regarded as possible, if less than certain. A problem arises over the interpretation of his career, for W. Eck argues that it would have been abnormal in the Trajanic-Hadrianic period for a man to proceed to the consulship with no other post than a legionary command and a proconsulship after being praetor.[4] If the identification is made, one should perhaps postulate that some other post was held after the proconsulship of Baetica.[5] At all events, if this legate is Cassius Agrippa (or Agrippinus), he must have preceded Aemilius Papus, whose consulship was probably some six or more years after 130, and who was legate of the XXth in 128.[6]

As far as the evidence of this inscription goes, his earlier career was relatively straightforward. No mention of a post in the vigintivirate survives, although one may be presumed. λεγιῶν[οϛ] is clearly a reference to a military tribunate, and ἐπαρχείαϛ to a provincial quaestorship. Either tribunate of the plebs or aedileship must have been mentioned in line 6. The next post may be restored as a legateship in Crete–Cyrene, evidently before the praetorship, which must have been mentioned in line 4.

If this man was a Cassius, it is natural to conclude that he was from the family of the historian Cassius Dio Cocceianus, and that he was a native of the city where his *cursus* was found.[7] If not, although he may have belonged to another local family, nothing in the surviving portion of his career connects him with the city or with the province of Bithynia. In conclusion, it must be stressed that, if this legate is not the consul of 130, there is no other reason to date the career to the Hadrianic period.[8]

**128(?)   M. (Cutius Priscus Messius Rusticus) Aemilius M. f.
Gal. Papus (Arrius Proculus Julius Celsus) (*cos. a. inc.*)**

II 1371, Callenses: *Imp. Caesari divi / Traiani Aug. cos. VI f. divi / Nervae cos. III trib. p. II nepoti Traiano* [4] / *Hadriano Aug. pont. max. / tribunic. potest. XII p. p. cos. III / M. Messius Rusticus / Aemilius Papus Ar[r]ius Proculus* [8] / *Iulius Celsus*

[2] *Arch. Esp. Arq.* 39 (1966) 15 ff., esp. 21.
[3] *ILS* 8784, Thasos: 'Ιουλίαν Μάρκου 'Αγ[ρ]ίππου θυγατέρα.
[4] *ANRW* II. 1, 202 n. 213; *RE* Supp. 14 (1974) 86 f.
[5] In that case, he could be the Hadrianic governor(?) of Thrace, Agrippa: *AE* 1937. 171, near Abdera.
[6] p. 243 below.
[7] Thus e.g. F. Millar, *A Study of Cassius Dio* (1964).
[8] The point is stressed by Eck, *RE* Supp. 14 (1974) 86 f.

sodal. Augustal. IIIIvir. / viarum curandarum tr. mil. leg. III Aug. / [q.] pr. pr. provinc. Africae trib. pleb. / pr. peregrinus curator viae Aureliae [12] */ leg. Aug. leg. XX V. V. / optimo principi*

II 1283, Salpensa: *M. Cutio M. f. Gal. Prisco Messio / Rustico Aemilio Papo Ar[r]io Proculo / Iulio Celso cos. sodal. Augustal.* [4] */ leg. pr. pr. imp. Caes. [T.] Aelii Hadriani / [Antonini] Aug. Pii provinc. D[e]lmat. curator[i] / operum publicorum praefecto / aerarii Saturni leg. leg. XX V. V.* [8] */ curator. viae Aureliae pr. peregrino / trib. pleb. [q.] pr. pr. provinc. Africae / trib. mil. leg. VII [sic] Aug. / IIIIvir. viarum curandarum* [12] */ Caesia Senil[l]a amico / optimo*

This legate can be dated securely to the year 128, when he made a dedication to Hadrian at Callenses in Baetica, near his home at Salpensa. The legateship of the XXth legion is the last office mentioned, and it is reasonable to suppose that he was holding the post at the time the inscription was set up—indeed, it is possible that his appointment was the occasion for the dedication. His principal names were Aemilius Papus, for he is named as such in his capacity as curator of public works at Rome ten years later.[1] As H.-G. Pflaum has shown,[2] he was the son of an Aemilius Papus mentioned in the *Historia Augusta* as a friend of Hadrian, along with Sosius Senecio and Platorius Nepos, at the time of Trajan's Parthian war.[3] The origin of these names, recalling a great family of the early republic, remains obscure.[4] An epitaph from Castelmadama near Tibur of a young man of similar names, presumably our legate's brother, was set up by Aemilius Papus and Cutia Prisca, his parents,[5] indicating that the family had property at or close to Tibur, like a number of other Spanish notables of the period.[6] Papus clearly acquired the names Cutius Priscus from his mother, while Messius Rusticus presumably derives by inheritance from the *cos.* 114.[7] The sources of the other two pairs, Arrius Proculus and Julius Celsus, are unknown.[8]

After service in the vigintivirate, Papus became tribune of III Augusta, probably towards the end of Trajan's reign, then quaestor of Africa, tribune of the plebs, and praetor. Before taking up his legionary command

---

[1] *AE* 1934. 146; note also II 1282c, VI 998.

[2] *Klio* 46 (1965) 331 ff.

[3] *HA Had.* 4. 2, cf. p. 103 above.

[4] *RE* I 1 (1893) 575 f. Aemilius was very common in Spain: Syme, *Tacitus* 783.

[5] XIV 3615: M. Messius M. f. Gal. Rusticus Aemilius Afer Cutius Romulus Priscianus Arrius Proculus.

[6] Syme, *Tacitus* 602 and n. 5; and cf. p. 215 above.

[7] Degrassi, *FC* 34.

[8] But note e.g. *PIR*² 1422 (Cn. Arrius Cornelius Proculus), J 258-9 (Julii Celsi). Further possible kinsmen are evoked by the nomenclature of his presumed brother (n. 5 above), e.g. Julii Romuli (*PIR*² J 521-3).

he was curator of a road in Italy,[9] while after his return from Britain he became prefect of the *aerarium Saturni*.[10] His consulship was probably *c.*136 or 137, and was followed by service as curator of public works at Rome.[11] Later he became governor of Dalmatia, being attested in this position in the year 147.[12] In spite of his father's friendship with Hadrian, his career shows no signs of particular favour: he was not *candidatus* of the emperor in any magistracy, nor did he hold a major priesthood, being merely a *sodalis Augustalis*.

No sons are attested, but the nomenclature of C. Julius Pisibanus Maximus Aemilius Papus, senatorial tribune of II Adiutrix, suggests that he may have had a daughter who married C. Julius Pisibanus, suffect consul in the 140s.[13]

L. Minicius L. f. Gal. Natalis Quadronius Verus (*cos.*139)

XIV 3599 = *ILS* 1061 = *Inscr. It.* IV 113, Tibur: *L. Minicio L. f. Gal. Natali / Quadronio Vero cos. procos. / prov. Africae leg. Aug. ⁴/ pr. pr. provinciae Moesiae infer. / curatori operum publicorum / et aedium sacrar. curat. viae / Flamin. praef. alimentor. leg. ⁸/ Aug. leg. VI Victr. in Britannia / praetori trib. pleb. candidato / quaestori candidato divi / Hadriani et eodem tempore legato ¹²/ prov. Afric. dioeceseos Carthaginien. / proconsulis patris sui trib. mil. leg. I / Adiut. p. f. item leg. XI Cl. p. f. item leg. XIIII Gemin. Martiae Victric. IIIviro ¹⁶/ monetali a. a. a. f. f. patrono municipii / curat. fani Herc. V. decuriones Tiburt. / ex aere collato q. q. maximi exempli.* (In latere) *curante / M. Tullio Blaeso*

II 4510, Barcino: *L. Minici[o L. fil.] / Gal. Nata[li] / Quadronio Vero Iu[niori] ⁴/ cos. augu[ri] / procos. provinc[iae Africae] / leg. Aug. pr. pr. [prov. Moesiae] / inferior. curator. [oper. public.] ⁸/ et aedium sacrar. [curator. viae] / Flamini. praef. alim. [leg. Aug.] / leg. VI Victric. in Br[itannia pr.] / tr. pl. candidato q. candid[ato divi] ¹²/ Hadriani A(u)g. et eodem tem[pore] / leg. prov. Africae di[oe]ceseos Ca[rthag.] / procos. patris sui tri. milit. leg. pr[im.] / Adiutr. p. f. item leg. XI Cl. p. f. item [leg.] ¹⁶/ XIIII Gem. Marti. Vict. triumviro / monetali a. a. a. f. f. / L. Sempronius Carpio clies / l. d. d. d.*

XI 3002, ager Viterbensis: [. . .] βαι [. . .]ριω [. . .]μω καὶ [. . .]ς θεοῖς / [L. Minicius L. f. Natalis cos. aug. pr]ocos. prov. A[fricae leg.] Aug. pr. pr. prov. Moesiae /

---

[9] As noted by Eck, *ANRW* II. 1, 192, there is no way of telling how long such *curae* lasted.
[10] Corbier, *L'aerarium* 189 ff.
[11] *AE* 1934. 146, of 13 Dec. 138; VI 998, from earlier in the same year, mentions a M. Aemilius . . ., evidently curator of public works (*PIR²* A 326 + add.).
[12] II 1282. There is no need to believe that he was governor from 141 to 147, as urged by W. Hüttl, *Antoninus Pius* I (1936) 329 n. 12, II (1933) 83 f., followed by Jagenteufel, *Dalmatia* 60 f. See A. R. Birley, *Corolla . . . Swoboda* 43 ff., esp. 48 f. Note that another governor is now attested from this reign, T. Prifernius Paetus (*cos.* 146): *AE* 1972. 153. Alföldy, *Konsulat* 224 f., suggests that Papus' governorship began in 147.
[13] *PIR²* J 463-4. See now Eck, *ZPE* 37 (1980) 41-4 for a possible son of Papus.

in [*ferioris curator oper. publicor. et ae*] *dium sacrar* [*um curator*] *viae Flaminiae* [4] /
[*praef. alimentor. leg. Aug. leg. VI*] *Vic* [*t*] *r. in Britannia* [*praetor trib. pleb.
candidatus* / *quaest. candid. Aug. et eodem tempore leg. pat*] *ris sui* [*pr*] *ovinc.*
[*Africae trib. mil. leg.*] / *I Adiut. p. f. item leg. XI Cl. p. f. item leg. XIIII Gem.*]
Mart. Vi [*ctr. IIIvir monet. a. a. a. f. f.*]

IGR I 658 = E. Ritterling, *JÖAI* 10 (1907) 307 ff., Callatis: [Λούκιον Μινίκιον
Λουκίου υἱὸν Γαλερίᾳ / Ναταλιν Κουαδρώνιον Οὐῆρον τριανδρι]κὸν μον[ηταλιν
χειλίαρχον πλατύσημον] [4] / λεγ. α' βο[ηθοῦ λεγ. ιά Κλαυδίας λεγ. ιδ' νεικη]/φόρου
τ[αμίαν κανδίδατον θεοῦ Ἀδριανοῦ] / καὶ τῷ αὐ[τῷ χρόνῳ πρεσβευτὴν τοῦ πατρὸς]/
ἀνθυπάτ[ου Ἀφρίκης δήμαρχον κανδίδατον] [8] / στρατηγὸ[ν καὶ πρεσβευτὴν Σεβαστοῦ λεγ. ς'] / νεικηφόρ[ου ἔπαρχον ἀλειμέντων ἐπιμελητὴν] / Φλαμινί[ας ὕπατον
ἐπιμελητὴν ἔργων καὶ τόπων / δημοσίων πρεσβευτὴν καὶ ἀντιστράτηγον 12/ Μυσίας
τῆς κάτω ...]

This legate can be dated with some precision, to the early 130s. A
native of Barcino in Hispania Tarraconensis, and one of several Spanish
senators with property at Tibur, he was the son of one of Trajan's
younger marshals, also called L. Minicius Natalis (*cos.* 106).[1] He began
his career in remarkable fashion, after a year as *monetalis* (befitting the
son of a consular), serving successively in three different legions, a feat
for which the career of Hadrian offers the only parallel.[2] All were
Danubian legions, and the third, XIV Gemina, was part of the army of
Pannonia superior at the time when that province was governed by the
elder Natalis, who is known to have been there in 113-17.[3] He entered
the senate as quaestor of Hadrian, and, although he would normally
have stayed at Rome to carry out his duties, was permitted instead to
serve as legate to his father, now the proconsul of Africa. This was
probably in 121-2.[4] There followed the tribunate of the plebs, in
which he was *candidatus* of the emperor, and then the praetorship,
which cannot have been later than 128. For in 129 he competed at the
Olympic Games, and the inscription which describes his victory in the
four-horse chariot race describes him as στρατηγικός, ex-praetor.[5] He
had hardly had time, however, to have commanded VI Victrix, his first
post after this, before his Olympic victory. It is more probable that he
came to Britain in 130, in which case he presumably served under the
orders of the governor Sex. Julius Severus. It is worth noting that Julius

---

[1] Groag, *RE* 15. 2 (1932) 1828 ff., discusses father and son in exemplary fashion.

[2] *ILS* 308; *HA Had.* 2. 2 ff. See Syme, *Danubian Papers* 204 ff., with comments on Natalis
207 f. Note also his remarks, ibid. 99, 107, 222. Natalis' tribunates were discussed by E. Ritterling in a fundamental paper, *JÖAI* 10 (1907) 299 ff., esp. 310.

[3] Eck, *Senatoren* 180 ff. XVI 64 shows him governor in 116 (after February), *ILS* 1029
shows that he was governor under Hadrian as well as Trajan. Eck kindly informs me that an
unpublished diploma shows him already in Pannonia in 113.

[4] Eck, *Senatoren* 192 n. 331.

[5] *SIG* II[3] 840, Olympia.

Severus had previously commanded XIV Gemina, shortly before 120,[6] Natalis may therefore have been nominated to the legionary command on Severus' recommendation. Normally, governors seem to have had no say in the appointment of legionary legates,[7] but Hadrian may have been prepared to waive regulations in exceptional cases.[8]

Natalis' later career, while not spectacular, was distinguished. After administrative duties in Italy,[9] he became consul in 139,[10] curator of temples and public works at Rome, and then governor of Moesia inferior,[11] in the area where he had served as a tribune. Finally, like his father, he became proconsul of Africa.[12] Although he is not mentioned in any literary source, his career is recorded by such a large number of incriptions that E. Groag justifiably felt able to give a sketch of his pesonality as well as an analysis of his official service.[13] He was clearly extremely wealthy, somewhat vain, and, in the manner of the age, a pious devotee of a number of religious cults. He was an augur, a distinction which he achieved as a quaestorian, a further indication of his high social standing, and of the influential patronage which he enjoyed. Later in his career, perhaps after his father's death, this patronage may have declined somewhat, but there are no real grounds for supposing that he fell from favour, even if his unusual degree of early military experience was not exploited to the full with a plurality of military governorships.[14]

[6] p. 108 above.

[7] p. 18 above.

[8] Cf. the case of the Mummii Sisennae, p. 000 below.

[9] As Thomasson, *Statthalter Nordafrikas* II 73 n. 278, notes, he may well have held the posts of *praefectus alimentorum* and *curator viae Flaminiae* simultaneously. But in that case, as Schumacher, *Priesterkollegien* 299 n. 64, comments, either his tenure of the combined post must have been rather prolonged, or his career must have been delayed by Hadrian; see also his remarks on p. 232. Pflaum, *J. des Savants* 1962. 119 f., gives a useful list of comparable cases (but erroneously dates Natalis' tenure 'vers 128'). Yet if Natalis were, e.g. legate of VI Victrix 130-3, and prefect and curator 134-7, there is no reason to suspect disfavour and delay. It must be recalled that the arrangements for the succession may have slightly disrupted Hadrian's dispositions for the consulship in 137-8.

[10] XVI 175. Thus Groag's assumption, *RE* 15. 2, 1838 (followed e.g. by Degrassi, *FC* 38) that he was *cos. c.*133 or 134 proved mistaken.

[11] Syme, *Danubian Papers* 219, suggests '142-144'. *AE* 1972. 547, Troesmis, shows him in office at some time after Antoninus Pius' third consulship (140), hence before 145.

[12] Thomasson, *Statthalter Nordafrikas* II 72 f. Syme, *REA* 61 (1959) 314, puts his proconsulship in 153 or 154.

[13] *RE* 15. 2, 1840 f.: 'Aus epigraphischem Material das Wesen einer Persönlichkeit zu erschliessen, scheint wohl ein vergebliches Beginnen; immerhin lassen sich vielleicht gerade in unserem Falle aus den Inschriften gewisse Schlüsse ziehen.'

[14] Groag, *RE* 15. 2, 1838, wondered whether the fact that he was not *candidatus* as praetor meant a loss of favour in the 120s (and suggested that the death of Natalis senior might be relevant), and suspected a fall from favour under Pius, 1839. But see Schumacher, *Priesterkollegien* 232.

Q. Antonius Isauricus (*cos. c.*143)

VII 233 = *RIB* 644, York: *Deae* / *Fortunae* / *Sosia*[4] / *Iuncina* / *Q. Antoni* / *Isaurici* / *leg. Aug.*

A *leg. Aug.* at York must be a legionary commander rather than a governor.[1] The date and hence the legion must be worked out from external evidence. It seems reasonable to suppose that this legate is the same man as one of the suffect consuls attested by fragment VII of the *Fasti Feriarum Latinarum*, Q. Antonius I..u....., whose *cognomen* may readily be completed as I[sa] u[ricus]. The year is not given directly, but A. Degrassi's reconstruction of the monument allows it to be worked out by measurement to *c.*142–4.[2] In that case, Isauricus may be assumed to have commanded his legion, which will have been VI Victrix, late in the reign of Hadrian, *c.*135.

Nothing else is known of his career, but a few comments may be made about his nomenclature. QQ. Antonii are rare in all parts of the empire, and only one other senator is so named.[3] Isauricus evokes the *cos. ord.* 79 BC and his son, *cos. II ord.* 41 BC. The latter, P. Servilius Isauricus, was said by Cicero to have had several children,[4] and apparent descendants may be detected as late as the second century AD.[5] Antonius Isauricus might perhaps descend from the Servilii through the female line. As for his wife, Sosia Juncina, it is possible that she was connected with another great, although much more recently ennobled, family, that of Q. Sosius Senecio (*cos. II ord.* 107).[6]

(?) Ignotus *AE* 1922. 36

AE 1922. 36, Salonae: [. . .*le*]*gat. l*[*eg. ?XX Val.* / *Vic*]*tric. praetori c*[*andidato* /

---

[1] Cf. pp. 431 f. below on the titulature of legionary legates.

[2] *Inscr. It.* XIII 1, 154 f., 158, and plates LV, LX. E. Birley, *Yorks. Arch. Journal* 41 (1966) 727, argues that this legate is more likely to belong to the Severan period, noting Hübner's comment on the lettering, ad VII 233, and citing L. C. Evetts, *Arch. Ael.*[4] 26 (1948) 162 ff. to show 'that the form of the G is most characteristic of the Severan age'. But so few of the inscriptions from York are precisely dated that arguments from the lettering are a little risky. Besides, the G in *RIB* 673 (the tombstone of a soldier from IX Hispana, which must be fairly early) is not unlike that on *RIB* 644.

[3] In *PIR*[2] there is only Q. Antonius Cassius Cassianus, consul in an unknown year (A 819).

[4] *Philipp.* 12. 5.

[5] Note Plotia Servilia(?) Isaurica, owner of a brick-works at Rome (*RE* 21. 1 (1951) 610 f.), and Caesennius Serviliu[s Isauricus] (*PIR*[2] C 175, cf. 171). The polyonymous Trajanic senator T. Julius Maximus (*PIR*[2] J 426) had the names Servilius Vatia among many others.

[6] No husband is known for his presumed daughter Sosia Frontina (VI 17461). She might have married a Juncus or Juncinus, and have had a daughter named Sosia Juncina—descendants of Senecio preferred to take Sosius as their *gentilicium*, cf. the consuls of 149, 169, and 193.

divi] Hadriani tri[b.] plebis [4]*/ candidato eiusdem q[uaestori / divi Ha]driani t[rib. mil. legion.] I Itali[cae . . .]*

This fragmentary inscription reveals part of the career of a senator of the Hadrianic period, perhaps a native of Salona or some other Dalmatian city, as G. Alföldy has suggested.[1] The same scholar rightly stressed the exceptional favour which the *ignotus* had received from Hadrian, being his *candidatus* as both tribune of the plebs and praetor, after being the emperor's quaestor. He suggests that the man might have been a son or close kinsman of Sex. Julius Severus, and that he could have served as tribune of I Italica in Moesia inferior when Severus was governing that province, *c.*128-30.[2] In that case, the three republican magistracies must have been held in the last five years or so of Hadrian's reign, and the legionary command should be dated *c.*140.[3]

However this may be, there is unfortunately no way of determining whether the legion was XXX Ulpia Victrix or XX Valeria Victrix.[4] G. Alföldy favours the former, on the grounds that three other former *candidati Caesaris* are known to have commanded it in this period.[5] Certainly, no *candidati Caesaris* are known to have gone on to be legate of the XXth at this or any other period. But the evidence is perhaps too limited to draw any conclusion.

P. Mummius P. f. Gal. Sisenna Rutilianus (*cos.* 146)

XIV 3601 = *ILS* 1101 = *Inscr. It.* IV 115, Tibur: *P. Mummio P. f. Gal. Si/sennae Rutiliano cos. / auguri procos.* [4]*/ provinc. Asiae legato Aug. / pr. pr. Moesiae superioris / praef. aliment. per Aemiliam / praef. aer. Saturni leg. leg. VI* [8]*/ Victric. praetori tr. pl. quaest. / trib. leg. V Maced. Xviro stli/tib. iudic. patrono munici/pii cur. fani H. V. salio Her*[12]*/culanii Augustales / L. d. s. c. dedicato kal. Iun. Maximo / et Orfito cos. curantibus P. Ragonio Satur/nino et C. Marcio Marciano q.* [16]*/ ordinis Augustalium Tiburtium*

XIV 4244 = *Inscr. It.* IV 116, ibid.; [*P.*] *Mummio P. f.* [*Gal. / S*]*isennae Rutili[ano / c]os. auguri procos. p[rov.* [4]*/ As]iae legato Aug. pr. pr.* [*Moesiae / sup*]*erioris praef. alimen[t. per / Aemilia]m praef. aer. Saturni* [*leg. leg. / VI*] *Victric. praetori tri[b. pleb.* [8]*/ quaest.] trib. leg. V Maced. X[viro / stlit. i]udicandis patron[o muni/cipii c]ur. fani H. V.* [*salio / senat*]*us populusque T[iburs]*

---

[1] *Ep. Stud.* 5 (1968) 119 f.
[2] pp. 106 ff. above.
[3] Alföldy, *Legionslegaten* 30 f., suggests '141-143', since another legate of XXX Ulpia must be accommodated *c.*140-2.
[4] Strictly speaking, I or II Adiutrix and VI Victrix are also possible: although all three had the additional titles *pia fidelis*, they are frequently mentioned without *p. f.* See pp. 284 f. below, for comparable cases.
[5] *Legionslegaten* 30 f.

The laconic phraseology of this man's *cursus* inscriptions sets forth an apparently conventional career, but there happens to be a vivid record of him in Lucian's *Alexander vel Pseudomantis*, the account of the bogus oracle-monger of Abonuteichus in Paphlagonia. Rutilianus, described by Lucian as 'a man of good family and tested in many Roman offices, but utterly sick as far as the gods were concerned', was only the most distinguished of the many who were taken in by Alexander. When he heard about the oracle established by Alexander, 'he very nearly abandoned the office entrusted to him in order to take wing to Abonuteichus'.[1] The other chronological data in Lucian[2] make it clear that the office in question must have been his last, the proconsulship of Asia, which he ought to have taken up about fifteen years after the consulship, in 160 or 161.[3] A little later, he was persuaded to marry the prophet's daughter, as a 'sexagenarian bridegroom'.[4] If this indication of his age is approximately correct, he must have been born *c*.105. Lucian also mentions that he died ('mad from melancholy') at seventy, in which case the inscription of June 172 must have been set up a few years before his death.[5]

He was probably the son of the *cos. ord.* 133, P. Mummius Sisenna, governor of Britain in 135;[6] and, since his own consulship, as suffect, came in 146, only thirteen years later,[7] it looks as if the father attained the *fasces* late in life. His close connection with Tibur, and enrolment in the tribe Galeria, strongly suggest that the family was of Spanish origin.[8]

---

[1] *Alex.* 30.

[2] e.g. the mention of Severianus, i.e. M. Sedatius Severianus *cet.* (*cos.* 153), the governor of Cappadocia who lost his life in the Parthian invasion of Armenia (*Alex.* 27, cf. *quom hist. conscr.* 21 ff., Dio 71. 2) and of the governor of Bithynia, Avitus, i.e. L. Hedius Rufus Lollianus Avitus (*PIR*[2] H 40), who persuaded Lucian not to prosecute Alexander (*Alex.* 57).

[3] Syme, *REA* 61 (1959) 319, comparing proconsuls of Africa, briefly states a preference for 160; likewise Alföldy, *Konsulat* 215.

[4] *Alex.* 35.

[5] *Alex.* 34.

[6] pp. 109 f. above.

[7] Degrassi, *FC* 41. The evidence for Rutilianus' consulship invalidates the discussion of the chronology in Groag's otherwise excellent treatment in *RE* 16. 1 (1933) 529 ff. (and the supposed grandfather disappears, 528, since X 6587 turns out to be a record of Rutilianus' own consulship). AD 146 is a suitable year for a man born *c*. 105 to have been consul, cf. p. 21 above.

[8] Suggested in *Ep. Stud.* 4 (1967) 71. Approved by Corbier, *L'aerarium* 218 n. 4, and by Alföldy, *Konsulat* 312; but it is doubted by Schumacher, *Priesterkollegien* 205, on the grounds that there are no PP. Mummii in Spain and only two Sisennae, evidently having overlooked *AE* 1952. 49, Emerita: P. Mummius P. f. Gal. Ursus, one of two *legati* involved in drawing up a *hospitium* agreement with Emerita, on behalf of the decurions and *municipes* of the *Martienses qui antea Ugienses* in AD 6. Ugia is not far from Hispalis. Note also, apart from II 1523 (Ipagrum: Sisennae) and 5450 (Sabora: Sisen[na]) which he cites, 2057 (Malaca: Sisanna). Sisenna is typical of the nomenclature of Roman Spain: see Syme, *Tacitus* 784 f. There is no reason why Mummius Ursus should not be an ancestor of our man. Note, finally, a firm Spanish connection for senatorial Mummii, the wife of L. Antistius Rusticus, Mummia Nigrina (p. 270 below).

The early stages of his career were straightforward. After service in the vigintivirate, he was tribune of V Macedonica in Moesia inferior. Then followed the three urban magistracies, the last of which was perhaps held c.134, shortly after his father's consulship. In that case, there is no obstacle to the view that he served as legate of VI Victrix under his father, c.135-8. Such close links between governors and legionary legates were abnormal,[9] but they could be interpreted as a sign of favour from Hadrian.[10] His next post was as prefect of the *aerarium Saturni*, early in the reign of Antoninus. He is generally reckoned to have served as *praef. aliment. per Aemiliam* after his consulship,[11] but the case of Minicius Natalis a few years earlier is a useful reminder that the post could well have been praetorian.[12] Otherwise, on this reconstruction a period of unemployment must be postulated. His only certainly consular post, apart from the proconsulship of Asia many years later, was the governorship of Moesia superior. There is no means of telling exactly when he took up this appointment, nor how long he held it, except that he cannot have been there later than 155 or 156, when another governor is attested.[13] His high social standing, revealed by Lucian, is confirmed by his membership of the college of augurs.

A. Claudius Charax (*cos.* 147)

E. Boehringer, *Neue deutsche Ausgrabungen im Mittelmeergebiet und im vorderen Orient* (1959) 138 ff. = *AE* 1961. 320 = *Istanbuler Mitteilungen* IX/X (1959-60), 109 ff., Pergamum: Πατρέων ἡ πόλις / ᾿Α. Κλ. Χάρακα / ὕπατον ῾Ρωμαίων [4] / ἡγεμόνα Κιλικίας / Λυκαονίας Ἰσαυρίας / ἡγεμόνα λεγιῶνος β᾿ Αὐγ. / ἐπιμελητὴν ὁδοῦ Λατείης [8] / [στ]ρατηγὸν ῾Ρωμαίων / [κατ]αλεχθέντα ὑπὸ τῆς / [συγ]κλήτου εἰς τοὺς ἀγορανομικοὺς / ταμίαν Σικελίας [12] / τὸν συγγραφέα / εἰσηγησαμένου / ᾿Οκταβίου Χρυσάνθου

The career of Claudius Charax, revealed by this inscription found at Pergamum, his home, can be dated with some precision, since he is known from the *Fasti Ostienses* to have been consul in 147.[1] If his

---

[9] p. 18 above. Alföldy, *Konsulat* 299 n. 111, prefers a date 138-41 for the legionary command, 'da er rasch zum Konsul aufstieg', rejecting the dating here proposed, as previously put forward in Butler (ed.), *Soldier and Civilian in Roman Yorkshire* 85.

[10] Cf. the case of Minicius Natalis, p. 246 above.

[11] e.g. by Groag, *RE* 16. 1 (1933) 529 f., followed by Stein, *Moesien* 44 Schumacher, *Priesterkollegien*, 52, Corbier, *L'aerarium* 218.

[12] See p. 246 n. 9 above.

[13] p. 252 below (C. Curtius Justus).

[1] See C. Habicht, *Ist. Mitt.* 9/10 (1959-60) 109 ff., Eck, *RE* Supp. 14 (1974), 99 ff., Thomasson, *SPQR* (1975) 29 f., conveniently lists the inscriptions referring to Charax.

government of Cilicia, which preceded his tenure of the *fasces*, occupied approximately a *triennium*,[2] his command over II Augusta must be assigned to the early 140s, during the campaigns of Lollius Urbicus in Scotland and the building of the Antonine Wall which followed them.[3] As far as his earlier career is concerned, it must be noted that there is no mention on the inscription of any preliminary post, either as a *vigintivir* or as military tribune. As the inscription stresses, he was an historian, known to have written Ἑλληνικά in forty books.[4] It is not unlikely that it was his literary qualities that won him entry to the senate as quaestor under Hadrian, and it might be unwise to assume that he was then aged only twenty-four or twenty-five, as was normal.[5] The description of his adlection *inter aedilicios*, by the formula [κατ]α-λεχθέντα ὑπὸ τῆς [συγ]κλήτου εἰς τοὺς ἀγορανομικούς, is peculiar. It might reflect ignorance of the role of the emperor in *adlectio* on the part of the persons who drew up the text of the inscription. It could perhaps indicate some special role for the senate at the time of Antoninus' accession.[6] But it is perhaps more plausible to suppose that at some stage two separate items have been conflated: καταλεχθέντα ὑπὸ θεοῦ Ἀδριανοῦ εἰς τοὺς ἀγορανομικούς and ἐπὶ τῶν ὑπομνημάτων τῆς συγκλήτου. Certainly, holders of the post *ab actis senatus* generally went on to be *aedilis curulis*.[7] Adlection was followed by the praetorship and the *cura viae Latinae*. Nothing in this series of posts, all of them in or near Rome except for the quaestorship of Sicily, could be construed as particularly suitable preparation for commanding troops in the far west.

His grandson is also attested at Pergamum and his name, A. Julius Charax, suggests that our man may have been polyonymous, as E. Birley points out.[8] The *praenomen* Aulus is not otherwise known to have been used by the Claudii. His full name may have been A. Julius Ti. Claudius Charax.

C. Curtius C. f. Pol. Justus (*cos. c.*150)

III 1458 = Stein, *Dazien* 23, Sarmizegethusa: *C. Curt*[*io C. f.* / *P*]*oll. Iust*[*o*] *c*[*o*]*s.*

---

[2] p. 21 above.
[3] p. 114 above.
[4] See *RE* 3. 2 (1899) 2122 f., *PIR*² C 831, Habicht, op. cit.
[5] p. 12 above.
[6] See e.g. A. R. Birley, *Marcus Aurelius* 63 ff.
[7] A. Stein, *Protokolle des römischen Senates* (1904) 16 ff.
[8] *Chiron* 7 (1977) 280, on *AE* 1961. 321.

[IIIIviro | v]iarum curandarum [trib. leg. . . .] ⁴*/ quaestori urbano [adlecto] / inter tribunicios a div[o H]ad[riano] / praetori peregrino IIIIIIviro [eq. R.] / turmis ducendis praef. [fr]umen[t.] da[n]di* ⁸*/ curatori via[r.] Clodiae Anniae Cassiae | [C]iminiae leg. imp. Antonini Augusti Pii | leg. X[X] Val. Vict. proco[s.] provinciae | [Si]çiliae leg. pr. [pr.] imp. Anton. Aug. Pii* ¹²*/ provinciae Daciae / col. Ulp. Traiana Dacic. | Sarmizeg. patrono*

This legate may be firmly dated to the reign of Pius. The main chronological indication is supplied by an inscription from Viminacium in Moesia superior, recording the discharge under his governorship of veterans of VII Claudia enlisted in successive years. Mommsen, who first published the stone, restored the names of the *ordinarii* of 134 and 135: *[vet le]g. VII [Cl. p. f., pr]obati [Servia]no et [Varo et Po]ntian. [et Attic]o cos.* This would give a date in 158 or 159 for their discharge, which has been universally followed.[1] But two further governors are known for this province in 159 and 160–1, which means an uncomfortable squeeze.[2] It does not seem to have been appreciated that the names of the consuls of 130 and 131 could equally well be restored: *[Catulli]no et [Apro et Po]ntian. [et Rufino] cos.*[3] This would date the inscription to 155 or 156, which relieves the congestion. Since the governor of the province in 159, M. Pontius Sabinus, had been consul in 153, it is reasonable to assume that Justus had held the *fasces* a little earlier. The year 152 is ruled out, as the lists are complete, which is also the case for AD 146–8. Hence one of the years 149–51 remains.[4]

As his *cursus* inscription shows, he had been *adlectus inter tribunicios* by Hadrian, after a conventional start as *vigintivir*, tribune of an unknown legion, and urban quaestor. Hence his praetorship cannot have been much after 138 at the very latest. He had a rather lengthy series of appointments between the praetorship and consulship.[5] The final post,

---

[1] T. Mommsen, *Arch.-epigr. Mitt. aus Oesterreich* (1883) 188 ff., followed by e.g. Dessau, *ILS* 2302, W. Hüttl, *Antoninus Pius*, II (1933) 130, Stein, *Moesien* 44, and most recently by Thomasson, *Laterculi praesidum. Moesia, Dacia, Thracia* (1977) 9. Groag, *PIR*² C 1613, was a shade hesitant ('vix etiamtum a. 159').

[2] M. Pontius Sabinus (*cos.* 153) in 159 and M. Statius Priscus (*cos. ord.* 159) in 160–1: Stein, *Moesien* 45 (and, for Priscus, p. 125 above); see also Syme, *Danubian Papers* 215, who shows that M. Valerius Etruscus (*cos.* 154, according to Alföldy, *Konsulat* 164 f.) might also have been governor in the later 150s.

[3] Degrassi, *FC* 37 ff. Mommsen had perhaps not appreciated, when writing the item cited in n. 1 above, that Pontianus was also the principal *cognomen* of the first *cos. ord.* 131 (Ser. Octavius Laenas Pontianus).

[4] Degrassi, *FC* 42 f.; and see now Alföldy, *Konsulat* 156, proposing the year 150.

[5] Stein, *Moesien* 43 n. 3, notes that the position of *sevir eq. R.* etc. was indeed held after the praetorship, as on the *cursus* inscription, in spite of Groag's doubts in *PIR*² C 1613. There is no way of telling how long the *cura viarum* and *praefectura frumenti dandi* lasted at this period. Eck, *ANRW* II.1 (1974) 192 f., notes that in the period which he was considering, AD 70–138, none of the ten holders of the latter post went on to consular employment. Perhaps

the governorship of Dacia superior, probably lasted about three years, at latest *c.*148–51, but perhaps as early as *c.*146–9, and was preceded by a year as proconsul, probably of Sicily.[6] His previous position, as legate of XX Valeria Victrix, may thus have coincided with the campaigns of Lollius Urbicus,[7] but, at all events, may be assigned to the early or mid-140s.

His origin is generally reckoned to be north Italian,[8] on the basis of his membership of the Pollia tribe, which is particularly well represented in that region.[9] C. Curtius C. f. Pollia Rufinus, *IIIvir monetalis* and *tribunus laticlavius* of XIII Gemina, known from inscriptions at both Mediolanium and Sarmizegethusa, may be regarded as his son, serving under Justus' command.[10] There are various other Curtii with whom our man might be connected. It is worth noting the celebrated figure of the Julio-Claudian era, Curtius Rufus, whose origin Tacitus found too shameful to put on record.[11] That senator might have been the product of a liaison between a legionary and a woman camp-follower. Such persons were customarily enrolled in the Pollia.[12] However this may be, our man's social standing was certainly respectable, as shown by his holding the post of *sevir*[13] and his son's selection as a *IIIvir monetalis*;[14] and, while not a member of one of the four major priestly colleges by the time of his last post, he was at least a *sodalis Augustalis*.[15] Finally, it may be noted that he could be identical with the Curtius Justus cited as a *scriptor rei rusticae* by Gargilius Martialis.[16]

L. Junius Victorinus Flavius Caelianus

VII 940 = *RIB* 2034, Kirkandrews upon Eden: [. . .] / *L. Iunius Vic/torinus Fl*[*av.*]

---

favourable reports on his conduct as legate of XX Valeria Victrix helped Curtius Justus to overcome this handicap, if it was one.

[6] The *cursus* inscription is known only in a sixteenth-century MS, and the first word of line 11 is given as COLLIAE. As Groag, *Achaia* 71, notes, the restoration [*Sici*] *liae*—or [*Si*] *ciliae* —is palaeolographically easier than [*Acha*] *iae*.

[7] p. 114 above.   [8] Thus e.g. *PIR*² C 1613.

[9] Kubitschek 271.

[10] *PIR*² C 1617. Mediolanium—where an inscription is also known to Justus himself, n. 15 below—was itself enrolled in the Oufentina, see Kubitschek 120 f. See also Alföldy, *Konsulat* 307.

[11] Tac. *Ann.* 11. 21. 1–2, cf. *PIR*² C 1618.

[12] Kubitschek 271; G. R. Watson, *The Roman Soldier* (1969) 39, 167 n. 77.

[13] See *RE* 2A 2 (1923) 2018.   [14] p. 5 above.

[15] As shown by V 5809, Mediolanium, which also records his consulship, full names and a governorship.

[16] Garg. Mart. 2. 1. 4, 7.

4/ Caelianus leg. / Aug. leg. VI Vic. / p. f. ob res trans / vallum pro⁸/spere gestas

The inscription is not directly datable, except that the period before the construction of Hadrian's Wall,[1] which is here described as *vallum*,[2] must be ruled out, likewise the periods when the Antonine Wall replaced it as the frontier. Unfortunately there is still some uncertainty over these, but the phrase *ob res trans vallum prospere gestas* would have been inappropriate from the time of Lollius Urbicus until the mid-150s.[3] He could be identified with the L. Ju..., consul in the reign of Antoninus, evidently in the year 158,[4] and with the Junius Victorinus who was governor of Germania Superior at an unknown date in the second or early third centuries.[5] If he is the same as the *cos.* 158, he must have been the immediate predecessor of Numisius Junior as legate of VI Victrix, if the latter's identification with the *cos.* 161 is accepted.[6]

Whatever his date, G. Alföldy has shown good grounds for supposing that he was a native of North Africa, where the names Junius Victorinus are particularly common.[7]

Q. Camurius Lem. Numisius Junior (*cos.* 161)

XI 5670, Attidium: [*Q. C*]*amurio* [*Q. f. Lem.*] / *Numisio Iu*[*niori*] / *IIIvir. a. a. a. f. f. tr*[*ib. mil.*] *4/ leg. VIIII Hi*[*sp.*] / *sodali Titiali* [*Flaviali*] / *qua*[*e*]*st. urb. ae*[*d. cur.*] / *pr.* [*le*]*g. Aug. leg.* [. . .] *8/ et* [*leg.*] *VI Victr.* [. . .] / *et* [*Iu*]*nior pa*[*tri* . . .]

Numisius Junior was evidently a native of Attidium in Umbria, where he is mentioned not only on this inscription, but on two further stones. One is the beginning of another *cursus* inscription, which supplies his *praenomen* and tribe,[1] while the other was set up in honour of two polyonymous persons by the *municipes et* [*decuriones*] of the place,

---

[1] p. 104 above.

[2] See Davies, *ZPE* 27 (1977) 244.

[3] pp. 114 ff. above. After the creation of Britannia inferior the legate of VI Victrix became the governor (p. 169 above), which excludes the period after *c.* 213.

[4] See Alföldy, *Konsulat* 170 ff.

[5] XIII 6638. Ritterling, *FRD* 36, noted that this inscription is one of a series at the *beneficiarius* station of Stockstadt which belongs to the years 166-208. See also *PIR*² J 848 and Alföldy, *Konsulat* 172, 229. Davies, *ZPE* 27 (1977) 244, argues that only the periods of Commodus and Caracalla are suitable for Victorinus' dedication in Britain. But there is no reason to exclude the period immediately following Julius Verus' reoccupation of Hadrian's Wall (or indeed the reign of M. Aurelius), or the period of Alfenus Senecio, pp. 120, 137, 159 f. above.

[6] See below.

[7] Alföldy, *Konsulat* 314.

[1] XI 5671.

while *Numisius Iunior sodalis Titi[alis Flavialis] aed. cur. desig[natus]*
is mentioned at the end, presumably because he had paid for the
monument.[2] Of the two persons honoured, the lady was presumably
his wife, Stertinia L. f. Cocceia Bassula Venecia Aeliana Iunioris,
while the man, Q. Corn[elius] Flaccus [Stertinius?] Noricus Numisius
[Junior?], was perhaps his son. Stertinia was doubtless a descendant of
the *cos.* 113, L. Stertinius Noricus,[3] while the man's nomenclature
suggests possible descent from the Neronian legionary. legate Cornelius Flaccus.[4] Our man's own first *gentilicium* points clearly to a
connection with the Trajanic procurator C. Camurius C. f. Lem. Clemens,
also known from an inscription at Attidium.[5] Finally, attention should
be drawn to a brick-stamp naming one Q. Numisius Aper Junior.[6]

The dating of Numisius Junior's career has had to be radically revised
in the light of the diploma of 8 February 161, issued during the consulship of M. Annius Libo and Q. Numisius Junior.[7] To be sure, the consul
of 161 might be a son of the legionary legate, since our man did indeed
have a son, called Junior, while the fact that the other consul, M.
Annius Libo, was the son of a homonym who had been *cos. ord.* in
128,[8] is a pertinent reminder. None the less, on present evidence it
seems reasonable to identify the Q. Numisius Junior *cos.* 161 with the
honorand of XI 5670.

The career opened auspiciously with the most favoured post in the
vigintivirate,[9] followed by a tribunate in IX Hispana. A consul of 161,
with one or more children, and a favoured start to his career, is unlikely
to have been born later than *c.*120, so the tribunate was probably held
*c.*140.[10] After the three urban magistracies came two legionary commands, the second of them over VI Victrix. As is generally recognized,
it was exceptional for a man to command more than one legion, and
the reason in this case may be sought in the dangerous military situation

---

[2] XI 5672.
[3] p. 271 below.
[4] *PIR*² C 1362, cf. 1354.
[5] XI 5669 = *ILS* 2728. See *PIR*² C 382 (where he is regarded as the father of Numisius
Junior) and Pflaum, *CP* no. 87.
[6] XI 6712, 295, Forli. See now Eck, *ZPE* 37 (1980) 31-40 on other kinsmen.
[7] B. Overbeck, *Chiron* (1972) 452 ff. The implications are fully discussed by Eck, 459 ff.,
whose views are summarized in *RE* Supp. 14 (1974) 287 f., where he cites another inscription
showing the pair still in office on 26 Apr. The diploma is now republished as Roxan no. 55,
where the possibility is kept open, p. 79 n. 4, that the *cos.* 161 was a son of the tribune of IX
Hispana.
[8] *PIR*² A 667–8.
[9] p. 5 above.
[10] By this time the legion was no longer in Britain, it would appear, see Eck, *Chiron* 2
(1972) 461 f., and pp. 220 f. above.

in Britain in the mid-150s.[11] It is not unlikely that Numisius Junior had been commanding a legion on the Rhine, and was appointed to VI Victrix on the recommendation of Cn. Julius Verus, when the latter went from Germania Inferior to Britain.[12]

Ignotus *Inscr. It.* IV 143

XIV 4249 = *Inscr. It.* IV 143, Tibur: [. . .] *cio* [. . . / . . .l] *eg. leg. II* | [*Aug. adlec*] *to ab* [4] | [*imp. Anto*] *nino* | [. . .]

Aug. must be restored at the beginning of line 3, for the other legions with the same number, existing under Pius, who is presumably the emperor mentioned in line 4,[1] did not have legates. II Traiana, in Egypt, was commanded by an equestrian prefect,[2] and II Adiutrix, in Pannonia inferior, by the praetorian governor of that province.[3] The surviving details of the career seem to preclude regarding this inscription as another one in honour of T. Marcius Cle[mens].[4] [. . .] cio is presumably the end of the man's *gentilicium*, but there are too many possible names with that termination to permit any restoration.[5]

...sus Cl. ...ilius Q. J[ul (?)] Haterianus

VII 108 = *RIB* 335, Caerleon: [. . . / . . .] *ņsus Cl.* [*Aem?/*] *ilius Q. I* [*ul.?*] [4] / *Haterianus* | *leg. Aug. pr. pr.* | *provinc. Cilic.*

As R. P. Wright comments in *RIB*, 'Haterianus was probably legate of the Second Legion, and on his appointment to the governorship of Cilicia set up this dedication without specifying the recent office.' For a parallel to this promotion of a commander of a western legion to the governorship of the praetorian province of Cilicia, one may point to the

---

[11] Eck, *Chiron* 2 (1972) 461.

[12] p. 120 above.

[1] See Pflaum, *Mélanges Carcopino* (1966) 717 ff.

[2] Ritterling, *RE* 12. 2 (1925) 1484 ff.

[3] Ibid. 1446 ff. There were of course exceptions, e.g. Q. Antistius Adventus commanded II Adiutrix when it was temporarily transferred to the east in the 160s (p. 130 above). After the reorganization of the Pannonian provinces by Caracalla, II Adiutrix must have been commanded by an ordinary legate again.

[4] p. 263 below.

[5] e.g. Anicius, Larcius, Minicius, Moscius, Sabucius, Sulpicius, etc. One man with a suitable name who received senatorial rank in the Antonine period was Tuticius Proculus, a former teacher of M. Aurelius, whom he 'usque ad proconsulatum provexit' (*HA Marcus* 2. 5, cf. 2. 3). See A. R. Birley, *H-A-C 1966/7* (1968) 39 ff., for the name, suggesting identification with the equestrian procurator M. Tuticius Proculus (VIII 1625, Sicca).

case of Q. Venidius Rufus, who made a dedication at Bonn, where he was commanding I Minervia, mentioning both his legionary legateship and the Cilician post.[1] One might suppose that Haterianus had already made dedications at Caerleon on which his style as legate of II Augusta was set forth, making it unnecessary to mention it again on this inscription. The stone itself is now lost, but there is a detailed drawing of it in Camden, and a report of its discovery, along with *RIB* 316, recording the reconstruction of a temple of Diana by the third century legionary legate T. Fl. Postumius Varus,[2] and a statue of the goddess. The full names of the man are lost beyond restoration. The first surviving traces, SVS preceded by an upright, must represent a name ending in -isus or -nsus. The former seems virtually impossible,[3] and examples of the latter are exceedingly rare.[4] Densus is known to have been borne by persons of higher rank: a Roman knight named Julius Densus was a friend of Claudius' son Britannicus,[5] and a centurion of the guard, Sempronius Densus, sacrificed his life in an attempt to save Galba's heir in AD 69.[6] The next name could be Cl., followed by the first part of the name terminating -ilius in line 3. This too is followed by an upright, but it is not possible to decide between Aemilius, Metilius, Quintilius, Rutilius, or Statilius, among the commoner names.[7] This is followed by Q. I[. . .], either Q. J[ul.] or Q. J[un.], and then by Haterianus. He might therefore be the same as the Virgilian scholar Julius Haterianus.[8] However, since several lines at the top of the stone are certainly missing, our man may have had other names by which he was mainly known. Hence the possibility cannot be excluded that he is identical with one of the legates of Cilicia otherwise recorded.[9] Nothing firm can be said about the date, except that joint reigns are excluded, i.e. the years 161-9, 177–80, 198–211.

---

[1] XIII 7994. See Alföldy, *Legionslegaten* 48.

[2] p. 266 below.

[3] Kajanto offers only Conisus (p. 350: one specimen only, a Christian: VIII 13580).

[4] Census, Consus, Densus, Sensus: Kajanto 350, 216, 289, 356.

[5] Tac. *Ann.* 13. 10. 2.

[6] Tac. *Hist.* 1. 43. 1. But note also C. (Flavius) Consus, a kinsman by marriage of the Augustan senator P. Paquius Scaeva (*PIR*² F 248).

[7] In *PIR*² H 21, E. Birley's restoration is noted: [De]nsus Cl.[Ae]milius Q. I[ul.] Haterianus.

[8] See Wessner, *RE* 7. 2 (1912) 2512 f., who dates him not later than the third century. See also Syme, *Ammianus and the Historia Augusta* 185, commenting on the Julius Aterianus, or Haterianus, in *HA tyr. trig.* 6. 2, 'perhaps fictitious in this role'.

[9] A list is supplied by Pflaum, *Corolla . . . Swoboda* 189 ff. Note e.g. Q. Gellius Longus (*AE* 1920. 72: AD 92-3), T. Vibius Varus (*Digest* XXII 5. 3. 1: before 134), Cornelius [Dex]-ter (or [Ni]ger) (*AE* 1960. 34: AD 157), and Rutilianus (*Cod. Iust.* IX 43. 1: 215), all otherwise unknown (except that Varus was *cos. ord.* 134), and possibly polyonymous.

---Fronto(?) Aemilianus --- Calpurnius --- Rufilianus

VII 98 = *RIB* 320, Caerleon: *Iovi, O. M. Dolich[e]n[o . . . / F[r]onto Aemilianus [. . .] / Calpurnius [. . .] ⁴/ Rufilianus [l]eg[atus] / Augustorum / monitu*

There can be no doubt that this man was legate of II Augusta and not governor of the province.[1] As the inscription is now lost, some doubt must attach to his nomenclature. If the five or six letters at the beginning of line 2, of which only ON are certain, may be restored as F[r]onto, it is probable that an abbreviated *nomen*, such as Iul., should be supplied at the end of line 1.[2] The drawing in *RIB* also indicates that two further names must be restored, before and after Calpurnius. E. Groag suggested[3] that the man might be a kinsman of L. Calpurnius Fidus Aemilianus of Utica,[4] and of C. Memmius Fidus Julius Albius, from Bulla Regia, whose daughter's names, apparently [Iul]ia Me[m]mia Ca[lp]u[rnia] Aemi[liana] Fidia[na], suggest that her mother belonged to a family of Calpurnii Aemiliani.[5] But the precise relationships, if any, elude definition. Groag suggested a third-century date, perhaps because of the apparent lack of initial *praenomen* and *nomen*.[6] But, as is noted in *RIB*, the writing out of *legatus Augustorum* in full suggests that joint emperors were still something of a novelty. In that case, the years 161-9, when M. Aurelius and L. Verus were co-rulers, seem a likely period. It may be noted that Memmius Fidus was tribune of II Augusta at that time:[7] the legionary legate might have been instrumental in obtaining the commission for him.

L. Cestius Gallus Cerrinius Justus Lutatius Natalis

X 3722, Volturnum: *L. Cestio Gallo Cerri/nio Iusto Lu[t]atio Natali / IIIIviro viar. curand. trib. ⁴/ laticlavio leg. VIII Aug. / quaestori urbano ab / actis [se]natus aedil. curul. / praetori leg. Augg. leg. ⁸/ XX V. V. procos. provin/ciae Narbonensis praef. / aerar. Saturn. cos. [des(?)] patrono colo[ni]ae d. d.*

The only chronological indication provided by the inscription from Volturnum is *Augg.* in line 7, which shows that his legionary command

---

[1] See appendix 2, pp. 431 f. below on the titulature.
[2] There are various Julii Frontones in *PIR*² J 323-8. No links with our man suggest themselves.
[3] *PIR*² C 310, cf. 264, A 427. Note also the Antonine senator Aemilius Fronto, ibid. A 349, cf. 345-8.
[4] VIII 25382.
[5] p. 278 below.
[6] Barbieri, *L'Albo* no. 1988, also assigns this man to the third century.
[7] p. 278 below.

cannot be dated earlier than 161–9. But the periods 177–80 and 198–209 are equally possible.[1] The career given on this *cursus*-inscription is a conventional one, the only problem being the gap after *cos.* in the last line. In *CIL*, the text offered is [*II*], but as E. Groag pointed out, it is unacceptable, since a second consulship would not have been given to a man who had held no consular office. It is preferable to postulate [*d.*] or [*des.*].[2]

An inscription from Salona, of which only a few letters at the beginning of six lines survive, has been restored as referring to our man.[3] The restoration is certainly possible, but doubt subsists. For one thing, the letters [. . .]*p. Sup*[. . .], which do not match anything in the stone from Volturnum, must necessarily—it appears—refer to the post of [*cur. r.*] *p. Sup*[*eraequanor.*]. Yet there seems no good reason why the post should have been omitted from the Volturnum *cursus*.

More powerful grounds for hesitation lie in the wide variety of alternative restorations that might be offered for every other line, except the last, where *pat*[*rono* . . .] is obvious enough. The solitary C which is the first surviving letter might be restored as, e.g. [*leg. VII*] *C*[*l. p. f.*], just as well as [*IIIIviro viar.*] *c*[*ur.*], and se in the next line could be *se*[*viro eq. R.* . . .] as well as [*ab actis*] *se*[*natus*]. Finally, val in the line that follows need not refer to [*leg. XX*] *Val*[*eriae Victricis*] : it could be [*cur. viae*] *Val*[*eriae*].[4]

Our man is otherwise unknown, and there are no links to connect him with the CC. Cestii Galli, consuls in AD 35 and 42.[5] The C. Cestius of the famous sepulchral pyramid at Rome was, however, L. f,[6] and two senators of the early Augustan period seem to have been called L. Cestius.[7] However this may be, he must have been a kinsman, perhaps the father or son, of L. Cestius L. f. Pom. Gallus Varenianus Lutatius Natalis Aemilianus, patron of the Sicilian town of Gaulus.[8] If our man shared the same tribe as this person, he must have been an Italian.[9]

---

[1] In *PIR*[2] C 692, Groag preferred the two earlier periods, whereas Ritterling, *RE* 12. 2 (1925) 1778, opted for the end of the second century.

[2] See Groag in *PIR*[2] C 692, Alföldy, *Ep. Stud.* 5 (1968) 136 f.

[3] *Bull. Dalm.* 27 (1914) 42. See Groag, *PIR*[2] C 692, and Alföldy, *Ep. Stud.* 5 (1968) 136 f., who offers a text, n. 246: [. . . *IIIIviro viar.*] / *c*[*ur. trib. mil. leg. VIII Aug., q. urb., ab actis*]/*se*[*natus, aed. cur., pr., leg. Augg. leg. XX*]/ *Val*[*eriae victricis, procon*]/*suli* [*provinc. Narbonensis, cur. r.*] / *p. Sup*[*eraequanor., r. p. Salonitan.*]/, *pat*[*rono praestantissimo, d. d.*]

[4] Cf. *ILS* 1080.

[5] *PIR*[2] C 690–1.

[6] *PIR*[2] C 686.

[7] *PIR*[2] C 687–8.

[8] X 7506, cf. p. 994, Gaulus; *PIR*[2] C 693.

[9] Kubitschek 271.

Priscus

Dio 72. 9. 2a (Petr. Patr. *exc. Vat.* 122): Ὅτι οἱ Βρεττανίᾳ στρατιῶται Πρίσκον ὑποστράτηγον εἵλοντο αὐτοκράτορα· ὁ δὲ παρῃτήσατο εἰπὼν ὅτι "τοιοῦτος ἐγώ εἰμι αὐτοκράτωρ οἷοι ὑμεῖς στρατιῶταί ἐστε."

This fragment of Cassius Dio is preserved only in Petrus Patricius' *excerpta Vaticana*. To judge from its position in the *excerpta*, it must describe an event later than 177 and earlier than 189-90.[1] The context demonstrates that it must be assigned to the early 180s, when the British army was in a mutinous state.[2] According to the *Historia Augusta*, 'Commodus was called Britannicus by flatterers when the Britons even wanted to choose another emperor in opposition to him'.[3] This looks like a reference to the Priscus affair, which could then be dated to 184, the year when Commodus took the title Britannicus as a result of the campaigns of Ulpius Marcellus.[4] Furthermore, it looks as if the *Historia Augusta* has also transmitted the government's response to this abortive coup, although the connection is not made: the praetorian prefect Perennis is said to have removed senators from their posts during the British wars and replaced them by equestrian commanders, a measure which was to lead to his own overthrow, in 185.[5] However, it must be noted that later in the *Historia Augusta*, Pertinax is said to have 'deterred the soldiers from mutiny, when they wanted anyone [else other than Commodus] as emperor, especially Pertinax himself',[6] shortly after his arrival as governor in 185.[7] This is another possible context for the episode of Priscus, but the nature of Perennis' measure makes the previous year rather more attractive. There is no way of deciding which legion Priscus was commanding.[8]

[1] U. P. Boissevain, *Cassii Dionis historiarum quae supersunt* III (1903) 290. *Exc. Vat.* 121 refers to M. Aurelius' return to Rome in 177, 123 to Julius Solon's entry to the senate through the agency of Cleander (Dio 71. 32. 1, 72. 12. 3).

[2] pp. 139, 145 above.

[3] *HA Comm.* 8. 4. Grosso, *La lotta politica* 453 n. 1, prefers to translate *cum voluerint* as a concessive clause, rather than as here, '*when* the Britons even wanted'. His arguments from *Comm.* 8. 1 and 8. 5 are not decisive, in my view. But even if *cum* is rendered 'although', it seems unnecessary to exclude 'il sincronismo tra le due proposizioni'. Certainly, it does not serve to· prove his case for assigning the Priscus affair to the governorship of Pertinax (n. 8 below).

[4] *PIR*² A 1482; p. 142 above.

[5] *HA Comm.* 6. 2. See p. 139 above, on the fall of Perennis. I cannot accept F. Kolb's inference from Dio 72. 9. 2² that a son of Perennis was a legionary commander in Britain (*Historia* 26 (1977) 467 n. 101).

[6] *HA Pert.* 2. 6.

[7] p. 145 above.

[8] Grosso, *La lotta politica* 451 ff., argues that the affair must date to the governorship of Pertinax, identifying it with the *seditio legionis* in which Pertinax nearly lost his life (*HA Pert.* 2. 8). Although this is attractive, it fails to provide an explanation for the dismissal of the

The *cognomen* is much too common[9] to make any sure identification, but it may be noted that the legate of III Augusta, *de facto* governor of Numidia, in 186, was one T. Caunius Priscus.[10] This is exactly the kind of post which a man who was legionary legate in 184 might be expected to have been holding in 186, and it is not impossible that the British legionary legate was rewarded for his loyalty by promotion to the Numidian command. A suffect consul named Priscus is recorded late in the reign of Commodus,[11] and could be identical with either or both of these men.

Q. Aurelius Polus Terentianus (*cos. a. inc.*)

Mainzer Zeitschr. 59 (1964) 56 = *AE* 1965. 240 = *Ep. Stud.* 3 (1967) 44 no. 229, Moguntiacum: *Libero et Apol/lini pro salute / [[im[p.] C[a]es. M. [Au]r. ⁴/ Commod[i] Pi[i] Fel. / Aug. [. . . / . . .]]] Q. Aurel. / Polus Terentianus ⁸/ cum Q. Aur. Polo / Syriaco filio / fetialis leg. / leg. XXII Pr. p. f. ¹²/ item leg. II Aug.*

Polus Terentianus was long known to have been consular governor of the III Daciae in the crucial year 193,[1] but two further elements in his career are now known, following the discovery of inscriptions at Moguntiacum in Germania superior and in the province of Asia. The Mainz inscription quoted above was one of a pair, the other, much more fragmentary, being a dedication to Mars and Victory.[2] The dedication to Liber and Apollo shows that Terentianus was successively legate of two legions, XXII Primigenia, stationed at Mainz itself, and II Augusta, and a member of the college of *fetiales*.[3] From the fact that

---

legionary legates by Perennis (*Comm.* 6. 2). For the equation ὑποστράτηγος = *legatus legionis*, see G. Vrind, *De Cassii Dionis vocabulis* (1923) 82 f., 88 ff. II Augusta, as the most southerly of the legions and therefore the best placed for a move on London and the Channel ports, is perhaps slightly more likely than the other two.

[9] Barbieri, *L'Albo* p. 745, indexes over thirty senators with this item in their nomenclature.

[10] *PIR²* C 590; Thomasson, *Statthalter Nordafrikas* II 192 f. But the date and identification are not quite certain: the governor in 186 was --cus (VIII 2697), thought to be the same as T. Caunius Priscus recorded on two undated inscriptions (*ILS* 3843, 3893), all three from Lambaesis. The *gentilicium* Caunius is extremely rare: Schulze 76. Note that a Caunia Firmina (V 6561, Gt St Bernard) has the same *cognomen* as Caunius Priscus' son.

[11] G. M. Bersanetti, *Athenaeum* 28 (1940) 113 ff., favours identity with the British legate. See also Barbieri, *L'Albo* nos. 830, 830a, Grosso, *La lotta politica* 573 f.

[1] III 1374, cf. p. 1402, Micia. See Stein, *Dazien* 56.

[2] *AE* 1965. 241.

[3] The *cursus* inscription of P. Septimius Geta, a more or less exact contemporary, shows that he was elected to the *fetiales* immediately after the praetorship (*IRT* 541, Lepcis Magna: see p. 278 below). The fact that this priesthood is the only item apart from the legionary legateships to be mentioned, suggests that it was a recent honour: see A. R. Birley, *Bonner*

Commodus bears the title Felix, the date cannot be earlier than 185.[4] Study of parallel cases, where men specify two posts on a dedication, suggests that it was common practice to do this on receipt of a letter of appointment to a new command.[5] It is also demonstrable that it was only when unusual circumstances prevailed that men were appointed to command more than one legion.[6] These may certainly be detected in Britain in the 180s.[7] It could be that Terentianus was sent from Mainz to replace the legionary legate Priscus, after the latter had rejected his soldiers' attempt to thrust the purple on him. On the other hand, that episode may have provoked Perennis' substitution of senatorial *legati* by equestrian prefects in the army of Britain.[8] In that case, Terentianus' appointment may have come shortly after Perennis' overthrow and the removal of his equestrian commanders. At all events, Terentianus ought to have taken up his command in 185 or 186.

He presumably held one further praetorian post,[9] followed by the consulship *c.*190. His appointment as legate of the III Daciae was probably made before the death of Commodus, and was perhaps engineered by Q. Aemilius Laetus, the praetorian prefect, as part of his preparations for the *coup d'état* of 31 December 192.[10] Like Septimius Severus, who had evidently served as legionary legate under Pertinax when the latter was governor of Syria, *c.*180,[11] Terentianus had probably been under Pertinax's orders in a similar capacity when in Britain. Terentianus' origin is nowhere recorded, but study of the distribution of QQ. Aurelii, and other elements in his nomenclature, suggest that he too, like other men in key positions at the end of 192, may have been an African.[12] His governorship of Dacia cannot have lasted later than

Jahrb. 169 (1969) 268, where it is pointed out that a vacancy occurred in 185 or 186. For a parallel inscription, recording present post, post to which news of appointment had just been received, and priesthood (*sodalis Hadrianalis*), see III 1071, cf. 1072 with p. 1390, Apulum.

⁴ *PIR*² A 1482, citing *HA Comm.* 8. 1.

⁵ Compare the cases quoted on pp. 95, 123 and 256 above, and n. 3 above. I am indebted to a study by E. Birley, 'Inscriptions indicative of impending or recent movements', *Chinon* 9 (1979) 495 ff. The view here taken, that Terentianus' British legateship followed that in Germania superior, was put forward in *Bonner Jahrb.* 169 (1969), 267 f., and is shared by F. Grosso, *Athenaeum* 45 (1967) 346 ff. For another view, see Alföldy, *Legionslegaten* 44 f.

⁶ p. 18 above.

⁷ pp. 139 ff. above.

⁸ pp. 139, 145 above.

⁹ Even the exceptional circumstances prevailing at Rome in the 180s are unlikely to have secured Terentianus the consulship immediately after a legionary legateship, see p. 20 above.

¹⁰ See A. R. Birley, *Bonner Jahrb.* 169 (1969) 247 ff.

¹¹ See A. R. Birley, op. cit., and *Septimius Severus* 106 ff.

¹² The evidence is set out in *Bonner Jahrb.* 169 (1969) 267. One non-African Q. Aurelius there cited, n. 140 (*IG* III 877 = *CIA* III 877) may be deleted, as the man was evidently an Aurelius Cotta, probably M. Aurelius Cotta Maximus Messalinus (*PIR*² A 1488), see Eck, *RE* Supp. 15 (1978) 76.

195, when the emperor's brother Geta is recorded in the province.[13] But Terentianus evidently remained in favour, for he was proconsul of Asia later in the reign.[14]

T. Marcius T. f. Fal. Cle[mens]

XIV 3595 = *Inscr. It.* IV 110, Tibur: *T. Marcio T. f. Fal. Cle[menti] / sacerdoti fetiali tr. [mil.] / leg. XIIII Gem. q[uaest. pro pr.] provinciae Achaiae a[b actis] / senat. aed. cur. praet. c[and.] / curatori viae Latinae [legato] / leg. II Aug. / Grania Tertull[. . .]*

There is no obvious means of dating this career, although E. Groag suggested that the sequence *ab actis senatus—aedilis curulis* ought to belong to the period from Antoninus Pius to Severus Alexander.[1] Unfortunately, evidence for the former post is too limited to determine the validity of this argument.[2] The man is otherwise unknown, but his membership of the tribe Falerna shows that he was of Italian origin,[3] although he probably had a residence at Tibur. Grania Tertull. . . was presumably his wife.

Claudius Hieronymianus (*cos. a. inc.*)

VII 240 = *ILS* 4384 = *RIB* 658, York: *Deo sancto / Serapi / templum a so⁴/lo fecit Cl. Hierony/mianus leg. / leg. VI Vic.*

An approximate dating of this fine dedication by the legate Claudius Hieronymianus may be arrived at from a consideration of the mention made of him by two early-third-century authors. The jurist Papinian, put to death by Caracalla in late 211 or early 212,[1] is quoted by Ulpian in the *Digest* for his legal opinion on a legacy left to Claudius Hieronymianus, 'clarissimus vir', by Umbrius Primus. The latter is said to have made various dispositions when about to set out for his

---

[13] Stein, *Dazien* 57; p. 278 below.

[14] *AE* 1964. 232, Menye. It was no doubt in this capacity that he received the rescript from Severus and Caracalla preserved in *Frag. Vat.* 200.

[1] Groag, *Achaia* 121. The apparent omission of any post in the vigintivirate is unusual. If not merely omitted in error, it might point to the 160s, cf. the case of C. Memmius Fidus, p. 278 below.

[2] See Eck, *ANRW* II. 1 (1974) 178 n. 84, for holders of the post in the period 70–138.

[3] Kubitschek 270: the main distribution was in regio I.

[1] *PIR*² A 388; Pflaum, *CP* no. 220. For the date of his death see now esp. Barnes, *JTS* N.S. 19 (1968) 574 f.

proconsulship.[2] This doubtless refers to his proconsulship of Africa, unfortunately undated, but perhaps held *c.* 202.[3] The second reference is slightly more helpful, and more interesting. Tertullian, addressing the proconsul of Africa Scapula, who is known to have been in office in August 212,[4] refers to dealings with Christians by other Roman officials.[5] Vigellius Saturninus is mentioned as 'the first to turn the sword against us here' (sc. in Africa).[6] He then relates how 'Claudius Lucius Hieronymianus',[7] in Cappadocia, angry that his wife had converted to Christianity, treated the Christians cruelly. But he was then the only one 'in praetorio suo' to be struck by the plague. Festering with worms, he said that no one should know about it, 'ne gaudeant Christiani'. Later, he saw the error of his ways, and died almost a Christian. Tertullian adds a third anecdote, of how one Caecilius Capella, 'in illo exitu Byzantino', which must refer to the fall of Byzantium to the army of Marius Maximus in 195,[8] shouted out, 'Christiani gaudete'. At first sight, this suggests that the Cappadocian governorship of Hieronymianus —for that is implied by the reference to his *praetorium*—must be dated between Vigellius Saturninus' proconsulship in Africa, 180-1, and the fall of Byzantium in 195. But, admittedly, the anecdote about Caecilius Capella's outburst at the fall of Byzantium, not strictly relevant to Tertullian's argument, was probably brought to his mind by association of ideas when he quoted the phrase 'ne gaudeant Christiani', and need not therefore be supposed to describe an event later than Hieronymianus' governorship of Cappadocia. On the other hand, the plague mentioned by Tertullian could well be the one that Cassius Dio and Herodian refer to, which seems to have reached Rome in 188-9.[9]

On this hypothesis, if Hieronymianus was governor of Cappadocia *c.* 188,[10] his command over VI Victrix probably fell in the reign of M. Aurelius, in the 170s. But it must be pointed out that Tertullian implies that he died not long after his affliction, even if it is not stated

---

[2] *Digest* 23. 7. 12. 40. The *cognomen* is given in the MSS as *Hieroniano.*

[3] See E. Birley, *JRS* 52 (1962) 222, referring to XV 7969. On the career, see also Barbieri, *L'Albo* no. 539 + *Agg.*, Alföldy, *Fasti Hispanienses* 129 f.

[4] Scapula, *cos. ord.* 195, was proconsul during the eclipse of 14 Aug. 212, see Thomasson, *Statthalter Nordafrikas* II 112 f., who also discusses the possibility that he had been proconsul in May 212.

[5] *ad Scapulam* 3. 4.

[6] Thomasson, *Statthalter Nordafrikas* II 87: proconsul 180-1.

[7] The *cognomen* is given in the MSS in various forms, but the emendation seems certain. 'Lucius' may have been his *praenomen*. See *PIR*[2] C 888; Barbieri, *L'Albo* no. 157.

[8] A. Birley, *Septimius Severus* 186 f.

[9] Dio 72. 14. 3-4, Herodian 1. 12. 1-2. See Grosso, *La lotta politica* 248 ff. (no reference to Hieronymianus).

[10] Only one governor is known during the reign of Commodus, in 184 (Caelius Calvinus: *PIR*[2] C 125).

that he died from the plague.[11] In that case, his governorship of Cappadocia should be placed some time between the death of Umbrius Primus, after *c.*202(?) and the death of Papinian, at the end of 211. His legionary command would then need to be assigned to the 190s.[12]

His origin is not recorded, but may be assumed to be from the Greek-speaking part of the empire, in view of his *cognomen.*

L. Julius L. f. Pal. Julianus (*cos. a. inc.*)

XI 4182, Interamna: *L. Iulio L. f. Pal. / Iuliano / praetori curatori* [4]*/ civitatis Interamna/tium Nartium praef. / Minicia. proconsuli / provinciae Achaiae* [8]*/ leg. legionis secund. / August. legato Aug. / pro pr. provinci/ae Aquitaniae con*[12]*/suli officiales / eius provinciae Aquita/niae optimo praesidi / homini bono.*

VII 480 = *RIB* 1138, the Hermitage, near Hexham: *Victoriae / Aug. / L. Iul. Iuli*[*anus leg.*(?) [4]*/ A*]*ug̣*[. . .]

If the ascending order of appointments—omitting, as of less interest, everything earlier than the praetorship—is in correct chronological sequence,[1] Julius Julianus only received command of II Augusta when of several years' standing after his praetorship.[2] The jurists quote two rescripts to a Julius Julianus who may be equated with our man. The first, in the *Digest*, was from Severus and Caracalla, cited by Aemilius Macer,[3] while the second was issued by *impp. Augg.* who are clearly the same emperors; and as it comes from Ulpian's *de officio proconsulis*, it suffices to date his proconsulship of Achaia to the joint reign, AD 198-209.[4]

Further precision in the dating is supplied by an incomplete inscription

[11] E. Birley, *Yorks. Arch. J.* 41 (1966) 729, refers to Hieronymianus having 'died as consular governor of Cappadocia'. But Tertullian, *Scap.* 3. 4, simply says, after a reference to his suffering from the plague, 'cum vivus vermibus ebullisset', and his attempt to keep his affliction secret so that the Christians should not rejoice, 'Postea cognito errore suo, quod tormentis quosdam a proposito suo excidere fecisset, pene Christianus decessit.' This may imply that he died soon after, but it is not completely certain.

[12] As E. Birley rightly notes, *Yorks. Arch. J.* 41 (1966) 729 f., the dating of Hieronymianus' legionary command has an important bearing on the vexed question of the division of Britain. Unfortunately, as has been seen, there is too much uncertainty for this to be decisive.

[1] Compare the case of A. Larcius Priscus, p. 236 above. Julianus might have been proconsul of Achaia after his legionary command.

[2] There is no way of telling how long that interval may have been. The proconsulship was for a single year, but the other posts were of indeterminate duration. Julianus is the second earliest known holder of the post *praefectus Miniciae*; see Pflaum, *Bonner Jahrb.* 163 (1963) 232 ff.; and *ILS* 1110, quoted on p. 278 below.

[3] *Digest* 48. 21. 2.

[4] *Frag. Vat.* 119: 'Ulpianus l. II de officio proconsulis, Impp. Augg. Iulio Iu[liano . . .]'. See Groag, *Achaia* 82.

found near Hadrian's Wall.[5] If, as seems reasonable, the dedicator may be identified with our man,[6] the governorship of Alfenus Senecio seems a likely period for II Augusta and its legate to have been involved in successful fighting.[7] At all events, the fact that his next post, as governor of Aquitania, was held under a single emperor, shows that he cannot have held it earlier than 212,[8] which accords reasonably enough with the suggested dating of his legionary command.

The tribe Palatina gives no help in finding the man's origin. His residence was obviously at Interamna, where he had been *curator civitatis* and where his Aquitanian staff set up the text in his honour. But it seems possible that he originally came from Ocriculum, not far away, where a municipal worthy of the same names and tribe is attested, perhaps his father or grandfather.[9]

Ti. Claudius Paulinus

EE IX 1012 = *RIB* 311, Caerwent: see pp. 189 f. above, under governors of Britannia Inferior, where Paulinus' legionary command is shown to date to the reign of Caracalla; he was probably the successor of L. Julius Julianus.

T. Flavius Postumius Varus (*cos. a. inc.*)

VII 95 = *RIB* 316, Caerleon: T. Fl. Postumius / [V]arus v. c. leg. / templ. Dianae [4] / restituit

A senator describing himself as *leg.* at a legionary fortress cannot well

---

[5] Davies, *Latomus* 35 (1976) 399 and n. 3, rightly points out that the provenance of this stone is misleadingly given by the editors. But I cannot follow him in his interpretation of the career of Julianus. He justifiably rejects the restoration *Iuli*[*anus leg. leg. II*] in line 3, where there is insufficient space for more than about six letters after the break. But it is not necessary to read *Iulia*[*nus leg.*]/ *Aug.* [*pr. pr.*], and make Julianus into a praetorian governor of Britannia superior. Apart from the fact that the findspot of the inscription is well over 100 miles north of the frontiers of Britannia superior, a restoration of the text as *Iulia*[*nus leg.*] *Aug.* [*leg. II Aug.*] would be quite adequate. In fact, I prefer to remain hesitant about the traces in lines 3 and 4, and to read *Iuli*[*anus leg.*(?)/*A*]*ug*[. . .], leaving open the possibility that Julianus was described as *leg. Augg.* or even *Auggg.* (But the traces at the beginning of line 4 might refer to *v*(*ir*) *c*(*larissimus*)).

[6] Thus *PIR*[2] J 367; Davies, *Latomus* 35 (1976) 399 ff.

[7] See pp. 159 f. above, on Senecio, and pp. 168 ff. on the division of Britain.

[8] Groag, *Achaia* 82 n. 334, comments that '*leg. Aug.* statt *Augg.* findet sich nicht selten in Inschriften dieser Zeit,' but Davies, *Latomus* 35 (1976) 400 and n. 9, rightly stresses that the *officiales* should have got this item right.

[9] Pflaum, *Rev. de phil.* 82 (1956) 72, quoting the views of E. Birley; *PIR*[2] J 367.

be anything but the *legatus legionis*.[1] The present man rose to be *prae-fectus urbi* in 271,[2] and probably held his legionary command some twenty years earlier. He was a great-grandson of the orator M. Postumius Festus, a friend and contemporary of Fronto and a fellow-African.[3] But the family seems to have been long domiciled in Italy. The nomen-clature of his brother or cousin T. Fl. Postumius Titianus (*cos. II ord.* 301)[4] suggests a link with the family of Pertinax's wife Flavia Titiana, although these names were common.[5] Our man's high social standing was enhanced by his membership of two of the great priestly colleges, the augurs and the *XVviri*.[6]

between 253 and 258	**Vitulasius Laetinianus**

VII 107 = *ILS* 537 = *RIB* 334, Caerleon: see p. 178 above.

This man is otherwise unknown. His names suggest Italian origin, as is certain for the governor Desticius Juba under whom he served.[1] So rare is the *gentilicium* that it would be unreasonable to doubt his descent from the Flavian consul Sex. Vitulasius Nepos (*cos.* 78).[2] This is the latest known instance of a legionary legate anywhere in the empire.[3]

II.9

TRIBUNI LATICLAVII OF THE BRITISH ARMY

(?) Ignotus XI 5173

XI 5173 = Alföldy, *Fasti Hispanienses* 154, Vettona: [. . . / . . . (?)*Procu*]*lo tr. mili*[*tum / legionum*] *IX et XXI* [*quaest.* [4]/ *provinc.* . . .]*ae aed. pl. Cer.* [*praet. leg. / pro pr. provinc.*] *Ponti et* [*Bithyniae / item Galliae N*]*arbonensis ter*(?) *ex s.* [*c. pro consule / in provin*]*cia Hisp*[*ania ulteriore* [8]/ . . .]

---

[1] See Appendix 2, pp. 431 f. below, on the titulature.

[2] *Chron. a.* 354, p. 66 Mommsen.

[3] *ILS* 2929, 2940, Rome. See Lambertz, *RE* 22. 1 (1953) 950 ff.

[4] *PLRE* I 919 f. For the probable grandparents suggested on p. 920, see now Alföldy, *RIT* 34, where the wife's name is read as Postumia S[i] ria (?).

[5] *PIR*[2] F 444, cf. 378–87 for Flavii Titiani.

[6] *ILS* 2940.

[1] p. 178 above.

[2] Schulze 153, who notes that the *cos.* 78 may have had property among the Vestini, citing IX 3587, 3617. Kajanto 261, knows only two other bearers of the *cognomen*, both women.

[3] Cf. pp. 35 and 200 above for senatorial governors of one-legion provinces still command-ing troops in the 260s.

The absence of title for the legion later known regularly as IX Hispana suggests a pre-Flavian date for this senator's career.[1] He probably held his military tribunate before the legion was transferred to Britain in 43.[2]

M. Ostorius P. f. Scapula (*cos.* 59)

Tac. *Ann.* 12. 31. 4; 16. 15. 1.

The younger Scapula's status when in Britain is not recorded, but it is most probable that he was a military tribune.[1] There is no evidence to suggest which legion he was attached to; only auxiliary units took part in the action during which he won his *corona civica*, early in his father's governorship, probably in the year 48. He became consul in 59, probably in his early thirties. Tacitus reports that Nero feared his 'vast size and skill at arms', and he committed suicide to avoid execution in 66.[2]

L. Cornelius L. f. Gal. Pusio Annius Messalla (*cos. a. inc.*)

VI 37056; Rome: *L. Cornelio L. f. / Gal. Pusioni / IIIIvir. viar. curandar.* [4] / *tr. mil. leg. XIIII Geminae / quaestori tr. pl. pr. legat. / Augusti leg. XVI / M. Vibrius Marcellus* [8] / *7 leg. XVI*

This man must have served with XIV Gemina before 60, when it received the additional titles Martia Victrix.[1] The *terminus ante quem* is 70, when the old legion XVI was reconstituted as XVI Flavia Firma.[2] G. Alföldy assigns his command over it to late in the reign of Nero, since he became consul under Vespasian.[3] He later became proconsul of Africa or Asia and was also a *VIIvir epulonum.*[4] He was evidently a Spaniard, probably from Gades, with a residence at Tibur.[5]

[1] See Alföldy, op. cit. 155 and n. 27. But it should be noted that *XXI*[. . .] might conceivably refer to *XXI*[*I*] (Primigenia) rather than to XXI (Rapax).

[2] Alföldy, op. cit. 155, notes that the man is almost certainly identical with the Proculus, proconsul of *Hispania* (Baetica) on another inscription from Vettona, XI 5172. Even the latest of the known Proculi of the Julio-Claudian period, P. Sulpicius Scribonius Proculus (*cos.* before 56), ought to have held his military tribunate before 43. But Pflaum, *Les Fastes de la province de Narbonnaise* (1978) 59, allows for the possibility that our man was tribune of IX Hispana either in Pannonia or in Britain.

[1] See pp. 42 f. above.

[2] For further details on his family, see p. 42 above.

[1] Ritterling, *RE* 12. 2 (1925) 1731.

[2] Alföldy, *Legionslegaten* 6 f.

[3] Degrassi, *FC* 121.

[5] *RE* IX 214, Gades; *Inscr. It.* IV 107, Tibur. See *PIR*[2] C 1425. His son was *cos.* 90, Degrassi, *FC* 27.

60   Cn. Julius L. f. Ani. Agricola (*cos.* 77)

Tac. *Agr.* 5: see pp. 74 f. above.

T. Flavius T. f. Quir. Vespasianus (Titus) (*cos. ord.* 70 etc.)

Suet. *D. Tit.* 4. 1.

The future emperor's service as military tribune in Britain is recorded
only by Suetonius—Cassius Dio's story of his having saved his father's
life in Britain, in 47, is clearly a mistake,[1] since Titus was born on
30 December 39.[2] His tribunate ought to fall *c.*60. Hence it seems
possible that his transfer to Britain coincided with the dispatch of
2,000 legionaries, eight auxiliary cohorts, and 1,000 cavalry, to bring
the British army up to strength after the Boudiccan war.[3] In that case
Titus may have been attached to IX Hispana, commanded by Q. Petillius Cerialis, a kinsman, perhaps his brother-in-law.[4] He went on to hold
the quaestorship and to bè appointed legate of XV Apollinaris under his
father, at the outbreak of the Jewish war.[5]

L. Antistius L. f. Gal. Rusticus (*cos.* 90)

JRS 14 (1924) 180 = *AE* 1925. 126, Antioch (Pisidia): [*L. Antistio L. f.*] *Gal.
Rustico cos. / leg. imp. Caes.* [[*Domi/tiani*]] *Aug.* [4]/ *pro pr. provinciarum / Capp.
Galat. Ponti Pisid. / Paphl. Arm. min. Lyca. praef. / aer. Sat. procos. provinc. Hisp.*
[8]/ [*ul*]*t. Baetic. leg. divi Vesp. et divi Titi / et imp. Caesaris* [[*Domitiani*]] *Aug. /*
[[*Germanici*]] *leg. VIII Aug. cura/tori viarum Aureliae et Corne*[12]/*liae adlecto inter
praetorios / a divo Vespasiano et divo Tito / donis militaribus donato ab iisdem /
corona murali cor. vallari* [16]/ *corona aurea vexillis III / hastis puris III trib. mil. leg.
II / [A]ug. X vir. stlitibus iudicand. / [p]atrono coloniae quod [ind]ustrie pros-
pexit annon.*

Adlection to the senate in the grade of ex-praetor was no doubt this
man's reward for the part played by II Augusta in swinging Britain to
the Flavian side in the latter part of 69.[1] His decorations, appropriate
to an ex-praetor, were perhaps given to him after he had attained that

---

[1] Dio 60. 30. 1; see Eichholz, *Britannia* 3 (1972) 154 f. for possible explanations.
[2] *PIR*[2] F 399.
[3] Tac. *Ann.* 14. 38. 1, see A. R. Birley, in Levick (ed.), *The Ancient Historian and his
Materials* 140, 149 f.
[4] pp. 67 f. above.
[5] *PIR*[2] F 399.
[1] Tac. *Hist.* 3. 44. See E. Birley, *Britannia* 9 (1978) 243 ff.

rank. It is worth asking whether he may not have been acting commander of II Augusta in the absence of a legate.[2] After adlection he held four praetorian posts, as *curator viarum*, legate of VIII Augusta, from 79–81, proconsul of Baetica and prefect of the *aerarium Saturni*. After his consulship, in 90, he was governor of Cappadocia-Galatia, where he died *c*.93. He seems to have been of Spanish origin, and was a friend of the poet Martial, who commemorated his death.[3]

83   L. Roscius M. f. Quir. Aelianus Maecius Celer (*cos.* 100)

XIV 3612 = *ILS* 1025 = *Inscr. It.* IV 129, Tibur: *L. Roscio M. f. Qui. | Aeliano Maecio | Celeri* [4] *| cos. procos. provinc. | Africae pr. tr. pl. quaest. | Aug. Xvir. stlitib. iudic. | trib. mil. leg. IX Hispan.* [8] *| vexillarior. eiusdem | in expeditione Germanica | donato ab imp. Aug. | militarib. donis corona* [12] *| vallari et murali vexillis | argenteis II hastis puris II | salio | C. Vecilius C. f. Pal. Probus | amico optimo | L. d. s. c.*

EE IX 612, Lanuvium: [. . . *Xvi*]*r. stliti*[*b. iudic. trib. mil. | leg.*] *VIIII His*[*pan. vexillarior. | legio*]*nis eiusd*[*em in expeditione* [4] */ Ger*] *ṃạṇịc*[*a . . .*]

The German expedition to which Roscius Aelianus took detachments of IX Hispana was clearly Domitian's Chattan war of 83. He was consul in 100, presumably in his late thirties. E. Groag suggested that Aelianus' friend Vecilius Probus gave only a selection of posts on the Tibur inscription.[1] Otherwise it would certainly be curious that he held a relatively early consulship, with no appointments in the imperial service to his credit, after the military tribunate, under Domitian, Nerva, and Trajan, and that he had no consular offices until the proconsulship of Africa *c*.117. His origin is unknown, but a descendant was honoured at Emerita by the province of Lusitania, and he might well be a Spaniard.[2] The first *gentilicium* and filiation suggest the possibility that he was a son or adopted son of M. Roscius Coelius, legate of XX Valeria Victrix in 69; and he was clearly also linked to the *cos.* 101, M. Maecius Celer.[3]

[2] See p. 231 n. 3 (on Roscius Coelius) above, for the possibility that either IX Hispana or II Augusta may have been without a legate in 69. See further Alföldy, *Legionslegaten* 13 ff.

[3] Mart. 9. 30. See *PIR*[2] A 765, Alföldy, *Legionslegaten* 13 ff., Schumacher, *Priesterkollegien* 192 f. His wife Mummia Nigrina was from a family connected with the Spanish Valerii Vegeti (II 2074, 2077).

[1] Groag, *RE* 1A 1 (1914) 117 ff.

[2] See Alföldy, *Fasti Hispanienses* 148 and n. 104, followed by Eck, *Senatoren* 228 n. 487. Schumacher, *Priesterkollegien* 207 f., prefers North Italy.

[3] See p. 231 above, on Roscius Coelius. For Maecius Celer (origin unknown), see M. Fluss, *RE* 14.1 (1928) 234 f.

L. Ster[tinius Noricus(?)]

VIII 5355 + 17493 = *ILAlg*. I 282, Calama: *L. Ster[tinio ...] / Hor.* [.../...*l*] *eg.*
VIIII Hispa[nae ... ⁴/...a] t census [accipiendos ... /... pro] vinciae [.../...
di] vi Traiani [Parthici... /... ?pro] cos. [...⁸/...] *m[.../...pa] trono* [...]

The precise nomenclature and career set forth on this inscription from
Calama must remain uncertain. The last letter before the break in line 1
is an upright, and theoretically I, N, etc. are also possible restorations.
But given that the career belongs to the Trajanic period, Ster[tinius]
appears the most probable *gentilicium*,[1] and he may provisionally be
identified with the *cos.* 113, L. Stertinius Noricus[2]—which raises the
question whether *Nor[ico...]* might be a possible reading in line 2.
Since the mention of VIIII Hispana comes so soon after the name, it
looks as if a tribunate rather than a legateship must be restored. Since
the exact length of the original lines cannot be calculated, it is impossible to judge at what stage in his career he took part in a census, but it
is possible that he did so as military tribune in Britain. A census is
known to have taken place in this province late in the reign of Trajan,[3]
in which case he would have to be identified with one of the other L.
Stertinii from the early second century.[4] The remainder of his career
cannot be reconstructed on the basis of this inscription, and it would be
hazardous to make any firm suggestions about his *origo*.[5]

L. Burbuleius L. f. Quir. Optatus Ligarianus (*cos. c.* 135)

X 6006 = *ILS* 1066, Minturnae: *L. Burbuleio L. f. Quir. / Optato Ligariano / cos.*
sodal. Aug. leg. imperat. ⁴/ Antonini Aug. Pii pro pr. prov. / Syriae in quo honor.
decessit leg. / eiusdem et divi Hadriani pro pr. prov. / Cappad. cur. oper. locor. q.
publ. praef. ⁸/ aerar. Saturn. procos. Sicil. logiste / Syriae legat. leg. XVI Fl. firm.
cur. rei p. / Narbon. item Anconitanor. item / Tarricin. curat. viar. Clodiae Cassiae
¹²/ Ciminae pr. aed. pl. q. Ponti et Bithyn. / trib. laticl. leg. IX Hispan. IIIvir. kapit.
patr. col. / Rasinia Pietas nutr. filiar. eius / s. p. p. L. d. d. d.

---

[1] Groag, *RE* 3A 2 (1929) 2452 f., who was unaware of the *cos.* 113, suggested L. Stertinius
Avitus (*cos.* 92).

[2] E. Birley, *JRS* 52 (1962) 223, Syme *REA* 67 (1965) 344.

[3] *ILS* 1338, Fulginiae (p. 302 below).

[4] e.g. L. Stertinius Quintilianus cet., the *cos.* 146, whose principal names were (or became)
Q. Cornelius Proculus: *PIR²* C 1423. Note also the *cos.* 162, D. Fonteius Frontinianus L.
Stertinius Rufus: ibid. D 472; and see p. 255 above.

[5] Q. Cornelius Proculus (see previous note) was from Carteia in Baetica. But Stertinius is
common in Africa, rare elsewhere, and the tribe Horatia—if the reading in the inscription from
Calama be accepted—is found at Assuras and Uthina in that province, as well as at four towns in
Italy (and nowhere else): Kubitschek 139, 161, 271.

Burbuleius Optatus succeeded the historian Arrian as governor of Cappadocia in 137 at the earliest,[1] and was there at the time of Hadrian's death in 138. His consulship, succeeded by the curatorship of public works at Rome, was therefore held c.135. He had probably been military tribune in Britain at least twenty years earlier.[2] Starting as *IIIvir capitalis*, he had to work his passage before achieving the consulship, with no fewer than eight praetorian posts, suggesting that he might never have held a consular command but for the fact that Hadrian, in the closing years of his reign, had come to distrust many of his former friends.[3] Since his funerary inscription is at Minturnae, and he was patron of the colony, it is clear that he had a residence there, but as that place was enrolled in the Teretina tribe it cannot have been his home.[4] Although the very rare *gentilicium* is not found outside Italy, he may have been a provincial.[5]

L. Annius Fabianus (*cos.* 141?)

III 1455 = 7972, Sarmizegethusa: *L. Annio Fabiano / IIIviro capital. trib. / leg. II Aug. quaest. urban.* [4]/ *trib. pl. praetori / curatori viae Latinae / legat. leg. X Fretensis / leg. Aug. pr. pr. provinc. Dac.* [8]/ *col. Ulp. Traia*[n.] *Sar*[m.].

The legionary command cannot be earlier than the reign of Hadrian, when Judaea became a two-legion province and X Fretensis regained a separate legate instead of being commanded by the praetorian governor,[1] while a *terminus ante quem* is supplied by his post in Dacia, which must have preceded the creation of the consular province of the III Daciae in

---

[1] Eck, *Senatoren* 213 ff.

[2] His quaestorship of Pontus-Bithynia cannot have been held during the years when the younger Pliny and his friend Cornutus Tertullus governed that province as imperial legates. Eck, *Senatoren* 13 n. 59, aware of this point, assigns Burbuleius' quaestorship to the first years of Hadrian. But he might perhaps have been there before Pliny's arrival, during the first decade of the second century—indeed, had he served as quaestor to one of the errant proconsuls, it might have caused his career to stagnate for a good many years. On the date at which Pliny took over the province, see Syme, *Tacitus* 659 f., and for a different view, Sherwin-White, *Letters of Pliny* 80 f., whose arguments for an earlier date are shown to be weak by Schumacher, *Priesterkollegien* 296 f. Thus the years 111–14/15 may be ruled out.

[3] See pp. 104 f. above.

[4] Kubitschek 24.

[5] See p. 216 n. 4 above, on rare *gentilicia* in provinces. Quirina is found in Africa more frequently than elsewhere, see Kubitschek 271 f. for the list. Although Burbuleius is not found outside Italy, Ligarius (and Ligarianus) and Rasinius are well attested in Africa, while Optatus falls into a category especially favoured there, see Kajanto 75 f. See now Syme, *Historia* 27 (1978) 597, drawing attention to Q. Ligarius, legate to a proconsul of Africa in 50 BC, and suggesting possible African derivation for our man.

[1] Eck, *Senatoren* 17 f.

the 160s.[2] Hence there is no difficulty in identifying him with the Fabianus attested as consul early in the reign of Pius, probably in 141.[3] His tribunate in Britain may therefore be assigned to the early Hadrianic period, when Pompeius Falco was governor.[4] Although his nomenclature is very indistinctive, he may well have been a son or kinsman of the *eques Romanus* L. Annius C. f. Quir. Fabianus, of Caesarea in Mauretania.[5] The *cos. ord.* 201 of the same names was presumably his grandson.[6]

M. Pontius M. f. Pup. Laelianus Larcius Sabinus (*cos.* 144)

VI 1497 + 1549 = *ILS* 1094 + 1100, Rome: *M. Pontio M. f. Pup. | Laeliano Larcio Sabino cos. pon/tifici sodali Antoniniano Veriano* [4]*| fetiali leg. Aug. pr. pr. prov. Syriae leg. Aug. | pr. pr. prov. Pannon. super. leg. Aug. pr. pr. Pan/non. infer. comiti divi Veri Aug. donato donis | militarib. bello Armeniaco et Parthico* [8]*| ab imp. Antonino et a divo Vero Aug. | [coron.] mu[rali vallari clas]sica aur[ea | hast. puris IIII vexill. IIII comiti imp. Anto/n]ini Aug. et divi Veri bello Germanic.* [12]*| item comiti imp. Antonini Aug. Germanici Sar/matici leg. leg. I Miner. curatori civit. Araus. | prov. Galliae Narb. praetori trib. pleb. candidato | imp. divi Hadriani ab act. senat. quaestor. prov.* [16]*| Narb. trib. mil. leg. VI Victr. cum qua ex Germ. in/ Brittan. transiit IIIIvir. viar. curandar. | Huic senatus auctore M. Aurelio Antonino Aug. | Armeniac. Medic. Parthic. maximo Germ. Sarmat.* [20]*| statuam poni habitu civili in foro divi Traiani | pecunia publica censuit.*

Both stones are now lost, but there is really no question but that they provide the two halves of a single text. The only serious argument brought forward against this view is that a marshal of the eminence of Pontius Laelianus would not have been honoured by a statue in civilian dress.[1] But that is best explained by assuming that he had died out of harness. His consulship is assignable to 144,[2] just over twenty years after his service as military tribune of VI Victrix, *cum qua ex Germ. in Brittan. transiit,* an event which logically ought to have coincided with Platorius Nepos' transfer from Lower Germany to Britain in 122.[3] Nearly twenty years after his consulship he was described by Fronto as 'vir

[2] Stein, *Dazien* 41 ff.
[3] Alföldy, *Konsulat* 141 f.
[4] p. 99 above.
[5] Thus Alföldy, *Konsulat* 312, citing VIII 9374.
[6] *PIR*[2] A 644, a patrician.
[1] The point was noted by Ritterling, *RE* 12. 2 (1925) 1605 n. See Alföldy, *Legionslegaten* 28 f., and Schumacher, *Priesterkollegien* 24 f. The break comes at the end of line 10.
[2] Alföldy, *Konsulat* 147.
[3] p. 101 above. See also A. R. Birley, in Butler (ed.), *Soldier and Civilian in Roman Yorkshire* 81 f.

gravis et veteris disciplinae' in connection with his position on L. Verus' staff in the Parthian war.[4] His tribe, Pupinia, is found only in Italy,[5] with the single exception of Baeterrae in Narbonensis,[6] where he served twice, as quaestor and as *curator* of Arausio. It is therefore possible that his home was there, as G. Alföldy suggests,[7] although Italian origin is slightly more likely.[8]

(?) Q. Licinius Q. f. Silvanus Granianus Quadronius Proculus

II 4609 = *ILS* 1028, Baetulo: *Q. Licinio / Q. f. Silvano / Graniano* [4]/ *Quadronio / Proculo III/viro ad mo/netam trib.* [8]/ *mil. leg. VI Vict. / p. f. d. d.*

This man appears to be the son of the *cos.* 106, Q. Licinius Silvanus Granianus.[1] The son of the latter's consular colleague L. Minicius Natalis was military tribune at the end of the reign of Trajan,[2] and hence it cannot be excluded that the younger Granianus was tribune in the 120s, after VI Victrix had moved to Britain. It should be noted that two of his kinsmen commanded the legion at that time, the first the polyonymous senator from Tarraco whose names included Grani[us] , the second the younger Natalis, already mentioned, whose names included Quadronius, from Barcino.[3]

L. Aemilius L. f. Cam. Karus (*cos.* 144?)

VI 1333 = *ILS* 1077, Rome: *L. Aemilio L. f. Cam. Karo co*[s.] *| leg. Aug. pr. pr. provinicae Cappadociae | leg. Aug. pr. pr. censitori provinciae Lugdunensis* [4]/ *leg. Aug. pr. pr. provinciae Arabiae | curatori viae Flaminiae leg. leg. XXX U.V. | praet. trib. pleb. quaest. Aug. trib. militum leg. VIII Aug.* [8]/ *trib. militum leg. VIIII*

---

[4] Fronto, *ad Verum imp.* 2. 1. 19 = Haines II 148.

[5] Kubitschek 271, lists only Forobrentani, Sassina, Tergeste, and Laus.

[6] Kubitschek 207.

[7] Alföldy, *Legionslegaten* 28 f.

[8] Schumacher, *Priesterkollegien* 241 f. Alföldy, *Konsulat* 312 and n. 97, maintains his previous view. However, caution is required, since no Pontii, Larcii, or Laelii are on record at Baeterrae. Our man's grandfather was probably the Pontius Laelianus, friend of the (so-called) 'testator Dasumius' (VI 10229). Larcia Sabina, owner of a small brickworks under Hadrian (XV 123-6), may be his mother. Tiles with his name have been found in Umbria (XI 6689, 190), where he presumably had an estate. For his son, *cos. ord.* 163, and later members of the family, see Hanslik, *RE* 22. 1 (1953) 39 f., 43 f.

[1] Pflaum, in *Les Empereurs romains d'Espagne* 90, followed by L. Petersen in *PIR*[2] L 249. The honorand of *ILS* 1028 was previously identified with the *cos.* 106 himself; thus Dessau, ad loc. I owe to G. Alföldy the revised reading of the last two lines.

[2] p. 245 above.

[3] pp. 240 f., 245 f. above.

Hispanae / Xviro stlitib. iudic. / sodali Flaviali XVviro s. f. / C. Iulius Erucianus Crispus praef. [12] */ alae primae Ulpiae Dacorum / amico optimo*

L. Aemilius Carus was governor of Arabia in April 143 and his consulship may be assigned with a strong degree of probability to 144.[1] His earlier posts may be assumed to have been approximately contemporary with those of M. Pontius Laelianus, also consul in 144, who was tribune of VI Victrix in 122.[2] If the order of his two tribunates is descending, as is the remainder of the *cursus*, he may have left IX Hispana in 122, when Platorius Nepos came to Britain.[3] It should, however, be recalled that IX Hispana may have been stationed outside Britain by the 120s.[4] His tribe, Camilia, is found only in Italy,[5] but circumstantial evidence suggests that his family may have migrated to Syria.[6] The man of the same names who was consular governor of the III Daciae in the 170s was no doubt his son.[7]

(?) Q. Fuficius Cornutus (*cos.* 147)

ILS 8975 = Alföldy, *Fasti Hispanienses* 81 ff., ager Histonii: [*Q. Fufi*] *cio Cornu* [*to cos. / sodali Titia*] *li Flaviali leg. Aug. pr.* [*pr. prov. Pann. inf. / leg. leg. . . .*] *quae est in Moesia* [*. . . leg. Aug.* [4] */ iurid. per As*] *tyriam et Callaecia* [*m praetori can/didato tri*] *b. pleb. candidato* [*quaest. . . . trib. / mil. leg. . . . d*] *onis militarib.* [*donato a divo Had/riano coron.*] *murali vexillo a* [*rgenteo leg. pr. pr.* [8] */ Antonini Au*] *g. Pii provinciae M* [*oesiae inferior. / l.*] *d. d.* [*d.*]

Q. Fuficius Cornutus is known to have been governor of Pannonia inferior in 145 and consul in 147. The dating of his earlier career can only be inferred from this information, but since, after the republican magistracies, he seems only to have held the posts of legionary legate in Moesia (probably Upper)[1] and *iuridicus* in Spain, it seems improbable that the military service, presumably as legionary tribune, for which he was decorated, could have been held as early as the Parthian war of Trajan. On the other hand, the Jewish war under Hadrian, 132–5, seems rather too late in date to allow for him to have been through the three

---

[1] Alföldy, *Konsulat* 147 f. See also *PIR*[2] A 338, for the spelling of the *cognomen*, elsewhere Carus, Karus only in this inscription (but Groag amalgamates the two L. Aemilii Cari; see n. 7 below, for the son).

[2] p. 273 above.

[3] p. 101 above.

[4] pp. 220 ff. above.

[5] Kubitschek 270.

[6] Thus Schumacher, *Priesterkollegien* 247 f., 262, approved by Alföldy, *Konsulat* 319 n. 156.

[7] Stein, *Dazien* 44 ff.

[1] Thus Alföldy, op. cit. 83 n. 75; see also p. 29 above.

magistracies at Rome, and three posts in the imperial service, before his consulship in 147. G. Alföldy therefore proposes that he may have gained his *dona* for service in another war under Hadrian, either in Britain or in the east.[2] The case must remain rather uncertain.[3]

[C. Fabius C. f. Vot. Agri] ppi [nus]   (*cos.* 148)

XIV 4129, Ostia: [*C. Fabio C. f. Vot. Agri*]*ppi*[*no* / *IIIIvir. vi*]*ar. cur*[*andar.* / *trib. mil. le*]*g. II Augu*[*stae* . . .]

There seems little reason to doubt J. Morris's identification[1] of the senator in this fragmentary inscription with C. Fabius Agrippinus, member of a well-known Ostian family.[2] It must remain slightly uncertain whether he is the *cos.* 148, previously governor of Thrace,[3] or the Fabius Agrippinus mentioned by Cassius Dio as governor of Syria Coele in 218 or 219,[4] or from an intervening generation. But it seems probable that he is the same as the honorand of another fragmentary *cursus* inscription from Ostia: *C. Fabio* [. . .]/ *praetori*[. . .]/ *provin*[. . .] [4]/ *pr. trib. p*[*l.?* . . . *IIIIvir./ v*]*iaru*[*m curand.* . . .].[5] If he is the *cos.* 148, his tribunate in Britain presumably fell in the late 120s.

L. Novius Crispinus Martialis Saturninus (*cos.* 150?)

VIII 2747 = *ILS* 1070 + *add.*, Lambaesis: *L. Novio Crispino* / *Martiali Saturnino* / *cos. desig. leg. Aug. pr. pr.* [4]/ *provinciae Africae procos. Galliae* / *Narbonensis leg. Aug. leg. I Italicae* / *leg. Aug. iuridico Astyriae et Callaeciae* / *praetori trib. pleb. quaestori pro praet.* [8]/ *provinciae Macedoniae trib. mil.* / *leg. VIIII Hisp. IIIIviro viarum* / *curandarum seviro eq. Romanorum* / *veterani* ⟦*leg. III*⟧ *Aug.* [12]/ *qui militare coeperunt Glabrione* / *et Torquato item Asiatico II et Aquilino cos.*

This inscription belongs to the year 149 or 150, since the veterans who erected it were enrolled in 124 and 125, and as Crispinus is also referred

---

[2] Alföldy, op. cit. 83; id., *Konsulat* 351 ff., with some refinements to the dating of the praetorian career.

[3] There do not seem to be any other certain cases of *dona* for a British or eastern (other than Jewish) war under Hadrian. That emperor was notably ungenerous with *dona* for the Jewish war, cf. pp. 113, 125 n. 4 above.

[1] Morris, thesis F 2.

[2] *PIR*[2] F 20.

[3] See now Alföldy, *Konsulat* 152, 258.

[4] Dio 79. 3. 4.

[5] *AE* 1955. 174, variously interpreted in *PIR*[2] F 20, where Groag prefers to read, from line 2, *praetori* [*tribuno plebis? legato pr. pr.*] *provin*[*ciae* . . .] *quaestori prov. Cy*]*pr. tribuno* [*militum legionis* . . . *IIIIviro v*]*iar*[*um curandarum*].

to as consul designate in another inscription, of 149, it is clear that he was consul in one of those years, probably 150.[1] Although his career shows no signs of undue retardation, with only four posts between praetorship and consulship, it appears from the careers of two other senators of the period who were also *iuridici* in Spain, that he cannot have held that post later than the last years of Hadrian, and hence must have been praetor *c.*135.[2] His tribunate of IX Hispana may thus be assigned to the mid-120s.[3] Several senatorial Novii are known in this period, but there is no particular reason to connect our man with any of them.[4] He seems to have owned property near the *via Labicana* close to Tusculum;[5] but this need not have been his original home. His daughter married Q. Antistius Adventus, who was to be governor of Britain in the 170s.[6]

(?) Q. Camurius Lem. Numisius Junior (*cos.* 161?)

XI 5670, Attidium: see p. 255 above.

(?) Ignotus *RIB* 1132

RIB 1132, Corbridge: for the text, see p. 118 above.

This tribune of VI Victrix is more likely to have been *angusticlavius*, but must be included here as a possible *laticlavius* for the sake of completeness. Only the *praenomen* L. is certain. The *nomen* could have begun either with C or O, to judge from the surviving portion of the letter.[1] He must be assigned to the second half of the 150s, in view of the dating of Julius Verus' governorship.[2]

---

[1] Alföldy, *Konsulat* 156 f.
[2] Ibid. 351 ff.
[3] On the movements of IX Hispana at this period, see pp. 220 ff. above.
[4] See Groag, *RE* 17. 1 (1936) 1216 ff.
[5] *EE* IX 704 = (*CIL*) XV 7843.
[6] p. 130 above.
[1] Known senators with *praenomen* L. whose *nomen* began with C are fairly numerous, even when the search is confined to the latter second century. One may note L. Octavius Felix (VI 35199, XV 7503) and L. Ovinius Rusticus Cornelianus (II 4126, *AE* 1935. 21). Q is also a possible reading, but no senators with names beginning with this letter seem to have the *praenomen* L. in this period.
[2] pp. 119 f. above.

P. Septimius P. f. Quir. Geta (*cos. a. inc.*, *II ord. 203*)

Epigraphica 4 (1942) 105 ff. = *AE* 1946. 131 = *IRT* 541, Lepcis Magna: *P. Septimio Getae c. v. X/vir. stlitibus iudican/dis trib. latic. leg. II Aug.* [4]/ *quaest. provin. Cretae et / Cyrenarum aed. cereali / curatori rei pub. Anconita/norum praet. hastario et tu*[8]/*telar. sacerdoti fetiali leg. / leg. I Italicae procos. Siliciae / les.* (sic) *Augg* ⟦*g*⟧ *pr. pr. provinciae / Lusitaniae cos. leg. Augg* ⟦*g*⟧ [12]/ *pr. pr. provinciae Mysiae inferioris leg. Au* [*ggg. p*]*r. pr. / provinc. Daciarum / curia Dacica ex voto pos.*

This is the brother of the emperor Severus. There is no evidence which of the two was the elder, but *a priori*, at least, Geta is more likely to have been the first-born, since he was named after their father. Severus was consul in 190, hence, on this assumption, Geta probably held the *fasces* a year or two earlier. Thus by dead reckoning his tribunate of II Augusta should be assignable to the late 160s. Apart from the offices listed on this inscription, he held a second consulship in 203.[1]

C. Memmius C. f. Quir. Fidus Julius Albius (*cos. a. inc.*)

VIII 12442 = *ILS* 1110, Vina: *C. Memmio C. f. Quir. / Fido Iulio Albio cons. sodali / Titio leg. Aug. pr. pr. prov. Noricae cur.* [4]/ *viae Flam. praef. Minic. procos. provin. / Baetic. leg. Aug. leg. VII Claudiae iuridico per / Italiam reg. Transpadanae praetori leg. / pr. pr. prov. Afric. aedil. Cerial. q. prov.* [8]/ *Asiae trib. laticl. leg. II Augustae / C. Annius Iulius Secundus* ⟦*et . . ./ . . .*⟧ *amico rarissimo ob eximiam eius er/ga se benivolentiam sua pec. posuer. et d.* [12]/ *d. d.*

Memmius Fidus was consul designate on 18 September 191[1] and his consulship may thus be assigned to that year or to 192, while his position as legate to the proconsul of Africa is also dated, to 175 or 176.[2] Since he held that appointment after the aedileship, his tribunate of II Augusta may be assumed with confidence to have fallen *c.*170.[3] No post in the vigintivirate is mentioned; it may have been omitted in error, but it is possible that the disturbed conditions of the period resulted in his exemption, to permit him to go more rapidly to his legion.[4] A fragmentary inscription from Bulla Regia, his home, shows that he went on to govern a consular province, evidently one of those on the Rhine or Danube, since it was either [*superio*]*ris* or [*inferio*]*ris*.[5]

---

[1] See A. R. Birley, *Bonner Jahrb.* 169 (1969) 261 ff., for discussion. The tribe Quirina may be supplied from the *tabula Banasitana*, see A. R. Birley, *H-A-C 1972-/4* (1976) 63 f.

[1] *ILS* 9082, Lauriacum.

[2] VIII 11928.

[3] See p. 258 above, for a legate of that legion at about this time, perhaps a kinsman.

[4] On the vigintivirate, see p. 5 above.

[5] Groag, *RE* 15. 1 (1931) 623, on VIII 25527. Ritterling, *FRD* 88, suggested that Fidus

M. Accenna M. f. Gal. Helvius Agrippa

II 1262, Hispalis: *M. Accenna M. f. Gal. Helvius | Agrippa praetorius trib. | pleb. leg. provinciae Africae dioecesis [4]/ Carthaginensium item quaesto/ri provinciae Africae IIIviro ca/pitali trib. laticl. Syriae leg. XVI Fla. | item trib. laticl. Brittanniae leg. XX [8]/ Val. Victricis curio minor vixit an/nis XXXIIII mensibus tribus dieb. XXIII | M. Accenna Helvius Agrippa [fil.] patri dul. f.*

The precise details of age at death smack of the second century rather than the first, as do the naming of the African diocese in which he was proconsular legate and the description of his military tribunate as *laticl.*[1] If the order of posts is descending throughout, he transferred to XVI Flavia in Syria from XX Valeria Victrix in Britain. No known governor of Britain proceeded direct to Syria, although L. Alfenus Senecio may have gone straight to Britain from Syria Coele in the first decade of the third century.[2] This senator is otherwise unknown, but several kinsmen are attested, including L. Helvius Agrippa, proconsul of Sardinia in 67–67-8[3] and M. Accenna L. f. Gal. Saturninus, proconsul of Baetica, who is known from an inscription at Tibur.[4] There seems no doubt that the family was from Spain, presumably from Hispalis.[5]

L. Aemilius L. f. Gal. Naso Fabullinus

VI 29683: *L. Aemilio | L. f. Gal. | Nasoni Fabullino [4]/ tribuno laticlavio | leg. XX V. V. | triumviro capitali | d. d. publice*

VI 29684 = XI 4083, Ocriculum: *L. Aemilio | L. f. Gal. Naso/ni Fabulli[4]/no trib. lat. | leg. XX Val. | Vict. IIIvir. capit. | d. d. publ.*

Ocriculum was enrolled in Arnensis, not Galeria,[1] so that it cannot have been his place of origin. Elements of his nomenclature occur further north in Italy, an Aemilius Naso at Milan and a Fabulla and a Naso at Verona.[2] But his tribe Galeria is found only at Genua in the Cisalpine

was the *ignotus* of VI 1546; but other candidates have been proposed, and see now Alföldy, *Konsulat* 361 ff.

[1] Ritterling, *RE* 12. 2 (1925) 1765 f., noted that XVI Flavia was not in Syria before Hadrian; he assigns this man's service to the reign of Pius, but gives no reasons.

[2] p. 159 above.

[3] *PIR*[2] H 64.

[4] *Inscr. It.* IV 97. See Alföldy, *Fasti Hispanienses* 171; see also ibid. 66 n. 321 for another senatorial member of the family (II 3108, cf. p. 944, near Madrid).

[5] M. Helvius M. f. M. n. Serg. Agrippa, who was given a public funeral by the *civitas Hispalensium* (II 1184) is an obvious connection, as noted in *PIR*[2] H 64. Presumably the Helvii were in Sergia and the Accennae in Galeria: both tribes are found at Hispalis, Kubitschek 174 f.

[1] Kubitschek, 74.

[2] V 5837, 3441, 3341 (the last a senator of first-century date, *trib. Pub.*).

region, whereas it is very common in Spain.³ His second *cognomen* Fabullinus is otherwise unattested,⁴ but Fabullus, from which it derives, itself fairly rare, is found in several parts of Spain,⁵ where Aemilius is one of the commonest *gentilicia*. It is therefore not improbable that he derived from the Iberian peninsula.

M. Caelius Flavius Proculus

XI 3883, Capena: *d. m. / M. Caeli Flavi Proculi / Xviri stlitibus iudicandis ⁴/ tribuni laticlavi leg. XX V. V. / VIvir. turmae equitum Romanor. / quaestoris tribuni plebis / candidati praetoris candidati ⁸/ curatoris rei publicae / Aquinatium*

This inscription is probably later than the time of Hadrian, since it does not name the emperor under whom the man was *candidatus*.¹ In that case it is not very likely that he was the Flavius Proculus, apparently an office-holder, to whom Hadrian addressed a rescript,² but he could be a descendant of that man, and one should also note the litigious *eques Romanus* of the same names under Claudius.³ E. Groag assumed that the third name was Flavus,⁴ but, although this is perfectly possible, the other genitives, *Caeli* and *laticlavi*, make it natural to suppose that the genitive of Flavius was intended. Although he was buried at Capena, there is no need to assume that this was his original home; but his names are rather too common to allow much scope for tracing kinsmen. Still, for the record one should note the legate of VI Victrix, L. Junius Victorinus Flavius Caelianus,⁵ the Severan couple of senatorial rank at Thamugadi, P. Fl. Pomponianus Pudens and Caelia Procilla,⁶ and Q. Caelius Flavianus, patron of Canusium in 223.⁷

(Rubrenus)

R. Stillwell (ed.), *Antioch on the Orontes. The Excavations of 1935–36* (1938)

---

³ Kubitschek 103, cf. his list, 270 f.

⁴ Kajanto 170.

⁵ Groag, *RE* 6. 2 (1909) 1770, on M. Fabius Fabullus, citing eight Spanish examples of that combination of *nomen* and *cognomen*. One might add II 3329, L. Postumius Fabullus. Kajanto 170, knows only twenty-two Fabulli/Fabullae.

¹ Barbieri, *L'Albo* 3 f. He includes our man as no. 673, not later than the early third century because of the sevirate and tribunate of the plebs.

² *Digest* 49. 14. 3. 9.

³ Pliny, *HN* 33. 33.

⁴ *PIR*² C 133.

⁵ p. 254 above.

⁶ *PIR*² C 146, F 346, Barbieri, *L'Albo* no. 240 + *Agg.*

⁷ *PIR*² C 338.

150, no. 61 = *AE* 1938. 177, Antioch (Syria): [. . . *praef. frumenti*] *dandi p* [*r*] *ae-* [*tori/ t*] *r. pleb. quaestori u* [*rb/a*] *no trib. milit. leg. II Au* [*g.* [4]/ *X*] *viro stlitib. iudicand* [*is* / *Ar*] *ria Magia Secundil* [*la* / *u*] *xor et M. Rubrenus Ma* [*g/i*] *anus filius fecerun.* / *v.*

This man may be assumed with some confidence to have been a Rub-renus in view of the nomenclature of his son. The third century patrician M. Rubrenus Virius Priscus Pomponianus Magianus Proculus, who held the consulship and the proconsulship of Africa,[1] could be identical with the son, but it seems preferable to regard him as a member of a later generation. However this may be, the patrician Rubrenus was described as *civis et patronus* at Atina,[2] which must be regarded as the *origo* of this family.[3] Our man's presence at Antioch suggests that he was holding office in Syria, either as legate of IV Scythica or as consu-lar governor. On the other hand, it should be noted that the compara-tively rare *nomen* Magius is fairly common at the colony of Berytus in that province, and it may be that the Rubreni were at Antioch in a private capacity. But neither hypothesis gives any assistance over the dating of this career, which remains uncertain.

L. Vettius L. f. Stel. Statura

XI 6054, Urvinum Mataurense: *L. Vettio L. f. Stel. Staturae* / [*X*] *vir. stlit. iudic. trib.* / *milit. leg. II Aug. quaestori* [4]/ *provinc. Narbonensis* / *trib. praetori IIIIvir.* / *quinq. i. d. patrono mu/nicipi decuriones ex*[8]/*aere conlato ob plenis/sima merita eius quod* / *primus omnium cum quin/quennalis esset annuum se* [12]/ *epulum municipibus suis* / *daturum pollicitus est*

The inscription makes it clear that Urvinum was this man's home, and his tribe Stellatina is the appropriate one for that community.[1] But he is otherwise unknown and there is no specific evidence for dating his career.

---

[1] Barbieri, *L'Albo* no. 2091, regards him as the son of our man.

[2] *ILS* 1197.

[3] Schumacher, *Priesterkollegien* 215 f., suggests a link with Q. Virius Egnatius Sulpicius Priscus, ibid. 38, a senator of the Severan period. This is possible, but not definite. Equally, it is hard to see just what link there should be between the polyonymous patrician Rubrenus and the Verona landowner P. Pomponius Cornelianus and his wife Julia Magia (V 3243–4, 3318, cf. 3106), ibid., since the Rubreni manifestly acquired the *cognomen* Magianus from our man's wife [*Ar*] ria Magia Secundil[la]. P. Pomponius Magianus, recorded at Puteoli (X 8180), might be a son of the Verona couple (and could be the governor of Thrace in the early 240s, Barbieri, *L'Albo* no. 1700).

[1] Kubitschek 78 f. It may be noted further that Kajanto (365) knows only two other bearers of the *cognomen* Statura, XI 5992, the Trajanic centurion L. Aconius L. f. Clu. Statura and his homonymous son from nearby Tifernum Mataurense.

An. Satrius Lem. Sal[---]

XI 6165, Suasa: *An. Satr* [*io . . .f.*] / *Lem. Sal* [. . .] / *Xvir. stlit. i* [*udic.*] [4]/ *trib. leg. XX V.* [*V.*] / *q. urb. q. prov.* [. . .] / *trib. pl. pr. de* [*sig.*] / *patrono mun* [*icipi*]

There is nothing closely datable in this inscription. The double quaestorship can be paralleled by more than half a dozen cases:[1] it must be assumed that the occasion for it must normally have been the death of one of the provincial quaestors during the interval between election and the start of the proconsular year.[2] This person's nomenclature requires some discussion. The first two letters appear to be an abbreviation for An(nius), here used as a *praenomen*, as in a few other inscriptions in Italy.[3] Of the various *gentilicia* beginning with the letters Satr--,[4] only Satrius is at all common, and this restoration is supported by an inscription from Sentinum set up by Satria An. f. Vera,[5] especially as Sentinum was enrolled in the Lemonia tribe,[6] as was our man—and several other Satrii are also recorded there.[7] Suasa, on the other hand, was in the Camilia,[8] so that Satrius, although patron of the town, was not a native. It seems probable that he came from Sentinum, also in *regio* VI. There are numerous possible *cognomina* beginning Sal..., of which only Salvius and Salvianus are found at all frequently.[9]

Ignotus XIV 182

XIV 182, Ostia: [. . .*viocu*]*ro tr* [*ib. mil.* / *le*]*g. II Augu* [*st. . . c*]*urat* [*ori?* [4]/ . . .] *c* [. . .]

The first two letters of this fragmentary inscription may be the end of

---

[1] L. Aquillius Florus *cet.* (*PIR²* A 993); Q. Gavius Fulvius Tranquillus (ibid. G 102); Q. Petronius Melior (Barbieri, *L'Albo* no. 1126); Cn. Pompeius Ant. Amoenas (*Forschungen in Ephesos* III p. 125, no. 8); [V]alerius Claud. Acilius Priscilianus (Barbieri, *L'Albo* no. 1173 + *agg.*); L. Septimius Severus (*HA Sev.* 2. 2-3); and perhaps P. Flavonius Paulinus (*PIR²* F 448).

[2] See Mommsen, *Staatsrecht* II³ 258.

[3] See Schulze 519 with n. 1.

[4] Schulze lists Satrenus, Satricanius, Satridius, Satrinius, etc., of which only Satrius is common. For senators of that name, see Groag, *RE* 2A 1 (1921) 190 f., Eck, *RE* Supp. 14 (1974) 656.

[5] XI 5761, mother of a *IIIIvir quinquennalis.*

[6] Kubitschek 75.

[7] XI 5782, 5749 (four numbers of a *collegium centonariorum*).

[8] Kubitschek 77.

[9] Schulze 93; Kajanto 177. Note also XI 833, Salvius Satrianus Minicius, senatorial patron of Suasa, and *curator* of Ocriculum and Blera. None of these communities were in the Lemonia, Kubitschek, 74, 77, 81. (In the commentary to XI 833 it is recalled that L. Minucius Basilus, one of Caesar's murderers, was M. Satrius before his adoption, and was perhaps an ancestor of the *curator*).

the word [*viocu*]*ro*, occasionally found in place of the more usual *IIIIviro viarum curandarum.*[1] In that case, there would be no doubt that this is the remains of a senatorial *cursus* inscription. It is, however, not absolutely certain that it is in ascending order, given that the military tribunate could precede as well as follow a post in the viginti-virate.[2] If it was ascending, it would be unusual to find a curatorship so early in the career,[3] and it may be that *q.* should be restored at the end of line 3—in which case, the post concerned could have been that of *curator actorum senatus* (normally referred to as *ab actis senatus*).[4]

Ignotus VI 31780

VI 31780, Rome: [. . .]*ṇṭium* [. . .] / *praet. candid.* [*Aug. quaest.*] / *candid. Aug.* [*trib. miL*] [4]/ *leg. VI Victr. p.* [*f. IIIvir.*] / *a. a. a. f. f. sevir.* [*eq. Rom. . . .*] / *sidii Masc*[. . .] / *filius ÇĮĮ*[. . .]

The first surviving line of this inscription mentions what seems to have been the curatorship of a town, the citizens of which were named in the genitive plural. There follows, in descending order, a patrician career, in which the senator proceeded direct from quaestorship to praetorship.[1] The term *candidatus Augusti*, not naming the emperor concerned, excludes a date earlier than the Hadrianic period.[2] As normal with patricians, the man's first post was as mint-master. This is the only certain instance of a patrician *tribunus laticlavius* serving in Britain. It is all the more unfortunate that his name is not recover-able.[3]

---

[1] See Pflaum, *J. des Savants* 1962. 117 f., on VI 1529, where he follows Borghesi in reading [*vioc*]*uro*, citing *AE* 1927. 173, *ILS* 8842, Keil and Premerstein, *Denkschr. Ak. Wien* 57 (1914) 92, 129, *Forschungen in Ephesos* III (1932) 165, 84–5, for Greek specimens (βιό-κουρος etc.) and *ILS* 6290, 6529, for *viocurus* and *vioc.* in municipal careers. Add now *Karthago* 11 (1961) 6 ff.: [. . . *Kar*]*thag. praet. trib. pL quaest. prov. Baeticae viocuro* etc.

[2] p. 8 above.

[3] p. 17 above.

[4] See *ILS* 1032 (L. Neratius Marcellus, p. 87 above).

[1] p. 14 above.

[2] See p. 13 and n. 15 above.

[3] It is hard to see what the last two lines mean, but [. . .]*sidii Masc*[. . .] *filius ÇĮĮ*[. . .] might be interpreted as 'the [. . .]*sidii, Masc*[. . .], the son, *ÇĮĮ*[. . ., the daughter]'. No sena-torial bearers of the various *cognomina* beginning *Masc.* . ., e.g. Mascellinus, Mascellio, Mascli-anus, Masculinus, seem to be known. Of the fairly numerous *gentilicia* ending *-sidius*, none is very common, and only Hosidius and Tusidius are attested for second-century senatorial families. The Mussidii are not recorded after the Augustan age (M. Fluss, *RE* 16. 1 (1933) 900 f.).

Ignotus X 525

X 525, Salernum: [. . .] / *pr. aed. cer. q. provinc.* / *C*[*y*]*pri pro pr.* [4] / *trib. mil. leg. II August.* / *IIIvir.* [*sic*] *viar. curand.* / *patrono col.* / *d. d. p.*

There appears to be no possibility either of dating this career or of identifying the man honoured. All that can be said is that by a mason's error *IIIvir.* is given instead of *IIIIvir.*

(?) [--] Julius T. f. Insteius Paulinus

XIV 2926, Praeneste: [. . .*I*]*ulio T. f. P*[*up.* (?) / *In*]*steio Pauli*[*no* / *IIIvir.*] *capital. trib.* [*mil.*] [4] / *leg.* [?*I*]*I Aug. quaest.* [. . .]

In *CIL*, the legion's number is restored as [*II*]*I*, but [*I*]*I* seems equally possible. E. Ritterling provisionally accepted the reading [VII]I,[1] but that seems to be too long. The man is otherwise unknown, but ought to be connected with Q. Insteius T. f. Pup. . . ., who was honoured by the town at Praeneste, together with his family. Part of this man's career is recorded: [. . .*tr*]*ib. pleb. pr. cos. leg. consularis prov*[. . .], but there is no indication of date.[2] Other Insteii were connected with Africa;[3] one of them was enrolled in the Horatia, but his daughter's name Praenestina suggests some connection with our man.[4] The Insteii continued to provide senators as late as the end of the fourth century.[5]

II.10

INCERTI

MEN WHO MAY HAVE SERVED AS LEGATE OR AS *TRIBUNUS LATICLAVIUS* IN A BRITISH LEGION

1. XIV 3518, Castelmadama: [. . .*leg. leg.* . . .] *tricis leg. leg. XI Claud. sodal. Titi*[*o* / *pr. trib. plebi*]*s quaest. urb. qui vix. annis X*[. . ./ . . .]*iani C*[. . .]

Either [*VI Vic*]*tricis* or [*XX Valeriae Vic*]*tricis* could be restored in

[1] Ritterling, *FRD* 141.

[2] XIV 2924, see *PIR*[2] I 29.

[3] See Alföldy, *Konsulat* 316 n. 127, on the *cos.* 162, M. Insteius Bithynicus, buried in Africa (*PIR*[2] I 30), as was Insteius Tertullus (ibid. 35).

[4] VI 1429 = 31652: he and his wife and daughter were honoured by Faustinus, *servus actor arkarius ex Africa*. The tribe Horatia is found in Africa: Kubitschek 139, 161.

[5] *PLRE* I 883 f.

line 1 of this inscription. But [*XXX Ulpiae Vic*]*tricis* and [*I* or *II Adiu*]*tricis* or even [*XIV Geminae Martiae Vic*]*tricis* are all equally possible.

2.*EE* IX 772 + 774 = Kolbe, *Chiron* 2 (1972) 405 ff.: see under *iuridici*, p. 217 above, for text and discussion.

3. *Bull. Dalm.* 37 (1914) 42 = Alföldy, *Ep. Stud.* 5 (1968) 137 n. 246 Salona: [. . .] / C[. . .] / SE[. . .] / VAL[. . .*con*] /*suli* [. . .] / P. SVP[. . ./*pat*[*rono* . . .]

See p. 259 above, for discussion of the suggestion that this inscription refers to L. Cestius Gallus cet., legate of XX Valeria Victrix. Unfortunately, it is not even certain that the stone refers to the legion, for VAL could be, e.g. [*cur. viae*] *Val*[*eriae*].

4. *Britannia* 1 (1970) 305 f. = *AE* 1971. 213, Caerleon:
(a) [. . .] G/[. . .] VM/[. . .] *et*⁴/ [. . .*A*] *ugg.* /[. . . *a so*] *lo* /[*restituit*(?)] Ṭ. EṢ[.]
(b) [. . .] N[. . .] / [*l*] *eg. A*{*ugg.*] / [.] RPḌ[.]

This inscription is unfortunately much too fragmentary for it to be certain whether a governor, [*l*] *eg. A* [*ugg. p*] *r*(*o*) *p*(*raetore*), or a legionary legate and *pr*(*imus*) *p*(*ilus*), were named. The former seems much more likely. See pp. 202 f. above, for a discussion.

5.   Ignotus *EE* VII 1267

XIV 4059 = *EE* VII 1267, Fidenae: [. . . *leg.*] XX Valeriae [*Victricis*/ . . .] *nares ex pr*[. . .] / *patr*[*ono*]

The restoration of line 2 offered in *EE* must be regarded as highly conjectural: [*Reü Apolli*] *nares ex pr*[*ovincia Narbonensis*]. Unfortunately there is no real indication what rank the honorand held in XX Valeria Victrix, but, if the inscription gave his career in descending order, a tribunate would have been mentioned last. But the possibility must not be excluded that it was in ascending order, with a legionary legateship the highest position held. At all events, the man was clearly being honoured by a community of which he was the patron, and may well have been of senatorial rank.

6.   Ignotus VI 37083

VI 37083, Rome: [. . .*Bit*] *hynia*[. . ./. . .] *iae Vict*[*ricis* . . ./. . .] *ioniu*[. . .]

One of the four legions with the title Victrix, VI, XIV Gemina Martia, XX Valeria, or XXX Ulpia, appears to be referred to in line 2. Either a tribune or a legate is equally possible.

7.   Ignotus *Corinth* VIII. 2, 64

Corinth VIII. 2. 64, Corinth: [. . .?*legi*]*on. II* [. . ./. . .]*es. pro*[. . ./. . .]*r. et* [. . . [4] / . . .]*at*[. . .]

This inscription is far too fragmentary to make any restoration at all certain.[1] Even [. . .*legi*]*on.* in line 1 can only be regarded as probable, for [. . .*expediti*]*on. II.* [. . .] cannot be excluded. But if a legion is in question, its number is certainly *II*, rather than *II*[*I*] or *II*[*II*], since there is a clear stop after the second upright. But II Augusta, II Adiutrix, and even II Traiana—for the inscription might refer to an equestrian career—are all possible. Equally, there is no way of determining whether a tribunate or legateship should be restored.

8.   Ignotus *ILAfr.* 324

AE 1909. 22 = *ILS* 8980 = *ILAfr.* 324, Sidi-Bou-Arkoub, near Vina: [. . . (?)*consuli ordin*]*ario a sena*[*tu* . . ./ *leg. Aug. pr. pr. prov. Aqui*]*tanicae sace*[*rdoti fetiali*(?) / *sodali Antoninia*]*no leg. leg. VII*[. . . [4] / *curatori viae Labica*]*nae et Latinae ve*[*teris / procos. prov. Sic*]*iliae praetori tribu*[*no plebis quaest.* / *trib. mil. leg.* . . .] *tricis p. f. Xviro s*[*tlitibus iudicandis* / *ob exi*]*miam eius in se a*[*dfectionem* [8] / *pec. pu*]*bl. ex decr. spl. o*[*rdinis*]

This man's tribunate could have been held in any one of six legions, I and II Adiutrix, and the four legions with the title Victrix, VI, XIV Gemina Martia, XX Valeria, and XXX Ulpia. The career probably belongs to the third century.[1]

9.   Ignotus *AE* 1961. 37

AE 1949. 61 = *Karthago* 2 (1951) 100 ff. = *AE* 1952. 95 = *AE* 1961. 37, Sufetula:

---

[1] Line 2 might be restored as [*qua*]*es. pro*[*vinc.* . . .], but there are numerous other possibilities, e.g. [*Phoenic*]*es pro*[*ces.* . . .]. In line 3, [*Cy*]*r. et* [*Cretae*] is possible, but so is e.g. [*Hispaniae citerio*]*r. et* [*Gallaeciae*], or [*curator viae Sala*]*r. et* [*alimentorum*] ; in line 4, [*ab actis sen*]*at*[*us*], [*cos. design*]*at*[*o*], [*cur*]*at*[*or*], etc.

[1] Thus Barbieri, *L'Albo* no. 2140.

[. . . *trib. leg.* . . .] *tricis quaestor* [*i.* . ./ . . .*i*] *uridico per Flaminiam et P* [. . . *XVviro*/
sa] *cris faciundis praes. prov. Pan* [*noniae* . . . ⁴/ *Ma*] *c* [*edo*] *niae Dalmatiae agenti
vice prae* [. . .] / *universus populus* [*curiarum*]

This *cursus* inscription has occasioned considerable debate. All that can
be affirmed with any certainty is that it must be assigned to the third
century. Any one of six legions may be restored in line 1, as pointed
out by H. Lieb:[1] I and II Adiutrix, VI, XIV Gemina Martia, XX Valeria,
and XXX Ulpia, Victrix.

II.11
EQUESTRIAN PROCURATORS OF BRITAIN

43   (?) P. Graecinius P. f. Pob. Laco

Dio 60. 23. 3.

The fact that Graecinius Laco was granted exceptional honours—including the *ornamenta consularia*—on the occasion of Claudius' triumph in
44, as Dio here records, strongly suggests that he had been to Britain
with the emperor.[1] Dio adds that at the time of the award he was 'procurator of the Gauls'.[2] It is possible that he had gone to Britain not
least to supervise the arrangements for taxing the new province, and
paying the army, and hence might be regarded as its first procurator,
albeit for a brief tenure.

Laco is otherwise known only as prefect of the *vigiles* in AD 31,
when he assisted Macro in the overthrow of Sejanus. On that occasion
he had received quaestorian *ornamenta.*[3] Nothing is known of his
activities in the interim. He may well have continued to command the
vigiles for some years. An inscription in his honour from Verona[4] suggests that his home was there, for he has the correct tribe for that city.[5]

---

[1] H. Lieb, in Reidinger, *Pannonien* 239 ff. See also Barbieri, *L'Albo* no. 550a (*post scrip-
tum*, p. 795); Fitz, *A. Ant. Hung.* 8 (1960) 405 ff., ibid. 11 (1963) 286 f., and in *RE* Supp. 9
(1962) 19. Fitz identifies the *ignotus* with L. Cassius Pius Marcellinus (*PIR²* C 507, cf. 516;
Barbieri, *L'Albo* nos. 123-4), but there is considerable room for doubt.
[1] Thus A. Stein, *RE* 7. 2 (1912) 1691 f., who offers no detailed suggestions. J. A. Crook,
Consilium Principis (1955) 44 n. 5, 166, suggests that he may have been a *comes* of Claudius
in Britain (but it is far from certain that non-senators could have such a title at this period).
[2] See *PIR²* G 202, where this is taken to mean—exceptionally—the *tres Galliae.*
[3] *PIR²* G 202.
[4] *ILS* 1336.
[5] Kubitschek 116. It may be noted that in spite of appearances to the contrary, both
gentilicium and *cognomen* are probably of Etruscan derivation: Schulze 81.

60   Decianus Catus

Tac. *Ann.* 14. 32. 2-3; 14. 38. 3; Dio 62. 2. 1.

Nothing is recorded of the origin and career of Decianus Catus apart from the brief accounts by Tacitus and Dio of his conduct as procurator of Britain, which evidently contributed in large measure to the outbreak of Boudicca's rebellion. If there is any truth in Suetonius' story that Nero contemplated abandoning Britain, the period following Catus' flight, after the severe mauling received by IX Hispana, is as likely a time as any. His report to Rome, explaining his panic-stricken arrival in Gaul, might have led Nero to believe that the province was irretrievably lost.[1]

Although he is called Catus Decianus in the *Annals*, this need not mean that Decianus was a second *cognomen*.[2] Tacitus not infrequently inverts *nomen* and *cognomen*,[3] and Decianus is attested as a *gentilicium*. M. G. Jarrett has suggested that he may have been an African, but the evidence is too limited to support this.[4]

61   C. Julius Alpinus Classicianus

VII 30 + p. 305 + *JRS* 26 (1936) 264 = *RIB* 12, London: *Dis* / [*M*]*anibus* / [*C. Iul. C. f. F*]*ab. Alpini Classiciani* [4]/ [. . . / . . .] / *proc. provinc. Brita*[*nniae*] / *Iulia Indi filia Pacata I*[. . .] [8]/ *uxor* [*f.*]

Tac. *Ann.* 14. 38. 3.

The brief record of Julius Classicianus' conduct in the aftermath of the Boudiccan revolt is a paradigm case for the tensions between legate and procurator which Augustus must have envisaged as a key element in his system.[1] Agricola, who no doubt witnessed the discord between Paullinus and Classicianus, was to be careful to avoid conflict with the

---

[1] Thus I. A. Richmond, *Arch. J.* 103 (1947) 61. For other views, cf. Stevens, *CR* 1 (1951) 4 ff.; E. Birley, *Roman Britain and the Roman Army* 1 ff.

[2] The view evidently taken in *PIR²* C 587 and in various other works where the Tacitean inversion is followed without comment.

[3] e.g. the previous Roman named before Catus is 'Paulinus Suetonius' (*Ann.* 14. 29. 2). Note also 'Quadratum Ummidium' (13. 8. 2), 'Sabina Poppaea' (13. 45. 1), 'Rufum Faenium' (14. 57. 1), etc.

[4] Jarrett, *Ep. Stud.* 9 (1972) 222 f., citing VI 1056 (a praetorian guardsman) and *AE* 1915. 22 (a man from Carthage). No other cases seeem to be extant, but for *gentilicia* in -ianus see W. Schulze 17f. Kajanto 249 gives no particular distribution for the small number of Cati known to him.

[1] See esp. Pflaum, *Bulletin de la Faculté des Lettres de Strasbourg* 37. 3 (1958) 1 ff., also id., *Les Procurateurs équestres* 157 ff.

procurators in his first gubernatorial post.[2] The discovery of Classicianus' funerary inscription at London reveals that he died in harness and sheds further light on his background.[3] As might have been deduced even from the names Julius Classicianus, he was clearly a member of the Gallic aristocracy. His name, Alpini in the genitive, may have been a second *gentilicium*, Alpinius, rather than the *cognomen* Alpinus; both names were characteristic of the Celtic parts of the empire.[4] His wife's names show her to have been the daughter of the Treveran noble Julius Indus, who helped to suppress the rebel Julius Florus in AD 21, and gave his name to the *ala Indiana*—her own *cognomen* Pacata suggesting that she was born soon after that campaign.[5]

Nothing is known of Classicianus' earlier career, but it should be noted that there is room, in the missing portion of the inscription, for several posts to have been recorded. Previous service as an equestrian officer is probable.[6] No descendants are known, but the equestrian officer in Vitellius' army in 69, Alpinius Montanus, a Treveran, might have been his son, as E. Birley has suggested.[7]

There may be some significance in Classicianus' place of burial, which might imply that London was his place of residence, and hence the procuratorial headquarters in the 60s.

Ti. Claudius Augustanus

V 3337, Verona: [*Ti*] *b. Claudio* / *Tib. f. Quir.* / *Augustano patri* [4] / *Bellici Sollertis* / *proc. Aug. prov. Britan.* / *Claudia Ti. f. Marcellina* / *socero optimo p* [. . .]

Ti. Claudius Augustanus' earlier career is unknown, and the procuratorship of Britain appears to have been the highest post which he achieved, to judge from this dedication by his daughter-in-law, Claudia Marcellina. An approximate indication of date is furnished by the career of his son, here called Bellicius Sollers, the names he took after adoption.[1] He had previously been named Ti. Claudius Alpinus, and another inscription at

[2] Tac. *Agr.* 9. 4: 'procul a contentione adversus procuratores'.
[3] See E. Birley, *Ant. J.* 16 (1936) 207 f.
[4] Pflaum, *Archivo español de arqueologia* 39 (1966) 5 ff.
[5] Tac. *Ann.* 3. 42. 3. See *PIR*[2] J 358, 685. On the *ala*, E. Birley, *Ancient Society* 9 (1978) 257, 267.
[6] It may be noted that residence at Rome for a time is suggested by VI 9363 = 33805: *dis manibus Diocharis Iuli Classiciani ser. Quietus disp.* The *cognomen* is very rare: Kajanto 319, knows only five examples, presumably including the procurator and the *dominus* of Diocharis as two individuals.
[7] *ap.* Jarrett, *Ep. Stud.* 9 (1972) 223.
[1] *PIR*[2] B 103; Pflaum, *CP* no. 68.

Verona set up by Claudia Marcellina records him, still under that name, as having been through the *tres militiae*, and having been decorated *bello Germ.*[2] This was presumably Domitian's campaign of 83, since he went on to be procurator of Dalmatia, where he is recorded under the name of Augustianus Bellicus,[3] and then to enter the senate, for he is evidently the 'vir praetorius Sollers' mentioned in a letter of Pliny from the year 105[4] (and he ultimately became consul[5]). H.-G. Pflaum assigns his procuratorship of Dalmatia to *c.*98,[6] and our man's post in Britain to *c.*80,[7] but it might be safer to assume that Augustanus had held a ducenary appointment rather more than eighteen years before his son reached this rank—and it is in any case not excluded that Bellicius Sollers was procurator of Dalmatia well before 98.[8] Hence the period *c.*65–*c.*80 might be regarded as the outside limits.

The family's close connection with Verona is guaranteed by three inscriptions,[9] while Augustanus' son Sollers is revealed by Pliny to have had estates at Vicetia.[10] But neither of those communities was enrolled in the Quirina,[11] which Augustanus must be assumed to have entered when he (or perhaps his father) received the citizenship by a viritane grant under Claudius or Nero.[12] It is probable that he was a leading man in one of the Alpine peoples.

Although Bellicius Sollers appears to have had a son, the direct line seems to have died out early in the second century, for the names Augustanus Alpinus Bellicius Sollers appear in the nomenclature of two

---

[2] *ILS* 2710. Complications are introduced by the inscription of a senator called [T]i. Claudius Ti. f. Qui. Alpi[nus?], recorded at Petra (*AE* 1968. 525), discussed by Eck, *Senatoren* 166 f. n. 231, and by an equestrian officer called Claudius Alpinus, serving in Moesia superior in 96: S. Dušanić, *Chiron* 7 (1977) 295. The relationships are uncertain and in any case, H. Halfmann, *Die Senatoren aus dem östlichen Teil des Imperium Romanum bis zum Ende des 2. Jh.n.Chr.* (1979) 135 identifies the man at Petra as C. Claudius Severus (*cos.* 112), regarding the reading of the *cognomen* as mistaken.

[3] *ILS* 5968, Burnum.

[4] Pliny, *ep.* 5. 4. 1, see Sherwin-White, *Letters of Pliny* 318 f.

[5] *ILS* 1031, Verona.

[6] *CP* pp. 162, 1061.

[7] *CP* p. 1050.

[8] Pflaum's dating of the career assumes that as procurator of Dalmatia Sollers could have been concerned with the [p]*rata leg*(*ionis*) long after the departure of the last legion from Dalmatia, viz. in 86 (for the date see J. J. Wilkes, *Dalmatia* (1969) 104, who, however, also takes Bellic(i)us to be Trajanic); and that his *dona* for the war of 83 were won as prefect of a cohort, since his tribunate was with the British legion II Augusta and the *ala Gallica* which he then commanded was in Syria in 88 (XVI 35). Even so, he could still have become procurator of Dalmatia well before 98.

[9] V 3337, *ILS* 1031, 2710.

[10] *ep.* 5. 4. 1.

[11] Kubitschek 116 f.

[12] Id. 272.

senators of the Antonine period, one being the polyonymous grandson of Q. Pompeius Falco.[13]

Cn. Pompeius Sex. f. Quir. Homullus Aelius Gracilis
Cassianus Longinus

VI 1626 = *ILS* 1385, Rome: *Cn. Pompeio Sex. f. | Quir. Homullo | Aelio Gracili Cassiano Longino* [4]*| pp. bis leg. II Aug. et leg. X Fretens. | trib. coh. III vig. trib. coh. X urb. | trib. coh. V pr. donis donato ab | imp. torq. phal. armill. cor. aur.* [8]*| hast. pur. proc. Aug. provinciae | B*[*ritt*]*aniae proc. Aug. provinc. | duarum Lugud. et Aquit. proc. | Aug. a rationibus* [12]*| heredes*

The only real clue to the dating of this career is provided by the mention of *dona* in lines 7–8 of the inscription. There seems no doubt that the unnamed *imp.* must be Domitian, and it is reasonable to suppose that Homullus won part of these *dona* as tribune of the guard in one of Domitian's wars in the 80s or early 90s.[1] Hence his British post may be assigned to the mid-90s at the latest. His heirs did not choose to give details of his early career, the first post mentioned being that of *primus pilus* of the British legion II Augusta. He may have begun as a soldier, and then as a centurion, in the Rome garrison, although B. Dobson has suggested that he may have entered the army as a *centurio ex equite Romano*.[2] At all events, after his post in II Augusta, he passed through the Rome garrison in three tribunates before going to Judaea as *pp. bis* with X Fretensis. H.-G. Pflaum notes that a further ducenary procuratorship was normally held between the first appointment in this grade and the post in Gaul, and that exceptional circumstances may perhaps have enabled him to omit this stage.[3] It is difficult to be certain—given that most of the evidence comes from the second century[4]—but it may be noted that during the period when Homullus could have served in

---

[13] *ILS* 1050 + *add.*, 1104; cf. p. 97 above. Cf. also Schumacher, *Priesterkollegien* 258 f., 417 f., Stemma Anlage VIII, whose suggestion that Pompeius Falco married a daughter of our man as his first wife seems implausible. Note the Hadrianic centurion of the XXth, Cl. Augustanus (VII 1268, *RIB* 1770, 1811, 1855), perhaps a descendant.

[1] Pflaum, *CP* no. 89, argues that he won them first as a soldier, 'ou plutôt *principalis* prétorien' and the remainder as a centurion in the guard, from which he goes on to assign the procuratorial career to the reign of Trajan. In the *addenda* he concedes the likelihood of B. Dobson's observation that Homullus' career began as a *centurio ex equite Romano*, without, however, drawing the consequences for the dating. A centurion of equestrian rank might, perhaps, have qualified for the 'nur dem *eques Romanus* gebührende *hasta pura*' (Domaszeski, *RO*[2] 110), but there is no reason why he should not have won it as a praetorian tribune. In any case, if he never served in the ranks, the time-scale is reduced.

[2] *ap.* Pflaum, *CP* no. 89, *add.* p. 967. See now Dobson, *Die Primipilares* 219 f., no. 97, who stresses the exceptional nature of this career, for a *primipilaris*.

[3] *CP* p. 187.   [4] Pflaum, *Les Procurateurs équestres* 246 ff., 250 ff.; *CP* p. 1053.

Britain, the governor Sallustius Lucullus was put to death.[5] Hence it is just possible that Homullus revealed accelerated promotion as a reward for loyalty—if not more—at the time of that episode. His final appointment, as *a rationibus*, was doubtless held under Trajan.

One item in his lengthy nomenclature, Aelius Gracilis, provides a clue to his origin, for there was a Spanish senator of that name in the 50s, a native of Dertosa.[6] Homullus' other names, and the tribe Quirina, would accord well with an *origo* in the Iberian peninsula, although not at Dertosa itself, which was enrolled in the Galeria.[7]

M. Maenius C. f. Cor. Agrippa L. Tusidius Campester

XI 5632 = *ILS* 2735, Camerinum: *M. Maenio C. f. Cor. Agrip/pae L. Tusidio Campestri / hospiti divi Hadriani patri* [4]/ *senatoris praef. coh. II Fl. / Britton. equitat. electo / a divo Hadriano et misso / in expeditionem Britan/nicam trib. coh. I Hispanor.* [8]/ *equitat. praef. alae / Gallor. et Pannonior. catafracta/tae proc. Aug. praef. classis / Brittannicae proc. provin/ciae Brittanniae equo pu/blico patrono municipi* [12]/ *vicani Censorglacenses / consecuti ab indulgentia / optimi maximique imp. Anto/nini Aug. Pii beneficio inter/pretationis eius privilegia quibus in p[e]r-petuum aucti / confirmatique sunt* [16]/ *L. d. d. d.*

The chronology of Maenius Agrippa's career is reasonably clear, thanks to the mention of *divus Hadrianus* in line 6 of the inscription from Camerinum; but there has been considerable discussion about the precise dating of the *expeditio Britannica* on which that emperor sent him. It would be natural, at first sight, to assign this to the occasion when Hadrian came to Britain, with the new governor, A. Platorius Nepos, and the legion VI Victrix, transferred from Lower Germany, in the year 122.[1] However, as E. Birley pointed out, the career of another officer, T. Pontius Sabinus, who was *praepositus vexillationibus milliaris tribus expeditione Brittannica*, is difficult to reconcile with that date.[2] Sabinus had been decorated for service as an equestrian officer in the Parthian war of 114–17, and had then transferred to the centurionate, holding commissions in XXII Primigenia in Upper Germany, XIII Gemina in Dacia, and—as *primus pilus*—in III Augusta in Numidia, before the appointment to take the vexillations to Britain. The time

---

[5] p. 82 above.

[6] *PIR*[2] A 776, noted by Pflaum, *CP* no. 89, who suggests that the senator might have been Homullus' maternal grandfather.

[7] Kubitschek 193, cf. 271 f. for the communities in the Quirina.

[1] pp. 101, 273 above.

[2] E. Birley, *ap.* Pflaum, *CP* nos. 118 + *add.* (Sabinus), 120 (Agrippa); see also *Roman Britain and the Roman Army* 28 f., 38.

available, 117-22, or 118-21, scarcely seems long enough for him to have held the three posts, in widely separated legions. Hence it is possible that there was a second British expedition, later in the reign, the need for which may be well understood in the light of the changes of plan in the course of the building of the Wall and its attendant works.[3] However, it must be admitted that, as M. G. Jarrett, among others, has pointed out,[4] T. Pontius Sabinus could, after all, have held three centurionates between 117 and 122,[5] and in the absence of further evidence it is perhaps best to assume that 122 was the year in which he and Maenius Agrippa came to Britain.

Agrippa had doubtless already met some natives of the province, for his first appointment had been as prefect of the *cohors II Flavia Brittonum equitata*, which probably still included Britons in its ranks, a unit then stationed in Moesia inferior.[6] As tribune of the *cohors I Hispanorum* he is attested by four out of the sixteen fine altars to Jupiter Optimus Maximus found at Maryport, suggesting that he held the appointment for at least four years, until 126.[7] He was then promoted to the third *militia*, as prefect of the *ala Gallorum et Pannoniorum catafractata*, an appointment which took him back to Moesia inferior.[8] On the chronology here adopted, the governor of that province during part at least of Agrippa's second tour of duty there was Sex. Julius Severus (*cos.* 127), and it would not be too fanciful to suppose that it was on the latter's recommendation that Agrippa received his next appointment, as prefect of the *classis Brittannica*, for it will be recalled that Severus himself proceeded from Moesia inferior to Britain *c.*130.[9] He doubtless went on to the further appointment as procurator of Britain without leaving the province. As H.-G. Pflaum points out, he thus omitted the sexagenary grade, and achieved ducenary rank after a single appointment in the centenary, which testifies to the favour which he enjoyed.[10] He had perhaps already had the opportunity of attracting the emperor's attention by acting as his host, although this must be a matter of guesswork. Likewise, there is no

---

[3] See e.g. Stevens, *The Building of Hadrian's Wall, passim.*

[4] Jarrett, *Britannia* 7 (1976) 145 ff.

[5] For comparison, one may note the extraordinary number of appointments held between 114 and 119 by T. Haterius Nepos (p. 302 below).

[6] XVI 45, of AD 99; the cohort was still in that province in the third century, see III 7473 etc.

[7] See now Jarrett, *Maryport, Cumbria: A Roman Fort and its Garrison* 17 ff. The altars are *RIB* 823-6, on which our man is called variously M. Maenius Agrip., M. Mae. Agripp., Mae. Agrippa, and Maen.[...].

[8] Attested in Moesia inferior in the year 134, XVI 78.

[9] p. 107 above.

[10] *CP* no. 120.

certainty about the moment or the circumstances when he obtained senatorial rank for his son. The latter was presumably the Campester who was consul in the 160s.[11]

Agrippa was clearly a native of the town where his inscription was found, which was enrolled in his tribe, the Cornelia,[12] and the imperial favour which he continued to enjoy under Antoninus Pius enabled him, as its patron, to obtain privileges from that emperor for one of its *vici*.

Q. Lusius Sabinianus

VII 1082 = *ILS* 4646 = *RIB* 2132, Inveresk: *Apollini / Granno / Q. Lusius / Sabinia⁴/nus proc. / Aug. / v. s. s. l. v. m.*

Britannia 8 (1977) 433, ibid.: [. . .] *Q. / Lusius / Sabinian⁴/us proc. Aug.* secondary text: [. . .] *a/ra ex nu/ntio dic. ar. ⁴/ pos. l. l. m.*

The only clear indication of the date of this procurator is afforded by the find-spot of his inscriptions, at Inveresk, a few miles east of Edinburgh, in territory which was occupied only from *c.*80 to 95 and for some decades in the second century, apart from the brief period of reoccupation under Septimius Severus. The third period appears to be ruled out, since the second inscription must have been *in situ* long enough for it to have been reused for another dedication. Further, none of the dedications to Apollo Grannus, a deity whose worship seems to have centred on the upper Danube, appears to be earlier than the second century.[1] A date in the Antonine period thus looks almost certain—probably the reign of Antoninus Pius, since he was procurator of a single emperor.

His nomenclature is insufficiently distinctive to provide information about his *origo*. The *gentilicium* is found widely in Italy. In the provinces there is a particular concentration of Lusii at Narona in Dalmatia, one of whom achieved senatorial rank.[2] A consular of the Severan period, Q. Lusius Laberius Gemin(i)us Rutilian[us], possibly African, might be a descendant.[3]

---

[11] See now Alföldy, *Konsulat* 179 f., who assigns him to 165. Note the homonym at Ricina, IX 5781, cf. 5730, 5761, 5772, *EE* VIII 208, 830, etc.; and M. Ulpius Puteolanus Tusidius Campester, tribune of X Gemina (VI 3544).

[12] Kubitschek 70.

[1] See Ihm, *RE* 7. 2 (1912) 1823 ff.

[2] Alföldy, *Die Personennamen in der römischen Provinz Dalmatia* 95 f.

[3] *PIR*² L 436.

C. Valerius C. f. Claud. Pansa

V 6513, Novaria: *C. Valerius C. f. Claud. Pansa flamen / divorum Vespasiani Traiani Hadrian. pp. bis / trib. coh. VIIII pr. proc. Aug. provinc. Britanniae* [4] / *balineum quod vi consumptum fuerat ampliatis solo / et operibus intra biennium pecunia sua restituit et dedicavit / in quod opus legata quoque rei p. testamento Albuciae Candidae / uxoris suae HS CC consensu ordinis amplius erogavit*   .

It seems reasonable to accept H.-G. Pflaum's conclusion that this inscription may be assigned to the reign of Antoninus Pius, since after the latter's death Pansa 'aurait certainement aussi été flamine du divin Pius', at his home town of Novaria.[1] Pflaum also notes Dobson's comment that Pansa was probably one of those who began his military career as a *centurio ex equite Romano*, since he is specifically described as [*e*]*q. R.* on another inscription from the town.[2] On the inscription quoted above Pansa has contented himself with specifying only two of the posts which he held, and his rank as *pp. bis*, but he may be assumed to have passed through the three tribunates of the Rome garrison as did Cn. Pompeius Homullus.[3]

No direct descendants are known, but the Severan consular M. Juventius Secundus Rixa Postumius Pansa Valerianus . . . Severus, of Brixia, may have acquired the relevant part of his nomenclature through inheritance of some kind from our man.[4] It is worth noting that Pansa's wife Albucia Candida was, no doubt, a distant descendant of the Augustan rhetor C. Albucius Silus of Novaria, 'non obscurus professor atque auctor'.[5]

193   (?)Heraclitus

HA Severus 6. 10: sed eos ipsos pertimescens, de quibus recte iudicabat, Heraclitum ad optinendas Brittannias, Plautianum ad occupandos Nigri liberos misit.

Cf. *HA Pesc. Nig.* 5. 2: Sane Severus Heraclitum ad optinendam Bithyniam [*sic*] misit, Fulvium autem ad occupandos adultos Nigri filios.

The mission of Heraclitus to Britain in 193 mentioned in the *Historia Augusta* is undoubtedly the same as that described by Cassius Dio, who tells how Severus, before marching on Rome from Pannonia, 'sent a

---

[1] Pflaum, *CP* no. 127.
[2] *ap.* Pflaum, *CP* no. 127, *add.* p. 974, referring to V 6514. See now Dobson, *Die Primipilares* 260 f., no. 142.
[3] p. 291 above.
[4] *PIR*[2] J 888.
[5] *PIR*[2] A 489. The quotation is from Quintil. 2. 15. 36.

letter to Albinus by the hand of one of his confidants'.[1] Heraclitus might conceivably have been intended to take up an appointment in Britain, but it is much more probable that he returned at once with Albinus' reply, and hence should be regarded merely as an emissary. However, J. Hasebroek, following a suggestion of Hübner, believed that Heraclitus was sent to Britain as procurator.[2]

There are several homonyms in the period, with whom he might be identified. The likeliest candidate is M. Aurelius Heraclitus, evidently centenarian procurator of the *portorium vectigalis Illyrici* in 201, later praesidial procurator of Mauretania Caesariensis, and perhaps the same as the prefect of Egypt in 215, Aurelius Septimius Heraclitus.[3] If he was the procurator of the *portorium* in 201, he could hardly have been made ducenary procurator of Britain eight years earlier.[4] The question must remain unresolved at present. Whatever his status in Britain, the name Heraclitus, at this period, unquestionably points to Greek origin, although he might have been the son of an imperial freedman.

Sex. Varius Marcellus

X 6569 = *ILS* 478, Velitrae: *Sex. Vario Marcello / proc. aquar. C proc. prov. Brit. CC proc. rationis privat. CCC vice praeff. pr. et urbi functo / c. v. praef. aerari militaris leg. leg. III Aug. [4]/ praesidi provinc. Numidiae / Iulia Soaemias Bassiana c. f. cum filis / marito et patri amantissimo /* Σέξτῳ Οὐαρίῳ Μαρκέλλῳ [8]/ ἐπιτροπεύσαντι ὑδάτων ἐπιτροπεύσαντι ἐπαρχείου / Βριταννείας ἐπιτροπεύσαντι λόγων πρειβάτης πιστευ/θέντι τὰ μέρη τῶν ἐπάρχων τοῦ πραιτωρίου καὶ Ῥώμης / λαμπροτάτῳ ἀνδρὶ ἐπάρχῳ ἐραρίου στρατιωτικοῦ [12]/ ἡγεμόνι λεγειῶνος γ' Αὐγούστης ἄρξαντι ἐπαρχείου / Νουμιδίας Ἰουλία Σοαμίας Βασσιανὴ σὺν τοῖς τέκνοις τῷ / προσφιλεστάτῳ ἀνδρὶ καὶ γλυκυτάτῳ πατρί

Sex. Varius Marcellus, a native of Apamea in Syria Phoenice, was married

---

[1] Dio 73. 15. 1, cf. Herodian 2. 15. 4.

[2] Hübner, *Rhein. Mus.* 12 (1857), 64 f., taking him to be a freedman procurator; 'procurator provinciae' in J. Hasebroek, *Untersuchungen zur Geschichte des Kaisers Septimius Severus* (1921), 29.

[3] See *PIR*[2] H 90, where identity with our man is rejected, and the prefect of Egypt is regarded as a third person. Note also H 88 (our man) and 89, . . .aclitus, legate of VI Ferrata in 196, whom L. Petersen regards as a possible candidate for the man who had the British mission in 193. Stein was prepared to identify the man of 193 with both the Illyrican procurator and the prefect of Egypt, in *RE* 8. 1 (1912) 406 f.; he does not discuss the question in *Die Präfekten von Ägypten* (1950) 117 ff., but suggests that he was a brother of a Septimius Heraclitus recorded as legate of Syria Phoenice under Severus and Caracalla (*IRT* 437, Lepcis Magna)—presumably the same as the legate of VI Ferrata of 196, mentioned above. See also Barbieri, *L'Albo* nos. 269, 754.

[4] Pflaum, *CP* no. 253, and Thomasson, *RE* Supp. 9 (1962) 145 ff., who identify the Illyrican procurator of 201 with the governor of Caesariensis, do not even explore the possibility.

to a niece of the empress Julia Domna and was the father of the emperor known as Elagabalus, whom he predeceased.[1] He is attested in the first office on his funerary inscription, that of *procurator aquarum*, by a lead pipe from Rome on which Caracalla is named *imp.* and Geta is Caesar, which can thus only be assigned to the period 198–209; but it is quite probable that he had held the post even before 198.[2] His second appointment was as procurator of Britain, a post which he cannot have taken up earlier than 198, so he can hardly be the first man to hold the procuratorship after Severus' recovery of Britain from Albinus early in 197.[3] His third post, as procurator of the *ratio privata*, was combined at some stage with the functions of acting prefect of both the guard and the city of Rome. Such a position can only have been held when the emperors were away from Rome, together with the prefects. H.-G. Pflaum suggested that this was during the *expeditio Britannica* of 208–11,[4] but it is now known that another man was in charge of the *ratio privata* at that time,[5] and it seems preferable to date Marcellus' tenure of the post to the years 202–4. His promotion to senatorial rank, indicated on the inscription by the letters *c.v.*, and appointment as prefect of the *aerarium militare*, could then be assigned to 204. His final post, as governor of Numidia—in which he evidently died, for he did not receive the consulship—may have lasted for a short time only, *c.*207.[6] But it must be admitted that this dating is hypothetical. He

[1] See esp. Pflaum, *CP* no. 237. I have already put forward the interpretation set forth here in *Septimius Severus* 304 ff.

[2] *ILS* 8687.

[3] Hence Frere has no warrant for his statement that 'in 197 Sextus Varius Marcellus . . . was despatched as Procurator to Britain; the reason behind this exceptional appointment of an oriental was no doubt to ensure that supporters of Albinus should be hunted out by an officer of unimpeachable devotion to the new ruler's interests', *Britannia*[2] 195, but is perhaps over-interpreting Pflaum's remarks in *CP* p. 610.

[4] *CP* pp. 610 f.

[5] Q. Cerellius Apollinaris, prefect of the *vigiles* on 13 Apr. 212, his predecessor still being in this post on 4 Apr. 211 (*PIR*[2] J 511), had been procurator of the *ratio privata* immediately before that post, sc. in 211 and for some while earlier: see J. M. Reynolds, *PBSR* 30 (1962) 33 ff., followed by A. R. Birley, *Septimius Severus* 305.

[6] It must be noted that the *Fasti* of Numidia are extremely congested in the years 201–10. See Thomasson, *Statthalter Nordafrikas* II 202 ff., to which another man (Pontius) must be added, *AE* 1967. 571. But Marcellus could be fitted in for a brief tenure before Subatianus Proculus (attested in 208 and 210), with the other three men occupying the first six or seven years after Q. Anicius Faustus. On this chronology Marcellus would have been in charge of the two prefectures at Rome while Severus and the court were visiting Africa. Pflaum discusses this possibility, *CP* p. 640 n. 7, only to reject it on the grounds that the prefects are not known to have gone with Severus. But Fulvius Plautianus' presence is guaranteed by his claim to have been *comes per omnes expeditiones eorum* (*ILS* 455) and he would hardly have missed the chance of returning to his native town. See A. R. Birley, *Septimius Severus* 294 ff. As Marcellus' wife Soaemias was still of equestrian status at the Secular Games of 204, Marcellus' promotion to senatorial rank must be assumed to have come after that, on this chronology (*PIR*[2] J 704).

might have been *proc. rationis privat.* and acting prefect for part of the period 208–11, and have held his senatorial posts under Caracalla. It must be stressed that this career is quite exceptional. Thanks to his relationship with the empress, this man held only one post in each of the three superior grades of procurator, omitting the sexagenary stage altogether—and possibly having had no previous service of any kind. Although his inscription mentions *filis*/τέκνοις, nothing is known of his children other than his universally reviled son.

between 205 and 207   M. Oclatinius Adventus

VII 1003 + *add.* = *ILS* 2618 = *RIB* 1234, Risingham: for text, see p. 157 above.

VII 1346 + *EE* VII 1020 + *EE* VII 1028 = *Arch. Ael.*[4] 16 (1939) 240 ff. = *RIB* 1462, Chesters: for text see p. 157 above.

This remarkable man was to rise higher than any of the other known procurators of Britain, becoming praetorian prefect under Caracalla, *consul ordinarius* and prefect of the city under Macrinus.[1] The notoriety which Adventus achieved at the end of his life prompted Cassius Dio to provide some details of his career. He began as a *speculator*, became a centurion in the *frumentarii*, or secret police, and then commander of that force as *princeps peregrinorum*. Later he became a procurator, but whether the post in Britain—which Dio does not mention by name —was his first in that rank is unknown.[2] But he presumably went on to other procuratorial appointments after being in Britain, since he cannot have become praetorian prefect earlier than 213.[3] He was holding that post, together with Macrinus, when the latter arranged the murder of Caracalla in April 217 and proclaimed himself emperor. Adventus then told the troops that 'the sovereignty belongs to me, because I am older than Macrinus, but since I am excessively old I yield it to him.'[4] Macrinus made him his colleague as *cos. ord.* for 218 and then sent him back to Rome as urban prefect, a task for which, according to Dio, he was manifestly unsuited, 'being unable to see by reason of his age nor to read for lack of education nor to do anything through lack of experience'. At all events he was soon replaced in the prefecture of Rome, but continued to be consul even after the overthrow of Macrinus by Elagabalus.[5]

---

[1] Pflaum, *CP* no. 247 + *add.* See p. 160 above, for Adventus' role in Britain.
[2] Dio 78. 14. 1, 3.
[3] Pflaum, *CP* p. 992.
[4] Dio 78. 14. 2.
[5] Dio 78. 14. 2–3; 79. 8. 2.

Nothing is known of his origin, except that it was humble. His *gentilicium* appears to be unique, although related to Oc(u)latius.[6] This does not exclude provincial extraction,[7] especially as his not very common *cognomen* is found more frequently in Africa than elsewhere.[8]

| between 212 and 217 | M. Cocceius Nigrinus |

VII 875 = *ILS* 9317 = *RIB* 2066, Brampton: *Deae Nymphae Brig. / quod [vo]verat pro/ sal[ute et incolumitate]* [4]*/ dom. nostr. invic. imp. M. Aurel. Severi / Antonini pii felic[i]s / Aug. totiusque do/mus divinae eius* [8]*/ M. Cocceius Nigrinus / [pr]oc. Aug. n. devo/[tissim]us num[ini / maies]tatique eius v. [s.] l. m.*

This procurator clearly belongs to the sole reign of Caracalla, 212–17. Nothing further is known of him, but it may be noted that the inscription, now lost, is preserved in variant readings, and the names Cocceius Nigrinus, although plausible enough, must be regarded as very uncertain. The admittedly very rough Cotton Julius MS drawing could be read as ACIDEVS NORINVS, and although Acideus appears unexampled as a *nomen*, various forms, such as Pacideius, Pacidaeus,[1] are attested in Italy. Norinus is equally unknown, but Nor[t]inus is possible.[2]

Even the exact findspot is in doubt, but the dedication clearly came from the western part of Hadrian's Wall.

(?)Valens

EE IX 1123 = *RIB* 752, Watercrook: *[Dis] deab[us/que sacru[m/ . . .] Valens* [4]*/ [?proc.] Aug. v. s. / l. m.*

R. P. Wright suggests, ad loc., that 'the dedicator may well have been *procurator Augusti*', but other interpretations are possible, e.g. [7 *leg. II*] *Aug.* The stone is now lost and the MS drawing is very sketchy. At all events, there is possibly room for a *nomen*, perhaps abbreviated, to be restored. The *cognomen* is very common, but one may note Valerius Valens, prefect of the Misenum fleet and later of the *vigiles* under Gordian III,[1] and P. Aelius Valens, presidial procurator or prefect of Sardinia in 248.[2]

---

[6] Schulze 151, 364. [7] See p. 216 n. 4 above.
[8] Kajanto (349) notes that twenty out of forty known examples come from Africa.
[1] Schulze 348.
[2] Kajanto 215.
[1] Pflaum, *CP* no. 323.
[2] Ibid. no. 332.

II.12

JUNIOR PROCURATORS AND CENSUS OFFICIALS

L. Didius Marinus

III 249 = III S 6753 = *ILS* 1396, Ancyra: *b. f. / L. Didio Marino v. e. / proc. Aug. n. provinc. Ara[b.] [4]/proc. Galatiae proc. fam. / glad. per Gallias Bret. Hisp/[a]nias German. et Raetiam / [pr]oc. Minuciae proc. alimen[8]/[to]r. per Transpadum Histriam / [et] Liburniam / proc. vectigalior. / [p]opul. R. quae sunt citra Padum [12]/ proc. fam. glad. per Asiam Bi/thyn. Galat. Cappadoc. Lyciam / Pamphyl. Cilic. Cyprum Pontum / Paflag. trib. coh. I praetor. [16]/ Marianus Aug. n. lib. pp. XX / lib. Bithyniae Ponti Paflag. / nutritor eius*

The career of Didius Marinus[1] touched Britain only marginally, in that as fifth and last in a series of sexagenary procuratorships he was in charge of recruiting and training gladiators from Gaul, Britain, Spain, Germany, and Raetia. Since he was procurator of Arabia of a single emperor (after a similar post in Galatia), whereas he is later attested as procurator of two emperors in Asturia–Callaecia[2] and as procurator of Caracalla in Asia,[3] H.-G. Pflaum concludes that his post in Arabia must be dated before 198, and that his career was interrupted between that date and 211. However this may be, it looks as if the post which concerns us here must have been held towards the end of the reign of Commodus, since it seems unlikely that it could have belonged to the years 193–7.

Pflaum suggests that Marinus may have been a Syrian.[4] He ultimately attained senatorial rank, having in the meanwhile married, as her second husband, M. Aurelius' daughter Cornificia.[5]

T. Statilius Optatus

VI 31863 = *ILS* 9011, Rome: *T. Statilio [. . .f.] / Optato p[raef. ann. ?] / proc. Aug. a [rationibus?] [4]/ flamini C[armentali] / proc. Aug. hered[itatium] / proc. Aug. ad patrim[onium] / proc. Aug. ferrariar[um] [8]/ proc. Aug. ad cens[us] / Gallorum / proc. Aug. ad census Brit. / praef. alae Afrorum / trib. leg. VI Victricis*

---

[1] *PIR*[2] D 71; Pflaum, *CP* no. 295 + *add.*

[2] *AE* 1911. 4–5.

[3] *Forschungen in Ephesos* III (1923) 137 f.; *AE* 1933. 282. He was also *a sacris cognitionibus*, evidently in conjunction with his post in Asia, Pflaum, *CP* pp. 768 f.

[4] Pflaum, *CP* p. 769, a suggestion based on the name Marinus and on his evident devotion to Julia Domna.

[5] Pflaum, *CP* pp. 996 f., *J. des Savants* 1961. 36 f. Cornificia was forced to commit suicide by Caracalla (Dio 77. 16. 6a).

12/ trib. leg. VI Ferratae / praef. coh. I Lucensium / Statilii Homullus / et Optatus
16/ patri optumo

The career of Statilius Optatus[1] began with a prefecture of a cohort in Syria,[2] from which he was promoted to a tribunate in VI Ferrata, probably in the same province.[3] He remained in the same grade with his next appointment as tribune of VI Victrix, in Germania inferior or Britain, and then became prefect of an *ala* in Germania inferior.[4] His first procuratorial appointment, which concerns us here, was *ad census Brit(tonum)* or *Brit(anniae)*. H.-G. Pflaum notes that before the time of Hadrian equestrian *censitores* did not have procuratorial rank, which makes it probable that his tribunate of VI Victrix had been in Britain. But Pflaum suggests further that he might have served successively in VI Victrix and as commander of the *ala Afrorum* in Germania inferior under Platorius Nepos, and that the latter selected him for the *census* post on his transfer to Britain in 122.[5] Unfortunately, there is not enough evidence to date the career precisely. One may only note that as Optatus was procurator of a single emperor the years 161–9 and 177–80 are ruled out, while the Severan period can evidently be excluded anyway on the grounds that the lettering looks early.[6]

After a second sexagenary procuratorship, also concerned with the census, Optatus held one centenary post, and then a series of ducenary ones, the third of which may have been that of *a rationibus*, his career culminating, perhaps, with the prefecture of the *annona*. Pflaum regards Optatus as a man of western origin, while G. Alföldy notes that Statilii are found much more frequently in Italy itself than in the provinces.[7]

M. Arruntius M. f. Serg. Frugi

Ath. Mitth. 1908. 150 = *AE* 1908. 200 = *ILS* 9013, Iconium: *M. Arruntio M. / fil. Serg. Frugi praef. / coh. III Ulp. Petraeor. 4/ trib. mil. leg. XIII Gem. / praef. alae Parthor. / sagit. proc. Aug. provin. / Britan. ad census provin. 8/ Cilic. prov. Cappad. et / Armeniae minoris / et Ponti mediterrani / M. Claudius Longus 12/ cognato suo ob me/rita*

Arruntius Frugi began his career as prefect of a cohort in Cappadocia,

---

[1] Pflaum, *CP* no. 119.
[2] *AE* 1939. 126.
[3] E. Ritterling, *RE* 12. 2 (1925) 1605.
[4] Alföldy, *Die Hilfstruppen der römischen Provinz Germania Inferior* 169 ff.
[5] Pflaum, *CP* p. 289 ff.
[6] Pflaum, *CP* p. 292, notes that the fine lettering inclined the first editor of the stone, C. Tomasetti, *BCR* 1893. 87, to assign it to the time of Claudius or Nero.
[7] Alföldy, op. cit. 169.

went on to a tribunate with XIII Gemina in Dacia, and completed the *tres militiae* as commander of an *ala Parthorum*, a unit of which the station is unknown.[1] He then commenced a procuratorial career, not as ducenary procurator of Britain—which would be an almost unparalleled promotion—but in the comparatively humble sexagenary post of procurator *ad census* of this province, here expressed slightly awkwardly.[2] He then proceeded to two procuratorships, one centenary and one ducenary, in Cilicia and Cappadocia. As H.-G. Pflaum points out, the two auxiliary units which Frugi commanded would have been composed of Greek-speaking soldiers, and, apart from the tribunate in Dacia, a province immediately adjacent to the Greek-speaking half of the empire, his sole truly western post was that in Britain. We may readily suppose, with Pflaum, that he owed that appointment to the recommendation of the governor of Britain, who may have come to know and appreciate Frugi's qualities in one of his previous posts. Frugi himself may be regarded as a native of one of the Roman colonies in Pisidia, if not of Iconium itself, where he was honoured by a kinsman.[3]

T. Haterius Nepos

XI 5213 = *ILS* 1338, Fulginiae: [. . .] *o prae* [*f.* / *coh*] *ortis trib. milit* [*um*] / *p*] *raef. equit. censito* [*ri*] [4] / *Brittonum Anavion* [*ens.*] / *proc. Aug. Armeniae mai* [*oris*] / *ludi magni hereditatium* / *et a censibus a libellis Aug.* [8] / *praef. vigilum praef. Aegy* [*pti*] / *M. Taminius Ce* [. . .]

The honorand of this inscription from Fulginiae in Umbria may be identified without difficulty as T. Haterius Nepos, a native of that town, who was prefect of Egypt in August 119.[1] He must have reached that position after a rapid series of promotions, since his first procuratorial post, as procurator of Armenia maior, can only have been held during the years 114–17. This establishes that his appointment as *censitor* in Britain must have been held shortly before the creation of the province of Greater Armenia, *c.*112. The *Brittones Anavion* [*enses*] with which Nepos was concerned are otherwise unattested, but I. A. Richmond proposed that the latter name derives from the River Annan, *Anava*, in Dumfriesshire.[2] At any rate, it is legitimate to assume that

[1] Pflaum, *CP* no. 157.

[2] Pflaum, *CP* p. 374, following a suggestion of E. Birley.

[3] Pflaum, *CP* p. 375, takes him to be a native of Iconium, but his tribe, Sergia, is that of Pisidian Antioch, see Kubitschek 253, while Iconium was probably in the Claudia, 254.

[1] *PIR*[2] H 29; Pflaum, *CP* no. 95.

[2] I. A. Richmond, *Archaeologia* 93 (1949) 22, a suggestion dismissed on inadequate grounds

Nepos had been serving as *praefectus alae* in Britain immediately before taking up the appointment—unless it coincided with the arrival of a new governor, who brought Nepos with him from his previous province.

Gn. Munatius M. f. Pal. Aurelius Bassus

XIV 3955 = *ILS* 2740, near Nomentum: *Gn. Munatius M. f. Pal.* / *Aurelius Bassus* / *proc. Aug.* [4]/ *praef. fabr. praef. coh. III* / *sagittariorum praef. coh. iterum II*/ *Asturum censitor civium*/ *Romanorum coloniae Victri*[8]/*censis quae est in Brittannia* / *Camaloduni curator* / *viae Nomentanae patronus eiusdem* / *municipi flamen perpetus* [12]/ *duumvirali potestate*/ *aedilis dictator IIII*

Munatius Aurelius Bassus had a modest career, the presentation of which is slightly perplexing. His three posts as an equestrian officer are straightforward enough, the first of them, as *praefectus fabrum*, perhaps involving little or no military duties.[1] Then came two prefectures of cohorts, the first in an unknown province, the second in Germania inferior or Britain. Either province would suit equally well, since it may readily be imagined that a governor of Germania inferior, on being promoted to Britain, might have taken an equestrian officer with him to act as a *censitor*, while if Bassus was already serving in Britain his selection would be natural. Our man's only other post was as curator of the minor road linking Nomentum, his home town, with the capital. Yet, although neither this post nor that of *censitor* formally ranked as a procuratorship, he is indeed described as *proc. Aug.* immediately after his name. H.-G. Pflaum concludes that, in a 'situation singulière et sans exemple', the curator was at the same time an imperial procurator.[2] One or two other possible interpretations are worth considering. It is conceivable that *proc. Aug.* refers to a further, unspecified, appointment which Bassus had just received, but omitted to name. Alternatively, it might be the post of *censitor* which is intended, perhaps for the good reason that, while Bassus himself had held the position before the reign of Hadrian, the inscription was set up later, after *censitores* had begun to be graded as procurators. Or it could be that he did indeed hold the post of *procurator ad census*, but preferred to separate the procuratorial title, for greater emphasis, from the specific duties attached to it,

by Frere, *Britannia*[2] 246 n. 9, as shown by A. L. F. Rivet, reviewing the first edition of Frere in *JRS* 59 (1969) 248 f.

  [1] See B. Dobson, in M. G. Jarrett and B. Dobson (edd.), *Britain and Rome* (1966) 61 ff., on the post.

  [2] Pflaum, *CP* no. 83, p. 181.

reserved for their proper chronological position in the *cursus*. By this means he could give more prominence to the highest position he achieved. In this case, there is no need to assume that the post in Britain was held before the time of Hadrian. It is worth noting that, although Bassus' home town was clearly Nomentum, of which he was not only patron but a magistrate at repeated intervals, his tribe, the Palatina, was one of the four *tribus urbanae* in which freedmen were enrolled.[3] Further, since he was M. f. and had Aurelius as his second *gentilicium*, it is worth asking the question whether he might have been the son of an imperial freedman of the Antonine or Severan dynasty, a M. Aurelius Aug. lib.

II.13

A FREEDMAN PROCURATOR OF BRITAIN

M. Aurelius Aug. lib. Marcio

III 348 = *ILS* 1477, Tricomia: *M. Aur. Aug. liber. / Marcioni proximo / rationum proc. marmorum proc.* [4] */ prov. Britanniae / proc. summi chorag. / proc. prov. Frgy. / Senecianus collib.* [8] */ ex tabular. / h. c.*

Career inscriptions of freedmen procurators are rare, as is evidence for freedmen with the title *procurator provinciae*,[1] so it is not surprising that Marcio is the only example of a freedman 'procurator of the province of Britain'. It is important to recognize that imperial *liberti* who had the title *proc. prov.* were not holding the same position as the equestrian financial procurators. Whether their duties were confined to the administration of imperial estates, or whether they served as assistants to the equestrian procurators in their province, cannot be established.[2] Nor is it known whether they were appointed regularly[3]—the paucity of evidence might suggest that they were not, although imperial freedmen and slaves were stationed in the provinces in a variety of subordinate capacities.[4]

---

[3] C. Koch, *RE* 28. 2 (1942) 2528 f.

[1] P. R. C. Weaver, *Familia Caesaris* (1972) 271, 276 ff.

[2] See Pflaum, *RE* 23. 1 (1957) 1277 f.; id., *Bull. Faculté de Lettres de Strasbourg* 1958, 194. The suggestion by F. Millar, *JRS* 53 (1963) 196, that freedmen procurators had access to the same posts as equestrians is quite mistaken, see P. R. C. Weaver, *Historia* 14 (1965) 460 f.; id., *Past and Present* 37 (1967) 17 f.; id., *Familia Caesaris* 276 ff.; G. Boulvert, *Esclaves et affranchis impériaux sous le Haut-Empire romain, rôle politique et administratif* (1970) 392 f.

[3] See the comments by G. P. Burton, *JRS* 67 (1977) 162.

[4] Boulvert, op. cit., *passim*; Weaver, *Familia Caesaris*, esp. 197 ff.

Marcio is also recorded by three other inscriptions in Phrygia, two of them mentioning his wife Ael. Maximilla,[5] and one from Rome, a dedication he made to Silvanus, *pro salute et incolumitate indulgentissimorum dominorum.*[6] This phrase, taken together with the description of him on the Greek inscriptions as ἐπίτροπον τῶν . . . αὐτοκράτορων, indicates that he served during a joint reign. Hence his presence in Britain can hardly have been much before 161, but might have been much later.[7] Beginning as assistant to the *a rationibus*, he went on to administer imperial marble quarries, before his spell in Britain, after which he took charge of the *summum choragium*, the stage machinery of the theatres and amphitheatre at Rome, and finally went to Phrygia, where, since it was under Roman rule only a district and not a true province, his duties must have been principally concerned with imperial estates and perhaps the collection of indirect taxes.[8]

II.14

PREFECTS OF THE *CLASSIS BRITANNICA*

(?)L. Valerius ---

III 8716 = Pflaum, *CP* no. 92, Salona: *D. [M.] / L. Valerio [. . .] / proc. Aug. p[rov. Dalmat.(?)]* [4]/ *praef. classis [Brit.* or *Germ. praef. alae] / Moesicae trib. [mil. . . .] / praef. coh. I Tyr[ior. . . .] / Gal. Niger pro [. . .]* [8]/ *consobr[ino posuit]*

H.-G. Pflaum has demonstrated that the restoration [*Flaviae*] formerly supplied in line 4 of this inscription is unsatisfactory, since the promotion from the sexagenary prefecture of the *classis Moesica* to the ducenary procuratorship of Dalmatia, which seems required in line 3, would be irregular. Hence he restores [*praef. alae*], giving a post in

---

[5] *IGR* IV 546, 676, 704. His name is not preserved on the first stone honouring his wife, [γ]υναῖκα το[ῦ κρα]τίστου ἐπιτ[ρόπου].

[6] VI 648 = *ILS* 3535, where he is just called *Marcio lib. proc.*, with no *gentilicium*.

[7] K. Wachtel, *Freigelassene und Sklaven in der staatlichen Finanzverwaltung der römischen Kaiserzeit von Augustus bis Diokletian* (1966) 119, cautiously assigns Marcio to the '2/3 Jh.'; Weaver, *Familia Caesaris* 271, will only accept 'under M. Aurelius or later'. Since the Latin inscription from Tricomia calls him *Aug. liber.*, whereas the Greek inscriptions from Phrygia and the Latin one from Rome show that he was a freedman of more than one emperor, his service in his last post ought to have fallen either in 169, or 180, or 211, years when a single emperor followed joint rule.

[8] On *proximi*, see Weaver, *Familia Caesaris* 252 ff., on the other posts, 276 ff. O. Hirschfeld, *Die kaiserliche Verwaltungsbeamten bis auf Diokletian*[2] (1905) 292 ff., is still worth consulting on the *summum choragium*, although his comments on Marcio's provincial appointments, 381 and n. 4, are misplaced.

the third *militia*, from which promotion to one of the centenary fleet prefectures, and then to the Dalmatian procuratorship, would be appropriate. The Pontic fleet is theoretically possible, but Pflaum prefers either the British or the German, on the reasonable grounds that the *ala Moesica* was stationed in Germania inferior, from which appointment to one of these fleets would be a logical move. He notes that the procuratorship of Dalmatia was only created as a separate appointment after the second Dacian war of Trajan, in 106, but that the fine lettering favours a date not much later than that period. L. Valerius' cousin Niger was enrolled in the Galeria tribe, found only in Italy, at Lugdunum, and in Spain, thus providing a clear pointer to these men's origin.[1]

M. Maenius C. f. Cor. Agrippa L. Tusidius Campester

XI 5632 = *ILS* 2735, Camerinum: see pp. 292 ff. above, for text and discussion.

L. Aufidius Pantera

VII 18 = *RIB* 66, Lympne: [*N*]*eptu*[*no*] / *aram* / *L. Aufidius* [4] / *Pantera* / *praefect.* / *clas. Brit.*

L. Aufidius Panthera is recorded as prefect of the *ala I Ulpia contariorum milliaria* on an Upper Pannonian diploma of 2 July 133.[1] Hence he will have proceeded shortly after this to his next appointment, as prefect of the *classis Britannica.*[2] Nothing else is known of his career, but his origin, Sassina in Umbria, is supplied by the diploma, and indeed the Aufidii are well attested in that place.[3] Further, his remarkable *cognomen* recalls an Aufidius who as tribune of the plebs in the second century BC was responsible for a law permitting the import of African wild beasts, including panthers.[4] Our man was no doubt a descendant of a freedman of the tribune.[5]

---

[1] Alföldy, *Die Hilfstruppen der römischen Provinz Germania Inferior* 179, while accepting Pflaum's basic reinterpretation of the stone, regards it as possible that the procurator was a native of Salona; but he does not discuss the question of the tribe. See Kubitschek 270 f., for the distribution of Galeria. Salona was in Tromentina, and Sergia is also found frequently, id. 236.

[1] XVI 76, where the *cognomen* is spelt with an H.

[2] Pflaum, *CP* no. 133.

[3] XI 6494, 6546, 6550-3, 6564.

[4] T. R. S. Broughton, *MRR* I 423 n. 6, assigns him to 170, noting that a date later in the second century BC is possible.

[5] Pflaum, *CP* no. 133, who notes that the suggestion goes back to Mommsen.

Q. Baienus P. f. Pup. Blassianus

XIV 5341 + 5353 + 5382 + further fragments = *Acta of Fifth Congress of Epigraphy*, 193 ff. = *Atti e memorie della Società istriana di archeologia e storia patria* 68 (1968) 5 ff. = *AE* 1972. 70 = *AE* 1974. 123, Ostia: [*Q. Baieno*] *P. fiL Pup. / Bla*[*s*]*sian*[*o*] */ praef. Aeg. praef. ann. p*[*raef. vig.*] [4]*/ proc. provinciar. Lu*[*gdunens.*] *et Aqu*[*itanicae / praef.*] *classis praetor. Rave*[*n*]*nat. pro*[*c. provin/ciae Rae*]*t. proc. Mauret. Tingitan.* [. . . */ . . . p*]*raef. class. Brittann*[*icae proc. ad cen*[8]*/sus accip.*] *Cappadoc. Armen. min*[*oris proc. / ludi matuti*]*ni functo tribus m*[*ilitiis equestrib. / sacer*]*dot*[*i*] *Caeninensium* [. . . */ c*]*olleg. fabr. t*[*ign. Ost.* [12]*/ opti*] *mo e*[*t s*]*anctissimo p*[*iissimoque patrono / c*]*ura. agent*[*ibus / . . .*] *Maximo C.* [*Iulio Tyranno / Iulio*] *Com*[*mune magistris qq. lustri XXII*]

The career of Baienus Blassianus, formerly thought to have reached its culmination in the reign of Hadrian,[1] is now known to belong a generation later, for his prefecture of Egypt can be assigned to the year 168, a papyrus date which accords with the period when he was honoured as prefect by the *collegium fabrum tignariorum* of Ostia, now shown to be between the years 164/5 to 168/9.[2] His service as an equestrian officer, not specified in the great Ostian *cursus* inscription, is detailed on other stones honouring him at his home, Trieste.[3] He began as prefect of the *cohors II Asturum*, probably the unit of that name in Britain. It would fit the chronology of his career if he obtained a commission from A. Platorius Nepos, governor of Britain 122-4, who was patron of Aquileia,[4] a city close to Blassianus' home and where he himself is also recorded.[5] He served as tribune in either VII Claudia, in Moesia superior, or VII Gemina, in Tarraconensis, and then became prefect of an *ala*, evidently *II Gallorum* in Cappadocia.[6] It was formerly assumed that he had gone directly from this command to the sexagenary procuratorship *ad census accipiendos* in the same province, but it now appears that he returned to Rome in the interim, as procurator of one of the gladiatorial training schools, the *ludus matutinus*, thus having two sexagenary appointments before he assumed command of the

---

[1] Pflaum, *CP* no. 126, who identified the man honoured in XIV 5341 as Blassianus for the first time, was inclined to date the career to the period 130-60, noting E. Birley's preference for the reign of M. Aurelius for most of his later posts, p. 313. In the *addenda*, p. 974, he noted that *P. Oxy.* 24 (1957) 2413, made it possible—as it then appeared—to date Blassianus' prefecture of Egypt to a short period in 133.

[2] See now *AE* 1974. 123, where the evidence for Blassianus having been prefect of Egypt in 168 is cited, together with F. Zevi's redating of the Ostian inscription, *RAL* 26 (1971) 472 ff. Pflaum's original dating, 130-60, was thus almost right.

[3] *Inscr. It.* X. iv 37-40, on which see Pflaum, *CP* no. 126, esp. pp. 309 ff.

[4] p. 101 above.

[5] E. Pais, *CIL Suppl. Ital.* I 229.

[6] *Inscr. It.* X iv 37, discussed by Pflaum, *CP* p. 311 f. In *AE* 1974. 123 it is noted that the tribunate is perhaps of VII Gemina, rather than VII Claudia.

British fleet. This appointment may be dated *c.*140.[7] His later career does not concern us in detail here, but it may be noted that his next post after that in Britain remains unknown. He went on to two presidial procuratorships, the command of the Ravenna fleet, and the senior financial procuratorship of two Gallic provinces, before attaining the series of prefectures.

Sex. Flavius Sex. f. Quir. Quietus

AJA 64 (1960) 274 = *AE* 1960. 28, Rome: D. M. / *Sex. Flavio Sex. f. Quir. Quieto / p. p. leg. XX V. V. misso cum* [4] / *exer. in exp. Maur. ab imp. / Antonino Aug. praef. classis / Brit. Varinia Crispinilla conig. / piẹnṭissimo et Fl. Vindex et Qui[8] /eṭus fiḷ. piissimi*

As H.-G. Pflaum notes, Flavius Quietus had doubtless risen from the ranks to become *primus pilus* of XX Valeria Victrix, after passing through the centurionate. His dispatch with an expeditionary force by Antoninus may be assigned to the year 145, or shortly afterwards, when the outbreak of hostilities in Mauretania led to a number of exceptional measures, including the reinforcement of the garrison there. Pflaum points out that he must have returned to Britain with the men under his command, in order to take up his next appointment, as prefect of the British fleet. This may therefore be dated *c.*150, or a little earlier. He presumably died not long after, before he could receive a further appointment.[1] The fact that he was buried at Rome gives no real clue to his origin.[2]

---

[7] *AE* 1974. 123.

[1] See Pflaum, *CP* no. 156 *bis*. D. Kienast, *Untersuchungen zu den Kriegsflotten der römischen Kaiserzeit* (1966) 41 n. 38 prefers Caracalla as the Antoninus, unconvincingly; see Pflaum, *Mélanges Carcopino* (1966) 717 ff., showing that *imp. Antoninus Aug.* should normally be Pius.

[2] The nomenclature Sex. Flavius is exceedingly rare. Even in VI, there are only three specimens (18145, 18405, 21019), and there is only one in VIII (220, Cillium). There is one at Narbo (XII 4821), where the names Varinia (XII 4964) and Quietus (4466, 4733), but not Vindex and Crispinilla, are also found; and another Sex. Flavius at Lugdunum (XIII 1857), likewise two Varenii, but they were natives of Cologne (XIII 2037), and several Quieti (XIII 1936, 2138, 2222, 2300, ?2138). But these cities were enrolled in the Papiria and Galeria respectively, not Quirina, see Kubitschek 210 f., 217 f. The question must remain open. Alföldy, *Die Personennamen in der römischen Provinz Dalmatien* 279, 329, notes that Quietus and Vindex were both widespread in Africa and the Celtic provinces. For what it is worth, a Flavius Quietus is on record at Auzia (VIII 9107) and there are Flavii Vindices at Caesarea (VIII 21193) and near Theveste (VIII 28001). See now Dobson, *Die Primipilares* 251, no. 130, who cites a freedman Sex. Flavius from ·Peltuinum Vestinum (IX 3467), which was in the Quirina (Kubitschek 60).

Ignotus VI 1643

VI 1643, Rome: [. . .] / *praef. class. Brit. et* [*German. et*] / *Moesic. et Pannonic.*
[. . .] ⁴/ *proc. et praesidi Alpium* [. . .] / *subpraef. class. praet.* [. . .] / *trib. leg.*
XVI Fl. et praep [*o*] *s. a* [*lae* . . .]

This man appears to have begun his career as an equestrian officer, and
it is reasonable to suppose that he held a prefecture of a cohort, of
which mention would have been made at the end of this descending
cursus inscription. His tribunate of XVI Flavia was combined with the
acting command of an *ala*, presumably in Syria, where XVI Flavia was
stationed. He went on to a sexagenary procuratorial post as sub-prefect
of one of the Italian fleets, and then became presidial procurator of one
of the Alpine provinces. H.-G. Pflaum points out that the description
proc. et praeses does not occur before the Severan period. Hence the
extraordinary post which followed, the joint command over the entire
Rhine and Danube fleets combined with the *classis Britannica*, may
reasonably be assigned to the year 208, when Severus launched his
British expedition. As Pflaum notes, such a command over all the naval
units which could be assembled in the Channel implies a British war.[1]
The fact that this inscription comes from Rome does not necessarily
indicate that the *ignotus* was a native of the capital.[2] He may well have
been promoted to a post at Rome later in his career. Hence nothing
much can be said of his origin or identity, except to point out that this
dating of his *cursus* makes it possible that he received his tribunate
from L. Alfenus Senecio, governor of Syria in the year 200,[3] and that
this influential senator's patronage helped to further his promotion.

II.15

THE BRITISH EMPERORS, AD 286-296

286-293   M. Aurelius Maus. Carausius

Panegyrici Latini Veteres 10 (2). 12. 1-2: Quid nunc animi habet ille pirata, cum

---

[1] Pflaum, *CP* no. 259. D. Kienast, *Untersuchungen zu den Kriegsflotten der römischen
Kaiserzeit* (1966) 44 f., argues that the career is earlier, and that the concentration of naval
forces was for a Danubian campaign during the Marcomannic wars. This cannot be disproved,
but it is unconvincing: the command of M. Valerius Maximianus over detachments of the
Misenum and Ravenna and British fleets, together with a cavalry force *electorum ad curam
explorationis Pannoniae*, as *praepositus* (*AE* 1956, 124, on which see Pflaum, *CP* no. 181 *bis*)
is not a true parallel.

[2] Thus Pflaum, *CP* p. 696: 'un Romain d'Italie, sinon de Rome'.

[3] p. 159 above.

fretum illud quo solo mortem suam hucusque remoratus est paene exercitus vestros videat ingressos, oblitosque navium refugum mare secutos esse qua cederet? 2. Quam nunc insulam remotiorem, quem alium sibi optet Oceanum? Quo denique pacto effugere poenas rei publicae potest, nisi si haustu terrae devoretur aut turbine aliquo in devia saxa rapiatur?

Ibid. 13. 5: . . .Adeo, sacratissime imperator, multis iam saeculis inter officia est numinis tui superare piratas.

Ibid. 8 (5). 12. 1-2: Isto vero nefario latrocinio abducta primum a fugiente pirata classe quae olim Gallias tuebatur, aedificatisque praeterea plurimis in nostrum modum navibus, occupata legione Romana, interclusis aliquot peregrinorum militum cuneis contractis ad dilectum mercatoribus Gallicanis, sollicitatis per spolia ipsarum provinciarum non mediocribus copiis barbarorum, atque his omnibus ad munia nautica flagitii illius auctorum magisterio eruditis, exercitibus autem vestris licet invictis virtute, tamen in re maritima novis malam coaluisse ex indignissimo latrocinio belli molem audibamus, licet de exitu fideremus. 2. Nam et accesserat diuturna sceleris impunitas quae desperatorum hominum inflarat audaciam, ut illam inclementiam maris, quae victoriam vestram fatali quadam necessitate distulerat, pro sui terrore iactarent, nec consilio intermissum esse bellum sed desperatione omissum crederent, adeo ut iam communis poenae timore deposito archipiratam satelles occideret et illud auctoramentum tanti discriminis putaret imperium.

Aur. Vict. *de Caes.* 39. 19-21: Sed Herculius in Galliam profectus fusis hostibus aut acceptis quieta omnia brevi patraverat. 20. Quo bello Carausius, Menapiae civis, factis promptioribus enituit; eoque eum, simul quia gubernandi (quo officio adulescentiam mercede exercuerat) gnarus habebatur, parandae classi ac propulsandis Germanis maria infestantibus praefecere. 21. Hoc elatior, cum barbarum multos opprimeret neque praedae omnia in aaerarium referret, Herculii metu, a quo se caedi iussum compererat, Britanniam hausto imperio capessivit.

Ibid. 39. 39-42: Per Africam gestae res pari modo, solique Carausio remissum insulae imperium, postquam iussis ac munimento incolarum contra gentes bellicosas opportunior habitus. 40. Quem sane sexennio post Allectus nomine dolo circumveniat. 41. Qui cum eius permissu summae rei praeesset, flagitiorum et ob ea mortis formidine per scelus imperium extorserat. 42. Quo usum brevi Constantius Asclepiodoto, qui praetorianis praefectus praeerat, cum parte classis ac legionum praemisso delevit.

Eutropius, 9. 13-14: Per haec tempora etiam, Carausius, qui, vilissime natus, in strenuae militiae ordine famam egregiam fuerat consecutus, cum apud Bononiam per tractum Belgicae et Armoricae parandum mare accepisset, quod Franci et Saxones infestabant, multis barbaris saepe captis, nec praeda integra aut provincialibus reddita, aut imperatoribus missa, cum suspicio esse coepisset consulto ab eo admitti barbaros, ut transenntes cum praeda exciperet, atque hac se occasione ditaret; a Maximiano iussus occidi, purpuram sumpsit, et Britannias occupavit. 14. Ita cum per omnem orbem terrarum res turbatae essent, et Carausius in Britanniis rebellaret, Achilleus in Aegypto, Africam Quinquegentiani infestarent, Narseus Orienti bellum inferret, Diocletianus Herculium ex Caesare fecit Augustum, Constantium et Maximianum Caesares . . . Cum Carausio tamen, cum bella frustra tentata essent contra virum rei militaris peritissimum, ad postremum pax convenit.

Eum post septennium Allectus, socius eius, occidit atque ipse post eum Britannias triennio tenuit;qui ductu Asclepiodoti, praefecti praetorio, est oppressus. Ita Britanniae decimo anno receptae.

Epit. de Caesaribus 39. 3: Hoc tempore Charausius in Galliis, Achilleus apud Aegyptum, Iulianus in Italia imperatores effecti diverso exitu periere.

Oros. *Hist. adv. paganos* 7. 25. 3: deinde Carausius quidam, genere quidem infimus sed consilio et manu promptus, cum ad observanda Oceani litora, quae tunc Franci et Saxones infestabant, positus plus in perniciem quam in provectum reipublicae ageret, ereptum praedonibus praedam nulla ex parte restituendo dominis sed sibi soli vindicando accendit suspicionem, quia ipsos quoque hostes ad incursandos fines artifici neglegentia permitteret: quamobrem a Maximiano iussus occidi, purpuram sumpsit ac Britannias occupavit.

Ibid. 7. 25. 6: Carausius, Britannia sibi per septem annos fortissime vindicata ac retenta, tandem fraude Allecti socii sui interfectus est, Allectus postea ereptam Carausio insulam per triennium tenuit : quem Aslepiodotus praefectus praetorio oppressit Britanniamque post decem annos recepit.

Johann. Antioch. fr. 164: Ὅτι ἐπὶ Διοκλητιανοῦ Καραύσιός ἀνὴρ τεχθεὶς μὲν ἐν ἀφανεστάτῃ πόλει, περὶ δὲ στρατιωτικὰ σπουδῇ καὶ γενναιότητι διαφέρων κατὰ μικρὸν δόξαν ἀρίστην κτησάμενος, ἐκ τοιαύτης αἰτίας νεωτερίζειν ἤρξατο. Βελγικὸν καλούμενον κλίμα, κατὰ τὴν τῆς ἁλμυρίδας θάλασσαν, Φράγκοι τε καὶ Σάξονες, ἔθνη Κελτικὰ, διετάραττον, ληϊζόμενοι τοὺς ἐμπόρους, καὶ τῶν χωρίων πορθοῦντες τὰ ἐπιθαλάσσια. Σταλεὶς τοίνυν οὗτος ἐκ Βονωνίας πόλεως Γαλατικῆς, ἐπειδὴ πολλοὺς μὲν τῶν βαρβάρων ἐχειρώσατο, τὴν δὲ λείαν τὴν ἐκ τοῦ πολέμου οὔτε τοῖς ἐποίκοις τῶν ἐθνῶν ἀπεδίδου οὔτε τοῖς βασιλεῦσιν ἀπέπεμπεν, ἑκουσίως προπέμπειν τοὺς πολεμίους ὑπωπτεύθη· ἀναιρεθῆναι τοίνυν ὑπὸ τοῦ Ἑρκουλίου προσταχθείς, τήν τε πορφύραν περιέθετο, καὶ τὴν Βρεττανίαν καταλαμβάνει. . . .

Zonar. 12. 31: Κράσσον δὲ Βρεττανίαν κατεσχηκότα ἐπὶ ἐνιαυτοὺς τρεῖς ὁ ἔπαρχος ἀνεῖλεν Ἀσκληπιόδοτος.

Carausius deserves attention in these *Fasti* on two counts, not only as the creator of the *insulae imperium* and ruler of Britain for seven years, but in his role as a military commander before his usurpation.[1] The exact nature of that command cannot be determined from the sources, but, since it fell at the moment of transition between the old system and the new, it need not have been exactly analogous to any known position.[2] He clearly controlled the fleet 'quae olim Gallias tuebatur', which might be construed as the prefecture of the *classis Britannica*. But few scholars have been inclined to suggest this,[3] partly because the

---

[1] See N. Shiel, *The Episode of Carausius and Allectus* (1977). His bibliography, 208–17, is particularly valuable; he also devotes some space to demolishing the fictions of Hector Boethius and others, given undeserved credence in *RIC* V 2, 426 ff. He could have been more severe.

[2] See the useful remarks by Mann, in Johnston (ed.), *Saxon Shore* 11 ff.

[3] D. Atkinson, *Hist. Essays . . . James Tait* (1933) 8, and C. G. Starr, *The Roman Imperial Navy*² (1960) 155 f., appear to imply that Carausius commanded the British fleet, but do not describe him as its prefect.

last recorded reference to this fleet dates to the reign of Philip, some forty years earlier.[4] Eutropius gives a fuller description: 'cum apud Bononiam per tractum Belgicae et Armoricae pacandum mare accepisset, quod Franci et Saxones infestabant.' It might be tempting to take this as indicating that Carausius was *dux tractus Armoricani et Nervicani limitis*,[5] but there is no reason to believe that this command already existed in the 280s, even if it had been established by the time that Eutropius was writing.[6] In fact, there is nothing against the assumption that the *classis Britannica* was still in being, with a base at Boulogne, during the late third century,[7] and in that case it will have come under the orders of Carausius. But he must have had a larger force at his disposal, and it is legitimate to infer that the nine legions later commemorated on his coinage were those from which detachments had been drawn for a special command.[8] Carausius' title may have been *dux* or *praepositus vexillationibus*[9]—but he might also have enjoyed the title and rank of *praefectus classis Britannicae*.

The date of his appointment was presumably 285, for it is a natural deduction that it was Carausius' initial successes, 'multis barbaris saepe captis', which led Diocletian to assume the title Britannicus in that year.[10] Eutropius indicates that it was Carausius' usurpation which led Diocletian to confer the rank of Augustus on Maximian. W. Seston, who first stressed this connection, dated Maximian's elevation to September 286.[11] Others would place it considerably earlier,[12] but at present no clear solution is in sight.[13] Eutropius' reference to Allectus' murder of Carausius *post septennium* i.e. in 293, is consistent with his account of the circumstances of the original usurpation; Victor's statement that Allectus disposed of Carausius *sexennio post* appears to

[4] XII 686 = *ILS* 2911, Arles.

[5] A. H. M. Jones, *The Later Roman Empire* (1964) 44, regards this as possible.

[6] See J. S. Johnson, in Goodburn and Bartholomew (edd.), *Aspects of the Notitia Dignitatum* 83 ff.

[7] Shiel, op. cit. 7, comments sensibly that 'there must have been such a fleet throughout the century, however run down it may have become.'

[8] Shiel, op. cit. 190 f.

[9] For some parallels, see R. Saxer, *Untersuchungen zu den Vexillationen des römischen Kaiserheeres von Augustus bis Diokletian* (1967) esp. 53 ff.; *PLRE* I 1125.

[10] W. Seston, *Dioclétien et la tétrarchie* (1946) 75 with n. 1. On p. 74 he hints at the possibility that Carausius had been appointed by Carinus—that emperor also took the title Britannicus (*PIR*[2] A 1473), along with his brother Numerianus (A 1564).

[11] Seston, op. cit. 65 ff., esp. 76. Seston's arguments are not discussed by Shiel, op. cit. 200, who, however, speculates that Carausius' 'dissatisfaction at [Maximian's elevation to the rank of Augustus] was presumably the primary reason why he proceeded to act in his own interests', thus directly contradicting Eutropius—earlier (p. 16) he seems to find evidence in Victor for his version, which is hardly warranted.

[12] e.g. R. E. Smith, *Latomus* 31 (1972) 1058 ff.

[13] See A. K. Bowman, *JRS* 66 (1976) 156 n. 33.

conflict with this.[14] But it must be admitted that both these authors give a very muddled account of these years.

Carausius remained ruler of Britain for seven years, extending his dominion to part of the Channel coast of Gaul, including Boulogne. It was evidently Constantius' capture of that base in 293 which provided the occasion for Allectus' *coup d'état*.[15] During Carausius' reign he seems to have awarded himself two consulships, to judge from the coinage.[16] Of his subordinates only Allectus is known, perhaps in charge of finances as *rationalis summae rei*.[17] There is no indication in the sources whether the British provinces continued to have separate *praesides*. All that can be said is that Carausius' control extended to the far north-west of Roman Britain, as shown by the single inscription recording his name, from near Carlisle.

His precise nomenclature is a matter of some uncertainty. On his coinage he is called CARAVSIVS, M CARAVSIVS, M AV M CARAV-SIVS, and M AVR M CARAVSIVS.[18] It may be assumed that he adopted the names M. Aurelius in imitation of Maximian. The other name, beginning with M., is apparently given more fully on the milestone from near Carlisle: *Imp. C. M. / Aur. Maus. / Carausio p. f. / invicto Aug*.[19] Mowat's suggestion that MAVS. is an abbreviated form of Mausaius or Mausaeus, a name attested on Gallic coins, although otherwise unknown, seems to have won general acceptance.[20] But it should be recalled that Haverfield was initially very doubtful about the reading, and preferred to regard it as a mason's error, brought about by confusion with M AVR immediately before and AVS in Carausio immediately afterwards.[21] Hence caution is required, especially in view of the eccentric orthography on other third century British milestones, e.g. *Mar. Casianio Latinianio Postimo, Exsuuvio Tetricus, Aesuio,*

---

[14] Unless *post* refers not to the usurpation itself, but to the phrase which precedes it, 'solique Carausio remissum insulae imperium'—but this *de facto* 'recognition' is usually referred to 289, see e.g. Pflaum, *Rev. num.*[6] 2 (1959-60) 71 ff.

[15] This may be assumed from *Pan. Lat.* 8 (5) 6. 1 ff., 12. 2, see p. 000 below. R. A. G. Carson, *JBAA* 22 (1959) 33 ff., argued that Carausius held part of Gaul from the start of his usurpation. But see now P. J. Casey, *Britannia* 8 (1977) 283 ff., reasserting the view that he only acquired a foothold in Gaul after the failure of Maximinian's expedition.

[16] P. J. Casey, in Munby and Henig (edd.), *Roman Life and Art in Britain* 225.

[17] p. 315 below. Shiel, op. cit., esp. 180 ff., disputes the commonly held view that Carausius' continental possessions extended as far as Rouen, and argues that his mint was not there but at Boulogne. See now Casey, *Britannia* 8 (1977) 283 ff. X. Loriot, *Bull. de la société française de numismatique* 34 (1979) 583, reasserts the case for Rouen.

[18] *RIC* 5. 2, 426 ff.

[19] *RIB* 2291.

[20] R. Mowat, *Arch. Ael.*[2] 17 (1895) 281 ff.; id., *Rev. num.*[3] 13 (1895) 129 ff. Followed e.g. in *RIB*; Pflaum, *Rev. num.*[6] 2 (1959-60) 53, is more cautious.

[21] F. Haverfield, *CW*[1] 13 (1895) 437.

Numoriano, Nuberiano.[22] It may be noted at least as a possibility that Carausius' first name was something other than Mausaeus, e.g. Maius, Magius, or Marius, botched by a rustic mason. His principal name certainly appears to be unique, at any rate before the sub-Roman period in Britain.[23] In origin it may simply be a 'fabricated' *gentilicium*, derived from Carosus/Carausus.[24] But names beginning with the element Car- were of course very common in the Celtic world.[25]

Carausius' earlier career before 285 is alluded to briefly by Victor and Eutropius. Victor calls him 'Menapiae civis', and there is no reason to doubt that he was a native of the region bounded by the Meuse and the Scheldt.[26] Eutropius, followed by Orosius, stresses his humble origin. This too may be accepted, but there is no reason to comment that he was 'nothing but a barbarian'.[27] The Menapii had been within the empire since Caesar's conquest of Gaul.[28] Like the tetrarchs,[29] he had served as a common soldier, but had perhaps also been a helmsman in the fleet, as Victor says.[30] No relatives or descendants are known.[31]

293–296   Allectus

See pp. 310 f. above, for the ancient sources.

Allectus is a figure even more shadowy than Carausius. But his dates, at least, are not in doubt. He was defeated and killed in 296,[1] three years after he had overthrown the 'archipirata' whose 'satelles' he had been.[2] Eutropius, more sober than the panegyrist, calls him Carausius' 'socius',

---

[22] *JRS* 55 (1965) 224, Kirkby Thore; *RIB* 2224, Bitterne; 2226, ibid. 2250, Kenchester; 2307, Hadrian's Wall, nr. m/c 42.

[23] V. E. Nash-Williams, *The Early Christian Monuments of Wales* (1950) 92, no. 101, Penmachno, Caerns.: *Carausius hic iacit in hoc congeries lapidum.*

[24] Kajanto 284. For the variation, cf. Prosius–Prausius, Rosius–Rausius, Cosinius–Causinius. Carausus is unattested, but Kajanto gives Carusus.

[25] Holder, *Alt-celtischer Sprachschatz* I 775 ff.

[26] E. Janssens, *Latomus* 1 (1937) 269 ff., argued unconvincingly that Carausius was a Manxman. Other fantasies are discussed by Shiel, op. cit. 15.

[27] Thus Seston, op. cit. 74.

[28] *RE* 15. 1 (1931) 766 f.

[29] Aur. Vict. *de Caes.* 39. 26: 'His sane omnibus Illyricum patria fuit: qui, quamquam humanitatis parum, ruris tamen ac militiae miseriis imbuti satis optime reipublicae fuere.'

[30] Shiel, op. cit. 15, seems to doubt the literalness of Victor's *gubernandi . . . gnarus*, skill at the helm gained by a nautical youth. There is nothing to object to in this.

[31] For 'Carausius II' (and Genseris) see *Ep. Stud.* 4 (1967) 99.

[1] W. Seston, *Dioclétien et la tétrarchie* (1946) 108: 'Tout était fini avant la fin de 296, car les monnaies qui célébrèrent la victoire de Constance le montrent revêtu du costume consulaire qu'il avait pris cette année-là.' The victory was celebrated by the Gallic panegyrist on 1 Mar. (*Pan. Lat.* 8 (5). 3. 1), the following year: see Seston, op. cit. 31, for the date of the speech.

[2] *Pan. Lat.* 8 (5). 12. 2.

but Victor is quite specific, introducing Allectus with the phrase 'qui cum eius permissu summae rei praeesset'. This was originally taken to mean that he had been Carausius' praetorian prefect.[3] But, if this is what Allectus had been, Victor should have been able to say so—after all, in the next sentence he introduces Asclepiodotus with the words 'qui praetorianis praefectus praeerat.'[4] Hence, it is argued, Victor's language must be taken literally and Allectus may be regarded as Carausius' chief financial officer, the *rationalis summae rei*[5] of the *insulae imperium*. Further, the frequently occurring mark on Carausius' coinage, R S R, is interpreted as the signature of the *rationalis*.[6] It may be recalled that under Aurelian the *rationalis* Felicissimus led a revolt of the mint-workers at Rome, 'poenae metu', as Victor puts it, after tampering with the 'nummaria nota'.[7] This is echoed by the phrase used about Allectus' motives for treachery, 'flagitiorum et ob ea mortis formidine'.

Constantius' capture of Carausius' naval base at Boulogne was perhaps a blow to the latter's prestige from which Allectus profited to stage his *coup*.[8] Allectus' coinage stressed peaceful themes,[9] but he survived for as long as three years only because the tetrarchs were concerned to ensure that potential German allies of the British state should be neutralized, and that a really powerful invasion fleet should be prepared, before crossing the Channel.[10]

The name Allectus—the only one he is known to have borne—is extremely uncommon.[11] It is presumably a form of Adlectus, likewise rare,[12] but it might conceal a Celtic original.[13]

II.16

THE SECOND DIVISION OF BRITAIN

The two British provinces of Superior and Inferior may be presumed to

---

[3] Thus e.g. O. Seeck, *RE* 1. 2 (1894) 1584.

[4] Elsewhere, too, Victor makes frequent references to prefects of the guard, e.g. 13. 9, 22. 1, 27. 1, 27. 8, 38. 1, 38. 6, in each case employing the normal title.

[5] E. Stein, *Geschichte des spätrömischen Reiches* I (1928) 116 n. 3, appears to have been the first to point this out.

[6] The point was apparently first made by P. H. Webb, *Num. Chron.* 7 (1907) 48 f.

[7] Aur. Vict. *de Caes.* 35. 6.

[8] Thus e.g. Seston, op. cit. 103. Casey, *Britannia* 8 (1977) esp. 292 ff., argues that Allectus continued to hold part of Gaul until 295.

[9] Seston, op. cit. 104.

[10] Seston, op. cit. 104 ff. For Allectus' overthrow, see Eichholz, *JRS* 43 (1953) 41 ff.

[11] Not in Kajanto, but see VI 241, an imperial freedman.

[12] Kajanto, 349: 'seven men + sl./fr. two'—most are in VI.

[13] See Holder, *Alt-celtischer Sprachschatz* I 95 ff., for names in All-.

have continued in existence from *c.*213[1] at least until the time of Carausius and Allectus. That there was more than one province in 296 is indicated by the panegyrist who thanked Constantius for supplying 'plurimos, quibus illae provinciae redundabant . . . artifices' to rebuild Autun, and elsewhere in the same oration speaks of 'Britanniae'.[2] But these passages do not make it explicit whether there were still two or already a greater number of provinces. Further subdivision might conceivably have taken place under the Gallic emperors during the years 260–74 or when Britain formed the *insulae imperium* of Carausius and Allectus. All that can be stated with confidence is that by the time that the Verona List was compiled, between 312 and 314,[3] there were four provinces, grouped together in a *dioecesis Britanniarum*: Prima, Secunda, Maxima Caesariensis, Flavia Caesariensis.[4] These names are also found in the *Notitia Dignitatum* and in the *Laterculus* of Polemius Silvius;[5] and Prima appears to be attested by an inscription at Cirencester.[6]

Bury put forward the hypothesis that there was a short-lived initial subdivision under the tetrarchy, by which portions of the Upper and Lower provinces were hived off to create a third province named Caesariensis. He argued that this name could only have derived from a town called Caesarea, and suggested that Verulamium might have had this name since before the Claudian conquest, much as the cities in the client-kingdoms of Mauretania and Judaea had been called Caesarea by their rulers to flatter Augustus. *A fortiori*, Caesariensis must have been applied in the first instance to a single province, later split into Maxima and Flavia.[7] If the substance of this theory be accepted, it is more plausible to follow E. Birley's alternative version, that it was London which had the name Caesarea, and that it received it from the Caesar Constantius when he recovered Britain in 296. Then, on his elevation to

---

[1] pp. 168 ff. above.

[2] *Pan. Lat.* 8 (5). 21. 2; he also refers to *Britannia*, 3. 3, 17. 2.

[3] See A. H. M. Jones, *JRS* 44 (1954) 21 ff., with the refinement added by Mann, *Antiquity* 35 (1961) 316 n. 1.

[4] *Laterculus Veronensis* p. 249 Seeck: 'Diocensis Brittaniarum habet provincias numero VI [*sic*]: 1. Primam. 2. Secundam. 3. Maxime Caesariensis. 4. Flaviae Caesariensis.'

[5] *Not. Dig. Occ.* 23: 'Vicarius Britanniarum. Sub dispositione viri spectabilis vicarii Britanniarum: consulares: Maximae Caesariensis. Valentiae. Praesides: Britanniae primae. Britanniae Secundae. Flaviae Caesariensis.' Polemius Silvius, *Laterculus* p. 260 Seeck: 'In Brittannia V: Prima: Brittannia (prima). Secunda: item Brittannia (secunda). Tertia: Flavia. Quarta: Maxima. Quinta: Valentiniana. [Sexta: Orcades].' See pp. 318 f. below, on Valentia, and n. 18 on Orcades.

[6] *RIB* 103: see pp. 178 ff. above, and 317 and n. 14 below.

[7] J. B. Bury, *Cambridge Historical Journal* 1 (1923) 1 ff. Bury also supposed that the third province was created *c.*286, which is implausible and unnecessary; and that it was named Maxima Caesariensis, not just Caesariensis.

the rank of Augustus in 305, he will have altered the name to Augusta[8] —and London certainly was called Augusta in 367, as Ammianus reveals.[9] This reconstruction cannot of course be regarded as conclusive, but it fits the available evidence better than any other.

However this may be, the names Maxima and Flavia must surely have been intended to honour Maximian and Flavius Constantius, and should therefore have been given before Maximian's abdication in 305.[10] Prima and Secunda, by analogy with other provinces of the empire, will have formed from portions of the old Superior and Inferior.[11] Of the four provinces only Maxima was to receive a governor with the rank of *consularis*, as shown by the *Notitia*. J. C. Mann points out that this makes it almost certain to have been the province of which London was the chief city.[12] Prima is generally supposed to have had its centre at Cirencester, where an inscription was set up by the *primae provinciae rector*.[13] But it is not excluded that Cirencester belonged to Maxima, and Prima might have been the area beyond the Severn.[14] Flavia Caesariensis may have comprised the areas to the east and north-east of London, while Secunda will then have been the rump of the old Inferior, north of the Humber.[15]

[8] E. Birley, in *Quintus Congressus . . . 1961* (1963) 83 ff. Frere, *Britannia*[2] 241, indicates cautious assent.

[9] Bury, op. cit. 10 n. 24 remarks that 'the ambiguous expression of Ammianus left it uncertain whether it was Valentinian I who named Londinium Augusta', but that coins with the mark L.A. 'leave no doubt'. However, the two statements of Ammianus, 'Lundinium, vetus oppidum quod Augustam posteritas appellavit', 27. 8. 7, and 'Augusta . . . quam veteres appellavere Lundinium', 28. 3. 1 make it perfectly possible that the name was given in 305.

[10] Thus E. Birley, *Quintus Congressus* 85; Frere, *Britannia*[2] 241. A less plausible alternative would be during the brief period when Constantine I, also Flavius, and Maximian were united, in 307–8 (against Maxentius: see W. Ensslin, *RE* 14. 2 (1930) 2512).

[11] E. Birley, *Quintus Congressus* 84.

[12] Mann, *Antiquity* 35 (1961) 318 f.

[13] *RIB* 103.

[14] The governor L. Septimius is discussed on pp. 178 ff. above. Mann, op. cit. 319, concedes that 'the one reason for which a governor was allowed to leave his province was to make a dedication' (citing *Digest* 1. 18. 15); but he adds that 'in the formal prose dedication the governor's province is not specified, as it certainly would have been if he had been dedicating in a province not his own. (The mention of the province in the verse dedication clearly has no force)'. This was based on the reading in *ILS* 5435, where no more letters are shown after *v. p. pr.* But R. P. Wright now reads *v. p. pr. β[r. pr.]*, so that Mann's case is no longer so compelling. On pp. 179 f. above, it is argued that this may in any case be a third century governor, using *primae provinciae* informally as the equivalent of *superioris* (which would not scan), following E. Birley, *Quintus Congressus* 84. It must be observed that if the *praesides* of the British diocese were not obliged to make their entry and departure into their province by sea, they would have found it hard to avoid traversing one another's provinces in some cases.

[15] E. Birley, *Quintus Congressus* 85. Mann, *Antiquity* 35 (1961) 316 ff., seems not to have expressed an opinion on the relative positions of Flavia and Secunda. M. W. C. Hassall, in Goodburn and Bartholomew (edd.), *Aspects of the Notitia Dignitatum* 109, assumes without discussion that Flavia was centred on York.

THE FIFTH PROVINCE

The *Notitia* and Polemius Silvius list a fifth province, Valentia. Ammianus' account of the elder Theodosius' mission in 367-8[16] indicates that this name was given in celebration of Theodosius' victory: 'recuperatamque provinciam, quae in dicionem concesserat hostium, ita reddiderat statui pristino, ut eodem et rectorem haberet legitimum, et Valentia deinde vocaretur arbitrio principis, velut ovantis.' J. G. F. Hind argues that Ammianus misunderstood the arrangement, and that, in reality, what was renamed was not a single province, but the entire diocese.[17] He is indeed right in pointing out that in Ammianus' account Valentia is not a newly created province; but it is impossible to discount the evidence of the *Notitia* and Polemius Silvius.[18] Nor is it acceptable to argue that these works derived their mention of Valentia as a province from Ammianus. The solution must surely be that Valentia already existed in 367 as a fifth province, but under another name. The sole obstacle to this view is constituted by the *Breviarium* of Festus, dedicated to the emperor Valens; for Festus gives only the four provinces of the Verona List. From this omission it has long been inferred that he wrote shortly before Valentia was created.[19] But since, as Hind so clearly pointed out, Ammianus does not describe the creation of a fifth province in 368, it is better to assume that Festus was simply ignorant or careless[20]—or that a name was missed out by a scribe.[21] Festus is not

[16] pp. 333 ff. below.

[17] J. G. F. Hind, *Historia* 24 (1975) 101 ff.

[18] C. E. Stevens, in Goodburn and Bartholomew, op. cit. 222 n. 31; and Polemius Silvius' extra province, *Orcades*, is dismissed as an interpolation from Eutropius 7. 13. 3, *contra* Hind op. cit., who tries to use this as evidence for that work's unreliability over Valentia.

[19] Festus, *Brev.* 6: 'Sunt in Gallia, Aquitania et Brittanniis provinciae decem et octo: . . . in Brittannia Maxima Caesariensis, Flavia Caesariensis, Brittannia prima, Brittannia secunda.' Whence Mommsen, *Gesammelte Schriften* V (1908) 587 (an item first published in 1862) inferred that Festus was writing shortly before 369; thus too A. H. M. Jones, *The Later Roman Empire* III (1964) 381; J. W. Eadie, *The Breviarium of Festus* (1967) 1. A. Cameron, *Class. Rev.* 19 (1969) 305 f., reviewing Eadie, points out that that date is too early anyway, and that the work was written with a view to Valens' projected war with Persia in 370. W. Den Boer, *Some Minor Roman Historians* (1972) 198, shows a healthy scepticism: 'Nevertheless I still have my doubts. Festus was no Mommsen. . . . Memories, however, being notoriously fallible, Valentia cannot be used as a clinching argument in establishing the date of writing.' Nor can Festus be used as a decisive *terminus* for the creation of the fifth British province.

[20] In the same chapter Festus lists two Aquitanias, although Ammian. 15. 11. 6 and Hilary of Poitiers, *de synodis*, *pr.*, give only one, both referring to a period shortly before 368-9. It is perfectly feasible that Festus, remembering that there had been two Aquitanias, left them as two to make his figures tally with the total of eighteen. Eadie, op. cit. 165 f., produces an elaborate hypothesis of the reunification and subsequent redivision of the Aquitanian provinces to save Festus' credit.

[21] Cf. the omission of 'superiorem Dardaniam' between 'Moesiam' and 'Daciarum duas' in *Brev.* 8.

an author who inspires confidence.[22] We must remain in ignorance of Valentia's previous name, but it is possible to infer when it could have been created. The winter expedition of Constans in 343 required him to take special measures on the northern frontier, involving the 'areani'.[23] It is plausible to suppose that in the course of this visit he subdivided Secunda. Certainly, the north of England is the area where Valentia must have been, for it is only there that traces of destruction and repair assignable to Count Theodosius can be detected; and the province that was 'recuperata' had fallen 'in dicionem . . . hostium'. Since, according to the Notitia, Valentia was under a *consularis*, it is tempting to locate its governor's residence at York,[24] but there is really no means of telling. At all events, the archaeological evidence, combined with Ammianus' description, makes it virtually certain that the forts 'per lineam valli' must have been within that province.[25]

MILITARY COMMAND IN THE LAST CENTURY OF ROMAN RULE

The *praeses* Aurelius Arpagius was still commanding troops in the north of the Lower province—or what had been the Lower province—at some time during the reign of Diocletian.[26] J. C. Mann has pointed out that the garrison of Britain will have continued to be commanded by *praesides* throughout that reign.[27] There is no evidence for a *dux* commanding troops here before the year 367, when the general Fullofaudes is referred to under this title.[28] But no doubt, as Mann notes, Britain had acquired a *dux* before the death of Constantine.[29] From then onwards the *praesides* will have ceased to have military authority in Britain, or so it may be assumed.[30] The *dux* is shown in the *Notitia* in command

[22] Cf. his error over Gallienus and Dacia, in *Brev.* 8, and his garbled account of Mesopotamia in 14.

[23] Amm. Marc. 28. 3. 8. One might also consider the year 315, when Constantine I took the title Britannicus (*ILS* 8942), or 360, when Lupicinus was sent to Britain to deal with trouble in the north (p. 372 below).

[24] Thus Hassall, in Goodburn and Bartholomew, op. cit. 109; E. Birley, *Quintus Congressus* 83, 85, prefers Carlisle as the seat of the *consularis*; cf. also Mann, *Antiquity* 35 (1961) 320 n. 22.

[25] See Frere, *Britannia*² 394 ff. for a survey of Theodosius' reconstruction. Note his comment on p. 396: 'In the south of Britain the damage inflicted by the invaders is hard to detect'. It may well be that there was none of any significance, except in the province later renamed Valentia. It is unfortunate that we have no idea what it was called before 368.

[26] p. 200 above.

[27] Mann, in Johnston (ed.), *The Saxon Shore* 11 f.; id., *Glasgow Arch. Journal* 3 (1974) 39.

[28] p. 344 below.

[29] Mann, in *The Saxon Shore* 12; id., *Glasgow Arch. Journ.* 3 (1974) 39 f.

[30] Mann, *The Saxon Shore* 12, suggests that 'such military forces as remained in Wales were left under the control of the praeses'; id., *Glasgow Arch. Journ.* 3 (1974) 39 n. 47.

of the northern garrison; and, since he was *dux Britanniarum*, his responsibilities must have extended into more than one province.[31]

The role of the *comites* is rather more complex. Logically there was no place for any *comes* as part of the regular military establishment of a frontier area such as the diocese of the Britains. The *comites* Gratianus and Theodosius clearly served in Britain on special missions, and Theodosius at least is known to have had a small field army under his command.[32] Yet in 367 there was a 'comes maritimi tractus' in post, apparently on a regular basis: doubtless Ammianus' description is a literary periphrasis for the title *comes litoris Saxonici* which appears in the *Notitia*.[33] The units listed under this Count in the *Notitia* are in some cases frontier troops.[34] Mann has argued convincingly that, as with some other *comites*, the post of the *comes litoris Saxonici* was 'an elevated frontier ducate'.[35] It may have originally spanned both sides of the Channel,[36] but whatever the truth behind that hypothesis, in the Notitia it extended into more than one province.[37]

As for the *comes Britanniarum*, whose title, like that of the *dux*, shows that he operated in more than one of the British provinces, he is assigned a small permanent field army in the *Notitia*.[38] Mann has shown that the post derives from an innovation of Stilicho, 'who began the practice of creating small permanent field-armies, too small to qualify for the appointment of a *magister*, and which were therefore put under the command of men with the next lowest rank, which was that of *comes*.'[39] There is thus no need to expect a Count of the Britains to have held office before the very end of the fourth century; and his post will of course only have survived until the expulsion of Roman officials by the Britons in the year 409.[40]

---

[31] Mann, *Antiquity* 35 (1961) 319, argues that when the *dux* was first appointed his command lay solely within a single province, but points out, 320 n. 22, that 'the title *dux Britanniarum* implies that by the time of the *Notitia* his command covered more than one province.'

[32] pp. 331 ff. below.

[33] p. 333 below.

[34] See Hassall, in Johnston (ed.), *The Saxon Shore* 7 ff., for a detailed discussion.

[35] Mann, in Johnston, op. cit. 13 f. Note his comment that 'the later elevation of what does not seem to have been a very important command to comitival rank is a puzzle, to which I see no obvious answer.'

[36] Thus J. S. Johnson, in Goodburn and Bartholomew (edd.), *Aspects of the Notitia Dignitatum* 87 ff.

[37] *Not. Dig. Occ.* 1, 5 have *per Britannias* (but 28 has *per Britanniam*).

[38] *Not. Dig. Occ.* 7, in the section on the *magistri militum*; no troops are listed in the *comes'* entry in 29, only his *officium*.

[39] Mann, in Goodburn and Bartholomew, op. cit. 6 f.; id., in Johnston op. cit. 13 f.

[40] Zos. 6. 5. 2-3.

II.17

VICARII

319   **L. Papius Pacatianus** (*cos. ord.* 332)

Cod. Theod. 11. 7. 2: Idem A. ad Pacatianum vic. Brittaniarum. Unusquisque decurio pro ea portione conveniatur, in qua vel ipse vel colonus vel tributarius convenitur et colligit; neque omnino pro alio decurione vel territorio conveniatur. Id enim prohibitum esse manifestum est et observandum deinceps, quo ixuta hanc provisionem nostram nullus pro alio patiatur iniuriam. dat XII kal. Decembr. Constantino A. et Licinio C. conss.

Constantine's rescript of 20 November 319 is the only evidence for Pacatianus' vicariate, which may be assumed to have lasted into the following year. C. E. Stevens has suggested that the need for an imperial decision may have arisen from a conflict between Celtic and Roman laws of land tenure.[1]

He is now known to have been *v. p. pr(a)eses* of Sardinia ten years earlier, in 308 or 309, under the usurper L. Domitius Alexander. The Sardinian inscription also supplies his *gentilicium*, Papius, in full.[2] Since the usurpation of Alexander was directed against Maxentius, rather than Constantine, this appointment probably assisted, rather than hindered, the progress of Pacatianus' career after 311,[3] and he may be assumed to have held one or more other posts before going to Britain as *vicarius*.

He is not heard of again after 319 until 332, when he was *consul ordinarius* with Maecilius Hilarianus, and was made a praetorian prefect, an appointment he continued to hold until 337, under the Caesars Constantine and Constans.[4] Again, he may be assumed to have held other posts during the intervening period.

His origin is unknown, but the *gentilicium* is found much more frequently in southern Italy than elsewhere.[5]

c.353-354   **Martinus**

Amm. Marc. 14. 5. 6-9: Inter quos Paulus eminebat notarius, ortus in Hispania

---

[1] Stevens, *JRS* 37 (1947) 132 ff.

[2] *AE* 1966. 169, a milestone on the Sulci–Carales road. For the *praenomen*, *ILTun.* 814, Tubernuc, which abbreviates the *nomen* to Pap. (interpreted as Papinius).

[3] See Pflaum, *Bull. arch. alg.* 1 (1962-5) 159 ff.

[4] *PLRE* I 656, 1048.

[5] There are some thirty Papii in X (more than in VI), compared with e.g. 11 in VIII and 8 in IX.

coluber quidam sub vultu latens, odorandi vias periculorum occultas perquam
sagax. is in Brittaniam missus, ut militares quosdam perduceret, ausos conspirasse
Magnentio, cum reniti non possent, iussa licentius supergressus, fluminis modo
fortunis conplurium sese repentinus infudit, et ferebatur per strages multiplices ac
ruinas, vinculis membra ingenuorum adfligens, et quosdam obterens manicis,
crimina scilicet multa consarcindando, a veritate longe discreta. unde admissum est
facinus impium, quod Constanti tempus nota inusserat sempiterna. 7. Martinus
agens illas provincias pro praefectis, aerumnas innocentium graviter gemens, saepe-
que obsecrans, ut ab omni culpa immunibus parceretur, cum non inpetraret, mina-
batur se discessurum: ut saltem id metuens, perquisitor malivolus tandem desineret,
quieti coalitos homines in aperta pericula proiectare. 8. per hoc minui studium
suum existimans Paulus, ut erat in conplicandis negotiis artifex dirus, unde ei
Catenae indutum est cognomentum, vicarium ipsum eos quibus praeerat defensan-
tem, ad sortem periculorum communium traxit. et instabat ut eum quoque cum
tribunis et aliis pluribus, ad comitatum imperatoris vinctum perduceret: quo
percitus ille, exitio urguente abrupto, ferro eundem adoritur Paulum. et quia
languente dextera letaliter ferire non potuit, iam destrictum mucronem in proprium
latus inpegit. hocque deformi genere mortis, excessit e vita iustissimus rector, ausus
miserabiles casus levare multorum. 9. quibus ita sceleste patratis, Paulus cruore
perfusus, reversusque ad principis castra, multos coopertos paene catenis adduxit, in
squalorem deiectos atque maestitiam, quorum adventu intendebantur eculei, un-
cosque parabat carnifex et tormenta. et ex his proscripti sunt plures, actique in
exilium alii, non nullos gladii consumpere poenales. nec enim quisquam facile
meminit sub Constantio, ubi susurro tenus haec monebantur, quemquam absolutum.

Nothing is known of the *vicarius Britanniarum* Martinus apart from this
vivid episode in Ammianus.[1] He was in office shortly after the fall of
Magnentius, who committed suicide on 10 August 353. Martinus,
having tried in vain to protect the innocent from being arrested by the
notary Paulus for complicity in Magnentius' usurpation, was himself
accused. He tried to kill Paulus, but failed, and killed himself. The affair
was a blot on the reign of Constantius.[2]

---

360   Alypius

Libanius, *ep.* 327 (324 Foerster): Διὰ μὲν τὸ μέγεθος τῆς ἀρχῆς εὐδαιμονίζω σε,
διὰ δὲ τὴν ἀρετὴν μεθ' ἧς ἄρχεις ἐπαινῶ. καί φημι μὲν τοῦτο κέρδος εἶναι τῇ ἡμετέρᾳ,
παρ' ἧς ἔχεις τὸ ἐπίστασθαι ἄρχειν, εἴπερ ἀπὸ μὲν τῶν λόγων ἐκεῖνο, παρὰ δὲ
ταύτης οἱ λόγοι, τῇ διδαξάσῃ δὲ κόσμος ὁ μαθών, πολὺ δ' ἂν αὐτῇ καλλίω τὰ τροφεῖα
γενέσθαι, εἰ τὴν πρόνοιαν εἰς αὐτὴν καταθεῖο λαχὼν ἄρχειν αὐτῆς. 2. ἀλλὰ τοῦτο

---

[1] The name was fairly common during the principate: Kajanto 162. Alföldy, *Die Personennamen in der römischen Provinz Dalmatia* 240, comments that it was widespread everywhere,
'besonders in den keltischen Gebieten.'

[2] It was no doubt satisfying for Ammianus to describe in a later book the fate of Paulus,
22. 3. 11: he was sentenced to death by burning, early in the reign of Julian. See *PLRE* I
683 f., for further details on this man.

μὲν ἀπαιτήσομεν τὴν Τύχην, καὶ δώσει γε, ἂν τὰ δίκαια ποίῃ· τὸν δὲ Ἰερκλέα σοι τρέφομεν ἀμείνω ἥκιστα τοῦ πατρός, ἴσον δὲ ἴσως τῷ πατρί. καί τοι σχίζεταί γε ἡ σπουδὴ τῷ νέῳ περί τε τὴν γλῶτταν καὶ τὸ τῆς χειρὸς ἔργον, ἀλλ᾽ ὅμως ἐστὶν ὀξὺς ἀμφότερα, ὧν τὸ μὲν ἄλλοις ἐγώ, τὸ δὲ παρ᾽ ἄλλω ἀκούω.

Julian, *ep.* 10 Bidez-Cumont (= 30 Hertlein = 7 Wright), 403d-404b: Περὶ δὲ τὴν διοίκησιν τῶν πραγμάτων ὅτι δραστηρίως ἅμα καὶ πράως ἅπαντα περαίνειν προθυμῇ, συνηδόμεθα· μῖξαι γὰρ πραότητα καὶ σωφροσύνην ἀνδρείᾳ καὶ ῥώμῃ, καὶ τῇ μὲν χρήσασθαι πρὸς τοὺς ἐπιεικεστάτους, τῇ δὲ ἐπὶ τῶν πονηρῶν ἀπαραιτήτως πρὸς ἐπανόρθωσιν, οὐ μικρᾶς ἐστι φύσεως οὐδὲ ἀρετῆς ἔργον, ὡς ἐμαυτὸν πείθω. Τούτων εὐχόμεθά σε τῶν σκοπῶν ἐχόμενον, ἄμφω πρὸς ἓν τὸ καλὸν αὐτοὺς συναρμόσαι· τοῦτο γὰρ ἁπάσαις προκεῖσθαι ταῖς ἀρεταῖς τέλος οὐκ εἰκῆ τῶν παλαιῶν ἐπίστευον οἱ λογιώτατοι. Ἐρρωμένος καὶ εὐδαιμονῶν διατελοίης ἐπὶ μήκιστον, ἀδελφὲ ποθεινότατε καὶ φιλικώτατε.

Id., *ep.* 9 (= 29 = 6), 402d-403b: Ἰουλιανὸς Ἀλυπίῳ ἀδελφῷ Καισαρίου. Ὁ Συλοσῶν ἀνῆλθε, φασί, παρὰ τὸν Δαρεῖον καὶ ὑπέμνησεν αὐτὸν τῆς χλανίδος καὶ ᾔτησεν ἀντ᾽ ἐκείνης παρ᾽ αὐτοῦ τὴν Σάμον· εἶτα ἐπὶ τούτῳ Δαρεῖος μὲν ἐμεγαλοφρονεῖτο [τὸ] μεγάλα ἀντὶ μικρῶν νομίζων ἀποδεδωκέναι, Συλοσῶν δὲ λυπρὰν ἐλάμβανε χάριν. Σκόπει δὴ τὰ ἡμέτερα νῦν πρὸς ἐκεῖνα· ἓν μὲν δὴ τὸ πρῶτον οἶμαι κρεῖσσον ἔργον ἡμέτερον· οὐδὲ γὰρ ὑπεμείναμεν ὑπομνησθῆναι παρ᾽ ἄλλου, τοσούτῳ δὲ χρόνῳ τὴν μνήμην τῆς σῆς φιλίας διαφυλάξαντες ἀκέραιον, ἐπειδὴ πρῶτον ἡμῖν ἔδωκεν ὁ θεός, οὐκ ἐν δευτέροις, ἀλλ᾽ ἐν τοῖς πρώτοις σε μετεκάλεσα. Τὰ μὲν οὖν πρῶτα τοιαῦτα· περὶ δὲ τῶν μελλόντων ἀρά μοι δώσεις τι (καὶ γάρ· εἰμι μαντικός) προαγορεῦσαι; μακρῷ νομίζω κρείττονα ἐκείνων (Ἀδράστεια δὲ εὐμενὴς εἴη)· σύ τε γὰρ οὐδὲν δέῃ συγκαταστρεφομένου πόλιν βασιλέως, ἐγώ τε πολλῶν δέομαι τῶν συνεπανορθούντων μοι τὰ πεπτωκότα κακῶς. Ταῦτά σοι Γαλλικὴ καὶ βάρβαρος Μοῦσα προσπαίξει, σὺ δὲ ὑπὸ τῇ τῶν θεῶν πομπῇ χαίρων ἀφίκοιο.

Καὶ τῇ αὐτοῦ χειρί—χῆς ἐρίφων καὶ τῆς ἐν τοῖς χειμαδίοις θήρας τῶν προβαταγρίων, ἧκε πρὸς τὸν φίλον, ὅς σε τότε, καίπερ οὔπω γινώσκειν ὅσος εἶ δυνάμενος, ὅμως περιεῖπον.

Amm. Marc. 23. 1. 2: et licet accidentium varietatem sollicita mente praecipiens, multiplicatos expeditionis apparatus flagranti studio perurgeret, diligentiam tamen ubique dividens, imperiique sui memoriam, magnitudine operum gestiens propagare, ambitiosum quondam apud Hierosolyma templum, quod post multa et internecina certamina, obsidente Vespasiano, posteaque Titio, aegre est expugnatum, instaurare sumptibus cogitabat inmodicis, negotiumque maturandum Alypio dederat Antiochensi, qui olim Brittanias curaverat pro praefectis.

Id. 29. 1. 44: ecce autem Alypius quoque, ex vicario Brittaniarum, placiditatis homo iucundae, post otiosam et repositam vitam, (quoniam huc usque iniustitia tetenderat manus,) in squalore maximo volutatus, ut veneficus reus citatus est, cum Hierocle filio adulescente indolis bonae, urgente Diogene quodam, et vili et solo, . . . omnique laniena excruciato, ut verba placentia principi, vel potius accersitori, loqueretur: quo cum poenis non sufficerent membra, vino exusto, ipse quoque Alypius, post multationem bonorum exulare praeceptus, filium miserabiliter ductum ad mortem, casu quodam prospero revocatum, excepit.

Alypius is the most interesting of the six known *vicarii* of Britain, since

324   *Vicarii*

he was a friend and correspondent of the orator Libanius and of the emperor Julian, whose letters, in each case, seem to have been directed to him while he was in the island. Ammianus Marcellinus mentions his appointment twice, in both cases retrospectively, and the passage in book 23 must be the starting point for this examination of Alypius' career. Under the year 363, Ammianus describes how Julian appointed Alypius, 'former *vicarius* of the Britains' ('qui olim Brittanias curaverat pro praefectis') to rebuild the temple at Jerusalem. Ammianus' choice of phrase indicates that the British post was at any rate the most important that Alypius had held, which makes it practically certain that it was his administration of the vicariate to which Libanius was referring in the letter quoted above, dated by O. Seeck to the year 357 or 358.[1] It is less clear, unfortunately, how the two letters from Julian to Alypius should be interpreted. In Seeck's view, letter 9 (29) was written shortly after Julian became Caesar, in late 355 or early 356, and the summons at the end, ἧκε πρὸς τὸν φίλον, resulted in Alypius' appointment to the British vicariate. Letter 10 (30), which opens with Julius thanking Alypius for sending him a map, and then continues, in the passage quoted above, with some flattering remarks about Alypius' administration, will thus be later.[2] But J. Geffcken pointed out that the mention of πόλιν and βασιλέως in letter 9 (29) is only really intelligible as referring to Constantinople and to Julian himself after his proclamation as emperor in 360. Likewise, the phrase Γαλλικὴ καὶ βάρβαρος Μοῦσα implies that Julian had been in Gaul long enough to become rather 'barbarized'. Hence the summons at the end of this letter will have marked the end of Alypius' vicariate, and he will have joined the new emperor's entourage.[3]

No further appointment is in fact known until the mission—abortive as it proved—to rebuild the temple, in which capacity he had the rank of *comes*.[4] Ammianus calls Alypius an Antiochene, but as Seeck showed,[5] this must be mistaken, for Libanius would certainly have mentioned it if he had been a native of his own city. Further, he had an uncle whom Libanius describes as a Cilician, who had the same name as

---

[1] O. Seeck, *Die Briefe des Libanius, zeitlich geordnet, Texte und Untersuchungen* 30 (n.F. 15) (1906) 56 f., assigns the letter to 357, but later, 177, 346, puts in in 358. He notes that the chronology of book 4 of the letters is the most awkward to establish, ibid. 338 ff.

[2] Seeck, op. cit. 56 f. Earlier, he had taken a different view, *RE* 1. 2 (1894) 1709.

[3] J. Geffcken, *Kaiser Julianus* (1914) 139, approved by U. v. Wilamowitz-Moellendorff, *Hermes* 69 (1924) 268 f., whose emendation I follow in 403 b.

[4] Rufin. *Hist. Eccl.* 10. 38 (omitting his name) gives the rank; the appointment is also described by Philostorg. *Hist. Eccl.* 7. 9.

[5] Seeck, op. cit. 56 f.

Alypius' son, Libanius' pupil Hierocles.[6] Alypius' brother Caesarius also held high rank at this time, being *comes rei privatae* in 363-4, having been, perhaps, *vicarius Asiae* immediately before.[7] One of Julian's letters reveals Alypius as a writer of verse,[8] and another from Libanius shows that he was a pagan.[9] In 371 or 372, this 'mild and charming man,[10] after living in leisured retirement, was plunged in the depths of wretchedness', as Ammianus puts it, when he was tried, together with his son, at Antioch on a charge of poisoning, and was sentenced to exile after confiscation of his property, while Hierocles was condemned to death—but then, by good fortune, was reprieved.[11] Nothing more is heard of the family.

367	Civilis

Amm. Marc. 27. 8. 10: for text, see p. 334 below.

Nothing is known of Civilis apart from this passage describing his appointment as *vicarius* ('recturum Britannias pro praefectis'), together with that of Dulcitius as *dux*, in response to the request by Count Theodosius. It should be noted that this item now be dated to 367, in the light of R. S. O. Tomlin's revised chronology for the 'barbarian conspiracy'.[1]

Ignotus Auson. *Mosella* 407-8

Auson. *Mosella* 392 ff.:

> tempus erit, cum me studiis ignobilis oti
> mulcentem curas seniique aprica faventem
> materiae commendet honos; cum facta viritim
> Belgarum patriosque canam decora inclita mores

[6] See *PLRE* I 46 f. (the uncle's full name was Fl. Ant. Hierocles; Libanius, *ep*. 30, mentions his origin).

[8] Julian, *ep*. 10 (30), immediately before the passage quoted above: he sent his poetry to Julian from Britain.

[9] Liban. *ep*. 1395.

[10] Gibbon's characterization is worth quoting: 'The humanity of Alypius was tempered by severe justice, and manly fortitude; and while he exercised his abilities in the civil administration of Britain, he imitated, in his poetical compositions, the harmony and softness of the odes of Sappho' (*Decline and Fall of the Roman Empire*, ch. xxiii).

[11] As Seeck noted, *RE* 8. 2 (1913) 1478, the reprieve of Hierocles from the hangman may be described in John Chrysostom, *de incompr. dei nat.* 3. 7—not cited in *PLRE* I 431; ibid. 47, Alypius is also said to have been reprieved; but Ammianus only speaks of Hierocles' life being spared, not of Alypius' sentence being set aside.

[1] See p. 337 below.

405   quique suas rexere urbes purumque tribunal
                       sanguine et innocuas inlustravere secures;
                       aut Italum populos aquilonigenasque Britannos
                       praefecturarum titulo tenuere secundo

All that can be said of this passage is that Ausonius implies that at least
one vicar of the British diocese came from Belgica.[1]

385   (?) Desiderius

Cod. Theod. 9. 36. 1: Imppp. Val(entini)anus, Theodosius, et Arcad(ius) AAA.
Desiderio vic. Quisquis accusatur reum in iudicium sub inscribtione detulerit, si
intra anni tempus accusationem coeptam persequi supersederit vel, quod est contu-
macius, ultimo anni die adesse neglexerit, quarta bonorum omnium parte multatus
aculeos consultissime legis incurrat, scilicet, manente infamia, quam veteres iusser-
ant sanctiones. dat. iiii id. ivl. Trev(eris) Arcad(io) A. I et Bautone conss.

This rescript issued from Trier on 12 July 385 must, if the date and place
are correct, have been subsequently doctored, for it was Magnus Maximus who then reigned in the west. Desiderius must be assumed to have
been the *vicarius* of one of the three dioceses under the usurper's control, Gaul, Spain, and Britain.[1] The name was favoured by Christians,[2]
and, for what it is worth, it may be noted that a small silver salver
found in the river Tyne near Corbridge bears the inscription *Desideri
Vivas.*[3]

                        Chrysanthus

Socr. *Hist. Eccl.* 7. 12. 1: Σισιννίου δὲ τελευτήσαντος, Χρύσανθος καθειλκύσθη εἰς
τὴν ἐπισκοπήν. Ὃς υἱὸς μὲν ἦν Μαρκιανοῦ τοῦ γενομένου Ναυατιανῶν ἐπισκόπου πρὸ
Σισιννίου. Ἐκ νέας δὲ ἡλικίας κατὰ τὰ βασίλεια στρατευσάμενος, ὕστερον ἐπὶ τοῦ
μεγάλου Θεοδοσίου τοῦ βασιλέως, ὑπατικὸς τῆς Ἰταλίας γενόμενος, μετὰ ταῦτα καὶ
βικάριος τῶν Βρεττανικῶν νήσων καταστὰς ἐθαυμάσθη ἐπὶ ταῖς διοικήσεσι. Προβὰς
δὲ τῇ ἡλικίᾳ, καὶ καταλαβὼν τὴν Κωνσταντινούπολιν, σπεύδων δὲ ἔπαρχος γενέσθαι
πόλεως, εἰς τὴν ἐπισκοπὴν ἄκων εἱλκύσθη.

    [1] Not registered in *PLRE* I. The date is of course very vague, earlier than the composition
of the *Mosella*, in the early 370s (line 450, referring to 'father and sons', shows that it was
written after the birth of Valentinian II, in 371 and before the death of Valentinian I in 375).
    [1] Thus *PLRE* I 250. O. Seeck, *RE* 5. 1 (1903) 250 took the contrary view: the date must
be wrong, 'da Ort und Tag nicht zu einander passen'. He also suggests identity with the brother
of Serenilla, recipient of a letter from Jerome in the year 394 (*ep.* 47), also mentioned by
Symmachus, *ep.* 4. 40, 5. 46, 94, 103.
    [2] Kajanto 363: 'CIL five men, one woman . . . CHRIST. eight men.'
    [3] VII 1287.

Chrysanthus' career is known only from this passage in Socrates.[1] Son of Marcianus, Novatianist bishop of Constantinople, he served as a palatine official in his youth.[2] Under Theodosius, i.e. during the years 379-95, he was *consularis* of an Italian province. 'After this'—which may mean 'after the death of Theodosius', and, if so, after 395[3]—he was vicar of the Britains. In old age he went to Constantinople in the hope of becoming city prefect there, but instead was compelled to become Novatianist bishop on the death of his father's successor Sisinnius. He occupied this position from 412 until his death on 26 August 419, as Socrates mentions in a later passage,[4] acquiring considerable fame by his refusal to accept a stipend from the church, while distributing his own funds to the poor.[5] His origin is unknown and no descendants are recorded.

Victorinus

Rut. Namat. *de reditu* 491–508:

	O quam saepe malis generatur origo bonorum!
	Tempestas dulcem fecit amara moram:
	Victorinus enim, nostrae pars maxima mentis
494	Congressu explevit mutua vota suo.
	Errantem Tuscis considere compulit agris
	Et colere externos capta Tolosa lares.
	Nec tantum duris nituit sapientia rebus:
498	Pectore non alio prosperiora tulit.
	Conscius Oceanus virtutum, conscia Thule
	Et quaecumque ferox arva Britannus arat,
	Qua praefectorum vicibus frenata potestas
502	Perpetuum magni foenus amoris habet.
	Extremum pars illa quidem discessit in orbem,
	Sed tamquam medio rector in orbe fuit.
	Plus palmae est illos inter voluisse placere,
506	Inter quos minor est disciplicuisse pudor.
	Illustris nuper sacrae comes additus aulae
	Contempsit summos ruris amore gradus.

[1] It is repeated with minor verbal changes by Nicephorus Callistus Xanthopoulus, *Hist. Eccl.* 4. 13.

[2] Marcianus also began his career with palatine service, and then became tutor to the daughters of Valens, Anastasia and Carosa, Socr. *Hist. Eccl.* 4. 9, Sozom. *Hist. Eccl.* 6. 9, before becoming bishop, Socr. 5. 21.

[3] The alternatives are noted in *PLRE* I 203, where 'after 395' is favoured.

[4] Socr. *Hist. Eccl.* 7. 17.

[5] Socr. *Hist. Eccl.* 7. 12.

On his journey home to Gaul from Rome in the late autumn of 417,[1] Rutilius Namatianus called on his friend Victorinus, whose career he describes in the lines quoted above. He had been *vicarius* of Britain,[2] where he had behaved in an exemplary fashion, doing his best to make himself popular, even though it hardly mattered ('minor . . . pudor') if one earned disfavour in that quarter—a revealing comment, perhaps reflecting a general anti-British prejudice,[3] although it might recall the activities of the three British pretenders, Marcus, Gratian, and Constantine III.[4] In line 507, Victorinus is referred to as 'illustris', showing that he had received some advancement, since *vicarii* were only 'spectabiles'.[5] It is, however, not clear whether he became an 'illustris' by the appointment as *comes* which he had recently received, but then resigned, preferring country life.[6] This retirement itself had been rudely interrupted by the capture of Toulouse, an event which cannot be precisely dated, but which must have fallen in the period 409–14.[7] The British vicariate is generally assigned to the reign of Honorius,[8] although nothing in these lines makes this certain and it could have been held before the death of Theodosius. At all events, J. F. Matthews's observation that 'it will have fallen before 406 (the proclamation of Marcus)' must be right.[9] Had Victorinus held office under one of the British pretenders he would hardly have received preferment from Honorius.

Rutilius' language makes it certain that Victorinus was a Gaul, with his home in or close to Toulouse.

[1] The date has been established by A. Cameron, *JRS* 57 (1967) 31 ff., approved by J. Matthews, *Western Aristocracies and Imperial Court A.D. 364–425* (1975) 325.

[2] This is the only possible interpretation of *praefectorum vicibus* in line 501, as pointed out by J.-R. Palanque, *REA* 36 (1934) 273 n. 1.

[3] Cf. Ausonius' sarcastic remarks about the British poet Silvius Bonus, *epigr.* 107–12 (e.g. 110, 1: 'Nemo bonus Brito est').

[4] pp. 341 ff. below.

[5] See O. Hirschfeld, *Kleine Schriften* (1913) 663 ff.; A. H. M. Jones, *The Later Roman Empire* (1964) 143, 378 f., 528 ff.

[6] Palanque, *REA* 36 (1934) 273 n. 1: 'Victorinus, *vir illustris*, a été nommé *comes consistorii* (membre du conseil impérial), mais a décliné cette dignité.' He is followed by K. F. Stroheker, *Der senatorische Adel im spätantiken Gallien* (1948) 227 no. 48. Matthews, *Western Aristocracies . . .* 326, avoids precision.

[7] See Matthews, op. cit. 307, 318, 326. The capture of Toulouse is frequently assigned to the year 412, thus e.g. Stroheker, op. cit. 227.

[8] Thus Stroheker, op. cit. 227; W. Ensslin, *RE* 8A 2 (1958) 2079, followed in *Ep. Stud.* 4 (1967) 94.

[9] *Western Aristocracies . . .* 326 n. 3. For Marcus see pp. 341 ff. below.

II.18

PRAESIDES

L. Septimius . . .

EE IX 997 = *ILS* 5435 = *RIB* 103, Cirencester: see pp. 178 ff., 317 above.

. . .rocles Perpetuus

VI 1223, Rome: [. . .] *conservator* [*em militum et provincialium* (?) / *pr*] *opagator-emque re* [*ipublicae Romanae* /. . .] *p. quod sacram quoque* [*viam* (?). . . [4] / *vet*] *ustate temporis desid* [*iaque priorum corruptam* / *ad s*] *plendorem pristinum res* [*tituerit* / . . .] *rocles Perpetuus v. c. cur* [*ator* . . ./ (?)*praes*] *es provinciae Brittanni* [*ae* . . .]

The language of this inscription, although rather fragmentary, is thought to indicate a late third- or early fourth-century date.[1] Perpetuus evidently carried out repairs to the *sacra via* in his capacity as *curator*, probably *aedium sacrarum*.[2] The latest known holder of this post held office under Constantine.[3] Earlier in his career, apparently, Perpetuus had been governor of one of the British provinces.[4] Although he was *v. c.* at the time the inscription was set up, he may well have been still *vir perfectissimus* as *praeses* in Britain.[5]

Perpetuus' first name is generally restored as Hierocles,[6] which is by far the commonest of names terminating -rocles, and the only one known to have been borne by senatorial or equestrian office-holders.[7] But there are several other possible restorations.[8] Nothing can be inferred about his origin from the nomenclature.

Flavius Sanctus

Auson. *Parentalia* 20:

[1] Thus *PLRE* I 689.   [2] Thus *PLRE* I 689.
[3] See the list in *PLRE* I 1058.
[4] In *PIR*[2] H 173, doubt is expressed whether Perpetuus is the same person as the [*praes*] *es*. But it is difficult to see why a British governorship should be mentioned on the inscription if it had not been held by Perpetuus himself.
[5] The possibility should not be excluded that the British governorship was mentioned because he had just received the appointment at the time the inscription was set up.
[6] Thus *PLRE* I 689, *PIR*[2] H 173, etc.
[7] See e.g. *PIR*[2] L 182, 202; *PLRE* I, 431 f. Our man might conceivably be identical with one of these fourth century persons. It should be noted that other names might have been recorded at the end of line 5.
[8] Most of the possible names are rather too long, but note Androcles; there was a rhetor of that name at Ancyra, a friend of Libanius, *ep.* 1242, 1340.

Qui ioca laetitiamque colis, qui tristia damnas
   nec mutuis quemquam nec metuendus agis,
qui nullum insidiis captas nec lite lacessis,
4   sed iustam et clemens vitam agis et sapiens,
tranquillos manes supremaque mitia Sancti
   ore pio et verbis advenerare bonis.
militiam nullo qui turbine sedulus egit,
8   praeside laetatus quo Rutupinus ager,
octoginta annos cuius tranquilla senectus
   nullo mutavit deteriore die.
ego precare favens, ut qualia tempora vitae,
   talia ad manes otia Sanctus agat.

Flavius Sanctus was married to Ausonius' sister-in-law Namia Pudentilla.[1] Since the *Parentalia* was written in the late 380s,[2] and Sanctus had already reached the age of eighty[3] by then, it may be assumed that his service as *praeses* in Britain had been accomplished many years earlier, perhaps c.350. It is not clear whether the untroubled 'militia' referred to in line 7 should be taken to mean some other post held before the British one,[4] or is intended to refer to the governorship itself.[5] *Rutupinus* might be thought to indicate which province was meant, the one which included Kent, namely Maxima Caesariensis.[6] But the adjective is probably poetic for 'British'.[7]

Sanctus may confidently be regarded as a Gaul;[8] he might be a descendant of the consul of that name who held office in the *imperium Galliarum* with the emperor Victorinus.[9]

383   (?) Leucadius

Sulp. Sever. *Dial.* 3. 11. 8: praeter multas, quas evoluere longum est, has principales habebat: pro Narseti comite et Leucadio praeside, quorum ambo Gratiani partium fuerant, pertinacioribus studiis, quae non est temporis explicare, iram victoris emeriti.

Count Narses and the *praeses* Leucadius, as men who remained loyal to

---

[1] Auson. *Parentalia* 20 tit., 21. 4. They had a son, ibid. 21. 9. See *PLRE* I 755, 801.
[2] F. Marx, *RE* 2. 2 (1896) 2573.
[3] Auson. *Parentalia* 20. 9. In *PLRE* I 801 he is said to have died at ninety.
[4] Thus O. Seeck, *RE* IA 2 (1920) 2252: 'Er diente in irgend einem Officium and wurde dann Praeses einer britannischen Provinz.'
[5] This interpretation appears to be intended in *PLRE* I 801.
[6] See p. 317 above, and *PLRE* I 801, cf. Auson. *Ordo urb. nob.* 72, on Magnus Maximus, quoted p. 383 below.
[7] Thus *PLRE* I 801.
[8] Thus K. F. Stroheker, *Der senatorische Adel im spätantiken Gallien* (1948) 215 no. 347.
[9] XIII 11976. For the date, see Degrassi, *FC* 72.

Gratian, had presumably held office in 383 in territories then taken over by Magnus Maximus. The choice for Leucadius is large, for the three western dioceses contained nearly twenty governors with the title *praeses* (as well as nearly a dozen *consulares*), to judge from the *Notitia*,[1] but the possibility at least deserves to be registered that he had been governing one of the three British provinces, Prima, Secunda, or Flavia Caesariensis, which were not under a *consularis*.

The date of St Martin's intervention on behalf of the two men was 385 or 386, after the executions of the Priscillianists.[2] Leucadius' name appears to be Greek, but could in fact derive from a place in Spain.[3]

II.19

COMITES

Gratianus

Amm. Marc. 30. 7. 2–3: Natus apud Cibalas, Pannoniae oppidum, Gratianus maior ignobili stirpe, cognominatus est a pueritia prima Funarius . . . 3. ob ergo validum corporis robur, et peritiam militum more luctandi, notior multis, post dignitatem protectoris atque tribuni, comes praefuit rei castrensi per Africam, unde furtorum suspicione contactus, digressusque multo postea pari potestate Brittanicum rexit exercitum, tandemque honeste sacramento solutus, revertit ad larem, et agens procul a strepitu, multatione bonorum adflictus est a Constantio, hoc nomine, quod civili flagrante discordia, hospitio dicebatur suscepisse Magnentium, per agrum suum ad proposita festinantem.

Gratianus, as the parent of the emperors Valentinian and Valens, is naturally referred to by a number of writers,[1] but Ammianus is the only one to provide full details of his career.[2] Of humble origin, he was a native of Cibalae, south of Mursa in Pannonia, a town that had been a *municipium* from Hadrian's reign and a *colonia* from the Severan period.[3]

---

[1] See the lists in A. H. M. Jones, *The Later Roman Empire* (1964) III 382 f.

[2] *PLRE* I 504.

[3] Cf. *AE* 1938. 30 = *RIT* 971, Tarraco, for a fifth- or sixth-century *primicerius notariorum* of this name, regarded by Alföldy, ad loc., as probably a native of the place. Note also the Spanish place-name 'Contrebia quae Leucada appellatur' (*RE* 4. 1 (1900) 1163).

[1] *PLRE* I 400 f. supplies references.

[2] Gibbon recasts Ammianus elegantly: 'Valentinian was the son of count Gratian, a native of Cibalis in Pannonia, who, from an obscure condition, had raised himself, by matchless strength and dexterity, to the military commands of Africa and Britain; from which he had retired with an ample fortune and suspicious integrity' (*Decline and Fall of the Roman Empire*, ch. xxv).

[3] A. Mócsy, *Pannonia and Upper Moesia* (1974) 143, 152, 225 f.

The chronology of his career depends on the fact that he was in retirement at Cibalae when he entertained the usurper Magnentius in 351, and on the date of birth of Valentinian, *c.* 321,[4] by which time Gratianus' military service may be assumed to have started. After a period in the ranks, his physical strength and skill in wrestling won him a commission as *protector* and then a command as tribune. If an inscription from Salonae refers to him, he also held an appointment as *praefectus* (and was a *protector domesticus* rather than one of the ordinary kind).[5] There followed two commands with the rank of *comes rei militaris*, in Africa and in Britain. J. C. Mann has stressed that 'possession of the title did not imply appointment to a particular post . . . it is very probable that, if indeed he served as a regular frontier commander, an inscription in either case would have referred to him as *v. p. comes et dux.*'[6] There is in fact no reason to suppose that the post of *comes Britanniarum* listed in the *Notitia Dignitatum* was a regular one before the late fourth century.[7] Hence it is reasonable to suggest that the dispatch of a *comes* to Britain some time before 351 was occasioned by some particular military threat, such as the one which caused Constans' winter expedition in 343.[8]

An inscription from Constantine (Cirta) in Numidia, set up in his memory during the years 364–7, indicates the latest possible date of his death.[9]

367   Nectaridus

Amm. Marc. 27. 8. 1: see p. 333 below.

---

[4] Amm. Marc. 30. 6. 6.

[5] III 12900. The identification is taken for granted by O. Seeck, *RE* 7. 2 (1912) 1831, regarded as possible in *PLRE* I 401. For the two sorts of *protectores*, see A. H. M. Jones, *The Later Roman Empire* (1964) 636 ff., and for tribunes and *praefecti*, ibid. 640 ff.

[6] Mann, in Johnston (ed.), *The Saxon Shore* 13.

[7] *Not. Dign. Occ.* VII, XXIX. For the problem, see p. 320 above; note also Frere, *Britannia*[2] (1974) 268 ff.; J. S. Johnson, in Goodburn and Bartholomew (edd.), *Aspects of the Notitia Dignitatum* 87 ff.; and the general discussion, taking Gratianus' career as a starting point, in Jones, op. cit. III 19 ff. (n. 26).

[8] Frere, op. cit. 387 f. The suggestion of D. Van Berchem, *AJP* 76 (1955) 146 n. 47, that Gratianus was *dux Britanniarum* with the rank of *comes*, is attractive. He compares *P. Lond.* 234, where the Duke of Egypt is *comes et dux*. K. M. Martin, *Latomus* 28 (1969) 413, argues from Ammianus' words *pari potestate* that Gratianus must have been *comes* in Britain since he could not have been other than *comes Africae*, citing Seeck, *RE* 4. 1 (1900) 637 f., for the proof that the latter officer was regularly of comitial status from the time of Constantine I. But see Mann, in Goodburn and Bartholomew, op. cit. 6, who argues that Taurinus (*PLRE* I 878 f.), *c.*345, was the first *comes Africae*. Gratian must have been in Africa before this. But even if Seeck's view were valid, it would not disprove Van Berchem's hypothesis about Gratian's rank in Britain. (See also Jones, op. cit. 125; III 19 ff., and the discussion on p. 320 above).

[9] *ILS* 758.

Nectaridus, killed by the invaders in the 'barbarian conspiracy' of the
year 367, is described by Ammianus as 'comes maritimi tractus', which
seems like a literary periphrasis for the post of *comes litoris Saxonici
per Britannias* attested in the *Notitia Dignitatum*.[1] Although this has
been disputed,[2] it remains the most natural interpretation.[3]

Nothing else is known of this man, whose name has been taken to
indicate German origin.[4]

367-368   Flavius Theodosius

Symmachus, *relat*. 9. 4 (287 Seeck): nam familiae vestrae et stirpis auctorem,
Africanum quondam et Brittannicum ducem statuis equestribus inter prisca nomina
consecravit, qui felici satu numen in imperium salutare progenuit.

Ibid. 43. 2 (314 Seeck): quorum auctor et parens, ut dudum v. c. et inlustri offici-
orum magistro scripsisse memini, statuarum equestrium honore decoratus est, quas
ei ordo venerabilis Africani et Brittannici belli recordatione decrevit ea scilicet
causa, et iustis superiorum ducum titulis praesentium circa vos devotio provocetur.

Panegyrici Latini Veteres 2 (12). 5. 1-2: Erat iustae compensationis occasio, ut qui
de patriae tuae laudibus pauca dixissem, patris saltem virtutibus praedicandis pro-
lixius immorarer. Sed quid faciam? Novam quandam patior ex copia difficultatem.
2. Quid, inquam, faciam? Quae Rhenus aut Vachalis vidit adgrediar? Iam se mihi
Sarmatica caede sanguineus Hister obiciet. Attritam pedestribus proeliis Britanniam
referam? Saxo consumptus bellis navalibus offeretur. Redactum ad paludes suas
Scotum loquar? . . .

Amm. Marc. 27. 8. 1-9. 1: Profectus itaque [sc. Valentinianus] ab Ambianis,
Treverosque festinans, nuntio percellitur gravi, qui Brittanias indicabat barbarica
conspiratione ad ultimam vexatas inopiam, Nectaridumque comitem maritimi
tractus, occisum, Fullofauden ducem hostilibus insidiis circumventum. 2. quibus
magno cum horrore conpertis, Severum etiam tum domesticorum comitem misit, si
fors casum dedisset optatum, correcturum sequius gesta: quo postea revocato,
Iovinus . . . ad eadem loca provectus . . .†idem caeleri gradu permisit, adminicula
petiturus exercitus validi; id enim instantes necessitates flagitare firmabant. 3.
postremo ob multa et metuenda, quae super eadem insula rumores adsidui per-
ferebant, electus Theodosius illuc properare disponitur, officiis Martiis felicissime
cognitus, adscitaque animosa legionum et cohortium pube, ire tendebat, praeeunte

---

[1] *Not. Dig. Occ.* I, V, XXVIII. See p. 320 above, for discussion of the post. A. H. M. Jones,
The Later Roman Empire (1964) 140, calls Nectaridus 'the *comes litoris Saxonici*' without
comment. Frere, *Britannia*[2] 242, calls Ammianus' words 'an obvious periphrasis'.

[2] By K. M. Martin, *Latomus* 28 (1969) 408 ff., who argues that the *maritimus tractus* was
on the west coast. See next note.

[3] See J. S. Johnson, in Goodburn and Bartholomew (edd.), *Aspects of the Notitia Dignitatum* (B.A.R. Supp. ser. 15, 1977) 81 ff., esp. 87 ff.

[4] Thus M. Waas, *Germanen in römischen Dienst im 4. Jahrhundert n. Chr.* (1965) 117, with
a mark of interrogation.

fiducia speciosa. 4. . . . 5. illud tamen sufficet dici, quod eo tempore Picti in duas gentes divisi, Dicalydonas et Verturiones, itidemque Attacotti, bellicosa hominum natio, et Scotti, per diversa vagantes, multa populabantur. Gallicanos vero tractus Franci et Saxones, isdem confines, quo quisque erumpere potuit, terra vel mari, praedis acerbis incendiisque, et captivorum funeribus omnium, violabant. 6. Ad haec prohibenda, si copiam dedisset fortuna prosperior, orbis extrema dux effica-cissimus petens, cum venisset ad Bononiae litus, quod a spatio controverso terrarum, angustiis reciproci distinguitur maris, attolli horrendis aestibus adsueti, rursusque sine ulla navigantium noxa, in speciem conplanari camporum, exinde transmeato lentius freto, defertur Rutupias, stationem ex adverso tranquillam. 7. unde cum consecuti Batavi venissent et Heruli, Ioviique et Victores, fidentes viribus numeri, egressus tendensque ad Lundinium, vetus oppidum quod Augustam posteritas appellavit, divisis plurifariam globis, adortus est vagantes hostium vastatorias manus, graves onere sarcinarum, et propere fusis, qui vinctos homines agebant et pecora, praedam excussit, quam tributarii perdidere miserrimi. 8. isdemque restituta omni praeter partem exiguam, inpensam militibus fessis, mersam difficultatibus †suis antehac civitatem, sed subito, quam salus sperari potuit recreatam, ovantis specie laetissimus introiit. 9. Ubi ad audenda maiora, prospero successu elatus, tutaque scrutando consilia, futuri morabatur ambiguus, diffusam variarum gentium plebem, et ferocientem inmaniter, non nisi per dolos occultiores, et inprovisos excursus, superari posse†, captivorum confessionibus, et transfugarum indiciis, doctus. 10. denique edictis propositis, inpunitateque promissa, desertores ad procinctum voca-bat, et multos alios per diversa libero commeatu dispersos. quo monitu rediere plerique, incentivo perciti, relevatusque anxiis curis, Civilem nomine recturum Brittanias pro praefectis, ad se poposcerat mitti, virum acrioris ingenii, sed iusti tenacem et recti, itidemque Dulcitium, ducem scientia rei militaris insignem. 9. 1. Haec in Brittaniis agebantur. . . .

id. 28. 3: 1. Theodosius vero, dux nominis inclyti, animi vigore collecto, ab Augusta profectus, quam veteres appellavere Lundinium, cum milite industria conparato sollerti, versis turbatisque Brittanorum fortunis, opem maximam tulit, opportuna ubique ad insidiandum barbaris praeveniens loca, nihilque gregariis inperans, cuius non ipse primitias, alacri capesseret mente. 2. hocque genere cum strenui militis munia et praeclari ducis curas expleret, fusis variis gentibus et fugatis, quas insolen-tia nutriente securitate, adgredi Romanas res inflammabat, in integrum restituit civitates et castra, multiplicibus quidem damnis adflicta, set ad quietem temporis longi fundata. 3. Evenerat autem eodem haec agente facinus dirum, erupturum in periculum grave, ni inter ipsa conatus principia fuisset extinctum. 4. Valentinus quidam natus in Valeria Pannoniae, superbi spiritus homo, Maximini illius exitialis vicarii, postea praefecti coniugis frater, ob grave crimen in Brittanias exsul, quietis inpatiens ut malefica bestia, ad res perniciosas consurgebat et novas, in Theodosium tumore quodam, quem solum resistere posse nefandis cogitationibus advertebat. 5. multa tamen clam palamque circumspiciens, crescente flatu cupiditatis inmensae, exules sollicitabat et milites, pro temporis captu ausorum inlecebrosas pollicendo mercedes. 6. iamque propinquante temptatorum effectu, doctus haec unde con-venerat, dux alacrior ad audendum, et corde celso ad vindictam compertorum erectus, Valentinum quidem, cum paucis arta ei societate iunctissimis, letali poena plectendos, Dulcitio dediderat duci: militari scientia vero, qua superabat praesentes, futura coniciens, de coniuratis quaestiones agitari prohibuit, ne formidine sparsa per multos, reviviscerent provinciarum turbines consopiti. 7. Hinc ad corrigenda plura conversus et necessaria, periculo penitus dempto, cum aperte constaret, nulla eius propitiam deseruisse fortunam, instaurabat urbes et praesidiaria (ut diximus) castra, limitesque vigiliis tuebatur et praetenturis, recuperatamque provinciam, quae in dicionem concesserat hostium, ita reddiderat statui pristino, ut eodem referente et rectorem haberet legitimum, et Valentia deinde vocaretur arbitrio principis, velut ovantis. 8. . . .tudio nuntio inest. haec etiam praecipua. Areanos genus hominum a veteribus institutum, super quibus aliqua in actibus Constantis rettulimus, paulatim prolapsos in vitia, a stationibus suis removit, aperte convictos, acceptarum promissarumque magnitudine praedarum allectos, quae apud nos agebantur, aliquotiens barbaris prodidisse. id enim illis erat officium, ut ultro citroque, per longa spatia discurrentes, vicinarum gentium strepitus nostris ducibus intimarent. 9. Ita spectatissime ante dictis rebus aliisque administratis similibus, ad comitatum accitus, tripudiantesque relinquens provincias, ut Furius Camillus vel Cursor Papirius, victoriis crebris et salutaribus erat insignis. et favore omnium ad usque fretum deductus, leni vento transgressus, venit ad conmilitium principis, cumque gaudio susceptus et laudibus, in locum Iovini ut lenti successit, qui equorum copias tuebatur.

Claud. *Epithalamium* 218–21:

> illic exuvias omnes cumulate parentum:
> quidquid avus senior Mauro vel Saxone victis,
> quidquid ab innumeris socio Stilichone tremendus
> quaesivit genitor bellis . . .

Id., *de III cons. Honorii* 51–8:

> quoque magis nimium pugnae inflammaret amorem,
> facta tui numerabat avi, quem litus adustae
> horrescit Libyae ratibusque impervia Thule:
> 54 ille leves Mauros nec falso nomine Pictos
> edomuit Scottorumque vago mucrone secutus
> fregit Hyperboreas remis audacibus undas
> et geminis fulgens utroque sub axe tropaeis
> 58 Tethyos alternae refluas calcavit harenas.

Id., *de IV cons. Honorii* 24–33:

> hinc processit avus, cui post Arctoa frementi
> classica Massylas adseruit Africa laurus,
> ille, Caledoniis posuit qui castra pruinis,
> qui medio Libyae sub casside pertulit aestus,
> 28 terribilis Mauro debellatorque Britanni
> litoris ac pariter Boreae vastator et Austri.
> quid rigor aeternus, caeli quid frigora prosunt
> ignotumque fretum? maduerunt Saxone fuso
> 32 Orcades, incaluit Pictorum sanguine Thyle;
> Scottorum cumulos flevit glacialis Hiverne.

Id., *laus Serenae* 37–46:

> non hoc privata dedere
> limina nec tantum poterat contingere nomen
> augustis laribus; patruo te principe celsam
> 40 bellipotens inlustrat avus, qui signa Britanno
> intulit Oceano Gaetulaque repperit arma.
> claram Scipiadum taceat Cornelia gentem,
> seque minus iactet Libycis dotata tropaeis:
> 44 cardine tu gemino laurus praetendis avitas:
> inde Caledoniis, Australibus inde parentum
> cingeris exuviis.

Byzantion 5 (1929–30) 9 ff. = *AE* 1931. 53, Stobi:
(a) [. . .] ΔΟ/[. . .] ΡΑ/[. . .] ΦΟ⁴/[. . .] ΣΤ/[. . .] ΣΤ/[. . .] Ω/[. . .] ΩΑ⁸/[. . .] ΙΟΥ
/[. . .] χάρμα / μέγα Βριττάνων καὶ / Μαυριτανίης μέγα δί¹²/μα Σαξωνείης λυτῆ/ρα
καὶ γένους Κελτῶν / φιλοτιμίας χρυσίον
(b) [. . .] / εἰσορᾷς ξῖϝε[. . .] / ἀντιμέτωπον εἰκόνα [μ]αρ⁴ /[μ]έρουσαν χρυσῷ
πᾶσαν ἠέλι/όν ὡς ἱππ[ικὴν καθ]ὼς ἵδρυται / θεῷ Κ[ωνσταντίνῳ πρ]ὸς τῷ / φω] . . .]
(The reading Βριττάνων in line 10 of (a) is supplied by N. Vulić *ap.* W. Ensslin, *RE*
5A 2 (1934) 1939, in place of the editor's Δαρδάνων.)

More is recorded about the activity in Britain of Flavius Theodosius
than about that of any other figure in the late Roman period. This
presumably results more from the elevation to the throne of his son
Theodosius I, emperor from 379 to 395 and founder of a dynasty
which lasted until the mid-fifth century,[1] than from the importance of
the crisis of 367 and the significance of Theodosius' measures, great
though these undoubtedly were.[2] But the only real evidence is in the
account of Ammianus, who 'has concisely represented the whole series of
the British war', as Gibbon remarked. The sycophantic effusions of Pacatus and Claudian are no more reliable than those of the Flavian poets who
sang of Vespasian's British exploits.[3] 'The voice of poetry and panegyric
may add, perhaps with some degree of truth,' says Gibbon, 'that the
unknown regions of Thule were stained with the blood of the Picts;
that the oars of Theodosius dashed the waves of the Hyberborean
ocean; and that the distant Orkneys were the scene of his naval victory

[1] See *PLRE* I 1131(stemma).
[2] J. Morris, *The Age of Arthur* (1973) 15 ff., comments that the prominence given to
Theodosius by Ammianus may be explained by the fact that his son was emperor at the time of
writing. (But Morris stresses that, even if the effect of the barbarian invasion on the south was
very limited, 'the northern assault was far more serious' and 'on the northern frontier, Theodosius devised a new policy, whose impact was felt for a thousand years.') See also Syme,
Ammianus and the Historia Augusta 14: 'There is a discrepancy between the praise and the
achievement: the historian was writing under the rule of Theodosius' son.'
[3] p. 227 above.

over the Saxon pirates.' But he comments, in a note, that 'it is not easy to appreciate the intrinsic value of flattery and metaphor.'[4]

Nothing is known in detail of Theodosius' career before his appointment to the British command. Ammianus only refers vaguely to his distinguished military service, 'officiis Martiis felicissime cognitus'. He was selected by Valentinian after the brief and abortive missions of Severus, *comes domesticorum*,[5] and Jovinus, the *magister equitum*,[6] when the latter returned, 'adminicula petiturus exercitus validi.' R. Tomlin has convincingly unravelled the confusion in Ammianus' account, created by his having described Valentinian's dangerous illness at Amiens in the summer of 367 in chapter 6 of book 27, before dealing with the invasion of Britain and its aftermath.[7] In fact, as Tomlin shows, Valentinian's journey to Amiens, soon after 3 June, must have been prompted by the first news of the 'barbarian conspiracy'. The dispatch of Severus, 'etiam tum domesticorum comitem', and his return, and then the sending of Jovinus, must all have occurred before Valentinian's illness, in the course of which Severus, by then promoted to *magister peditum*, was thought of as a possible successor to the throne, Jovinus, senior in rank, being still absent.[8]

In the light of this reinterpretation of Ammianus, Theodosius can be seen to have dealt with the British emergency 'in not much more than a year', with additional forces of only some 2,000 men.[9] Arriving before the campaigning season of 367 was over,[10] he reached London and wintered there, after dispersing bands of raiders and recapturing booty. From London he prepared for an offensive, regrouping the scattered Roman troops and offering an amnesty to deserters; and he sent for Civilis to be *vicarius* and Dulcitius to be *dux*.[11]

In 368 he campaigned vigorously, ambushing enemy bands, defeating and putting to flight several *gentes*, restoring towns and forts. In the meantime he had to deal with an added problem, an attempt at usurpation by the exile Valentinus, the suppression of which was left to Dulcitius,

---

[4] *Decline and Fall of the Roman Empire*, ch. xxv.

[5] p. 372 below.

[6] p. 373 below.

[7] Tomlin, *Britannia* 5 (1974) 303 ff.

[8] As Tomlin, op. cit. 305 n. 19, notes, A. Demandt, *RE* Supp. 12 (1970) 596, implausibly solves the problem by postulating the two Severi, one the *comes domesticorum* sent to Britain, the other the *magister peditum* and possible emperor. Tomlin's solution is far neater.

[9] Tomlin, op. cit. 307.

[10] As Tomlin, op. cit. 306 and n. 25, reasonably infers from Ammian. Marc. 27. 8. 6, on the calmness of the Channel crossing—had it been already past the equinox, the fact would have been mentioned, as with earlier expeditions.

[11] See pp. 325 above, 345 below, for these men.

while Theodosius forbade any inquisition to find accomplices.[12] Finally, he strengthened the frontiers, and the province which had fallen into enemy hands was so thoroughly restored to its former condition that it could be given a regular governor, and was renamed Valentia—a statement which causes some difficulty of interpretation.[13] His final action was the removal of the *areani* from their posts,[14] and he then returned—before the end of 368, it would seem[15]—to the emperor's side, where he was appointed *magister equitum* in place of Jovinus.

It must be noted that although he is always called 'Count Theodosius', as he is in the summary of Ammianus' book 27,[16] that writer nowhere explicitly mentions his rank. He calls him *dux*, in the non-technical sense of 'general' or 'leader', on four occasions.[17] It has to be deduced that he was *comes rei militaris*,[18] a rank appropriate for one promoted to be *magister equitum*, who commanded field-army troops in Britain.[19] Among those who served under him were his son, the future emperor,[20] and a distant kinsman, a 'poor relation' one might call him, Magnus Maximus.[21]

Theodosius continued to be *magister equitum* until his death. In 370 he fought the Alamanni *per Raetias*,[22] and in 372 participated in Valentinian's campaign against the Alamannic king Macrianus on the Rhine.[23] In 373 he was sent to Africa, after collecting troops from

[12] It may be mentioned that Zosimus 4. 12. 2 and Jerome, *chron. s. a.* 371, only describe the Valentinus affair (getting the name wrong, and the date too, in Jerome's case), although Zosimus does have a muddled reference to the campaign in 4. 35. 3. This might arouse the unworthy suspicion that the campaign was not thought significant except by those writing under Theodosius I (see n. 2 above).

[13] J. G. F. Hind, *Historia* 24 (1975) 101 ff., argues that in this passage Ammianus meant that the whole diocese of Britain was renamed Valentia, comparing Constantius' renaming of the Asian diocese Pietas after his wife Eusebia (Amm. Marc. 17. 7. 6). Stevens, in Goodburn and Bartholomew (edd.); *Aspects of the Notitia Dignitatum* 222 n. 31, accepts this interpretation of Ammianus, but regards it as a mistake on the latter's part. See pp. 315 ff. above, for a discussion of the fourth century provinces. Hind, incidentally, imports some gratuitous confusion by his statement, 101, about 'a passage in Eutropius to the effect that Theodosius conquered Britain as far as *Orcades insulae*'. Eutrop. 7. 13. 2–3 refers to A. Plautius (quoted p. 37 above).

[14] See Stevens, *Latomus* 14 (1955) 395, for the explanation of this term; also I. A. Richmond, *Roman and Native in North Britain* (1958) 114 ff.

[15] Ammianus' account certainly does not imply that he wintered in Britain after his second campaign, but this might be concealed in the phrase 'Ita spectatissime ante dictis rebus aliisque administratis similibus'—*aliisque* could cover a great deal.

[16] Quoted p. 345 n. 2 below.   [17] See p. 345 n. 4 below.

[18] W. Ensslin, *RE* 5A 2 (1934) 1938, suggests *comes litoris Saxonici* or *comes Britanniarum*. But see Mann, in Johnston (ed.), *The Saxon Shore* 14 and n. 16; and p. 320 above.

[19] Tomlin, *Britannia* 5 (1974) 307 n. 31.

[20] Zos. 4. 35. 3 etc.; see *PLRE* I 904.

[21] pp. 346 ff. below.

[22] Amm. Marc. 28. 5. 15; *Pan. Lat.* 2 (12). 5. 2.

[23] Amm. Marc. 29. 4. 5. *PLRE* I 903 refers to a campaign against 'the Alani', which is presumably a misprint.

Illyricum,[24] to suppress the rebellious Moorish prince Firmus, a campaign which lasted until the beginning of 375.[25] Valentinian died on the Danube on 17 November of that year, and shortly afterwards Theodosius, still in Africa, was arrested, taken to Carthage, and beheaded. The circumstances of his death are mysterious—even the date is uncertain, but it was probably in January or February 376.[26] Ammianus does not record the affair, although by his comparison of Theodosius to Corbulo and Lusius Quietus, great generals of earlier days—who were executed by ungrateful emperors—he delicately alludes to it. Explicit details would have been too painful, no doubt, when the great man's son was emperor.[27]

Theodosius was a native of Spain, born into an orthodox Christian family. Later, it was alleged that the family was descended from Trajan, and hence that they came from Italica. But he had property at Cauca, on the road between Emerita and Caesaraugusta, where his wife Thermantia bore their second son, the future emperor.[28]

370   (?)Nannienus

Amm. Marc. 28. 5. 1–2: Erupit Augustis ter consulibus Saxonum multitudo, et Oceani difficultatibus permeatis, Romanum limitem gradu petebat intento, saepe nostrorum funeribus pasta: cuius eruptionis primae procellam, Nannenus sustinuit comes, regionibus isdem adpositus, dux diuturno bellorum labore conpertus. 2. sed tunc ad mortem destinatae plebi congressus, cum milites quosdam ruisse, et se vulneratum, inparem fore certaminibus adverteret crebris, docto imperatore quid agi deberet, id est adeptus, ut magister peditum Severus, opitulatum rebus dubiis adveniret.

The context makes it clear that the Saxon invasion of 370 described here was of northern Gaul,[1] not of Britain. G. Macdonald and others

---

[24] *Pan. Lat.* 2 (12). 5. 2, referring to a Sarmatian campaign, may be explained by his presence in Illyricum—to collect the troops which Zosimus 4. 16. 3 says he took from Pannonia and Moesia. Thus Ensslin, *RE* 5A 2 (1934) 1938.

[25] See *PLRE* I, 903, for references, and for a thorough discussion, J. F. Matthews, in Goodburn and Bartholomew (edd.), *Aspects of the Notitia Dignitatum* 157 ff.

[26] See Demandt, *Historia* 18 (1969) 598 ff.

[27] Thus Ensslin, *RE* 5A 2 (1934) 1943 f. Ammianus also compares him with a whole series of republican worthies—Camillus and Papirius Cursor (28. 3. 9), Curio (29. 5. 22), Fabius Cunctator (29. 5. 32), and Pompey (29. 5. 33).

[28] See *PLRE* I 902 ff. for details.

[1] The early editor of Ammianus who wrote the summary of 28. 5 took this to be the case: 'Saxones in Gallia, post factas indutias, a Romanis insidiis circumventi.' W. Ensslin, *RE* 16. 2 (1935) 1682, regards Nannienus as having been perhaps successor of Charietto as *comes per utramque Germaniam*, killed in 365, Amm. Marc. 27. 1. 2 ff., an office otherwise unknown, *PLRE* I 200.

described the general Nannienus,[2] who met the first wave of the attackers, as *comes Britanniae* or *Britanniarum*,[3] but it is unlikely that the post had been created at this date.[4] More plausible is the suggestion by J. S. Johnson that he was *comes litoris Saxonici*, and that this officer's responsibilities at this time covered both sides of the Channel.[5] But he may simply have been commanding a small *ad hoc* field army, as Theodosius had in Britain three years earlier.[6] The question cannot be decided on present evidence.

The details of Nannienus' earlier career, alluded to by Ammianus in the phrase 'dux diuturno bellorum labore conpertus', are unknown. He must have made a good recovery from the wounds which obliged him to hand over command to Severus,[7] since he is found in 378 participating in Gratian's campaign on the Upper Rhine, described by Ammianus on this occasion as 'virtutis sobriae ducis', with the same rank as Mallobaudes, *comes domesticorum*.[8] He turns up finally as *magister militum* of Magnus Maximus in Gaul, in 387-8, when he was left behind, with Quintinus, under the nominal control of Maximus' son Victor. He apparently refused to join his colleague in a campaign against the Franks, but was then dismissed, in any case, after the fall of Maximus and the death of Victor.[9]

His origin is not recorded, but he may have been a German, although the name is Celtic.[10]

383   (?)Narses

Sulp. Sever. *Dial.* 3. 11. 8: see p. 330 above, for the text.

Narses, the *comes*, and Leucadius the *praeses* were two of those for whom St Martin petitioned Magnus Maximus. It is reasonable to infer

---

[2] The MSS of Ammianus spell the name 'Nannenus', but Nannienus is evidently the correct form. J. S. Johnson, in Goodburn and Bartholomew (edd.), *Aspects of the Notitia Dignitatum* 90, gives no reason for preferring the former spelling. Amm. Marc. 31. 10. 6-7 has 'Nannieno'; he is called 'Nanninus' by Gregory of Tours, *Hist. Franc.* 2. 9.

[3] G. Macdonald, *RE* 16. 2 (1935) 1682, where, curiously, there are two entries for the same man. Ensslin, ibid., in the second entry, cites other writers who have described Nannienus as *comes* of Britain.   [4] p. 320 above.

[5] Johnson, in Goodburn and Bartholomew (edd.), op. cit. 90 f.

[6] p. 337 above.   [7] p. 373 below.

[8] Amm. Marc. 31. 10. 6. See *PLRE* I 616, where it is thought he may have been *comes utriusque Germaniae*; Ensslin, *RE* 16. 2 (1935) 1682, regards him as *magister equitum praesentalis*.

[9] Ensslin, *RE* 16. 2 (1935) 1682 f.; *PLRE* I 616.

[10] M. Waas, *Germanen im römischen Dienst im 4 Jh. n. Chr.* (1965) does not discuss him. For this name, and related ones, see Holder, *Alt-celtischer Sprachschatz* II 682 f.

that they had held appointments in one of the territories taken over by Maximus in 383, when they clearly remained loyal to Gratian, 'Gratiani partium fuerant' and thus incurred Maximus' wrath, 'iram victoris emeriti'. It is more probable that Narses (if he was a military *comes*) held a command in Gaul or on the Rhine than in Britain.[1] But it is not impossible that he was *comes litoris Saxonici*[2] in 383, and failed to support Maximus. Martin's intervention on behalf of the two men was probably in 385 or 386, soon after the trial and execution of the Priscillianists.[3] The name Narses clearly indicates Iranian origin.[4]

406   (?)Marcus

Olympiodor. frag. 12 (*FHG* 4. 59): Καὶ βασιλεὺς διὰ τὰ ἐνεστηκότα δυσχερῆ τέως καταδέχεται τὴν τῆς βασιλείας κανωνίαν, κατὰ τὰς Βρεττανίας δὲ ὁ Κωνσταντῖνος ἐτύγχανεν ἀνηγορευμέονος, στάσει τῶν ἐκεῖσε στρατιωτῶν εἰς ταύτην ἀνηγμένος τὴν ἀρχήν · καὶ γὰρ ἐν ταύταις ταῖς Βρεττανίαις, πρὶν ἢ Ὀνώριον τὸ ἕβδομον ὑπατεῦσαι, εἰς στάσιν ὁρμῆσαν τὸ ἐν αὐταῖς στρατιωτιπόν, Μάρκον τινὰ ἀνεῖπον αὐτοκράτορα. τοῦ δὲ ὑπ᾽ αὐτῶν ἀναιρεθέντος, Γρατιανὸς αὐτοῖς ἀντικαθίσταται. ἐπεὶ δὲ καὶ οὗτος εἰς τετράμηνον, αὐτοῖς προσκορὴς γεγονώς, ἀπεσφάγη, Κωνσταντῖνος τότε εἰς τὸ τοῦ αὐτοκράτορος ἀναβιβάζεται ὄνομα.

Sozom. *Hist. Eccl.* 9. 11. 1-2: Ὑπὸ τοῦτον τὸν χρόνον, πολλῶν ἐπανισταμένων τυράννων ἐν τῇ πρὸς Δύσιν ἀρχῇ, οἱ μὲν πρὸς ἀλλήλους πίπτοντες, οἱ δὲ παραδόξως συλλαμβανόμενοι, οὐ τὴν τυχοῦσαν ἐπεμαρτύρουν Ὀνωρίῳ θεοφίλειαν. 2. Πρῶτον μὲν γὰρ οἱ ἐν Βρεττανίᾳ στασιάσαντες στρατιῶται ἀναγορεύουσι Μάρκον τύραννον · μετὰ δὲ τοῦτον Γρατιανόν, ἀνελόντες Μάρκον · ἐπεὶ δὲ καὶ οὗτος οὐ πλέον τεσσάρων μηνῶν διελθόντων ἐφονεύθη παρ᾽ αὐτῶν, πάλιν Κωνσταντῖνον χειροτονοῦσιν, οἰηθέντες καθότι ταύτην εἶχε προσηγορίαν, καὶ βεβαίως αὐτὸν κρατήσειν τῆς βασιλείας. Ἐκ τοιαύτης γὰρ αἰτίας φαίνονται καὶ τοὺς ἄλλους εἰς τυραννίδα ἐπιλεξάμενοι. (A garbled version of the above appears in Nicephorus Callistus Xanthopoulus, *Hist. Eccl.* 14. 5).

Zos. *Hist. Nov.* 6. 2. 1-2: Ἔτι βασιλεύοντος Ἀρκαδίου, καὶ ὑπάτων ὄντων Ὀνωρίου τὸ ζ᾽ καὶ Θεοδοσίου τὸ β᾽, οἱ ἐν τῇ Βρεττανίᾳ, στρατευόμενοι στασιάσαντες ἀνάγουσι Μάρκον ἐπὶ τὸν βασίλειον θρόνον, καὶ ὡς κρατοῦντι τῶν αὐτόθι πραγμάτων ἐπείθοντο. ἀνελόντες δὲ τοῦτον ὡς οὐχ ὁμολογοῦντα τοῖς αὐτῶν ἤθεσιν, ἄγουσι Γρατιανὸν εἰς μέσον, καὶ ἁλουργίδα καὶ στέφανον ἐπιθέντες ἐδορυφόρουν ὡς βασιλέα. 2. δυσαρεστήσαντες δὲ καὶ τούτῳ τέτταρσιν ὕστερον μησὶ παραλύσαντες ἀναιροῦσι,

---

[1] No *comites* seem to be recorded in the Spanish diocese in the fourth century (except for Tingitana: *Not. Dig. Occ.* 26; *PLRE* I 595, Fl. Memorius). By contrast, *comites rei militaris* are frequently found in Gaul (*PLRE* I 1117 f.) and Gratian's presence in 383 will have ensured this. But, equally, Narses could have been a civil *comes*, *rei privatae*, *sacrarum largitionum*, etc.
[2] See p. 320 above, on fourth-century British *comites*.
[3] See H. Chadwick, *Priscillian of Avila* (1976) 111 ff.
[4] Thus *PLRE* I 617, cf. Narses 1 and 2, ibid. 616.

Κωνσταντίνῳ παραδόντες τὴν βασιλείαν. ὃ δὲ Ἰουστινιανὸν καὶ Νεβιογάστην
ἄρχειν τῶν ἐν Κελτοῖς τάξας στρατιωτῶν ἐπεραιώθη, τὴν Βρεττανίαν καταλιπών ·
Ibid. 6. 3. 1: ἐν τοῖς προλαβοῦσι χρόνοις, ἕκτον ἤδη τὴν ὕπατον ἔχοντος ἀρχὴν
Ἀρκαδίου καὶ Πρόβου, Βανδίλοι Συήβοις καὶ Ἀλανοῖς ἑαυτοὺς ἀναμίξαντες τούτους
ὑπερβάντες τοὺς τόπους τοῖς τὰς Ἄλπεις ἔθνεσιν ἐλυμήναντο, καὶ πόλυν ἐργασά-
μενοι φόνον ἐπίφοβοι καὶ τοῖς ἐν Βρεττανίαις στρατοπέδοις ἐγένοντο, συνηνάγκασαν
δέ, δέει τοῦ μὴ κἀπὶ σφᾶς προελθεῖν, εἰς τὴν τυράννων ὁρμῆσαι χειροτονίαν, Μάρκου
λέγω καὶ Γρατιανοῦ καὶ ἐπὶ τούτοις Κωνσταντίνου ·

Polemius Silvius, *Laterculus* (*Chron. min.* i. 523. 79): Honorius. Sub quo Gratianus
et Constantinus, bisque Attalus, Constans, Maximus atque Servatus, Marcus,
Magnus et Maximus, Iovinus, Sebastianus ac Victor tyranni fuerunt.

Apart from the bare mention of his name in a jumbled list in Polemius
Silvius, the short-lived British usurper Marcus is mentioned only in a
fragment of Olympiodorus and by the two historians who drew on him,
Sozomen and Zosimus. He was speedily replaced by Gratianus, a *municeps tyrannus*, who in turn was suppressed, after four months' rule, in
favour of Constantinus, *ex infima militia*. On both of these, particularly
Constantine III, there are more ample sources, and clearly neither of
them were generals.[1] But it is reasonable to suppose that Marcus may
have been one of the three commanders who ought to have been in
Britain at the time, *comes Britanniarum*, *comes litoris Saxonici*, or *dux
Britanniarum*.[2] This may be the meaning behind Zosimus' phrase that
the soldiers in Britain obeyed Marcus 'as the man commanding affairs
there', although on the face of it this applies to his position after the
proclamation.[3]

Olympiodorus gives no reason for the coup, other than στάσις by
the British soldiers, but Sozomen and Zosimus both provide explanations. The latter, in the second passage quoted above, describes how in
406 the Vandals, Suebi, and Alans had invaded the empire and were
wreaking havoc in the transalpine provinces. Their behaviour terrified
the forces in Britain and compelled them, 'through fear that the invaders
would turn against them, too, to proceed to elect *tyranni*, I mean
Marcus and Gratianus, and in addition to these Constantinus.' Olympiodorus likewise dates the usurpation of Marcus to 406, but Prosper Tiro

[1] See on these two O. Seeck, *RE* 7. 2 (1912) 1840; id., *RE* 4. 1 (1900) 1028 ff. It should
be noted that although Constantine may have started in the *infima militia*, this is not proof
that he was a common soldier at the time of his elevation, cf. Val. Max. 7. 8. 6. for a similar
case. See also p. 353 below, for one of his officers.
[2] p. 320 above. Frere, *Britannia*² 407, suggests that Marcus may have been *comes Britanniarum*, a possibility overlooked in *Ep. Stud.* 4 (1967) 97 f.
[3] J. B. Bury, *History of the Later Roman Empire*² I (1923) 188, alludes to this by remarking that 'we can easily conceive that the troops longed for a supreme responsible authority on
the spot'. But Zosimus' source (see n. 7) might have described Marcus' status *before* his usurpation in the phrase ὡς κρατοῦντι τῶν αὐτόθι πραγμάτων.

puts the crossing of the Rhine by the Vandals and Alans—he omits the
Suebi—on the last day of that year, 'ii k. Ian.'[4] If this date is rigidly
adhered to, then Zosimus can hardly be right, it might seem, since the
British army could not have had reason to be afraid of these invaders
when Marcus was proclaimed. For this reason, N. H. Baynes suggested
that Prosper's sentence should be interpreted to mean that the Vandals
and Alans invaded in 406, having crossed the Rhine on 31 December
405.[5] But even if this interpretation be rejected, there is no difficulty in
postulating that there was an awareness of impending invasion well before
31 December 406.[6] Certainly, it would be foolish to reject the evidence of
Zosimus, derived from a sound historian like Olympiodorus of Thebes,[7]
in favour of a wretched chronicler.[8] There are further possibilities, for
Prosper does not mention the Suebi, who, it could be argued, had
entered Gaul earlier in 406; alternatively, one might emend Prosper's
text to 'ii k. I*un*.' But neither of these expedients is really necessary.[9]

Sozomen gives a different explanation for the usurpation. 'They
appear to have chosen Constantine,' he says, 'thinking that as he had
this name, he would master the imperial power firmly [βεβαίως = *con-
stanter*], since it was for a reason such as this that they appear to have
chosen the others for usurpation as well.' The magic of the name of
Constantine, in Britain above all, does not require documentation, but
the attractions of the other names are less obvious. In the case of
Gratian, C. E. Stevens observed that 'in 378 the emperor Gratian had
defeated and virtually annihilated a host of Germans who, like the
invaders of 406, crossed the Rhine in winter.'[10] This explanation is
thoroughly acceptable,[11] As for Marcus, Stevens's reference to 'Marcus

---

[4] Prosper Tiro, *Chron.* 1230 (*Chron. min.* I 465).

[5] N. H. Baynes, *JRS* 12 (1922) 417 ff.

[6] E. A. Freeman, *EHR* 1 (1886) 54 f., makes this point, as does E. A. Thompson, *Antiquity* 30 (1956) 163, although favouring Baynes's suggestion.

[7] On Zosimus' sources, see F. Paschoud, *RE* 10A (1972), esp. 822 ff.; on the excellence of
Olympiodorus, J. F. Matthews, *JRS* 60 (1970) 79 ff.

[8] See the stern comments by Mommsen, *Chron. min.* I 348: 'In summa re minore studio et
diligentia liber conscribi vix potest quam hunc conscripsit homo Aquitanus . . . In narrandis
rebus a. 379–455 auctorem non maiore diligentia versatum esse'.

[9] Freeman, *EHR* 1 (1886) 54, mentions the possibility of emending Prosper. The invaders
were certainly already creating mayhem in Gaul when Gratian was proclaimed, according to
Oros. 7. 40. 4: 'His per Gallias bacchantibus apud Britannias Gratianus, municeps eiusdem
insulae, tyrannus creatus est.' E. A. Thompson, *Britannia* 8 (1977) 303 ff., abandoning the
views which he expressed in 1956 (n. 6 above), which he does not 'find it necessary to refer to'
(303 n. 2), attacks the article by Stevens, *Athenaeum* 35 (1957) 316 ff., where it is argued that
events on the continent precipitated the British coups. Yet Thompson refuses to pay any attention to Zosimus 6. 3. 1, and insists on sticking rigidly to Prosper; he also renders the last sentence of Sozomen by a translation that deprives it of any real meaning (see n. 11 below).

[10] Stevens, op. cit. 320, citing Amm. Marc. 31. 10. 10.

[11] Thompson, *Britannia* 8 (1977) 318, renders ἐκ τοιαύτης αἰτίας as 'For this reason', which

Carausius' is less satisfactory, although Carausius ruled Britain for seven years and defeated Saxons and other Germans, for the simple reason that he was hardly thought of as 'Marcus'—the M. in his original name seems to have been something else, and he called himself 'M. Aur. M. Carausius' later, only as a gesture towards Maximian.[12] It would be more plausible to suggest that the troops had some recollection of Marcus Aurelius, whose valiant repulse of a German invasion of Italy, led by the Suebic Quadi and Marcomanni, had been recalled by Ammianus a few years earlier.[13] The great Stoic emperor had no special association with Britain, but he spent ten years fighting the northern barbarians, and his name was much revered in late antiquity.[14]

Marcus was removed, according to Zosimus, 'because he did not agree with the soldiers' character'—if that is what ὡς οὐχ ὁμολογοῦντα τοῖς αὐτῶν ἤθεσιν means. This does not really tell us much, and certainly gives no help in discovering the man's origin. The name is far too common to provide any clue.[15]

II.20

DUCES

Fullofaudes

Amm. Marc. 27. 8. 1: see p. 333 above, for this text.

Nothing further is known about the *dux* Fullofaudes apart from this mention in Ammianus. The only slight uncertainty concerns his ultimate fate. The phrase 'hostilibus insidiis circumventum' appears to mean that he was 'surrounded by an enemy ambush'.[1] He is not referred to

---

he explains as 'so as to gain control of the empire'. This would surely have been tautologous—besides, τοιαύτης does not mean 'this', but 'of this kind'. I see no justification for criticising the interpretation of Stevens, op. cit. 320 f., on these grounds. Baynes, *JRS* 12 (1922) 219, took a similar view to Stevens about Sozomen's meaning (though he spoilt his discussion by confusing Marcus with Gratian). Orosius 7. 40. 4 also comments on Constantine's name, but ignores Marcus.

[12] Stevens, op. cit. 321. See pp. 313 f. above, on the names of Carausius.

[13] See Amm. Marc. 29. 6. 1 (Quadi and Marcomanni); also 31. 5. 13-14. The Suebi who invaded in 406 were Quadi: Schönfeld, *RE* 4A 1 (1931) 572; P. Goessler, *RE* 24 (1963) 645.

[14] See e.g. Aur. Vict. *de Caes.* 16. 2. 13; Oros. 7. 15; etc.

[15] According to Stevens, op. cit. 321 n. 36, 'the language of Sozimus suggests, according to the manners of the time, that Marcus was of barbarian origin and hence unpopular with the Roman soldiery.' This seems unconvincing; as a matter of fact, the majority of the Marci in this period were clerical and in many cases Greek, *RE* 14. 2 (1931), 1644-8.

[1] J. C. Rolfe, in the Loeb edition, vol. 3 p. 51, renders this as 'had been ambushed by the

again and probably lost his life.[2] His name clearly reveals his German origin.[3]

Dulcitius

Amm. Marc. 27. 8. 10: see p. 334 above, for this text.

Id. 28. 3. 6: see p. 334 above, for this text.

Late in 367,[1] after his initial successes in clearing the invaders, Theodosius asked for Civilis to be sent, as *vicarius*,[2] and also for Dulcitius, 'ducem scientia rei militaris insignem'. In the following year, Dulcitius, again described as *dux*, was entrusted by Theodosius with the task of executing the accomplices of the conspirator Valentinus. It is natural to assume that Dulcitius replaced the *dux Britanniarum* Fullofaudes, but this cannot be regarded as certain, given Ammianus' stylistic habits.[3] After all, Count Theodosius himself is called *dux* four times, never *comes*, in the narration of the British campaign.[4] Unfortunately, nothing else is known of Dulcitius,[5] before or after 367–8, which might help to resolve the question of his status at this time. It must be accepted, therefore, that he might have been *comes* rather than *dux*, although the

---

enemy and taken prisoner'. Cf. I. A. Richmond, *Roman Britain* (1955) 62 ('immobilizing the Duke of the Britains'); A. H. M. Jones, *The Later Roman Empire* (1964) 140 ('capturing the *dux Britanniarum*'); Frere, *Britannia*[2] 391 ('was besieged or captured').

[2] The editor who wrote the summaries certainly assumed this: '8. Pictis, Attacottis, et Scottis, post Ducem et Comitem interfectos, Britanniam impune vastantibus, Theodosius Comes fusis praedam excussit'—but he was probably just being careless. Ammianus has an enormous variety of expressions for killing and death: see H. Hagendahl, *Studia Ammianea* (1921) 101, who does not, however, include *circumventus est* among them. None the less, *PLRE* I 375 writes: 'killed during disturbances in Britain in 367.'

[3] M. Waas, *Germanen im römischen Dienst im 4. Jahrhundert n. Chr.* (1965) 99. The name is given as Bulchobaudes in one MS of Ammianus, but Fullofaudes is preferred by the editors. Waas does not discuss this point, but notes that Fullobaudes was probably the original German form.

[1] Following the revised chronology established by Tomlin, *Britannia* 5 (1974) 303 ff. See also p. 337 above.

[3] p. 337 above.

[3] See e.g. Tomlin, in Goodburn and Bartholomew (edd.), *Aspects of the Notitia Dignitatum* 207 n. 63: 'The description . . . is literary and need not mean he was actually a *dux*.' J. S. Johnson, ibid. 88 f., is less sceptical, though noting, 89, that 'Ammianus is notorious for not using technical terms'; more cautiously ibid. 101 n. 85, he comments that 'Ammianus' usage of such technical terms is admittedly slack'. See Syme, *Ammianus and the Historia Augusta* 129: 'Nor was Ammianus able to achieve a desirable harmony of language. Poetic and archaic words, Graecisms, standard rhetoric and technical terms, it is a strange mixture.'

[4] 27. 8. 6 ('dux efficacissimus'), 28. 3. 1 ('dux nominis inclyti'), 28. 3. 2 ('praeclari ducis curas'), 28. 3. 6 ('dux alacrior ad audendum'). He is called *comes* in the summary of 27. 8.

[5] There is no evidence to link him with the other Dulcitii in *PLRE* I 273 f.

latter may be regarded as more probable in the absence of further evidence.[6]

383   Magnus Maximus

Pacatus, *Pan. Lat. Vet.* 2 (12) 23. 3: Quis non ad primum novi sceleris nuntium risit? Nam res infra dignitatem iracundiae videbatur, cum pauci homines et insulani totius incendium continentis adolerent et regali habitu exsulem suum illi exsules orbis induerent.

Id. 31. 1-2: An sustinere te coram et solum oculorum tuorum ferre coniectum ille quondam domus tuae neglegentissimus vernula mensularumque servilium statarius lixa potuisset? Non statim totum subisset hominem praeteriti sui tuique reputatio? Non sibi ipse obiecisset te esse triumphalis viri filium, se patris incertum; te heredem nobilissimae familiae, se clientem; te omni retro tempore Romani exercitus ducem, libertatis patronum, se orbis extorrem patriaeque fugitivum? 2. Iam vero te principem in medio rei publicae sinu, omnium suffragio militum, consensu provinciarum ipsius denique ambitu imperatoris optatum; se in ultimo terrarum recessu, legionibus nesciis, adversis provinciarum studiis, nullis denique auspiciis in illud tyrannici nominis adspirasse furtum?

Id. 38. 2: Quotiens sibi ipsum putamus dixisse: 'Quo fugio?... Repeto Britanniam, quam reliqui?... sed notus sum...'

Auson. *Ordo urbium nobilium* 64–72:

> 64   Non erat iste locus: merito tamen aucta recenti
>   nona inter claras Aquileia cieberis urbes,
>   Itala ad Illyricos obiecta colonia montes,
>   moenibus et portu celebrrima: sed magis illud
> 68   eminet, extremo quod te sub tempore legit,
>   solveret exacto cui sera piaculi lustro
>   Maximus, armigeri quondam sub nomine lixa.
>   felix, quae tanti spectatrix laeta triumphi
> 72   punisti Ausonio Rutupinum Marte latronem.

Epit. de Caes. 47. 7: Hoc tempore cum Maximus apud Britanniam tyrannidem arripuisset et in Galliam transmisisset, ab infensis Gratiano legionibus exceptus Gratianum fugavit nec mora exstinxit.

Claud. *de IV cons. Honorii*, 72–7:

> 72   per varium gemini scelus erupere tyranni
>   tractibus occiduis: hunc saeva Britannia fudit;
>   hunc sibi Germanus famulum delegerat exul:
>   ausus uterque nefas, domini respersus uterque

---

[6] K. M. Martin, *Latomus* 28 (1969) 419, argues that Ammianus meant *comes* in this passage, as part of his thesis that the *comes Britanniarum* (but not the *comes litoris Saxonici*) was an established post at this time. See J. S. Johnson, in Goodburn and Bartholomew, op. cit. 100 n. 71, for a more restrained conclusion.

76 insontis iugulo. novitas audere priori
    suadebat cautumque dabant exempla sequenter.

Rufin. *Hist. Eccl.* 2. 14: Verum is postquam multa religiose ac fortiter gessit, a Maximo tyranno. . apud Britannias exorto . . . peremptus est.

Sulp. Sever. *Chron.* 2. 49. 5: iam tum rumor incesserat clemens, Maximum intra Britannias sumpsisse imperium ac brevi in Gallias erupturum.

id. *v. Martini* 20. 3: postremo, cum Maximus se non sponte sumpsisse imperium adfirmaret, sed impositam sibi a militibus divino nutu regni necessitatem armis defendisse. . .

Oros. 7. 34. 9: interea. . . Maximus, vir quidem strenuus et probus atque Augusto dignus nisi contra sacramenti fidem per tyrannidem emersisset, in Britannia invitus propemodum ab exercitu imperator creatus in Galliam transiit . . .

Prosper Tiro, *s. a.* 384: In Brittania per seditionem militum Maximus imperator est factus.

Sozom. *Hist. Eccl.* 7. 13. 1: Ὑπὸ δὲ τοῦτον τὸν χρόνον . . . ἐπανέστη Μάξιμος ἐκ τῆς Βρετανίας, καὶ ὑφ᾽ ἑαυτὸν Ῥωμαίων ἀρχὴν ποιήσασθαι ἐσπούδαξεν.

Socr. *Hist. Eccl.* 5. 11. 2: Μάξιμος ἐκ τῶν περὶ τὰς Βρεττανίας μερῶν ἐπανέστη τῇ Ῥωμαίων ἀρχῇ καὶ κάμνοντι Γρατιανῷ εἰς τὸν κατὰ Ἀλαμανῶν πόλεμον ἐπιτίθεται. (Cf. Nicephorus Callistus Xanthopoulus, *Hist. Eccl.* 12. 19-20).

Zos. *Hist. Nov.* 4. 35. 3-4: τοῦτο τοῖς στρατιώταις κατὰ τοῦ βασιλέως ἔτεκε μῖσος, ὅπερ ὑποτυφόμενον κατὰ βραχὺ καὶ αὐξανόμενον εἰς νεωτέρων πραγμάτων ἐκίνησε τοὺς στρατιώτας ἐπιθυμίαν, τούς τε ἄλλους καὶ κατ᾽ ἐξαίρετον τοὺς ταῖς Βρεττανικαῖς νήσοις ἐνιδρυμένους οἷα τῶν ἄλλων ἁπάντων πλέον αὐθαδείᾳ καὶ θυμῷ νικωμένους. ἔκυει δὲ πρὸς τοῦτο πλέον αὐτοὺς Μάξιμος Ἴβηρ τὸ γένος, Θεοδοσίῳ τῷ βασιλεῖ κατὰ τὴν Βρεττανίαν συστρατευσάμενος. 4. οὗτον δυσανασχετῶν ὅτι Θεοδόσιος ἠξίωτο βασιλείας, αὐτὸς δὲ οὐδὲ εἰς ἀρχὴν ἔντιμον ἔτυχε προελθών, ἀνήγειρε πλέον εἰς τὸ κατὰ τοῦ βασιλέως ἔχθος τοὺς στρατιώτας.

narratio de imperatoribus domus Valentinianae et Theodosianae (Chron. min. i. 629): [Gratianus] victus a Maximo tyranno, qui intra Brittanias Augusti nomen adsumpsit. . .

Chronographer of AD 452 (Chron. min. i. 646):
Maximus tyrannus in Britannia a militibus constituitur.
Incursantes Pictos et Scottos Maximus strenue superavit.

Gregory of Tours, *Hist. Franc.* 1. 43: Maximus vero cum per tyrannidem oppressis Brittannis sumpsisset victoriam, a militibus imperator creatus est.

Gildas, *de excidio Britanniae*, 13: Itidem tandem tyrannorum virgultis crescentibus et in immanem sylvam iam iamque erumpentibus, insula nomen Romanum, nec tamen mores legesque tenens, quin potius abiiciens, germen suae plantationis amarissimae ad Gallias, magna comitante satellitum caterva, insuper etiam imperatoribus insignibus; quae nec decenter usquam gessit, nec legitime, sed ritu tyrannico et tumultuante initiatum milite, Maximum mittit.

John, Bishop of Nikiou (Nicium), *Chronicle* 83. 14 (translated from Zotenberg's Ethiopic text by R. H. Charles, 1916, 86): And during the stay of the emperor Theodosius in Asia there arose a usurper named Maximus, of British descent, who slew the blessed emperor Gratian through treachery and seized his empire by force and made his residence at Rome.

Nennius, *Hist. Brittonum*, 26-7, 29: Sextus Maximus imperator regnavit in Brittannia . . . 27. Septimus imperator regnavit in Brittannia Maximianus. ipse perrexit cum omnibus militibus Brittonum a Brittannia, et occidit Gratianum regem Romanorum . . . 29. Dum Gratianus imperium regebat in toto mundo, in Brittannia, per seditionem militum, Maximus imperator factus est.

Bede, *Hist. Eccl. gentis Angl.* 11 = Oros. 7. 34. 9 (above).

Johann. Antioch. fr. 186: Ὅτι ἐπὶ Θεοδοσίου τοῦ βασιλέως Μάξιμος ἐκ τῶν περὶ τὰς Βρεττανίας μερῶν ἐπαναστὰς τῇ Ῥωμαίων ἀρχῇ, κάμνοντι τῷ Γρατιανῷ εἰς τὸν κατὰ Ἀλαμανῶν πόλεμον ἐπιτίθεται καὶ δι᾽ Ἀνδραγαθίου τοῦ τῆς τυραννίδος κοινωνοῦ . . . ἐπιβουλεύεται δολίως. Ἐτελεύτα μὲν οὖν Γρατιανὸς βιώσας ἔτη κδ᾽, βασιλεύσας ἔτη ιε᾽. 2. Αἰτία δὲ τῆς κατὰ Γρατιανοῦ κινήσεως τῷ Μαξίμῳ γέγονεν ἥδε. Οὗτος Θεοδοσίῳ τῷ βασιλεῖ κατὰ τὴν Βρεττανίαν συστρατευσάμενος ἐν τοῖς Οὐάλεντος χρόνοις, δυσανασχετῶν ὅτι Θεοδόσιος ἀπὸ Γρατιανοῦ βασιλείας ἠξιώθη, αὐτὸς δὲ οὐδὲ εἰς ἀρχὴν ἔντιμον ἔτυχε προελθών, ἤγειρε τοὺς ἐν Βρεττανίᾳ στρατιώτας εἰς τὸ κατὰ τοῦ βασιλέως ἔχθος · καὶ ἀνηγορεύθη παρ᾽ αὐτῶν βασιλεύς.

Georg. Cedrenus (*PG* 121, 599): Μαξιμιανὸς δέ τις Βρεττανός, ὅτι τὸν Θεοδόσιον ὁ Γρατιανὸς βασιλέα ἐποίησεν αὐτοῦ μηδεμίας τυχόντος τιμῆς, διήγειρε τοὺς ἐν Βρεταννίᾳ ἀντᾶραι Γρατιανῷ. (Cf. Georg. Monachus Hamartolus, *Chron.* 4. 196. 3; *Anec. Gr.* 2, 304).

Magnus Maximus'[1] proclamation as emperor in midsummer 383[2] is recorded by variety of sources from late antiquity, and he is also a potent figure in early British literature.[3] First, his origin and earlier career require examination. Zosimus calls him a Spaniard, Ἴβηρ τὸ γένος,[4] and he seems to have been some kind of kinsman of Theodosius—he was a 'poor relation', if there is any substance in the sneering remarks of Pacatus, who also says that Maximus boasted of his relationship.[5] One may accept that his father was not a public figure,

---

[1] He was formerly thought to have been called Magnus Clemens Maximus, through a mistaken reading of Sulp. Sever. *Chron.* 2. 49. 5 and of his name in the consular Fasti; see Ensslin, *RE* 14. 2 (1930) 2546. He is called Flavius on *ILS* 787, Gigthis, in common with Valentinian II, Theodosius, and Arcadius. On *AE* 1967. 561, he is called Magnius Maximus.

[2] V. Grumel, *Rev. Ét. Byz.* 12 (1954) 18, puts his proclamation in the autumn of 382, 'with neither evidence nor likelihood', as J. F. Matthews, *Western Aristocracies and Imperial Court A.D. 364-425* (1975) 173 n. 1, rightly comments. See further n. 23 below.

[3] See especially Stevens, *Études celtiques* 3 (1938) 86 ff.; R. Bromwich, in H. M. Chadwick *et al.*, *Studies in Early British History* (1954) 97, 107 ff.

[4] Cedrenus and John of Nikiu call him British, which has no more value than Ausonius' description, *Ordo urb. nob.* 72, of Maximus as *Rutupinum . . . latronem*. II 4911, Siresa, showing that a Spanish province acquired a governor of enhanced rank, *consularis*, under Maximus, is thought to indicate favour by him towards his native province—taken to be Gallaecia by Ensslin, *RE* 14. 2 (1930) 2546, but·Chastagnol, in *Les Empereurs romains d'Espagne* 285 f., who offers an improved reading of the stone, prefers Tarraconensis; likewise Palanque, ibid. 255.

[5] Pacat. *Pan. Lat.* 2 (12). 31. 1, 24. 1 ('tua se et adfinitate et favore iactanti'); cf. n. 34.

even if Maximus was not really *patris incertum*.[6] At all events, he served in Britain under the elder Theodosius in 367-8, as Zosimus specifically mentions.[7] No details are given of his rank or activity there, although C. E. Stevens argued that the strange sentence in Gregory of Tours was a reference to his having suppressed the usurper Valentinus at that time[8]—Ammianus says that Count Theodosius entrusted this task to Dulcitius, the *dux*.[9]

The next part of his career is obscure, but it is reasonable to suppose that he is the otherwise unidentified Maximus mentioned by Ammianus as serving under the elder Theodosius in the war against Firmus: together with Firmus' brother Gildo, he was sent to arrest Vincentius, an associate of Romanus.[10] J. F. Matthews has shrewdly suggested that our man may also be the general Maximus mentioned by Ammianus in book 31, in connection with the transfer of the Goths across the Danube into Thrace in 376-7.[11] Through some misfortune, Ammianus says, the Roman forces were commanded by 'homines maculosi', 'persons of ill repute', Lupicinus, 'per Thracias comes', and Maximus, 'dux exitiosus', 'the deadly general'. Ammianus goes on to describe the 'insidiatrix aviditas' of these two. It is tempting to take Matthews's point further, for it does not stretch the imagination too far to detect here a subtle echo of the passionate denunciation of the fallen Maximus, delivered at Rome, a few years before Ammianus wrote, by Pacatus, with its repeated reference to the insatiable greed of the 'carnifex', the 'publicus spoliator', who, at the last, is called 'homo funebris'.[12]

However this may be, if our man was indeed on the Danube in 377, he could, as Matthews notes, have played some part in the deliberations of the following year, after the disaster to Valens, which led Gratian to

---

[6] O. Seeck, *Geschichte des Untergangs der antiken Welt* V[2] (1928) 165, line 34, interprets this to mean that he was a bastard, unnecessarily.

[7] It may be that Zosimus confuses father and son, as e.g. Stevens, *Études celtiques* 3 (1938) 91 n. 6, believes, but, whether or not this is so, there is every reason to believe that the future emperor accompanied his father in 367, cf. Pacat. *Pan. Lat.* 2 (12). 8. 3 ff. and Zosim. 4. 24. 4; he was already *dux Moesiae primae c.* 373-4, Amm. Marc. 29. 6. 14 ff., Zosim. 4. 16. 6.

[8] Stevens, *Études celtiques* 3 (1938) 92, who translates 'after achieving victory for the Britains who were oppressed by tyranny'. But it may be impossible to recover what Gregory really meant by this sentence. See also n. 23 below.

[9] Amm. Marc. 28. 3. 6, pp. 334 f., 337 f. above.

[10] Amm. Marc. 29. 5. 6 and 21; accepted in *PLRE* I 588, and by Matthews, *Western Aristocracies* . . . 95.

[11] Amm. Marc. 31. 4. 9 ff. (see *PLRE* I 585, Maximus 24, where the identification is not made, for other references), interpreted by Matthews, op. cit. 96.

[12] Note also Amm. Marc. 31. 4. 11, 'insatiabilitas', 5. 1, 'dissimulatione perniciosa', and cf. Pacat. *Pan. Lat.* 2 (12), esp. 25. 5 ff., on Maximus' insatiate greed; the word 'aviditas' occurs, 25. 7; 'homo funebris', 43. 4. For the time of writing, see Syme, *Ammianus and the Historia Augusta* 17 ff.; Pacatus' speech was delivered in 389, R. Hanslik, *RE* 18. 2 (1942) 2058.

choose the younger Theodosius as his new colleague.[13] This must remain a matter for conjecture, but it is readily understandable that, as Zosimus stresses,[14] Maximus, a fellow-countryman and comrade-in-arms—and, we may add, a kinsman—of the new emperor, may have been jealous, or may at least have hoped for high office, an ἀρχή ἔντιμος. Instead, he found himself in Britain. But in what capacity? Zosimus gives no hint. Pacatus calls him an 'exile' and a 'fugitive'— 'exulem', 'orbis extorrem patriaeque fugitivum'. In the Welsh genea-logies he is called *guletic*, which is thought to be 'connected with *gwlad* = land, evidently conveying some idea of command'.[15] Gibbon commented that 'this provincial rank might justly be considered as a state of exile and obscurity; and if Maximus had obtained any civil or military office, he was not invested with the authority of either governor or general.'[16] C. E. Stevens, following Gibbon's lead, argued that Maximus could not have been either *comes* or *dux*, but must have had some inferior function. He suggests that he was *consularis* of Valentia, which he identifies as Wales, 'an appointment which involved residence in the reconstructed fort of Carnarvon, and supervision of the local militia.'[17] The evidence seems too slender for this view to be accepted.[18] Others have argued that he was *dux*[19] or *comes Britan-niarum*.[20] If it be accepted that the latter post had not been created in the 380s, but was first instituted by Stilicho,[21] then it looks very probable that he was *dux Britanniarum*; but he might conceivably have been *comes litoris Saxonici*.[22] In either case, he would have been commanding low-grade troops, and could well have felt that this ἀρχή

---

[13] Matthews, op. cit. 96. For Theodosius' return to public life—he had withdrawn to Spain after his father's death, *Pan. Lat.* 2 (12). 9. 1—see *PLRE* I 904; he became emperor on 19 Jan. 379.

[14] He is followed by Cedrenus and John of Antioch, of whom the former exaggerates—it would seem—by saying that he had no office at all.

[15] Stevens, *Études celtiques* 3 (1938) 89.

[16] *Decline and Fall of the Roman Empire*, ch. xxvii.

[17] Stevens, op. cit. 87 ff.; the quotation is from p. 94.

[18] Gibbon wrote that 'the prudent reader may not be satisfied with such Welsh evidence', but it is unfair to Stevens to fling Gibbon back at him—the reference was to the legends for the marriage which Maximus 'is said to have contracted with the daughter of a wealthy lord of Caernarvonshire'. Stevens, op. cit. 86 ff., is careful to discount this aspect of the early British tradition. More pertinent is the criticism of Matthews, *Western Aristocracies*... 175 n. 6, that *consularis Valentiae* would be 'an anomalous civilian office in a military career.' R. Tomlin, in Goodburn and Bartholomew (edd.), *Aspects of the Notitia Dignitatum*, esp. 195 ff., does produce some evidence for the blurring of the distinction, however; so Stevens's theory cannot be totally ignored.

[19] Thus Frere, *Britannia*[2] 404; preferred, with some hesitation, in *Ep. Stud.* 4 (1967) 96.

[20] Matthews, *Western Aristocracies* ... 175 n. 6; also favoured by Ensslin, *RE* 14. 2 (1930) 2546 f.; Palanque, in *Les Empereurs romains d'Espagne* 255 and Chastagnol, ibid. 286.

[21] Mann, in Goodburn and Bartholomew (edd.), op. cit. 6.

[22] See p. 320 above, on this post. His very rapid crossing (Zos. 4. 35. 4) might fit this, but

was insufficiently ἔντιμος—especially if he had already been *dux Thraciarum* in 377.

Before his departure for Gaul, probably, in fact, before his elevation, Maximus vigorously repelled the Picts and Scots, 'Pictos et Scottos incursantes strenue superavit', as the Gallic Chronicler put it.[23] The successful conclusion of this campaign might well have provided a suitable occasion for the *pronunciamento*. It appears possible that he assumed the title Britannicus, if the restoration of a fragmentary Italian inscription is correct: [*d.n. Ma*]*gnus M*[*aximus / Brita*]*nnicus m*[*aximus / pi*]*us felix* [*Augustus* [4] */ . . .i*]*ssimi.*[24]

Maximus' motives are treated variously in the miserable sources. Sulpicius Severus, quoting Martin, who knew him, reports Maximus' claim to have taken on the 'regni necessitatem' imposed on him by the soldiers through the divine will, not to have seized the imperial power of his own accord. Orosius goes some way towards accepting this. Both men may have had some sympathy for a pious Catholic—Maximus was baptized in 383, 'going straight from the font', he told the Pope, 'to the throne'.[25] The Greeks ascribe base motives—jealousy of Theodosius and resentment at his lack of promotion. Modern writers have searched for other reasons, for example, discontent among Roman officers at the favours bestowed on barbarian troops by Gratian. J. F. Matthews stresses cogently that Maximus and his supporters may simply have tried to replace the rule of 'a dilettante youth and a child', Gratian and Valentinian II, by a western emperor of tried military worth, to match Theodosius in the east. They did indeed claim to have Theodosius' backing.[26]

---

not the northern campaign (see next note), which would have been waged by the *dux*. See also p. 341 above, on the possible *comes* Narses.

[23] Seeck, *Geschichte des Untergangs der antiken Welt* V[2] 166 n., points out that Gratian was at Verona on 16 June 383 (*C. Th.* 1. 3. 1) and after that left for the Alamannic campaign—which he would not have done if he had heard of Maximus' rising; he was engaged with the Alamanni when Maximus moved against him (Socrates 5. 11. 2 etc.), and was dead by 25 Aug. Hence the usurpation cannot have been earlier than mid-June, but Maximus can hardly have had time for a northern campaign between then and his crossing to Gaul, hence the northern campaign must have been before his usurpation. Stevens, *Études celtiques* 3 (1938) 91 f., noting Seeck's argument, puts the successes against Picts and Scots at the time of the 'barbarian conspiracy', but this is surely going too far.

[24] L. Braccesi, *La parola del passato* 23 (1968) 279 ff., reinterpreting XI 6327, Pisaurum. (I cannot follow this author in all other respects.)

[25] See J. Ziegler, *Zur religiösen Haltung der Gegenkaiser im 4 Jh. n. Chr.* (1970) 76 on the attitude of Sulpicius Severus and Orosius. Maximus stresses the significance of his baptism in his letter to Pope Siricius, *Collectio Avellana* 40 (*CSEL* 35. 1, 90). Matthews, *Western Aristocracies . . .* 165 and n. 2, says that he was baptized after his usurpation, at Trier, but Maximus' words, 'ad imperium ab ipso statim salutari fonte conscenderim', must mean that he was baptized first, then proclaimed, in Britain.

[26] Matthews, op. cit. 175 f. Theodosius forced a retraction from Maximus by torture (*Pan. Lat.* 2(12). 43. 4).

Maximus' five years as emperor do not require detailed discussion here.[27] Nothing is known of his treatment of Britain, except that he appears to have withdrawn troops from the island in his bid to extend his power.[28] One may note also that the Scilly Isles were chosen as the place of exile for two of the Priscillianist heretics,[29] to whose suppression Maximus devoted much of his energies as emperor.[30] If he had hoped that Theodosius would welcome him as a colleague, he was soon disappointed. He gained control of the Gauls and the Spains with ease, but he had to wait until 386 for grudging recognition. In late 387 he lost patience and invaded Italy. Theodosius, who had not moved against him earlier, now made preparations, and in 388 marched rapidly through Illyricum. Maximus was trapped at Aquileia and executed,[31] as was his son Victor shortly afterwards.[32] The day of his death, 28 July, was evidently celebrated annually thereafter.[33] But the female members of his family were treated well. His mother was given a pension, and his daughters were entrusted to a relation of Theodosius to be brought up—which may, perhaps, confirm that Maximus was some kind of kinsman.[34] One of the daughters may have made a brilliant marriage, if there is any truth in a romantic story in Procopius, which makes of Petronius Maximus, born in 396, and emperor for a few weeks in 455 after a glittering senatorial career, a descendant of the usurper.[35]

[27] See Ensslin, *RE* 14. 2 (1930) 2547 ff.; Palanque, in *Les Empereurs romains d'Espagne* 255 ff.; Matthews, op. cit. 223 ff.

[28] As revealed by the presence of the (*pedites*) *Seguntienses* in Illyricum, *Not. Dig.*, *Occ.* V 65 (= 213), see Stevens, *Arch. J.* 97 (1940) 134; V. E. Nash-Williams, *The Roman Frontier in Wales* (2nd edn. by M. G. Jarrett, 1969) 28, 62 f. See also p. 326 above, for a possible *vicarius* of Britain under Maximus. [29] Sulp. Sever. *Chron.* 2. 51. 4.

[30] See Matthews, *Western Aristocracies* . . . 165 ff. and H. Chadwick, *Priscillian of Avila* (1976) 42 f., 111 ff. Doubtless his fervent orthodoxy had political motives.

[31] Details in Ensslin, *RE* 14. 2 (1930) 2554. He was tortured first (n. 26 above).

[32] The boy had been made Augustus by Maximus in 383: Ensslin, *RE* 8A 2 (1958) 2060 f.; *PLRE* I 961. One may also note Maximus' brother Marcelinus, *PLRE* I 547, who served as his *comes*, along with an unnamed uncle.

[33] Procop. *bell. Vand.* 1. 4. 16. For 28 July rather than 28 Aug. see Chadwick, *Priscillian of Avila* 122 n. 3.

[34] Ambrose, *ep.* 40. 32, from which Ensslin, *RE* 14. 2 (1930) 2546, infers that Maximus' claim to be a kinsman of Theodosius was probably genuine.

[35] Procop. *bell. Vand.* 1. 4. 16 etc.; see Ensslin, *RE* 14. 2 (1930) 2543 ff. He reigned from 17 Mar.-31 May 455. The Greek historians make him responsible for the downfall and death of Aëtius and the murder of Valentinian III, Theodosius' grandson—and it all began with a game of draughts (which uncannily recalls the game of chess in the dream of Maxen Wledig in the 'White Book of Rhydderch'). All 'Klatschgeschichte' in the view of Ensslin, *RE* 14. 2, 2544; and Chastagnol, *Les Fastes de la préfecture de Rome sous le bas-empire* 283, refuses to believe the descent from Magnus Maximus—although J. B. Bury, *History of the Later Roman Empire*[2] I (1923) 324, was less sceptical. I cannot subscribe to J. H. Ward's acceptance, *Britannia* 3 (1972) 277 ff., of the British legends regarding Maximus' marriages and relationships, e.g. that enshrined in the Valle Crucis Pillar, recording a marriage between Maximus' daughter Sevira and Vortigern (nor does Ward's theory that Vortigern was *vicarius* of Britain from 426-30 seem plausible; it certainly cannot be proved).

II.21
A POSSIBLE *PRAEPOSITUS LIMITIS*

Justinianus

VII 268 = *Ant. J.* 32 (1952), 185 = *RIB* 721, Robin Hood's Bay (Ravenscar): *Iustinianus p. p. / Vindicianus / magister turr*[e][4] */ m castrum fecit / a so.*

There seems little doubt that Justinianus was *p(rae)p(ositus)* and that Vindicianus was a *magister* of relatively low rank, 'perhaps a garrison engineer or a pioneer sergeant', as R. G. Goodchild suggested.[1] It is less certain what Justinianus was in charge of. He might have been simply a regimental commander,[2] although Goodchild, citing North African examples, suggested that he was a *praepositus limitis*.[3] However this may be, the inscription probably dates to the period soon after the 'barbarian conspiracy', when a system of signal stations was set up along the Yorkshire coast.[4] It was long ago proposed[5] that he might be the same person as the Justinianus, appointed by Constantine III, together with Neviogastes, to command troops in Gaul, shortly before the usurper left Britain in 407.[6] The name is not particularly common,[7] but the lapse of time that must be assumed between the two appointments is rather large,[8] and the identification can only be regarded as a slight possibility.

---

[1] *Ant. J.* 32 (1952) 186, comparing V 8750, 8988c, Concordia, XIII 8262, Cologne. See now also A. Demandt, *RE* Supp. 12 (1970) 553–6, for examples of these low-grade *magistri*.

[2] See e.g. A. H. M. Jones, *The Later Roman Empire* (1964) 620, and the list in *PLRE* I 1125 ff.

[3] See now *IRT* 880 for the earliest African example, and note the comments of Jones, op. cit. 652, and J. F. Matthews, in Goodburn and Bartholomew (edd.), *Aspects of the Notitia Dignitatum* (1976) 167 ff.

[4] Frere, *Britannia*[2] 395 f., 462; J. Morris, *The Age of Arthur* (1973) 16 f.

[5] By A. J. Evans, *Num. Chron.*[3] 7 (1887) 191 ff. = *Arch. Camb.*[5] 5 (1888) 152 ff.

[6] Zos. 6. 2. 2–3; Olympiodorus, fr. 12 = *FHG* IV 59 (called Justinus).

[7] For the principate, see Kajanto 252. Only two others in *PLRE* I 489.

[8] R. G. Goodchild, op. cit. 188 n. 3, suggests that the Ravenscar inscription could be as late as *c.*375, which still leaves a gap of over thirty years. The general of Constantine might of course have been extremely old.

II.22

COMITES OF THE EMPERORS IN BRITAIN, AND SENIOR OFFICERS SENT TO THE ISLAND ON SPECIAL MISSIONS

1. CLAUDIUS' RETINUE IN 43 (IN ALPHABETICAL ORDER)

L. Coiedius Candidus

ILS 967 = XI 6163, Suasa: *L. Coiedio L. f. Ani. / Candido / tr. mil. leg. VIII Aug. IIIv. capital. quaest.* [4]*/ Ti. Claud. Caes. Aug. Ger. / quaest. aer. Satur. cur. tab. p. / Hunc Ti. Cl. Caes. Aug. Germ.* [8]*/ revers. ex castr. don. m* [*il.*] *don. / cor. aur. mur. val. hast* [*p*]*ura / eund.* [*q.*] *cum ha* [*be*]*r. inter suos q. / eod. ann.* [*e*]*t a* [*e*]*r. Sat. q. esse ius.* [12] */ Pub* [*lice*] .

It would surely have seemed appropriate for the antiquarian emperor Claudius to have taken his quaestor with him on the British expedition, and there seems no reason to doubt that Coiedius Candidus was in the imperial entourage in 43. *eod(em) ann(o)* in line 11 of the Suasa inscription will then refer to 44, when Claudius transferred control of the *aerarium Saturni* back to quaestors.[1] It has been suggested that Candidus' decorations were received as tribune of VIII Augusta, but there is no good reason to believe that this legion went to Britain,[2] nor is the alternative suggestion, that it took part in the suppression of Scribonianus' revolt in Dalmatia in 42, particularly plausible.[3]

Groag noted that the *nomen* Coiedius appears to be confined to Umbria, but Suasa was enrolled in the Camilia tribe;[4] it is possible, therefore, that Candidus' home was Ariminum, not far away, the only Umbrian town known to have been in Aniensis.[5]

---

[1] See Tac. *Ann.* 13. 29. 2, Dio 60. 24. 1 f.; Suet. *D. Claud.* 24.

[2] See e.g. L. J. F. Keppie, *Britannia* 2 (1971) 149 ff.

[3] This is argued by Keppie, op. cit. 154 f., following Groag in *PIR*[2] C 1257 and more fully in *Wien. Stud.* 54 (1936) 192 ff., but he concedes that it is unproved. The possibility that the *dona* were awarded to Candidus as quaestor is overlooked—they 'must have been awarded during his Tribunate, as the inscription was set up before he had reached the Praetorship and so obtained a position where as *legatus legionis* he could earn more' (p. 154). Apart from the fact that legionary legates at that period were often appointed before the praetorship (p. 000 above), there is no reason why quaestors could not have received *dona*. One may note the exceptional *dona* awarded to L. Nonius Asprenas (*IRT* 346). Cébeillac, *Les quaestores* 46, is happy to assign Candidus' quaestorship of the emperor to 43, but ascribes his *dona* to the Scribonianus revolt. One difficulty is that it is unclear whether *revers(us)*—meaning Claudius—or *revers(um)*—meaning Candidus—should be understood in line 8. The former is preferred here, the latter in *PIR*[2] C 1257.

[4] Groag, *RE* 4. 1 (1900) 360. See Kubitschek 77.

[5] Kubitschek 94 (cf. 270); noted by Keppie, op. cit. 154.

Julius Planta

V 5050 = *ILS* 206, Cles: *M. Iunio Silano Q. Sulpicio Camerino cos. | idibus Martis, Bais in praetorio, edictum | Ti. Claudi Caesaris Augusti Germanici propositum fuit id* [4]/ *quod infra scriptum est. | Ti. Claudius Caesar Augustus Germanicus pont. | maxim. trib. potest. VI imp. XI p. p. cos. designatus IIII dicit:|*
Cum ex veteribus controversis pe[*nd*]*entibus aliquamdiu etiam* [8]/ *temporibus Ti. Caesaris patrui mei, ad quas ordinandas | Pinarium Apollinarem miserat, − quae tantum modo | inter Comenses essent (quantum memoria refero) et | Bergaleos, − isque primum apsentia pertinaci patrui mei,* [12]/ *deinde etiam Gai principatu, quod ab eo non exigebatur | referre, non stulte quidem, neglexserit; et posteac | detulerit Camurius Statutus ad me, agros plerosque | et saltus mei iuris esse: in rem praesentem misi* [16]/ *Plantam Iulium amicum et comitem meum, qui | cum, adhibitis procuratoribus meis qu*[*i*]*que in alia | regione quique in vicinia erant, summa cura inqui/sierit et cognoverit, cetera quidem, ut mihi demons/trata commentario facto ab ipso sunt, statuat pronun*[20]/*tietque ipsi permitto | . . .* etc.

Julius Planta, *amicus* and *comes* of Claudius, is so described in the emperor's famous edict on the status of the Anauni, Tulliasses, and Sinduni,[1] into which he had enquired, on Claudius' behalf, and reported, *summa cura*, before the imperial pronouncement of 15 March 46. Mommsen was in no doubt that Planta had acquired the title *comes* as a participant in the British expedition of 43. He suggested, plausibly enough, that Planta had still been with Claudius when the emperor passed through north Italy on his return to Rome in 44, and that, when Claudius was approached by the Anauni and others, he seconded Planta to enquire into the controversy.[2] Mommsen was followed by A. Stein, who stressed that Planta must have been a senator.[3] This latter point has been doubted by some, but seems reasonable.[4] At any rate, Planta may be listed as one of those who formed Claudius' entourage in Britain.

He is otherwise completely unknown. A high-ranking Julius at this period, particularly one thought suitable to investigate questions of land-ownership and citizenship in the Alpine regions of Italy, might be supposed to have derived from Cisalpine Italy; but perhaps south Gaul is more likely a home.[5]

---

[1] See U. Schillinger-Häfele, *Hermes* 95 (1967) 353.

[2] Mommsen, *Gesammelte Schriften* IV (1906) 299 ff.

[3] A. Stein, *RE* 10. 1 (1917) 773.

[4] Planta is not registered in De Laet, *De Samenstelling van den romeinschen Senaat (28 v.C.-68 n.C.)*, while J. A. Crook, *Consilium Principis* (1955) 168 doubts his senatorial status on grounds found inadequate in *PIR²* J 471—where participation in the British expedition is accepted.

[5] Note the comments of Syme, *Tacitus* 801: 'Now the *nomen* 'Iulius' suggests an origin from Narbonensis or from Tres Galliae. It is a material fact that not a single specimen of the numerous Transpadane senators in the early Empire is a Julius.'

L. Junius Silanus

XIV 2500 = *ILS* 957, Tusculum: [*L. Iunius M.*] *f. M. n. Silanu* [*s . . . / honoratus an*] *n. XVIII* [*triumphalib. ornam. / q. pr. inte*] *r civis e* [*t peregrinos gener* [4] / *Ti. Claudi C*] *aesaris Augus* [*ti*]

Tac. *Ann.* 12. 3. 2; Suet. *D. Claud.* 24. 3; Dio 60. 21. 5; 60. 31. 7.

L. Junius Silanus, son of M. Silanus Torquatus (*cos. ord.* 19) and Aemilia Lepida, a great-granddaughter of Augustus, was betrothed to Claudius' younger daughter Octavia soon after the emperor's accession in 41.[1] If the inscription in Silanus' honour is correctly restored, he was probably aged at least sixteen when he went to Britain with Claudius in 43, although both Suetonius and Dio stress that he was still a boy when he received the *ornamenta triumphalia* in 44. It may have been normal to assume the *toga virilis* in the eighteenth year.[2] At all events, his presence on the expedition was doubtless purely honorific, although he and Pompeius Magnus were given the task of taking the news of victory to Rome, as Dio records.

The selection of the younger Agrippina as Claudius' wife in 48 spelt Silanus' doom. Agrippina wanted his betrothed as a bride for her son Nero. Silanus was accused of incest with his sister and removed from his office as praetor at the end of December 48. He committed suicide early in 49, on the day of Claudius' marriage to Agrippina.[3]

M. Licinius Crassus Frugi (*cos. ord.* 27)

Suet. *D. Claud.* 17. 3.

Crassus Frugi, son of the consul of 14 BC of the same names, and married to a descendant of Pompey, possessed a pedigree second to none.[1] The prestige attaching to it was duly utilized by Claudius, who married his elder daughter Antonia to Crassus' son Pompeius Magnus,[2] and gave Crassus himself a military appointment recorded on

---

[1] See *PIR*[2] J 829 (he is sometimes incorrectly called Torquatus, an additional *cognomen* borne by his father, a brother, and a nephew, ibid. 839, 837, 838). His mother Lepida had once been betrothed to Claudius (*PIR*[2] A 419).

[2] J. Regner, *RE* 6A 2 (1937) 1452.

[3] See *PIR*[2] J 829 for details. Silanus was replaced as praetor by Eprius Marcellus (p. 229 above).

[1] Syme, *JRS* 50 (1960) 12 ff., esp. 18 f.; *PIR*[2] L 190. Both these discussions supersede earlier accounts, in the light of *IRT* 319, Lepcis Magna and *AE* 1957. 317, Pollentia, showing that his father was also called Frugi.

[2] p. 359 below.

an inscription from Rome with the words *leg. Ti. Claudi Caesaris Aug. Ge[r]manici in M[........]a*,[3] for which he won *ornamenta triumphalia*, as may be deduced from Suetonius' words quoted above. Either *M[acedoni]a* or *M[auretani]a* are theoretically possible, but the latter is more probable, since military operations are known to have been conducted there at the beginning of Claudius' reign.[4] Even though Crassus is not mentioned among the generals who took part, there is no evidence for any fighting in Macedonia at this time.

Crassus' presence with Claudius in Britain is attested only by this mention in Suetonius, describing the special honour he received at the triumph in 44, since he was receiving the *ornamenta triumphalia* for the second time. Some two years later Crassus, his wife, and eldest son, were all put to death at the instigation of Messalina.[5] Crassus is described in the *Apocolocyntosis* as 'so stupid that he was even capable of being emperor' and—which amounts to the same thing—'as similar to Claudius as an egg is to an egg.'[6] His surviving children included Galba's ill-fated heir Piso Licinianus,[7] and among his descendants were the much exiled Calpurnius Crassus, put to death by Hadrian,[8] and, it would seem, the emperor Marcus Aurelius.[9]

Ti. Plautius Silvanus Aelianus (*cos.* 45, II 74)

XIV 3608 = *ILS* 986 = *Inscr. It.* IV 125, near Tibur: *Ti. Plautio M. f. Ani. | Silvano Aeliano | pontif. sodali Aug.* [4]*| IIIvir. a. a. a. f. f. q. Ti. Caesaris | legat. leg. V in Germania | pr. urb. legat. et comiti Claud. | Caesaris in Brittannia consuli* [8]*| procos. Asiae legat. pro praet. Moesiae | . . . Hunc legatum in | {in} Hispaniam ad praefectur. urbis remissum* [28]*| senatus in praefectura triumphalibus | ornamentis honoravit, auctore imp. | Caesare Augusto Vespasiano verbis | ex oratione eius q. i. s. s.:* [32]*| Moesiae ita praefuit ut non debuerit in | me differri honor triumphalium eius | ornamentorum, nisi quod latior ei | contigit mora titulus praefecto urbis.* [36]*| Hunc in eadem praefectura urbis imp. Caesar | Aug. Vespasianus iterum cos. fecit.*

Since he was closely related to Claudius' former wife Urgulanilla and more distantly to the commander-in-chief of the invasion army, A. Plautius,[1] Silvanus Aelianus was an obvious choice to accompany the

---

[3] *ILS* 954.
[4] See J. Gascou, *Mel. Boyancé* (1074) 299 ff., arguing in favour of Mauretania.
[5] See *PIR²* L 190.
[6] *Apoc. divi Claudii* 11. 2 and 5.
[7] *PIR²* C 300. He was married to Q. Veranius' daughter Gemina (p. 54 above).
[8] *PIR²* C 259.
[9] A. R. Birley, *Historia* 15 (1966) 249 f.
[1] pp. 37 ff. above.

emperor to Britain. His career before 43 displays all the hallmarks of the patrician: the post as *monetalis*, service as Tiberius' quaestor, and, the conclusive point, the absence of tribunate of the plebs or aedileship.[2] Thus he clearly had patrician rank well before his consulship in 45, yet his brother or uncle, P. Plautius Pulcher, had to wait until 48 to achieve it.[3] The solution must be what is implied by his second *cognomen*, that he had been adopted from a patrician family of Aelii by a M. Plautius Silvanus, either the consul of 2 BC or his son, who committed suicide while praetor in 24. Since descendants also bear the name Lamia, there can be no doubt that he was by birth an Aelius Lamia—perhaps Ti. Aelius Lamia, although the *praenomen* is a puzzle, and may point to his mother or grandmother ·being a Claudia.[4]

His quaestorship cannot have been later than 37, the year of Tiberius' death, which indicates that he was born at the latest in 12. He was made a legionary commander before the praetorship, as was not uncommon in the pre-Flavian period.[5] This could be said to have equipped him to make himself useful as well as decorative in the emperor's entourage in Britain—although he seems not to have received the *ornamenta triumphalia*, he became consul in 45, the year after the triumph, as suffect to another *comes*, M. Vinicius.[6] His later career does not require detailed discussion here, but it may be noted that the great honour he received from Vespasian in the 70s may reflect in part a friendship formed in 43. Apart from a year as proconsul of Asia he had no further employment under Claudius—he may well have been out of favour with Agrippina.[7] But in the latter part of Nero's reign he was governor of Moesia, as the successor of Flavius Sabinus;[8] his achievements in that post are described at length in lines 9–26 of the Tibur inscription. Finally, when he must have been in his sixties, he held office as governor of Tarraconensis,[9] prefect of the city, and consul *iterum*.[10]

[2] p. 14 above.

[3] *ILS* 921 (from the same mausoleum as the inscription of Silvanus Aelianus).

[4] See esp. L. R. Taylor, *MAAR* 24 (1956) 28 ff. and n. 60. On the MM. Silvani and the Lamiae Aeliani, see also p. 40 and n. 34 above.

[5] p. 14 above.

[6] p. 363 above.

[7] Cf. the experience of Vespasian, p. 228 above.

[8] p. 225 above.

[9] Alföldy, *Fasti Hispanienses* 17 f.

[10] Syme, *Tacitus* 594, comments that 'Easy credit accrued to a government when it brought back some worthy consular who had been shabbily treated by an earlier ruler.' Still, one might allow some place for sentiment on Vespasian's part.

Cn. Pompeius Magnus

Dio 60. 21. 5.

Cn. Pompeius Magnus, eldest of four sons of M. Licinius Crassus Frugi (*cos. ord.* 27)[1] and Scribonia, a descendant of Pompey, advertised his glorious ancestry by his names—a rather dangerous procedure, and Caligula had in fact ordered him to surrender the *cognomen*.[2] Claudius allowed him to resume it, and then gave him his elder daughter Antonia[3] as his bride in 41, a 'matrimonial stratagem' that was 'timely and expedient', as was demonstrated the following year when another descendant of Pompey, the governor of Dalmatia Scribonianus, attempted a coup.[4] As an inscription from Rome shows,[5] Magnus was Claudius' quaestor after the marriage, perhaps in 44.[6]

His presence with Claudius in Britain is attested only by the mention in Dio, but could have been deduced even without this, in view of the participation of his father and of other kinsmen of the Julio-Claudian house.[7] It doubtless gave Claudius particular pleasure, even amusement, to have a Pompeius Magnus with him in a subordinate capacity, and to use him as one of his messengers of victory. He was put to death on false charges brought by Messalina at the same time as his parents, presumably in 46.[8]

Rufrius Pollio

Dio 60. 23. 2

Rufrius Pollio, whose previous career and origin are unknown, was appointed prefect of the guard by Claudius immediately after his accession in 41.[1] He evidently commanded that portion of the praetorians which escorted Claudius to Britain,[2] while his colleague Catonius

[1] p. 356 above.
[2] Dio 60. 5. 8.
[3] *PIR²* A 886.
[4] Syme, *JRS* 50 (1960) 18.
[5] *ILS* 955.
[6] Cébeillac, *Les quaestores* 48—but Dio does not make it clear how old he was. *ILS* 955 was presumably set up before Magnus received his decorations for the British war, which are not mentioned.
[7] pp. 356 f. above.
[8] p. 357 above.
[1] Joseph. *Ant. Jud.* 19. 267.
[2] *ILS* 2648, 2701, show guardsmen decorated by Claudius *bello Britannico*. See L. J. F. Keppie, *Britannia* 2 (1971) 149 ff., reaffirming the men's status at the time they were in Britain.

Justus remained at Rome, where he was put to death by Messalina in the emperor's absence.[3] Pollio was rewarded in 44 by a statue, doubtless a *statua triumphalis*,[4] and the right to have a seat in the senate whenever he accompanied the emperor there. He was later put to death, although no details are recorded in the *Apocolocyntosis*, the sole source of this information, where his execution is mentioned together with that of Justus.[5]

It is not known whether he was related to Rufrius Crispinus, first husband of Poppaea Sabina, and also praetorian prefect, from 47 to 51, who was ordered to commit suicide by Nero in 66.[6] But 47 is presumably the latest date at which Pollio can have commanded the guard, since Crispinus' colleague was Lusius Geta.[7]

Cn. Sentius Saturninus (*cos. ord.* 41)

C. Giordano, *Rend. Acc. Arch. Napoli* 41 (1966) 113, Pompeii: *Vadimonium factum / Truphoni Potamonis f. Alex. / in X K. Apriles Romae [4] / in foro Augusto ante statuam / Cn. Senti Saturnini triumpha/[l]em hora quinta HS MMM / fide rogavit C. Sulpicius [8] / [Cinnamus] fidem promisit [. . .]*

Eutrop. 7. 13: Britanniae bellum intulit [sc. Claudius], quam nullus Romanorum post Iulium Caesarem attigerat, eaque devicta per Cn. Sentium et A. Plautium, illustres et nobiles viros, triumphum celebrem egit.

Only this curious notice in Eutropius records that Cn. Sentius Saturninus (*cos. ord.* 41) participated in the conquest of Britain, evidently in an important role, since he alone is named with the commander-in-chief A. Plautius, and indeed is mentioned first. A wax tablet found at Pompeii reveals incidentally that he had a *statua triumphalis* at Rome, in the Forum of Augustus—in other words, he must have received the *ornamenta triumphalia* for his service.[1] Although a number of other persons involved in the expedition received a like honour, including *comites* of the emperor[2] and legionary legates,[3] Sentius Saturninus

---

[3] Dio 60. 18. 3, one of the things which happened at Rome while Plautius invaded Britain etc., ibid. 60. 19. 1.

[4] See Eichholz, *Britannia* 3 (1972) 158 ff.

[5] 13. 5. See A. Stein, *RE* 1A 1 (1914) 1202.

[6] Stein, *RE* 1A 2 (1914) 1201 f.

[7] *PIR²* L 435.

[1] Degrassi, *Mem. Acc. Linc.* 14 (1969) 136 f., pointed out that this referred to the consul of 41. On the significance of a triumphal statue, see Eichholz, *Britannia* 3 (1972) 158 ff. Groag, *RE* 2A 2 (1923) 1536, had already deduced that Saturninus must have been awarded *ornamenta triumphalia*.

[2] pp. 356 ff. above.

[3] pp. 222, 227 above.

would hardly have been singled out, with Plautius, for mention by Eutropius unless he had had some special function. It may be suggested that he was deputy to Plautius, enjoying a position relative to the commander-in-chief analogous to that of L. Pomponius Flaccus (*cos. ord.* 17) under C. Poppaeus Sabinus (*cos. ord.* 9) in the Balkans in the years 18 and 19[4]—for Sentius was already consular at the time of the expedition, and indeed it may be said that it was to his tenure of the *fasces*, rather than to his role in Britain, that he owed his fame. He was the colleague of Caligula in the office and, for a matter of hours, after the emperor's assassination, was obliged to fulfil the republican consul's role as head of state.[5]

His involvement in the momentous transactions of January 41 might have made him an obnoxious figure in the eyes of Claudius, but his appointment to a command in 43 suggests that this was not so—although he might have been sent in order to ensure his absence from Rome when the emperor was to be away himself.[6] He was a grandson of the *cos. ord.* of 19 BC, one of Augustus' staunchest allies and a kinsman of the *princeps*'s former wife Scribonia. The family appears to derive from Atina in *regio* I.[7] Not much is known of our man's earlier career, although an inscription from Saepinum is thought to record his quaestorship, tribunate of the plebs and praetorship.[8] His later fortunes are not recorded in detail. He is said to have been a friend of Vespasian—and clearly will have come to know him in Britain if at no other time—and to have lost his life at the orders of Nero.[9] No descendants are known.

L. Livius Ocella Ser. Sulpicius Galba (*cos. ord.* 33, *II ord.* 69)

Suet. *Galba* 7. 1.

---

[4] Flaccus' career is summarized by Eck, *RE* Supp. 14 (1974) 439 f. Note also L. Nonius Asprenas (*cos.* 6) and L. Apronius (*cos.* 8), who served under Quintilius Varus and Germanicus respectively in Germany: E. Ritterling, *FRD* 122. C. F. C. Hawkes, in E. Clifford, *Bagendon. A Celtic Oppidum* (1961) 65, following a suggestion by C. E. Stevens, suggested that Saturninus had a diplomatic mission before the invasion; but Eutropius says 'devicta per Cn. Sentium . . .'

[5] See Groag, *RE* 2A 2 (1923) 1532 ff. Two future governors of Britain played minor roles in the dramatic events of 24-5 Jan. 41: see pp. 52 (Q. Veranius) and 59 (M. Trebellius Maximus) above.

[6] This seems to have been the case with one or two of the emperor's *comites* in 43, see pp. 363 f. below. The point is made by D. R. Dudley and G. Webster, *The Roman Conquest of Britain* (1965) 61.

[7] See esp. Syme, *Historia* 13 (1964) 156 ff.

[8] IX 2460; *praenomen* and *gentilicium* are erased, *Cn. f. Saturninus* survives.

[9] This is an inference from Tac. *Hist.* 4. 7. 2, where he is named as a friend of Vespasian with Thrasea Paetus and Barea Soranus. The erasure of the Saepinum inscription (n. 8) would thus be readily explained. See Groag, *RE* 2A 2 (1923) 1536 f.

The participation of the future emperor Galba in the British expedition of 43 is not explicitly mentioned in this passage, although generally assumed.[1] Claudius may have taken him because he could not safely be left behind, as in the case of several others among his *comites* in 43.[2] But Galba could have been a valuable military adviser, for he had commanded the army of Upper Germany from 39 until 41 or later. He had imposed stern discipline on his men and campaigned with success against the Chatti in 41.[3] Two of the legions in the invasion force had been under his orders in the Upper German army, II Augusta and XIV Gemina.[4]

Galba's career is too well known to require more than a brief summary here.[5] Descendant of a patrician family, the Sulpicii, he had been adopted by his stepmother Livia Ocellina, a kinswoman of Augustus' wife, who also showed him favour.[6] He was consul in 33, at an early age, after a year as governor of Aquitania. After his Upper German command and the British expedition, already mentioned, he had a special appointment as proconsul of Africa for two years. He received *ornamenta triumphalia* for his achievements in Germany and Africa, Suetonius records; he does not mention any honour for service in Britain.[7] After many years in retirement, he was appointed governor of Hispania Tarraconensis in 60, and it was there that he became emperor in 68, 'omnium consensu capax imperii, nisi imperasset'.

D. Valerius Asiaticus (*cos.* 35, *II ord.* 46)

Tac. *Ann.* 11. 3. 1.

Valerius Asiaticus was a remarkable figure. A native of Vienna in Gallia Narbonensis, and thus almost certainly of ultimately Gallic extraction, he was the first person from that province to become consul, late in the reign of Tiberius. Nothing is known of his public service other than his two consulships and his 'adversus Britanniam militia', mentioned only in this passage of Tacitus. But several sources, including the *Annals*,

---

[1] Suetonius may just have meant that Claudius delayed his own departure until he was assured of Galba's return to health.

[2] pp. 363 f. below.

[3] Suet. *Galba* 6. 2-3, 8. 1; Dio 60. 8. 7.

[4] Ritterling, *RE* 12. 2 (1925) 1459, 1730.

[5] See M. Fluss, *RE* 4A 1 (1931) 772 ff.

[6] *PIR²* L 305.

[7] See p. 364 below for the suggestion that V 7165, an inscription referring to a senator decorated by Claudius, and a member of his *cohors amicorum*, may belong to Galba, and cf. also p. 365 n. 6 below.

combine to provide a full picture of his personality. He was enormously rich, possessing the famous Gardens of Lucullus at Rome, and was married to a sister of Caligula's wife Lollia Paullina. It was allegedly her adultery with Caligula that caused Asiaticus to become a prime mover in the plot to assassinate the emperor in January 41. After the murder he is said to have been a candidate for the throne. It was doubtless partly because of his conduct at this time that Claudius took him to Britain, although Asiaticus' prestige, especially in Gaul, through which Claudius travelled on his way to the campaign, probably helped to enhance Claudius' popularity. His appointment to a second consulship, only eleven years after his first, and as *ordinarius*, is a sign that he enjoyed the emperor's favour to the full—Tacitus' account makes it clear that Asiaticus, who, with Claudius' chief senatorial ally L. Vitellius, had once cultivated the emperor's mother, must have been an old friend. Yet in 47 it was possible for Messalina to have him condemned to death, out of greed and jealousy, and when Claudius alluded to him in his famous speech the following year the hatred that he felt was made plain by his violent language.[1]

M. Vinicius (*cos. ord.* 30, *II ord.* 45)

Not. Scav. 1929, 31 = *AE* 1929. 166, Cales: *M. Vinicius P. f. M. n. | L. pron. cos. II VIIvir | [epu]lonum sodalis*[4] *| Augustalis thriumphalibus* [sic] *| ornamentis quinq. | viam ab angiporto aedi[s] | Iunonis Lucinae usque* [ad][8] *| aedem Matutae et [clivom] | ab ianu ad g[isiarios portae] | Stellatin[ae et viam patulam] | ad porta[m laevam et ab foro]*[12] *| ad port[am domesticam | sua pecunia stravit]*

R. Syme and A. v. Premerstein deduced that the above inscription from Cales, home of the Vinicii, must be in honour of the *cos. II ord.* 45 rather than of his grandfather the *cos. suff.* 19 BC, and that the *ornamenta triumphalia* must have been bestowed for participation in the expedition of 43.[1] Nothing is known of his career before the first consulship in 30, repeatedly referred to by the historian Velleius Paterculus, who dedicated his work published in that year to Vinicius.[2] In 33 Tiberius selected him as the husband of Germanicus' youngest daughter, the beautiful Julia Livilla. This marriage became dangerous on the accession of Caligula, whose unnatural fondness for his sisters was

---

[1] The evidence is assembled and discussed by P. Weynand, *RE* 7A 2 (1948) 2341 ff. The first consulship is dated by the *Fasti Ostienses*, not available to Weynand. See also Syme, *Tacitus* 414 f., 455, 602.
[1] Syme, *CQ* 27 (1933) 142 ff.; A. v. Premerstein, *JÖAI* 29 (1934) 60 ff.
[2] Vell. Pat. 1. 8. 1, 1. 12. 6, 2. 7. 5, etc.

notorious but turned to hatred in the case of Livilla and the younger
Agrippina, who were both exiled for adultery and alleged treason in 39.
Livilla was recalled by Claudius, but soon exiled again, through the
influence of Messalina, on a charge of adultery with Seneca, and killed
not long afterwards, probably in 42.[3] In the meantime Vinicius himself
had been involved in the successful plot to assassinate Caligula in
January 41, and had been nominated as emperor by his kinsman Annius
Vinicianus before Claudius seized power.[4] All this meant that, as Syme
puts it, for Claudius 'to have omitted Vinicius from his retinue would
have been a gratuitous insult and a gratuitous risk.'[5] As with the other
candidate for the throne in 41, Valerius Asiaticus,[6] Claudius was
apparently doing his best to forgive and forget. Both men were given
the honour of a second consulship, Vinicius in 45 and Asiaticus in 46,
but both of them were put to death within a year of holding office, at
the instigation of Messalina.[7]

Ignotus V 7165

V 7165, Piedmont (exact provenance unknown): [. . .] GI [. . . / *donis dona*]*t. ab
Ti. Claud*[*io Caesare Augusto Germanico / corona aur*]*ea classica val*[*lari* . . . [4]/
. . . *coh*]*ort. amicorum* [*h*]*ospitium cum leg. V*[. . . / *tab*]*ula argent. ae*[. . . / . . .]
o[. . .]

The *dona* awarded to this unknown senator are said to be those appropriate to a consular.[1] This person might be identifiable with the future
emperor Galba, since the phrase in line 4 recalls Suetonius' statement
that soon after Claudius' accession Galba was received 'in cohortem
amicorum'. Further, although Galba received *ornamenta* from Claudius
for his achievements in Germany and Africa, according to the *vita*,
there is no mention of any honour for the British expedition.[2] The
legion in line 4 was presumably the Ninth.[3]

[3] *PIR*[2] J 674.
[4] Joseph., *Ant. Jud.* 19. 102. For Vinicianus, see *PIR*[2] A 701: he was involved in the failed
coup of Scribonianus in 42, and committed suicide.
[5] Syme, *CQ* 27 (1934) 143.
[6] p. 363 above.
[7] Dio 60. 27. 4.
[1] Thus Domaszewski, *RO*[2] 184 and n. 1 (although n. 8 seems to imply the possibility that
the man was only a *tribunus laticlavius*). Ritterling, *RE* 12. 1 (1924) 1250, 12. 2 (1925) 1666,
takes him to be a consular.
[2] p. 362 above.
[3] Thus Ritterling, *RE* 12. 2 (1925) 1666.

Ignotus *AE* 1947. 76

Hesp. 10 (1941) 239 ff. = *AE* 1947. 76, Athens:
(a) [. . .] EI[. . . / . . .] *o inter* [. . . / . . .] *quit* [. . .⁴/. . .] R[. . .]
(b,c,d,e) [. . .*le*] *ga* [*to i*] *n Brittan* [*nia?* . . . / *leg*] *ato Cae* [*s*] *aris* / [*leg*] *ato div* [*i*]
Clau [*dii* ⁴/ *le*] *gato* [. . . / *le*] *gato* [. . .] *prov* [. . . / *le*] *gat* [*o* . . . *pr*] *ovin* [*c.* . . . /
. . .] V[. . .]

J. H. Oliver, who first published the above fragments, identified the
person honoured with A. Didius Gallus (*cos.* 39), governor of Britain
under Claudius and Nero, and assumed to have been with the invasion
force in 43; but there are serious objections to this view.[1] A more
plausible suggestion is that they refer to Cn. Hosidius Geta (*cos.* 47?),[2]
to whom another fragment with similar lettering found in the same
place has been assigned: *Cn.* [*Hosidio?* . . .] *f. Ar* [*n. Getae*] / *co* [*s.
procos. provinciarum? Afr*] *icae* / [*et? Cretae et C*] *yrenar* [*um*].[3] It is
argued above that the Hosidius Geta mentioned by Cassius Dio as
playing a part in the campaign of 43 is this man's brother C. Hosidius
Geta.[4] It is not impossible that both brothers accompanied Claudius to
Britain, Gaius perhaps as legionary legate and Gnaeus as *comes et
legatus Augusti*.[5] But it must be borne in mind that several members
of the high command might have been honoured in a group of inscriptions set up at Athens at the same time. This inscription might refer to
another *comes*.[6]

2. TWO MEN WHO MAY HAVE ACCOMPANIED HADRIAN IN 122

C. Septicius Clarus

HA Hadrian 11. 2–3: Ergo conversis regio more militibus Brittaniam petit, in qua
multa correxit murumque per octoginta milia passuum primus duxit, qui barbaros
Romanosque divideret. 3. Septicio Claro praefecto praetorii et Suetonio Tranquillo
epistularum magistro multisque aliis, quod apud Sabinam uxorem in usu eius

[1] See Petersen and Vidman, *Eirene Congress 1972* 656 f., 667. For Gallus, see p. 45 above.
[2] *PIR*² H 216 (for the date of his consulship see p. 225 above). I owe this suggestion to
Morris, thesis H 42.
[3] *Hesperia* 10 (1941) 237 f. = *AE* 1947. 74. For the identification, see *PIR*² H 216, citing
Morris.
[4] pp. 222 f. above. Morris, thesis H 42, prefers to assume that there was only one Hosidius
Geta, Cnaeus, who served in both Mauretania and Britain.
[5] For the phrase, cf. *ILS* 986 (cited p. 357 above: *legat. et comiti Claud. Caesaris in Brittannia*).
[6] Galba cannot be ruled out—QVIT in line 3 of fragment (a) might refer to [*A*] *quit* [*ania*],
which he governed (p. 362 above).

familiarius se tunc egerant, quam reverentia domus aulicae postulabat, successores dedit, uxorem etiam ut morosam et asperam dimissurus, ut ipse dicebat, si privatus fuisset.

Septicius Clarus is best known for his literary friendships, as the recipient of the opening letter of the younger Pliny, in which Pliny gracefully attributes his decision to publish to Clarus' frequent encouragement, and, according to Johannes Lydus, as the person to whom Suetonius addressed his *Lives of the Caesars*.[1] None of Pliny's *Letters* to him reveal any details of his career. He first emerges in public service with the mention of his appointment as prefect of the guard. The *Historia Augusta* states that Hadrian made him the successor of Sulpicius Similis in that office, at the same time as Acilius Attianus was replaced by Marcius Turbo, evidently in 119.[2]

The *Historia Augusta* also records his dismissal, together with that of Suetonius and 'many others', in the passage quoted above. Since, after further remarks about Hadrian's practice of spying on his friends, the author continues with the remark 'conpositis in Brittania rebus trangressus in Galliam etc.',[3] it seems a legitimate inference that this took place at the time of Hadrian's visit to Britain in 122, and, further, that the two men were with the emperor at the time.[4] It would certainly be natural that one of the prefects of the guard should have been in attendance on the emperor.[5]

Nothing is known for certain of Clarus' origin, but he may have derived from northern Italy.[6] His nephew, Sex. Erucius Clarus, also known from Pliny's *Letters*, ultimately rose to the prefecture of the city and a second consulship in 146, in which year he died.[7]

C. Suetonius Tranquillus

HA Hadrian 11. 2-3: see above.

The career of the celebrated biographer was known only from this

[1] Pliny, *ep.* 1. 1; Joh. Lydus, *de mag.* 2. 6.

[2] *HA Had.* 9. 4-5. See Syme, *Tacitus* 246; Pflaum, *CP* no. 94 (Marcius Turbo). The new diploma found in Rumania (Roxan no. 21) need not mean that Turbo was still in the Danubian area in August 123 (with implications for the careers of Septicius Clarus and Suetonius): see further p. 367 and nn. 6-10 below. Literary references to Clarus are collected and discussed by A. Stein, *RE* 2A 2 (1923) 1557 f.

[3] *HA Had.* 12. 1.

[4] Thus Syme, *Tacitus* 779. See further below.

[5] Cf. the cases of Rufrius Pollio (p. 359 above) and Aemilius Papinianus (p. 368 below).

[6] Syme, *Historia* 9 (1960) 374, citing *ILS* 1348 and Valerius Maximus 7. 7. 4.

[7] *PIR*² E 96; Syme, *Historia* 9 (1960) 362 ff.

passage of the *Historia Augusta* until the discovery of an inscription in his honour at Hippo Regius.[1] From this it emerges that he had been one of the *iudices selecti*, and had then held two posts in the secretariat, [*a*] *studiis* and *a byblio* [*thecis*], presumably under Trajan, before being appointed *ab epistulis* by Hadrian.[2] The context of the story of his dismissal, along with the prefect of the guard Septicius Clarus and 'many others', places it during Hadrian's visit to·Britain in 122.[3] It seems probable that the two men were with the emperor at the time[4]— certainly the empress Sabina, on account of whom the sackings took place, is likely to have been with Hadrian, and it would have been highly appropriate for a guard prefect to have accompanied the emperor abroad.[5]

Some doubt has been cast on the chronology of the affair—and hence on the presence of Septicius and Suetonius in Britain—by the diploma discovered in Rumania dating to August 123.[6] In that document reference is made to men serving in Dacia Porolissensis and Pannonia inferior who had been discharged by Marcius Turbo. Yet Turbo, so the *Historia Augusta* informs us, had governed Pannonia and Dacia temporarily, *ad tempus*, with the status equivalent to a prefect of Egypt, shortly after Hadrian's accession,[7] later to be appointed prefect of the guard at the same time as Septicius Clarus.[8] But the answer ought to be that Turbo had relinquished his appointment some years prior to the issue of the diploma. Certainly, another man was by then governing the Dacian province,[9] while the *ala* prefect under whom the recipient of the diploma had served was no longer in post.[10]

[1] *AE* 1953. 73.

[2] Correspondence with G. B. Townend, whose views were published in *Historia* 10 (1961) 99 ff., persuaded H.-G. Pflaum to accept, in the *addenda* to *CP* no. 96, that Suetonius held his earlier positions in the secretariat under Trajan.

[3] Thus e.g. Funaioli, *RE* 4A 1 (1931) 596 f., puts the dismissal at the time of Hadrian's absence on his travels, wavering between 121 and 122 (but assuming that Suetonius was left behind in Rome). For the date of Hadrian's visit to Britain, see W. Weber, *Untersuchungen zur Geschichte des Kaisers Hadrians* (1907) 109 ff.

[4] Thus Syme, *Tacitus* 779 f. J. A. Crook, *Proc. Cambridge Phil. Soc.* 4 (1956-7) 18 ff., took a different view. Syme was more cautious in *Emperors and Biography* (1971) 114 f. New evidence (see below) led J. Gascou, *Latomus* 27 (1978) 436 ff., to support Crook enthusiastically.

[5] Sabina is known certainly to have accompanied Hadrian only on his visit to the east in 120/30: *SEG* 716-18. The presence of guard prefects on imperial expeditions is too well attested to require documentation, but note p. 359 above (Rufrius Pollio with Claudius in Britain), p. 368 below (Aemilius Papinianus with Severus in Britain).

[6] See now Alföldy, *ZPE*.

[7] *HA Had.* 6. 7, 7. 3.

[8] *HA Had.* 9. 4-5.

[9] Livius Grapus (perhaps Gratus is the correct form) is named on Roxan no. 21. Sex. Julius Severus (pp. 108 f. above) was governor of Dacia superior from 120 to 126.

[10] As shown by the form *praefuit*: see Mrs Roxan's note ad loc.

If Suetonius did, after all, go to Britain, it may have been then that he made the observation, recorded in the *Life* of Titus, that the latter's memory was still green in the province, 'sicut apparet statuarum et imaginum eius multitudine ac titulis'.[11] As it happens, a letter of Pliny reveals that Suetonius had declined an opportunity to go to Britain much earlier in his career: Pliny had obtained for him a commission as an equestrian officer from the governor Neratius Marcellus, but Suetonius turned it down.[12]

Suetonius' origin is a matter of some debate. Africa seems probable, in view of the dedication at Hippo, for which no other reason may readily be offered. That his priesthood as *pontifex Volcani*, recorded on the stone, was held at Ostia, now seems improbable.[13] But wherever he saw the light of day, as the son of Suetonius Laetus, who served as an equestrian tribune under Otho in 69,[14] it is probable that the family's *ultima origo* was the town of Pisaurum in Italy.[15]

3. MEN WHO ACCOMPANIED SEVERUS, CARACALLA, AND GETA
208-211

Aemilius Papinianus

Dio 76. 14. 5-6: καὶ [sc. ὁ Σεουῆρος] καλέσας τόν τε υἱὸν καὶ τὸν Παπινιανὸν καὶ τὸν Κάστορα ξίφος τέ τι τεθῆναι ἐς τὸ μέσον ἐκέλευσε, καὶ ἐγκαλέσας αὐτῷ ὅτι τε ἄλλως τοιοῦτόν τι ἐτόλμησε καὶ ὅτι πάντων ὁρώντων τῶν τε συμμάχων καὶ τῶν πολεμίων τηλικοῦτον κακὸν δράσειν ἔμελλεν, τέλος ἔφη · "ἀλλ' εἴγε ἀποσφάξαι με ἐπιθυμεῖς, ἐνταῦθά με κατάχρησαι · 6. ἔρρωσαι γάρ, ἐγὼ δὲ καὶ γέρων εἰμὶ καὶ κεῖμαι. ὡς εἴγε τοῦτο μὲν οὐκ ἀναδύῃ, τὸ δὲ αὐτόχειρ μου γενέσθαι ὀκνεῖς, παρέστηκέ σοι Παπινιανὸς ὁ ἔπαρχος, ᾧ δύνασαι κελεῦσαι ἵνα με ἐξεργάσηται · πάντως γάρ που πᾶν τὸ κελευσθὲν ὑπὸ σοῦ, ἅτε καὶ αὐτοκράτορος ὄντος, ποιήσει."

The presence of the praetorian prefect Aemilius Papinianus in Britain during the Severan expedition of 208-11 is revealed only by this story in Cassius Dio about Severus' reaction to an attempt on his own life by Caracalla.[1] It is a little surprising that Papinian, best known as a jurist, should have been the prefect chosen for this campaign.[2] The only previous post he is known to have held was that of *a libellis*. He had

---

[11] *D. Titus* 4. 1, pointed out by Syme, *Tacitus* 779.
[12] Pliny, *ep.* 3. 8. For Marcellus see p. 88 above.
[13] See R. Meiggs, *Roman Ostia*[2] (1973) 515, 584, 597.
[14] Suet. *Otho* 10. 1.
[15] See p. 55 and n. 6 above (on Suetonius Paullinus).
[1] For the context, see A. R. Birley, *Septimius Severus* 261 f.
[2] His colleague Maecius Laetus (Pflaum, *CP* no. 219) had at least been prefect of Egypt.

become prefect of the guard in 205, with Q. Maecius Laetus, after the murder of Plautianus.[3] Of particular importance, apart from his great reputation as a lawyer, was his relationship to Julia Domna.[4] After the death of Severus he was dismissed by Caracalla, perhaps before leaving Britain,[5] and was put to death less than a year later, shortly after the murder of Geta.[6]

C. Julius Avitus Alexianus (*cos. a. inc.*)

JÖAI 19/20, Bbl. 318 ff. = *AE* 1921. 64 = *Bayerische Vorgeschichtsblätter* 27 (1962) 95 = *AE* 1963. 42, Salonae: *C. Iulio [Avito Ale]/xiano [praef. coh. . . Ulp.] / Petraeo [r. trib. leg. . . .] [4]/ praef. eq. [al. . . .proc.] / ad anno [nam Augg. Ostiis] / c. v. prae [t. sodali Titiali] / leg. leg. III[. . . leg. pro pr. pro] [8]/vinciae [Raetiae cos. co]/miti imp [p. Severi et Anto]/nini in B[ritannia praef.] / aliment[orum comiti imp.] [12]/ Antonin[i in . . .] / praef. ali[ment. II leg. pro pr.] / provin[ciae Dalmatiae] / procon[suli prov. Asiae(?)] [16]/ praesidi [clementissimo(?) / M. Aure[lius . . .] / trib. coh. [. . .] / Anto [ninianae]*

Julius Avitus Alexianus was a native of Emesa in Syria and very probably the nephew of the empress Julia Domna. His connection is revealed by the dedication he made, while governor of Raetia *c.*207, to the Emesene god Elagabalus.[1] Alexianus began his career as an equestrian officer, but entered the senate after holding a minor procuratorial post. After a legionary command, the governorship of Raetia, and the consulship, he accompanied Severus and his party to Britain in 208. His presence on Severus' staff illustrates the dominance of the empress Julia's Syrian kinsmen at this time.[2]

After the British expedition he became prefect of the *alimenta*, accompanied Caracalla as *comes*, probably on his German expedition of 213,[3] and had a second spell as prefect of the *alimenta*. His last two

---

[3] For details, see *PIR*[2] A 388; Pflaum, *CP* no. 220.

[4] Mentioned only by *HA Carac.* 8. 2: 'Papinianum amicissimum fuisse imperatori Severo et, ut aliqui loquuntur, adfinem etiam per secundam uxorem, memoriae traditur.' See A. R. Birley, *Septimius Severus* 336.

[5] Dio 77. 1. 1.

[6] See *PIR*[2] A 388 for references, and, for the date of Geta's death, Barnes, *JTS* N.S. 19 (1968) 514 ff.

[1] *Germania* 39 (1961), 383 ff. = *Bayer. Vorgesch.-Bl.* 27 (1962) 82 ff. = *AE* 1962. 229, Augusta Vindelicorum. The correct dating of this inscription and the career of Alexianus as revealed by the Salonae inscription, were worked out by H.-G. Pflaum, *Bayer. Vorgesch.-Bl.*, loc. cit. His conclusions are summarized in *PIR*[2] J 192, and followed, with some minor divergences, in A. R. Birley, *Septimius Severus* 298 f.

[2] Cf. the praetorian prefect Papinian (above), and Sex. Varius Marcellus, pp. 297 f. above.

[3] Pflaum, op. cit. 93, prefers to restore *Mesopotamia* in line 12 of the Salonae inscription, but the German expedition is slightly more attractive, since Alexianus' previous service as governor of Raetia should have made him a useful adviser for a campaign against the Alamanni.

posts were as governor of Dalmatia and proconsul of Africa or Asia. The latter post would normally have been held about fifteen years after the consulship, *c.*222,[4] and the Dalmatian appointment probably preceded it fairly closely. His names were erased, although still legible, on the Salonae inscription, indicating that he suffered *damnatio memoriae*. This might have occurred when his elder presumed nephew Elagabalus was overthrown in 222 and replaced by the younger, Severus Alexander.

C. Junius Faustinus [Pl] a[ci] dus Postumianus (*cos. a. inc.*)

VIII 597, cf. 11764, near Thugga: see pp. 161 f. above, for the text of this inscription.

It is generally assumed that this man is the same as the former *praeses* of Spain and Britain C. Junius Faus[ti]nus Postumianus commemorated on another inscription from the same area. However this may be, since the Postumianus of VIII 597 was *comes* of more than one emperor after being *leg. Augg. pr. pr.* of three provinces, two praetorian and one consular, it was almost certainly at the time of the British expedition of 208-11 that he was attached to the imperial staff.[1]

4. A PRAETORIAN PREFECT IN 296

Julius Asclepiodotus (*cos. ord.* 292)

Jerome, *Chron. s. a.* 300: Post decem annos per Asclepiodotum praefectum praetorio Britanniae receptae.

For Aur. Vict. *Caes.* 39. 42, Eutrop. 9. 14, Oros. 7. 25. 6, Zonar. 12. 31, see pp. 310 f. above, under Carausius.

The above passages appear to indicate that, in spite of the panegyrist's rhetoric,[1] the real victor in the campaign against Allectus in 296 was not Constantius but his praetorian prefect Asclepiodotus. He is uniformly referred to in the literary sources by a single name; Jul(ius) is supplied by an inscription from Oescus.[2] The *Historia Augusta* lists him, with

---

[4] p. 32 above.
[1] See the discussion on pp. 162 ff. above.
[1] *Pan Lat.* 8 (5), esp. 11 ff.
[2] *ILS* 8929, set up in honour of Diocletian by himself and Afranius Hannibalianus, *v*[v.] *eemm. prae*[*ff. praet.*] *d. n.* [*m. q. e.*].

others, among the generals trained by Probus—'ex eius disciplina',[3] but nothing is known of his earlier career. He was already prefect when the Oescus inscription was dedicated, early in the reign of Diocletian, between the years 286 and 290. He was *consul ordinarius* in 292, and received rescripts in 292 and 293.[4] Nothing certain is known about his origin, nor are any descendants recorded.

5. A *MAGISTER EQUITUM* IN 360

Flavius Lupicinus (*cos. ord.* 367)

Julian, *ep. ad Ath.* 283A: . . . ἀνέμενον δὲ Φλωρέντιον παραγενέσθαι καὶ τὸν Λουππικῖνον· ἦν γὰρ ὁ μὲν περὶ τὴν Βιένναν, ὁ δὲ ἐν ταῖς Βρεττανίαις . . .

Amm. Marc. 20. 1. 1–3: . . . consulatu vero Constantii deciens, terque Iuliani, in Brittaniis cum Scottorum Pictorumque gentium ferarum excursus, rupta quiete condicta, loca limitibus vicina vastarent, et inplicaret formido provincias, praeteritarum cladium congerie fessas, hiemem agens apud Parisios Caesar distractusque in sollicitudines varias, verebatur ire subsidio transmarinis, ut rettulimus ante fecisse Constantem, ne rectore vacuas relinqueret Gallias, Alamannis ad saevitiam etiam tum incitatis et bella. 2. ire igitur ad haec ratione vel vi conponenda, Lupicinum placuit, ea tempestate magistrum armorum, bellicosum sane et castrensis rei peritum, sed supercilia erigentem ut cornua, et de tragico (quod aiunt) coturno strepentem, super quo diu ambigebatur, avarus esset potius an crudelis. 3. moto igitur velitari auxilio, Aerulis scilicet et Batavis, numerisque Moesiacorum duobus, adulta hieme dux ante dictus Bononiam venit, quaesitisque navigiis, et omni inposito milite, observato flatu secundo ventorum, ad Rutupias sitas ex adverso defertur, petitque Lundinium, ut exinde suscepto pro rei publicae consilio, festinaret ocius ad procinctum.

Id. 20. 4. 3: Et super auxiliariis quidem et trecentenis, cogendis ocius proficisci, Lupicinus conventus est solus, transisse ad Brittanias nondum conpertus . . .

Id. 20. 4. 6: Et quia sollicitus Caesar, quid de residuis mitti praeceptis agi deberet, perque varias curas animum versans, adtente negotium tractari oportere censebat, cum hinc barbara feritas, inde iussorum urgueret auctoritas, maximeque absentia magistri equitum augente dubietatem, redire ad se praefectum hortatus est, olim Viennam specie annonae parandae digressum, ut se militari eximeret turba.

Id. 20. 4. 9: Inter has tamen moras absentis Lupicini, motusque militares timentis praefecti, Iulianus consiliorum adminiculo destitutus, ancipitique sententia fluctuans, id optimum factu existimavit: et sollemniter cunctos e stationibus egressos, in quibus hiemabant, maturare disposuit.

---

[3] *HA Probus* 22. 3. Note also the Asclepiodotus cited as a (second-hand) source for remarks of Diocletian about Aurelian and Maximian, *HA Aurelian.* 44. 2–3.

[4] *PLRE* I 115 f.

Id. 20. 9. 9: Et quoniam cum haec ita procederent, timebatur Lupicinus, licet absens agensque tum apud Brittanos, homo superbae mentis et turgidae, eratque suspicio (si haec trans mare didicisset) novarum rerum materias excitaret, notarius Bononiam mittitur, observaturus sollicite, ne quisquam fretum oceani transire permitteretur. quo vetito, reversus Lupicinus antequam horum quicquam sciret, nullas ciere potuit turbas.

Flavius Lupicinus[1] was *magister equitum* in Gaul under Julian, having been appointed in 359.[2] Early in 360 news reached Julian at Paris of an invasion of the Britains by the Scots and Picts. Reluctant to go in person, for fear of an Alamannic attack on the Gauls, Julian dispatched Lupicinus with reinforcements. Ammianus adds a characterization of the man, on which Gibbon's comment is worth quoting: 'The valour of Lupicinus and his military skill, are acknowledged by the historian, who, in his affected language, accuses the general of exalting the horns of his pride, bellowing in a tragic tone, and exciting a doubt whether.he was more cruel or avaricious.'[3] When Constantius asked Julian for more troops, Lupicinus was instructed to take them, but was still in Britain. After Julian's proclamation as emperor, Constantius sacked Lupicinus, but Julian doubted whether he would support him and evidently arrested him on his return to Gaul.[4]

He was reappointed *magister equitum*, in the east, by Jovian, and continued in office under Valens, being rewarded for his assistance in the suppression of the usurper Procopius by the consulship for 367. His origin is not recorded and no relatives are mentioned; he is known to have been a Christian.[5]

6. A *COMES DOMESTICORUM* AND A *MAGISTER EQUITUM* IN 367

Severus

Amm. Marc. 27. 8. 2: see p. 333 above, for this text.

When Valentinian heard the news of the 'barbarian conspiracy' in the summer of 367, he sent Severus, 'etiam tum domesticorum comitem' to restore the situation, but he was recalled shortly afterwards and the

---

[1] His full name is known only from an inscription at Rome: *Inscr. Christ. Urb. Rom.* 193.
[2] Amm. Marc. 18. 2. 7.
[3] *Decline and Fall of the Roman Empire*, ch. xxii.
[4] *PLRE* I 520. It is difficult to·calculate how long he had been in Britain from the indications in Amm. Marc. 20. His departure was during the winter ('adulta hieme', 20. 1. 3).
[5] See *PLRE* I 520 f. for details.

magister equitum Jovinus was sent instead. Severus had been *comes domesticorum* since at least 365.[1] Soon after his return to Gaul he was promoted to *magister peditum*, since he is described as such by Ammianus when mentioned as a possible successor to Valentinian during the latter's illness, in the same summer.[2] R. Tomlin, who has made sense of Ammianus' muddled narrative, also notes that Severus could be thought of as a possible successor because his senior and more distinguished colleague Jovinus was absent in Britain.[3]

Severus continued to be master of the soldiers for several years, the latest evidence coming from the year 372.[4] His subsequent history is unknown.

Nothing can be discovered about his origin or family, and his name is one of the commonest.[5] Ammianus characterises him as 'asper . . . et formidatus', although preferable in every way to his potential rival at the time of Valentinian's illness, Rusticus Julianus.[6]

Flavius Jovinus (*cos. ord.* 367)

Amm. Marc. 27. 8. 2: see p. 333 above, for this text.

Flavius Jovinus,[1] whose earlier career is unknown, was *magister equitum* from 361 until he was replaced by Theodosius, having been consul with Lupicinus[2] in 367.[3] In the summer of that year he was sent to Britain, following the recall of the *comes domesticorum* Severus.[4] Ammianus' text is defective at this point,[5] but there seems little doubt that he did go to Britain, and that it is his absence, while the emperor was dangerously ill, that explains why he was not thought of, rather than Severus, as a possible successor to Valentinian.[6] His report on the state of the island led to the dispatch of Theodosius. When the latter returned to

---

[1] *PLRE* I 833. For Jovinus, see below.
[2] Amm. Marc. 27. 6. 3. The chronology has been explained by Tomlin, *Britannia* 5 (1974), 303 ff. See further above, p. 337.
[3] Tomlin, op. cit. 305.
[4] *Cod. Theod.* 7. 1. 11 (24 Apr. 372).
[5] See *PLRE* I 831 ff., which lists thirty-one Severi, fifteen of them with no other name.
[6] Amm. Marc. 27. 6. 3. For Julianus, see *PLRE* I 479 f.
[1] The first name is known only from *Inscr. Christ. Urb. Rom* 193.
[2] p. 372 above.
[3] His appointment was a reward for his successes against the Alamanni in 366, Amm. Marc. 27. 3. 10; see *PLRE* I 463 for other references.
[4] Cf. above.
[5] See p. 333 above, where the text follows the 'more conservative emendation' favoured by Tomlin, *Britannia* 5 (1974) 306 f.
[6] Tomlin, op. cit. 305.

the emperor's side, he took the place of Jovinus as *magister equitum*. Jovinus was apparently dismissed for 'sluggishness', if the emendation *ut lenti* may be accepted.[7] The date can now be seen to have been 368, rather than 369, as shown by R. Tomlin.[8]

Jovinus had spent many years on the Rhine frontier, and it was perhaps because he had come to know and like Rheims that he chose to settle there on his retirement, building the church of St Agricola in the town.[9] He may of course have been of Gallic origin.[10]

7. STILICHO'S SUPPOSED VISIT TO BRITAIN

Flavius Stilicho

Claud. *in Eutrop.* 1. 391–3:

> Quantum te principe possim,
> non longinqua docent, domito quod Saxone Tethys
> mitior aut fracto secura Britannia Picto.

Id., *de cons. Stil.* 2. 247–55:

> Inde Caledonio velata Britannia monstro,
> 248   ferro picta genas, cuius vestigia verrit
> caerulus Oceanique aestum mentitur amictus:
> 'me quoque vicinis pereuntem gentibus' inquit
> 'munivit Stilicho, totam cum Scottus Hivernen
> 252   movit et infesto spumavit remige Tethys.
> illius effectum curis, ne tela timerem
> Scottica, ne Pictum tremerem, ne litore toto
> prospicerem dubiis venturum Saxona ventis.

The two passages from Claudian quoted above, published in 399 and 400 respectively,[1] represent the sole evidence[2] for the *magister militum* and father-in-law of Honorius, Stilicho,[3] having taken measures for the defence of Britain. Earlier in the second poem, and in the *de IV consulatu*

---

[7] Amm. Marc. 28. 3. 9 (quoted p. 335 above), where the MSS have 'in locum ut lentis Iovini', 'in locum Valentis Iovini'.

[8] Tomlin, *Britannia* 5 (1974) 303 ff.

[9] XIII 3256. See S. Applebaum, *Latomus* 23 (1964) 782; J. F. Matthews, *Western Aristocracies and Imperial Court A.D. 364–425* (1975) 51; and for Jovinus' career as a whole *PLRE* I 462 f.

[10] As seems to be assumed by K. F. Stroheker, *Der senatorische Adel im spätantiken Gallien* (1948) 185 no. 203.

[1] Vollmer, *RE* 3. 2 (1899) 2654.

[2] D. P. S. Peacock, *Antiquity* 47 (1973) 138 ff., has demonstrated that the tiles with the stamp *Hon. Aug. Andria.* allegedly found at Pevensey are modern forgeries.

[3] See *PLRE* I 853 ff.

Honorii,[4] of 398, Claudian refers to a visit to the Rhine frontier by the great general, which took him to the mouth of the river and involved the renewal of treaties with the barbarians. The date was evidently 396, and it might seem plausible that it was at this time that he was in some way involved with the defence of Britain against Scots, Picts, and Saxons.[5] However, it is more probable that his British measures were taken in 398—although it is unlikely that more was involved than the despatch of troops. No campaign need have taken place, let alone a personal expedition of Stilicho.[6] Had anything of the kind occurred, Claudian would not have failed to devote a lengthy panegyric to it.

Whatever Stilicho did in the late 390s, a few years later he allegedly weakened Britain by withdrawing troops to protect Italy, including 'a legion which was stationed in far off Britain' and which had had to fight the Scots and Picts. But this whole picture is a poet's fantasy.[7] It has been suggested that Stilicho established the post of *comes Britanniarum* at this time, in 402, to compensate for the withdrawal of large numbers of frontier troops.[8] But it is more plausible to suppose that the post had already been created *c.*398, if not earlier.[9] Any troop withdrawals—and the *Notitia Dignitatum* does indeed show traces of these—may be ascribed to Constantine III in 407.[10]

[4] *de cons. Stil.* 1. 189-231; *de IV cons.* Hon. 439-59.

[5] O. Seeck, *RE* 8. 2 (1913) 2278 f.

[6] Seeck, *RE* 8. 2 (1913) 2278 ff., assigns the British measures to 398, after the fall of Gildo, as do D. Hoffmann, *Das spätrömische Bewegungsheer und die Notitia Dignitatum* (1969) I 365 f., and M. Miller, *Britannia* 6 (1975) 141 ff. But whether there was any 'Pictish war', as Miller believes, is another matter.

[7] Claud. *de bello Gothico* 416-18. For the date, Seeck, *RE* 8. 2 (1913) 2281, *PLRE* I 856. But Hoffmann, op. cit. I 364 f. and II 159 f. nn. 473-4, shows quite clearly that Claudian need no more be taken literally here than in the *In Rufinum* 2. 148-50, where British troops are also alleged to have participated, in the campaign of 395 against Rufinus. As he stresses, the British troops could not possibly have arrived in Italy in 401-2 in time to cope with Alaric. (Miller, op. cit. 144, appears to be unaware of Hoffmann's discussion.) Furthermore, the mention of a *legio* is purely poetic language and could mean any military force, as Hoffmann points out.

[8] Thus Frere, *Britannia*[2] 269, 407.

[9] Hoffmann, op. cit. I 166 f., believes that the post was established immediately after Count Theodosius' mission, but see p. 320 above, where Mann's view, in Johnston (ed.), *Saxon Shore* 14, that it was created by Stilicho *c.*398, is followed.

[10] See Hoffmann, op. cit. I 364 f.

III

III.1

THE ORIGINS AND CAREERS OF THE GOVERNORS
OF UNDIVIDED BRITAIN

ORIGINS

From AD 43 until the reign of Trajan the vast majority of the governors were of Italian origin. Thereafter provincials preponderated. Of the first nine all but M. Trebellius Maximus, whose home may have been in southern Gaul, came from Italy. Sex. Julius Frontinus probably came from Gallia Narbonensis, as was certainly the case with his successor Cn. Julius Agricola. But the next five governors attested after Agricola all seem to have been Italian. The first Hadrianic governor, Q. Pompeius Falco, was a man with multifarious connections in different parts of the empire, whose precise origin seems undiscoverable. A. Platorius Nepos was almost certainly a provincial, from southern Spain or perhaps Dalmatia, the latter province being the home of Sex. Julius Severus and his kinsman Cn. Julius Verus. P. Mummius Sisenna may well have come from Spain, as did Cn. Papirius Aelianus. But none of these three areas outside Italy so far mentioned, Gaul, Spain, and Dalmatia, is known to have supplied any other governors. By contrast, several came from North Africa, starting with Q. Lollius Urbicus in the late 130s. Sex. Calpurnius Agricola may be another North African. Four further governors undoubtedly derived from that quarter: Q. Antistius Adventus, D. Clodius Albinus, L. Alfenus Senecio, and C. Junius Faustinus Postumianus. The only other men for whom probable provincial origin may be asserted are Ulpius Marcellus, who perhaps came from the east, and C. Julius Marcus. The future emperor Pertinax is the only certain Italian in the period from Hadrian to c. 213, but Italian origin appears probable for Caerellius, Virius Lupus, and Pollienus Auspex, and quite possible for M. Statius Priscus. Priscus is the only man for whom there is even a remote chance of derivation from Britain itself—but Italy or Dalmatia look more probable. Finally, the Severan governor C. Valerius Pudens has nomenclature so featureless that he could have come from anywhere in the empire.

Thus twelve if not thirteen out of the first sixteen governors were Italian, as against a maximum of nine—and perhaps as few as two or

Table 7

Name	Origin	Dates attested
A. Plautius	Italy (Trebula Suffenas)	43–47
P. Ostorius Scapula	Italy	47–52
A. Didius Gallus	Italy (Histonium)	52–7
Q. Veranius	Italy	57–8
C. Suetonius Paullinus	Italy (Pisaurum?)	58–61
P. Petronius Turpilianus	Italy	61–3
M. Trebellius Maximus	Italy or Gaul (Toulouse?)	63–9
M. Vettius Bolanus	Italy	69–71
Q. Petillius Cerialis	Italy (Novaria)	71–3
Sex. Julius Frontinus	southern Gaul?	73–7
Cn. Julius Agricola	southern Gaul (Forum Julii)	77–84
Sallustius Lucullus	Italy	84/96
P. Metilius Nepos	Italy (Novaria)	98
T. Avidius Quietus	Italy (Faventia)	98
L. Neratius Marcellus	Italy (Saepinum)	103
M. Atilius Bradua	Italy	c.117
Q. Pompeius Falco	unknown	122
A. Platorius Nepos	Spain or Dalmatia	122–4
Sex. Julius Severus	Dalmatia (Aequum)	c.130–3
P. Mummius Sisenna	Spain?	135
Q. Lollius Urbicus	North Africa (ager Cirtensis)	139–42
Cn. Papirius Aelianus	Spain (Iliberris)	146
Cn. Julius Verus	Dalmatia (Aequum)	158
M. Statius Priscus	Italy or Dalmatia (or Britain)?	c.161–2
Sex. Calpurnius Agricola	North Africa?	163
Q. Antistius Adventus	North Africa (Thibilis)	c.173
Caerellius	Italy (or North Africa)?	c.178
Ulpius Marcellus	east?	184
P. Helvius Pertinax	Italy (Alba Pompeia)	185
D. Clodius Albinus	North Africa (Hadrumetum)	192–7
Virius Lupus	Italy?	197–8
C. Valerius Pudens	unknown	205
L. Alfenus Senecio	North Africa (Cuicul)	205/7
Ulpius Marcellus jr	east?	211–12
C. Julius Marcus	east?	213
Pollienus Auspex	Italy?	under Severus?
C. Junius Faustinus	North Africa	under Severus or Caracalla?

three—out of the next twenty-one. The details are recapitulated in Table 7.

Only four of the governors belonged to families that were already senatorial at the beginning of the principate: A. Plautius, A. Didius Gallus, P. Petronius Turpilianus, and Q. Petillius Cerialis. A further four were patricians: Q. Veranius, Cn. Julius Agricola, L. Neratius

Marcellus, and M. Atilius Metilius (Appius) Bradua; but these men were of course 'new patricians'. At the other end of the social scale, M. Statius Priscus and P. Helvius Pertinax had entered the senate after an equestrian career, Pertinax's humble origin as the son of a wealthy freedman being known from the *Historia Augusta*. Sex. Julius Frontinus may also have had service as an equestrian officer and procurator before becoming a senator. With a few of the other governors it is known that they were not the first senator of their family—this certainly applies to Cn. Julius Verus, presumed to be the son or nephew of Sex. Julius Severus; and, if his existence be accepted, it applies *a fortiori* to the younger Ulpius Marcellus. But with many of these men it is impossible to say. Apart from Priscus and Pertinax, only of Sex. Julius Severus, Q. Lollius Urbicus, and L. Alfenus Senecio, can it be said with confidence that they were of non-senatorial parentage. P. Ostorius Scapula may have been the son, rather than grandson, of the praetorian prefect under Augustus, and Alfenus Senecio was probably the son of the homonymous high-ranking procurator (if not identical with him), but these two are the only identifiable specimens among the governors of a distinct group under the principate, senatorial sons of prominent equestrians.

THE CAREER OF BRITISH GOVERNORS UP TO THE PRAETORSHIP

The first ten to twelve years in the career of a future governor of Britain must in many cases have been of great significance for their future success, but it is hard to deduce much from the evidence of career inscriptions alone. It might have been inferred from Q. Veranius' start as *IIIvir monetalis*, tribune of IV Scythica, and quaestor of the emperor, that he enjoyed powerful patronage; and his successful *quinquennium* as first governor of Lycia, as mentioned on his unusually lengthy memorial inscription, would no doubt have made it possible to predict, even were it not otherwise known, that he would receive a major consular command such as that in Britain. But what is known of his father, and of his own role as tribune of the plebs in 41, helps to explain his success very much more satisfactorily. Even in Tacitus' biography of Agricola, much is left unsaid. What is said about his career up to the praetorship does not indicate any particular distinction: it was undoubtedly Agricola's early adherence to the Flavian *partes* in 69 which made the real difference. In the case of Platorius Nepos, his start as *IIIvir capitalis* suggests, in the light of what is known about other former holders of his post, that his career would not have been nearly so successful as it was, but for his personal friendship with Hadrian.

In all cases where there is any information governors of Britain had served as legionary tribune—except for Junius Faustinus Postumianus; but he may have been legate of Britannia superior anyway. On the other hand, the early stages of the career are known for only nine governors. The significance of an appointment as quaestor of the emperor, and his backing for election to this office or to the tribunate of the plebs and praetorship, cannot be denied. But it may be remarked that Julius Verus, after being *quaestor Augusti*, was apparently not *candidatus* in his next two magistracies; yet clearly continued to enjoy a highly successful career. One may, indeed, wonder whether senators always troubled to mention that they had been *candidatus*, for Sex. Julius Severus' fragmentary inscription from Aequum omits to record it, although it does appear on the fuller *cursus* from Burnum. However, in the cases of Lollius Urbicus and Junius Faustinus, for example, the fact that they were *candidatus* as tribunes of the plebs and as praetor, after an ordinary quaestorship, does allow one to infer that they had acquired useful favour or patronage in the interval. Urbicus may perhaps have found a patron in the shape of the proconsul of Asia whom he served as legate after the quaestorship. Only a handful of governors held appointments other than the tribunate of the plebs between the quaestorship and praetorship. No doubt it was mostly available ex-praetors who became proconsular legates. It is hard to say whether there is any significance in the fact that no governors of Britain are known to have been aedile, while eleven were tribunes of the plebs.

The vigintivirate

Only in the case of nine governors is it known which post they held in the vigintivirate. Three were *IIIviri monetales*, three *IVviri viarum curandarum*, two *Xviri stlitibus iudicandis*, and one *IIIvir capitalis*. The number is perhaps too small to make any firm inferences.

Q. Veranius	τριῶν ἀνδρῶν ἐπὶ χαράξεως νομίσματος (*IGR* III 703)
L. Neratius Marcellus	*IIIvir a. a. a. f. f.* (*ILS* 1032)
Q. Pompeius Falco	*decemviro stli[tibu]s iudicandis* (*ILS* 1936)
A. Platorius Nepos	*IIIvir. capitali* (*ILS* 1052)
Sex. Julius Severus	*[I]IIIviro [v]iarum c[ura]nd[ar]um* (*ILS* 1056)

Q. Lollius Urbicus	*IIIIviro viarum curand.* (VIII 6706)
Cn. Julius Verus	*triumviro a. a. a. f. f.* (*ILS* 1057)
Q. Antistius Adventus	*IIIIvir. viarum curandarum* (*ILS* 8977)
C. Junius Faustinus Postumianus	*d*[*ec*]*emviro stlitibus iud*[*ic.*] (p. 162 above)

The military tribunate

Again, only nine governors are known with certainty to have served as *tribunus laticlavius*, the first eight of those listed above as *XXviri*—the ninth, Faustinus Postumianus, seems not to have held a commission as tribune—together with Julius Agricola. In addition, we know the equestrian *militiae* of M. Statius Priscus and P. Helvius Pertinax.

Q. Veranius	χειλιάρχου λεγιῶνος τέταρτης Σκυθικῆς (Moesia)
Cn. Julius Agricola	'prima castrorum rudimenta in Britannia, Suetonio Paulino, diligenti ac moderato duci, approbavit' etc. (Tacitus, *Agr.* 5. 1–3) (AD 60)
L. Neratius Marcellus	*trib. mil. leg. XII Fulminat.* (Cappadocia)
Q. Pompeius Falco	*trib. mil. leg. X* [*Gem.*] (Germania inferior; see p. 98 and n. 16 above)
A. Platorius Nepos	*trib. mil. leg. XXII Primigen. p. f.* (Germania superior)
Sex. Julius Severus	*trib. leg. XIIII* [*Gem.*] (Pannonia superior)
Q. Lollius Urbicus	*trib. laticlavio leg. XXII Primigeniae* (Germania superior)
Cn. Julius Verus	*tribuno laticlav*[*i*] *o leg. X Fretensis* (Judaea)
Q. Antistius Adventus	*tribuno mil. leg. I Minerviae p. f.* (Germania inferior)

In two cases, those of Marcellus and Verus, it appears that the tribunates were served under close kinsmen, probably the fathers. It is hard to say whether there is any significance in the fact that four out of nine served in German legions. Perhaps more important is the fact that only Agricola served in a British legion.

The quaestorship

Service as quaestor is attested for fourteen governors. Four of these were quaestor of the emperor. Julius Severus was *candidatus* of Trajan, although he served in Macedonia. Four served at Rome, in addition to the *quaestores Augusti,* the remaining six in the provinces. Faustinus' province is unknown; Agricola served in Asia, Papirius Aelianus in Achaia, and the three others were all in Macedonia.

A. Didius Gallus	[?*quaestori impe*]*ratoris* [*Ti. Caesaris Aug.*] (p. 45 above)
Q. Veranius	ταμίαν Τιβερίου καὶ Γα[ἰ]ου Σεβαστοῦ (*IGR* III 703)
Cn. Julius Agricola	'sors quaesturae provinciam Asiam, proconsulem Salvium Titianum dedit' (Tac. *Agr.* 6. 3)
L. Neratius Marcellus	*quaest. Aug.* (*ILS* 1032)
M. Atilius Bradua	ταμίαν (*ILS* 8824a)
Q. Pompeius Falco	[*q*]*uaestori* (*ILS* 1036)
A. Platorius Nepos	*quaest. provinc. Maced.* (*ILS* 1052)
Sex. Julius Severus	[*q*]*uaestor. pro*[*vin*]*cia*[*e*] *Macedoniae* [*c*]*an-dida*[*t*]*o div*[*i Tr*]*ai.* [*P*]*artici* (*ILS* 1056)
Q. Lollius Urbicus	*quaest. urbis* (VIII 6706)
Cn. Papirius Aelianus	*q. prov*[*inciae*] *Achaiae* (II 2078)
Cn. Julius Verus	*quaestori Aug.* (*ILS* 1057)
M. Statius Priscus	· *quaes*[*t.*] (*ILS* 1092)
Q. Antistius Adventus	*q. pr. pr. provinc. Macedoniae* (*ILS* 8977)
C. Junius Faustinus	[*qu*]*ae*[*s*]*tori provinc*[*iae . . .*]*ae* (p. 162 above)

The tribunate of the plebs

This stage in the *cursus honorum* was omitted, owing to possession of patrician rank, by L. Neratius Marcellus and—it seems—by M. Atilius Metilius Bradua. Eleven governors are known to have served as tribune of the plebs, but none as aedile. P. Helvius Pertinax was presumably *adlectus inter tribunicios* or *inter aedilicios*, since the *Historia Augusta*, after saying that he 'lectus est in senatu', records that M. Aurelius 'postea . . . praetorium eum fecit' (*Pert.* 2. 5-6).

Q. Veranius	[δήμ]αρχ[ον] (*IGR* III 703) (AD 41) καὶ οἱ μὲν πρεσβευταὶ Οὐηράνιός τε καὶ Βρόγχος, δήμαρχοι δὲ ἦσαν ἀμφότεροι (Jos. *AJ* 19. 234)
Cn. Julius Agricola	'tribunatus annum quiete et otio transiit, gnarus sub Nerone temporum, quibus inertia pro sapientia fuit' (*Agr.* 6. 3)
Q. Pompeius Falco	*trib. pleb.* (*ILS* 1036) 'consulis an existimem te in tribunatu causas agere debere', etc. (Pliny, *ep.* 1. 23) (AD 97?)
A. Platorius Nepos	*trib. pleb.* (?*candidato divi Traiani*) (*ILS* 1052)
Sex. Julius Severus	*trib. pleb. candidat*[*o ei*]*usdem* [sc. *Traiani*] (*ILS* 1056)

Q. Lollius Urbicus	*trib. pleb. candidat. Caes.* (VIII 6706)
Cn. Papirius Aelianus	*tribuno plebi*[*s*] (II 2078)
Cn. Julius Verus	*tribuno plebis* (*ILS* 1057)
M. Statius Priscus	*tr. pl.* (*ILS* 1092)
Q. Antistius Adventus	[*t*]*r. pl.* (*ILS* 8977)
C. Junius Faustinus	[*tri*]*buno pl*[*e*]*b. candida*[*to*] (p. 162 above)

Other posts

A handful of the governors held other appointments at various stages before the praetorship.

L. Neratius Marcellus	*curat. actorum senatus* (presumably between quaestorship and praetorship) (*ILS* 1032)
Sex. Julius Severus	[*se*]*v*[*iro*] *t*[*u*]*rma*[*e*] *V eq.* [*R.*] (apparently before the vigintivirate, but see p. 108 n. 14 above) (*ILS* 1056)
Q. Lollius Urbicus	*leg. procos. Asiae* (between quaestorship and tribunate) (VIII 6706)
Q. Antistius Adventus	*leg. pr. pr. Africae* (between tribunate and praetorship) (*ILS* 8977)
C. Junius Faustinus	[*leg. pr*]*ovinciae* [*Africae dio*]*eceseos* [*K*]*ar-*[*tha*]*g.* (?) (between tribunate and praetorship) (p. 162 above)

The praetorship

Sex. Julius Frontinus	'Kalendis Ianuariis in senatu, quem Iulius Frontinus praetor urbanus vocaverat . . . et mox eiurante Frontino Caesar Domitianus praeturam cepit' (Tacitus, *Hist.* 4. 39. 1-2) (AD 70)
Cn. Julius Agricola	'idem praeturae tenor et silentium; nec enim iurisdictio obvenerat. ludos et inania honoris medio rationis atque abundantiae duxit, ut longe a luxuria, ita famae propior' (*Agr.* 6. 4) (AD 68)
L. Neratius Marcellus	*pr.* (*ILS* 1032)
M. Atilius Metilius Bradua	στρατηγόν (*ILS* 8824a)
Q. Pompeius Falco	*pr. inter civ*[*es et*] *peregrinos* (*ILS* 1036)
A. Platorius Nepos	*praet.* (?*candidato divi Traiani*) (*ILS* 1052)
Sex. Julius Severus	*praetor.* (*ILS* 1056)
Q. Lollius Urbicus	*praet. candidat. Caes.* (VIII 6706)
Cn. Papirius Aelianus	*pr.* (II 2078)

Cn. Julius Verus	*praetor.* (*ILS* 1057)
M. Statius Priscus	*pr. inter cives et peregrinos* (*ILS* 1092)
Q. Antistius Adventus	*praetori* (*ILS* 8977)
P. Helvius Pertinax	'Marcusque imperator . . . praetorium eum fecit' (*HA Pert.* 2. 6)
C. Junius Faustinus	*praetori* [*c*]*andi*[*dato*] (p. 162 above)

The praetorian career of British governors

In all cases where information is available, save that of L. Neratius Marcellus, future governors of Britain held a military command, in most cases as legate of a legion, after the praetorship. In some cases the exact nature of their military role is not clear: Didius Gallus' post as *pr*[*aefectu*]*s equitat*(*us*); Q. Veranius' mission in Lycia; Suetonius Paullinus' campaign in Mauretania; Julius Frontinus' status in the Rhineland in 70; Clodius Albinus' status in the wars against 'barbarians beyond Dacia'; all these are slightly uncertain. The last three may all have been legionary legates. But fifteen of the governors commanded legions, in Antistius Adventus' case two in succession. Only Cerialis and Julius Agricola commanded a legion in Britain. The others are fairly well distributed round the frontier provinces: three certainly in the east (Trebellius Maximus, Vettius Bolanus, and Antistius Adventus), perhaps four if Platorius Nepos' legion was temporarily there for Trajan's Parthian war while he was in command, and five if Papirius Aelianus' legion was *XII* [*Fulminata*] rather than *XII*[*II Gemina*]; Avidius Quietus and Julius Verus commanded German legions; Pompeius Falco the Moesian legion V Macedonica. As many as six or seven commanded a Pannonian legion: Platorius Nepos, Julius Severus, Lollius Urbicus, possibly Papirius Aelianus, Statius Priscus, Pertinax, and Junius Faustinus. In all cases the legions in question were of course in Upper Pannonia, since the sole legion in the Lower province, II Adiutrix, was commanded by the governor—although Antistius Adventus commanded it when it was in the east for L. Verus' Parthian war. It is significant that no governors of Britain are known to have been legates of Upper Pannonia as well.

Two future governors held some other appointment before the legionary command: Julius Agricola had a special assignment from Galba and a recruiting mission in 69–70 and Platorius Nepos was curator of a road-network. The others whose careers are known in detail became legionary legates as their first post after the praetorship. Of particular interest are the men whose main appointments between praetorship and consulship were solely a legionary command and a

Table 8
From praetorship to consulship†

	date of praetorship	praetorian posts	date of consulship
A. Plautius	24?	*(missus) in Apulia [ad servos to]rquendos (ILS* 961)	29
*A. Didius Gallus	?	*pr[aefectu]s equitat. [leg. pr. pr. ?A]siae proco[s.] . . . Siciliae curator aquarum* (AD 36) (p. 45 above)	39
*Q. Veranius	42?	*[Lyciae . . .] quinq[ue]nnio pr[a]efui[t]* (*AE* 1953. 251) (*c.*AD 43–8)	*ord.*49
C. Suetonius Paullinus	?	Σουητώνιος μὲν γὰρ Παυλῖνος, ἐκ τῶν ἐστρατηγηκότων ὤν, τὴν χώραν αὐτῶν μέχρι τοῦ Ἄτλαντος ἀντικατέδραμε. (Dio 60. 9. 1) (AD 42)	?
M. Trebellius Maximus	?	'M. Trebellius legatus a Vitellio praeside Suriae cum quattuor milibus legionariorum et delectis auxiliis missus,' etc. (Tac. *Ann.* 6. 41, 1; see p. 59 above) (AD 36)	56
M. Vettius Bolanus	?	'legiones duas cum Verulano Severo et Vettio Bolano subsidium Tigrani mittit [sc. Corbulo]' (Tac. *Ann.* 15. 3. 1, cf. Stat. *Silv.* 5. 2. 31 ff.) (AD 62) ?proconsul of Macedonia (see p. 63 above)	66
Q. Petillius Cerialis	?	'et victor Britannus Petilio Ceriali legato legionis nonae in subsidium adventanti obvius fudit legionem et quod peditum interfecit' etc. (Tac. *Ann.* 14. 32. 3) (AD 60) 'propinqua adfinitas Ceriali cum Vespasiano, nec ipse inglorius militiae, eoque inter duces adsumptus est' (Tac. *Hist.* 3. 59. 2; also 3. 78–80) (AD 69)	70
Sex. Julius Frontinus	70	']ello quod Iulius Civilis in Gallia moverat, Lingonum opulentissima civitas . . . ad obsequium redacta septuaginta milia armatorum tradidit	73

Table 8 (*Continued*)

	date of praetorship	praetorian posts	date of consulship
		mihi' (Frontin. *Strat.* 4. 3. 14; cf. p. 70 above) (AD 70)	
*Cn. Julius Agricola	68	'tum electus a Galba ad dona templorum recognoscenda diligentissima conquisitione fecit' (Tac. *Agr.* 6. 5) 'is [sc. Mucianus] missum ad dilectus agendos Agricolam integreque ac strenue versatum (AD 69–70) vicesimae legioni . . . praeposuit' etc. (*Agr.* 7. 3–9. 1) (AD 70–3) 'Revertentem ab legatione legionis divus Vespasianus . . . deinde provinciae Aquitaniae praeposuit, splendidae inprimis dignitatis administratione ac spe consulatus, cui destinarat. . . . minus triennium in ea legatione detentus ac statim ad spem consulatus revocatus est.' (*Agr.* 9. 1–5) (AD 73–6)	77
T. Avidius Quietus	?	*leg. Aug.* [sc. *leg. VIII Aug.*] (*ILS* 6105) (at latest AD 82) ἀνθύπατον Ἀχαΐας (Dittenberger, *Syll.*[3] 882)	93
L. Neratius Marcellus	?	?*curat. aquarum urbis* (*ILS* 1032) (perhaps held as consular, see p. 90 above)	95
*Q. Pompeius Falco	c.99?	*leg. leg. V Macedonic.* *leg. pr. pr. prov. Lyciae* [*et Pamphyl*]*iae leg. Aug. pr. pr. provinc.* [*Iudaeae e*]*t leg. X Fret.* (*ILS* 1035)	108
*A. Platorius Nepos	c.111?	*curat. viarum Cassiae Clodiae Ciminiae novae Traianae* *leg. legion. I Adiutricis* *leg. pro pr. provinc. Thrac.* (*ILS* 1052)	119
*Sex. Julius Severus	c.117?	*leg. leg. XIIII Geminae* *leg. pr. pr. imp. Traiani Hadria* [*n*]*i Aug. p*[*r*]*ovinciae Dacia*[*e*] (*ILS* 1056) (AD 120–6)	127
P. Mummius Sisenna	?	διέποντος τὴν ἐπαρχείαν Ποπνίου [?Μουμμίου Σεισέννα?] [sc. τὴν	ord.133

Table 8 (*Continued*)

	date of praetorship	praetorian posts	date of consulship
		Θρακῶν] (*IGR* I 785) (between 129 and 136)	
*Q. Lollius Urbicus	*c.*128?	*leg. leg. X Geminae legato imp. Hadriani in expedition. Iudaica* (VIII 6706) (*c.*AD 132–5)	*c.*136
Cn. Papirius Aelianus	?	*leg. Aug. leg. XII*[. . .] (II 2078) *legat. eius pr. pr.* [sc. *Daciae superioris*] (III 1078) (AD 132)	*c.*136
*Cn. Julius Verus	?	*leg. leg. XXX Ulpiae praef. aerari Saturni* (*ILS* 1057)	*c.*151
*M. Statius Priscus	?	*leg. leg.* [*X*]*IIII Gem. Martiae Victricis leg. Aug. prov. Daciae* (*et*) *leg. leg. XIII G. p. f.* (*ILS* 1092)	*ord.*159
*Q. Antistius Adventus	?	*leg. Aug. leg. VI Ferratae et secundae Adiutricis . . . expeditione Parthica leg. Aug. pr. pr. provinc. Arabiae* (*ILS* 8977)	*c.*166
Ulpius Marcellus	?	?*leg. Aug. pr. pr.* (sc. *Pannoniae inferioris*) (*ILS* 3795, but see p. 141 and n. 4 above)	*c.* 174?
*P. Helvius Pertinax	*adl. c.*170	'Marcusque imperator . . . praetorium eum fecit et primae legioni regendae imposuit' etc. (*HA Pert.* 2. 6) (*c.*AD 170) ?governor of Moesia superior (but see p. 144 and n. 17 above)	175
D. Clodius Albinus	?	Ἐγένοντο δὲ καὶ πόλεμοί τινες αὐτῷ πρὸς τοὺς ὑπὲρ τὴν Δακίαν βαρβάρους, ἐν οἷς ὅ τε Ἀλβῖνος καὶ ὁ Νίγρος . . . εὐδοκίμησαν (*c.*AD 182) (Dio 72. 8. 1)	*a. inc.*
*C. Junius Faustinus	?	[*leg. Augg. leg*]*ion*[*i*]*s* [*pri*]*ma-* [*e Ad*]*iu*[*tr*]*icis* [*pi*]*a*[*e*] *fidelis* [*leg.*] *Augg. pr. pr. provinciae Lusetani*[*ae*] [*leg.*] *Augg. pr. pr. provinc*[*iae Be*]*lgica*[*e*] (p. 162 above)	*a. inc.*

* Cases where the record is complete are marked with an asterisk.

praetorian governorship of an imperial province. Those in this category certainly included Julius Agricola, Julius Severus, Lollius Urbicus, Julius Verus, Statius Priscus, and Antistius Adventus—with Urbicus' staff appointment in the Jewish war and Verus' prefecture of the *aerarium Saturni* being the equivalent of a praetorian province. Papirius Aelianus probably also belonged in the same group, while Platorius Nepos' career lagged only a little behind, delayed by his road curatorship. Pompeius Falco's governorship of two praetorian provinces is anomalous for the early second century—by the third it was not uncommon, Junius Faustinus Postumianus being an example. Finally, there are the especially striking cases of men achieving the consulship with only one praetorian post, Veranius, Frontinus (so it appears), and Pertinax.

By contrast, some of the governors must have had a fairly slow progress. This presumably applies to Trebellius Maximus, if he was the legionary commander in the east in AD 36—even if he was then in his twenties and had not yet been praetor—since he did not become consul until early in the reign of Nero. Avidius Quietus may have been legionary legate as late as AD 82, in which case his consulship in 93 does not seem unduly retarded; but he must have been well over the theoretical minimum age, forty-two.

The consulship

The consulship was an essential prerequisite for governors of Britain, as made plain by Tacitus with the first word of his account of Agricola's predecessors, 'consularium primus Aulus Plautius praepositus' (*Agr.* 14. 1). The majority of the British governors had been *suffecti*, but five were former *ordinarii*: Q. Veranius (49), P. Petronius Turpilianus (61), M. Atilius Metilius Bradua (108), P. Mummius Sisenna (133), and M. Statius Priscus (159). Turpilianus and Bradua, as sons of consulars, belonged to a group that tended to monopolize this position. Veranius and Priscus were relatively rare cases, of oustanding military men rewarded for their success in war—and Veranius had two additional advantages, his father having been a trusted associate of Claudius' brother, and his own role in AD 41. Sisenna remains unexplained, since his earlier career is unknown.[1]

The path from the consulship to Britain

As the list shows, the great majority of those whose career is known governed at least one other province between their consulship and

---

[1] Unless he was governor of Thrace, p. 110 n. 2 above.

their appointment to Britain. Only in two cases can it be said categorically that a governor came to Britain immediately after holding the *fasces*, P. Petronius Turpilianus (61 *ord.*) and Cn. Julius Agricola (77); but Sex. Julius Frontinus (73?) is also a likely case, and P. Mummius Sisenna (133 *ord.*) may be another. The first three were certainly exceptional. Turpilianus was clearly appointed to inaugurate a new policy in the aftermath of the Boudiccan revolt. Agricola, the sole real 'British specialist' among the governors, may have owed his appointment in any case to personal friendship with Titus. The career of Frontinus had clearly been abnormal, since his consulship came only three years or so after his praetorship, suggesting that he had become praetor late, perhaps after adlection to senatorial rank, and hence that he was no younger than the normal age for the consulship, 42; indeed he may have been older. This may also apply to Mummius Sisenna, although the sole evidence is the unusually short interval between his consulship in 133 and that of his presumed son in 146. These considerations make the career of L. Neratius Marcellus all the more unusual, since his *cursus* inscription credits him with no posts other than the compulsory magistracies, apart from the military tribunate and charge over the *acta senatus*, before his British command (unless the *cura aquarum* was held earlier than 103). Either the *cursus* is incomplete on the stone from Saepinum, or the choice of Marcellus as governor of Britain may reflect special circumstances. There may have been a shortage of suitably qualified persons; or a changed assessment of the importance of the province.

The list also demonstrates what has long been recognised, that the largest single group of British governors were former legates of Germania inferior. Of the Julio-Claudian governors whose earlier career is at all known, A. Plautius had governed Pannonia (it appears); Q. Veranius' only post was the *cura aedium sacrarum*—apart from presiding over Nero's games; A. Didius Gallus, on the other hand, must have been continuously employed between his consulship in 39 and his arrival in Britain, continuing his *cura aquarum*, with a short break to command in Moesia, and being proconsul of Asia. From 71 to *c.*213 some twenty-nine governors may be identified (excluding really uncertain cases). For nine of these there is no evidence for their employment immediately before the British post,[2] while a further three—Frontinus, Julius Agricola, and Neratius Marcellus—evidently held no appointment

---

[2] Sallustius Lucullus, P. Metilius Nepos, T. Avidius Quietus, P. Mummius Sisenna, Cn. Papirius Aelianus, Sex. Calpurnius Agricola, the Ulpii Marcelli, and C. Julius Marcus.

between the consulship and Britain. Of the remaining seventeen, six definitely governed Lower Germany (Cerialis, Platorius Nepos, Urbicus, Verus, Adventus, and Pudens); Virius Lupus certainly campaigned there, probably as governor; and Albinus may also have held this post. This makes it probable that it was the Lower province which is meant by Γερμανίας, unqualified, on the inscription of Bradua at Olympia, for otherwise there is only the case of the man known as Caerellius who proceeded from Upper Germany to Britain.[3] Of the remaining seven governors in this period, Falco, Julius Severus, and Junius Faustinus (whose British province may have been Superior) had governed Moesia inferior before Britain, and Statius Priscus had governed Moesia superior; Pollienus Auspex governed one of the Moesian provinces before Britain —although if his career is placed later he may have governed Upper Britain, conceivably before Moesia. L. Alfenus Senecio governed Syria Coele shortly before going to Britain. The final case, P. Helvius Pertinax, is anomalous: he had governed four consular provinces, both Moesias, the III Daciae, and Syria, and was living in enforced retirement, when he was recalled to quell the turbulent British legions.

It is clear that in most cases there was an interval of several years between the consulship and the British command. With a number of men for whom no specific evidence of employment after the consulship is recorded, namely Suetonius Paullinus, Avidius Quietus, Neratius Marcellus, Papirius Aelianus, Calpurnius Agricola, and the elder Ulpius Marcellus, enough is nevertheless known to establish that there was an appreciable gap. As for the few cases of men who went to Britain more or less immediately after their consulship, Turpilianus, Frontinus, and Sisenna all seem to have been at least as old when they arrived in the province as those governors who had consular employment before governing Britain. This makes the case of Julius Agricola, appointed governor at the age of thirty-six or thirty-seven, all the more remarkable. Most governors must have been at least forty-five at the time of appointment, and a few were doubtless as old as Pertinax, born in 126 and governor in 185.

The choice of governors

The information available indicates that it was normally men with military background who were selected as consular legates of Britain. In a few early cases it could be argued that Claudius and Nero looked

---

[3] Note also Ti. Claudius Quartinus, perhaps governor of Britain after being in Upper Germany, pp. 110 ff. above.

Table 9

The career between consulship and Britain†

	date of consulship	consular posts before Britain	interval between consulship and Britain	dates in Britain
A. Plautius	29	legato Ti. Claudi Caesaris Aug. Germ. [sc. Pannoniae(?) ILS 5889]	14	43–7
*A. Didius Gallus	39	curator aquarum (AD 38–49) [leg]atus [Tib.] Claudi Caes[aris] Aug. Ger[mani]ci [sc. prov. Moesiae] (c.AD 44) proco[s. Asia]e(?) (p. 45 above)	13	52–7
*Q. Veranius	ord. 49	[curator] aedium sacrarum, etc. (praefectus) ludis (AE 1953. 251)	8	57–8
P. Petronius Turpilianus	ord. 61	nil	nil	61–3
M. Trebellius Maximus	56(?)	?	7(?)	63–9
M. Vettius Bolanus	66	?	3	69–71
*Q. Petillius Cerialis	70(?)	legate in Germania inferior (p. 68 above) (AD 70–1)	1(?)	71–3
Sex. Julius Frontinus	73(?)	nil(?)	nil(?)	73–7
*Cn. Julius Agricola	77	nil	nil	77–84
P. Metilius Nepos	91	censitor in Gaul (Tac. Ann. 14. 46)	c.5(?)	c.96(?)–98
T. Avidius Quietus	93	?	c.5	98–c.100(?)
L. Neratius Marcellus	95	nil(?)	c.5(?)	c.100(?)–c.104(?)
*M. Atilius Metilius Bradua	ord.108	ὑπατικὸν Γερμανίας (ILS 8824a)	c.3(?)	c.111–c.114(?)
*Q. Pompeius Falco	108	curator. viae Traianae leg. Aug. pr. pr. prov. Moes. inf. (ILS 1036) (AD 116, 117)	c.10	c.118–22

Table 9 (Continued)

	date of consulship	consular posts before Britain	interval between consulship and Britain	dates in Britain
*A. Platorius Nepos	119	leg. pro pr. provinc. German. inferior. (ILS 1052)	3	122–c.125(?)
*Sex. Julius Severus	127	leg. pr. p[r.] provinciae Moesia[e] inferioris (ILS 1056)	c.3	c.130–c.133(?)
P. Mummius Sisenna	ord.133	nil(?)	nil(?)	135
*Q. Lollius Urbicus	c.136	leg. Aug. provinc. Germ. inferioris (VIII 6706)	c.3	139–42
Cn. Papirius Aelianus	c.136	?	c.9	c.145(?)–c.148(?)
*Cn. Julius Verus	c.151	leg. Aug. pr. pr. provinciae German. inferioris (ILS 1057)	c.	c.154(?)–c.158(?)
*M. Statius Priscus	ord. 159	curato[ri] alvei Tiberis leg. Aug[g.] pr. pr. prov. Moesiae super. (ILS 1092) (AD 161)	c.2	c.161–2
Sex. Calpurnius Agricola	154(?)	?	c.8(?)	c.162–c.165(?)
*Q. Antistius Adventus	c.166	cura. operum locorumq. publicorum leg. Aug. at prae[t]enturam Italiae et Alpium expeditione Germanica (AD 168?) leg. Aug. pr. pr. provinc. Germaniae inferioris (ILS 8977)	c.7(?)	c.173–c.176(?)
*Caerellius	c.173(?)	[leg. Augg.] pr. pr. pro[vi]n[c.] . . . Rae[t.] Germ. sup. (XIII 6806)	c.5(?)	c.178–c.180(?)
Ulpius Marcellus	c.174(?)	?	c.8(?)	c.182–5

Table 9 (*Continued*)

	date of consulship	consular posts before Britain	interval between consulship and Britain	dates in Britain
*P. Helvius Pertinax	175(?)	'inde Moesiae utriusque, mox Daciae regimen accepit. bene gestis his provinciis Syriam meruit' (*HA Pert.* 2. 10–11)	10	185–c.187
D. Clodius Albinus	c.178(?)	governor of Germania inferior(?) (p. 148 above)	c.4(?)	c.191(?)–197
Virius Lupus	?	governor of Germania inferior(?) (p. 150 above)	?	197–c.200(?)
*C. Valerius Pudens	c.194	leg. Aug. pr. pr. [sc. *Germaniae*] *inferior.* (*ILS* 9178)	c.8(?)	c.200(?)–c.205(?)
L. Alfenus Senecio	?	leg. Augg. pr. pr. [sc. *Syriae Coelae*] (*ILS* 5899) (AD 200)	more than 5	c.205–c.208(?)
*C. Junius Faustinus Postumianus	?	leg. Augg. pr. pr. provinciae Mysiae inferior[is] adlecto inter co[m]i[t]es Augg. nn. (p. 162 above)	?	?

† Cases where the record is complete are marked with an asterisk.

particularly for men with previous experience of mountain warfare, at a time when the main campaigning area in Britain was Wales. Thus Didius Gallus, Veranius, and Paullinus, are all known to have conducted mountain campaigns, in the Balkans, Taurus, and Atlas respectively; and even Trebellius Maximus, although appointed at a time when a policy of non-aggression prevailed, could be said to have had similar experience. Vettius Bolanus may have been chosen by Vitellius partly on the strength of his service as a legionary legate under Corbulo in the east. On the other hand, it was probably qualities of a different kind in the background of Petronius Turpilianus that made him particularly suitable when a policy of reconciliation was required after the Boudiccan revolt. In some cases, without doubt, it will have been personal connections with the emperor, and political reliability, that were the deciding factors. Thus A. Plautius' influential family network and Petillius Cerialis' kinship with Vespasian were probably of overriding importance, outweighing, in Cerialis' case, his service as commander of IX Hispana in the province. Cerialis and Julius Agricola are indeed exceptions, the only men among the governors who had previously commanded British legions; and Agricola is the sole known example of a man who had been *tribunus laticlavius* in the province later returning as governor. Two second-century governors, Statius Priscus and Pertinax, had, however, held equestrian military appointments in Britain at the beginning of their careers.

To some extent it may appear that the selection of British governors was predetermined, in view of the frequent progress from Lower Germany to Britain. Unfortunately, not enough is known about the inner working of imperial appointments to assess exactly what was involved. It could perhaps be argued that, if no other factors intervened, the governor of Britain would be replaced by the governor of Lower Germany. On the other hand, it might be asked whether men earmarked to govern Britain a few years later were sent to Lower Germany specifically to give them suitable experience. Another noteworthy trend, observable during the period 120–65 when the province of Upper Dacia was in existence, is that three men who governed it went on to Britain some years afterwards: Julius Severus, Papirius Aelianus, and Statius Priscus. One or two of the other eight men known to have governed Upper Dacia may have governed Britain later in their careers. This province, with its large auxiliary garrison,[4] may well have been deemed

---

[4] See Syme, *Danubian Papers* 102, 109 f., 167 f.; note also his comment, ibid. 241, that 'In the dearth of active warfare in this age the praetorian legates of Dacia might seem to command a high premium when the government needed, for example, a general in Britain . . . It would be

especially suitable for men who were proving themselves to be of above average military talent.

It is at any rate manifest that a number of the known governors showed themselves, whether in Britain or at other stages in their career, to be accomplished generals. There is no reason not to accept Tacitus' verdict on Plautius and Scapula, 'uterque bello egregius', whether it was intended to apply to their careers before they went to Britain or to their performance in the province. Suetonius Paullinus likewise receives Tacitus' approbation, as do, of course, Agricola and his two predecessors, although Tacitus' assessment of Cerialis may be tinged with dislike. More valuable, perhaps, because completely unbiased, is Cassius Dio's reference to Sex. Julius Severus. When the great crisis occurred in Judaea, 'Hadrian sent against them his best generals, of whom the first was Julius Severus, despatched from Britain, which he was governing, against the Jews'. Dio's word, $\pi\rho\hat{\omega}\tau\sigma\varsigma$, here surely means first in the sense of 'foremost', not merely first in time.[5] The very fact that Julius Severus was further away from the theatre of war than any other general who might have been selected is surely significant. Precisely the same phenomenon occurred in 161 or 162, when disaster struck in Armenia, with the ignominious defeat and suicide of the governor of Cappadocia. The man chosen to restore the situation was M. Statius Priscus, who had only just been appointed to Britain—an appointment which was itself perhaps in answer to an emergency, for he had not long been in Moesia superior before that. Other second century governors may also be regarded as leading military men. Cn. Julius Verus is not mentioned in the literary sources, but his record speaks for itself. Pertinax and the elder Ulpius Marcellus both enjoyed reputations which are transmitted in the surviving literature. Not all the governors were good generals, to be sure: one whose name is unknown was defeated and killed in Britain in the early 180s; and Virius Lupus lost a battle in the Civil War against Albinus—who himself was no mean commander.

The governors' titulature

The various titles, official and unofficial, by which the governors were described, either in the literary sources or on inscriptions—or, in the case of Neratius Marcellus, in a letter preserved on a writing tablet, are best looked at in detail in an appendix, in which the style of the

---

a temptation to look for some of the missing legates of Britain on the roll of Dacia.' One possibility is Calpurnius Julianus: p. 123 n. 13 above.

[5] Dio 69. 13. 2. Dio's plural 'generals' presumably includes Q. Lollius Urbicus also, praetorian *leg. Aug. pr. pr.* in Judaea, perhaps to be regarded as Julius Severus' chief of staff there.

governors of Upper and Lower Britain is also shown, for comparison.[6]
Here it will be sufficient to draw attention to the main points. Tacitus
uses a very great variety of terms: *consularis, legatus, dux, rector
pro praetore*, even *imperator Romanus* on one occasion, as well as
verbs such as *praeesse, praeponi, obtinere*, and phrases such as *rebus
gerundis*, or *curandi provinciam*. Suetonius is much less rich, using
only *legatus consularis*. The Greek writers use the nouns ἡγεμών,
ἄρχων, and στρατηγός, and related verbs. The poet Statius is predictably flowery, referring to Bolanus entering Thule, *mandata gerens*,
and to Britain as the *tellus frenata* by the young Crispinus' great
parent.

Epigraphic usage shows a fairly clear development. The first governor
recorded as such on stone, Q. Veranius, was probably called [*legatus
pro praetore imp. Neronis Caesaris German*]*ici provinciae Britanniae*,
while the first governor recorded in the province, Julius Agricola, is
called *leg. Aug. pr. pr.*, by far the commonest formula, on the lead
pipes from the legionary fortress at Chester. But the term *consularis*
appears with L. Neratius Marcellus, called *clarissi*[*mum virum*] *consularem meum* on a wooden writing tablet found at Vindolanda, which
nicely echoes Pliny's reference to him at the same time as *clarissimo
viro*. On his *cursus* inscription Marcellus is called [*leg. pr. pr.*] *divi
Traiani Aug. prov. Britanniae*. At about the same time a slightly later
governor, Bradua, is referred to as ὑπατικὸν . . . Βρεταννίας on the
incription in his honour at Olympia. Pompeius Falco exhibits both the
full length and the abbreviated Latin style, *leg. pr. pr. imp. Caes.
Traiani Hadriani Aug. provinc. Brittanniae* and *leg. Aug.* [*pro p*]*r.
provinciae Britanniae*, as well as the standard Greek version for governors
of imperial provinces, πρεσβευτὴν Σεβαστοῦ καὶ ἀντιστράτηγον . . .
Βρεταννίας. Platorius Nepos, one of the best attested governors, is
called *leg. Aug. pr. pr.* or simply *leg. pr. pr.* on building inscriptions
from the Wall, with the fuller version *legat. Aug. pro praet. provinc.
Britanniae* coming on his *cursus* inscription at Aquileia.

The later Hadrianic governor Julius Severus, and the governors Urbicus, Aelianus, and Verus under Antoninus Pius, are all more or less
uniformly described as *leg. Aug. pr. pr.*, with slight variations in the
abbreviation. A change inevitably came about with the installation of
joint Augusti in 161. Statius Priscus is called [*leg. August*]*or.* [*provin*]*c.
Britan*[*niae*] on a stone set up in Moesia superior shortly after his
appointment. His successor Calpurnius Agricola is [*legati Augustoru*]*m*

---

[6] Appendix 1 pp. 425 ff.

pr. pr. on one stone, in Britain, but on another he is *leg. Aug. pr. pr.* still, and on a third simply *cos.*, the first case on stone in Britain. As for the Severan governors, Lupus is *leg. eorum pr. pr.*, perhaps [*v. c. cos.*], and, more traditionally *leg. Aug. pr. pr.*; in the *Digest* he is called *Brittaniae praesidem.* C. Valerius Pudens is *amplissimi cosularis* on his only inscription, a form found for his successor Alfenus Senecio as well. Senecio is also *leg. Augg. pr. pr.*, *leg. eorum pr. pr.*, *v. c. cos.*, and just *cos.* The remaining governors who may belong to the period before the division into Upper and Lower provinces exhibit most of these forms: Pollienus Auspex is called ὑπατικοῦ Βριταννίας; Ulpius Marcellus is *cos.* and [*leg. Aug.* or *Augg.*] *pr. pr.*, C. Julius Marcus is *leg. Aug. pr. pr.* or *leg. eius* (with no *pr. pr.* on one occasion). Finally, C. Junius Faustinus Postumainus is a portent of the future, with the title *praesidis provinciaru*[*m His*]*pani*[*ae*] *et Britanniae.*

The length of the governorship and the number of governors

Thanks to Tacitus, the list is complete for the first four decades of the province's existence, 43–84. The length of tenure of these eleven governors varied markedly, from the single year of Veranius to Trebellius Maximus' six years and Julius Agricola's seven. None the less it may be postulated that eleven governors in forty-one years may have been close to the average for an imperial consular province. In the succeeding generations, up to the province's division *c.*213, a calculation based on this figure would require there to have been a further thirty-five governors, or thereabouts. In fact, a maximum of some thirty-two governors can be identified in the period 84–*c.*213, although this includes five *ignoti*[7] and the rather uncertain cases of Pollienus Auspex and C. Junius Faustinus Postumianus, who may belong later as governors of Upper Britain, and of the younger Ulpius Marcellus, whose existence may seem doubtful. But even if all thirty-two could be accepted, it would be certain that more than three names are missing, and hence that the average length of tenure must have declined a little from about three years and eight months to a round three years apiece. This can be seen from a consideration of particular parts of the period where gaps can be identified.

Between Agricola's replacement in 84 (or at latest in 85), and Metilius

---

[7] viz. the men whose names are imprecisely or incompletely recorded by XVI 88; *RIB* 995; 1997–8; 2313 = *Britannia* 4 (1973) 336 f.; XVI 130; and the man whose death is reported by Dio 72. 8. 2. See also the *incerti* discussed on pp. 284 ff. above, one or two of whom may be governors of the undivided province otherwise unrecorded. But some of the evidence listed in the present footnote may in fact refer to men already attested, e.g. Dio's man might be the same as (Caerellius) of XIII 6806.

Nepos, who was replaced at latest in 98 and may be assumed to have been appointed not later than 96, we know the name of only one governor, Sallustius Lucullus. It must be accepted that there were at least two other governors in those years, especially as Lucullus' appointment was abruptly terminated by his murder. The next obvious gap lies between Neratius Marcellus, attested in 103, and Pompeius Falco, replaced in 122. During the period of fifteen years at most between the departure of Marcellus and the arrival of Falco only Atilius Bradua can be supplied. Once again, at least two, probably three, more governors must be postulated. It is difficult to be certain that there are any real gaps between 122 and 146, for no fewer than four *ignoti* appear to belong there.[8] But between Papirius Aelianus, attested in 146, and Julius Verus, attested in 158—both of whom may have been at the end of their term of office in those years—one must reckon with another two governors if not more. Another definite gap comes in the 160s and early 170s, between Calpurnius Agricola and Antistius Adventus, allowing sufficient time for two or three more governors. Finally, it seems probable that Albinus was not the direct successor of Pertinax, which allows room for one further governor *c.* 187–91. From *c.* 191 to *c.* 213 it is possible that all the governors are known—except that Albinus may well have appointed one of his supporters to govern Britain when he was proclaimed Augustus in 195.[9]

The gaps in the *Fasti* may thus be seen in Table 10.

Table 10

	number of governors known	estimated number missing
84–*c.*96	1	2 or 3
*c.*104–*c.*119	1	3
*c.*146–*c.*155	nil	2
*c.*165–*c.*173	nil	2
*c.*187–*c.*191	nil	1

At least ten or eleven further governors must be postulated, and if this is added to the maximum number of identifiable governors for the years 84–*c.*213, one must reckon with there having been at least forty-three governors in the period, an average tenure of exactly three years.

As far as the actual tenure of office is concerned, we are badly served by the evidence after 84. None the less, it is possible to note a few hints.

---

[8] XVI 88; *RIB* 995; 1997–8; 2313 = *Britannia* 4 (1973) 336 f.

[9] In that case one would imagine that he would be one of the men listed by *HA Severus* 13. 1–8 as having been put to death by Severus after the battle of Lugdunum. See Alföldy, *H-A-C 1968/69* (1970) 1 ff. for a careful analysis of the names, some of them bogus, but some thirty-two genuine.

For example, at the end of the first and beginning of the second centuries the governors Metilius Nepos, Avidius Quietus, and Neratius Marcellus had been consuls at intervals of two years from one another, in 91, 93, and 95. This suggests that the first two held office for only two years in Britain. Under Hadrian, Platorius Nepos is attested in 122 and 124, showing that he was governor for at least two years, while Julius Severus can hardly have stayed much longer than two years, given the known facts about his posts before and after the British governorship. Lollius Urbicus is attested in 139 and 140, and indirect evidence points firmly to his having still been in Britain in 142, the year when Antoninus Pius took an imperatorial acclamation—for the victory with which Urbicus is credited in the *Historia Augusta*. Statius Priscus' tenure of the British command must have been exceedingly brief, perhaps only a few months, given that he was still in Moesia superior in 161 and won a victory in Armenia in 163. Pertinax was appointed to Britain in 185 and must have left in 187, if the posts recorded by the *Historia Augusta* are all to be fitted in.

The above considerations may indeed make it appear that a full three years may be a rather generous estimate of the average length of tenure. However this may be, it is clear that roughly three-quarters of the governors of undivided Britain are known,[10] over the period 43–c.213, even if some of them are little more than names at best.

The further career of governors after being in Britain

Five governors may be excluded at once, the four who died in office, together with Julius Agricola, who is known not to have received further employment after leaving Britain. In the case of nearly a dozen governors, no information is available—in some cases they are not heard of again. But something is known about the subsequent appointments of the following men:

C. Suetonius Paullinus	*dux* of Otho, AD 69
P. Petronius Turpilianus	*curator aquarum*, 63–4
	dux of Nero, 68
M. Vettius Bolanus	proconsul of Asia
Q. Petillius Cerialis	*cos. II* 74; *cos. III ord.* 83(?)
Sex. Julius Frontinus	*comes* of Domitian(?), 83
	proconsul of Asia, 86
	member of economy commission, 97

---

[10] viz. forty-three out of an estimated total of fifty-four. The first figure could of course be slimmed down, but it is doubtful whether the second figure could be inflated much higher.

[Sex. Julius Frontinus]	*curator aquarum*, 97–103/4
	cos. II 98, *III ord.* 100
P. Metilius Nepos	*cos. des. II ord.* for 128
L. Neratius Marcellus	proconsul of Africa(?)
	cos. II ord. 129
M. Atilius Metilius	*comes* of Hadrian
Bradua	proconsul of Africa(?)
Q. Pompeius Falco	proconsul of Asia, 124
Sex. Julius Severus	governor of Judaea, *c.*133–5
	governor of Syria
P. Mummius Sisenna	proconsul of Asia, 150–1
Q. Lollius Urbicus	*praefectus urbi*
Cn. Julius Verus	governor of Syria, *c.*164
	in charge of *dilectus leg. II Italic.*
	comes of the emperors
	cos. des. II ord. for 180
M. Statius Priscus	governor of Cappadocia, 163
Sex. Calpurnius Agricola	governor of III Daciae(?), *c.*165–6
Ulpius Marcellus	proconsul of Asia(?), 189
P. Helvius Pertinax	*praefectus alimentorum*
	proconsul of Africa
	praefectus urbi
	cos. II ord. 192
	Augustus, 193
D. Clodius Albinus	Caesar, 193–5 (and *cos. II ord.* 194)
	Augustus, 195–7
C. Valerius Pudens	proconsul of Africa
C. Junius Faustinus	governor of Hispania citerior
Postumianus	

The career of Pollienus Auspex is too uncertain in its interpretation to decide whether he held any appointments after being in Britain.

Priesthoods

Membership of one or more of the priestly colleges is recorded for sixteen governors:

A. Didius Gallus	*XVvir. s. f.*
Q. Veranius	*augur*
M. Trebellius Maximus	*frater Arvalis* (*magister* 72)
Sex. Julius Frontinus	*augur*
Cn. Julius Agricola	*pontifex*

L. Neratius Marcellus	*salius Palatinus*
M. Atilius Metilius Bradua	*pontifex, sodalis Hadrianalis*
Q. Pompeius Falco	*XVvir s. f.*
A. Platorius Nepos	*augur*
Sex. Julius Severus	*XVvir s. f.*
Q. Lollius Urbicus	*fetialis*
Cn. Julius Verus	*augur*
M. Statius Priscus	*sacerdos Titialis Flavialis*
Q. Antistius Adventus	*fetialis*
C. Junius Faustinus Postumianus	*sacerdos Flavialis Titialis*

It is probable that most if not all the other governors obtained some priesthood; but it is striking, in the case of Pollienus Auspex, that although his granddaughter's inscription mentions the pontificate of her other grandfather Fl. Latronianus and the quindecimvirate of her great-grandfather, the elder Auspex, no priesthood at all is mentioned for the former governor of Britain. The above list is instructive to the extent that it brings out the social differentiation between the men who enjoyed membership of one of the four great colleges and the others. Urbicus, Statius Priscus, and Junius Faustinus, perhaps failed to achieve from their fellow-senators the same kind of support that they obtained from the emperors. This underlines the importance of Sex. Julius Severus' quindecimvirate.

Julius Agricola received his pontificate immediately after the consulship, at the time of his appointment to Britain, and Q. Veranius was made an augur, on the nomination of Claudius, during his consulship. The implication of the placing of the priesthoods in the *cursus* inscriptions of Pompeius Falco and Lollius Urbicus is that they too received their priesthoods at this stage in their career. Statius Priscus, on the other hand, presumably became a priest of the deified Flavian emperors after his praetorship. In all the other cases, the priesthood is evidently mentioned out of chronological order.

III.2

THE GOVERNORS OF BRITANNIA SUPERIOR

Only three senatorial governors of the Upper province are known with any certainty, ---r--ius Rufinus, M. Martiannius Pulcher, and Desticius Juba. Besides them, there is only the unnamed governor, presumed to have been an equestrian *praeses* of Britannia superior, who rebelled unsuccessfully against Probus. Three other men may have governed the province, Pollienus Auspex, C. Junius Faustinus Postumianus, and L. Septimius. But the first two could possibly have governed Britain before its division *c.*213, while the equestrian *praeses* L. Septimius is generally thought to have governed the fourth century province of Britannia Prima. Nothing is known of the careers of Pulcher, Juba, and L. Septimius, nor of course of the unnamed governor under Probus. Detailed speculation is possible about various senators called Rufinus, who might be identifiable with the British governor; and the careers of Postumianus and Auspex are known in considerable detail. But, in view of the doubtful nature of their connection with Britannia superior, it is preferable to leave discussion of these cases to the entries in part II.

All that remains to be said here concerns the governors' origin. Desticius Juba undoubtedly derived from the Italian town of Concordia, and must be presumed a descendant of the Antonine procurator T. Desticius Severus. Martiannius Pulcher's *gentilicium* points strongly to the north-western provinces, where this type of name is particularly common, above all in the Rhineland. Pollienus Auspex was probably Italian, while Faustinus Postumianus must be presumed an African, in view of the find-spots of his two inscriptions.

The titulature of these governors is analysed in the appendix, together with that of the other governors.

III.3

THE ORIGINS AND CAREERS OF THE GOVERNORS OF BRITANNIA INFERIOR

Some fifteen *legati Augusti pro praetore* of Britannia inferior are attested, in all cases but that of Ti. Claudius Paulinus only from inscriptions within the province. The earliest appears to be M. Antonius Gordianus, in 216, the latest Octavius Sabinus during the reign of Postumus, 260-9. There are in addition a number of fragmentary inscriptions recording governors, a few of which may be of other governors of the Lower province. The equestrian *praeses* Aurelius Arpagius, who was responsible for rebuilding work at Birdoswald on Hadrian's Wall under the tetrarchy, between 296 and 305, may well have been the governor of Britannia inferior, rather than of a further divided and renamed province.

The origin of more than half these men is unknown, although in a few of these cases suggestions can be made: Ti. Claudius Paulinus is likely to have been provincial rather than Italian, in view of his nomenclature; while Egnatius Lucilianus may well have been Italian, for his names suggest kinship with the family of Valerian and Gallienus. Three of the others were from the Greek-speaking provinces: M. Antonius Gordianus probably from Cappadocia or Galatia; Claudius Apellinus from Pamphylia; and Claudius Xenophon, to judge from his name, from anywhere in the east. At least two may have come from North Africa, Valerius Crescens Fulvianus and [T]uccianus; and it is a reasonable assumption that Octavius Sabinus derived from somewhere in Postumus' Gallic empire.

Only in two cases is any career known, M. Antonius Gordianus and Ti. Claudius Paulinus. Gordian must have gone on to the consulship, since he became proconsul of Africa; calculation from his dates there gives a probable approximate date of 222. He may have been proconsul of Achaia between his British post and the consulship; and he may even have governed the consular province of Syria Coele in the reign of Severus Alexander. He is said to have been aged seventy-nine when he was proclaimed emperor in the spring of 238, and must therefore have been in his mid-fifties when appointed governor of Britannia inferior, rather older than most known governors of the undivided province of Britain, and an age well beyond that of most consuls. He is indeed the only governor of Inferior known to have become consul. The other legate whose career is at all known, Paulinus, may never have achieved the *fasces*, although his career is not unlike that of a number of second- and third-century senators who became consul. After service as legate of II Augusta, at Caerleon, close to Caerwent where his *cursus* inscription was set up, he was successively proconsul of Narbonensis and legate of Lugdunensis, before going to Britannia inferior in 219 or 220, for what must have been a short term of office.

In spite of other deficiencies in the evidence, we are unusually well supplied with names and dates for the first few decades of the Lower province's existence. For the years 216–44 no fewer than thirteen governors are recorded. This makes it quite certain that the average duration of the governorship had been reduced from the three years or more of the undivided province. A succession of dated governors, Gordian in 216, Modius Julius in 219, Paulinus in 220, Marius Valerianus in 221 and 222, Xenophon in 223, and Maximus in 225, demonstrates that about two years was, for a while at least, the norm. A further three governors are recorded during the remainder of Severus Alexander's reign, 226-35, one is recorded under Maximinus, and three under Gordian (AD 238-44).

The titulature of these men is analysed in the appendix, together with that of the other governors.

III.4

THE ORIGINS AND CAREERS OF THE *IURIDICI* OF BRITAIN

Seven holders of this post are attested,[1] ranging from C. Salvius Liberalis, in office during the governorship of Julius Agricola, to M. Antius Crescens Calpurnianus, whose most probable date is *c.*184. Hispania citerior evidently had a *iuridicus* from the time of Augustus, although the earliest holders of the post are simply called *legatus* or *legatus Augusti* and the earliest *iuridicus* with that title is found under Trajan.[2] But it seems unnecessary to suppose that the post existed in Britain from the time of the Claudian conquest, for the consular governor and his four legionary legates could surely have dealt with whatever legal business was required. During the northward advance under Vespasian, however, particularly when Agricola began penetrating deep into Scotland during his third campaign, it must have become increasingly difficult for any of the five military *legati* to devote attention to civil administration in the south of the province, at any rate in summer. At the same time, the death of the client king Cogidubnus, especially if he was not, as once thought, himself a *legatus Augusti*, may have created particular problems of a legal nature.[3] Meanwhile Vespasian had created another *iuridicus*—although not specifically so called—in the new consular province of Cappadocia-Galatia.[4] Hence it seems logical to accept that Salvius Liberalis was one of the earliest, if not the first of all *iuridici.*

---

[1] It should be noted that there are a number of men known to have been *iuridici* but whose inscriptions are too fragmentary to restore the name of the province or region concerned, e.g. VI 1471 (*iuridic*[. . .]); VI 1551 ([*i*]*uridico* [. . .] before two legionary commands); 1518 (*iu*[*rid.* (?) . . .]); but in view of the far greater number of *iuridici* in the Italian regions, from the time of M. Aurelius onwards, it is pointless to discuss them: cf p. 218 above for the texts.

[2] Alföldy, *Fasti Hispanienses* 236 ff.

[3] p. 210 above.

[4] Eck, *Senatoren* 3 with n. 9. (But 'the enigmatic Sospes' of *ILS* 1017 is reinterpreted by Syme, *JRS* 67 (1977) 38 ff.)

It has been suggested that the *iuridicus* may not have been regularly appointed. The relative epigraphic poverty of Britain cannot be the explanation for so few holders of the post being attested during the span of over a hundred years when it existed; for most of the very many more Spanish *iuridici* are known from inscriptions outside their province.[5] It could indeed be the case that a *iuridicus* was only sent when the governors and legionary legates were occupied in the far north. This certainly applies at the periods when the datable *iuridici* were in Britain: Liberalis and Javolenus Priscus during the Flavian campaigns in Scotland; Vettius Valens under Hadrian, when the construction of the frontier was still in progress; Sabucius Major Caecilianus and—it seems—Antius Crescens Calpurnianus when there was trouble in the north under M. Aurelius and Commodus. But the small number of known *iuridici* may be a matter of chance.[6] For one thing, as will be seen, they were mostly men of no great distinction, whose chances of commemoration were doubtless inferior to those of the Spanish *iuridici*, more than two of whom went on to consular governorships.[7]

It may well be that after the division of Britain into Upper and Lower provinces no further *iuridici* were appointed. The legate of Superior thereafter had no occasion to travel further north than Cheshire, and ought to have been able to handle the business without such assistance.

All seven *iuridici* may well have been of Italian origin. This was certainly the case with C. Salvius Liberalis, from Urbs Salvia, M. Vettius Valens, from Ariminum, and M. Antius Crescens Calpurnianus, from Ostia. Italian origin is also probable for L. Javolenus Priscus, although his undoubted links with Iguvium in Umbria may have been owed to adoption rather than birth; and it has been suggested that he derived from Dalmatia. C. Sabucius Major Caecilianus has a *gentilicium* only recorded in Italy, but origin in North Africa cannot be excluded. As for the two *ignoti*, their attestation at Tibur and Praeneste no doubt indicates that they had a residence in those towns; but since both were favoured by provincial notables, it would be premature to pronounce on their origins, particularly the man from Tibur, whose tribe was Quirina.

No pre-senatorial career, in vigintivirate or military tribune, is known for any of the seven. In the case of Liberalis and perhaps of Javolenus

[5] Eck, *ANRW* II. 1 (1974) 194 n. 166.

[6] See the remarks of Syme, *JRS* 67 (1977) 49, on the supposed abolition of the *praefectura frumenti dandi* between Claudius and the end of Domitian's reign.

[7] Alföldy, *Fasti Hispanienses* 251 f.

also this was because entry to the senate had come about by adlection. Liberalis was *allecto . . . inter tribunicios* and then [*promoto*] *inter praetorios* by Vespasian and Titus, while Javolenus' *cursus* inscription lists no posts before his legionary command. Vettius Valens' career opened with the quaestorship—but mention of a post in the vigintivirate was perhaps omitted. The *cursus* inscriptions of the other four are all fragmentary. Only Sabucius Major is known to have been tribune of the plebs—Valens is said on his stone, presumably by a lapicide's error, to have been *quaestori pleb.* as well as quaestor of Macedonia; either *tribuno* or *aedili* can be substituted.

However, although almost nothing can be said about the early career of the *iuridici*, an important observation can be made about the later stages, after the praetorship. The first two *iuridici*, Liberalis and Javolenus, were appointed after service as legionary legate; and Javolenus had also gone on to command the Numidian legion III Augusta, as *de facto* governor of Numidia, before being sent to Britain. Both men were also distinguished practicioners of law, Javolenus being ultimately head of one of the two schools of jurisprudence and both men obtained the consulship, while Javolenus later governed both Upper Germany and Syria. By contrast, the second century *iuridici* were more junior at the time of appointment and less distinguished in their later careers. Vettius Valens had only served as legate to the proconsul of Narbonensis before going to Britain; and he went on to command the legion XV Apollinaris, his only other recorded post. The unknown man from Tibur may have held posts before being *iuridicus*, but he went on to be a legionary legate and proconsul of Cyprus. The man from Praeneste seems to have had posts as a proconsular legate and perhaps as proconsul himself; but after the iuridicate he commanded two legions in succession and was prefect of the *aerarium militare*. Sabucius Major, who was *iuridicus* of an Italian region before holding the British post, went on to be prefect of the *aerarium militare*, governor of Belgica, and proconsul of Achaia, before he reached the consulship in 186. The final *iuridicus*, Antius Crescens, had only been proconsular legate and curator of a town before coming to Britain. The fact that he obtained the consulship after only one further office, as proconsul of Macedonia, was probably due to his having had to act as governor of Britain in an emergency; the early consulship can be construed as a reward for this.

Thus the status of the later *iuridici* must be interpreted as junior to that of the legionary legates, whereas Liberalis and Javolenus had clearly been of higher rank, and must have been regarded as deputy-governors. The reason why Antius Crescens was none the less acting governor may indeed have been that the legionary legates had at the time been replaced by equestrian prefects.

No *iuridici* appear to be recorded in Britain,[8] nor are any mentioned in the literary sources. Their titulature on the seven *cursus* inscriptions in Italy is as follows:

C. Salvius Liberalis	[*iuridi*] *c. Britann. (ILS* 1011)
L. Javolenus Priscus	*iuridic. provinc. Brittaniae (ILS* 1015)
M. Vettius Valens	[*iuridic.*] *provinc. Britan.* (XI 383)
ignotus, Tibur	[*iuri*] *dic. Britan* [*niae*] (*Inscr. It.* IV 137)
ignotus, Praeneste	[*iuridic.*] *prov. B* [*ritanniae*] (*AE* 1973. 133)
C. Sabucius Major	*leg. iurid. prov. Britanniae (ILS* 1123)
M. Antius Crescens	*iurid. Brit. vice leg. (ILS* 1151)

III.5

THE ORIGINS AND CAREERS OF THE LEGIONARY LEGATES OF THE BRITISH ARMY

The legions stationed in Britain, four from 43 to *c.*85 and thereafter three,[1] may be assumed to have been commanded by senatorial legates up till the end of the Gallic empire in 274 at the latest.[2] But VI Victrix, as the sole legion of Britannia inferior from *c.*213 onwards did not require a separate commander, being under the governor of Inferior for that period.[3] Taking all these factors into consideration, one may assume that well over 200 senators ought to have held the post of legionary legate in Britain, if the average tenure of the appointment was no more than three years.[4] The number of known legates actually amounts to thirty-nine, a few of whom are a little uncertain, either because the name or number of the legion is incomplete on their

---

[8] On *RIB* 8, see p. 206 above.

[1] See pp. 219 ff. above, on the movements of legions.

[2] The case of Octavius Sabinus, p. 200 above, governor of Britannia inferior under Postumus, demonstrates that the Edict of Gallienus did not apply in the Gallic empire.

[3] See pp. 168 ff. above, on the date of the division.

[4] p. 412 below. If Alföldy's conclusions on the legates of the Rhine legions, *Legionslegaten* 85 ff., also apply to Britain, an average of only two and a half years must be assumed. For the forty-two years from 43 to *c.*85 there were four legions (except for about three years out of the period *c.*66-71, p. 219 above). One must assume that between fifty-five and sixty-six legates were required in this period. From *c.*85 to *c.*213, when there were three legions, one must allow for between 128 and 154 legates. All but four of the known legates appear to belong to the period up to *c.*213, during which the estimated total is between 183 and 220: thus the number known is between *c.*16 per cent and 19 per cent.

inscriptions,[5] or because it is not completely clear whether the legion was in Britain when they commanded it.[6] This proportion compares not unfavourably with other armies.[7]

Ten legates are recorded by inscriptions in Britain, only one of whom is also attested as such elsewhere:

T. Pomponius Mamilianus	(*RIB* 445)
Q. Antonius Isauricus	(*RIB* 644)
L. Junius Victorinus Fl[av.] Caelianus	(*RIB* 2034)
F[r]onto Aemilianus ... Calpurnius ... Rufilianus	(*RIB* 320)
Haterianus	(*RIB* 335)
Claudius Hieronymianus	(*RIB* 658)
L. Julius Julianus	(*RIB* 1138; X 4182)
Ti. Claudius Paulinus	(*RIB* 311)
T. Flavius Postumius Varus	(*RIB* 316)
Vitulasius Laetinianus	(*RIB* 334)

Junius Victorinus and Julius Julianus are known from stones found close to Hadrian's Wall, and Claudius Paulinus by a *cursus* inscription from Caerwent, close to the base of his legion II Augusta. The others are all recorded on inscriptions at the legionary fortresses, Chester, Caerleon, and York.

A further ten are mentioned in the literary sources, in the main Tacitus and Dio, although Vespasian's command of II Augusta is not surprisingly referred to elsewhere as well, and Hosidius Geta's legateship appears to be recorded by an inscription in his honour at his home town Histonium:

C. Hosidius Geta	(Dio 60. 20. 4; *ILS* 971)
T. Flavius Sabinus	(Dio 60. 20. 3)
T. Flavius Vespasianus	(Tac. *Hist.* 3. 44; Dio 60. 30. 1; etc.)

---

[5] Namely T. Clodius Eprius Marcellus (XIV Gemina or a *legio* IV); C. Calpurnius Flaccus (II or VIII Aug.); the unknown from Salona (XX V.V. or XXX U.V.). Some even more uncertain cases are listed on pp. 284 f. above, but are excluded from consideration here.

[6] Namely Fabius Priscus (XIV Gemina); P. Tullius Varro and Grattius (VI Victrix). The even more dubious case of Sex. Julius Frontinus (II Adiutrix?) is excluded from the present discussion, but is dealt with on p. 70 above.

[7] Alföldy, *Legionslegaten* 2, 85 ff., makes the following estimates: Upper Germany 11 per cent (1st cent.), 15 per cent (2nd cent.), 20 per cent (3rd cent.); Lower Germany 10 per cent (1st cent.), 25 per cent (2nd cent.), 18 per cent (3rd cent.). The British figure for the last period, *c.*213–74, when between forty-one and forty-nine legates may have served in the two legions of Upper Britain, is much less favourable, for only four are known, i.e. between 8 per cent and 10 per cent.

C. Manlius Valens	(Tac. *Ann.* 12. 40. 1)
Caesius Nasica	(Tac. *Ann.* 12. 40. 4)
Q. Petillius Cerialis	(Tac. *Ann.* 14. 32. 3)
M. Roscius Coelius	(Tac. *Hist.* 1. 60)
M.(?) Fabius Priscus	(Tac. *Hist.* 4. 68. 4, 4. 79. 3)
Cn. Julius Agricola	(Tac. *Agr.* 7. 3-9. 1)
Priscus	(Dio 72. 9. 2a)

As well as L. Julius Julianus and C. Hosidius Geta, already listed above, there are nineteen further legates whose command over British legions is certain or probable, on the evidence of *cursus* inscriptions in other parts of the empire.

The origin of the legates is known in most cases, or can be inferred with a fair degree of probability. Fourteen were Italian: Geta and the two Flavii, Eprius Marcellus, Caesius Nasica, Q. Petillius Cerialis, A. Larcius Priscus, P. Tullius Varro, C. Curtius Justus, Q. Camurius Numisius Junior, L. Cestius Gallus, T. Marcius Clemens, L. Julius Julianus, and Vitulasius Laetinianus. Four certainly came from Spain: Fabius Priscus, Grattius, M. Aemilius Papus, and L. Minicius Natalis. Spanish origin is also probable for a further three: T. Pomponius Mamilianus, Calpurnius Flaccus, and P. Mummius Sisenna Rutilianus. Agricola is the only Gaul, and the only man whose family came from North Africa is T. Flavius Postumius Varus; but similar origin is likely for L. Junius Victorinus, Rufilianus, and Q. Aurelius Polus Terentianus. The unknown honoured at Salona may well have been a native of Dalmatia, but no others from this province may be found. Finally, there are four men from the east: C. Caristanius Fronto from the Latin-speaking colony of Antioch towards Pisidia, [Cas]sius [?Agri]ppi f. perhaps from Nicaea, A. Claudius Charax from Pergamum, and Claudius Hieronymianus from somewhere in the Greek-speaking provinces. Only in eight cases is there insufficient information to decide: C. Manlius Valens, M. Roscius Coelius, L. Aninius Sextius Florentinus, Q. Antonius Isauricus, Haterianus, Priscus, Ti. Claudius Paulinus, and the unknown from Tibur. Thus provincials just outnumber Italians by fifteen to fourteen among the legates whose origin can be determined; the proportion of Italians predictably declines after the first few decades from 43.

THE CAREER OF LEGIONARY LEGATES UP TO THE PRAETORSHIP

The pre-senatorial stages are known for sixteen legates, although only in ten cases are both vigintivirate and military tribunate recorded. The biographers of Vespasian and Agricola do not mention the former, and it is omitted on the inscription of T. Marcius Clemens and missing from that of [Cas]sius. A. Larcius Priscus did not hold a tribunate (although he had an unusual military post as a quaestorian), and in four cases the legion in question cannot be read on the inscription. Of eleven known vigintivirates, three were *IIIviri monetales*, five were *IVviri viarum curandarum*, three *Xviri stlitibus iudicandis*.[8] The total is of course too small a sample to permit any inferences, but it is none the less striking that no *IIIviri capitales* are recorded and relatively so few *Xviri*. The legion, or at least the army, where the tribunate was held is known in twelve cases. Only Cn. Julius Agricola served with a British legion, for Q. Camurius Numisius Junior's tribunate in IX Hispana must surely belong to the period after it had left Britain and was probably in the east.[9] Only one other man is known to have served with an eastern legion, P. Tullius Varro, and only M. Aemilius Papus served in the Numidian legion III Augusta. The others all held commissions in a legion of the Rhine or Danube armies, three in Germany,[10] two in Pannonia,[11] and four in Moesia.[12] Most remarkable of all is L. Minicius Natalis, with his three tribunates unequalled save by the emperor Hadrian; two were in Upper Pannonia, one in Lower Moesia.

Seventeen legates are also known to have served as quaestor, while C. Caristanius Fronto was adlected *inter tribunicios* by Vespasian in 69 or later and Eprius Marcellus may have entered the senate via the tribunate of the plebs. Nine were provincial quaestors[13] and eight served at Rome,[14] only two of them being quaestors of the emperor, the unknown from Salona and L. Minicius Natalis. Six served as aedile,[15] although one of these, A. Claudius Charax, may have been *adlectus*

---

[8] *Monetales*: L. Aninius Sextius Florentinus, L. Minicius Natalis, Q. Camurius Numisius Junior. *IVviri*: Fabius Priscus, C. Calpurnius Flaccus, M. Aemilius Papus, C. Curtius Justus, L. Cestius Gallus. *Xviri*: A. Larcius Priscus, P. Tullius Varro, P. Mummius Sisenna Rutilianus.

[9] p. 255 above.

[10] Fabius Priscus, L. Aninius Sextius Florentinus, L. Cestius Gallus.

[11] L. Minicius Natalis, T. Marcius Clemens.

[12] Vespasian, L. Minicius Natalis, the unknown from Salona, P. Mummius Sisenna Rutilianus.

[13] Vespasian (Crete-Cyrene), Fabius Priscus (Achaia), Agricola (Asia), A. Larcius Priscus (Asia), [Cas]sius (unknown province), L. Aninius Sextius Florentinus (Achaia), M. Aemilius Papus (Africa), A. Claudius Charax (Sicily), T. Marcius Clemens (Achaia). It may be observed that Africa and Asia, with consular proconsuls, must have seemed preferable to the other eight (p. 15 above); and perhaps Achaia was favoured among the others for sentimental reasons.

[14] C. Calpurnius Flaccus, P. Tullius Varro, L. Minicius Natalis (but he went to Africa to be legate to his father), the unknown from Salona, P. Mummius Sisenna Rutilianus, C. Curtius Justus, Q. Camurius Numisius Junior, L. Cestius Gallus.

[15] Vespasian, P. Tullius Varro, A. Claudius Charax(?), Q. Camurius Numisius Junior, L. Cestius Gallus, T. Marcius Clemens.

inter aedilicios. Nine were tribunes of the plebs,[16] including the doubtful case of Eprius Marcellus, while Caristanius Fronto was adlected into that rank, as was C. Curtius Justus. Only the two former quaestors of the emperor received backing in the next stage, both as *tribuni plebis*. Minicius Natalis was not *candidatus* as praetor, but the Salona man continued to enjoy imperial backing, and T. Marcius Clemens now obtained it for the first time. Caristanius Fronto was allowed to omit the praetorship, by further adlection. A few of the legates held additional posts. L. Minicius Natalis acted as legate to his father when the later was proconsul of Africa—exceptionally, during his quaestorship—and [Cas]sius was legate in Crete before his praetorship. Two were *ab actis senatus* between the quaestorship and aedileship;[17] and A. Claudius Charax may also have held this post. Finally, there is the exceptional post given to A. Larcius Priscus, who was made legate of the Syrian legion IV Scythica while serving as quaestor in Asia, and was also acting governor of Syria: this was clearly a result of the crisis of the year 97.

THE LEGIONARY COMMAND

As has been seen, only Agricola is known to have served in Britain before his appointment to command XX Valeria Victrix, and evidence from other provinces suggests that it was the exception rather than the rule to appoint as legionary legates men who had served in the same legion, or even in the same army, as tribune.[18] There is some evidence to suggest that the governor normally had no say in the choice of legionary commanders,[19] but in a few cases it appears that his wishes may have been consulted. At any rate, L. Minicius Natalis may have had links with the governor under whom he probably served, Sex. Julius Severus, while P. Mummius Sisenna Rutilianus could well have held his command during the governorship of his father. Four men, apart from Larcius, commanded another legion as well as the one in Britain. C. Manlius Valens, who is in any case a remarkable exception, is the only one who commanded the British legion first, *c.*52; his second legionary legateship was that of I Italica during the year 69. The other three, P. Tullius Varro, Q. Camurius Numisius Junior, and Q. Aurelius Polus

---

[16] T. Clodius Eprius Marcellus(?), Agricola; A. Larcius Priscus, C. Calpurnius Flaccus, L. Aninius Sextius Florentinus, M. Aemilius Papus, L. Minicius Natalis, the unknown from Salona, P. Mummius Sisenna Rutilianus.
[17] L. Cestius Gallus and T. Marcius Clemens.
[18] pp. 17 f. and Table 3 above.
[19] pp. 18 f. and Table 4 above.

Terentianus, all took over a British legion after experience commanding one elsewhere. In all three cases one may infer particular problems, requiring men with proven abilities. Nine men are known to have been made legionary legates immediately after the praetorship, or at any rate without holding any other post first.[20] Another nine held one or more intermediate appointments. Agricola had two special missions, from Galba to investigate temple treasures and from Mucianus to levy troops. Caristanius Fronto was legate to a proconsul and Larcius Priscus was *praefectus frumenti dandi*. Aemilius Papus, Claudius Charax, and Marcius Clemens were curators of roads. Calpurnius Flaccus was both a proconsular legate and a road curator, and Curtius Justus was *praefectus frumenti dandi* as well as being a road curator. Finally, the latest man whose full praetorian career is known, Julius Julianus, was successively curator of a town, *praefectus Miniciae*, and proconsul of Achaia, before becoming legate of II Augusta.

Information about the length of the command is directly available only for Julius Agricola: Tacitus' account implies that he was legate for three years, from 70–3. The careers of a few other legates are known in sufficient detail to make it appear that this period was not uncommon. M. Aemilius Papus was perhaps appointed commander of XX Valeria Victrix in 128, and was consul *c*.136 or 137, allowing eight or nine years for the legionary command and the prefecture of the *aerarium Saturni*. L. Minicius Natalis, legate of VI Victrix *c*.130, was consul in 139, which allows the same number of years for his command and the appointment in Italy concerned with the *alimenta*. In the case of P. Mummius Sisenna Rutilianus a rather longer tenure might be possible, or a gap before or after his prefecture of the *aerarium Saturni*; but this is admittedly because of the temptation to date his legateship of VI Victrix *c*.135, when his father was governor, rather than a year or two later, which it could be argued accords better with the date of his consulship, 146, and his career as a whole.[21]

THE LATER CAREER OF THE BRITISH LEGIONARY LEGATES

Twenty-six legates evidently reached the consulship,[22] and one more can be added if the Junius Victorinus who governed Upper Germany was the same man as the legate of VI Victrix of that name. Further, L.

---

[20] Eight are shown in the table on p. 414; the other is Vespasian.

[21] See also n. 4 above, where the possibility is allowed for that the average tenure was only two and a half years.

[22] The case of [Cas]sius (Agrippa?) is a little doubtful.

Cestius Gallus was evidently consul designate, perhaps dying before holding the *fasces*; and L. Aninius Sextius Florentinus would surely have become consul if he had not died during his governorship of Arabia. Of the remaining ten not known to have been consul, the *ignotus* from Salona, quaestor of the emperor and *candidatus* in two further posts, must surely have achieved the office, if he survived, and Haterianus, appointed governor of Cilicia while still legate of II Augusta at Caerleon, may likewise be regarded as a probable consul. If the Commodan legionary legate Priscus, who rejected an offer of the purple from the British army, was the same man as the Numidian army commander T. Caunius Priscus, he was designated to the consulship while in the latter post. The other cases are completely uncertain—even Ti. Claudius Paulinus, with his two praetorian governorships, may not have reached the consulship given the circumstances of the early 220s.

The example of Manlius Valens, consul forty-four years after his legionary command, is of course a salutary reminder that progress through the *cursus honorum* may not always have been smooth and uninterrupted. A less extreme case is that of Caristanius Fronto, governor of Lycia–Pamphylia in 81, who had to wait for nine more years for his consulship. In contrast, Julius Agricola became consul less than ten years after his praetorship. Two or three of the earliest legates, the two Flavii and Hosidius Geta, evidently became consul with no other posts after their legionary command. The special circumstances of the campaign of conquest were no doubt enough to make the difference; but in any case, in the time of Claudius there were not all that many praetorian provinces available, only the III Galliae, Lusitania, Lycia, and III Augusta. By the Flavio-Trajanic period this had changed, and it is possible to detect something like a standard pattern: praetor, legionary legate, governor of a praetorian imperial province, consul. Julius Agricola seems to exemplify this type of career, but he did not in fact proceed directly from his praetorship to a legion, having had two other functions, albeit brief ad hoc ones. Perhaps Eprius Marcellus is a better specimen of what was to be found quite often with legates of British legions— although it must be remembered that he may have commanded one of the two *legiones IV*, rather than XIV Gemina. The accompanying list shows another seven legates who proceeded direct to the legionary command from the praetorship. Eight legates gained the consulship after one other post—if one includes Minicius Natalis, on the assumption that he held his *cura viae* and alimentary prefecture jointly, and Mummius Sisenna Rutilianus, if his prefecture of the *alimenta* was held after the consulship, not before. The same number held two posts, an

Table 11

T. Clodius Eprius Marcellus	48	—	XIV Gem.(?)	Lycia Cyprus	62
Cn. Julius Agricola	68	temples, *dilectus*	XX V.V.	Aquitania	77
C. Caristanius Fronto	adl. 73/4	*leg. procos.*	IX Hisp.	Lycia-Pamph.	90
A. Larcius Priscus	c.101	*leg. procos.* *praef. frum.* *dand.*	II Aug.	'Numidia' Narbonensis	110
C. Calpurnius Flaccus	a. inc.	*cur. viae Aur.*	II (?) Aug.	Lusitania	124(?)
L. Aninius Sextius Florentinus	a. inc.	—	IX Hisp.	Cyprus Narbonensis Arabia	(d.)
P. Tullius Varro	a. inc.	—	XII Fulm.	Baetica *aerarium Sat.*	127
Grattius [Cas]sius (Agrippa?)	a. inc. c.126(?)	— —	VI Vic. XX V.V.	Aquitania Baetica Thrace(?)	126(?) 130(?)
M. Aemilius Papus	a. inc.	*cur. viae Aur.*	XX V.V.	*aerarium Sat.* *cur. viae Flam.*	c.136
L. Minicius Natalis	c.126(?)	—	VI Vict.	*praef. aliment.*	139
P. Mummius Sisenna Butilianus	a. inc.	—	VI Vict.	*aerar. Sat. praef.* *aliment.* (?)	146
A. Claudius Charax	a. inc.	*cur. viae Lat.*	II Aug.	Cilicia Sicily(?)	147
C. Curtius Justus	a. inc.	*praef. frum dand.* *cur. viae Clod.*	XX V.V.	Dacia sup. Narbonensis *aerarium Sat.*	150(?)
L. Cestius Gallus	a. inc.	—	XX V.V.	Cilicia	des. a. inc.
Haterianus	?	?			?
L. Julius Julianus	a. inc.	*cur. civit. praef.* Minic. Achaia	II Aug.	Aquitania	a. inc.
Ti. Claudius Paulinus	?	?	II Aug.	Narbonensis Lugdunensis Britannia inf.	?

imperial province, or its equivalent, the *aerarium Saturni*, and a senatorial province—and Claudius Paulinus, at the end of the list, held two
imperial provinces as well as a senatorial one without necessarily
becoming consul. It is not certain to which category Haterianus belongs.

Thirteen legates are known to have governed imperial consular
provinces:

T. Flavius Sabinus	Moesia
T. Flavius Vespasianus	Judaea
Q. Petillius Cerialis	Germania inferior; Britain
Cn. Julius Agricola	Britain
P. Tullius Varro	Moesia superior
Grattius	Germania inferior
M. Aemilius Papus	Dalmatia
L. Minicius Natalis	Moesia inferior
P. Mummius Sisenna Rutilianus	Moesia superior
C. Curtius Justus	Moesia superior
L. Junius Victorinus	Germania superior(?)
Q. Aurelius Polus Terentianus	III Daciae
Claudius Hieronymianus	Cappadocia

It may not mean much that as many as five are found to have governed
a Moesian province, but the absence of Pannonia superior from the list
is probably not mere coincidence. None of the legates is known to have
governed Pannonia inferior either. It should be observed also that
Cerialis and Agricola are the only men known to have served twice in
Britain while it was a single province, although Ti. Claudius Paulinus
returned to govern Inferior after being legate of II Augusta in Superior.

None of the legates is known to have been patrician (Agricola became
one later). Only Manlius Valens was *consul ordinarius*—unless Cerialis is
identified with the *cos. III ord.* of 83. Several enjoyed the distinctions
of senior senators, Sabinus and Postumius Varus being prefect of the
city, and seven being attested as proconsuls of Africa or Asia.[23] Finally,
nine became members of one of the great priestly colleges—or two in
the case of the third century legate T. Flavius Postumius Varus, who was
both augur and *X Vvir*—while two were *fetiales*, and three were *sodales*
of deified emperors.[24]

[23] Vespasian, Tullius Varro, Minicius Natalis (Africa); Eprius Marcellus, Grattius, Rutilianus, Terentianus (Asia).

[24] Hosidius Geta (*rex sacr.*); Agricola (*pont.*); Marcellus, Varro, Natalis, Rutilianus, Postumius Varus (*aug.*); Grattius, Varus (*X Vviri*); Larcius Priscus (*VIIvir*); Marcius Clemens, Terentianus (*fet.*); Papus, Justus, Numisius Junior (*sod.*); Vespasian had two unspecified priesthoods (Suet. *D. Vesp. 4. 2*).

III.6

THE *TRIBUNI LATICLAVII* OF THE BRITISH ARMY

Since there were four legions in the garrison for the first forty years of Roman rule, and never less than three thereafter—with the possible exception of a few years under Trajan—several hundred *laticlavii* must be presumed to have served in Britain. Unfortunately, there is little certainty about the length of service for these tribunes, so that it is quite impossible to estimate the total with any greater precision. It is, however, clear that only a small proportion is known. Twenty-eight are listed in part I, but a few are very doubtful, because their rank is uncertain, because it is not really clear whether the legion was in Britain when they served in it, or because the legion's number is fragmentary;[1] for most of the evidence is epigraphic, and, with a single possible exception, all from inscriptions outside Britain; three tribunes only are mentioned by Roman writers, the younger Scapula and Agricola by Tacitus, Titus by Suetonius.

The tribunes owed their appointment to the governor, but only in a few cases can it be established that a particular tribune owed his appointment to a specific governor: Scapula was clearly appointed by his father; Agricola by Suetonius Paullinus—but Paullinus presumably had no say over the secondment of Titus from Germany to Britain; L. Roscius Aelianus must have served under Agricola; and M. Pontius Laelianus was presumably commissioned by Platorius Nepos. Otherwise, one can only add that the tribune of VI Victrix imperfectly recorded by *RIB* 1132 was no doubt appointed by Julius Verus, mentioned on the same stone; but the tribune may have been *angusticlavius*.

Something can be said about the origin of eighteen tribunes. Julius Agricola was the only Gaul. There are five Spaniards, L. Cornelius Pusio, L. Antistius Rusticus, L. Roscius Aelianus, Q. Licinius Silvanus (but his presence in Britain is highly doubtful), and M. Accenna Helvius Agrippa. Two were from N. Africa, P. Septimius Geta and C. Memmius Fidus. Ten were Italian: Scapula, Titus, M. Pontius Laelianus, L. Aemilius Karus, C. Fabius Agrippinus, Q. Camurius Numisius Junior, L. Aemilius Naso Fabullinus, Rubrenus, L. Vettius Statura, An. Satr[ius] Sal.... Then there are six men whose names are known in whole or in part, but whose origin is uncertain;[2] and four *ignoti*.[3]

---

[1] For a number of even more uncertain cases see pp. 284 ff. above. they are excluded from consideration here.

[2] L. Burbuleius Optatus Ligarianus, L. Annius Fabianus, L. Novius Crispinus, M. Caelius Flavius Proculus, Julius Insteius Paulinus, and L. Ste. . .

[3] *RIB* 1132; VI 31780; X 525; XIV 182.

The distribution of these men between the legions is very uneven. Not surprisingly, no tribunes of II Adiutrix, which was only here for fifteen years at the most, are recorded, and there is only one for XIV Gemina, L. Cornelius Pusio. The two referred to by Tacitus, Scapula and Agricola, cannot be associated with a particular legion, nor does Suetonius tell us to which legion Titus was attached, although one may infer that it was IX Hispana.

II Augusta

L. Antistius Rusticus	*ignotus* X 525
L. Annius Fabianus	*ignotus* XIV 182
C. Fabius Agrippinus	Julius Insteius Paulinus (?or *III* or *VIII Aug.*)

P. Septimius Geta
C. Memmius Fidus Julius Albius
Rubrenus
L. Vettius Statura

IX Hispana

L. Roscius Aelianus
L. Ster...
L. Burbuleius Optatus Ligarianus
L. Aemilius Karus
L. Novius Crispinus Martialis Saturninus

Q. Camurius Numisius Junior	(?almost certainly after the legion had left Britain)

XX Valeria Victrix

M. Accenna Helvius Agrippa
L. Aemilius Naso Fabullinus
M. Caelius Flavius Proculus
An. Satr[ius] Sal...

VI Victrix

M. Pontius Laelianus Larcius Sabinus
ignotus VI 31780

ignotus RIB 1132	(?not necessarily *tr. laticl.*)
Q. Licinius Silvanus Granianus	(?not necessarily in Britain)

Twelve of the tribunes are simply called *tribunus*, or *tribunus militum*, variously abbreviated,[4] while for six the adjective *laticlavius* is

---

[4] L. Cornelius Pusio, L. Antistius Rusticus, L. Roscius Aelianus, L. Annius Fabianus, M. Pontius Laelianus, Q. Licinius Silvanus, L. Aemilius Karus, L. Novius Crispinus, Rubrenus, L. Vettius Statura, An. Satr[rius] Sal. . ., *ign.* X 525.

employed.[5] Information is lacking for the others. Twenty-two tribunes are known to have held posts in the vigintivirate. In two cases, Q. Licinius Silvanus Granianus and L. Aemilius Naso Fabullinus, it is not certain in which order the two posts were held, since no further career is recorded, but it is probable that the vigintivirate preceded the military tribunate, as it did with eighteen other tribunes. Only L. Roscius Aelianus and M. Accenna Helvius Agrippa are shown on their *cursus* inscriptions to have held the tribunate before becoming a *XXvir*, and in the former's case this may well be misleading—the tribunate being placed at the end of the *cursus*, perhaps out of order, together with the decorations received in Domitian's German campaign of 83. Three of the tribunes had been *IIIviri monetales*, but two of these are men whose presence in Britain is highly doubtful.[6] Five were *IIIviri capitales*;[7] six were *IVviri viarum curandarum*;[8] and eight were *decemviri stlitibus iudicandis*.[9] No inferences may be drawn from these figures. One man, C. Memmius Fidus, apparently did not serve as *XXvir*. Mention of a post may have been omitted from his inscription in error; but it is possible that the drain on manpower created by war and plague in the 160s, when his tribunate of II Augusta may be dated, resulted in his being exempted. Three of the tribunes are known to have held commissions in other legions. Titus was in a German as well as a British legion, probably transferred from the former to the latter in 60 or 61. It is not certain whether L. Aemilius Karus went from IX Hispana to VIII Augusta, as the order on his *cursus* suggests, or whether M. Accenna Helvius Agrippa served first in Britain and then in Syria with XVI Flavia; sometimes the order of two posts of the same rank may be in reverse order to that of the *cursus* as a whole.

Only three out of twenty-eight are known to have become quaestor of the emperor, L. Roscius Aelianus, L. Aemilius Karus, and the *ignotus* of VI 31780, a patrician who also became *praetor candidatus*. M. Pontius Laelianus and M. Caelius Flavius Proculus were the only other *candidati*, Laelianus as tribune of the plebs, Proculus as tribune and as

---

[5] L. Burbuleius Optatus, P. Septimius Geta, C. Memmius Fidus, M. Accenna Helvius Agrippa, L. Aemilius Naso Fabullinus, M. Caelius Flavius Proculus.

[6] The *ignotus* VI 31780 was almost certainly in Britain with VI Victrix, but Q. Licinius Silvanus was probably with the legion before it left Germania inferior, and Q. Camurius Numisius Junior was tribune of IX Hispana long after it had left Britain, if he is the *cos.* 161.

[7] L. Burbuleius Optatus, L. Annius Fabianus, M. Accenna Helvius Agrippa, L. Aemilius Naso, Julius Insteius Paulinus.

[8] L. Cornelius Pusio, M. Pontius Laelianus, C. Fabius Agrippinus, L. Novius Crispinus, and the *ignoti* of X 525 and XIV 182.

[9] L. Antistius Rusticus, L. Roscius Aelianus, L. Aemilius Karus, P. Septimius Geta, M. Caelius Flavius Proculus, Rubrenus, L. Vettius Statura, An. Satr[ius] Sal. . .

praetor. Twelve of the British tribunes are known to have commanded legions subsequently, four in Germany, three in Moesia, two in Judaea, one in Syria,[10] and two in Britain. But the latter pair, Julius Agricola and Q. Camurius Numisius Junior, is deceptive, for Numisius' tribunate was probably served after IX Hispana had left Britain; he also, it may be noted, commanded a further legion, the identity of which is unknown. Finally, it is worth noting that six or seven of these men subsequently governed consular imperial provinces. Three governed Cappadocia, and one of them later governed Syria as well.[11] M. Pontius Laelianus governed Pannonia superior and Syria, while P. Septimius Geta governed Moesia inferior and the III Daciae. The case of C. Memmius Fidus is uncertain, and Julius Agricola governed Britain, the only one of these tribunes known to have served in Britain more than once.

III.7

THE PROCURATORS OF BRITAIN

Ten procurators are certainly known, the earliest being Decianus Catus at the time of Boudicca's revolt in 60, and the latest M. Cocceius Nigrinus under Caracalla.[1] The salary enjoyed by this official is recorded only by the inscription of Sex. Varius Marcellus, on which the letters *CC* show that he received 200,000 sesterces. Only in five cases is any career recorded, but the four other than Marcellus accord well enough with this grading. H.-G. Pflaum categorizes the procuratorship of Britain as one of the junior posts in the ducenary grade, equivalent in status to that of Gallia Narbonensis, Lusitania, or Cappadocia, to cite a few examples.[2] At particular periods, of course, more senior men may have been assigned to Britain, for example at the time of the province's annexation in 43, when P. Graecinius Laco possibly served briefly as first procurator. It is not known what arrangements were made after the division of Britain into Superior and Inferior *c*.213. Analogy from elsewhere shows that the two provinces could either have had separate procurators or have been dealt with by a single official responsible for

---

[10] L. Cornelius Pusio, L. Antistius Rusticus, M. Pontius Laelianus, L. Aemilus Karus (Germany); L. Novius Crispinus, P. Septimius Geta, C. Memmius Fidus (Moesia); Titus and L. Annius Fabianus (Judaea); L. Burbuleius Optatus (Syria).

[11] L. Antistius Rusticus, L. Burbuleius Optatus (also Syria), L. Aemilius Karus.

[1] The doubtful cases of P. Graecinius Laco, Valens, and Heraclitus are excluded from consideration here.

[2] See Pflaum, *Les Procurateurs équestres, passim.*

the finances of both.[3] But as yet no procurators of Superior or Inferior are attested. However this may be, it seems clear that these officials must have been superseded during the later third century, when the prcuratorial career appears to have come to an end.[4]

The origin of four procurators is unknown: Decianus Catus, Q. Lusius Sabinianus, M. Oclatinius Adventus, and M. Cocceius Nigrinus may each have derived from a number of areas, but their nomenclature does not provide sufficient clues. C. Julius Alpin(i)us Classicianus, on the other hand, can be assigned to northern Gaul without hesitation on the basis of his names and those of his wife Julia Pacata. Ti. Claudius Augustanus doubtless belonged to a Celtic people of North Italy, presumably not far from Verona where he is attested. Cn. Pompeius Homullus probably had links with Spain, to judge from two of his other names, Aelius Gracilis. C. Valerius Pansa was certainly a citizen of Novaria in north-west Italy, and M. Maenius Agrippa came from Camerinum in Umbria. Finally, Sex. Varius Marcellus, father of the emperor Elagabalus, was a native of the Syrian town of Apamea.

The first two procurators, Catus and Classicianus, are known from the accounts of the Boudiccan uprising by Tacitus and Dio, the former being mentioned by both writers. Classicianus died in Britain and was buried at London by his widow, as fragments of the commemorative inscription reveal. The other procurators are known as such from epigraphic evidence only. Q. Lusius Sabinianus, M. Oclatinius Adventus, and M. Cocceius Nigrinus are recorded as procurator by inscriptions in the province, Sabinianus and Nigrinus being otherwise unknown, while Adventus' career is summarized in an unfriendly fashion by his contemporary Cassius Dio. Adventus is the only procurator recorded 'on duty', for he is associated with the governor L. Alfenus Senecio on two military building-inscriptions. Sabinianus and Nigrinus are known from religious dedications, although these are also in the frontier area. The remaining five procurators are known from commemorative or *cursus* inscriptions in Italy.

Their titulature is as follows:

Decianus Catus	*procurator* (Tac. *Ann.* 14. 32. 2, 3)
	ὁ τῆς νήσου ἐπιτροπεύων (Dio 62. 2. 1)
C. Julius Alpin(i)us	
Classicianus	*proc. provinc. Brita*[*nniae*] (*RIB* 12)

---

[3] Thus a single procurator was responsible for Belgica and the two Germanies. But the Upper and Lower provinces of Pannonia evidently had separate procurators after the division.

[4] Pflaum, op. cit.

Ti. Claudius Augustanus   *proc. Aug. prov. Britan.* (V 3337)
Cn. Pompeius Homullus   *proc. Aug. provinciae B*[*ritt*]*aniae* (*ILS* 1385)
M. Maenius Agrippa   *proc. provinciae Brittanniae* (*ILS* 2735)
Q. Lusius Sabinianus   *proc. Aug.* (*RIB* 2132, *Britannia* 8 (1977) 433)
C. Valerius Pansa   *proc. Aug. provinc. Britanniae* (V 6513)
Sex. Varius Marcellus   *proc. prov. Brit. CC*
    ἐπιτροπεύσαντι ἐπαρχείου
    Βριταννείας (*ILS* 478)
M. Oclatinius Adventus   *proc. Augg. nn.* (*RIB* 1234)
    [*p*]*roc.* (*RIB* 1462)
M. Cocceius Nigrinus   [*pr*]*oc. Aug. n.* (*RIB* 2066)

Two procurators started their careers in the centurionate. Pompeius Homullus' first recorded post was as *primus pilus* of the British legion II Augusta, from which he passed through the three Rome tribunates to a second primipilate, attached to X Fretensis in Judaea. Britain was his first procuratorial appointment; from this he went on to be procurator of Lugdunensis and Aquitania, and *a rationibus*. C. Valerius Pansa was *primus pilus*, legion not specified, tribune of a praetorian cohort, and *p. p. bis*, before coming to Britain, which was evidently his last appointment. This was also the case, it seems, with M. Maenius Agrippa, but the earliest part of his career was quite different. He began as an equestrian officer in the *tres militiae*. His first appointment was as prefect of a cohort of Britons stationed in Lower Moesia, from which he moved to be tribune of a milliary cohort in Britain—in which capacity he is recorded by several altars at Maryport. His third *militia* was back in Lower Moesia as prefect of an *ala*, from which he was appointed to the prefecture of the British fleet, and then the procuratorship of the province. Thus he was something of a British specialist, and served for longer in Britain than any other Roman known except Julius Agricola. Agrippa is the only procurator of Britain who started in the equestrian *militiae*, but it is probable that several of the others had similar careers. But Oclatinius Adventus rose from the ranks, having started as a *speculator*, and entered the procuratorial career after 'chief of the secret police' as the post of *princeps peregrinorum* is somewhat misleadingly rendered. He later rose to be prefect of the guard, and, in the extraordinary circumstances of the year 217–18, was made a senator, *consul ordinarius* and prefect of Rome. The final man whose career is known is Sex. Varius Marcellus, but his widow does not reveal what posts, if any, he had had before he became *procurator aquarum*, a centenary appointment. Since she was the niece of the empress Julia Domna it may well be that he secured the post without previous experience in public service. Britain was his second procuratorship, followed by that of the *ratio privata*, in the trecenary grade; in that he deputized for both the praetorian and urban prefects. Finally he was made a senator, and held two appointments in that capacity before his death.

III.8

THE PREFECTS OF THE *CLASSIS BRITANNICA*

Tacitus refers to but does not name Agricola's prefect of the fleet.[1] The only certainly known holders of the post[2] all belong to a period of some twenty years, *c.*130–*c.*150. The first three were all Italian: M. Maenius Agrippa came from Camerinum in Umbria, L. Aufidius Panthera from Sassina in Umbria, and Q. Baienus Blassianus from Tergeste. The origin of the fourth prefect, Sex. Flavius Quietus, is unknown. The first three all rose through the equestrian *militiae*. Agrippa and Blassianus both served in Britain during their period as army officers, and both probably obtained commissions from the governor A. Platorius Nepos, a tribunate in Agrippa's case, the prefecture of a cohort in that of Blassianus. Aufidius Panthera's only other known post was the prefecture of a milliary *ala* in Pannonia, a command in the *quarta militia*. Nothing is known of him subsequently, but Agrippa went on to be procurator of Britain, while Blassianus who had already held two sexagenary procuratorships before the fleet prefecture, went on to a long and distinguished career, culminating in the prefecture of Egypt in the 160s. Sex. Flavius Quietus, on the other hand, was a former chief centurion of the British legion XX Valeria Victrix, who returned as prefect of the fleet after conducting troops on expedition to Mauretania. It is obviously impossible to generalize on the basis of these four careers, but it is certainly striking that three out of four had served in Britain in other capacities before commanding the fleet.

III.9

HIGH OFFICIALS AND SENIOR OFFICERS FROM
THE LAST CENTURY OF ROMAN RULE

About twenty of the men who served in Britain during its last century

---

[1] *Agr.* 39. 3.
[2] The uncertain case of L. Valerius (pp. 305 f. above) is excluded from consideration here.

in the empire are recorded, mostly in literary sources. British inscriptions contribute only the *praeses* L. Septimius at Cirencester and the *praepositus* Justinianus on the Yorkshire coast. The origin of some of these men is clearly attested. Of the *vicarii*, Alypius came from Cilicia, Victorinus from Tolosa in southern Gaul, and at least one unnamed man referred to by Ausonius from Belgica. Three of the others, L. Papius Pacatianus, Martinus, and Civilis have names which look western, while Chrysanthus' name suggests a native Greek-speaker. But these criteria are rather unreliable in the late empire. One of the *praesides*, Flavius Sanctus, was a Gaul, related by marriage to Ausonius, and another, [?Hie]rocles Perpetuus, might have come from the eastern half of the empire. As for the military men, Gratianus and Theodosius, as the fathers of emperors, are well documented, the former deriving from Cibalae in Pannonia, the latter from Spain, probably from the small town of Cauca, between Emerita and Caesaraugusta. Magnus Maximus was also from Spain, and was evidently a kinsman of Theodosius. The *dux* Fullofaudes was clearly German, from his name, and the same may apply to his colleague the *comes* Nectaridus. The *dux* Dulcitius probably came from the western provinces.

It is difficult to say much about the careers of these men. They appear to conform to the pattern which became regular under Constantine I, of a separation between civil and military office. L. Papius Pacatianus is known to have been *praeses* of Sardinia about ten years before he was vicar of the Britains, and over ten years after that he became praetorian prefect, also achieving the honour of the ordinary consulship. Alypius had one other post after his British vicariate, the assignment to rebuild the Temple at Jerusalem, with the rank of *comes*. Chrysanthus had been *consularis* of an Italian province before his British appointment, and after it had hoped to become prefect of Constantinople, an ambition thwarted by his election as Novatianist bishop of that city. The final *vicarius*, Victorinus, evidently became a *comes* after leaving the island, but in what capacity is unknown. The *praeses* Perpetuus was also a *curator* at Rome.

The career of Count Gratianus, as described by Ammianus, led him from the ranks through the protectorate to a tribunate—perhaps also to an appointment as *praefectus*, and finally to two posts as *comes rei militaris*, in Africa and Britain. Theodosius' career before his British mission is only vaguely described by Ammianus with the words 'officiis Martiis felicissime cognitus'. After his return from Britain, where he evidently held the rank of *comes*, he was promoted to *magister equitum*, a position he held from 368 until his death in 376. Finally, something is known about Magnus Maximus: he served under Count Theodosius in Britain in 367-8, and perhaps also in Africa in the war against Firmus; and he may be the *dux* called Maximus involved in disgraceful dealings in Thrace in 376-7. But quite what his post in Britain was at the time of his *coup* in 383 is unfortunately unknown: that of *dux* appears most likely.

APPENDIX I

The titulature of governors

1. LITERARY REFERENCES

A. Plautius
'consularium primus' (Tac. *Agr.* 14)
'legati consularis' (Suet. *D. Vesp.* 4. 1)
βουλευτὴς λογιμώτατος ἐς τὴν Βρεττανίαν ἐστράτευσε (Dio 69. 19. 1); στρατηγήσας (19. 2); καὶ τὰ ὅπλα αὐτῶν ἀφελόμενος ἐκείνους μὲν τῷ Πλαυτίῳ προσέταξεν (60. 21. 5)

P. Ostorius Scapula
'pro praetore' (Tac. *Ann.* 1. 31. 1); 'ducem' (31. 1); 'duci' (31. 2); 'legati' (31. 4); 'ducem Romanum' (35. 1); 'imperatoris Romani' (39. 2); 'ducem haud spernendum' (39. 3); 'at Caesar cognita morte legati, ne provincia sine rectore foret, A. Didium suffecit' (40. 1); 'haec, quamquam a duobus pro praetoribus [*sc.* Ostorio et Didio] plures per annos gesta, coniunxi' (40. 5)

A. Didius Gallus
'legatus' (Tac. *Ann.* 14. 29. 1)

C. Suetonius Paullinus
'duci' (Tac. *Agr.* 5. 1); 'ducem' (5. 3); 'legati' (15. 1); 'legatus' (15. 2); 'ducem' (15. 5); 'legato' (16. 2); 'tum . . . obtinebat Britannos' (*Ann.* 14. 29. 2); 'ducis' (30. 2, 36. 3, 37. 3); 'dux' (39. 2); 'detentusque rebus gerundis' (39. 3); τὸν ἡγεμόνα σφῶν (Dio 62. 7. 1)

Paullinus and his predecessors
'ducibus nostris' (Tac. *Ann.* 14. 31. 4)

P. Petronius Turpilianus
'legatum' (Tac. *Ann.* 14. 38. 3)

M. Trebellius Maximus
'comitate quadam curandi provinciam tenuit' (Tac. *Agr.* 16. 3); 'praefuit, ducis' (16. 4);

M. Vettius Bolanus
'Thulen intrarit mandata gerens' (Stat. *Silv.* 5. 2. 55 f.); 'magno tellus frenata parenti' (ibid. 140); 'praeerat' (Tac. *Agr.* 8. 1)

Trebellius and Bolanus
'legatis . . . consularibus' (Tac. *Agr.* 7. 3)

Q. Petillius Cerialis
κελεύων ἄρχοντα Βρεττανίας ἀπιέναι (Joseph. *BJ* 7. 82); 'consularem' (Tac. *Agr.* 8. 2); 'ducem' (8. 3)

Cerialis and Frontinus
'magni duces' (Tac. *Agr.* 17. 1)

Agricola's predecessors
'veterum legatorum' (Tac. *Agr.* 33. 3)

Cn. Julius Agricola	'comitante opinione Britanniam ei provinciam dari' (Tac. *Agr.* 9. 5); 'Britanniae praepositus est' (9. 6); 'legati' (18. 2); 'ducis' (18. 4); 'provinciam regere' (19. 2); 'ducem' (22. 2); 'sextum officii annum' (25. 1); 'ducis' (27. 2, 33. 6, 37. 2); 'etiam tum . . . Britanniam obtinebat' (39. 3); 'tradiderat . . . successori suo provinciam quietam tutamque' (40. 3); ἅτε καὶ μείζονα ἢ κατὰ στρατηγὸν καταπτάξας (Dio 66. 20. 3)
Sallustius Lucullus	'aliquot consulares . . . ex quibus Sallustium Lucllum Britanniae legatum' (Suet. *Domit.* 10. 2-3)
Sex. Julius Severus	τοὺς κρατίστους τῶν στρατηγῶν ὁ Ἀδριανὸς ἐπ' αὐτοὺς ἔπεμψεν, ὧν πρῶτος Ἰούλιος Σεουῆρος ὑπῆρχεν, ἀπὸ Βρεττανίας ἧς ἦρχεν ἐπὶ τοὺς Ἰουδαίους σταλείς (Dio 69. 13. 2)
Q. Lollius Urbicus	'legatum' (*HA Ant. Pius* 5. 4)
Sex. Calpurnius Agricola	'et adversus quidem Brittannos . . . missus est' (*HA M. Ant. Phil.* 8. 8)
ignotus	στρατηγόν τέ τινα (Dio 72. 8. 2)
Ulpius Marcellus	ἀϋπνότατος δὲ τῶν στρατηγῶν γενόμενος . . . τὸν στρατηγόν (Dio 72. 8. 4)
P. Helvius Pertinax	'veniam legationis petit' (*HA Pert.* 3. 10)
D. Clodius Albinus	τῆς Βρεττανίας ἄρχων (Dio 73. 14. 3) ἦρχε δ' αὐτῆς [sc. τῆς ἐν Βρεττανίᾳ δυνάμεως] (Herodian 2. 15. 1); 'cum . . . in Britannos, quam provinciam a Commodo meruerat, transmittere niteretur' (Vict. *de Caes.* 20. 9); 'cum Britannicos exercitus regeret iussu Commodi' (*HA Clod. Alb.* 3. 4)
Virius Lupus	'Brittanniae praesidem' (*Digest* 28. 6. 2. 4)
ignotus	ὁ τῆς Βρεττανίας ἡγούμενος (Herodian 3. 14. 1)
the division	διοικήσας δὲ τὰ κατὰ Βρεττανίαν καὶ διελὼν ἐς δύο ἡγεμονίας τὴν τοῦ ἔθνους ἐξουσίαν (id. 3. 8. 2)
ignotus	τῆς Βρεττανίας ἄρχοντα (Zos. 1. 66. 2) ἕτερος δέ τις ἐν Βρεττανίαις ἀποστασίαν διεμελέτησεν, ὃν ἐπὶ τῆς ἀρχῆς ὁ βασιλεὺς ἐποιήσατο (Zonar. 12. 29)

2. EPIGRAPHIC TITULATURE[1]

Cn. Julius Agricola	*leg. Aug. pr. pr.* (*ILS* 8704a etc.)
L. Neratius Marcellus	*clarissi*[*mum virum*] *consularem meum* (*Vindolanda tablet* 29 + 31)
	[leg. pr. pr.] divi Traiani prov. Britanniae (*ILS* 1032)
M. Atilius Metilius Bradua	*ὑπατικὸν . . . Βρεταννίας* (*ILS* 8824a)
Q. Pompeius Falco	*leg. Aug. [pro p]r. provinciae [B]ritanniae* (*AE* 1957. 336

[1] Inscriptions from outside Britain are marked with an asterisk.

	leg. pr. pr. imp. Caes. Traiani Hadriani Aug. provinc. Brittanniae (ILS 1035)
	πρεσβευτὴν Σεβαστοῦ καὶ ἀντιστράτηγον Βρεταννίας *(AE* 1972. 577)
A. Platorius Nepos	[*l*] *eg. Aug. pr. p* [*r.*] *(RIB* 1340; similarly in 1427)
	leg. pr. p [*r.*] *(RIB* 1637, 1638)
	legat. Aug. pro praet. provinc. Britanniae (ILS 1052)
Sex. Julius Severus	*leg.* [*Aug. pr. p*] *r. (RIB* 1550)
	leg. pr. pr. provinciae Brittaniae (ILS 1056)
ignotus	[*leg. A*] *u* [*g.*] *pr. pr. (RIB* 995)
ignotus	[*leg. Aug.*] *pro* [*pr.*] *(RIB* 419)
ignotus	[*le*] *g. Aug. p* [*r.*] *pr. (JRS* 55 [1965] 222)
Q. Lollius Urbicus	*leg. Aug. pr. pr. (RIB* 2191, and, more or less complete, in 1147, 1148, 2192)
	leg. Aug. pro prae. (RIB 1276)
Cn. Papirius Aelianus	*[*l*] *eg. Au* [*g. pr. pr. prov. B*] *rittan* [*iae*] (II 2075)
Cn. Julius Verus	*leg. Aug. pr. pr. (RIB* 2110 and somewhat restored in 283)
	leg. Aug. pr. p. (1322)
	leg. Aug. pr. pr. provinc. Brittaniae (ILS 1057)
ignotus	*leg.* (XVI 130)
M. Statius Priscus	*[*leg. August*] *or.* [*provin*] *c. Britan* [*niae*] *(AE* 1910. 86, amended)
	leg. Aug [*g.*] *pr. pr. prov. Brittanniae (ILS* 1092)
Sex. Calpurnius Agricola	*cos. (RIB* 1809)
	[*legati Augustoru*] *m pr. pr.* (1149)
	leg. Aug. pr. pr. (1137 and, slightly restored, 1792)
Q. Antistius Adventus	*leg. Aug. pr. p* [*r.*] *(RIB* 1083)
Caerellius	*[*leg. Aug.* or *Augg.*] *pr. pr. pro* [*vi*] *n* [*c.*] . . . *Britt.* (XIII 6806)
M. Antius Crescens Calpurnianus	*iurid. Brit. vice leg. (ILS* 1151)
ignotus	[*l*] *eg. A* [*ugg. p*] *r. p* [. . .] *(AE* 1971. 213)
ignotus(?)	[*leg.*] *Aug.* [*pr. pr.*(?)] *(RIB* 2212)
Virius Lupus	*leg. eorum pr. pr. (RIB* 637)
	leg. Aug. pr. pr. (730)
Pollienus Auspex	ὑπατικοῦ Βριταννίας *(ILS* 8841)
C. Junius Faustinus	*praesidis provinciaru* [*m His*] *pani* [*ae*] *et Britanniae* (VIII 11763)
C. Valerius Pudens	*amplissimi cosularis (AE* 1963. 281)
L. Alfenus Senecio	*amplissimi* [*cos.*] *(RIB* 722, 723)
	v. c. cos. (1234)
	cos. (1337, 1909, incomplete in 1462)
	leg. Augg. pr. pr. (740)
	leg. eorum pr. pr. (746)
ignotus	[*leg.*] *Au* [*gg. pr. pr.*(?)] (591)
ignotus	[*cosul*] *are*(?) (430)
Ulpius Marcellus jr.	*cos.* (1329)

	[leg. Aug.] pr. pr. (976)
C. Julius Marcus	*leg. Aug. pr. pr.* (1265, and incomplete on 977, 2298)
	leg. [pr. pr. eiu]s (?) *pr. Br.* (1205)
	leg. eius (905)
ignotus (---cus)	*[leg. Aug.* or *eius pr. pr. prov. Bri] tann [i] ae* (8)

BRITANNIA SUPERIOR

Rufinus	*cos.* (*AE* 1962. 258)
M. Martiannius Pulcher	*v. c. leg. Augg. pro praet.* (*Britannia* 7 (1976) 378 f.)
Desticius Juba	*v. c. legatum Augg. pr. pr.* (*RIB* 334)
L. Septimius	*v. p. pr. B [r. . .] ; primae provinciae rector* (103)

BRITANNIA INFERIOR

M. Antonius Gordianus	*leg. Aug. pr. pr.* (*RIB* 1279, incomplete on 1049)
Modius Julius	*leg. Aug. pr. pr.* (980, 1914)
Ti. Claudius Paulinus	*[le]g. Aug. pr. pr.* (1280)
	*[l]eg. Aug. p. p. in Brit.; leg. Aug. pr. pr. prov. [B]ritanniae (XIII 3162)
Marius Valerianus	*leg. Aug. pr. pr.* (*RIB* 978)
	leg. eius pr. pr. (1060)
Cl. Xenophon	*leg. Aug. pr. praet.* (2299, 2306)
	[l]eg. [Aug.] n. pr. [pr.] (1706)
Paulinus or Xenophon	*leg. pr. [pr.]* (1467)
Maximus	*leg. Aug. pr. p [r.]* (1738)
Val. Crescens Fulvianus	*leg. eius pr. [pr.]* (587)
Cl. Apellinus	*le [g.] Augg.* (1281)
ignotus	*[l]eg. Au[g.* or *gg. pr. pr.]* (*AE* 1967. 260)
ignotus	*[praes]es* (?) (*RIB* 1922)
[T]uccianus	*v. c. leg. [Aug. pr. pr.]* (1553)
Maecilius Fuscus	*leg. Aug. pr. pr.* (1092)
Egnat. Lucilianus	*leg. Aug. pr. pr.* (1091, 1262)
Nonius Philippus	*leg. Aug. pro pre [to.]* (897)
ignotus	*[l]eg. Aug.* (883)
ignotus	*leg. Aug. p. p.* (1999)
ignotus	*[l]e [g.] Aug. pr. pr.* (1468)
Octavius Sabinus	*v. c. praeside n.* (605)
Aur. Arpagius	*v. p. . . . pr.* (1912)

3. THE FORMS IN WHICH GOVERNORS' NAMES ARE GIVEN ON ON BRITISH INSCRIPTIONS[1]

NOMINATIVE CASE

Virius Lupus	730

---

[1] Numbers refer to *RIB*, unless otherwise stated.

C. Julius Marcus	1265
M. Martiannius Pulcher	*Britannia* 7 (1976) 378 f.
L. Septimius	103
Egnat. Lucilianus	1262
Aemilianus	741
ignotus (--cus)	8
ignotus (?)(--imus Di--)	1922

ABLATIVE CASE

Cn. Julius Agricola	*ILS* 8704a etc.
A. Platorius Nepos	1340, 1427, 1634, 1637
C. Julius Marcus	2298

DATIVE CASE

L. Alfenus Senecio	1337

SUB CURA WITH GENITIVE CASE

Q. Lollius Urbicus	1147, 1148
Sex. Calpurnius Agricola	1137, 1149
Virius Lupus	1163
C. Valerius Pudens	*AE* 1963. 281
L. Alfenus Senecio	722, 746, 723 (? or *iussu*)
C. Julius Marcus	977
M. Antonius Gordianus	1049 (?or *iussu*), 1279, 590 (?or *sub* with ablative)
Modius Julius	980
Ti. Cl. Paulinus	1280
Marius Valerianus	978
Valerius Crescens Fulvianus	587
Cl. Apellinus	1281
Nonius Philippus	897
ignotus	1051
ignotus	1596
ignotus	1932 (?perhaps not a governor)
ignotus	1999

SUB WITH ABLATIVE CASE

ignotus (--dius)	1997 + 1998
Q. Lollius Urbicus	1276, 2191, 2192
Cn. Julius Verus	283, 1322, 2110

Sex. Calpurnius Agricola	589, 1792, 1703 (?or *sub cura* with genitive)
Q. Antistius Adventus	1083
Ulpius Marcellus	1329, 1463
L. Alfenus Senecio	1909
Rufinus	*AE* 1962. 258
M. Antonius Gordianus	590 (?or *sub cura* with genitive)
Modius Julius	1914
Cl. Xenophon	1706
Calvisius Ru--	929
[T]uccianus	1553
Octavius Sabinus	605
Aur. Arpagius	1912
ignotus	1151 (?or *sub cura* with genitive)

CURANTE WITH ABLATIVE CASE

Virius Lupus	637
L. Alfenus Senecio	1462
Marius Valerianus	1060
Cl. Xenophon	2299, 2306

IUSSU WITH GENITIVE CASE

L. Alfenus Senecio	740, 1234, 723 (?or *sub cura*)
M. Antonius Gordianus	1049 (?or *sub cura*)

PER WITH ACCUSATIVE CASE

Desticius Juba	334
Cl. (Paulinus or Xenophon)	1467
Marius Valerianus	1465
Maecilius Fuscus	1092
Egnat. Lucilianus	1091
ignotus(?) (Sa------)	2060

PROVINCIAM REGENTE WITH ABLATIVE CASE

Maximus	1738
ignotus	1751

The titulature of legionary legates of the British army [1]

T. Flavius Vespasianus	'illic [sc. in Britannia] secundae legioni a Claudio praepositus et bello clarus egerat' (Tac. *Hist.* 3. 44)
Vespasian and T. Flavius Sabinus	ὑποστρατηγοῦντά<ς> οἱ [sc. τῷ Πλαυτίῳ] (Dio 60. 20. 3, amended)
T. Clodius Eprius Marcellus	[πρεσβ]ευτῇ λεγιῶνος τε[σσαρακαιδεκάτης(?) Τιβερίου Κλαυδ]ίου Καίσαρος Σεβαστοῦ (*SEG* XVIII 587)
C. Manlius Valens	'adversa interim legionis pugna, cui Manlius Valens praeerat' (Tac. *Ann.* 12. 40. 1)
Caesius Nasica	'legione, cui Caesius Nasica praeerat' (Tac. *Ann.* 12. 40. 4)
Q. Petillius Cerialis	'legato legionis nonae' (Tac. *Ann.* 14. 32. 3)
M. Roscius Coelius	'legatus vicensimae legionis' (Tac. *Hist.* 1. 60)
	'legatus praetorius' (Tac. *Agr.* 7. 3)
M. Fabius Priscus	'sed legionem [sc. quartam decimam] terrestri itinere Fabius Priscus legatus in Nervios Tungrosque duxit' (Tac. *Hist.* 4. 79. 3, cf. 4. 68. 4)
Cn. Julius Agricola	'is [sc. Mucianus] ... Agricolam ... vicesimae legioni praeposuit' (Tac. *Agr.* 7. 3)
C. Caristanius Fronto	*leg. imp. divi Vespasiani Aug. leg. IX Hispanae in Britann.* (*ILS* 9485)
T. Pomponius Mamilianus	†*leg. Aug.* (*RIB* 445)
A. Larcius Priscus	*legatus Augus. legionis II Aug.* (*AE* 1908. 237)
	leg. Aug. leg. II Aug. (*ILS* 1055)
C. Calpurnius Flaccus	[ἡγεμόνα λεγ. β' (?)Σεβ]αστῆς (*IGR* III 991)
L. Aninius Sextius Florentinus	*leg. leg. VIIII Hisp.* (III 87 + 14148[10])
P. Tullius Varro	*leg. leg. .... VI Victricis p. f.* (*ILS* 1047)
Grattius	*lega[to Aug.] leg. VI Victricis [piae fid.]* (*RIT* 149)
[Cas]sius	πρεσ[βευτὴν αὐτοκράτορος λεγ]ιῶνος κ' Οὐαλε[ρίας Νικηφόρου] (*AE* 1950. 251)
M. Aemilius Papus	*leg. Aug. leg. XX V. V.* (II 1371)
	leg. leg. XX V. V. (II 1283)
L. Minicius Natalis	*leg. Aug. leg. VI Victr. in Britannia* (*ILS* 1061, II 4510, XIV 4244)

[1] Inscriptions found in Britain are marked with an obelisk.

[πρεσβευτὴν Σεβαστοῦ λεγ. ς´] Νεικηφόρ[ου] (*JÖAI* 10 (1907) 307 ff.)

Q. Antonius Isauricus   †*leg. Aug.* (*RIB* 644)

ignotus   [*le*]*gat l*[*eg. XX Val.* (?)*Vic*]*tric.* (*AE* 1922. 36)

P. Mummius Sisenna
Rutilianus   *leg. leg. VI Victric.* (*ILS* 1101; XIV 4244)

A. Claudius Charax   ἡγεμόνα λεγιῶνος β´ Αὐγ. (*AE* 1961. 320)

C. Curtius Justus   *leg. imp. Antonini Augusti Pii leg. X*[*X*] *Val. Vict.* (III 1458)

L. Junius Victorinus
Flav. Caelianus   †*leg. Aug. leg. VI Vic.* (*RIB* 2034)

Q. Camurius Numisius
Junior   [*le*]*g. Aug.* . . . [*leg.*] *VI Victr.* (XI 5670)

ignotus   [*l*]*eg. leg. II* [*Aug.*] (XIV 4249)

Rufilianus   † [*l*] *eg* [*atus*] *Augustorum* (*RIB* 320)

L. Cestius Gallus   *leg. Augg. leg. XX V. V.* (X 3722)

Priscus   ὑποστράτηγον (Dio 72. 9. 2a)

Q. Aurelius Polus
Terentianus   *leg.* . . . *leg. II Aug.* (*AE* 1965. 240)

T. Marcius Clemens   [*legato*] *leg. II Aug.* (XIV 3595)

Cl. Hieronymianus   †*leg. leg. VI Vic.* (*RIB* 658)

L. Julius Julianus   † [*leg. leg. II A*]*ug.* (*RIB* 1138)
     leg. legionis secund. August. (XI 4182)

Ti. Claudius Paulinus   †*leg. leg. II Aug.* (*RIB* 311)

T. Fl. Postumius Varus   †*v. c. leg.* (*RIB* 316)

Vitulasius Laetinianus   †*leg. leg. II Aug.* (*RIB* 334)

APPENDIX III

A patron of the province of Britain

XIV 2508, near Tusculum: [*C.*] *Iulio Aspro* / *cos.* / *praetori curatori*[4] / *viae Appiae soda*[*l.*] *August*[*al.*] / *trib.* [*pleb.*] *quaestori* / *provinc. Africae curat.* / *aedium sacrarum* [8]/ *provincia Britannia* / *patrono*

The above inscription is one of a group from the same place honouring the younger of the *consules ordinarii* of 212, who held the office with his father, prefect of the city and *cos. II.*[1] Another inscription was set up by Mauretania Tingitana, of which he was also patron, a little earlier, when he was *cos. des.*[2] Since his *cursus* displays no direct link by service with either province, it is assumed that he must have inherited the office of patron. An acephalous inscription found nearby is generally assigned to the elder Asper: here the honorand is described as patron of 'five provinces, three Spains and two Mauretanias, outstanding orator and most faithful defender of clients'.[3]

Although the only other known patron of the province of Britain, M. Vettius Valens, had indeed served there himself, as *iuridicus*,[4] parallel cases are few—only three other senatorial *patroni provinciae* are epigraphically recorded.[5] On the other hand, Pliny's correspondence demonstrates that men like himself were likely to be chosen as *patronus* for their qualities as orators.[6] Hence the putative service in Britain of a kinsman of Julius Asper must remain a pure hypothesis.

Much more important, perhaps, is the fact that after our man's consulship he could still be honoured by *provincia Britannia*, suggesting that Britain had not yet been divided.[7]

---

[1] See *PIR*[2] J 334, 182. It must be noted that the younger consul of 212 is named as C. Julius Camilius Asper in a diploma of 212: see Roxan no. 74. Previously only his son (J 232) was thought to have had the name Camilius, although Barbieri, *L'Albo* no. 295 allowed for the possibility that he had the same five names as his son.

[2] XIV 2509.

[3] XIV 2516.

[4] p. 215 above.

[5] L. Harmand, *Le Patronat sur les collectivités publiques* (1957) 413 (misleadingly assigning both Asper and Valens to the 'fin IIIe s.').

[6] See e.g. Pliny, *ep.* 3. 4, describing how envoys from Baetica sought his services as advocate in the prosecution of Caecilius Classicus. A decree of the senate was passed 'ut darer provincialibus patronus'—the *legati* reminding Pliny of the *patrocini foedus* that existed since the trial of Baebius Massa.

[7] Since XIV 2509 specifies Mauretania Tingitana and 2516 refers to the three Spanish and two Mauretanian provinces, it is clear that *provincia Britannia* must be taken as an accurate description of a single province. If the *cura aedium sacrarum* in Asper's *cursus* inscription could be taken to mean that at Rome, then the inscription might be later than 212, since, to judge

Although the family had a home at Tusculum, it appears to have derived from the Augustan colony of Antioch towards Pisidia, where probable ancestors are on record, as they are at the port of Attaleia.[8]

from the period 139–80, it looks as if *curatores* were generally appointed a year or two after holding the *fasces*: see Alföldy, *Konsulat* 289 ff. However, Pflaum suggests (*ap. PIR*[2] J 334) that in Asper's *cursus* this was a local office of the town of Tusculum. [M. Beard, *Britannia* 11 (1980) 313 f., discusses an inscription from Rome, first published by H. Solin, *Epigraphische Untersuchungen* . . . (1975) 6 ff.: [. . .] *devotissimae votorum* [*compotes*] *provinciae Britann*[*iae* . . .]. The plural here underlines the value of the singular in the Tusculum inscription.

[8] See *PIR*[2] J 182.

ADDENDUM

V. Saladino, 'Iscrizioni latine di Roselle (1)', *ZPE* 38 (1980) 159–176, includes, pp. 173–5 with photograph pl. XI, 40, a fragmentary inscription from Rusellae in Etruria:

[. . .]*o Q. f. Ar*[*n.* . . . / . . .]*no cos.* I[. . . / . . . *exe*]*rcitus Br*[*it.* . . .[4] / . . .] *Narbone*[*ns.* . . . / . . . *leg. XX Vale*]*riae vi*[*ctricis* . . . / . . .]*o or q.* [. . .]

Saladino notes that in line 1 *Ar* [*n*], already known as the probable tribe of Rusellae, may be restored in preference to *Ae*[*m.*] or *An*[*i.*]; that in line 2 the upright after *cos.* may derive from *d*[*es.*] or *I*[*I*] although other possibilities remain; that in line 5 [*pr. Etru*]*riae VI*[*viro eq. R.*], while theoretically possible, appears to be ruled out, since these posts generally receive mention only at the beginning or the end of a *cursus*-inscription; and that in line 6 there are traces which could belong either to an 0 or to a Q. There is no obvious candidate for identification with this *ignotus* either in these *Fasti* or in Pflaum's *Fastes de la Narbonnaise*. Q. Caecilius Q. f. Arn. Marcellus is attractive at first sight, since he served in Narbonensis both as quaestor and as proconsular legate, *ILS* 1045, *ager Tusculanus*, discussed by Pflaum 62. His filiation and tribe fit those of the *ignotus*, and his presumed son, *cos.* 167, had the additional *cognomen* Dentilianus, which would accord with the termination -*no* before *cos.* in line 2. But the career of Marcellus himself appears to have terminated with the proconsulship of Sicily; and even if it did continue after *ILS* 1045 was set up, it seems impossible to reconcile the items there recorded with the Rusellae fragment. The *cos.* 167, whose career is fully recorded before his consulship, in *ILS* 1096, served neither in Narbonensis nor in Britain; and in any case these men's tribe probably denotes an *origo* at Carthage (thus Groag in *PIR*[2] C 55). The titles *Valeria victrix* for *leg. XX* give no assistance with dating, since it remains uncertain when they were awarded, see Ritterling, *RE* 12.2 (1925) 1780, J. J. Wilkes, *Dalmatia* (1969) 71 and n. 1. The [*exe*]*rcitus Br*[*it.*] in line 3 is puzzling, for the lists supplied by H.-G. Pflaum, *Rec. de Constantine* 69 (1957) 3 ff. indicate that such a formula is only found, with one exception, on records of soldiers or lower-ranking officers, particularly when serving in a detachment outside their province, e.g. *Sim*[*p*]*licius Super dec. alae Vocontior. exerci*[*t*]*us*

Britannici, ILS 2536, Germ. inf. By contrast, officers who wished to show where the unit in which they had served was stationed expressed this in the form *in provincia* . . ., or *provinciae* . . . The one exception is when a senator commanded a task-force outside the province from which it was drawn, e.g. L. Marius Maximus, described as *duci exerciti* (sic) *Mysiaci aput Byzantium et aput Lugudunum, ILS* 2935, referring to the campaigns of 193–7. *Narbone*[*ns.*] on the Rusellae stone might then have been preceded by e.g. [*in prov.*]. But a historical context for such a mission is hard to conceive, unless one were to suppose that Severus entrusted the initial regrouping of Albinus' defeated forces to a former commander of the XXth. As an alternative, one might suggest that Roscius Coelius, after taking the lead in expelling Trebellius Maximus from Britain in 69, was selected to command the 8000 legionaries summoned from the province by Vitellius, and that he commanded them [*in prov.*]*Narbone*[*ns. et in Italia Transpadana*] (cf. p. 61 above). It would be necessary to assume that he had a *cognomen* terminating in -nus, and was *Q.f. Ar*[*n.*] (unless *AI* in line 1 represents the beginning of a *cognomen*, and no tribe was in fact given). But it must be conceded that all this is too speculative to carry any weight. After all, it cannot be certain whether the *cursus* was in ascending or descending order. If the former were the case, with *cos.* out of order as so often, the man might, after all, simply have been a *laticlavius* in a legion of the *exercitus Britannicus*, a *XXvir* (before or after the tribunate), and quaestor of *Narbone*[*nsis*] ; then, after the other republican magistracies, legate of the XXth; etc. Nothing indicates how long the original lines were and judgement must be suspended.

Select bibliography

A high proportion of the books and articles cited in the notes, including all entries in *PIR* and *RE*, are omitted, in an attempt to reduce this list to reasonable dimensions. Some of the works below are cited in the notes by short title, mentioned in brackets after the entry in cases where this may not be quite clear; and a few works are cited by author's name only.

ALFÖLDY, G. *Bevölkerung und Gesellschaft der römischen Provinz Dalmatien* (1965)
— Review of *RIB*, *Bonner Jahrb.* 166 (1966) 638
— *Die Legionslegaten der römischen Rheinarmeen* (1967) (*Legionslegaten*)
— *Die Hilfstruppen in der römischen Provinz Germania inferior* (1968)
— 'Septimius Severus und der Senat', *Bonner Jahrb.* 168 (1968) 112
— 'Senatoren in der römischen Provinz Dalmatia', *Ep. Stud.* 5 (1968) 99
— 'Herkunft und Laufbahn des Clodius Albinus in der Historia Augusta', *Historia-Augusta-Colloquium Bonn 1966/67* (1968) 19
— *Die Personennamen in der römischen Provinz Dalmatia* (1969)
— 'Die Generalität des römischen Heeres', *Bonner Jahrb.* 169 (1969) 233
— 'Ein *praefectus* der *cohors VI Nerviorum* in *Britannia*', *Hommages M. Renard* II (1969) 3
— *Fasti Hispanienses. Senatorische Reichsbeamte und Offiziere in den spanischen Provinzen des römischen Reiches von Augustus bis Diokletian* (1969)
— 'P. Helvius Pertinax und M. Valerius Maximianus', *Situla* 14/15 (1974) 199
— *Die römischen Inschriften von Tarraco* (1975) (*RIT*)
— *Konsulat und Senatorenstand unter den Antoninen. Prosopographische Untersuchungen zur senatorischen Führungsschicht* (1977)
—, and HALFMANN, H. 'M. Cornelius Nigrinus, General Domitians und Rivale Trajans', *Chiron* 3 (1973) 331
ATKINSON, D. 'The governors of Britain from Claudius to Diocletian', *JRS* 12 (1922) 60
AVOTINS, I. 'The date and recipient of the Vitae sophistarum of Philostratus', *Hermes* 106 (1978) 242
BARBIERI, G. *L'Albo senatorio da Settimio Severo a Carino (193-285)* (1952)
— 'Didius Gallus e Ti. Iulius Iulianus', *Rendic. Accad. Lincei* 29 (1974) 259
BARNES, T. D. 'Philostratus and Gordian', *Latomus* 27 (1968) 581
— 'A senator from Hadrumetum and three others', *Historia-Augusta-Colloquium Bonn 1968/1969* (1970) 45

BASTIANINI, G. 'Lista dei prefetti d'Egitto dal 30^a al 299^p, *ZPE* 17 (1975) 263

BERTRANDY, F. 'Une grande famille de la conféderation Cirtéenne: les Antistii de Thibilis', *Karthago* 17 (1973/1974) 195

BIRLEY, A. R. 'The status of Moesia superior under Marcus Aurelius', *Acta antiqua Philippopolitana. Studia historica et philologica* (1963) 109

— *Marcus Aurelius* (1966)

— 'The duration of provincial commands under Antoninus Pius', *Corolla Memoriae E. Swoboda Dedicata* (1966) 43

— 'The origins of Gordian I', in M. G. Jarrett and B. Dobson (edd.), *Britain and Rome. Essays presented to E. Birley* (1966) 45

— 'The Roman governors of Britain', *Ep. Stud.* 4 (1967) 63

— 'The invasion of Italy in the reign of M. Aurelius', *Festschr. R. Laur-Belart* (1968) 214

— 'The coups d'état of the year 193', *Bonner Jahrb.* 169 (1969) 247

— *Septimius Severus the African Emperor* (1971)

— 'VI Victrix in Britain', in R. M. Butler (ed.), *Soldier and Civilian in Roman Yorkshire* (1971) 81

— 'Virius Lupus', *Arch. Ael.*^{4} 50 (1972) 179

— 'Petillius Cerialis and the conquest of Brigantia', *Britannia* 4 (1973) 179

— 'Tacitus, Agricola, and the Flavian dynasty', in B. M. Levick (ed.), *The Ancient Historian and his Materials. Essays in honour of C. E. Stevens* (1975) 139

— 'The origin and career of Q. Pompeius Falco', *Arheološki Vestnik* 28 (1977) 360

BIRLEY, E. 'A new inscription from Chesterholm', *Arch. Ael.*^{4} 11 (1934) 127

— 'Roman Kirkby Thore and an African inscription', *Trans. Cumb. and Westm. Arch. and Ant. Soc.*^{2} 34 (1934) 116

— 'The epitaph of Julius Classicianus', *Ant. Journ.* 16 (1936) 207

— review of H. Nesselhauf, *CIL* XVI, *JRS* 28 (1938) 224

— 'Roman inscriptions from Chesters (Cilurnum), a note on *Ala II Asturum*, and two milestones', *Arch. Ael.*^{4} 16 (1939) 237

— 'The governors of Numidia, A D 193–268', *JRS* 40 (1950) 60

— 'The Roman governors of Britain', in G. Askew, *The Coinage of Roman Britain* (1951) 81

— *Roman Britain and the Roman Army* (1953)

— 'Senators in the emperors' service', *Proc. Brit. Acad.* 39 (1953) 197

— 'A Hadrianic inscription from Castlesteads', *Trans. Cumb. and Westm. Arch. and Ant. Soc.*^{2} 52 (1953) 184

— 'The Beaumont inscription, the *Notitia Dignitatum*, and the garrison of Hadrian's Wall, *Trans. Cumb. and Westm. Ant. and Arch. Soc.*^{2} 39 (1939) 190

— 'The Roman milestone at Middleton in Lonsdale', ibid. 53 (1954) 52

— 'Beförderungen und Versetzungen im römischen Heere', *Carnuntum Jahrb.* 1957, 3

— *Research on Hadrian's Wall* (1961)

— review of B. E. Thomasson, *Statthalter Nordafrikas*, *JRS* 52 (1962) 219

— 'The fourth-century subdivision of Britain', in *Quintus Congressus Internationalis Limitis Romani Studiosorum* (1963) 83

— review of *RIB*, *JRS* 56 (1966) 226

— 'The Roman inscriptions of York', *Yorks. Arch. Journ.* 41 (1966) 103

BIRLEY, E. 'Troops from the two Germanies in Roman Britain', *Ep. Stud.* 4 (1967) 10
— 'The fate of the Ninth Legion', in R. M. Butler (ed.), *Soldier and Civilian in Roman Yorkshire* (1971) 71
— 'The adherence of Britain to Vespasian', *Britannia* 8 (1977) 243
BOGAERS, J. E. 'De bezettingstroepen van de Nijmeegse legioensvesting in de 2de eeuw na Chr.', *Nugama* 12 (1965) 10 =
— 'Die Besatzungstruppen des Legionslagers von Nijmegen im 2. Jahrhundert nach Christus', in *Studien zu den Militärgrenzen Roms* (1967) 54
— 'Die Nijmegener Legionslager seit 70 n. Chr.', in *Studien zu den Militärgrenzen Roms* II (1977) 93
— 'King Cogidubnus: another reading of *RIB* 91', *Britannia* 10 (1979) 243.
BRACCESI, L. 'Una nuova testimonianza su Magno Massimo', *Parola del passato* 23 (1968) 279
BRASSLOFF, S. 'Patriziat und Quaestur in der Kaiserzeit', *Hermes* 39 (1904) 618
— 'Die Grundsätze bei der Commendation der Plebejer', *JOAI* 8 (1905) 60
— 'Die Provinzialstatthalter in der Kaizerzeit', *Wien. Stud.* 29 (1907) 321
BROMWICH, R. 'The character of the early Welsh tradition', in H. M. Chadwick et al., *Studies in Early British History* (1954) 83
BRUNT, P. A. 'The fall of Perennis: Dio-Xiphilinus 72. 9. 2', *CQ* N.S. 23 (1973) 172
BÜCHNER, K. 'Reicht die Statthälterschaft des Agricola von 77–82 oder von 77–83 n. Chr.?', *Rhein. Mus.* 103 (1960) 172
BURY, J. B. 'A lost Caesarea', *Camb. Hist. Journ.* 1 (1923) 1
CAMODECA, G. 'La carriera del giurista L. Neratius Priscus', *Atti dell' Acc. di scienze morali e politiche* 87 (1976) 1
CAMPBELL, B. 'Who were the *viri militares*?', *JRS* 65 (1975) 11
CASEY, P. J. 'Tradition and innovation in the coinage of Carausius and Allectus', in J. Munby and M. Henig (edd.) *Roman Life and Art in Britain* (1977) 217
— 'Carausius and Allectus—rulers in Gaul?', *Britannia* 8 (1977) 283
CÉBEILLAC, M. *Les quaestores principis et candidati aux Ier et IIIème siècles de l'empire* (1972)
CHAMPLIN, E. 'Hadrian's heir', *ZPE* 21 (1976) 79
CHASTAGNOL, A. *Les Fastes de la préfecture de Rome sous le Bas-Empire* (1962)
— 'La naissance de l'*ordo senatorius*', *MEFR* 95 (1973) 583
— 'Le laticlave de Vespasien', *Historia* 25 (1976) 255
CORBIER, M. *L'aerarium Saturni et l'aerarium militare* (1974)
DAVIES, R. W. 'A note on a recently discovered inscription from Carrawburgh', *Ep. Stud.* 4 (1967) 108
— 'Military decorations and the British war', *Acta Classica* 19 (1976) 115
— '*Singulares* and Roman Britain', *Britannia* 7 (1976) 134
— 'The *ala I Asturum* in Roman Britain', *Chiron* 6 (1976) 357
— 'L. Julius Julianus in Roman Britain', *Latomus* 35 (1976) 399
— '*Cohors I Cugernorum*', *Chiron* 7 (1977) 385
— 'Roman Cumbria and the African connection', *Klio* 59 (1977) 155
— 'A lost inscription from Bowness', *ZPE* 27 (1977) 241
DEGRASSI, A. *I Fasti Consolari dell'impero romano dal 30 a.C. al 613 d.C.* (1952) (*FC*)

DEGRASSI, A. 'Le nuove tavolette cerate di Pompei', *Mem. Acc. Lincei* 14 (1969) 136

DE LAET, S. J. *De Samenstelling van den romeinschen Senaat gedurende de eerste eeuw van het Principat (28 vor Chr.-68 na Chr.)* (1941)

DEMANDT, A. 'Der Tod des älteren Theodosius', *Historia* 18 (1969) 598

DESSAU, H. 'Le consulat sous les empereurs des Gaules', *Mélanges Boissier* (1903) 165

DOBSON, B. *Die Primipilares. Entwicklung und Bedeutung, Laufbahnen und Persönlichkeiten eines römischen Offizierranges* (1978)

v. DOMASZEWSKI, A. *'Praefectus equitatus', Römische Mitteilungen* 6 (1891) 163

— *Die Rangordnung des römischen Heeres. 2. durchgesehene Auflage. Einführung, Berichtigungen und Nachträge* von B. Dobson (1967) (RO^2)

DUDLEY, D. R. and WEBSTER, G. *The Roman Conquest of Britain* (1965)

ECK, W. *Senatoren von Vespasian bis Hadrian. Prosopographische Untersuchungen mit Einschluss der Jahres- und Provinzialfasten der Statthalter* (1970)

— 'Zur Verwaltungsgeschichte Italiens unter Mark Aurel. Ein iuridicus per Flaminiam et Transpadanam', *ZPE* 8 (1971) 71

— 'Zum Ende der legio IX Hispana', *Chiron* 2 (1972) 459

— 'Zu den prokonsularen Legationen in der Kaiserzeit', *Ep. Stud.* 9 (1972) 24

— 'Über die prätorischen Prokonsulate in der Kaiserzeit. Eine quellenkritische Überlegung', *Zephyrus* 23/4 (1972/3) 233

— 'Sozialstruktur des römischen Senatorenstandes der hohen Kaiserzeit und statistiche Methode', *Chiron* 3 (1973) 375

—'Beförderungskriterien innerhalb der senatorischen Laufbahn, dargestellt an der Zeit von 69 bis 138 n. Chr.' *ANRW* II 1 (1974) 158

— *Die staatliche Organisation Italiens in der hohen Kaiserzeit* (1979) *(Organisation Italiens)*

EICHHOLZ, D. E. 'How long did Vespasian serve in Britain?', *Britannia* 3 (1973) 158

EVANS, A. J. 'On a coin of a second Carausius, Caesar in Britain in the fifth century', *Num. Chron.*[3] 7 (1887) 191 = *Arch. Camb.*[5] 5 (1888) 152

FITZ, J. 'Legati legionum Pannoniae superioris', *A. Ant. Hung.* 9 (1961) 159

— 'Prosopographica Pannonica', *Epigraphica* 23 (1961) 65

— *Il soggiorno di Caracalla in Pannonia nel 214* (1961)

— 'Legati Augusti pro praetore Pannoniae inferioris', *A. Ant. Hung.* 11 (1963) 245

— *Die Laufbahn der Statthalter in der römischen Provinz Moesia Inferior* (1966) *(Moesia Inferior)*

— 'The governors of Britain', *Alba Regia* 10 (1969) 179

— 'L. Ulpius Marcellus', *Alba Regia* 16 (1978) 369

FRERE, S. S. *Britannia* (2nd edn., 1974)

FREEMAN, E. A. 'The tyrants of Britain, Gaul, and Spain, A.D. 406-411', *Eng. Hist. Rev.* 1 (1886) 53

GILLIAM, J. F. 'The governors of Syria Coele from Severus to Diocletian', *AJP* 79 (1958) 225

GOODBURN, R., and BARTHOLOMEW, P. (edd.) *Aspects of the Notitia Dignitatum* (1976)

GOODCHILD, R. G. 'The Ravenscar inscription', *Ant. Journ.* 32 (1952) 185

GORDON, A. E. *Quintus Veranius Consul A.D. 49* (Univ. of California Pub. in Class. Arch. 2. 5, 1952, 231 ff.)

GORDON, A. E. 'A. Platorius Nepos as *Tribunus Plebis*', *JRS* 48 (1958) 47

GRAHAM, A. J. 'The division of Britain', *JRS* 56 (1966) 92

GRASBY, K. D. 'The age, ancestry, and career of Gordian I', *CQ* N.S. 25 (1975) 123

GRIFFIN, M. T. *Seneca. A philosopher in politics* (1976)

— 'Nero's recall of Suetonius Paullinus', *Scripta Classica Israelica* 3 (1976/7) 138

GROAG, E. 'Patrizier und IIIviri monetales', *Arch.-ep. Mitt. aus Oesterreich-Ungarn* 19 (1896) 146

— 'Zur Ämsterlaufbahn der Nobiles in der Kaiserzeit', *Strena Buliciana* (1924) 143

— 'Zum Konsulat in der Kaiserzeit', *Wiener Studien* 47 (1929) 143

— 'Zu neuen Inschriften', *JÖAI* 29 (1935) Bbl. 177

— *Die römischen Reichsbeamten von Achaia bis auf Diokletian* (1939) (*Achaia*)

GROSSO, F. *La lotta politica al tempo di Commodo* (1964)

— 'Q. Aurelio Polo Terenziano', *Athenaeum* 45 (1967) 346

HABICHT, C. 'Zwei neue Inschriften aus Pergamon', *Istanbuler Mitteilungen* 9/10 (1959/60) 109

HARTLEY, B. R. 'The Roman occupation of Scotland: the evidence of Samian ware', *Britannia* 3 (1972) 1

HASSALL, M. W. C. 'Britain in the *Notitia*', in R. Goodburn and P. Bartholomew (edd.), *Aspects of the Notitia Dignitatum* (1976) 103

— 'The historical background and military units of the Saxon Shore', in D. E. Johnston (ed.), *The Saxon Shore* (1977) 7

HAVERFIELD, F. 'On a milestone of Carausius', *Trans. Cumb. and Westm. Ant. and Arch. Soc.* 13 (1895) 437

HIND, J. G. F. 'The British "provinces" of Valentia and Orcades (Tacitean echoes in Ammianus Marcellinus and Claudian)', *Historia* 24 (1975) 101

HOLDER, A. *Alt-Celtischer Sprachschatz* (1894–1916)

HÜBNER, E. 'Die römischen Legaten von Britannien', *Rhein. Mus.* 12 (1857) 46

JAGENTEUFEL, A. *Die Statthalter der römischen Provinz Dalmatien* (1958) (*Dalmatien*)

JARRETT, M. G. 'Legio II Augusta in Britain', *Arch. Camb.* 113 (1964) 47

— 'Legio XX Valeria Victrix in Britain', ibid. 117 (1968) 77

— (ed.) V. Nash-Williams, *The Roman Frontier in Wales* (2nd edn., 1969)

— *Maryport, Cumbria: A Roman Fort and its Garrison* (1976)

— 'An unnecessary war', *Britannia* 7 (1976) 145

— 'The case of the redundant official', ibid. 9 (1978) 289

—, and MANN, J. C. 'Britain from Agricola to Gallienus', *Bonner Jahrb.* 170 (1970) 178

JOHNSTON, D. E. (ed.) *The Saxon Shore* (1977)

JONES, C. P. 'A new commentary on the Letters of Pliny', *Phoenix* 22 (1968) 111

KAJANTO, I. *The Latin Cognomina* (1965)

KEPPIE, L. J. F. 'Legio VIII Augusta and the Claudian invasion', *Britannia* 2 (1971) 149

KOLBE, H.-G. 'Der cursus honorum eines unbekannten Senators aus Praeneste', *Chiron* 2 (1972) 405

KREILER, B. *Die Statthalter Kleinasiens unter den Flaviern* (1975) (*Statthalter Kleinasiens*)

KUBITSCHEK, W. *Imperium Romanum tributim discriptum* (1889)

MACALINDON, D. 'Entry to the senate in the early empire', *JRS* 47 (1957) 191
MANN, J. C. 'The administration of Roman Britain', *Antiquity* 35 (1961) 316
— 'The northern frontier after A.D. 369', *Glasgow Arch. Journ.* 3 (1974)
— 'What was the *Notitia Dignitatum* for?', in R. Goodburn and P. Bartholomew
(edd.), *Aspects of the Notitia Dignitatum* (1976) 1
— '*Duces* and *comites* in the fourth century', in D. E. Johnston (ed.), *The Saxon
Shore* (1977) 11
— 'The Reculver inscription—a note', ibid. 15
—, and JARRETT, M. G. 'The division of Britain', *JRS* 57 (1967) 61
MORRIS, J. 'The Roman Senate A.D. 69–193' (unpublished London Ph.D. thesis,
1955)
— 'Changing fashions in Roman nomenclature in the early empire', *Listy fil.* 86
(1963) 34
— '*Leges annales* under the principate. I. Legal and constitutional', ibid. 87 (1964)
316
— '*Leges annales* under the principate. II. Political effects', ibid. 88 (1965) 22
MOWAT, R. 'The names of Carausius on the Roman milestone discovered near
Carlisle', *Arch. Ael.*[2] 17 (1895) 281
— 'Les noms de l'empereur Carausius', *Rev. num.*[3] 13 (1895) 129
NESSELHAUF, H. and PETRIKOVITS, H. v. 'Ein Weihaltar für Apollo aus Aachen-
Burtscheid', *Bonner Jahrb.* 167 (1967) 268
OLIVER, J. H. 'Greek and Latin inscriptions', *Hesperia* 10 (1941) 237
OGILVIE, R. M., and RICHMOND, I. A. (edd.) *Cornelii Taciti de Vita Agricolae*
(1967) (*vita Agricolae*)
PALANQUE, J.-R. 'L'empereur Maxime', in *Les Empereurs romains d'Espagne*
(1965) 255
PETERSEN, L. and VIDMAN, L. 'Zur Laufbahn des A. Didius Gallus', *Actes de la
X.e Conférence internationale d'études classiques Eirene Cluj-Napoca 2–7 octobre
1972* (1975) 653
PFLAUM, H.-G. *Le Marbre de Thorigny* (1948)
— *Les Procurateurs équestres sous le haut-empire romain* (1950)
— *Les Carrières procuratoriennes équestres sous le haut-empire romain* (1961)
(*CP*)
— 'Émission au nom des trois empereurs frappée par Carausius', *Rev. num.*[6] 2
(1959–60) 53
— 'Un nouveau gouverneur de la province de Rhétie, proche parent de l'impératrice
Julia Domna, à propos d'une inscription récemment découverte à Augsbourg',
Bayerische Vorgeschichts-Blätter 27 (1962) 82
— 'Augustanius Alpinus Bellicius Sollers, membres de la gens Cassia', *Archivo es-
pañol de Arqueología* 39 (1966) 5
— *Les Fastes de la province de Narbonnaise* (*Gallia*, Supp. 30, 1978)
PISO, I. 'Zur Laufbahn des Calpurnius Julianus', *Römische Oesterreich* 3 (1975) 178
— 'Carrières sénatoriales (1)', *Revue roumaine d'histoire* 15 (1976) 465
POLOTSKY, H. J. 'The Greek papyri from the Cave of the Letters', *Israel Explora-
tion Journal* 12 (1962) 258
REIDINGER, W. *Die Statthalter des ungeteilten Pannonien und Oberpannoniens
von Augustus bis Diokletian* (1956) (*Pannonien*)

RÉMY, B. 'La carrière de Q. Aradius Rufinus Optatus Aelianus', *Historia* 25 (1976) 458

RICHMOND, I. A. 'The Romans in Redesdale', *Northumberland County History* 15 (1940) 65

— 'A new building-inscription from the Saxon Shore fort at Reculver, Kent', *Ant. Journ.* 41 (1961) 224

RITTERLING, E. 'Die Statthalter der pannonischen Provinzen', *Arch.-ep. Mitt. aus Oesterreich-Ungarn* 20 (1897) 1

— 'Zu zwei griechischen Inschriften römischer Verwaltungsbeamten', *JÖAI* 10 (1907) 299

— 'Sextus Julius Frontinus am Niederrhein?', *Bonner Jahrb.* 133 (1928) 48

— *Fasti des römischen Deutschland unter dem Prinzipat, mit Beiträgen von E. Groag*, ed. E. Stein (1932) (*FRD*)

ROXAN, M. M. *Roman Military Diplomas 1954-1977* (1978)

— 'A note on *CIL* XVI 130 and the review in *JRS* 28 (1938) by Eric Birley', *Britannia* 11 (1980) 335

SCHNEIDER, A. M. 'Die römischen und byzantinischen Denkmäler in Iznik-Nicaea', *Istanbuler Forschungen* 16 (1943) 1

SCHULZE, W. *Zur Geschichte lateinischer Eigennamen* (1904)

SCHUMACHER, L. *Prosopographische Untersuchungen zur Besetzung der vier hohen römischen Priesterkollegien im Zeitalter der Antonine und der Severer (96-235 n. Chr.)* (1973) (*Priesterkollegien*)

— 'Propinquo et Ambibulo cos. Methodische Überlegungen zur Datierung eines Ziegelstempels', *ZPE* 24 (1977) 155

SHERWIN-WHITE, A. N. *A Historical and Social Commentary on the Letters of Pliny* (1966) (*Letters of Pliny*)

SHIEL, N. *The Episode of Carausius and Allectus* (1977)

SMALLWOOD, E. M. *Documents Illustrating the Principates of Nerva, Trajan and Hadrian* (1966) (Smallwood II)

— *Documents Illustrating the principates of Gaius, Claudius and Nero* (1967) (Smallwood I)

STEIN, A. 'Zwei lykische Inschriften', *Arch.-ep. Mitt. aus Oesterreich-Ungarn* 19 (1896) 147

— *Römische Reichsbeamte der Provinz Thracia* (1920) (*Thracia*)

— *Die Legaten von Moesien* (1940) (*Moesien*)

— *Die Reichsbeamte von Dazien* (1955) (*Dazien*)

STEVENS, C. E. 'Magnus Maximus in British history', *Études celtiques* 3 (1938) 86

— 'The British sections of the *Notitia Dignitatum*', *Arch. Journ.* 97 (1940) 125

— 'The will of Q. Veranius', *CR* 1 (1951) 4

— 'Marcus, Gratian, Constantine', *Athenaeum* 35 (1957) 316

— *The Building of Hadrian's Wall* (1966)

SYME, R. 'M. Vinicius, *cos.* 19 B.C.', *CQ* 27 (1933) 142

— *The Roman Revolution* (1939)

— 'Antonine relatives: Ceionii and Vettuleni', *Athenaeum* 35 (1957) 306

— 'The origin of the Veranii', *CQ* N.S. (1957) 123

— review of W. Reidinger, *Pannonien*, *Gnomon* 29 (1957) 515 = *Danubian Papers* 177

SYME, R. 'The jurist Neratius Priscus', *Hermes* 85 (1957) 480
— *Tacitus* (1958)
— 'Consulates in absence', *JRS* 48 (1958) 1
— Review of A. Jagenteufel, *Dalmatia*, *Gnomon* 31 (1959) 510 = *Danubian Papers* 192
— 'Pliny's less successful friends', *Historia* 9 (1960) 362
— 'Proconsuls d'Afrique sous Antonin le Pieux', *REA* 61 (1959) 310
— 'Governors of Pannonia inferior', *Historia* 14 (1965) 342 = *Danubian Papers* 225
— 'Les proconsuls d'Afrique sous Hadrien', *REA* 67 (1965) 342
— *Ammianus and the Historia Augusta* (1968)
— 'Pliny the procurator', *Harv. Stud. Class. Phil.* 73 (1968) 201
— 'People in Pliny', *JRS* 58 (1968) 135
— *Ten Studies in Tacitus* (1970)
— *Danubian Papers* (1971)
— *Emperors and Biography* (1971)
— 'The enigmatic Sospes', *JRS* 67 (1977) 38
TAYLOR, L. R. 'Trebula Suffenas and the Plautii Silvani', *Mem. Amer. Acad. Rome* 24 (1956) 9
THOMASSON, B. E. *Die Statthalter der römischen Provinzen Nordafrikas* I–II (1960) (*Statthalter Nordafrikas*)
— 'The one-legion provinces of the Roman empire during the principate', *Opuscula Romana* 9 (1973) 61
THOMPSON, E. A. 'Britain AD 406–410', *Britannia* 9 (1978) 303
TOMLIN, R. 'The date of the "barbarian conspiracy"', *Britannia* 5 (1974) 303
TORELLI, M. 'The *cursus honorum* of M. Hirrius Fronto Neratius Pansa', *JRS* 58 (1968) 170
WARD PERKINS, J. B. 'The career of Sex. Julius Frontinus', *CQ* 31 (1937) 102

Index

1. *Persons*

Individuals given biographical entries in part II are listed in capitals. The first page reference in these cases is to the main entry; details there discussed are not listed separately, nor are the individual items which are dealt with in part III. Most persons are listed by *gentilicium*, except for emperors, persons from after *c.*300, and a few cases, such as Macro, Perennis, Sejanus, where only the *cognomen* has been used. Entries for emperors are somewhat selective, and most authors are omitted (but see Index 3), except where they have been mentioned in connection with their public service.

Abascantus, *ab epistulis*, 3 n.
ACCENNA HELVIUS AGRIPPA, M., *tr. lat.*, 279; 416 ff.; iterated *tr.*, 10
Accenna Saturninus, M., 279
Acilii Glabriones, consulships of, 142 n.
Acilius Attianus, P., *praef. praet.*, 365
Acilius Aviola, M'. (*cos. ord.* 54), *curator aquarum*, 27 n.
Aconius Statura, L., 281 n.
Ael. Maximilla, wife of freedman proc., 305
Aelian, visited Julius Frontinus, 69
Aelius Aelianus Archelaus Marcus, P., 168 n.
Aelius Aurelius Theo, M. (*cos. a. inc.*), iterated *tr.*, 10
Aelius Gracilis, Spanish senator, 292
Aelius Hadrianus, *see* HADRIAN
Aelius Lamia, L. (*cos. ord.* 3), consular command, 6
Aelius Optatus, *leg. leg.*, 176 n.
Aelius Paullus, P., high-priest of Asia, 141
Aelius Valens, P., governor of Sardinia, 299
Aemilia Lepida, descendant of Augustus, 356
AEM[ILIAN]US, gov. Brit. inf., 199, 429
Aemilianus, *praeses* of Tarraconensis, 199 n.
Aemilii, in Spain, 243 n.
Aemilius Aemilianus, M., emperor, 199 n.
Aemilius Berenicianus Maximus, C. (*cos. a. inc.*), iterated *tr.*, 10
Aemilius Crispinus, equest. officer, 198
Aemilius Fronto, senator, 258 n.
Aemilius Juncus, L. (*cos.* 127), 106
AEMILIUS KARUS, L. (*cos.* 144?), *tr. lat.*, 274 f.; 416 ff.; *censitor*, 27 n.; consular command, 7; iterated *tr.*, 10; military service, 18, 220

Aemilius Karus, L. (*cos. a. inc.*), 275
Aemilius Laetus, Q., *praef. praet.*, 146, 262
Aemilius Lepidus, M. (*cos. ord.* 6), *procos. Asiae*, 46
AEMILIUS NASO FABULLINUS, L., *tr. lat.*, 279 f.; 416 ff.
Aemilius Papus, M., friend of Hadrian, 103, 243
AEMILIUS PAPUS, M. *cet.* (*cos.* 136?), 242 ff.; family, 116 n.; origin and career, 409 ff.; cf. 7, 431
Aemilius Salvianus, equest. officer, 160
Aëtius, death of, 352 n.
Agricola, St, church of, 374
AGRICOLA, *see* Julius, Calpurnius
Agrippa II, M. Julius, Jewish king, 210 n.
Agrippina, the younger, 40, 42 n., 53, 228, 356, 358, 364
Aiacius Modestus Crescentianus, Q. (*cos. II ord.* 228), 175 n.
Alaric, Visigoth, 375 n.
Albucia Candida, wife of proc., 295
Albucius Silus, C., *rhetor*, 295
Alexander of Abonuteichus, charlatan, 249
ALFENUS SENECIO, L. (*cos. a. inc.*), gov. Brit., 157 ff.; 156, 163, 169, 170, 203, 204, 205, 206, 208, 254 n., 266, 279, 420; gov. Syria Coele, 29 n., 309, 390, 393; origin and career, 377 ff.; titulature 397, 427, 429 ff.
Alfenus Senecio, L., proc., 158
Alfius Maximus, *puer senatorius*, 193 n.
ALLECTUS, ruler of Britain, 314 f.; 200, 312 f., 316, 370
Alpinius Montanus, equest. officer, 289

ALYPIUS, *vicarius* of Brit., 322 ff.; 423

Anastasia, daughter of Valens, 327 n.

Androcles, friend of Libanius, 329 n.

Anicius Faustus, Q. (*cos.* 198?), family, 151 n.; gov. Numidia, 297 n.

ANINIUS SEXTIUS FLORENTINUS, L., *leg. leg.*, 327 ff.; 220; gov. Arabia, 241 n.; origin and career, 409 ff.; titul. 431

Annia Regilla, senator's wife, 92

Annianus, iterated *tr.*, 10

Annius Atilius Bradua, Ap. (*cos. ord.* 160), 94

ANNIUS FABIANUS, L. (*cos.* 141?), *tr. lat.*, 272 f.; 416 ff.; gov. Dacia sup., 117 n.

Annius Fabianus, *eq. R.*, 273

Annius Fabianus, L. (*cos. ord.* 201), 273

Annius Gallus, Ap. (*cos. a. inc.*), command in Rhineland, 68

Annius Gallus, Ap. (*cos. ord.* 108), 92

Annius Italicus, L. (*cos. a. inc.*), cons. command, 7

Annius Libo, M. (*cos. ord.* 128), 84

Annius Libo, M. (*cos.* 161), gov. Syria, 120, 255

Annius Verus, M. (*cos. III ord.* 126), 240

Annius Vinicianus (*cos. a. inc.*), conspirator, 364

Annius Vinicianus, *pro leg. leg.*, 19

ANTISTIUS ADVENTUS *cet.*, Q. (*cos.* 167?), gov. Brit. 129 ff.; 203, 277; gov. Germ. inf., 31; iterated legionary command, 18; *leg. leg.* II Adiut., 256 n.; origin and career, 377 ff.; *praetentura* command, 144 n.; titul., 427, 430

Antistius Agathopus, Q., freedman, 130

Antistius Asiaticus, L., *praef. montis Beren.*, 130 n.

Antistius Asiaticus, Q., of Thibilis, 130 n.

Antistius Burrus, L. (*cos. ord.* 181), son-in-law of M. Aurelius, 131 f.; fall of, 145 n.

Antistius Burrus Adventus, L., *salius*, 131 n.

Antistius Mundicius Burrus, L., 132 n.

ANTISTIUS RUSTICUS, L. (*cos.* 90), *tr. lat.*, 269 f.; 416 ff.; cons. command, 7; *leg. leg.* VIII Aug., 86 n.; wife, 249 n.

Antistius Thallus, A., brickmaker, 105 n.

Antistius Vetus, L. (*cos. ord.* 56), *procos. Asiae*, 75 n.

ANTIUS CRESCENS CALPURNIANUS, M., *iurid.* Brit., 137 ff.; 142 n.; origin and career, 404 ff.; titul., 427

Antius Gratillianus, M., *q.* of Sicily, 140

Antonia, d. of Claudius, 356, 359

Antoninus Aquila, *rhetor*, 185 n.

Antoninus Pius, emperor, and Britain, 100, 399; careers under, 18, 29, 240, 250, 273, 295; conservatism, 125; death, 120, 143; gov. Brit. under, 112-23, 203; *leg. leg.*, 250-7; *q. Aug.* not found after, 13 n.; s.-in-law, 40 n.

Antonius, M., the Triumvir, alleged ancestor of Gordian I, 185 n.; persons enfranchised by, 186

Antonius Antius Lupus, M., victim of Commodus, 140; predeceased by wife, 186 n.

Antonius Cassius Cassianus, Q. (*cos. a. inc.*), 247 n.

Antonius Gordianus, *see* GORDIAN

ANTONIUS ISAURICUS, Q. (*cos. c.* 143), *leg. leg.*, 247; origin and career, 408 f.; titul. 432

Antonius Naso, L., *primipilaris*, 219 n.

Antonius Primus, M., general, 76

Antonius Rufus, A. (*cos.* 45), 41 n.

Antonius Saturninus, L. (*cos. a. inc.*), rebel, 82

Antonius Zeno, M. (*cos.* 148), 186 n.

-ANUS, gov. Brit., 121 ff.; 117 f.

'Appius' Bradua, M., *see* ATILIUS METILIUS BRADUA

Apronia, murdered by husband, 38 n.

Apronius, L. (*cos.* 8), cons. command of, 6, 361 n.

Aquila, sophist, 185 n.

Aquila Romanus, *rhetor*, 185 n.

'Aquillius' Bradua, *see* ATILIUS METILIUS BRADUA

Aquillius Florus, L., iterated *q.* of, 282 n.

Aradii Rufini, of Bulla, 175 n.

Aradius Rufinus Optatus Aelianus, Q. (*cos. a. inc.*), career of, 34, 174 f.; praet. provs. of, 22 n.

Aristo, philosopher, 74

Armenius Peregrinus, L. (*pr.* 213), family of, 153

Arpagius Lupus, *v.c.*, 201 n.

Arrecinus Clemens, *praef. praet.*, 55

Arria, widow of Thrasea, 86

Arria Magia Secundilla, wife of former *tr. lat.*, 281

Arrian (L. Flavius Arrianus, *cos. a. inc.*), gov. Cappadocia, 215, 272; and Syria (?), 30 n.

Arrius Antoninus, C. (*cos. c.* 173), not *leg. leg.*, 29 n.; cons. commands, 7, 31 n.; fall of, 145 n.; gov. Dalmatia, 154 n.

Arruntius, M. (*cos.* 66), 63

Arruntius Camillus Scribonianus, L. (*cos. ord.* 32), rebel, 39, 354, 359, 364 n.

ARRUNTIUS FRUGI, M., *censit.* in Brit., 301 f.

Arrius Cornelius Proculus, Cn., 243 n.

Artemidorus, philosopher, 9 n.

Arulenus Rusticus, (*tr. pl.* 66), 75 n.

ASCLEPIODOTUS, JULIUS (*cos. ord.* 292), *praef. praet.*, in Brit., 370 f.; 315

Asellius Aemilianus (*cos. a. inc.*), *procos. Asiae*, 133 f., 149; gov. Syria, 147 n., rel. of Clodius Albinus, 149

Atilius Bradua, C. of Libarna, 92 n.

ATILIUS METILIUS BRADUA, M. (*cos. ord.* 108), gov. Brit., 92 ff.; 106 n., 201; origin and career, 377 ff.; titul. 396, 426; uncle (?), 85

Atilius Postumus Bradua, M. (*cos. a. inc.*), *procos. Asiae*, 92

Atilius Rufus, T. (*cos. a. inc.*), gov. Syria, 28 n.

Atilius Rufus Titianus, T. (*cos. ord.* 127), rebel, 116

Atrius Clonius, Q. (*cos. a. inc.*), gov. Thrace, 174 n.

Attidius Cornelianus, L. (*cos.* 151), gov. Syria, 30 n.

Attius Macro, L., iterated leg. command (?), 18

Aufidius, Cn. (*tr. pl.* 170 BC (?)), 306

Aufidius Fronto, M. (*cos. ord.* 199), and *procos.*, 183 n.

AUFIDIUS PANTHERA, L., *praef. class. Brit.*, 306; 422

Aufidius Victorinus, C. (*cos. II ord.* 183), Chattan campaign, 128 n.; death, 138; *procos. Africae*, 121 n.

Augustus, emperor, careers under, 198, 359, 361, 379; and consulship, 24; created new posts, 16 n., 33; favoured Plautii, 37 f.; and *leges annales*, 3 f.; praetorian provs., 21

Aurelian, emperor, mint-workers revolt against, 315; recovered west, 180, 199

Aurelius, Marcus, emperor, *adlecti* by, 24 n.; ancestor, 357; careers under, 6 n., 29 n., 131, 154 n., 162, 264; changed status of provs., 17 n., 22, 26 n., 28, 132 f., 134; *comites* of, 32, 121; created new posts, 33; friend, 125; gov. Brit. under, 121-35; and Italian *iuridici*, 23; *leg. leg.* under, 256-9; wars, 20 n., 109, 120, 121, 125, 126, 129 n., 130, 131, 143, 144, 249 n., 274, 344, 384

Aurelius Agaclytus, L., married d. of M. Aurelius, 132 n.

AURELIUS ARPAGIUS, *praeses* in northern Brit., 200 f.; 319; 402 f.; titul. 428, 430

Aurelius Cotta Maximus Messalinus, M., 262 n.

Aurelius Heraclitus, M., proc., 296

AURELIUS AUG. LIB. MARCIO, M., freedman proc. Brit. 304 f.

AURELIUS POLUS TERENTIANUS, Q. (*cos. a. inc.*), *leg. leg.*, 261 ff.; 18, 126 n.; iterated leg. command, 18; origin and career, 409 ff.; titul. 432

Aurelius Quietus, T. (*cos. c.* 82), gov. Lycia-Pamph., 234

Aurelius Quirinus, equest. officer, 197

Aurelius Septimius Heraclitus, *praef. Aeg.*, 296

Aurellius, spelling of, 207

Avidii, of Faventia, 85

Avidius Cassius, C. (*cos.* 166?), consulship of, 20 n.

Avidius Nigrinus, C. (*cos.* 110), killed by Hadrian, 87

AVIDIUS QUIETUS, T. (*cos.* 93), gov. Brit., 85 ff.; 83; origin and career, 378 ff.

Baebius Massa, trial of, 433 n.

BAIENUS BLASSIANUS, Q., *praef. class. Brit.*, 307 f., 422

Barea Soranus, Q. Marcius (*cos. a. inc.*), friend of Vespasian, 361 n.; *procos. Asiae*, 75 n.

Bar-Kokhba, Jewish leader, 107

Bellicius Sollers, son of proc. Brit., 389 ff.

Bolana Secunda, of Milan, 62

Bolanus, M., friend of Cicero, 62 n.

Boudicca, Queen, 40, 56, 67, 67, 74, 269, 288, 389, 394, 419, 420

Britannicus Caesar, friend of, 257; name of, 78 n.; and Titus, 227

Brocchus (*tr. pl.* 41), 52

Bruttii Praesentes, consulships of, 142 n.

Bruttius Praesens, C. (*cos. II ord.* 139), friend of Hadrian, 5 n., 102; governor of Syria (?), 32 n.; *IIIvir cap.*, 5 n.

'Bulchobaudes', *see* FULLOFAUDES

Burrus, Sex. Afranius, *praef. praet.*, 74

BURBULEIUS OPTATUS, L. (*cos. a. inc.*), *tr. lat.*, 271 f.; 416 ff.; in Syria, 30 and n.; *IIIvir cap.*, 5 n.

Caecilius Capella, at Byzantium, 264

Caecilius Classicus, trial of, 433

Caecilius Marcellus, Q. (*cos. a. inc.*), 434

Caecilius Marcellus Dentilianus, Q. (*cos.* 167), 434

Caecilius Rufinus Crepereianus, Q. (*cos. a. inc.*), gov. Pannonia inf., 11

Caecilius Rufinus Marianus, Q., *tr. lat.* of IV Fl., 11

Caecina Largus, C. (*cos. ord.* 42), 41 n.

Caelia Procilla, senator's wife, 280

Caelius Calvinus (*cos. a. inc.*), gov. Cappadocia, 264 n.

Caelius Flavianus, Q., patron of Canusium, 280

CAELIUS FLAVIUS PROCULUS, M., *tr. lat.*, 280; 416 ff.

Caenis, Antonia, mistress of Vespasian, 3 n.

Caerellia Germanilla, d. of gov. Brit., 132, 135 n.

CAERELLIUS (*cos. a. inc.*), gov. Brit., 132 ff.; 126 n.; origin and career, 377 ff.; praetorian provs. of, 22 n.

Caerellius Marcianus, son of above, 132, 134, 135 n.

Caerellius Priscus, *pr.* under M. Aurelius, 134

Caerellius Sabinus, C., gov. Raetia, 134
Caesar, Julius, conquest of Gaul, 314; quaestors, 12 n.
Caesarius, brother of ALYPIUS, 325
Caesennius Paetus, L. Junius (*cos. ord.* 61), in Cappadocia, 136; gov. Syria, 30
Caesennius Silvanus, kinsman of Suetonius, 88
Caesennius Servilius Isauricus, 247 n.
Caesennius Sospes, L. (*cos.* 114), in Cappadocia-Galatia, 404; *praef. frum. dandi*, 23 n.
Caesernius Statianus *cet.*, T. (*cos.* 141), consular command, 7
Caesius Aper, C., of Sentinum, 66 n.
CAESIUS NASICA, *leg. leg.*, 231; 49; 66; origin, 409; titul. 431
Caesius Propertianus, Sex., patron of Mevania, 66 n.
Caesius Sabinus, C., of Sassina, 66 n.
Caesonius Macer Rufinianus, C., *IIIvir cap.*, 5 n.
Caesonius Ovinius . . . Bassus, L. (*cos. a. inc.*), *IIIvir cap.*, 5 n.
Caligula, emperor, careers under, 51, 73 f.; *leg. III Aug.*, 22; murder of, 52, 59, 361, 363, 364; sister, 363 f.
Calpurnia Fidiana Aemiliana, senator's wife, 175 n.
Calpurnia Marcella, 105
CALPURNIUS AGRICOLA, SEX. (*cos.* 154?), gov. Brit., 127 ff.; 122, 123 n., 126 n., 151 n., 144, 151 n., 203; and Dacia, 28 n.; origin and career, 377 ff.
Calpurnius Crassus, exile, 357
Calpurnius Fidus Aemilianus, L., of Utica, 258
Calpurnius Flaccus, friend of Pliny, 237
CALPURNIUS FLACCUS, C. (*cos. c.* 124), *leg. leg.*, 237; origin and career, 409 ff.
Calpurnius Flaccus, C., *flamen* in Spain, 237
Calpurnius Julianus, possible gov. Dacia sup., 123, 133 n., 395 n.
Calpurnius Julianus, Sex., friend of Fronto, 127, 151 n.
Calpurnius Piso, Cn. (*cos.* 7 BC), consular command, 6; trial of, 51
Calpurnius Proculus, L., *tr.* of XIII Gem., 11
Calpurnius Proculus, P. (*cos. a. inc.*), governor of Dacia sup., 11
CALPURNIUS . . . RUFILIANUS, AEMILIANUS, *leg. leg.*, 258; origin, 408 f.; titul., 432
Calpurnius Salvianus, of Corduba, 105 n.
Calvina, 42
Calvisii Rusones, 193
CALVISIUS RU[FUS?], gov. Brit. inf., 193 f.; titul. 430
Calvisius Rufus, C., friend of Pliny, 194

Calvisius Ruso Julius Frontinus, P. (*cos.* 79), consular command, 6, 32 n., 194 n.; and Frontinus, 72
Calvisius Sabinus, C. (*cos. ord.* 26), governor of Pannonia, 39, 51 n.
Camillus, M. Furius, elder Theodosius compared to, 339 n.
Camurius Clemens, C., proc., 255
Camurius Numisius Junior, *see* Numisius Junior
Caracalla, emperor, careers under, 154, 184, 299; 369; German wars, 206, 369; gov. Brit. under, 164–8, 205 f.; of Brit. inf. 181–6; provincial boundaries changed, 17 17 n., 18, 22, 26 n., 28, 170, 172
Caratacus, British leader, 41, 43, 44
CARAUSIUS, M. AUR. MAUS., ruler of Brit., 309 ff.; 180, 315, 316, 343 f.
'Carausius II', 314 n.
Carinus, emperor, became Britannicus, 312 n.
CARISTANIUS FRONTO, C. (*cos.* 90), *leg. leg.*, 233 f.; adlected, 211; origin and career, 409 ff.; titul. 431
Caristanius Fronto, son of above, 234
Caristanius Julianus, C., *procos. Achaiae*, 234
Caristanius Fronto Caesianus Julius, C., 234
Caristanius Paulinus, 234
Carosa, d. of Valens, 327 n.
Cartimandua, Queen, 48, 64
CASSIUS AGRIPPI F. (?), *leg. leg.*, 241 f.; origin and career, 409 ff.; titul. 431
Cassius Apollinaris, M. (*cos.* 150), gov. Syria, 30 n.
Cassius Apronianus (*cos.* 185?), gov. Dalmatia, 166 n.
Cassius Dexter, P., *tr. lat.* of III Aug., 11
Cassius Dio Cocceianus (*cos. II ord.* 229), the historian, consular provs of, 185; family, 242; gov. Dalmatia, 166 n.; *procos. Africae*, 183 n.
Cassius Marcellinus (*cos. a. inc.*), gov. Pannonia inf., 11
Cassius Pius Marcellinus, *tr.* of II Ad., 11; identification of, 287 n.; in Pannonia inf., 31
Cassius Secundus, P. (*cos.* 138), *leg. leg.* III Aug., 11
Catilii Severi, 193 n.
Catilius Severus, L. (*cos.* 110), gov. Syria, 30 n.
Catius Celer, L. (*cos. a. inc.*), gov. Thrace, 174 n.
Catonius Justus, *praef. praet.*, 359 f.
Caucidia Tertulla, 92 n.
Caunia Firmina, 261 n.
Caunius Priscus, T. (*cos. a. inc.*), *leg. leg.* III Aug. (?), 261, 413
Ceionii Albini, 149
Ceionii Commodi, consulships of, 142 n.

Ceionius Commodus, L. (*cos. ord.* 136), brickworks of, 105 n.; consulship, 142 n.; heir of Hadrian, 87

Celer, senator, 38

Censor, consul in Gallic empire, 200

Cerellius Apollinaris, Q., *praef. vigil.*, 297 n.

Cerellius Macrinus, victim of Severus, 134

Cestii, LL., 259

Cestius Gallus, C. (*cos.* 35), 259

Cestius Gallus, C. (*cos.* 42), 259; legate of Syria, 60 n.

CESTIUS GALLUS CERRINIUS JUSTUS *cet.*, L., *leg. leg.*, 258 f., 285; origin and career, 409 ff.; titul. 432

Cestius Gallus Varenianus *cet.*, L., patron of Gaulus, 259

Charietto, *comes* in Germany, 339 n.

CHRYSANTHUS, *vicarius* of Brit., 326 f., 423

CIVILIS, *vicarius* of Brit., 325, 337, 423

Civilis, Julius, rebel, 64 f.

Claudia Marcellina, d.-in-law of proc., 289 f.

Claudia Regilla, senator's wife, 186 n.

Claudii Apellini, of Perge, 195

Claudii Nerones, 60

Claudii Pulchri, 38 n., 176

Claudius, emperor, accession of, 52, 227, 364; aqueduct, 47; alphabet, 225; Britannicus, 78 n.; careers under, 52, 60 n., 229, 401; *comites*, 41, 55, 287, 354 ff.; consulships of, 42 n., 227; friends, 38, 57; gov. Brit. under, 37–49; invasion of Brit. by, 37 ff., 209, 215, 222 ff., 387, 354 ff.; *leg. leg.* under, 222–31; quaestor of, 5, 6 n., 354; triumph, 78 f.

Claudius Alpinus, equest. officer, 290 n.

Claudius Alpinus, Ti., son of proc. 290 f.

CLAUDIUS APELLINUS, gov. Brit. inf., 195 f.; origin 403; titul. 428, 429

Claudius Attalus Paterculianus, Ti., supporter of Niger, 184 n.

Claudius Atticus Herodes, *see* Herodes Atticus

Claudius Augustanus, centurion, 291 n.

CLAUDIUS AUGUSTANUS, TI., proc. Brit., 289 ff.; origin and titul. 420 f.

Claudius Caecus, Ap. (censor 312 BC), 37 n.

Claudius Candidus, Ti. (*cos. a. inc.*), *adlectus*, 158 n.

CLAUDIUS CHARAX, A. (*cos.* 147), *leg. leg.*, 250 f.; early career unknown, 5 n.; possible adlection, 15 n.; origin and career 409 ff.; titul. 432

Claudius Claudianus, Ti. (*cos. c.* 199), iterated legionary command, 19

CLAUDIUS COGIDUBNUS, TI., *rex magnus* (?), 208 ff.; 40 n., 212, 404

Claudius Fronto, M. (*cos.* 165?), consular command, 7, 129 n.; iterated legionary command, 19; gov. Moesia sup. 133n.; monument of, 34 n.; recruiting mission, 121 n.

Claudius Gallus (*cos. a. inc.*), *adlectus?*, 158 n.; children's names, 134 n.

Claudius Gordianus, Ti. (*cos. a. inc.*), 185

CLAUDIUS HIERONYMIANUS (*cos. a. inc.*), *leg. leg.*, 263 ff.; origin and career 408 ff.; titul. 432

Claudius Julianus, Ti. (*cos.* 154?), 127 f.

Claudius Maximus (*cos. a. inc.*), gov. Pannonia sup., 125

Claudius Menander, M., equest. officer, 187 n.

Claudius Modestus, gov. Arabia, 130 n.

Claudius Paulinus, of Cibyra, 190

CLAUDIUS PAULINUS, TI., gov. Brit. inf., 187 ff.; 169; 191, 196 n.; *leg. leg.* II Aug., 266, 413 ff.; origin and career, 403, 409 ff.; titul. 428, 429, 430, 432

Claudius Pompeianus, Ti. (*cos. II ord.* 173), 143, 144

CLAUDIUS QUARTINUS, TI. (*cos.* 130), poss. gov. Brit., 110 ff., iterated legionary command, 19; gov. Germania sup. 390 n.

Claudius Saethida Caelianus, Ti., senator, quaestorship of, 14 n.

Claudius Severus, C. (*cos.* 112), gov. Arabia, 290 n.

Claudius Val. Menander, of Paros, 187 n.

CLAUDIUS XENOPHON, gov. Brit. inf., 191 f.; 188 n., 193; origin 403 f.; titul. 428, 430

Claudius Xenophon, philosopher, 192

Claudius Xenophon, T., proc., 192

Claudius Xenophon, Ti., of Cos, 192

Cleander, M. Aurelius, imperial freedman, bribery under, 3 n., 260 n.

CLODIUS ALBINUS, D. (*cos. II ord.* 194), gov. Brit., emperor, 146 ff.; 153, 296, 297; death of, 169 f.; defeated Virius Lupus, 150; origin and career, 377 ff.

Clodius Celsinus, alleged kinsman of preceding, 149

Clodius Crispinus, C. (*cos. ord.* 113), perhaps son of Vettius Bolanus, 65 n.

Clodius Marcellinus, iterated *tr.*, 10

Clodius Pulcher, P. (*tr. pl.* 58 BC), 38 n.

Clodius Saturninus Fidus, T. (*cos. c.* 237), gov. Thrace, 174 n.

Cluvius Maximus, P. (*cos.* 152), consular command, 7; consulship, 119 n.

Cluvius Rufus, 62

Cocceius Nerva, M., father of Nerva, 54 n.

COCCEIUS NIGRINUS, M., proc. Brit., 299; 419 ff.

COIEDIUS CANDIDUS, L., *q.* of Claudius in Britain (?), 354; 5, 6 n.

Commodus, emperor, Britain invaded under, 133, 135 ff., 140, 142, 405; Britannicus, 139, 142, 260; gov. Brit. under, 135–48, 165; *leg. leg.* under, 260–3; and senate, 34; victims of, 132, 140

Constans, emperor, British expedition of, 319, 332; as Caesar, 321

Constantine I, the Great, emperor, army changes under, 319; Britannicus, 319 n., *cur. aed. sac.* under, 329; provincial govs under, 35; rescript of, 321

Constantine II, emperor, as Caesar, 321

Constantine III, usurper, 328, 342, 343; a general of, 353; withdrew troops from Brit., 375

Constantius I Chlorus, emperor, Brit. recovered by, 200, 315, 316, 370; captured Boulogne, 313; and names of Brit. provs, 316 f.

Constantius II, emperor, distinction between civil and military under, 35; and Julian, 372; *vicarii* of Brit. under, 372

Consus, rare *cognomen*, 257 n.

Corbulo, *see* Domitius Corbulo

Corellia Hispulla, 91

Corellius Pansa (*cos. ord.* 122), 91

Corellius Rufus, friend of Pliny, 91

Cornelia Valentina Tucciana, of Thamugadi, 196 n.

Cornelius . . .er, gov. Cilicia, 257 n.

[Cornelius Dola] bella Verania[nus], descendant of Q. Veranius?, 54 n.

Cornelius Flaccus, *leg. leg.*, 255

Cornelius Flaccus . . .Noricus Numisius . . ., Q., 255

Cornelius Fuscus, later *praef. praet.*, 76

Cornelius Nigrinus Curiatius Maternus, M. (*cos. c.* 83), *leg. leg.* VIII Aug., 86 n.

CORNELIUS PRISCIANUS, possible gov. Brit.?, 116

Cornelius Priscianus, advocate, 116 n.

Cornelius Priscus, L. (*cos. c.* 104), 116

Cornelius Proculus, Q., names of, 271 n.

CORNELIUS PUSIO ANNIUS MESSALLA, L. (*cos. a. inc.*), *tr. lat.*, 268; 416 ff.

Cornelius Restitutus *cet.*, C., of Saguntum, 240 n.

Cornificia, d. of M. Aurelius, 300

Cornutus, *procos. Africae*, 90 n.

Cornutus Tertullus, C. Julius (*cos.* 100), friend of Pliny, gov. Pontus-Bithynia, 272 n.; *procos. Africae?*, 90 n.

Cossonius Gallus, L., iterated legionary command, 19

Cotys, ruler of Bosporus, 48, 49

Curtius Justus, agrarian writer, 253

CURTIUS JUSTUS, C. (*cos. c.* 150), *leg. leg.*, 251 ff.; consular command of, 7, 250; gov. Dacia sup. 11, 117 n.; origin and career, 409 ff.; *sevir*, 14 n.; titul. 432

Curtius Rufinus, C., son of preceding, father, 173 n.; *tr.* of XIII Gem., 11, 253

Curtius Rufus (*cos. a. inc.*), shameful origin, 253

Curio, C. Scribonius (*cos.* 76 BC), elder Theodosius compared to, 339 n.

Cutia Prisca, mother of M. Aemilius Papus, 243

'Dasumius the testator', 274 n.

Dasumius Rusticus, P. (*cos. ord.* 119), 239

Dasumius Tullius Tuscus, L. (*cos.* 152), consular command, 6; no legionary command, 29 n.; *tr.* of IV Fl., 11

DECIANUS CATUS, proc. Brit., 288; 67, 420

Decidius Domitianus, T., proc., 75 n.

Decius, emperor, 105 n., 177 n.

DESIDERIUS, *vicarius*, 326

Desticia Sallustia Plotina, of Concordia, 178

DESTICIUS JUBA (*cos. a. inc.*), gov. Brit. sup., 178, 267; origin, 402; titul., 428, 430

Desticius Sallustius Juba, of Concordia, 178

Desticius Severus, T., proc., 178

Didia, 45 n.

Didia Galla, 45 n.

DIDIUS GALLUS, A. (*cos.* 39), gov. Brit., 44 ff.; 54, 61, 67, 229, 231, 365; canvassed for post, 2, 44, 53; *curator aquarum*, 27 n.; inscription of, 93 n.; origin and career, 378 ff.

Didius Julianus, M. (*cos.* 175), emperor, consular command, 7, 31 n.; consulship, 144; gov. Belgica, 163 n.; links with Clodius Albinus; quaestorship, 13 n.

DIDIUS MARINUS, L., junior proc. in Brit., 300

Didius Postumus, A., *procos. Cypri*, 45

Didius Rufus, C. Pomponius Gallus, *procos. Cret. et Cyren.*, 49

Diocletian, emperor, abdication of, 200 f.; Britannicus, 312; *praeses* of northern Brit. under, 200 f.; provincial reorganisation, 178 f.; *praef. praet.* under, 371

Dolabella, 49 n.

Domitia Calvina, 42 n.

Domitia Decidiana, w. of Julius Agricola, 75

Domitian, emperor, accession of, 80; Athens under, 60; books burnt under, 4; careers under, 4 n., 86 n., 89, 92, 98, 102, 135, 211, 223 f., 234 f.; consuls under, 25 n., 88, 230; Germanicus, 78; govs. of Brit. under, 77–85; *leg. leg.* under, 234 f.; murder of, 86, 236; victims of, 82

Domitii brothers, 8 n., 66 n.

Domitilla, Flavia, d. of Vespasian, 67 f.

Domitius Afer, Cn. (*cos.* 39), *pr.*, 45 n.; *cos.* 44, 47; mocked Didius Gallus, 44

Domitius Alexander, L., usurper, 321

Domitius Antigonus, iterated legionary command, 19

Domitius Calvinus, Cn. (*cos.* 53 BC), 42 n.

Domitius Corbulo, Cn. (*cos. a. inc.*), consular command, 3 n.; campaigns, 53; officers of, 19, 63, 70 n., 394; elder Theodosius compared to, 339

Domitius Decidius, presumed father-in-law of Julius Agricola, 75 n.

Domitius Dexter, C. (*cos. II ord.* 196), gov. Syria, 147 n.

Domitius Lucanus, Cn. (*cos. a. inc.*), in Africa, 26 n.

Domitius Valerianus, M. (*cos. c.* 239), iterated legionary command, 19

DULCITIUS, *dux* in Britain, 345 f.; 325, 337, 349, 423

Egnatia Mariniana, mother of Gallienus, 197

EGNATIUS LUCILIANUS, gov. Brit. inf., 197; origin, 403; titul. 428, 429, 430

Egnatius Marinianus (*cos. a. inc.*), gov. Moesia sup., 11

Egnatius Proculus, C. Luxilius Sabinus, *tr.* of IV Fl., 11

Egnatius Tuccianus, *curator* of Thugga, 196

Elagabalus, emperor, gov. of Brit. inf. under, 186–91; father of, 296 ff.; murder of, 190, 370; nomenclature, 207; senators under, 154

Elpinice, d. of Herodes Atticus, 186

EPRIUS MARCELLUS, T. CLODIUS (*cos. II* 74), *leg. leg.*, 228 ff.; 223 n.; *cos.* 66, 229; *pr.*, 356 n.; origin and career, 409 ff.; titul., 431

Erucius Clarus, Sex. (*cos. II ord.* 146), death of, 114, 366

Esuvius, T., supposed name of *leg. leg.* II Aug., 202 f.

Euphrates, philosopher, 9 n.

Fabia Numantina, 38 n.

FABIUS AGRIPPINUS, C. (*cos.* 148), *tr. lat.*, 276; 416 ff.

Fabius Cilo, L. (*cos.* 193, *II ord.* 204), consular commands, 7, 31 n., 162 n.

Fabius Cunctator (Maximus), Q. (*cos. V* 209 BC), elder Theodosius compared to, 339 n.

Fabius Fabullus, M., iterated legionary command, 19; service with XIII Gem., 18; nomenclature, 280 n.

Fabius Magnus Valerianus, M., service in Moesia inf., 18

FABIUS PRISCUS, M.(?), *leg. leg.*, 232 f.; 219 n.; origin and career 409 f.; titul. 431

Fabius Valens (*cos.* 69), 75 n., 76

Fabricius Veiento, A. Didius Gallus (*cos. II* 80), 49

Fabulli, in Spain, 280

Falco, rare name, 97 n.

Falconilla, d. of Q. Tryphaena, 98 n.

Fannia, d. of Thrasea Paetus, 86

Felicissimus, *rationalis*, 315

Firmus, rebel Moor, 339, 349, 423

Flavia Silva Prisca, w. of Claudius Gallus, 134 n.

Flavia Titiana, w. of Pertinax, 146 n., 267

Flavii, Sexti, 308 n.

Flavius Catulus Munatianus, *c.p.*, son of Claudius Gallus, 134 n.

Flavius Latronianus, grandf. of Polliena Honorata, 152, 401

Flavius Petro, debt-collector, 226

Flavius Pomponianus Pudens, P., senator, 280

FLAVIUS QUIETUS, SEX., *praef. class. Brit.*, 308, 422

Flavius Sabinus, f. of Vespasian, 226

FLAVIUS SABINUS, T. (*cos.* 47?), *leg. leg.*, 224 f.; consulship, 20 n., 55 n.; entered senate, 226; and Gallic census, 211 n.; gov. Moesia, 358; titul. 431

Flavius Secundus Philippianus, T., iterated legionary command, 19

Flavius Sempronius Aquila, T., 185 n.

Flavius Silva Nonius Bassus, L. (*cos. ord.* 81), kinsman, 213; rise of, 6 n.; *IIIvir cap.*, 6 n., 102

Flavius Vindex, s. of Flavius Quietus, 308

Flavonius Paullinus, P., iterated *tr.*, 10; possible iterated *q.*, 282 n.

Flavus, date of consulship, 122

Fonteius Frontinianus *cet.*, D. (*cos.* 162), 271 n.

Frontina, of Nemausus, 70 n.

Frontinius Mercator, Q., 176 n.

Fronto, M. Cornelius (*cos.* 143), the orator, friend of, 267; influence of, 114

FUFICIUS CORNUTUS, Q. (*cos.* 147), *tr. lat.*, (?), 275 f.

Fufidia Pollitta, senator's wife, 134

FULLOFAUDES, *dux* in Brit., 344 f.; 319, 423

Fulvius Fuscus Granianus, *q. Augg.*, 13 n.

Fulvius Kastus Ful[vianus], L., of Mustis, 194

Fulvius Maximus, consular commands of, 31 n.

Fulvius Plautianus, C., *praef. praet.*, 297 n.

Funisulanus Vettonianus, L. (*cos.* 78?), kinsman, 235; XXvirate, 5 n.

GALBA, emperor, *comes Aug.* in Britain (?), 361 f.; 364, 365 n.; choice of heir, 54, 257, 357; gov. Tarraconensis, 60 n.; senators under, 75, 384; supporters of, 70; victim of, 58

Gallienus, emperor, army reforms, 35; and Dacia, 319 n.; edict, 34 f.

Gallus, senator, 49 n.

Gavius Fulvius Tranquillus, Q., iterated *q.*, 282 n.

Gellius Longus, Q., gov. Cilicia, 257 n.

Geminia Restituta, Spanish lady, 240 n.

Geminius Marcianus, Q., of Cirta, 135 n.

Geminius Modestus, of Cirta, 135 n.

'Genseris', 314 n.

Germanilla, rare name, 135 n.

Germanicus Caesar, campaigns of, 38; in east, 51; son, 5

Geta, emperor, not governor of Britain, 161; murdered, 165, 172, 360

Gildo, Moorish prince, 349

Glitius Atilius Agricola, Q. (*cos.* 97, II 103), consular command of, 7

GORDIAN I, emperor, gov. Brit. inf., 181 ff.; 165 n., 169; origin and career, 402 f.; proclaimed, 198; titul., 428, 429, 430

Gordian II, emperor, 183, 186

Gordian III, emperor, careers under, 174, 299; govs. of Brit. inf. under, 196-8, 207

Gracchi, Gordian I alleged descendant, 185

GRAECINIUS LACO, P., proc. Brit.(?), 287 f.; 419

Grania Honorata, m. of Lollius Urbicus, 113

Grania Tertull. . ., w. of Marcius Clemens, 263

Granius Paulus, P., uncle of Lollius Urbicus, 113

Gratian, emperor, 'dilettante youth', 351; German wars, 340, 343; men loyal to, 331, 341; selected Theodosius, 349 f.

Gratian, British usurper, 328, 342, 343

GRATIANUS, *comes* in Brit., 331 f.; 320, 423

GRATTIUS . . .GEMINIUS . . . (*cos.* 126?), *leg. leg.*, 240 f.; origin and career, 409 ff.; titul., 431

Hadrian, emperor, in Britain, 104, 365 ff.; career, 7; choice of heir, 87; *comes* of, 94; consulships of, 103, 239; Dacia, 99, 108 f.; death, 114; *dona*, 109, 113, 118 n.; in east, 112; equestrian *censitores*, 301, 303; friends, 5 n., 9, 11, 245, 410; gov. Brit. under, 93, 95-112, 202, 205; Jewish war, 17 n., 107, 109, 113, 124, 220, 275, 280, 283, 395; kinsmen, 81; 105; lawyers, 214; legions, 219 f.; *leg. leg.* in Brit., 237-50; in Pannonia, 31; provincial changes, 17 n., 22, 26 n., 28; senators under, 83, 113, 252, 272, 276, 277, 290 f., 307; in Spain, 111, 237, 238; thrice *tr.*, 9, 11; see also General Index, under Hadrian's Wall

Hannibalianus, Afranius, *praef. praet.*, 370 n.

Harpagius, 201 n.

HATERIANUS, *leg. leg.*, 356 f.; origin and career, 408 ff.

Haterius Latronianus, iterated *tr.* (?), 10

HATERIUS NEPOS, T., *censitor* in Brit., 302 f.; rapid promotion, 293 n.

Hedius Rufus *cet.*, Q., *see* Lollianus Gentianus

Helvidia Priscilla, w. of proc., 63 n.

Helvidius, Stoic senator, 86

Helvidius Priscus, C. (*pr.* 70), buried Galba, 58 n.

Helvius Agrippa, L., *procos. Sardiniae*, 279

Helvius Pertinax, emperor, *see* Pertinax

Helvius Pertinax, P., s. of emperor, 146

Helvius Successus, f. of Pertinax, 143

HERACLITUS, mission to Brit., 295 f., 419 n.

Herennius Faustus, M. (*cos. a. inc.*), consular command, 7

Herennius Saturninus, L. (*cos.* 100), 235

Hermogenes of Tarsus, sophist, 168

Herodes Atticus, Ti. Claudius (*cos. ord.* 143), descendant, 185, 186; son, 94 n.; wife, 92, 94

Hierocles, s. of Alypius, 325

Hierocles, persons called, 329

Hierocles, Fl. Ant., uncle of Alypius, 325 n.

Hirrius Fronto, *see* Neratius Pansa

Honorius, emperor, and Stilicho, 374; possible *vicarius* of Brit. under, 328

Hosidii, of Histonium, 45, 222 ff., 365

HOSIDIUS GETA, C., *leg. leg.*, 222 ff.; 43, 365; origin and career, 408 ff.

Hosidius Geta, C. Vitorius (*cos.* 130?), 223, 224 n.

Hosidius Geta, Cn. (*cos.* 47?), *comes* of Claudius?, 365; consulship, 225; in Mauretania, 55, 222

Hosidius Mauricus, Cn. (*cos. a. inc.*), 223 n.

Iasdius Domitianus (*cos. a. inc.*), in Dacia, 30

Insteia Praenestina, 284

Insteius . . ., Q., of Praeneste, 384

Insteius Bithynicus, M. (*cos.* 162), 284 n.

INSTEIUS PAULINUS, JULIUS, *tr. lat.*, 284; 416 ff.

Insteius Tertullus, 284 n.

JAVOLENUS PRISCUS, C. OCTAVIUS cet . . . L. (*cos.* 86), *iurid.* Brit., 213 f.; 405 ff.

Jovian, emperor, 372

JOVINUS, FLAVIUS (*cos. ord.* 367), mission to Brit., 373 f.; 337, 338

Julia, grandd. of Tiberius, 38, 40

Julia Domna, empress, 165, 297, 369, 421 f.

Julia Livilla, w. of M. Vinicius, 363

Julia Magia, 281 n.

Julia Mamaea, empress, 195, 206

Julia Memmia Calpurnia Aemiliana Fidiana, 175 n., 258

Julia Pacata, w. of Julius Classicianus, 288 f., 420

Julia Procilla, m. of Julius Agricola, 73, 75n., 81 n.

Julia Soaemias, empress, 297

Julian, emperor, friend, 324 f.; ideology, 179; Paulus condemned by, 322 n.; sent Lupicinus to Brit., 371 f.

Julianus, Sextius Rusticus, *mag. mem.*, 373

Julii, Sexti, 70

Julii Celsi, 243 n.

Julii Romuli, 243 n.

JULIUS AGRICOLA, CN. (*cos.* 77), gov. Brit., 73–81; 48 n., 61, 71, 101, 136 n.; age when *cos.*, 21 n., 232 n.; British specialist, 18, 30, 31, 189 n., 389 n., 394, 410, 415; death, 65, 82; descendants, 81 n., 151; gov. Aquitania, 288 f.; *leg. leg.*, 64, 69, 97, 232, 330; modesty, 3; origin, 2, 107; origin and career, 377 ff., 409 ff.; praet. career, 125; *q.*, 12 n.; recruits troops, 17 n.; attitude to Suetonius Paullinus, 57; to Syrian command, 28 n.; titul., 426, 429, 431; treatment by Domitian, 135; *tr. lat.*, 9 n., 269, 416 ff.; *tr. pl.*, 15 n., 61 n.

Julius Apronius . . . Salamallianus, L. (*cos. c.* 226), military service, 18

Julius Asper, C. (*cos. II ord.* 212), 433 f.

Julius (Camilius Galerius) Asper, C. (*cos. ord.* 212), patron of Brit., 215 n., 433 f.

Julius Auspex, Gallic notable, 155 n.

JULIUS AVITUS ALEXIANUS, C. (*cos. c.* 207), *comes* of Severus in Brit., 369 f.; *praef. aliment.*, 27 n.

Julius Bassus, C. (*cos.* 139), gov. Dacia sup., 117

Julius Charax, A., 251

JULIUS (ALPIN(I)US) CLASSICIANUS, C., proc. Brit., 288 f.; 56, 420

Julius Cottius, M., *praef. civitatium*, 209

Julius Donnus, C., king, 209

Julius Densus, friend of Britannicus, 257

Julius Eurycles *cet.*, C., Spartan, 96

Julius Florus, Gallic rebel, 289

Julius Frontinus, Q. Valerius Lupercus, of Vienna, 70

JULIUS FRONTINUS, SEX. (*cos. III ord.* 100), gov. Brit., 69 ff.; 77, 80 n.; *curat. aq.*, 27 n., 90; grandd., 96; *leg. leg.*, 219 n., 233; origin and career, 377 ff.; titul. 425

Julius Gavinianus, Sex., Gallic writer, 70 n.

Julius Geminius Marcianus, P. (*cos. a. inc.*), iterated *tr.*, 10

Julius Graecinus, L., f. of Julius Agricola, 73 f.

Julius Graecinus, M., kinsman of above, 73 n.

Julius Haterianus, Virgilian scholar, 257

Julius Indus, Gallic notable, 289

Julius Insteius Paulinus, *see* Insteius

Julius Julianus, gov. Arabia, 241 n.

JULIUS JULIANUS, L., *leg. leg.*, 265 f.; 172 n., 190; origin and career, 408 ff.; titul. 432

Julius Major, Sex. (*cos.* 126?), gov. Syria (?), 32 n.

Julius Marcus, notable, 168

JULIUS MARCUS, C., gov. Brit., 166 ff.; 164, 165, 182, 206; downfall, 184; loyalty dedications, 172; origin and career, 378 ff.; titul., 397, 428, 429

Julius Maximianus, *tr.* of V Mac., 11

Julius Maximianus, C. (*cos. a. inc.*), gov. III Daciae, 11

Julius Maximus Manlianus *cet.*, T. (*cos.* 112), *iurid.* in Spain, 210 n.; iterated legionary command, 19; and Julius Frontinus, 70 n.; names, 247 n.

Julius . . . Paternus, C. (*cos. a. inc.*), withdrew from proconsulship, 211 n.

JULIUS PLANTA, *comes* of Claudius, in Brit. (?), 355

Julius Pisibanus, C. (*cos.* 144?), 244

Julius Pisibanus Maximus Aemilius Papus, C., *tr.* of II Ad., 244

Julius Pompilius Piso, A. (*cos.* 178?), in Dacia, 18; iterated legionary command, 19; iterated *tr.*, 10

Julius Proculus, C. (*cos.* 109), consular command, 6; possible kinsman of Agricola, 81 n.; in Syria, 18; tr., 8 n.

Julius Quadratus, C. Antius A. (*cos.* 94, *II ord.* 105), gov. Syria, 11

Julius Quadratus Bassus, C. (*cos.* 105), consular commands, 6, 30 n., 31

Julius Quadratus Bassus, P. Manilius Vopiscus *cet.* (*cos. ord.* 114), *tr.* of IV Scyth., 11

Julius Sallustius Saturninus Fortunatianus, C., senatorial army commander, 35

Julius Saturninus, C. (*cos. c.* 183), gov. Syria, 147 n.; praet. career, 98 n.

Julius Scapula Tertullus Priscus, P. (*cos.* 195), *procos. Africae*, 156, 264

Julius Septimius Castinus, C. (*cos. a. inc.*), iterated *tr.*, 10; service in Dacia, 31

Julius Servatus, Sex., at Nemausus, 70 n.

Julius (Ursus) Servianus, Ser. (L.) (*cos. III ord.* 134), consular command, 9 n.; kinsman of Trajan, 102; victim of Hadrian, 105

Julius Severus, C. (*cos.* 138?), acting gov. Syria, 11; gov. Germania inf., 19

Julius Severus, C. (*cos.* 155), consular command, 7; *leg. leg.* XXX Ulp.; *tr.* of IV Scyth., 11

JULIUS SEVERUS *cet.*, SEX. (*cos.* 127), gov. Brit., 106 ff.; 22 n., 104, 110, 114, 166 n., 245, 293; consular commands, 7, 31 n.; gov. Dacia sup., 117 n., 123, Judaea, 11, 113, 114, 124, 125 n., 220, Moesia inf., 248, 293, Syria, 28 n., 30 n.; military experience, 33; not on Walcot diploma, 94; origin and career, 377 ff.; praetorian career, 21 n., 125; *q.*, 14 n.; related to Julius Verus, 118, 119; service with XIV Gem., 18, 245; *VIvir*, 15 n.; titul., 427

Julius Silvanus, Sex., of Aequum, 107 n.

Julius Sohaemus, C., *rex magnus*, 210 n.

Julius Solon, senator, 260 n.

Julius Sparsus, Sex. (*cos.* 88), 69 n.

JULIUS VERUS, CN. (*cos.* 151?), gov. Brit., 118 ff.; 107, 122 n., 133, 166n., 203; consular commands, 6, 31 n.; gov. Germania inf., 130; Syria, 28 n.; origin and career, 377 ff.; praetorian career, 21 n.; recruited new legions, 27 n.; related to Sex. Julius Severus, 109; titul., 396, 427, 429; *tr.* of X Fret., 11

Julius Victor Modianus, L., proc., 187

[Ju]lius [. . .] vianus, C., iterated *tr.*, 10

Junia Calvina, 42 n.

Junia Faustinilla, *c.f.*, 164 n.

Junius Aurelius Neratius Gallus, L., iterated *tr.*, 10

Junius Avitus, iterated *tr.*, 9 n., 10

Junius Blaesus, served under father, 19

Junius Blaesus, Q. (*cos.* 10), *procos. Africae*, 19

Junius Caturicus Faustinus, 164 n.

Junius Faustinus, *puer senatorius*, 164 n.

JUNIUS FAUSTINUS POSTUMIANUS, C. (*cos. a. inc.*),, gov. Brit., 161 ff.; 169 n., 203; *comes Augg.*, in Brit.(?), 370; consular commands, 7, 31 n.; gov. Tarraconensis, 29 n.; origin and career, 377 f.; praetorian career, 22 n.; titul., 307, 427

Junius Pastor, A. (*cos. ord.* 163), recruited troops (?), 121 n.

Junius Postumianus, senator, 164

Junius Silanus, M. (*cos. ord.* 15), 73, 74 n.

Junius Silanus Torquatus, M. (*cos. ord.* 19), 42 n., 73, 74 n., 356

JUNIUS SILANUS, L., s.-in-law of Claudius, his *comes* in Brit., 359; death, 229 n.

Junius Victorinus (*cos. a. inc.*), gov. Germania sup., 254, 412 f.

JUNIUS VICTORINUS FLAV. CAELIANUS, L., *leg. leg.*, 253 f.; origin and career, 408 ff.; titul. 432

JUSTINIANUS, *praepositus* (*limitis*?), 423

Juventius Secundus *cet.*, M. (*cos. a. inc.*), 295

Laberius Camerinus, A., and son, clients of Pompeius Falco, 96, 97

Lappius Maximus, A. Bucius (*cos.* 86), *leg. leg.* VIII Aug., 86 n.

Larcia Sabina, brickwork owner, 274 n.

Larcius Lepidus Sulpicianus, A., *leg. leg.* in Judaea, 237

LARCIUS PRISCUS, A. (*cos.* 110), *leg. leg.*, 235 ff.; iterated leg. command, 19; *pro. leg. leg.* IV Scyth., 14 n.; origin and career, 409 ff.; praetorian career, 265 n.; titul., 431

Lartia, w. of a Plautius, 38 n.

Latinius Macer, L., *pp.* of IX Hisp., 221 n.

Lepidus, *cos.* in Gallic empire, 200

LEUCADIUS, *praeses*, in Brit. (?), 341

Licinii Nepotes, 102 n.

LICINIUS (?), gov. Brit. inf. (?), 208

Licinius C. . ., L., iterated *tr.*, 10

Licinius Clemens, equest. officer, 126 n.

LICINIUS CRASSUS FRUGI, M. (*cos. ord.* 27), *comes Claudii* in Brit., 356 f.; in Mauretania, 55; son, 359

Licinius Mucianus, C. (*cos. II* 70, *III* 72), gov. Syria, 30 n.; in year 69, 76

Licinius Nigrinus, equest. officer, 126 n.

Licinius Pollio, C., possibly identical with Platorius Nepos, 102 f.

Licinius Silvanus Granianus, Q. (*cos.* 106), 274

Licinius Silvanus Granianus, Q., Spanish notable, 240 n.

LICINIUS SILVANUS GRANIANUS QUADRONIUS PROCULUS, Q., *tr. lat.* 274; 416 ff.

Licinius Sura, L. (*cos. III ord.* 107), death, 103 n.

Ligarius Q., legate in Africa 50 BC, 272 n.

Livia, w. of Augustus, 39, 362

Livia Ocellina, stepm. of Galba, 362

Livius Grapus, proc., 267 n.

Lollia Paulina, w. of Caligula, 363

Lollianus Avitus, L. Hedius Rufus (*cos. ord.* 144), gov. Bithynia, 249 n.; patron of Pertinax, 143

Lollianus Gentianus, Q. Hedius Rufus (*cos. a. inc.*), consular command, 6; consulship, 20 n.; gov. Tarraconensis, 19

Lollianus Plautius Avitus, Q. (Hedius) (*cos. ord.* 209), gov. Tarraconensis, 31; *tr.* of VII Gem., 19, 31

Lollius Honoratus, M., br. of Lollius Urbicus, 113

Lollius Senecio, M., f. of Lollius Urbicus, 113

Lollius Senis, L., br. of Lollius Urbicus, 113

'Lollius Urbicus', invented writer, 115

LOLLIUS URBICUS, Q. (*cos. c.* 135) gov. Brit., 112 ff.; 116; 117, 201; 202; 205 n., 206, 251, 253, 254; consular commands, 7; Jewish war command, 17 n., 109 n., 124; military experience, 33; origin and career, 377 ff.; titul., 396, 427, 429

Luccianus, rare *cognomen*, 196 n.

Lucillus (*cos. ord.* 265), kinsman of Gallienus, 197

Lupicinus, *comes* in Thrace, 349

LUPICINUS, FLAVIUS (*cos. ord.* 367), mission to Brit., 371 f.; 319; *cos.*, 373

Lusius Geta, *praef. praet.*, 360

Lusius Laberius Gemin(i)us Rutilianus, Q. (*cos. a. inc.*), 294

Lusius Quietus (*cos.* 117?), elder Theodosius compared to, 339

LUSIUS SABINIANUS, Q., proc. Brit., 294; 420

Macius (?) Valerianus, gov. Numidia, 191 n.

Macrianus, king of Alamanni, 338

Macrinius Avitus Catonius Vindex, M. (*cos.* 175?), gov. Moesia sup., 133 n.; nomenclature, 66 n.

Macrinius Vindex, M., *praef. praet.*, 66 n.

Macrinus, emperor, 115, 127, 189, 298

Macro, Naevius Sutorius, *praef. praet.*, 287 n.

MAECILIUS FUSCUS, gov. Brit. inf., 197; 207; titul., 428, 430

Maecilius Hilarianus (*cos. ord.* 332), 321

Maecius Celer, M. (*cos.* 101), kinsman, 270; in Syria, 18

Maecius Laetus, Q., *praef. praet.*, 368 n., 369

MAENIUS AGRIPPA *cet.*, M., *praef. class.* and proc. Brit., 292 ff.; 306; 420 ff.

Magnentius, usurper, 322, 332

Manilii Vopisci, 102 n.

Manilius Fuscus, Ti. (*cos. II ord.* 225), gov. Syria Phoen., 171 n.

MANLIUS VALENS, C. (*cos. ord.* 96) *leg. leg.*, 230; 43, 67; *cos.*, 25, 224 n.; iterated legionary command, 19; origin and career, 409 ff.; titul., 431

Mantennius Sabinus, L. (*cos. a. inc.*), gov. Moesia inf., 163 n.

Marcellinus, br. of Magnus Maximus, 352 n.

Marcellus, *procos. Africae*, 90 n.

Marcianus, rescript to, 177 n.

Marcianus, schismatic bishop, 327

Marcii Philippi, 198

Marcilius Tusculus, Spanish notable, 105 n.

MARCIUS CLEMENS, T., *leg. leg.*, 263; 256; origin and career, 409 ff.; titul., 432

Marc[ius] Gallus, P., iterated *tr.*, 10

Marcius Turbo, Q., *praef. praet.*, 366, 367

MARCUS, *comes* Brit. (?), usurper, 341 ff.

Maria Lucina, of Mustis, 194

Marinus, Syrian name, 300 n.

Marius Celsus, A. (*cos.* 69), gov. Germania inf., 70 n.; in year 69, 46 n.

Marius Maximus, L. (*cos. II ord.* 229), at Byzantium, 265, 425; consular commands, 7; gov. Syria Coele, 159; grandfather, 90 n.; iterated *tr.*, 10; nomenclature, 161 n.

Marius Perpetuus, C., of Thugga, 216 n.

Marius Perpetuus, L., *scriba*, 90 n.

Marius Perpetuus, L. (*cos. a. inc.*), in Syria, 18

Marius Priscus (*cos. a. inc.*), trial of, 213

MARIUS VALERIANUS, gov. Brit. inf., 190 f.; 188 n., 189, 192, 193; 493 f.; titul., 428, 429, 430

Marlianius Ripanus, M., 177 n.

Martialius Frontinus, Q., 176 n.

MARTIANNIUS PULCHER, M. (*cos. a. inc.*), gov. Brit. sup., 176 f., 203; origin, 402; titul., 428, 429

Martin, St, 331, 341, 351

MARTINUS, *vicarius* of Brit., 321 f.; 423

Martius Macer, commanded two legions, 19

Martius Verus, P. (*cos. II ord.* 179), gov. Syria, 30 n.

Maxentius, emperor, 317 n., 321

Maximian, emperor, 200 f., 312, 313; British provinces named after, 317

Maximinus, emperor, 184 n., 185 n.; Brit. inf. under, 195 f.

Maximus, consular command, 7; in Pannonia sup., 30

MAXIMUS, gov. Brit. inf., 192 f.; 404; titul., 428, 430

MAXIMUS, MAGNUS, *dux* (?) in Brit., 346 ff.; 330 n.; *comes* under, 340 f.; *mag. mil.*, 340; *praeses*, 330 f., 341; *vicarius*, 326; origin, 423; Theodosius related to, 338

Maximus, Petronius, emperor, 352

Maximus Caesar, 195

MEMMIUS FIDUS JULIUS ALBIUS, C. (*cos. c.* 191), *tr. lat.*, 278; kinsmen, 175 n., 258; no XXvirate, 5 n., 263 n.; origin and career, 416 ff.

Memorius, Flavius, *comes*, 341 n.

Messallina, empress, 3 n., 40, 215 n., 357, 359, 360, 363, 364

Messius Rusticus, L. (*cos.* 114), 243

Messius Rusticus Aemilius Afer, M., 243 n.

METILIUS NEPOS, P., (*cos.* 91), gov. Brit., 83 ff.; 86, 92, 93 n.; origin and career, 378 ff.

Metilius Regulus, M. (*cos. ord.* 157), 85

Metilius Sabinus Nepos, P. (*cos.* 103), 83 f.

Metilius Secundus, P., *leg. leg.* III Aug., 6 n.; possible iterated *tr.*, 10; possible kinsmen, 83, 85

Minicius Faustinus, Cn. (*cos.* 116), 107

Minicius Fundanus, C. (*cos.* 107), gov. Dalmatia, 108 n.; mil. service, 18

Minicius Natalis, L. (*cos.* 106), consular command, 7; *cos.*, 274; *leg. leg.* III Aug., 236; gov. Pannonia sup., 11, 108 n., 245

MINICIUS NATALIS jr., L. (*cos.* 139), *leg. leg.*, 244 ff.; 108 n.; consular command, 6; names, 274; origin and career, 409 ff. *praef. aliment.*, 250; *q.*, 13 n.; service in Moesia inf., 31; thrice *tr.*, 9, 10, 274; titul., 431; *tr.* of XIV Gem., 11

Minicius Opimianus (*cos.* 155), 123

Minucius Basilus, murderer of Caesar, 282 n.

Modestiana, w. of gov. Brit., 132, 135 n.

MODIUS JULIUS, gov. Brit. inf., 186 f.; 173 n., 189, 403; titul., 428, 429, 430

Modius Justus, C. (*cos.* 172), *leg. leg.* III Aug., 187

Mummia Nigrina, w. of *tr. lat.*, 249 n., 270 n.

MUMMIUS SISENNA, P. (*cos. ord.* 133), gov. Brit., 109 f.; 19, 106, 249, 250; cos., 25 n.; origin and career, 377 ff.

MUMMIUS SISENNA RUTILIANUS, P. (*cos.* 146), *leg. leg.* 248 ff.; 19, 110; consular command, 7; origin and career, 409 ff.; titul., 432

Mummius Ursus, P., Spanish notable, 249 n.

MUNATIUS AURELIUS BASSUS, CN., *censit.* in Brit., 303 f.

Munatius Plancus Paulinus, L. (*cos. ord.* 13), long governorship, 47 n.

Munatius Sulla Cerealis, M. (*cos. ord.* 215), consular command, 174

NANNIENUS, alleged commander in Brit., 339 f.

Narcissus, imperial freedman, 2, 227, 228

NARSES, *comes*, in Brit.(?), 340 f.; 330

NECTARIDUS, *comes* in Brit., 332 f.; 423

Nenolaus Campanianus, Sal., iterated *tr.*, 10

Neratius Bassus, L., 90 n.

Neratius Corellius, 91

Neratius M. . . , *iurid.*, probably in Italy, 218

NERATIUS MARCELLUS, L. (*cos.* 95), gov. Brit., 87 ff.; 93, 368; consular command, 6, 29, *curat. act. senat.*, 14 n., 283 n.; *curat. aquarum*, 27 n.; origin and career, titul., 395, 396, 426; *tr.* of XII Fulm., 11

Neratius Pansa, M. Hirrius Fronto (*cos. a. inc.*), in Armenia (?), 11, 89; *cos.*, 71 n.; governorships, 89, 91; f. of Neratius Marcellus (?), 88

Neratius Priscus, L. (*cos.* 87), 88, 89, 166 n.

Neratius Priscus, L. (*cos.* 97), 88, 89, 90, 91, 166 n.

Neratius Proculus, L. (*cos.* 145?), iterated *tr.*, 10

Nero, emperor, careers under, 5 n., 19, 40, 49, 58, 228 f., 231, 255, 268, 338; consuls under, 4, 59, 388; freedmen, 56, 112; frontier policy, 53 f., 61; gov. Brit. under, 50–62; *leg. leg.* under, 231–2; proc. under, 63, 288 f.; victims, 40, 44, 268, 360, 361; withdrew XIV Gem. from Brit., 61, 119, 231 n., 232

Nerva, emperor, adopts Trajan, 9 n., 72 n.; economy commission, 72; *praef. frum. dandi*, 16 n.; *pr.*, 98 n.; reign of, 86, 236

Neviogastes, general of Constantine III, 353

Niger, kinsman of a *praef. class.*, 305 f.

Niger, *see* Pescennius Niger

Nonii, of Cisalpina, 198

Nonii Asprenates, 198

Nonia Phili[ppa], 198

Nonius (Calpurnius) Asprenas, L. (*cos. a. inc.*), received *dona*, 354 n.

Nonius Asprenas, L. (*cos.* 6), command in Germany, 361 n.

Nonius Paternus (*cos. II ord.* 279), 198

Nonius Macrinus, M. (*cos.* 154), consular command, 7; praetorian career, 21 n.; service in Pannonia, 30

NONIUS PHILIPPUS, gov. Brit. inf., 198; 197, 207; titul., 428, 429

Nonius Proculus, C. (*cos. a. inc.*), perhaps gov. Brit., 106

Nortinus, possible *cognomen* of proc., 299

Novia Crispina, w. of Antistius Adventus, 130, 132 n., 277

NOVIUS CRISPINUS, L. (*cos.* 150), *tr. lat.*, 276 f.; 130, 220, 415 ff.

Numerianus, emperor, title Britannicus, 312 n.

Numerianus, schoolmaster, posed as senator, 3 n.

Numisius Aper Junior, Q., 255

NUMISIUS JUNIOR, Q. CAMURIUS, *leg. leg.*, 254 ff.; iterated legionary command, 6 n., 18; origin and career, 409 ff.; *tr.* of IX Hisp., 220, 277, 416 ff.; *IIIvir. mon.*, 6 n.

Numisius Junior, Q. (*cos.* 161), presumably identical with foregoing, 220, 255

Numisius Lupus, *leg. leg.* VIII Aug., 86 n.

Nummius Umbrius Primus, M. (*cos. ord.* 206), consular command, 6, 162 n., 173 f.; death, 263 f., 265

Oc. Sabinus, L. veteran, 200 n., 200 n.

OCLATINIUS ADVENTUS, M. (*cos. ord.* 218), proc. Brit., 298 f.; 132 n., 160, 170, 420 f.

Octavia, possible name of w. of Q. Veranius, 54

Octavia, d. of Claudius, 356

Octavius Felix, L., senator, 277 n.

Octavius Laenas, C. (*cos.* 33), 54 n.

Octavius Laenas Pontianus, Ser. (*cos. ord.* 131), 252 n.

[Octa]vius Sabinus (*cos.* 160), 200 n.

OCTAVIUS SABINUS, gov. Brit. inf., 200; 173 n., 402, 403, 407 n.; titul., 428, 430

Octavius Sabinus, Cn., *Cvir* of Veii, 200 n.

Oppius Sabinus, C. (*cos. ord.* 84), defeat of, 79 n., 220 n.

Ostorii, distribution of, 42 n.

Ostorius Eugrafianus, 42 n.

Ostorius Euhodianus (*cos. a. inc.*), 44 n.

Ostorius Pharnaces, P., freedman, 42

OSTORIUS SCAPULA, M. (*cos.* 59), *tr. lat.*, 268; 42, 43, 44, 416 ff.

OSTORIUS SCAPULA, P. (*cos. a. inc.*), gov. Brit., 41 ff.; 48, 53, 67, 136 n., 229, 230, 378, 395, 416, 425

Ostorius Scapula, Q., *praef. praet.*, 42

Otho, emperor, 55 n., 56, 57, 75 f.

Ovidius, Q., elderly Stoic, 87 n.

Ovinius Rusticus Cornelianus, L. (*cos. a. inc.*), 277 n.

PACATIANUS, L. PAPIUS (*cos. ord.* 332),

[PACATIANUS, L. PAPIUS] *vicarius* of Brit.. 321; 423

Pacideius, rare *nomen*, 299

Pactumeius Clemens, P. (*cos.* 138), legate of *procos. Africae*, 26 n.

Palfurius, P. (*cos.* 56?), 59

PAPINIAN (M. AEMILIUS PAPINIANUS), *praef. praet.*, in Brit., 368 f.; death of, 263, 265, 366 n., 367 n.

PAPIRIUS AELIANUS, CN. (*cos. c.* 136), gov. Brit., 116 ff.; gov. Dacia sup., 109 n., 123; origin and career, 377 ff.; titul., 396, 427

Papirius Cursor, L. (*cos. V* 313 BC), elder Theodosius compared to, 339 n.

Paquius Scaeva, P., senator, 45 n., 257 n.

Paulus, notary, 322

Pedanius Fuscus Salinator, Cn., grandnephew of Hadrian, 105

Perennis, Sex. Tigidius, *praef. praet.*, 139, 145, 260, 262

PERPETUUS, . . .ROCLES, *praeses* of Brit. province, 329, 423

PERTINAX (P. Helvius Pertinax), emperor, gov. Brit., 142 ff.; 34 n., 134 n., 260, 262; adlected, 138, 158 n.; attempted coup against 174; equest. posts, 31; gov. Moesia sup., 133 n.; Syria, 29 n.; military experience, 33; more than two consular provs., 31 n.; origin, 2, 11; origin and career, 377 ff.; praetorian career, 20 n.

Pescennius Niger, C., emperor, civil war of, 133, 146; *leg. leg.* (?), 147; gov. Syria, 147 n.

Petillia Modesta, of Aquileia, 66 n.

Petillius Capitolinus, *IIIvir mon.*, 67 n.

PETILLIUS CERIALIS CAESIUS RUFUS, Q. (*cos. II* 74), gov. Brit. 66 ff.; 64, 71, 77, 80 n.; British service, 30; command in 69, 17 n., 46 n.; command in Rhineland, 64 f.; kinsman of Flavians, 269; *leg.leg.* IX Hisp., 231, 269; origin and career, 378 ff., 409 ff.; Tacitus on, 57; titul., 425, 431

Petillius Cerialis, Tironis *lib.*, 66 n.

Petillius Rufus, shameful conduct of, 66, 67

Petillius Rufus, Q. (*cos. II ord.* 83), perhaps identical with Petillius Cerialis, 69

Petillius Spurinus, Q. (*cos.* 176 BC), 66 n.

Petronius, P. (*cos.* 19), br.-in-law of A. Plautius, 38; gov. Syria, 39, 58; old friend of Claudius, 38, 57; *procos. Asiae*, 46

Petronius Gallianus, *qui et* Harpagius, 201 n.

Petronius Melior, Q. (*cos. a. inc.*), iterated legionary command, 19; service in Germania inf., 18

Petronius Probatus, Cn., iterated legionary command, 19

PETRONIUS TURPILIANUS, P. (*cos. ord.* 61), gov. Brit. 57 f.; 40, 56, 166 n.;

[PETRONIUS TURPILIANUS, P.] consulship, 110; origin and career, 378 ff.; titul., 425

Philip, emperor, 198

Piso, C. Calpurnius (*cos. a. inc.*), conspiracy of, 40, 58

Piso Licinianus, L. Calpurnius, Galba's heir, 54, 357

Platorius Nepos, *IIvir* of Corduba (?), 101 n.

PLATORIUS NEPOS cet., A. (*cos.* 119), gov. Brit., 100 ff.; 95, 99, 202, 205, 239, 273, 275, 293; *candidatus Caes.*, 14 n.; friend of Hadrian, 243; origin and career, 377 ff.; titul., 396, 427, 429; *IIIvir cap.*, 5

Platorius Nepos Calpurnianus, A. (*cos.* 160?), iterated *tr.*, 10; son of foregoing, 105

Platorius Trebianus, C., of Gades, 101

Plautia, sister of A. Plautius (*cos.* 29), 38, 57

Plautia, Antonine ancestress, 41 n.

Plautia Urgulanilla, w. of Claudius, 38, 357

Plautius, A., legate in Social War, 37 n.

Plautius, A. (*cos.* 1 BC), 38 n.

PLAUTIUS, A. (*cos.* 29), gov. Brit., 37 ff.; 41, 44, 58, 166 n., 224, 227, 338 n., 357, 360 f.; lacked *cognomen*, 57 n.

Plautius, A., the younger, 40

Plautius, Q. (*cos.* 36), 39

Plautius Lamia Silvanus, s.-in-law of Antoninus Pius, 40 n.

Plautius Lateranus, death of, 40

Plautius Pulcher, P., br. of Plautia Urgulanilla, 38 n., patrician, 358

Plautius Silvanus, M. (*tr. pl.* 89 BC), 37 n.

Plautius Silvanus, M. (*cos. ord.* 2 BC), 37, 358

Plautius Silvanus, M. (*pr.* 24), defenestrated wife, 38; suicide, 358

PLAUTIUS SILVANUS AELIANUS, TI. (*cos.* 45, *II* 74), *comes* of Claudius in Brit., 357 f.; consular commands, 6; gov. Moesia, 60 n.

Plautius Venox, C. (*censor* 312 BC), 37 n.

Plinius Secundus, C. (*cos.* 100), consular governorship, 7, 272 n.

Plotia Servilia Isaurica, brickworks owner, 247 n.

Plotius Faustus, M., equest. officer, 196 n.

Plotius Romanus, P. (*cos. a. inc.*), iterated *tr.*, 10

Poblicius Marcellus, C. Quinctius Certus (*cos.* 120), 91 n.

Poenius Postumus, *praef.* of II Aug., 74

Polliena Honorata, grandd. of Pollienus Auspex jr., 152, 153 n.

Pollienus Armenius Peregrinus, Ti. (*cos. ord.* 244), 152, 153

Pollienus Auspex sr. (*cos. a. inc.*), 151 ff.; *praef. aliment.*, 27 n.; *XVvir s. f.*, 401; *vice sacra iudicans*, 32 n.

POLLIENUS AUSPEX jr (*cos. a. inc.*), gov.
Brit. or Brit. sup., 151 ff., 172 f.; 163 n.,
169 n., 3203; gov. Tarraconensis, 29 n.;
more than two consular provs., 31 n.;
origin and career, 378 ff.; titul., 397, 427
Pollienus Auspex, Ti. Julius (*cos. a. inc.*), gov.
Numidia, 153, 154
Pollienus Sebennus, gov. Noricum, 155
Polyclitus, imperial freedman, 56
Pompeius Ant. Amoenas, Cn., iterated *q.*,
282 n.
POMPEIUS FALCO cet., Q. (*cos.* 108?), gov.
Brit., 95 ff.; 101, 126 n., 133 n., 232, 273;
consular commands, 7; consular *curator
viae*, 16 n.; gov. Judaea, 125 n.; gov. more
than one praetorian prov., 22; grandson,
291; military service, 31; origin and career,
377 ff.; *procos. Asiae*, 113 n.; service in
Moesia inf., 30; titul., 396, 426
POMPEIUS HOMULLUS cet., CN., proc.
Brit., 291 f.; 295, 420 f.
Pompeius Magnus, Cn. (*cos. III* 52 BC), army
of, 226; descendants of, 357 f., 359;
eastern clients of, 97; elder Theodosius
compared to, 339 n.; house of, 185 n.
POMPEIUS MAGNUS, CN., s.-in-law of
Claudius, his *comes* in Brit., 359; 356, 357
Pompeius Silvanus, M. (*cos.* 45), consulships,
41 n., 55 n.; gov. Dalmatia, 60 n.;
recruited troops, 76 n.
Pomponia Germanilla, w. of senator, 135 n.
Pomponia Graecina, w. of A. Plautius (*cos.*
29), 38, 40
Pomponius Antistianus cet., T. (*cos.* 121),
235
Pomponius Atticus, T., friend of Cicero, 38 n.
Pomponius Bassus (*cos. ord.* 211?), in Moesia,
19, 174
Pomponius Bassus, T. (*cos.* 94), 235 n.
Pomponius Cornelianus, P. (*cos. a. inc.*),
281 n.
Pomponius Flaccus, L. (*cos.* 17), deputy com-
mander in Balkans, 361; kinsman of A.
Plautius (*cos.* 29), 38
Pomponius Graecinus, C. (*cos.* 16), kinsman
of A. Plautius (*cos.* 29), 38
Pomponius Magianus, P., gov. Thrace, 281 n.
POMPONIUS MAMILIANUS cet., T. (*cos.*
100), *leg. leg.* 234 f.; 408 f.; titul., 431
Pomponius Rufus, Q. (*cos.* 95), service in
Moesia inf., 30
Pomponius Rufus Marcellus, Q. (*cos.* 121),
procos. Asiae, 90 n.
Pontius, *leg. leg.* III Aug., 297 n.
Pontius Laelianus, legatee of 'Dasumius',
274 n.
Pontius Laelianus, M. (*cos. ord.* 163), 274 n.
PONTIUS LAELIANUS LARCIUS SABINUS
(*cos.* 144), *tr. lat.*, 273 f.; 275, 416 ff.;

[PONTIUS LAELIANUS LARCIUS
SABINUS] consular commands, 7; military experience, 33; relatives, 66 n.;
service in Germania inf., 18
Pontius Pontianus (Ti.) (*cos. a. inc.*), service
in Pannonia inf., 11, 31
Pontius Sabinus, M. (*cos.* 153), gov. Moesia
sup., 252
Pontius Sabinus, T., *primipilaris*, brought
reinforcements to Brit., 292 f.
Popilius Carus Pedo, C. (*cos.* 147), consular
command, 7; *dona*, 118 n.; not *candidatus
Caes.*, 119 n.; withdrew from legionary
command, 18, 29 n., 211 n.
Popillius Priscus, P. (*cos.* 132?), *procos. Asiae*,
110 n.
Poppaea Sabina, empress, 360
Poppaeus Sabinus, C. (*cos. ord.* 9), Balkan
command, 361
Porcius Cato, M. (*cos.* 36), disgrace, 47
Postumia Siria, 267 n.
Postumius Fabullus, L., 280 n.
Postumius Festus, M. (*cos.* 160), 122 n., 267
Postumius Titianus, T. Flavius (*cos. II ord.*
301), 267
POSTUMIUS VARUS, T. FLAVIUS (*cos. a.
inc.*), *leg. leg.* 266 f.; 57, 408 f.; 415;
titul., 432
Postumus, emperor, 176, 200
Prifernius Paetus cet., T. (*cos.* 146), consular
command, 7, 244 n.
'Princus', invented son of Clodius Albinus,
149 n.
PRISCUS, *leg. leg.*, 260 f.; 34 n., 139, 262;
origin, 409; possibly *leg. leg.* III Aug., 413;
titul., 432
Probus, emperor, revolt in Brit. under, 180 f.;
trained generals, 371
Procopius, usurper, 372
Proculus, *procos. Baeticae*, 268 n.
Propinquus, persons called, 240; and see
Grattius . . .
Prosius Celer, P., *praef. cast.*, 174 n.
Prosius Rufinus, L., gov. Thrace, 174
Prosius Tertullianus (*cos. a. inc.*), gov. Moesia
inf., 174
Publicius Certus, debate on, 98 n.
Pudens, proconsul, 156 n.
Pudentilla, Namia, w. of Sanctus, 330
Pulcher, recipient of rescript, 177 n.

Quintilii, victims of Commodus, 136
Quintilius Valerius Maximus, Sex., iterated
tr., 10
Quintilius Varus, P. (*cos. ord.* 13 BC),
command in Germany, 361 n.
Quintinus, served under Magnus Maximus, 340

Regillus, *praef. praet.*, 186 n.

Regulus, M'. Aquillius, fortune-hunter, 54
Romanus, *comes Africae*, 349
ROSCIUS AELIANUS MAECIUS CELER, L. (*cos.* 100), *tr. lat.*, 270; 81 n., 416 ff.
ROSCIUS COELIUS, M. (*cos.* 81), *leg. leg.*, 231 f.; 61, 77, 97, 409; possible son, 270; titul., 431, 432
Rubellia Bassa, grandd. of Tiberius, 54 n.
RUBRENUS, *tr. lat.*, 280 f.; 416 ff.
Rubrenus Virius Priscus *cet.*, M. (*cos. a. inc.*), 281
Rubrius Gallus (*cos. a. inc.*), command in 68, 58
RUFINUS (*cos. a. inc.*), gov. Brit. sup., 173 ff.; 203, 402; titul., 428, 430
Rufinus, Flavius (*cos. ord.* 392), *praef. praet.*, 375 n.
Rufrius Crispinus, *praef. praet.*, 360
RUFRIUS POLLIO, *praef. praet.*, in Brit., 359 f.; 366 n., 367 n.
Rutilianus, gov. Cilicia, 257 n.
Rutilius Gallicus, C. (*cos. II* 85), service in Pannonia, 18
Rutilius Pudens Crispinus, (*cos. a. inc.*), consular command, 7; gov. Thrace, 174

SABUCIUS MAJOR CAECILIANUS, C. (*cos.* 186), *iurid.* Brit., 216; 138, 405 ff.
Sabucius Major Plotinus Faustinus, C., 216
Sabucius Perpetuus, C., 216
Sabucius Sabinus, S., 216
Saevinius Proculus, L., gov. two praetorian provs., 22 n., 98 n.
Sallustia Calvina, hypothetical kinswoman of P. Ostorius Scapula, 42
Sallustia Plotina, kinswoman of Desticii, 178
Sallustius, P., 82 n.
Sallustius, Cn., friend of Cicero, 82 n.
Sallustius Blaesus, P. (*cos.* 89), 82
Sallustius Crispus, C., adviser of Augustus, 42 n.
Sallustius Lucullius, P., of Lanuvium, 82 n.
SALLUSTIUS LUCULLUS (*cos. a. inc.*), gov. Brit., 82 f.; 81 n., 292, 378, 389 n., 398
Sallustius Phosphorus, freedman, 42
Sallustius Utilis, freedman, 42
Salvius Julianus, P. (*cos. ord.* 148), *cos. ord.*, 126; consular command, 7, 119; gov. Germania inf., 130; Javolenus his teacher, 214; no legionary command, 29 n.; *procos. Africae*, 121 n.
SALVIUS LIBERALIS NONIUS BASSUS, C. (*cos. a. inc.*), *iurid.* Brit., 211 ff.; 214; 404 ff.; adlected (?), 15 n.; legionary command, 11; promotion, 234
Salvius Satrianus Minicius, senator, 282 n.
Salvius (Otho) Titianus, L. (*cos. ord.* 52, *II* 62), *procos. Africae*, 12 n., 75
Salvius Vitellianus, C., s. of Salvius Liberalis, 213; *tr.* of V. Mac., 11

Sanctus, consul in Gallic empire, 330
SANCTUS, FLAVIUS, *praeses* of Brit. prov., 329 f.; 423
Satria Vera, 282
Satrius, M., murderer of Caesar, 282 n.
SATR[IUS] SAL[. . .], AN., *tr. lat.*, 282; 416 ff.; iterated *q.*, 14 n.
Scapula, *see* Julius, Ostorius
Scapula, M., *procos. Asiae*, 44
Scribonia, w. of M. Licinius Crassus Frugi, 359
Scribonia, w. of Augustus, 361
Scribonii brothers, 66 n.
Scribonius Proculus, P. Sulpicius (*cos. a. inc.*), 66 n., 286 n.
Sedatius Severianus *cet.*, M. (*cos.* 153), gov. Cappadocia, 249 n., Dacia sup., 117 n.; link with Metilius Nepos, 85
Seius Oceanus, subject of lawsuit, 214
Seius Saturninus, naval officer, 214
Sejanus, L. Aelius, *praef. praet.*, 39, 287
Sempronia Romana, d. of *ab epistulis*, 185
Sempronius Aquila, *ab epistulis Graecis*, 185
Sempronius Densus, guard centurion, 257
Seneca, L. Annaeus (*cos.* 56), *cos.*, 59 f.; influence, 61, 74
Sennius Sollemnis, T., *assessor* of gov. Brit. inf., 169, 189 f.
Sentius Saturninus, C. (*cos. ord.* 19 BC), 361
SENTIUS SATURNINUS, CN. (*cos. ord.* 41), unknown role in Brit., 360 f.; *cos.*, 59
SEPTICIUS CLARUS, C., *praef. praet.*, in Brit., 365 f.; 367; sacking, 104
SEPTIMIUS . . ., L., *praeses* of Brit. prov., 178 ff.; 80, 317 n., 329, 402, 423; titul., 428, 429
SEPTIMIUS GETA, P. (*cos. II ord.* 203), *tr. lat.*, 278; 416 ff.; consular commands, 7; *fetialis*, 261 n.; gov. III Daciae, 263; origin, 2; service in Moesia inf., 30
Septimius Heraclitus, *leg. leg.* VI Ferr., 296 n.
Septimius Nilus, equest. officer, 188 n.
Septimius Rufus, *magister summae rei*, 180 n.
Septimius Severus, C. (*cos.* 160?), *cos.*, 122 n.; consular commands, 7
Serenilla, correspondent of Jerome, 326 n.
Serenus, iterated legionary command, 20
Sergia Paulla, w. of Caristanius Fronto, 234
Servaeus Fuscus Cornelianus, Q., iterated legionary command, 20
Servilius Fabianus Maximus, M. (*cos.* 158), consular command, 7
Servilius Isauricus, P. (*cos.* 79 BC), 247
Servilius Silanus, M. (*cos.* 152), 123
Severus, L. Septimius, emperor, biography of, 147; brother, 2, 278; careers under, 22, 31 n., 137, 152, 198, 294, 295; civil wars, 133, 147 ff., 295 f.; division of Britain, alleged, 169 ff.; gov. Brit. under, 149-64,

[Severus, L. Septimius] 203–5; grandfather, 90 n.; in Britain, 159 ff., 170 f., 309, 368 ff.; iterated *q.*, 14 n.; knowledge of senators, 3 n.; *leg. leg.* in Brit. under, 265 f.; new legions raised by, 8; proc. Brit. under, 296–9; prov. changes under, 22, 171; raised to purple in Pannonia, 146, 157; victims of, 134

Severus, consul, 122

SEVERUS, *comes domesticorum*, mission to Brit., 372 f.; 337; in Gaul, 340

Severus Alexander, emperor, careers under, 154, 403; gov. Brit. inf. under, 191–6; murder, 195 f.; name, 207; succeeds Elagabalus, 370; *XXviri* under, 5, 102

'Sevira', alleged d. of Magnus Maximus, 352 n.

Sextius Africanus, T. (*cos. ord.* 59), 59

Sextius . . . M. Vibius . . . Secundus, T., *iurid.* in unknown area, 218

Silius, C., lover of Messalina, 40

Silius Decianus, L. (*cos.* 94), *curator aquarum*, 90; linked with Pompeius Falco, 96 f.

Silius Italicus, Ti. Catius (*cos. ord.* 68), 97 n.

Silvius Bonus, British poet, 328 n.

Simonius Proculus Julianus, D., gov. Thrace, 174 n.

Siricius, Pope, Magnus Maximus wrote to, 351 n.

Sisinnius, schismatic bishop, 327

Soaemias, Julia, empress, 194 n., 297

Sosia Frontina, d. of Sosius Senecio, 247 n.

Sosia Juncina, w. of Antonius Isauricus, 247

Sosia Polla, w. of Pompeius Falco, 96

Sosius Falco, Q. (*cos. ord.* 193), 247 n.

Sosius Laelianus Pontius Falco, M., nomenclature of, 66 n.

Sosius Priscus, Q. (*cos. ord.* 149), date of birth, 99 n.; names, 247 n.

Sosius Priscus cet., Q. (*cos. ord.* 169), grands. of Pompeius Falco, 97, 291; names, 97, 291; *q.*, 13 n., 247 n.

Sosius Senecio, Q. (*cos. ord.* 99, *II ord.* 107), family, 247; f.-in-law of Pompeius Falco, 96; friend of Hadrian, 243; influence, 99 n.; origin, 97 f.; s.-in-law of Julius Frontinus, 72

Statilius Barbarus, T. (*cos. a. inc.*), consular command, 7

STATILIUS OPTATUS, T., *proc. ad census* in Brit., 300 f.

Statius Longinus, M. (*cos. a. inc.*), descendant of Statius Priscus

STATIUS PRISCUS LICINIUS ITALICUS, M. (*cos. ord.* 159), gov. Brit. 123 ff.; 122, 128, 133 n., 206; *cos.*, 25 n.; entry to senate, 12 n., 158 n.; gov. Cappadocia, 28 n., Dacia sup., 117 n., Moesia sup., 252 n.; more than two consular provs., 31 n.; not on Bewcastle inscription, 105;

[STATIUS PRISCUS LICINIUS ITALICUS, M.] origin and career, 377 ff.; praetorian career, 21 n.; service in Brit., 31, in Jewish war, 109 n.; titul., 396, 427

STEI. . ., L., *tra. lat.*, 271

Stertinia Cocceia Bassula *cet.*, 255

Stertinius Avitus, L. (*cos.* 92), 271 n.

Stertinius Noricus, L. (*cos.* 113), 255, 271

Stertinius Quintilianus, L. (*cos.* 146), 271 n.

STILICHO, FLAVIUS, *magister mil.*, alleged mission to Brit., 374 f.; military reforms, 320, 350

Subatianus Proculus, Ti. Claudius (*cos. c.* 210), *leg. leg.* III Aug., 297 n.

Sueto, rare name, 55

Suetonius Laetus, f. of Suetonius Tranquillus, 368

SUETONIUS PAULLINUS, C. (*cos. a. inc.*), gov. Brit., 54 ff.; 50, 61; appointed Julius Agricola *tr.*, 74, 416; command in Mauretania, 222; *dux* of Otho, 399; origin, 368 n., 378; praetorian career, 384, 385, 395; titul., 425

Suetonius Paullinus, C. (*cos. ord.* 66), 54 n.

SUETONIUS TRANQUILLUS, C., *ab epistulis*, in Brit., 366 ff.; declined commission in Brit., 88; origin, 55 n.

Suetrius Sabinus, C. Octavius Ap. (*cos. ord.* 214), consular command, 7; gov. Pannonia inf., 168 n.; judge of appeal, 153; name, 200 n.; vigintivirate, 5 n.

Suillius Rufus, P. (*cos. a. inc.*), 41

Sulla, L. Cornelius, dictator, and quaestorship, 12 n.

Sulpicius Apollinaris, teacher of Pertinax, 143

Sulpicius Rufus, P., *censor* 42 BC, 62 n.

Tacitus, Cornelius (*cos.* 97), s.-in-law of Julius Agricola, 77, 81

Tampius Flavianus (*cos. a. inc.*), gov. Pannonia, 60 n.

Taurinus, *comes Africae*, 332 n.

Terentius Tullius Geminus, C. (*cos.* 45), 41 n.

Tetricus, emperor, 203 n.

Tettius Julianus, L. (*cos.* 83), service in Moesia sup., 30

THEODOSIUS, FLAVIUS, *comes* in Brit., 333 ff.; 318, 319, 320, 325, 340, 345, 349, 373 f., 423

Theodosius I, emperor, accession, 336, 349 f.; alleged descent from Trajan, 339; death, 327, 328; defeat Magnus Maximus, 352; Maximus his kinsman, 348, 352

Theophanes of Mytilene, client of Pompeius Magnus, 97

Thermantia, w. of elder Theodosius, 339

Thrasea Paetus, P. Clodius (*cos.* 56), family, 86; friend of Avidius Quietus, 85, of Vespasian, 361 n.

Tiberius, emperor, *ab actis senatus* under, 14 n.; *arcana imperii*, 3 n.; campaigns, 38, 46; careers under, 31, 38, 45, 51, 57, 358, 362; reign of, 47, 48

Tineius Longus, equest. officer made senator, 165

TITUS, emperor, *tr. lat.*, 269; 9 n., 10, 67, 75, 416 ff.; birth, 227; careers under, 80, 211, 234; iterated *tr.*, 10; service in Judaea, 79 n.

Trajan, emperor, adopted, 9 n., 72 n.; British legions under, 219 ff.; careers under, 5 n., 44 n., 81 n., 85, 87, 96, 102, 198, 111, 214, 243, 245, 255, 271, 274, 292, 367; *curae viarum* under, 26 n.; Dacian wars, 90, 98, 221, 306; gov. Brit. under, 83–95; and Julius Frontinus, 72; *leg. leg.*, 16 n., 20 n.; *leg. leg.* in Brit. under, 235–7; and Neratius Priscus, 90; Parthian war, 20 n., 103, 221, 239, 275; provincial status changed by, 22; *tr. mil.*, 9, 10; and tribe Papiria, 238; Theodosius allegedly descendant, 339

Trebellius, M., *leg. leg.* in Syria, 59

Trebellius Catulus, Q., senator, 60 n.

TREBELLIUS MAXIMUS, M. (*cos.* 56?), gov. Brit., 59 ff.; 19, 63, 80 n., 138, 201, 231 f., 397; Gallic census, 27 n.; in year 41, 361 n.; origin and career, 378 ff.; titul., 425

Trebellius Rufus, Q., of Tolosa, 60

Trebius Germanus (*cos. a. inc.*), 237 n.

Trebius Verus, equest. officer, 123

Trebonius Mettius Modestus (*cos. c.* 102), gov. Lycia-Pamphylia, 98 n.

Triarius Maternus Lascivius (*cos. ord.* 185?), 174

Triarius Rufinus, A. (*cos. ord.* 210), 173 f.

Tryphaena, invented queen, 98 n.

[T]UCCIANUS, gov. Brit. inf., 196; 207, 403; titul., 428, 430

TULLIUS VARRO, P. (*cos.* 127), *leg. leg.*, 239 f., 241; consular command, 7; gov. Moesia sup., 11; iterated legionary command, 20; origin and career, 409 ff.; service in Syria, 18; titul., 431

Turpilius, Sex., poet, 57

Tusidius Campester, L. (*cos.* 165?), s. of Maenius Agrippa, 294

Tuticius Proculus, M., proc., 256 n.

Ulpia Marcella, persons called, 141

Ulpian (L. Domitius Ulpianus), *praef. praet.*, 184

Ulpius Aelianus Severus, C., 141 n.

Ulpius Marcellus, centurion's grands., 141

Ulpius Marcellus, jurist, 141

ULPIUS MARCELLUS sr (*cos. a. inc.*), gov. Brit., 140 ff.; 134 n., 135, 139, 250;

[ULPIUS MARCELLUS sr] origin and career, 377 ff.; titul., 397, 430

ULPIUS MARCELLUS jr (*cos. a. inc.*), gov. Brit., 164 ff.; 141; 389, 397; origin, 378; titul., 397, 427, 430

Ulpius Marcellus, third century consular, 142 n., 166 n.

Ulpius Marcellus, L., gov. Pannonia inf., 141, 157 n.

Ulpius Marcellus, M., *Aug. lib.*, 141

Ulpius Marcellus, Q., of Mauretania, 141 n.

Ulpius Marcellus Polybianus, C., *c.i.*, 141

Ulpius Maximus, M., gov. Numidia, 193 n.

Ulpius Puteolanus, M., *tr.* of X Gemina, 294 n.

Ulpius Tatianus Marcellus, 141

Ulpius Traianus, M. (*cos.* 72?), 92 n.

Umbrius Primus, *see* Nummius Umbrius

Ummidius Quadratus, C. (*cos. a. inc.*), consular command, 7

Urgulania, friend of Livia, 37, 39

Vagellius, L. (*cos.* 47?), 225

VALENS, proc. Brit.(?), 299

Valens, emperor, 318; daughters, 327 n.; father, 331 f.

Valentinian I, emperor, death, 326 n., 339; father, 331 f.; illness, 337, 373; sends men to Brit., 333 ff., 372 ff.

Valentinian II, emperor, birth, 326 n.; boy-emperor, 351

Valentinian III, emperor, murder, 352 n.

Valentinus, exile, 337, 338 n., 345, 349

Valerian, emperor, 164, 178

Valerianus, recipient of rescripts, 191 n.

Valerii Vegetii, Spanish family, 270 n.

VALERIUS . . ., L., possible *praef. class.* Brit., 305 f.; 422

VALERIUS ASIATICUS, D. (*cos. II ord.* 46), *comes Claudii* in Brit., 362 f.; conduct in, 41, 364

Valerius Claud. Acilius Priscillianus, iterated *q.*, 282 n.

VALERIUS CRESCENS FULVIANUS, gov. Brit. inf., 194 f.; 193, 403; titul., 428, 429

Val. Crescentia(nus), *eq. R.*, 195 n.

Valerius Etruscus, M. (*cos.* 154?), gov. Moesia sup.(?), 252 n.

Valerius Festus, C. (*cos.* 71), consular command, 7

Valerius Florus, M., *tr.* of III Aug., 11

Valerius Fulvianus, M., equest. officer, 194

Valerius Maternus, *c.i.*, 195 n.

Valerius Maximianus, M. (*cos. a. inc.*), adlected, 216 n.; commanded task force, 309 n.; iterated legionary command, 20

VALERIUS PANSA, C., proc. Brit., 295; 420 f.

Valerius Paulinus, proc. of Narbonensis, 76

Valerius Propinquus, L., *flamen* of Tarraconensis, 240 n.

Valerius Propinquus Grattius Cerealis, M., equest. officer, 240 n.

VALERIUS PUDENS, C. (*cos. c.* 194), gov. Brit., 155 ff.; 159, 169, 203, 204, 205; origin and career, 377 ff.

Valerius Senecio, M. (*cos. a. inc.*), gov. Numidia, 11

Valerius Valens, *praef. vigilum*, 299

Varinia Crispinilla, w. of Sex. Flavius Quietus, 308

Varius Ambibulus, L. (*cos.* 133?), *leg. leg.*, 20 n.

VARIUS MARCELLUS, SEX., proc. Brit., 296 ff.; 419 ff.

Vecilius Probus, friend of Roscius Aelianus, 270

Velleius Blaesus, rich consular, 82 n.

Velleius . . . Sertorius . . . Pedanius Fuscus *cet.*, 81

Venidius Rufus *cet.*, Q. (*cos. a. inc.*), gov. Cilicia, 257; service in Germania inf., 30

Venuleius Apronianus, L. (*cos. II ord.* 168), consular command, 6

Venutius, Brigantian leader, 48, 64, 231

Verania Gemina, d. of Q. Veranius, 54, 357 n.

Verania Octavilla, d. of Q. Veranius, 54

Veranius, friend of Catullus, 51

VERANIUS, Q. (*cos. ord.* 49), gov. Brit., 50 ff.; 44, 49, 61; *cos. ord.*, 25 n.; consular command, 6; daughter, 357 n.; lacked *cognomen*, 57 n.; monument, 3; origin and career, 378 ff.; *pr.*, 55; *tr. pl.*, 361 n.

Verica, British prince, 209

Verus, L., emperor, 120, 128 n., 129 n.

Vespasia Polla, m. of Vespasian, 226

VESPASIAN, emperor, *leg. leg.*, 225 ff.; 2, 64, 210, 224, 230, 336; accession, 6 n., 76, 228, 232, 233, 269; *adlecti* by, 24, 125, 234; careers under, 62, 65, 72 n., 86, 2211 f., 229, 268; consulship of, 20 n.; death, 212, 230; early career, 52 n.; friends, 76, 358, 361; gov. Brit. under, 62–81, 404; *iuridici* created, 210, 404; in Judaea, 60 n., 136, 269; *latus clavus* of, 4 n.; *leg. leg.* in Brit. under, 232; mistress, 3 n.; origin and career, 409 ff.; *pr.*, 223 n.; s.-in-law, 67 f.; titul., 431; Titus commanded legion under, 19; triumph, 79 n.

Vettilla, w. of Neratius Marcellus, 88, 91

VETTIUS BOLANUS, M. (*cos.* 66), gov. Brit., 62 ff.; 76 n., 77; nomenclature, 232; origin and career, 378 ff.; son, 9 n.; titul., 425, 63 n., 65

Vettius Bolanus, M. (*cos. ord.* 111), 63 n., 65

Vettius Crispinus, s. of Vettius Bolanus (*cos.* 66), 9 n., 63, 65, 396

Vettius Marcellus, M., proc., 63 n.

Vettius Philo, M., of Derriopus, 63

Vettius Sabinianus, C. (*cos. a. inc.*), consular commands, 31 n.; iterated legionary command, 20; service with XIV Gem., 30

VETTIUS STATURA, L., *tr. lat.*, 281; 416 ff.

Vettius Valens, amorous doctor, 215 n.

Vettius Valens, M., of Ariminum, 215

VETTIUS VALENS, M., *iurid.* Brit., 215; 405 ff.; patron of prov., 433

Vettulenus Cerialis, Sex. (*cos. a. inc.*), service with V Mac., 30

Vibia Aurelia Sabina, d. of M. Aurelius, 132

Vibius Marsus, C. (*cos.* 17), gov. Syria, 39 n.

Vibius Varus, T. (*cos. ord.* 134), gov. Cilicia, 257 n.

Victor, Flavius, s. of Magnus Maximus, 340, 352

Victorinus, emperor, 330

Victorinus, Moor, 181; perhaps *cos. ord.* 282, 181 n.

VICTORINUS, *vicarius* of Brit., 327 f.; 423

Vigellius . . . Saturninus *cet.*, P. (*cos. a. inc.*), nomenclature, 94 n.; *procos. Africae*, 264

Vincentius, associate of Romanus, 349

Vindex, C. Julius, rising of, 58, 61 n.

Vindicianus, low-ranking officer, 353

VINICIUS, M. (*cos. ord.* 30), *comes Claudii* in Brit., 363 f.; 358

Vinicius Pius, L., equest. officer, 156

Vipsania, first w. of Tiberius, 38 n.

Virius Agricola, L. (*cos. ord.* 230), 150, 151

Virius Egnatius Sulpicius Priscus, Q. (*cos. a. inc.*), 281 n.

VIRIUS LUPUS (*cos. a. inc.*), gov. Brit., 149 ff.; 137, 153, 169, 199, 204, 205; 208 n.; in Germania inf., 156; origin and career, 377 ff.; titul., 397, 426, 427, 428, 429, 430

Virius Lupus Julianus, L. (*cos. ord.* 232), 150, 151

Vitellia, m. of A. Plautius (*cos.* 29), 38

Vitellia Rufilla, w. of Salvius Liberalis, 213

Vitellius, emperor,, army and supporters of, 56, 66, 68, 75 n., 289; at Lugdunum, 57, 61, 62, 76 f., 230; Germanicus, 78; proconsular legate in Africa, 26 n.; returned XIV gem. to Brit., 232; withdrew troops from Brit., 61, 63 f.

Vitellius, L. (*cos. III ord.* 47), gov. Syria, 39; influence, 42; a son, 38; Vespasian a client, 227

Vitellius, P., on staff of Germanicus, 51

Vitorius Marcellus, M. (*cos.* 105), 223

Vitrasius Pollio, T. Pomponius Proculus (*cos. II ord.* 176), consular command, 6

VITULASIUS LAETINIANUS, *leg. leg.*, 267; 408 f.; titul., 432

Vitulasius Nepos, Sex. (*cos.* 78), 267
Voconius Saxa Fidus, Q. (*cos.* 146), iterated *tr.*, 10; military service, 18
Volasenna Severus, C. (*cos.* 47?), 225

Volusius Saturninus, Q. (*cos. ord.* 56), 59 f., 152
Vortigern, legendary sub-Roman Briton, alleged *vicarius* of Brit., 352 n.

2. *Geographical*

(Britain, Britannia, etc., Rome, and Italy are omitted)

Aachen, 221 n.
Aballava, 198 n.
Abila, 120
Abonuteichus, 249
Achaia, 17 n., 48, 86, 183, 216, 234, 238, 265, 381, 382, 405, 410, 412, 414
Aedui, 209
Aequum, 107, 118, 121, 378, 380
Africa, 17 n., 22, 23, 26, 31, 32, 47, 48, 70 n., 84, 90, 93, 94, 121, 126 n., 130, 134, 135 n., 145, 147, 152, 155 n., 156, 161, 163, 169, 175, 177 n., 179 n., 183, 185 n., 192, 194, 196, 197, 198, 201, 214, 216 n., 228, 238, 240, 243, 245, 246, 254, 262, 264, 267, 268, 270, 271 n., 272 n., 278, 279, 281, 284, 288, 294, 297 n., 299, 306, 308 n., 331 n., 339, 353, 362, 364, 365, 368, 370, 377, 378, 383, 400, 402, 403, 405, 409, 410 n., 411, 415, 416, 423, 424
Alamanni, 338, 351 n., 369 n., 373 n.
Alani, 215 n., 220, 342 n.
Alba, 172 n.
Alba Pompeia, 143, 378
Alexandria, 177 n.
Alpes Cottiae, 209
Alpes Graiae, 66 n.
Alpes Juliae, 131
Amiens, 337
Anatolia, 185
Anauni, 355
Anavionenses, 302
Ancyra, 9 n., 185, 329
Anglesey (Mone), 56, 79
Annan, R., 302
Antioch (Pisidia), 141, 192, 234, 302 n., 409, 434
Antioch (Syria), 159, 185, 281, 324 f.
Antium, 237
Apamea, 296, 420
Aphrodisias, 142 n.
Apulia, 38
Aquileia, 66 n., 101, 131, 307, 352
Aquincum, 201
Aquitania, 16 n., 21 n., 60 n., 77, 241, 266, 318 n., 362, 414, 421
Arabia, 6 n., 16 n., 17 n., 22, 30 n., 33, 84, 98, 130, 220, 238, 241, 275, 413, 414
Arausio, 274
Arelate, 60 n.
Argentorate, 227

Ariminum, 215, 354, 405
Armenia, 63, 89 n., 236 n., 395
Armenia maior, 302
Armorica, 312
Asia, 12 n., 17 n., 23, 26, 31, 32, 44, 46, 48, 57, 65, 71, 72 n., 75, 84 n., 87, 90 n., 92, 100, 110, 111, 113, 141, 142, 177 n., 185 n., 190, 192, 211, 226, 229, 236, 241, 249, 250, 263, 268, 300, 338 n., 358, 370, 380, 381, 382, 383, 389, 399, 400, 410 n., 411, 415
Assuras, 271 n.
Asturia-Callaecia, 17 n., 300
Athens, 60, 185, 365
Atina, 281, 361
Attidium, 254 f.
Augusta (London), 317
Atlas, Mt, 54 f., 394
Attaleia, 394
Autun, 316
Auzia, 158, 308 n.

Baebiani Ligures 91
Baeterrae, 274
Baetica, 17 n., 101, 102 n., 116, 236, 239, 241, 242, 243, 270, 271 n., 279, 414, 433 n.
Bainbridge, 156, 160
Balkans, 361, 394
Barcino, 245, 274
Batavians, 61
Bedriacum, 57, 62, 75 n., 232
Belgica, 16 n., 60 n., 139, 163 n., 216, 312, 326, 406, 423
Beneventum, 91, 99
Benwell, 140 f., 159, 165
Berytus, 281
Bewcastle, 104, 105 n.
Binchester, 194, 199
Birdoswald, 160, 187, 402
Birrens, 119, 120, 208 n.
Bithynia, 242; *see also* Pontus-Bithynia
Blemmyes, 132 n.
Blera, 282 n.
Boresti, 77
Bosporus (Crimea), 48, 49
Bostra, 130
Boulogne, 313, 315
Bowes, 107, 111 n., 151, 160, 199
Brigantes, 39 n., 48, 49, 64, 69, 71, 120, 151, 231

Brigetio, 103
Brixia, 116 n.
Brough-on-Noe, 120
Brühl, 143
Brundisium, 99
Bulla Regia, 175, 176 n., 258, 278
Burnum, 108, 109, 213, 380
Byzantium, 264, 425

Caerleon, 128 n., 172, 19, 257, 403, 408, 413
Caerwent, 189, 190, 403, 408
Caesaraugusta, 339, 423
Caesarea, London called?, 316 f.
Caesarea (Capp.), 185 n.
Caesarea (Mauret.), 273, 308 n., 316
Caesarea (Palest.), 183 n., 186, 316
Calama, 271
Caledonia, 80 n., 81, 136 n., 227
Callenses, 243
Cales, 363
Camerinum, 292, 420, 422
Campania, 45, 151
Camulodunum (Colchester), 67, 117, 121, 123, 124n., 219
Canusium, 280
Capena, 280
Cappadocia, 9 n., 17 n., 18, 26, 28, 29, 30 n., 51, 117, 125, 126, 136, 174 n., 185, 186 n., 215 n., 220, 236 n., 239, 264, 265, 272, 301, 302, 307, 381, 395, 400, 403, 415, 519
Cappadocia-Galatia, 17, 89, 210, 270, 404
Capua, 228
Carlisle, 71, 170, 191, 219, 221, 222 n., 313, 319 n.
Carnarvon, 350
Carnuntum, 125
Carrawburgh, 107
Carteia, 271 n.
Carthage, 195 n., 288 n., 339, 434
Caspian Gates, 224, 232
Cassandrea, 192
Castlecary, 123
Castlesteads, 111, 208 n.
Cauca, 339, 423
Caucasus, 61, 219
Chatti, 77, 128 n., 270, 362
Cheshire, 405
Chester (Deva), 170, 172, 220, 235, 396, 408
Chester-le-Street, 182
Chesters, 117, 141, 160
Chichester, 209 f.
Cibalae, 331 f.
Cibyra, 190
Cilicia, 17 n., 96, 97, 98 n., 222 n., 251, 256 f., 302, 324, 413, 414
Cirencester, 316, 317, 423
Cirta, 113, 114, 127, 135 n., 332, 378
Cisalpina, 62, 92, 198, 355

Clyde, Firth of, 80
Cologne, 143, 308 n.
Comum, 194
Concordia, 178, 402
Constantinople, 324, 327, 423
Corbridge, 120, 128, 151, 326
Corduba, 101, 105 n.
Cornovii, 40 n.
Cos, 192
Crete-Cyrene, 17 n., 49, 217, 226, 242, 365, 410 n., 411
Cuicul, 158, 378
Cyane, 51
Cyprus, 17 n., 45, 215, 228, 229, 237, 405, 414
Cyzicus, 192

Dacia, 26 n., 28, 31, 87, 103, 136, 144, 147, 292, 302, 319 n., 384
Dacia Apulensis, 129 n.
Dacia Porolissensis, 367
Dacia superior, 9 n., 17 n., 21 n., 22, 33, 108, 109 n., 116 f., 123, 125, 126, 134, 253, 272, 367 n., 394 f., 414
Daciae, III, 22, 26 n., 28, 29, 30, 31, 129, 144, 152, 153, 154 n., 155 n., 261, 262, 272, 275, 390, 400, 415, 419
Dalmatia, 17 n., 26 n., 28, 39, 55, 60 n., 76 n., 107, 108 n., 109, 118, 124, 135, 152, 154 n., 177 n., 214, 244, 248, 290, 294, 305 f., 354, 359, 370, 377, 378, 405, 409, 415
Danube, R., 79 n., 83, 121, 128, 144, 190 n., 220, 221, 224, 245, 278, 294, 309, 339, 349, 366 n., 410
Deceangli, 43
Derriopus, 63
Dertosa, 292
Deultum, 86
Dumfriesshire, 302
Dura-Europus, 121

Ebusus, 240 n.
Edinburgh, 294
Egypt, 8, 16 n., 42, 76 n., 147 n., 192, 256, 296, 302, 307, 332 n., 422
Elegeia, 220
Emerita, 249 n., 270, 339, 423
Emesa, 369
Ephesus, 81, 96 n., 170, 192
Etruria, 62 n., 103, 239, 434

Falacrina, 226
Faventia, 85, 87, 378
Felixstowe, 172 n.
Fishbourne, 210
Florence, 216
Formiae, 69
Forth, Firth of, 80

Forum Julii, 73, 76, 107 n., 378
Forum Novum, 51
Fulginiae, 302

Gades, 101, 268
Galatia, 16 n., 17 n., 34, 98 n., 162 n., 186, 223 n., 300, 403
Gallaecia, 348 n.
Galliae, III, 207 n., 223 n., 355 n., 413
Gallic empire, 35, 177, 178, 200, 316, 330, 403, 407
Gaul, Gauls, 47, 59 f., 70, 125, 149, 177, 180, 211 n., 225 n., 287, 288, 289, 291, 300, 308, 311, 313 ff., 324, 326, 328, 330, 339 f., 341, 343, 351, 352, 353, 355, 363, 372, 373, 377, 378, 409, 416, 420, 423
Gaulus, 259
Genua, 279
Ger, R., 55
Gerasa, 130
Germania inferior, 19, 28, 29, 30, 31, 68, 70 n., 71, 93, 98, 101, 103 f., 114, 117, 119, 120, 129, 131, 142, 148, 149, 150, 156, 219, 221, 238, 239, 241, 256, 273, 292, 301, 303, 306, 381, 389, 390, 394, 408 n., 415
Germania superior, 6 n., 28, 29, 82, 85, 93, 102, 111, 132, 133, 134, 159 n., 170 f., 214, 219, 227, 254, 261, 292, 362, 381, 390, 406, 408 n., 412, 415
Germanies, the, 26 n., 28, 29, 55, 93, 158
Germans, Germany, 9, 18, 38, 56, 67, 79, 81 n., 171, 172, 384, 410, 416, 418, 419
Glevum (Gloucester), 121, 219, 230
Goths, 549
Graupius, Mons, 78, 79, 81
Greece, 45, 86
Greta Bridge, 160

Hadrumetum, 147, 378
Herculaneum, 225
Hierapolis, 71
Hierapolis Castabala, 96, 97
High Rochester, 167, 182, 189, 196 n.
Hippo Regius, 367, 368
Hispalis, 249 n., 279
Hispania citerior, *see* Tarraconensis
Histonium, 45, 223, 378
Humber, R., 317

Iceni, 39 n., 43
Iconium, 302
Iguvium, 38 n., 214, 405
Iliberris, 116 f., 378
Ilkley, 150, 151
Illyricum, 38, 131, 296, 339, 352
Inchtuthil, 220
Interamna, 266

Intimilium, 75
Inveresk, 294
Ireland, 80
Italica, 101 n., 339

Jerusalem, 79 n., 324, 423
Judaea, 16 n., 17 n., 22, 26 n., 28, 29, 30, 31, 60 n., 98, 109, 125, 220, 222 n., 228, 237, 272, 291, 316, 381, 395, 400, 414, 419, 421; *see also* Syria Palaestina

Kent, 330
Kintyre, 80

Lambaesis, 120, 261 n.
Lancaster, 35, 131 n.
Lanchester, 129, 131 n.
Lanuvium, 216
Latium, 69
Leicester, 219
Libarna, 92 n.
Liguria, 42, 75, 143, 145
Lincoln, 172, 219, 220, 231
Lingones, 70
Lombardy, 65
London, 289, 316 f., 337, 420
Lugdunensis, 16 n., 60 n., 188, 403, 414, 421
Lugdunum, 57, 62, 149, 150, 169, 230, 306, 308 n., 398 n.
Lusitania, 16 n., 215, 223 n., 237, 270, 413, 414, 419
Lycia, 17 n., 30 n., 51, 52, 152, 229, 379, 384, 413, 414
Lycia-Pamphylia, 17 n., 21 n., 22, 89, 98, 156 n., 234, 413, 414
Lystra, 141 n.

Macedonia, 17 n., 48, 63, 137, 138, 192, 212, 213, 217, 357, 381, 382, 406
Maeatae, 136 n., 150 f.
Mainz, *see* Mogontiacum
Marcianopolis, 162
Marcomanni, 131, 344
Marsi, 45
Maryport, 293, 421
Mauretania, 54, 55, 171, 178 n., 222, 223 n., 273, 308, 316, 357, 384, 422
Mauretania, 54, 55, 171, 178 n., 222, 223 n., 273, 308, 316, 357, 384, 422
Mauretania Caesariensis, 126 n., 158, 296, 330
Mauretania Tingitana, 171, 341 n., 433
Mediolanium (Milan), 62, 253, 279
Medway, R., 227
Menapii, 314
Mesopotamia, 16 n., 319 n., 369
Meuse, R., 314
Mevania, 66
Milan, *see* Mediolanium

Minturnae, 272
Misenum, 158, 222 n., 299, 309 n.
Moesia, 26 n., 30, 38, 47, 48, 51, 60 n., 79,
    143, 147, 152, 225, 339, 358, 384, 389,
    410, 415, 419
Moesia inferior, 29, 30, 31, 99, 106, 127,
    129, 144, 152, 153, 154, 162, 163, 174,
    177 n., 195 n., 246, 248, 250, 293, 390,
    410, 415, 419, 421
Moesia superior, 9 n., 30, 122, 129 n., 133,
    144, 235, 239, 240 n., 250, 252, 275,
    290 n., 307, 390, 395, 396, 399, 415
Moesias, the, 26 n., 28, 29, 174 n.
Moguntiacum (Mainz), 79 n., 102, 132, 134,
    261, 262
Mona, 56, 79
Moors, 181, 339
Mursa, 331
Mustis, 194 f.
Mytilene, 97

Naples, 102
Narbo, 308 n.
Narbonensis, 17 n., 60, 70, 73, 81 n., 107,
    189, 220, 236, 238, 274, 285, 355 n.,
    362, 377, 403, 406, 414, 419, 434
Narona, 294
Nedinum, 213, 214
Netherby, 165, 167, 187
Newcastle upon Tyne, 119, 165 n.
Nicaea, 241 f., 409
Nicopolis, 162
Nijmegen, 219, 221
Nomentum, 303 f.
Noricum, 16 n., 17 n., 22, 193 n.
Novaria, 83, 295, 378, 420
Numidia, 16 n., 17 n., 22, 33, 35, 113, 114,
    127, 129, 130, 153, 154, 155, 158,
    191 n., 193 n., 196 n., 214, 223 n., 236,
    261, 292, 332, 405, 410, 413, 414
Nursia, 226

Ocriculum, 266, 279, 282 n.
Oescus, 370 f.
Old Carlisle, 167
Olympia, 47, 92, 396
Orcades, 318 n., 336, 38 n.
Ordovices, 43
Ostia, 112, 124 n., 137, 139, 187, 276, 307,
    368, 405
Oxyrrhynchus, 183 n.

Paeligni, 45
Pamphylia, 195, 403; *see also* Lycia-Pamphylia
Pannonia, 18, 26 n., 28 n., 39, 55, 60 n., 131,
    135 n., 219, 221, 268 n., 295, 331,
    339 n., 384, 389, 410, 422, 423
Pannonia inferior, 16 n., 17 n., 18, 22, 26 n.,
    28, 31, 33, 130 n., 141, 142 n., 144 n.,

[Pannonia inferior] 156, 157, 168, 170,
    174 n., 201, 256, 275, 367, 384, 415
Pannonia superior, 18, 26 n., 28, 29, 30, 103,
    113, 117, 125, 146, 157, 162 n., 163,
    245, 306, 381, 384, 410, 415, 419
Pannonias, the, 168, 170
Papcastle, 198 n.
Paphlagonia, 249
Paphos, 228, 229
Paros, 187 n.
Parthia, Parthians, 29, 120, 126, 220 n.
Peltuinum Vestinum, 308 n.
Pennines, 69, 120, 129, 151
Pergamum, 251, 409
Perge, 195
Persia, 318 n.
Petra, 238, 290 n.
Pevensey, 374 n.
Phrygia, 41, 71, 305
Picenum, 45
Pietas, 338 n.
Picts, 336, 351, 372, 375
Pisaurum, 55, 368, 378
Pisidia, 177 n., 302
Pompeii, 41, 360
Pontus-Bithynia, 17 n., 26 n., 28, 68 n., 217,
    272 n.
Praeneste, 37, 284, 405, 406
Puteoli, 112, 281 n.

Quadi, 131, 344

Raetia, 9 n., 16 n., 17 n., 22, 132, 133, 134,
    178, 300, 369
Ravenna, 76 n., 308, 309 n.
Ravenscar, 353 n.
Reate, 51, 226
Reculver, 173, 175
Reii Apollinares, 285
Remi, 180
Rheims, 374
Rhine, R., Rhineland, 64, 68, 70, 81, 120,
    144, 148, 156, 177, 219, 221, 224, 233,
    237, 256, 278, 309, 338, 340, 341, 343,
    374, 375, 402, 407 n., 410
Rhone, R., 70
Ribchester, 128, 169, 182, 204
Risingham, 159, 160
Rouen, 313 n.
Rumania, 367
Ruseilae, 434
Rusicade, 135 n.

Sabines, 51, 57, 66 n., 231
Saepinum, 88, 99 n., 91, 134 n., 361, 378, 389
Saguntum, 240 n.
Salamis (Cyprus), 237
Salona, 248, 259, 369 n., 370, 408, 409, 410,
    411, 413

Samnium, 45, 88
Sardinia, 17 n., 85, 279, 299, 321, 423
Sarmatians, 131
Sarmizegethusa, 117, 253
Sassina, 66 n., 306, 422
Savaria, 156 n.
Saxons, 339, 344, 375
Scalesceugh, 221 n.
Scheldt, R., 314
Scilly, 352
Scots, 351, 372, 375
Sentinum, 282
Severn, R., 43
Sicily, 12 n., 17 n., 47, 140, 155, 251, 253,
  259, 410 n., 414, 434
Side, 142 n.
Silures, 43, 48, 54, 71, 190, 230
Sinduni, 355
Sirmium, 144 n.
Smyrna, 71
Snowdonia, 61
Solway Firth, 100
Sopianae, 141
Spain, 62, 70, 101, 102, 110, 155 n., 161,
  171, 235, 239, 240, 243, 349, 368, 270,
  277, 279, 280, 300, 326, 331, 339,
  341 n., 348, 352, 370, 377, 378, 405,
  409, 416, 420, 423, 433; *xee also* Baetica,
  Lusitania, Tarraconensis
Sparta, 96
Spoletium, 155
Stainmore, 107
Stanwick, 64
Strathearn, 137 n.
Suasa, 282, 354
Suebi, 342 f.
Syria, 9, 18, 26 n., 28, 29, 30, 39, 52, 57, 58,
  59, 60 n., 81, 109, 120, 121, 126, 133,
  134, 141, 143, 144, 145, 146, 147 n.,
  159, 171, 214, 236, 262, 270, 275, 279,
  281, 290 n., 300, 301, 306, 309, 369,
  390, 400, 406, 411, 419
Syria Coele, 29 n., 159, 185, 276, 390, 403
Syria Palaestina, 18, 22, 26 n., 28, 29, 130,
  216 n.
Syria Phoenice, 16 n., 17 n., 22, 34, 171 n.,
  296

Tampium, 190
Tarquinii, 239
Tarracina, 69, 96
Tarraco, 49 n., 233, 237, 240 n., 274
Tarraconensis, 17, 26 n., 27, 28, 29, 31,
  60 n., 111, 116, 152, 153, 154 n., 155 n.,
  162, 163, 164, 174 n., 195 n., 199, 210,
  218, 240 n., 245, 307, 348 n., 358, 362,
  400
Tarsus, 168
Taurus, Mts, 59, 61, 395

Tay, R., 80
Teanum Sidicinum, 174 n.
Teate Marrucinorum, 63 n.
Tergestinus, ager, 39
Tern, R., 43 n.
Thamugadi, 196, 236, 280
Theveste, 141 n., 308 n.
Thibilis, 129, 130, 131, 378
Thorigny, 169, 189 f.
Thrace, 17 n., 21 n., 47, 48, 86, 103, 110 n.,
  133, 134, 147 n., 174, 226, 242 n., 276,
  349, 388 n., 414, 424
Thuburnica, 176 n.
Thugga, 161, 196, 216 n.
Thule, 64, 224, 227, 336, 396
Thyateira, 141
Thysdrus, 198
Tiber, *see General index, under curatores
  alvei Tiberis*
Tibur, 37, 102 n., 104 n., 110, 215, 243, 245,
  249, 263, 268, 270, 279, 405, 405, 409
Ticinum, 75 n.
Tiddis, 113
Tifernum Mataurense, 281 n.
Tigranocerta, 70 n.
Tolosa (Toulouse), 60, 328, 378, 423
Trebula Suffenas, 37, 378
Trent, R., 43
Treveri, 289
Tricomia, 305 n.
Trier, 326, 351 n.
Trieste, 307, 422
Tucci, 101 n.
Tulliasses, 355
Tusculum, 171, 277, 434
Tyana, 185
Tyne, R., 100, 326

Ugia, 249 n.
Umbria, 51, 56, 66, 155, 214, 231, 254,
  274 n., 302, 306, 354, 405, 420, 422
Urbs Salvia, 211, 213, 405
Urvinum Mataurense, 281
Usipi, 79 n.
Uthina, 271 n.
Utica, 258

Valentia, 318 f., 338, 350
Valle Crucis, 352 n.
Vandals, 342 f.
Vectio, 131
Verona, 51, 279, 281 n., 87, 290, 351 n., 420
Verulamium, 80, 316
Vestini, 267 n.
Vetera, 70, 239
via Aemilia, 22, 85, 144
via Appia, 22
via Flaminia, 22 246 n.
via Labicana, 277

via Latina, 251
via Salaria, 217, 226
via Triana, 99
via Valeria, 259, 285
Vicetia, 290
Vienna (Vienne), 70, 362
Viminacium, 126, 252
Vindobona (Vienna), 113
Vindolanda, 87, 88, 396
Volturnum, 258f.

Walcot, 107
Whitley Castle, 167
Wight, I. of, 227
Wroxeter, 43n, 219

Xanthus, 54n, 89, 152, 154

York, 81n, 170, 219, 221, 222, 239, 247,
317n, 319, 408
Yorkshire, 353, 423

3. *Sources quoted* in extenso
(a) Literary

Amm. Marc.	14.5.6–9	321f.
	20.1.1–3	371
	20.4.3,6,9	371
	20.9.9	372
	21.16.2	35
	25.1.2	323
	27.8.1–9.1	333f.
	27.8.7	317n
	28.3.1–9	334f.
	18.3.1	317n
	28.5.1–2	339
	29.1.44	323
	30.7.2–3	331
	31.4.9–10	349
	31.5.14	34n
Anec. Gr. 2.291		181
Aur. Vict. *de Caes.* 20.18		206n
	29.8–9	146
	33.33	35
	39.19–21	310
	39.26	314n
	39.39–42	310
Auson.	*Mosella* 392–5	325
	405–8	326
	Ordo urbium nobilium 64–72	346
	Parentalia 20	330
Catullus 81.3		55n
Chronographer of AD 452 (*Chron. min.* i.646)		347
Cic. *ad fam.* 13.77.2–3		62n
Claud. *in cons. Stil.* 2.247–55		374
	de III cons. Honorii 51–8	335
	de IV cons. Honorii 24–33	335
	72–7	346f.
	Epithalamium 218–21	335
	in Eutroph. 1.391–3	374
	laus Serenae 37–46	336
Cod. Just. 4.15.2		168n
Cod. Theod. 9.36.1		326
	11.7.2	321
Collectio Avellana (*CSEL* 35.1.90)		351n
Digest. 1.13.1.2,4		13n
	28.3.6.7	95
	28.6.2.4	150

Digest. (*cont.*) 33.7.12.43		88
	36.1.48	214
Dio 60.9.1		385
	60.20.3	224
	64.4.1	135n
	66.20.3	135
	69.13.2	135n
	72.8.1–2	135
	72.9.2a	260
	75.5.1–3	3n
	76.12.1	136n
	76.14.5–6	368
Epit. de Caes. 39.3		311
	47.7	346
Eutropius 7.13		37, 60
	9.13–14	310f.
Festus *Brev.* 6		318n
Frag. Vat. 119		265n
Frontin. *Strat.* 4.3.14		385f.
Fronto *ad Verum imp.* 2.1.19		273f.
Georg. Cedrenus, *PG* 121,599		348
Gildas, *de excidio Brit.* 13		347
Gregory of Tours, *Hist. Franc.* 1.43		347
HA *Ant. Pius* 5.4		112
	Carac. 8.2	369n
	Clod. Alb. 1.3	147
	3.4	146
	6.3	148
	Comm. 3.8.	136n
	6.2, 8.4	139n
	Gord. 9.1	183n
	Had. 1.3	9n
	4.1–1	103
	5.1–2	99n
	8.5	103n
	11.2–3	365f.
	15.2	104
	15.4	91
	23.4	105
	M. Ant. Phil. 2.5	256n
	8.8	127
	9.1	126n

HA M.Ant. Phil. (*cont.*) 10.3		33
14.6		131
Pert. 2.6		384, 387
2.10-11		393
3.5-4.1		142f.
12.8		146n
Pesc. Nig. 5.2		295
Severus 6.10		295
18.2		206n
Verus 7.1		126n
Herodian 7.5.2		183n
Jerome, *Chron. s.a.* 300		370
Johann. Antioch, *fr.* 164		311
fr. 186		348
John of Nikiou, *Chron.* 83.14		348
Joseph., *BJ* 3.4		225f.
7.82-3		66
Julian *ep. ad Ath.* 283A		371
epp. 9, 10		323
Libanius, *ep.* 327		322f.
Mart. 10.58.1-2		69n
narratio de imperatoribus domus		
Valentinianae et Theodosianae		
(*Chron. min.* i 629)		347
Nennius, *Hist. Brittonum* 26-7, 29		348
Not. Dig. Occ. 23		316n
Olympiodor. fr. 12		341
Oros. *Hist. adv. paganos* 7.25.3,6		311
7.34.9		347
7.40.4		343n
Pan. Lat. Vet. 2 (12).5.1-2		333
2 (12).23.3		346
2 (12).24.1		348n
2 (12).31.1-2,38.2		346
8 (5).12.1-2		310
10 (2).12.1-2		309f.
10 (2).15.5		310
Philo, *Leg.* 243		58n
Pliny, *ep.* 3.3.1		91
7.16.2		13n
8.12.1		3n
9.2.4		84
9.25.2		235
Polemius Silvius *Laterculus* 260		316n
Laterculus, Chron.		
min. i.523,79		342
Prosper Tiro *s.a.* 384		347
Quint. 2.15.36		295
6.3.38		44n
Rufin. *Hist. Eccl.* 2.14		347
Rut. Namat. *de reditu* 491-508		327

Senec. *Apoc.* 14.2		38n
Sil. Ital. 3.597-8		226
Socr. *Hist. Eccl.* 5.11.2		347
7.12.1		326
7.13.1		347
Sozom. *Hist. Eccl.* 9.11.1-2		341
Stat. *Silv.* 5.2.31-2		63n
5.2.54-6, 140-9		62
Suet. *D. Aug.* 37.1		33
Domit. 10.2-3		82
Nero 35.4		40n
D. Titus 4.1		368
D. Vesp. 2.2		226
Sulp. Sever. *Chron.* 2.49.5		347
Dial. 3.11.8		330
v. Martini 20.3		347
Symmachus *relat.* 9.4, 43.2		333
Tac. *Agr.* 5.1		9n, 74
5.1-3		381
6.3	61, 75n,	382
6.4		383
6.5		386
7.2		232
7.3	76, 386,	431
9.1-5		386
9.4		289n
14.1	38n,	41n
16.3	58, 59,	60
18.6		79
20.3	79,	80n
20.1, 23, 24		80
26.2		81
38.2-4		77f.
39.2		77
40.3, 41.3		81
Ann. 2.36.1		3n
6.41.1		385
12.31.2		41
12.39.2		53
13.6.4, 13.8.1		3n
14.32.2, 15.3.1		385
Hist. 2.57.1		61
3.44		431
3.50.1		76n
3.59.2	67,	385
3.75.1		225n
4.39.1-2		383
4.69.1		155n
4.79.3		431
5.3.1, 23.3		65n
Tertullian *ad Scap.* 3.4		264f.
Val. Flacc. 1.7-9		226
Laterculus Veronensis 249 Seeck		316
Zonar. 12.29		180f.
12.31		311

Zosim. *Hist. Nov.* 1.66.2, 68.3 — 180   Zosim. (*cont.*)   6.2.1-2 — 341f.
                4.35.3-4 — 347   6.3.1 — 342

(b) Epigraphic

Acta... *Fifth Congress of Epigr.*,
     193ff. — 307
AE 1897.78 — 151f.
     1908.200 — 301
     1908.237 — 235
     1909.22 — 286
     1910.86 — 123
     1911.112 — 158
     1921.64 — 369
     1922.36 — 247
     1925.126 — 269
     1929.166 — 363
     1931.53 — 336
     1938.177 — 281
     1946.94 — 73n
     1946.131 — 278
     1947.74, 76 — 365
     1949.61 — 286f.
     1950.251 — 241
     1952.95 — 286f.
     1953.251 — 50
     1955.174 — 276
     1956.123 — 120
     1956.186 — 228
     1957.123 — 134n
     1957.169 — 73
     1957.336 — 95
     1960.28 — 308
     1961.37 — 286f.
     1961.320 — 250
     1962.258 — 173
     1963.52 — 143n
     1963.281 — 155
     1965.240 — 261
     1967.260 — 206
     1968.145 — 89n
     1971.218 — 182
     1971.475 — 183n
     1971.490 — 175
     1972.70 — 307
     1972.577 — 95
     1973.133 — 217
     1973.152 — 41n
     1974.123 — 307
AJA 64 (1960) 274 — 308
Alföldy, *Fasti Hispanienses* 50 — 161f.
                    81ff. — 275
                    154 — 267
Alföldy, *Hommages Renard* II 3ff. — 155
                    4ff. — 157
Ant. J. 36 (1956) 8ff. — 73
     41 (1961) 22 — 173
Arch. Camb. 119 (1970) 37ff. — 202, 285
Arch.-ep. Mitt. 19 (1896) 147ff. — 151f.
Ath. Mitt. 1908. 150 — 301

Britannia 1 (1970) 305f. — 202, 285
     1 (1970) 307 — 182
     2 (1971) 292f. — 73
     3 (1972) 363 — 118
     4 (1973) 336f. — 115
     7 (1976) 378f. — 176
     8 (1977) 432 — 158
     8 (1977) 433 — 294
     10 (1979) 243ff. — 209
     11 (1980) 313f. — 434
Bull. Comm. 1940.180 — 105n
Bull. Dalm. 27 (1914) 42 — 259n, 285
Byzantion 5 (1929-30) 9ff. — 336
Chiron 2 (1972) 405ff. — 217
     6 (1976) 357ff. — 157
CIL II 1262 — 279
     II 1283 — 243
     II 1371 — 242f.
     II 1861 — 101n
     II 2075 — 117
     II 2078 — 116
     II 4117 — 233
     II 4510 — 244
     II 4609 — 273
     II 6084 — 240
     II 6259^{19} — 65n
     III 87 + 14148^{10} — 237f.
     III 249 — 300
     III 348 — 304
     III 1061 — 126n
     III 1455=7972 — 272
     III 1458 — 251ff.
     III 2830 + 9891 — 106
     III 2864 — 213
     III 4354=11082 — 160n
     III 4796 — 179n
     III 7247 + 12278 — 45
     III 8598 — 148
     III 8714 + 2732 — 118
     III 8716 — 305
     III 12117 — 96
     V 877 — 101
     V 3337 — 288
     V 5050 — 355
     V 5849 — 62n
     V 6513 — 295
     V 7165 — 364
     V 8112^{69} — 42n
     VI 452 — 103n
     VI 773 — 180n
     VI 1223 — 329
     VI 1333 — 273f.
     VI 1336 — 137
     VI 1471 — 218

CIL VI 1497 + 1549 — 273
VI 1510 — 216
VI 1518 — 218
VI 1523 — 124
VI 1551 — 218
VI 1567 — 111n
VI 1626 — 291
VI 1643 — 309
VI 2151 — 164n
VI 9363=33805 — 289n
VI 23601 — 42n
VI 29683–4 — 279
VI 31719 — 211n
VI 31780 — 283
VI 31863 — 300f.
VI 33805 — 289n
VI 37056 — 268
VI 37083 — 285
VII 1287 — 326
VIII 597, cf. 11754 — 161f.
VIII 1578 — 194
VIII 2747 — 276
VIII 5355 + 17493 — 271
VIII 5349 — 125n
VIII 6706 — 113
VIII 8826 — 179n
VIII 11763 — 161
VIII 12442 — 278
VIII 17891 — 235f.
VIII 18931 — 130n
VIII 21665 — 179n
IX 2456 — 87f.
IX 2847 — 222
IX 5533 — 211
IX 9335 — 38
X 525 — 284
X 3364 — 239
X 3722 — 258
X 5178 — 153
X 5398 — 153
X 6006 — 271
X 6321 — 95
X 6569 — 295
XI 383 — 215
XI 3002 — 244f.
XI 3883 — 280
XI 4083 — 279
XI 4182 — 265
XI 5173 — 267
XI 5213 — 302
XI 5632 — 292
XI 5670 — 254
XI 5672 — 254f.
XI 6054 — 281
XI 6163 — 354
XI 6165 — 282
XI 6327 — 351
XII 3656 — 70n
XIII 3162 — 188

XIII 6806 — 132
XIII 8598 — 148
XIV 182 — 282
XIV 2500 — 356
XIV 2508 — 433
XIV 2612 — 229n
XIV 2926, 3518 — 284
XIV 3595 — 263
XIV 3599 — 244
XIV 3955 — 303
XIV 3601 — 248
XIV 3608 — 357
XIV 3612 — 270
XIV 4059 — 285
XIV 4129 — 276
XIV 4244 — 248
XIV 4248 — 215
XIV 4249 — 256
XIV 4473 — 111n
XIV 5341 + 5353 + 5382 — 307
XV 1363–6 — 104
XV 8088 — 175n
XVI 43 — 83
XVI 48 — 87
XVI 69 — 95
XVI 70 — 100
XVI 82 — 109
XVI 88 — 94
XVI 93 — 116
XVI 130 — 121
Corinth VIII.2.64 — 286

Dittenberger & Purgold, *Inschriften von Olympia* 620 — 92

EE VII 1267 — 285
IX 612 — 270
IX 722 + 774 — 217
IX 1039 — 73
Epigraphica 4 (1942) 105ff. — 278
Ep. Stud. 3 (1967) 44 no. 229 — 261
4 (1967) 91f. — 199
5 (1968) 136f. — 259n, 285

Gordon, *Quintus Veranius* — 50

Hesp. 10 (1941) 237f., 239ff. — 365

IGR I 658 — 245
III 188 — 186n
III 618 — 151f.
III 703 — 51
III 991 — 237
ILAfr. 324 — 286
ILAlg. I 282 — 271
II 3605 — 113
ILS 206 — 355
216 — 43n
455 — 297n

ILS 478	296	9485	233f.
626	180n	9489	158
954	357	*Inscr. It.*IV 110	263
957	356	IV 113	244
961	38	IV 115–16	248
967	354	IV 125	357
970	45	IV 129	270
971	222	IV 137	215
986	357	IV 143	256
990–1	46	XIII.1 p. 205, cf. 235	116
1011	211	*IRT* 541	278
1015 + add.	213	*Istanbuler Mitt.* 9/10 (1959–60) 109ff.	250
1025	270		
1028	273	*JHS* (1896) 253	96
1032	87f.	*JÖAI* 10(1907) 307ff.	245
1035	95	12 (1909) Bbl. 149	123
1036	96	19/20 (1919) Bbl. 318 ff.	369
1047	239	49 (1968–71) Bbl. 29ff.	95
1052	101	*JRS* 3 (1913) 260	233f.
1055	235f.	14 (1924) 180	269
1056 + add.	106	45 (1955) 147	172n
1061	244	46 (1956) 146f.	73
1066	271	51 (1961) 191	173
1070 + add.	276	51 (1961) 192	155
1071	211n	55 (1965) 220	173
1077	273f.	55 (1965) 222	202
1092	117n, 124	57 (1967) 205f.	206
1094 + 1100	273	58 (1968) 170ff.	89n
1098	34n, 121n, 129n		
1101	248	*Karthago* 2 (1951) 100ff.	286f.
1110	278	11 (1961) 6ff.	283n
1123	216		
1151	137	*Mainzer Ztschr.* 59 (1964) 56	261
1159	153	Mitford, *Report of Dept. of Ant.,*	
1338	302	*Cyprus* (1954) 4	228
1385	291		
1396	300	Nash-Williams, *Early Christ. Mon.*	
1477	304	*of Wales* (1950) 92 no. 101	314n
2302	252	*Not. Scav.* 1929. 31	363
2536	434		
2735	292	Pflaum, *Arch. Esp. Arq.* 39 (1956)	
2740	303	15ff.	241
2935	425	Pflaum, *CP* no. 92	305
3620	103n	Pflaum, *Le Marbre de Thorigny* 7ff.	188f.
3891	123n		
4006	126n	*Rend. Acc. Arch. Napoli* 41 (1966)	
4197, 4452, 4501	179n	113	360
6043	225n	*REG* 59–60 (1946–7) 350f.	241
8704a	73	*RIB* 8	167n, 172, 206
8784	242n	12	288
8824a	92	66	306
8841	151f.	91	208f.
8929	370n	103	178
8974 + 1057 + add.	118	152	179n
8975	275	283	118
8977	129f.	311	187
8980	286	316	266
9011	300f.	320	258
9013	301	334	178

RIB 335 — 256
419 — 201
430 — 204
445 — 234
518 — 101n
587 — 194
589 — 127
590 — 181
591 — 204
605 — 200
637 — 149
644 — 247
658 — 263
721 — 353
722–3 — 157
730 — 149, 199
739 — 106
740 — 157
741 — 199
746 — 157
752 — 299
793 — 127
883 — 198n
897 — 198
905 — 167
929 — 193
976 — 164f., 166
977 — 166
978 — 191
980 — 187
995 — 105
1049 — 181
1051 — 205
1060 — 191
1083 — 129
1091–2 — 197
1132 — 118
1137 — 127
1138 — 265
1147–8 — 112
1149 — 127
1151 — 202
1163 — 150
1205 — 166
1234 — 157
1262 — 197
1265 — 166
1276 — 112
1279 — 181
1280 — 187f.
1281 — 195
1322 — 118
1329 — 140, 164
1337 — 157
1340, 1427 — 100

1462 — 157
1463–4 — 140, 164
1465 — 190
1467 — 188
1468 — 208
1470 — 188n
1550 — 106
1553 — 196
1596 — 208
1634, 1637 — 100
1638, 1666, 1702 — 101
1703 — 127
1706 — 191
1738 — 192
1751 — 197n
1792, 1809 — 127
1909 — 157f.
1912 — 200
1914 — 187
1922 — 207
1932 — 202
1935 — 101
1997–8 — 110
1999 — 207
2034 — 253
2060 — 206
2066 — 299
2110 — 118
2132 — 294
2191–2 — 112
2212 — 203
2291 — 313
2298 — 166
2299 — 191
2306 — 192
2313 — 115
RIT 134 — 233
140 — 240
Röm. Österreich 3 (1975) 178 — 123

Schneider, *Istanbuler Forsch.* 16
(1943) no. 2 — 241
SEG XVIII 587 — 228
Solin, *Epigraphische Untersuchungen*
(1975) 6ff. — 434
Stein, *Dazien* 23 — 251f.
Stillwell, *Antioch on the Orontes*
(1938) 150 no. 61 — 281

TAM II 278 — 151f.
Tesser. Urb. Rom. et sub. Syll. 230 — 56

Vindolanda Tablet, Inv. no. 29 + 31 — 83

ZPE 38 (1980) 173ff.

(c) Numismatic

A.S. Robertson, *Roman Imperial Coins in the Hunter Coin Cabinet*, I (1962) 284 no. 13 — 78n

4. *General*

ab actis senatus, 14, 89, 251, 259, 263, 283, 383, 389, 411

ab epistulis, 3 n., 367

acting governors, 137 ff., 236, 406 f.

adlectio, 14, 15, 24, 25, 68, 158, 211, 212, 213, 234, 240, 251, 252, 382, 406, 410 f.

aedileship, 3 f., 14, 263

aerarium militare, 16, 23 f., 34, 138, 216, 217, 297, 406

aerarium Saturni, 13, 16, 19, 23 f., 34, 239, 241, 250, 270, 354, 388, 412, 415

alae:
  Afrorum, 301; *II Asturum*, 141; *I Ulpia contariorum*, 306; *II Gallorum*, 307; *Gallorum et Pannoniorum*, 293; *Indiana*, 289; *Moesica*, 305 f.; *Parthorum*, 302; *Sebosiana*, 200; *Tampiana*, 190

alimenta, 16, 24, 26, 27, 144, 145, 152, 246 n., 250, 369, 400, 413, 414

Antonine Wall, breaching of, 135 ff.; building of, 100, 112, 114, 251, 254; evacuation of, 120, 128; possible reoccupation, 123, 128

aqua Claudia, 47

a rationibus, 292, 301, 305

Armeniacus, title, 120 n., 126, 128 n.

Arval Brethren, 32, 62, 83 f., 211 ff., 400

augurs, 32, 53, 119, 246, 267, 400 f., 415

Britannicus, title, 78 n., 139, 142, 260, 312 n., 319 n., 351

candidati Caesaris, 13 f., 15, 25, 75, 102, 108, 117, 163, 245, 248, 280, 283, 380, 382, 383, 411, 418

canvassing for office, 2 f., 44

censitores:
  equestrian, 300 ff., 307; senatorial, 27, 59 f., 225 n., 268

census, senatorial, 4

classis Britannica, 293, 305 ff., 311 f., 422

classis Germanica, 144, 306

classis Moesica, 305

cohortes:
  II Asturum, 307; *I Dalmatarum*, 141; *VII Gallorum eq.*, 143; *I Lingonum*, 197; *I Thracum*, 199; *II Tungrorum*, 208; *I fida Vardullorum*, 123, 195

comites:
  Africae, 322 n.; *Augustorum*, 32, 41, 71, 93 f., 120, 121, 129 n., 163, 164, 223 n., 354 ff.; *Britanniae*, 320, 338 n., 346 n.; *domesticorum*, 337, 373 f.; *litoris Saxonici*, 320, 333, 338 n., 341, 346 n., 350; *rei militaris*, 320, 332, 338, 341 n., 345, 423; *rei privatae*, 325

congiaria, 50, 78 f.

consular career, 26 ff., 384 ff., 413 ff., and *passim*

consularis, 319, 327

consulships: 3 f., 21, 24 f.
  iterated, 32, 66, 72, 84, 114, 145, 148, 151, 229, 267, 362, 363; ordinary, 24, 42, 53, 56, 65, 73, 84, 91, 92, 96, 110, 126, 131, 148, 150, 151, 152, 156, 173 f., 181 n., 230, 249, 255, 267, 321, 361, 363, 369, 373, 388, 415; suffect, 24, and *passim*

cuneus Frisionum, 198 n.

curatores:
  aedium sacrarum operumque publ., 26, 117, 119, 243, 246, 272, 329, 389, 433 n.; *alvei Tiberis*, 21 n., 26, 27, 239, 241; *aquarum*, 26, 27, 32, 46 f., 58, 72, 90, 389, 399 f.; *civitatium*, 17, 259, 274; *viarum*, 16, 22 f., 99, 103, 244, 245 n., 251, 252 n., 270, 272, 412; *see also alimenta, Minicia*

curio, 112

Dacian wars, of Trajan, 20 n., 90, 98, 221, 306

damnatio memoriae, 115, 165, 167, 182, 187, 195, 199, 200, 204, 206, 370

Danubian wars, of M. Aurelius, 24 n., 109, 121, 125, 128 f., 130 f., 133, 144, 309 n.

Xviri stlitibus iudicandis, 4 ff., 98, 163, 380, 410, 418

dona militaria, 113, 118, 125 n., 220 n., 269, 270, 276, 354

duces, 312, 319 f., 325, 337, 344 ff., 349, 350

epistrategus, 192

fetiales, 32, 114, 131, 361 f., 401, 415

Hadrian's Wall, building of, 100, 104, 107, 111, 160, 221, 254, 293; crossed by enemy (?), 135 ff.; forts on, 114; hinterland, 129; outposts of, 119, 120, 160; reoccupied (?), 120, 128; restoration by Constantius I, 200; etc.

iuridici, 16, 23, 111, 137 ff., 210 ff., 275, 277, 404 ff., 433

ius liberorum, 4, 21

Jewish war, of Hadrian, 17 n., 107, 109, 113 f., 118, 119, 125, 276 n., 384

latus clavus, 4, 226

leges annales, 3 f.

legates, proconsular, 15, 17, 23, 111, 113, 242, 278, 279, 383, 411, 412
legati Augusti pro praetore, passim; *see esp.* praetorian, 21 ff., consular, 26 ff.
legionary command, 6 n., 17 ff., and *passim*; iterated, 18 f. (list), 230, 239, 241, 262, 411 f.
legions:
    I Adiutrix, *tr. lat.*, 9 n., 10; *leg. leg.*, 18, 19, 20, 30, 103, 144, 163, 386, 387; assigned to Pannonia inf., 28, 168
    I Italica, *tr. lat.*, 10, 248; *leg. leg.*, 18, 19, 20, 30, 230, 411; raised, 219 n.
    I Minervia, *tr. lat.*, 10, 18, 31, 130, 381; *leg. leg.*, 18, 19, 31, 251
    II Adiutrix, *tr. lat.*, 10, 11, 31, 417; *leg. leg.*, 18, 20, 70, 130, 233, 384, 387; commanded by gov. Pannonia inf.; in Brit., 219, 220; soldier of, 156 n.
    II Augusta, *tr. ang.*, 290 n.; *tr. lat.*, 74 f., 269 f., 273, 278, 281, 282 f., 284, 417; *leg. leg.*, 18, 19, 117 189 f., 203, 230, 235 f., 237, 256 ff., 260 n., 261 f., 263, 265 ff., 403, 408, 412, 413, 414, 422, 423; *praef. castr.*, 74; *primus pilus*, 291, 421; in Brit., 219; Brit. sup., 219 ff., Germany, 362; Vespasian commanded it, 2, 64, 227 f., its support for him, 233
    II Italica, raised, 131
    II Parthica, 172 n.
    II Traiana, *leg. leg.*, 19, 112; normally under *praef.*, 256
    III Augusta, *tr. lat.*, 10, 11, 243, 410, 413; *leg. leg.*, 6 n., 17 n., 20 n., 22, 130, 179 n., 214, 223 n., 261, 406; *primus pilus*, 292
    III Cyrenaica, *tr. ang.*, 111; *tr. lat.*, 10, 18, 118 n.; *leg. leg.*, 19, 112
    III Gallica, *tr. ang.*, 124; *tr. lat.*, 9 n.
    III Italica, *leg. leg.*, 20; raised, 131
    IV Flavia firma, *tr. lat.*, 11; *leg. leg.*, 19, 20, 213
    IV Macedonica (?), *leg. leg.* (?), 229 n.
    IV Scythica, *tr. lat.*, 10, 11, 18, 51, 379, 381; *leg. leg.*, 18, 19, 229(?), 236, 281, 411
    V Alaudae, *tr. lat.*, 8 n.; *leg. leg.*, 19; in German exped., 128 f.
    V Macedonica, *tr. lat.*, 9 n., 10, 11, 31, 213, 250; *leg. leg.*, 11, 19, 20, 30, 96, 98, 147, 211, 212, 384, 386; soldier, 128 f.; veteran, 156 n.
    VI Ferrata, *tr. ang.*, 301; *leg. leg.*, 18, 20, 130, 296 n., 387
    VI Victrix, *tr. ang.*, 59, 143, 277, 301, 417; *tr. lat.*, 18, 273, 274, 275, 277?, 283, 417; *leg. leg.*, 18, 19, 20, 110, 189, 239, 240 f., 244 f., 247, 250,

254, 255 f., 263 f., 280, 412, 413, 414, 422, 423; transfer to Brit., 101, 104, 273, 292; in Brit., 219 ff.; in Brit. inf., 168 ff., 183, 407
    VII Claudia, *tr. ang.*, 307; *tr. lat.*, 10; *leg. leg.*, 19, 30; veterans, 252
    VII Gemina, *tr. ang.*, 307; *tr. lat.*, 10, 31; *leg. leg.*, 16 n., 18, 19, 20 n., 217 n.; in Spain, 27
    VIII Augusta, *tr. lat.*, 10, 355, 418; *leg. leg.*, 19, 20 n., 85 f., 237(?), 270, 386
    IX Hispana, *tr. lat.*, 10, 18, 81 n., 220, 255, 267 f., 269, 270, 271, 271 f., 275 f., 276 f., 410, 417, 418, 419; *leg. leg.*, 30, 66 f., 220, 231, 234, 238, 269, 385, 394, 414, 422; transfer to Brit., 39, 364; in Boudiccan revolt, 67, 288; detachment in Germany, 81 n.; end of, 99 n., 219 ff., 247 n.
    X Fretensis, *tr. lat.*, 10, 11, 31, 98, 118, 381; *leg. leg.*, 18, 98; *pp. bis*, 291, 421; recruits to, 222 n.
    X Gemina, *tr. lat.*, 9 n., 10, 18, 31, 98, 381; *leg. leg.*, 113, 272, 387; movements of, 221
    XI Claudia, *tr. lat.*, 10, 18, 31; *leg. leg.*, 19, 20
    XII Fulminata, *tr. lat.*, 10, 11, 18, 89, 381; *leg. leg.*, 18, 19, 20, 117, 239, 384, 414
    XIII Gemina, *tr. ang.*, 302; *tr. lat.*, 10, 11, 18, 31, 253; *leg. leg.*, 18, 19, 20, 21 n., 30, 125 n., 134; centurion, 292
    XIV Gemina, *tr. lat.*, 9 n., 10, 11, 18, 108, 245, 268, 381, 417; *leg. leg.*, 18, 19, 20, 30, 108, 117, 125, 228 f., 232 f., 246, 384, 386, 387, 413; withdrawn from Brit., 61, 231 n.; canvassed by Flavians, 64; returned to Brit., 63; withdrawn again, 64, 219; in Germany, 362; reputation of, 57
    XV Apollinaris, *tr. lat.*, 10; *leg. leg.*, 18, 19, 20, 215, 269, 406; movements of, 221
    XVI, *leg. leg.*, 60 n., 268
    XVI Flavia firma, *tr. ang.*, 309; *tr. lat.*, 10, 279, 418; *leg. leg.*, 18, 20, 30
    XX Valeria Victrix, *tr. lat.*, 10, 279 f., 280, 282, 285, 417, 434; *leg. leg.*, 18, 30, 61, 64, 76 f., 230, 231 f., 234 f., 242, 243, 248, 253, 258 f., 270, 285, 386, 411, 412, 414, 422, 423, 434; gives trouble, 63; in Brit., 219; in Brit. sup., 168 ff.; centurion, 291 n.; *primus pilus*, 308, 422
    XXII Primigenia, *tr. lat.*, 10, 102, 113, 381; *leg. leg.*, 18, 19, 20, 261; centurion, 292
    XXX Ulpia victrix, *tr. lat.*, 10; *leg. leg.*, 18, 19, 30, 119, 248, 387

ludi, 53
ludus matutinus, 307

magistri:
  equitum, 337, 338, 371 f., 373; *militum*, 320, 330, 374; *peditum*, 373
Minicia, curator or prefect of, 16 n., 265 n., 278, 412

nomenclature, 2, 62 f., 66, 97, 104 n., 110, 155, 174, 176, 179, 232, 282, 299, and *passim*

origo, 2, and *passim*
ornamenta:
  consularia, 287; *quaestoria*, 287; *triumphalia*, 43, 47, 53, 55, 58, 81, 109, 223, 227, 356, 358, 360, 362, 363, 364
ovatio, 39 f.

Parthian wars:
  of Trajan, 103, 239, 275, 384; of L. Verus, 120, 126 f., 130, 143, 384; of Severus, 128 n.
patricians, 5, 13 ff., 17, 53, 65, 77, 79, 89, 92, 131, 193, 281, 283, 362, 378 f., 382, 415
pedites Seguntienses, 352 n.
pedites singulares Britannici, 83
pontifices, 32, 79, 92, 152, 400 f., 415
praefecti:
  civitatium, 209; *frumenti dandi*, 16, 23, 33, 236, 252 n., 412; *montis Berenicidis*, 130 n.; *urbi*, 26, 32, 114 f., 152, 225, 267, 297, 415, 433; *see also aerarium militare* and *Saturni, alimenta, Minicia,* praetorians
praesides:
  equestrian, 162 n., 177, 178 ff., 199, 200, 309, 313, 317 n., 319 f., 321, 329 ff., 402, 423; senators called, 161, 169, 397
praetentura Italiae et Alpium, 130 f.
praetorian career, 15 ff., 384 ff., 412 ff.
praetorian provinces, imperial, 21 f.
praetorians, prefects of the, 139, 145, 146, 297, 298, 321, 359 f., 365 f., 368 f., 370 f.
praetorship, 3 f., and *passim*
primipilares, 170, 192, 221, 291, 292, 295, 308
Priscillianists, 331, 341, 352
proconsuls, 17, 26, 31 f., 183, and *passim*
procurators, 35, 56, 73, 160, 387 ff., 419 ff.
protectores, 332

quaestorship, 3, 122 ff.; of the emperor, 13, 45, 51, 119, 358, 379, 380, 381;

  iterated, 282
IVviri viarum curandarum, 4 f., 108, 283, 380, 410, 418
XVviri sacris faciundis, 32, 47, 99, 108, 137 f., 217, 400 f., 415

ratio privata, 297 f.
rationalis summae rei, 313, 315
recruiting of troops, 17 n., 27, 76, 111, 120 f., 384, 412
rex magnus, 210

Secular Games, 47, 137 f., 152, 155 n.
VIIviri epulonum, 32, 112, 268, 415
VIviri equitum Romanorum, 14 f., 108, 130, 252 n., 253, 280 n.
sodales:
  Antoniniani, 32; *Augustales*, 32, 175, 244, 253; *Flaviales Titiales*, 32; *Hadrianles*, 94; *Titii*, 32
specialization, 17 ff., 29 f., 73, 119, 293, 394, 421
Stoics, 85 ff.
summum choragium, 305

tenure of office, length of, 21, 30 f., 34, 73, 397 ff., 403, 407
IIIviri capitales, 4 f., 102, 272, 379, 410, 418
IIIviri monetales, 4 f., 51, 89, 118, 238, 245, 253, 255
tribes, Roman:
  Aniensis, 37, 73 n., 215, 354; Arnensis, 279, 434; Camilia, 215 n., 275, 282, 354; Claudia, 83, 124, 302 n.; Clustumina, 51; Cornelia, 294; Falerna, 263; Galeria, 103 n., 110, 117, 235, 249, 279, 292, 366 n.; Horatia, 271 n., 284; Lemonia, 254, 282; Oufentina, 134, 253 n.; Palatina, 112, 266, 304; Papiria, 192, 238, 308 n.; Poblilia, 279 n., 287; Pollia, 253; Pomptina, 259; Pupinia, 274; Quirina, 215, 216, 272 n., 278 n., 290, 292, 308 n., 405; Sergia, 101, 279 n., 302 n., 306 n.; Stellatina, 281; Teretina, 60 n., 272; Tromentina, 306 n.; Voltinia, 88 n.
tribunate, military, 8 ff., and *passim*
tribunate of the plebs, 3 f. and *passim*
triumphs, 78 f.

vex. Brit., 221 n., 434
vice sacra iudicans, 32, 152, 153 f.
vigintivirate, 4 ff., and *passim*; omission of, 5, 74, 163, 251, 278
viri militares, 20 f., n.